Asylum-Seeker and Refugee Protection in Sub-Saharan Africa

It is not often acknowledged that the great majority of African refugee movement happens within Africa rather than from Africa to the West. This book examines the specific characteristics and challenges of the refugee situation in Sub-Saharan Africa, offering a new and critical vision about the situation of asylum-seekers and refugees in the African continent. Cristiano d'Orsi considers the international, regional and domestic legal and institutional frameworks linked to refugee protection in Sub-Saharan Africa, and explores the contributions African refugee protection has brought to the cause on a global scale.

Key issues covered in the book include the theory and the practice of *non-refoulement*, an analysis of the phenomenon of mass-influx, the concept of burden-sharing, and the role of freedom fighters. The book goes on to examine the expulsions of refugees and the historical role played by the UNHCR in Sub-Saharan Africa.

As a work which follows the persecution and legal challenges of those in search of a safe haven, this book will be of great interest and use to researchers and students of immigration and asylum law, international law, human rights and African studies.

Cristiano d'Orsi is a Post-Doctoral Fellow at the Centre for Human Rights, Faculty of Law, University of Pretoria. He holds a Ph.D. in International Relations (International Law) from the Graduate Institute of International and Development Studies in Geneva (Switzerland), a two-year master in International Relations (International Law) from the same institution and a master in Diplomacy from the Italian Society for the International Organization in Rome (Italy). He has been, among other achievements, a Europaeum Fellow at the Refugee Studies Centre in Oxford (UK), a DAAD Fellow at the Max Planck for International and Comparative Law in Heidelberg (Germany), an Albert Gallatin Fellow at the University of Virginia School of Law in Charlottesville (USA) and a Hugo Grotius Fellow at the University of Michigan Law School in Ann Arbor (USA).

Routledge Research in Asylum, Migration and Refugee Law

Available titles in this series include:

Refugee Protection and the Role of Law
Conflicting Identities
Edited by Susan Kneebone, Dallal Stevens, Loretta Baldassar

Gender in Refugee Law
From the Margins to the Centre
Efrat Arbel, Catherine Dauvergne, Jenni Millbank

Asylum-Seeker and Refugee Protection in Sub-Saharan Africa
The Peregrination of a Persecuted Human Being in Search of a Safe Haven
Cristiano D'Orsi

Forthcoming titles in this series include:

European Asylum Law and the Rights of the Child
Ciara Smyth

Asylum Law in the European Union
Francesco Cherubini

The Socio-Economic Rights of Asylum Seekers
Liam Thornton

Migrant Rights at Work
Law's Precariousness at the Intersection of Immigration and Labour
Laurie Berg

Asylum-Seeker and Refugee Protection in Sub-Saharan Africa

The Peregrination of a Persecuted Human Being in Search of a Safe Haven

Cristiano d'Orsi

Routledge
Taylor & Francis Group
LONDON AND NEW YORK

First published 2016
by Routledge
711 Third Avenue, New York, NY 10017

and by Routledge
2 Park Square, Milton Park, Abingdon, Oxon, OX14 4RN

Routledge is an imprint of the Taylor & Francis Group, an informa business

Library of Congress Cataloging in Publication Data
A catalog record for this book has been requested

ISBN: 978-1-138-02542-4 (hbk)
ISBN: 978-1-315-76956-1 (ebk)

Typeset in Baskerville
by Florence Production Ltd, Stoodleigh, Devon, UK

To Bruno and Elisa, My Parents

In loving memory of
Major General Raffaello Parri

To all the asylum-seekers and refugees
in Sub-Saharan Africa

'The ideal place for me is the one in which it is most natural to live as a foreigner.'
('Il luogo ideale per me è quello in cui è piú naturale vivere da straniero')

Italo Calvino, *Eremita a Parigi. Pagine autobiografiche.*
Milano: Palomar-Mondadori, 1994, vii

Contents

Acknowledgements

I am at the end of a long journey. This journey was, however, not possible without the support, the encouragement and the help of many people that I had the good fortune to meet over these past few years. I am only sorry for the many that I could not cite here but that I will never forget.

First of all, I would like to thank everyone at the Centre for Human Rights, Faculty of Law, University of Pretoria, where they gave me the time and the consideration to complete this work in a great work environment, letting me feel part of their big family since my arrival in South Africa.

In particular, I would like to thank Professor Frans Viljoen, Director of the Centre; Associate Professor Magnus Killander, Head of the Research at the Centre; and Professor Michelo Hansungule, with whom I shared wonderful and interesting conversations that taught me a lot about Africa. I would like to dedicate a special mention also to Professor Andre Boraine, Dean of the Faculty of Law, and to Mr Norman Taku, Assistant Director and Project Manager at the Centre, who have always been very supportive to me and to my work.

I would like to thank my primary sources of academic inspiration, Professor James Hathaway at the University of Michigan Law School, where this book started to take shape; Professor David Martin at the University of Virginia School of Law; Professor Jennifer Moore, at the University of New Mexico School of Law; and Doctor Gino J. Naldi, former senior lecturer in Law at the University of East Anglia in Norwich.

I would like to thank also Emeritus Professor Vera Gowlland-Debbas, with whom I started this journey at the Graduate Institute of International and Development Studies, for the big opportunity she gave me to pursue my studies on a topic that interested and thrilled me even before my arrival in Geneva.

My heartfelt thanks go also to Professor Andrea Bianchi from the same institution; Doctor Catherine-Amelie Chassin at the University of Caen, Basse-Normandie; Extraordinary Professor Giovanni Di Stefano at the University of Neuchatel, Associate Professor Tarcisio Gazzini at Vrije University in Amsterdam; Emeritus Professor Thomas Green at the University of Michigan Law School, Doctor Susan Isiko-Strba; Senior Research Affiliate, IP and Development Program, WIPO, at the University of Minnesota; Doctor John Kotsopoulos, Consultant at the Centre for the Study of Governance Innovation, University of

Pretoria; Professor Galya Ruffer at Northwestern University; and to Professor Hennie Strydom at the University of Johannesburg. Thank you very much for your help at various stages of this work.

Can I omit in this shortlist Ms. Grace Mukulwamutiyo who suddenly and very agreeably appeared in my life? Thank you for caring for me so much.

Last, but certainly not least, I would like to warmly thank my parents, Elisa and Bruno (to whom this work is first dedicated), because – without them – I simply could not have achieved everything that I have in my life until now.

In addition, I would like to remember Major General Raffaello Parri, who passed away more than ten years ago but whose teachings remain essential for my education.

Finally, I would like to think that this work will be appreciated by its main protagonists: the millions of asylum-seekers and refugees in Sub-Saharan who are daily struggling for the well-being that has been denied to them. I strongly hope that they will reacquire it soon and start to lead the 'normal' life that should not be denied to any human being.

Cristiano
Pretoria 26 June 2015

Acronyms

AALCO
Asian-African Legal Consultative Organization
AALCO Principles
Bangkok Principles on the Status and Treatment of Refugees ('Bangkok Principles')
AALCO Principles
Final Text of the AALCO's 1966 Bangkok Principles on Status and Treatment of Refugees, as adopted on 24 June 2001 at the AALCO's 40th Session, New Delhi
ACHPR
African Commission on Human and Peoples' Rights
AHC
Assistant High Commissioner
AI
Amnesty International
ANC
African National Congress
AU
African Union
AU Charter
Constitutive Act of the African Union
Banjul Charter (1981 African Charter)
African Charter on Human and Peoples' Rights
BDP
Botswana Democratic Party
BPEAR
Bureau for the Placement and Education of African Refugees
CAR
Central African Republic
CAT
United Nations Convention against Torture and Other Cruel, Inhuman, or Degrading Treatment or Punishment

CNRS
National Commission for the Rehabilitation of Sinistrés
COREDA
Angolan Committee on Recognition of the Right of Asylum
COSATU
Congress of South African Trade Unions
CPA
Comprehensive Plan of Action
DHA
South African Department of Home Affairs
DRC
Democratic Republic of Congo
DTA
United Nations Declaration on Territorial Asylum
ECOSOC
Economic and Social Council of the United Nations
ECOWAS
The Economic Community of West African States
ERC
Emergency Relief Coordinator
ExCom
Executive Committee of the High Commissioner's Program
FDLR
Democratic Forces for the Liberation of Rwanda
Geneva Conventions
The four conventions at the core of international humanitarian law
Handbook
Handbook on procedures and criteria for determining refugee status under the 1951 Convention and the 1967 Protocol relating to the status of refugees
Handbook on voluntary repatriation
UNHCR Handbook on voluntary repatriation
HRC
United Nations Human Rights Council
HRW
Human Rights Watch
IASC
Inter-Agency Standing Committee
ICARA I
International Conference on Assistance to Refugees in Africa (Geneva, June 1981)
ICARA II
The Second International Conference on Assistance to Refugees in Africa (Geneva, July 1984)
ICCPR
International Covenant on Civil and Political Rights

ICJ
: International Court of Justice

ICRC
: International Committee of the Red Cross

ICRC Statutes
: Statutes of the International Committee of the Red Cross

IDPs
: Internally Displaced Persons

ILC
: International Law Commission

IOM
: International Organization for Migration

IPK
: Islamic Party of Kenya

Johannesburg Principles
: Johannesburg Principles on National Security, Freedom of Expression and Access to Information

JRS
: Jesuit Refugee Service

Kampala Convention
: African Union Convention for the Protection and Assistance of Internally Displaced Persons in Africa

LHR
: South African League for Human Rights

LRRRC
: The Liberia Refugee Repatriation and Resettlement Commission

MAFREMO
: Malawian Freedom Movement

MMD
: The Movement for Multi-Party Democracy (Zambia)

MoU
: Memorandum of Understanding

NGO
: Non-Governmental Organization

New York Protocol (Protocol)
: Protocol Relating to the Status of Refugees

OAU
: Organization of African Unity

OAU Charter
: Organization of African Unity Charter

OAU Convention (1969 African Convention)
: Convention Governing the Specific Aspects of Refugee Problem in Africa

OCHA
: Office for the Coordination of Humanitarian Affairs

Protocols
Protocols additional to the Geneva Conventions
Refugee Convention (1951 Geneva Convention)
The United Nations Convention Relating to the Status of Refugees REC
Ugandan Refugee Eligibility Committee
RPF
Rwandan Patriotic Front
RSD
Refugee Status Determination
SACP
South African Communist Party
SADC
Southern African Development Community
SWAPO
The South West Africa People's Organization
TRSP
Tanzanian Revolutionary State Party
UDHR
Universal Declaration of Human Rights
UN
United Nations
UN Charter (UN Charter)
Charter of the United Nations
UNDP
United Nations Development Program
UNGA
United Nations General Assembly
UNHCR (High Commissioner)
Office of the United Nations High Commissioner for Refugees (or the High Commissioner for Refugees)
UNHCR Statute (UNHCR Statute)
Statute of the Office of the United Nations High Commissioner for Refugees
UNICEF
The United Nations Children's Fund
UNITA
The National Union for the Total Independence of Angola
UNSC
United Nations Security Council
UNSG
United Nations Secretary General
VRI
Burundi's Rural Integrated Villages
WFP
World Food Program

Introduction

Defining key concepts

The term 'refugee' itself was invented at the end of the seventeenth century, when the revocation of the Edict of Nantes in 1685 forced between 200,000 and 300,000 Huguenot *réfugiés*, for their safety, to flee France for other countries.[1]

This work, conceived as an imaginary journey in stages that an individual fleeing persecution in his/her country of origin will undertake, represents a contribution to the analysis of an immense and deeply-rooted plight which concerned 2,932,960 refugees and 418,110 asylum-seekers and spanned across four 'macro-regions' in Sub-Saharan Africa[2] in 2013. The total figure of 3,351,070 individuals accounted for the 26 per cent of the people protected by refugee law worldwide, a total which comprised 12,863,728 individuals in the same year.[3] In this panorama, Kenya (534,900), Chad (434,500) and Ethiopia (433,900) were placed, at the end of 2013, at the sixth, seventh and eighth position in the list of the major refugee-hosting countries in the world while Somalia (1,121,800), Sudan (648,900), Democratice Republic of Congo (DRC) (499,600) and Eritrea (308,200) were, at the end of the same year, the third, fourth, fifth and tenth major source countries of refugees in the world.[4] At the end of 2013, Chad had 33 refugees per 1,000 inhabitants, while Mauritania 24, Djibouti 23, South Sudan 20, Liberia and Kenya 12. These six countries all occupied the top-ten of world countries with the major number of refugees per 1,000 inhabitants, with Chad being the third worldwide.[5] Kenya was also the first Sub-Saharan African country with

1 Dowty, A. and Loescher, G. 'Refugee flows as grounds for international action', *International Security*, vol. 21, 1996, p. 58. In this regard, see also the definition of 'refugee' provided in AA.VV., *The Oxford English Dictionary*, Oxford: Clarendon Press, 1978, vol. VIII, p. 357: 'One who, owing to religious persecution or political troubles, seeks refuge in a foreign country; originally applied to the French Huguenots who came to England after the revocation of the Edict of Nantes in 1685.'

2 The four 'macro-regions', analyzed by the UNHCR, are: Central-Africa (Great Lakes), East and horn of Africa, Southern Africa and Western Africa.

3 UNHCR, UNHCR Statistical Yearbook 2013, 13th edn, Country Data Sheets, 2 February 2015, Table 1, p. 81.

4 Ibid., p. 29.

5 Ibid., p. 34.

the highest new asylum claims registered at a UNHCR office in the region (third worldwide) in 2013, with 19,200 new asylum applications.[6]

Beyond these figures, the importance of the phenomenon of asylum-seeker and refugee protection in the region is also exemplified by the fact that Sub-Saharan Africa is the only macro-region in the world where the UNHCR has four central bureaux, correspondent to the four, aforementioned, 'macro-regions', their presence representing yet another sign of how delicate and closely-observed the refugee situation is there.[7] However, following the UNHCR's example, we will not take into consideration the situation of asylum-seekers and refugees in Northern Africa in this work, as the agency has excluded this region, choosing instead to categorize it with the Near and Middle East.[8] In addition, several countries which have been more seriously affected by the refugee phenomenon, like Tanzania,[9] Uganda and Kenya – although the Kenyan government has not been actively involved in management of asylum-seekers and refugees in past decades,[10] and has recently adopted measures to limit the number of refugees on its soil[11] – will be mentioned throughout this work for the sake of juxtaposing them to others such as Burkina Faso and Gabon, which historically have been less affected by the refugee situation.

If someone were to dismiss the gravity of this situation by pointing out that refugees and asylum-seekers represented 'only' 0, 36 per cent of the 2014 estimated population in Sub-Saharan Africa of 924,701,000,[12] we would call attention to

6 Ibid., p. 57. In this special ranking, Cameroon occupied the eighth position worldwide with 5,800 asylum claims submitted to the local UNHCR offices.

7 According to the studies undertaken by the UNHCR, apart from the four aforementioned, the other bureaux of the agency represent the following geographical regions: Asia and Pacific, Middle East and North Africa, Europe, and Americas.

8 We exclude from the study Algeria, Egypt, Libya, Morocco and Tunisia and we consider other countries, such as Sudan and Mauritania which are not entirely located below the Sahara Desert.

9 For instance, Tanzania legislation has always been considered in Africa quite liberal and one of the leading legislations on the protection of human rights and, therefore, of refugees. Tanzania is one of the African countries where the 'bill of rights' is incorporated into the constitution as noted by Lubuva, D.Z., 'Reflections on Tanzania's Bill of Rights', in *Commonwealth Law Bulletin*, vol. 14, 1988, p. 853.

10 Odhiambo-Abuya, E., 'United Nations High Commissioner for Refugees and status determination imtaxaan in Kenya: an empirical survey', in *Journal of African Law*, vol. 48, 2004, p. 206.

11 In this regard, see for instance, The Conversation, 'Kenya's harsh new security laws put hundreds of thousands of refugees at risk' 30 December 2014, available at: http://theconversation.com/kenyas-harsh-new-security-laws-put-hundreds-of-thousands-of-refugees-at-risk-35789, accessed 28 April 2015. In detail, we can read: 'The Security Laws (Amendment) Act 2014 changes Kenya's 2006 Refugee Act in two vital ways: it seeks to limit the number of refugees and asylum seekers in the country to 150,000, and it further enforces an encampment policy, limiting refugees to the country's two sprawling, remote camps in Dadaab and Kakuma.'

12 UN Department of Economic and Social Affairs, Population Division, World Population Prospects, The 2012 Revision, vol. I: Comprehensive Tables, Table A.18. Annual interpolated mid-year population by major area, region and country: medium variant, 2011–2030, p. 180, United Nations: New York, 2013, available at: http://esa.un.org/unpd/wpp/Documentation/pdf/WPP2012_Volume-I_Comprehensive-Tables.pdf, accessed 10 February 2015.

the UNHCR slogan that even 'one refugee without hope is too many', and therefore assert that the international community should continue to work towards defeating this plight.

We now draw attention to the fact that this study will not take into consideration the Internally Displaced Persons IDPs, whose legal protection on the continent has recently been strengthened through the adoption of the 2009 Kampala Convention.[13] This instrument is considered to be far more prescriptive than the 1969 Organization of African Unity (OAU) Convention (1969 African Convention).[14]

In addition, it is necessary to explain both the terms and the conceptual aspects of 'asylum-seekers' and 'refugees' as they are used throughout our analysis.

13 This convention has been adopted on 23 October 2009 and, to date, 20 February 2015, has been ratified by 22 countries and, therefore, it has entered into force. Article 1 k) of the convention defines the IDPs as the following: '[p]ersons or groups of persons who have been forced or obliged to flee or to leave their homes or places of habitual residence, in particular as a result of or in order to avoid the effects of armed conflict, situations of generalized violence, violations of human rights or natural or human-made disasters, and who have not crossed an internationally recognized State border.' According to its Article 17 1): 'This Convention shall enter into force thirty (30) days after the deposit of the instruments of ratification or accession by fifteen (15) Member States.' The 15 countries that have permitted the convention to enter into force are: Benin, Burkina Faso, CAR, Chad, Gabon, Gambia, Guinea-Bissau, Lesotho, Mali, Niger, Nigeria, Sierra Leone, Togo, Swaziland (15th to ratify, on 6 November 2012), Uganda (1st to ratify, on 29 January 2010), and Zambia. For a recent IDP situation in Sub-Saharan Africa (specifically in Mali), see the news: 'UN refugee agency prepares to assist possible returnees in Mali', 29 January 2013, available at: www.unhcr.org/5107abe26.html, accessed 30 January 2015: 'From interviews with internally displaced people (IDP) over the past few days in the Mali capital, Bamako, it appears that many civilians are hoping to return to their home in areas formerly or still under rebel control, including Gao, Timbuktu and Kidal soon. The process of spontaneous returns has already started in some places. In the central Mali town of Konna, for example, a UN security evaluation mission has confirmed that people are coming back. Up to half the town's population of 10,000 was earlier reported as having fled into the surrounding countryside when Konna was overrun on January 10, prompting the French military to intervene. While the mood among IDPs may be shifting towards returns, conditions in the north of the country are difficult. People recently displaced from the north have reported serious shortages of food, clean water and fuel. Electricity, transport, communications, access to health and education is said to have been severely disrupted.'

14 Email received by G.J. Naldi on 10 February 2011, on file with author. For an analysis of the 2009 Kampala Convention, see, for instance, Abebe, A.M., 'The African Union Convention on Internally Displaced Persons: its codification background, scope, and enforcement challenges', in *Refugee Survey Quarterly*, vol. 29, 2010, pp. 28–57; Solomon, A., 'Introductory note to African Union Convention for the Protection and Assistance of Internally Displaced Persons in Africa', in *International Legal Material*, vol. 49, 2010, pp. 83–100; Zorzi Giustiniani, F., 'New Hopes and Challenges for the Protection of IDPs in Africa: The Kampala Convention for the Protection and Assistance of Internally Displaced Persons in Africa', in *Denver Journal of International Law and Policy*, vol. 39, 2010–2011, pp. 347–70. See also Taddele Maru, M., *The Kampala Convention and Its Contribution to International Law*, The Hague: Eleven International Publishing, 2014. About the application of this convention, at p. 333, the author noted that: 'Currently, the most binding constraint in the AU system is the gap between the norms contained in treaties and policies on the one hand, and their effective implementation on the other. It is for this reason that implementation of the existing legal and policy frameworks should take priority.'

In effect, asylum describes '[a] place of refuge and the right of the state to give protection in the exercise of its sovereign power over territory and regarding the admission and removal of foreign nationals',[15] and has an effect which allows foreign nationals to remain in host countries. Refugee status, on the other hand, 'confers on the recipient particular rights going beyond the right to remain'.[16] In other words, according to the UNHCR, a 'refugee' is someone who meets the definition enshrined in Article 1 of the 1951 Geneva Convention (1951 Refugee Convention),[17] and modified by the definition provided by the 1967 New York Protocol,[18] whether he/she is formally recognized or not; while an 'asylum-seeker'

15 Goodwin-Gill, G., 'Asylum', in Cane, P. and Conaghan, J. (eds), *The New Oxford Companion of Law*, Oxford: Oxford University Press, 2008, p. 57.

16 UNGA, Second report on the expulsion of aliens, International Law Commission, 20 July 2006, document No. A/CN.4/573, paragraph 98, p. 30.

17 Article 1 of the 1951 Geneva Convention stipulates as follows: 'A) For the purposes of the present Convention, the term "refugee" shall apply to any person who: 1) Has been considered a refugee under the Arrangements of 12 May 1926 and 30 June 1928 or under the Conventions of 28 October 1933 and 10 February 1938, the Protocol of 14 September 1939 or the Constitution of the International Refugee Organization; Decisions of non-eligibility taken by the International Refugee Organization during the period of its activities shall not prevent the status of refugee being accorded to persons who fulfill the conditions of paragraph 2 of this section; 2) As a result of events occurring before 1 January 1951 and owing to well-founded fear of being persecuted for reasons of race, religion, nationality, membership of a particular social group or political opinion, is outside the country of his nationality and is unable or, owing to such fear, is unwilling to avail himself of the protection of that country; or who, not having a nationality and being outside the country of his former habitual residence as a result of such events, is unable or, owing to such fear, is unwilling to return to it. In the case of a person who has more than one nationality, the term "the country of his nationality" shall mean each of the countries of which he is a national, and a person shall not be deemed to be lacking the protection of the country of his nationality if, without any valid reason based on well-founded fear, he has not availed himself of the protection of one of the countries of which he is a national. B) 1) For the purposes of this Convention, the words "events occurring before 1 January 1951" in Article 1, section A, shall be understood to mean either: a) "events occurring in Europe before 1 January 1951"; or b) "events occurring in Europe or elsewhere before 1 January 1951", and each Contracting State shall make a declaration at the time of signature, ratification or accession, specifying which of these meanings it applies for the purpose of its obligations under this Convention. 2) Any Contracting State which has adopted alternative a) may at any time extend its obligations by adopting alternative b) by means of a notification addressed to the Secretary-General of the United Nations.'

18 The Protocol to the 1951 Refugee Convention was signed in 1967 in New York. It is a treaty that incorporates the 1951 Refugee Convention's rights regime by reference and extends those protections to all refugees by eliminating the convention's temporal and geographical limitations. The UNHCR collaborated in the removal of these limitations for those countries that are bound by the convention. Given the temporal and geographical limitations present in the 1951 Geneva Convention, it was very difficult to assure a complete protection to the African refugees based on the existing mechanisms in place. In effect, the new independent states of Sub-Saharan Africa had little incentive to become parties to the 1951 Refugee Convention because of the non-universality of the refugee definition in that treaty. Being non-parties to this convention, they were therefore not bound by the duty to cooperate with the UNHCR through Article 35 of the 1951 Geneva Convention. From this time on, the UNHCR lacked an important instrument to guide its work for refugee protection on the African continent. See Protocol Relating to the Status of

is defined as someone who would like to have asylum granted, and normally someone who is applying for asylum through a formal process.[19] Therefore, an 'asylum-seeker' is by definition someone who is 'seeking' something, whose legal status is still pending and whose claim for asylum has yet to be accepted or rejected by the authorities of the host country. A 'refugee' differs in the sense that he/she is an individual whose situation has already been assessed and, therefore, he/she should normally be an individual with an established living situation in a new country, temporarily or permanently, other than his/her country of origin. Therefore, as deducted from my previous affirmations:

Refugees, done at New York, on 31 January 1967, UNTS, vol. 606, No. 8791, p. 267. Article I1 of the protocol reads: 'The States Parties to the present Protocol undertake to apply articles 2 to 34 inclusive of the Convention to refugees as hereinafter defined.' In regard to the difference between the 1951 Convention and the 1967 Protocol, S.E. Davies affirmed as follows: 'The key difference between the 1951 Convention and the 1967 Protocol was the removal of the 1951 Convention's time and geographic constraints.' See Davies, S.E., 'Redundant or essential? How politics shaped the outcome of the 1967 Protocol', in *International Journal of Refugee Law*, vol. 19, 2007, p. 703.

19 Moore, J., personal correspondence with the author, March 2011, on file with author. See also, the definition provided by D. Martin in a personal document, March 2012, on file with author: 'It is important [. . .] to recognize that the terms "asylum" and "refugee" are not always used consistently. But [. . .] the most common and most helpful way of understanding these concepts is to consider refugee status as closely linked only to the most minimal requirements imposed by the 1951 Convention and Protocol, while "asylum" refers to a more ample status with additional rights – ideally including full settlement rights, full access to the labor market, etc. The distinction arises because the 1951 Convention actually guarantees far less to persons adjudged "refugees" than initially meets the eye. The most complete rights guaranteed under the Convention pertain only to persons "lawfully in" or "lawfully staying in" the state of refuge. The *Travaux Préparatoires* make it reasonably clear that the drafters intended a decision about lawful presence or residence to be a separate discretionary decision by the host government, not something that followed automatically from a determination of refugee status [. . .] Hathaway [. . .] in his more recent The Rights of Refugees, argues that persons determined to be refugees (or accepted into the process of adjudication) are at least lawfully staying in the country. I disagree with that reading (though not necessarily with the policy preference), because this interpretation would take away the discretionary authority over status that was quite important to acceding states. It simply is neither what the drafters intended nor what acceding countries agreed to, and I am very skeptical of "dynamic evolution" theories of interpretation. In rough terms, then, asylum connotes the full range of rights that would apply under the Convention to a refugee lawfully staying in the country of refuge, whereas a person who is a "refugee" is shielded from *refoulement*, but will not necessarily enjoy the wider range of rights associated with asylum. The enjoyment of the latter depends on a discretionary determination by the host state. [. . .] [P]ersons given asylum by a state could include persons who are not "refugees" under the 1951 Convention (or a broader regional definition, such as the OAU Convention) – though in countries with highly developed adjudication systems, they are highly likely to link asylum to the Convention definition. If the asylum granted was purely discretionary and based on no treaty criteria [. . .], then it's true that there is no international obligation not to return that person. But most states are not providing asylum regularly beyond the bounds of what they conceive to be international obligations – and the absolute minimum protection owed to someone within the relevant criteria is almost always *non-refoulement*.' Lastly, see also Vierdag, E.W., '"Asylum" and "Refugee" in International Law', in *Netherlands International Law Review*, vol. 24, 1977, pp. 287–303.

> The formal recognition of refugee character is of a declaratory nature – whether a person is a refugee depends on his fulfilling the conditions of the definition.[20]

In Sub-Saharan Africa, many countries often make no real distinction between the two categories of 'asylum-seeker' and 'refugee', making use of both terms interchangeably throughout their domestic legislation. For instance, the 2011 Kenyan Refugees Bill, in its Article 15, provides for the measures of *non-refoulement* for both asylum-seekers, refugees, and their respective families. In addition, Article 20 of the same law lumps the two categories together under the topic of 'vulnerable groups', so as not to subject them to discrimination.[21] The 1998 Tanzanian Refugee Act uses the formulation 'asylum-seeker and/or refugee' throughout to mean that, in practice, the protection assured to one category is also assured to the other.[22] Similar is the situation in the DRC, where the 2002 domestic law takes the same approach in terms of terminology.[23] In effect, for several concepts such as the cessation clauses (whose analysis is not provided in this monograph),[24] we need explicitly to talk about 'refugees', this being the only category subjected to cessation of 'refugee status'; whereas an asylum-seeker's situation is not dissimilar to that of a refugee in the case of, for instance, *refoulement*. In this situation, both categories are subject to limits which are not valid in reference to the expulsion of a foreigner who does not pertain to either of the two categories.[25]

It is true, however, that the 1969 OAU Convention, which is the instrument of reference for refugee protection in Africa, specifically addresses 'refugees', reserving Article II for discussion of the institution of 'asylum'. Article II represents one of the most important innovations and legal contributions to refugee protection in Africa, considering that its 1951 UN predecessor did not include a similar provision. This important innovation and contribution will be highlighted in the rest of this work and, most importantly, in the chapter appositely dedicated to the institution of asylum, which explicates how it is perceived and applied in Sub-Saharan Africa. However, we would like to make it clear from the beginning, that the language used in Article II of the 1969 African Convention is exclusively recommendatory. This instrument only advances, but does not protect, any

20 Weis, P., 'Development of international refugee law', in *Michigan Yearbook of International Legal Studies*, vol. 3, 1982, p. 38.

21 Kenya, The Refugees Bill 2011, 15 July 2011. In this regard, see also section 10) 3) p) of the same law: 'Without prejudice to the generality of subsection 2) the Commissioner shall: [. . .] p) protect and assist vulnerable groups, women, and children.'

22 Tanzania, Refugees Act (1998), Act No. 9, 15 April 1999.

23 DRC, Law No. 021/2002, portant statut des réfugiés en République Démocratique du Congo, 16 octobre 2002.

24 For an institutional analysis of the cessation clauses, see UNHCR, Handbook on procedures and criteria for determining refugee status under the 1951 Convention and the 1967 Protocol relating to the status of refugees, 2nd edn, Geneva: UNHCR, 1992, paragraphs 111–39, pp. 18–23.

25 UNGA, Second report on the expulsion of aliens, International Law Commission, 20 July 2006, document No. A/CN.4/573, paragraph 99, p. 30.

individual right to asylum.[26] Nor is this right protected in the national constitutions where it is mentioned, such as in Article 25 1) of the 2003 Rwandan Constitution, where the right to asylum in the country is simply 'recognized under conditions determined by the Law'.[27]

For the sake of clarity, the author will be attentive to specifying when his analysis refers to 'asylum-seekers' or 'refugees' throughout this entire work, rather than both categories jointly.

Presentation of the study

This study constitutes an attempt to assemble a comprehensive framework for the different legal and practical aspects linked to refugee protection in Sub-Saharan Africa, considering that, to our knowledge, very few complete and accurate studies have been conducted on this topical issue before. It highlights specific characteristics particular to the refugee situation in the region, negative aspects included, and elucidates the challenges and contributions that African refugee protection has brought and continues to bring to the cause of refugee protection on a global scale. In our opinion, the works conducted in the past have often been merely descriptive, without sufficient analysis of all the instruments applicable to the African asylum-seeker and refugee in Africa, comprising national legislations. Otherwise, these studies have limited themselves to analysis of only several particular features of the refugee plight on that continent. As we have mentioned above, this study will explore the challenges which are presently before asylum-seeker and refugee protection in Sub-Saharan Africa, the cradle of mankind, where the state of affairs is continuously changing. This latter point has been made apparent through Africa's 54th country, South Sudan, which was proclaimed on 9 July 2011, although, to date,[28] this state is still not part of the main instruments which guarantee the protection of the categories of individuals, which is the object of this work.

Moreover, this is first and foremost a legal study. Therefore, the reader should not expect any particular reference to the anthropological, political or sociological aspects of this topic although in several passages of the work it will be difficult not

26 Sharpe, M., 'The 1969 African Refugee Convention: innovations, misconceptions, and omissions', in *McGill Law Journal*, vol. 58, 2012, pp. 104–5.

27 Rwanda's Constitution of 2003 with Amendments through 2010, available at: www.constituteproject.org/constitution/Rwanda_2010.pdf, accessed 1 February 2015.

The Rwandan authorities have also adopted, in 2014, a new Refugee Law which, among other aspects, establishes the Refugee Status Determination Committee (Article 3), grant refugee status to refugees in mass-influx situations (Article 13), and deal with the question of refugee camps and their management (Chapter V, Articles 23 through 26), these last two representing aspects not commonly concerning the African domestic refugee laws. For the text of the law, see Rwanda: Law No. 13 ter/2014 of 21/05/2014 relating to refugees, 30 June 2014, available at: www.refworld.org/docid/53fb08cd4.html, accessed 1 April 2015.

28 20 February 2015. However, South Sudan signed the four 1949 Geneva Conventions on Monday 16 July 2012.

to draw upon some such reflections on the present situation of asylum in Sub-Saharan Africa for the purpose of context.[29] This situation does not constitute a thing of the past, but continues to challenge the cultural tendency towards hospitality traditionally associated with African civilization.[30]

At first glance, asylum-seeker and refugee protection in Sub-Saharan Africa is composed of both positive and negative elements. The existence of international, regional and domestic legislation, which provide a legal theoretical framework for asylum-seeker and refugee's protection, is beneficial for these categories of persons. On the contrary, the presence of such legal instruments whose provisions are not – or cannot be – properly enforced represents a challenge which remains to be resolved. Other negative elements are the lack of consistent jurisprudence by regional courts, as well as the shortcomings and incoherencies in domestic legislation and jurisprudence, which are not always clearly in favour of genuine asylum-seeker and refugee protection. Referring to this last point just mentioned, it is worth adding that, apart from the available documentation being quite fragmentary, it is not always easy to enter into material possession of domestic African legislation and jurisprudence from abroad. On this point, for instance, we were very disappointed to ascertain that it was not possible to have access in any way to the preparatory works of the 1969 OAU Convention because they are unpublished. If we had been able to study the preparatory works which, surely, must have been conducted, we most likely would have a better understanding of the positions adopted by given countries on specific issues concerning refugee protection on the continent. An inattentive reader of the 1969 OAU Convention may in fact have the impression that we are talking about a document that was approved unanimously and without any particular discussion whereas, in contrast, it was the result of much debate and compromise, as always occurs when a legal document requires the many governments to agree upon its contents in order to be adopted.

The fragmentation of the law is one of the main reasons why this work takes into consideration all of Sub-Saharan Africa, given that, perhaps with the exception of South Africa, there are generally insufficient legal references to permit the writing of an original work on refugee protection regarding a specific country/geographic area on the continent from a legal perspective. In addition, we are aware of the risks incurred by focusing our analysis on a very broad area. In fact, one of the ideas at the foundation of this work was to consider the similarities and the differences of approaches to asylum-seeker and refugee protection in the different states of this area, to underline – once again, if possible – that Africa is not as homogeneous as 'a country', a message often passed along

29 In this regard, E. Haddad clearly affirmed that: 'The refugee domain is a highly politicized and internationalized area.' See Haddad, E., *The Refugee in International Society: Between Sovereigns*, Cambridge: Cambridge University Press, 2008, p. 2.

30 Viljoen, F., *International Human Rights Law in Africa*, Oxford/New York: Oxford University Press, 2007, p. 257.

by media of so-called 'developed countries', but incarnates a set of different visions and responses concerning the question of refugees as well.

In Sub-Saharan Africa we also often witness a contradictory description of the practice of refugee protection, with governmental officials providing a version of facts that is not always shared by international actors present on the 'field' – such as international and/or regional organizations, as well as NGOs. Another challenge for asylum-seeker and refugee protection in the region is to try to convince national governments to eliminate propagandistic versions of refugee protection which mislead international public opinion and mask the problem, and to address the issue at hand as directly as possible to give a clear indication of governmental views regarding what constitutes effective protection.

To add to the list of weaknesses, there is a scarcity of laws by a single country dedicated to this problem – likewise regarding the correlated problem of migrants – in comparison to the number of laws that national legislators dedicate to other aspects of daily life in a state. For instance, we were disappointed to ascertain that many countries – for instance Nigeria, Kenya and Uganda – dedicate one, two or at most three 'laws', 'bills', and/or 'decrees' to safeguard the rights of refugees, while at the same time, these countries reserve plenty of space on their agenda for the adoption of a multitude of detailed national laws dealing with topics such as trade and investment. In principle, the topic of these highly prioritized laws are relevant for very few people in an African country compared to the multitude of those with an interest in refugee law in the region. Challenging these states to take better care of these vulnerable groups on their territory represents a step towards better protection of asylum-seekers and refugees.

E. Haddad has noted that the refugee problem is inevitably part of the international society.[31] This is particularly true in the African context because of the continuous intra-territorial fights but also because of the steady tradition of hospitality and solidarity that has characterized the entire continent through the past centuries.

There are lacunae in the legal protection available to asylum-seekers and refugees. Nonetheless, according to our analysis, breaches are more related to state practice than to a lack of legal instruments, considering that the existing instruments, although not as detailed as those in force in other geographical contexts, in our opinion suffice to protect asylum-seekers' and refugees' basic rights. On this purpose, should there be a doubt as to our meaning of 'state practice', we would like to clarify this concept with the following:

> The obvious way to find out how countries are behaving is to read the newspapers, consult historical records, listen to what governmental authorities are saying and peruse the many official publications. There are also memoirs of various past leaders, official manuals on legal questions, diplomatic

31 Haddad, E., op. cit. note 29, p. 7.

> interchanges and the opinions of national legal advisors. All these methods are valuable in seeking to determine actual state practice.[32]

The instruments just evoked will be the ones taken into consideration when referring to the 'practice' of governments. The analysis elaborated in this work will demonstrate that some African countries, despite practices that often differ from the rules established by international legal instruments, do not use these different practices as a source to create a new customary law, nor do they aspire to. In fact, these Sub-Saharan African countries are simply showing disrespect towards the law because they often transgress customary norms that have been accepted by the majority of the doctrine and endorsed by jurisprudence, such as the one of *non-refoulement*. The same is true of peremptory norms (*jus cogens*) by the international community, norms to which no derogation would be permitted as a matter of principle. Respect of the norms regarding asylum-seeker and refugee protection undoubtedly represents the biggest challenge faced on the continent. Despite efforts by the different organizations present there, this goal remains far from being reached.

The questions that we raise in the following chapters provide possible solutions as to how to fill these lacunae, given that in most of the countries, there is a legal and institutional framework for asylum-seeker and refugee protection put into place appositively to contribute to the respect of these categories of people in need. In many cases, however, states seem rather to act against the interests of refugees and asylum-seekers, or, simply, to not act at all. The institutional framework will be analyzed through the study, systematically, in conjunction with a close look into the practical application of the norms set in the legal instruments applicable to states. We will ascertain how this institutional framework is at times even too detailed to work properly, given the present reality of some states. This is, for instance, the case in the DRC, where Décret No. 03/14, Portant Organisation et Fonctionnement de la Commission Nationale pour les Réfugiés et de la Commission des Recours, of 5 August 2003,[33] is too detailed to be properly enforced in a country where political problems are still pervasive.[34] The decree is composed of 27 articles and the procedure of eligibility and recourse it has established is described in a very meticulous manner,[35] so overly meticulous that it undermines the country's ability to achieve credible results given that, at the beginning of 2015, the DRC still hosted 207,130 among asylum-seekers and refugees and where, according to the UNHCR, [the situation]

32 Shaw, M.N., *International Law*, 6th edn, Cambridge: Cambridge University Press, 2008, p. 82.

33 DRC, Décret No. 03/014 du 5 août 2003 portant organisation et fonctionnement de la Commission nationale pour les réfugiés et de la Commission des Recours.

34 See, for instance, HRW, World Report 2015 – Democratic Republic of Congo, 29 January 2015, available at: www.refworld.org/docid/54cf83af25.html, accessed 23 February 2015.

35 For a description of the procedures see, above all: Articles 2 through 24 of the DRC's decree.

> [i]s characterized by ongoing conflict, poor or non-existent infrastructure and highly challenging logistics, all of which make access to refugees and other populations of concern quite difficult.[36]

In any event, problems with the institutional framework concern both countries where Refugee Status Determination (RSD) is carried out mostly or exclusively by the central authorities, such as in Ethiopia,[37] Malawi,[38] Nigeria[39] or Zimbabwe,[40] and where RSD is conducted directly by the UNHCR, as delegated by central governments, such as in Central African Republic (CAR), Chad, Eritrea, Sudan and Burundi. This last country constitutes a particular example, due to legislation on the institutional aspect of the protection of asylum-seekers and refugees[41] which, evidently, still needs to find a means of practical enforcement, although the UNHCR strongly supported the set-up of the National Office for the Protection of Refugees and Stateless Persons and trained its personnel.[42]

In this regard, if it is true that where the UNHCR determines refugee status, procedures are fairer and the needs of asylum-seekers are taken more closely into consideration, it is also true that a UNHCR-recognized refugee can still be considered 'illegal' by local governments and durable solutions remain elusive, having little tangible outcome. The truth is that the significance of this kind of recognition varies from country to country, from one individual to another over

36 UNHCR, 2015 UNHCR country operations profile – Democratic Republic of the Congo, available at: www.unhcr.org/pages/49e45c366.html, accessed 10 February 2015.

37 Ethiopia, Refugee Proclamation No. 409, 19 July 2004, particularly Articles 13 through 19. However, particularly in the last few years, the UNHCR is sensibly replacing governmental authorities in this work, although most of the determination of refugee status is still carried out by the central government. For further information, see www.unhcr.org/refworld/country/ETH.html, accessed 10 October 2014.

38 Malawi, Refugee Regulations, 8 June 1990, particularly sections 2 through 6. Specificaly about this country, S. Getahun noted that: 'Malawi had been "warehousing" refugees and asylum-seekers from Somalia, Ethiopia, DRC, Burundi, Rwanda, and Eritrea at its Dzaleka refugee camp in Dowa (Northern district of Malawi).' See Getahun, S., 'Charting refugee and migration routes in Africa', in Gold, S.J. and Nawyn, S.J. (eds), *Routledge International Handbook of Migration Studies*, London/New York: Routledge, 2013, p. 92.

39 Nigeria, Decree, National Commission for Refugees, 29 December 1989, particularly sections 3 through 13.

40 Zimbabwe, Refugee Regulations, 1985, particularly sections 3 through 8.

41 Burundi, Ordonnance ministérielle No. 530–442 du 7/4/2009 sur les mesures d'application de la Loi n. 1/32 du 13 novembre 2008 sur l'asile et la protection des réfugiés au Burundi et portant sur les procédures de demande d'asile, No. 530–442, 7 April 2009; Ordonnance No. 530–443 du 7/4/2009 portant mesures d'application de la Loi n. 1/32 du 13 novembre 2008 sur l'asile et la protection des réfugiés au Burundi et portant composition, organisation et fonctionnement de la Commission consultative pour les étrangers et réfugiés et du Comité de recours, No. 530–443, 7 April 2009. All this information is available at: www.unhcr.org/cgi-bin/texis/vtx/refworld/rwmain, accessed 10 October 2014.

42 See the news: UNHCR, 'Asylum system in Burundi established with UNHCR's support', 16 April 2009, available at: www.unhcr.org/49e733de2.html, accessed 10 October 2014.

time.[43] 'Solutions' like the 2009 'voluntary' repatriation of Burundians from the Mtabila camp in Tanzania where Tanzanian authorities put pressure on the Burundians by closing down all the refugees' businesses, burning their houses and imprisoning the camp leaders in order to oblige refugees to flee the country, do not constitute a veritable exception to the current refugee situations in Sub-Saharan Africa. And, in spite of its efforts, on this occasion the UNHCR could not do anything more than verbally 'condemn' the behaviour of the Tanzanian government, the agency being incapable of doing anything more to preserve the rights of the Burundians, most of them having already acquired the official status of 'refugee'.[44] Such an attitude is by no means characteristic of the African panorama, because 'disincentives' such as these are used in other geographic areas of the world, as well. Nonetheless, there are some extremely pressing issues that must be dealt with in order to improve asylum-seeker and refugee protection in Sub-Saharan Africa. African countries must be persuaded not only to adopt norms more closely aligned with the real necessities of asylum-seekers and refugees but, more importantly, to convince them that unjust treatment of these vulnerable groups on their territory constitutes a legal and ethical breach detrimental to their own country – because it can, for instance, enhance tensions with the country of origin of the individuals concerned.

Structure of the study

This study will attempt to follow a linear path in order to clearly illustrate relevant situations, highlighting several pivotal concepts which are essential to understanding the coherence of the work, as well as the specific characteristics of the protection of asylum-seekers and refugees in Sub-Saharan Africa. At the same time, it will consider African contributions to refugee protection, as well as the challenges that refugee protection poses specifically in this region.

First of all, however, it is indispensable to briefly stress the root causes of the current refugee flow throughout the continent. These causes basically are to be found in ethnic conflicts (Ogden in 1977, Rwanda in 1994) sometimes coupled with religious undercurrents (Sudan in 1983); political intolerance or struggle for political power (Nigeria in 1993, Zimbabwe in 2002, Ivory Coast in 2010–2011, Mali 2012–2013); and natural and ecological disasters – although in doctrine it is still questionable whether the latter situations can legally generate refugees, while in converse, UNHCR categorically excludes this situation.[45] In addition, external

43 Alexander, M., 'Refugee status determination conducted by UNHCR', in *International Journal of Refugee Law*, vol. 11, 1999, p. 285.

44 See the news: Pambazuka, 'Burundi are being forcibly repatriated from Tanzania', 28 June 2009, available at: www.pambazuka.org/actionalerts/index/2009/06/, accessed 10 October 2014.

45 For a denial of the existence of such a category of refugees see, for instance, Crisp, J., 'Beyond the nexus: UNHCR's evolving perspective on refugee protection and international migration', in UNHCR, *New Issues in Refugee Research*, research paper No. 155, 2008, pp. 6–7: '*While UNHCR has firmly rejected the notion of "environmental refugees" and opposes any extension of the 1951 UN Refugee Convention to include people who have been displaced for reasons unrelated to persecution or armed conflict*', a draft position paper observes that 'UNHCR's own mandate has progressively and pragmatically

factors also contributed to the emergence of refugee protection in several countries by means of the colonial experience, which entailed the flight of freedom fighters who struggled for the liberation of their own countries.[46] In effect, historically speaking, the African refugee problems in the terms that we understand today are the product of the 1960s, the most significant decade for decolonization, with asylum-seekers and refugees originating both from the colonial and dependent states and the independent African countries. More than half of these individuals came mainly from the Portuguese colonies (Angola, Cape Verde, Guinea Bissau, Mozambique and Sao Tome and Principe).[47]

been extended over the years to persons considered to be in a "refugee-like" situation [. . .] UNHCR could be called upon to become involved with those displaced for environmental reasons who find themselves in a "refugee-like" situation, should this be deemed necessary by the international community.' Emphasis added. A similar opinion is shared, for instance, in Kaelin, W., 'Conceptualizing climate-induced displacement', in McAdam, J. (ed.), *Climate Change and Displacement*, Oxford/Portland, OR: Hart Publishing, 2010, pp. 88–9, where the author contended that climate-induced displacement was '[n]either covered by the wording and purpose of [the 1951 Geneva Convention] definition nor was it considered by the drafters of the treaty'. The author also excluded that the 1969 OAU Convention covers this kind of situation. For the question related to the displaced persons because of climate change, natural and man-made disasters, see also *infra*, next chapters where the debate will be explored in different sections of this study. For UNHCR's position, see: *UNHCR, Handbook on Procedures and Criteria for Determining Refugee Status under the 1951 Convention and the 1967 Protocol relating to the status of refugees*, 2nd edition, Geneva: UNHCR, 1992, paragraphs 39, p. 11.

46 Okogbule, N.S., 'The legal dimensions of the refugee problem in Africa', in *East African Journal of Peace and Human Rights*, vol. 10, 2004, pp. 177–81. For the causes of refugee flows in Sub-Saharan Africa see also, for example: Hofmann, R., 'Refugee law in the African context', in *Zeitschrift für Ausländisches Öffentliches Recht und Völkerrecht*, vol. 52, 1992, pp. 319–21; Oyelade, O.S., 'A critique of the rights of refugees under the OAU Convention governing the specific aspects of refugee problems in Africa', in *East African Journal of Peace and Human Rights*, vol. 12, 2006, pp. 164–168; Van Garderen, J. and Ebenstein, J., 'Regional developments: Africa', in Zimmermann, A. (ed.), *The 1951 Convention Relating to the Status of Refugees and its 1967 Protocol: A Commentary*, Oxford: Oxford University Press, 2011, pp. 187–8.

47 AALCO, *Yearbook of the Asian-African Legal Consultative Organization*, New Delhi: AALCO, vol. VII, 2009, p. 402. About the causes generating flows of refugees, more specifically M. Wiener explained: 'The four categories [of mass-refugee exodus] are: inter-state wars (including anti-colonial wars), ethnic conflicts, non-ethnic civil conflicts, and flights from repressive authoritarian and revolutionary regimes. The categories enable us to identify the principal determinants in ways that give us an improved handle for thinking about policy intervention.' See Weiner, M., 'Bad neighbors, bad neighborhoods: an inquiry into the causes of refugee flows', in *International Security*, vol. 21, 1996, p. 9. Particularly regarding ethnic-conflicts, very common in Sub-Saharan Africa, at ibid., p. 10, the author clarified: 'Ethnic conflicts include those in which linguistic or racial groups, tribes, or religious communities are in conflict with the state or with other ethnic groups in their own country. The distinctive feature of such conflicts is that individuals participate in such conflicts or are at risk because they belong to specific linguistic, racial, tribal, or religious communities. Two types of ethnic conflicts generate refugee flows: 1) where territorially based ethnic groups are engaged in secessionist or autonomy struggles against the central government; or 2) where territorially dispersed ethnic groups are persecuted by the state or are in conflict with other ethnic groups in the society. Conflicts between different religious communities are classified as ethnic; conflicts within religious communities are also classified as ethnic [. . .], but are not so classified if the conflict is primarily ideological.'

The analysis of this work will begin in Part I, and will constitute the pivotal axis of the work, taking into consideration the specific characteristics of refugee protection in Sub-Saharan Africa, the stages that the persecuted man needs to go through in search of his/her safe haven, underlining the contributions that the specific characteristics bring to universal refugee protection and the challenges they pose to its international and domestic actors.

This part starts with Chapter 1 by offering an analysis of the fundamental concept of *non-refoulement*, an area in which the African legislators have further demonstrated their desire to address the specific situation of refugees and asylum-seekers on the continent through regional interpretation. This can be noted in their use of the *non-refoulement* for both categories of individuals, considering that the 1969 African Convention provision applies to 'persons'. Under the circumstances of Article II3 of the 1969 OAU Convention, the ban of *refoulement* permits the countries concerned to 'temporarily' protect individuals fleeing their countries of origin, having enlarged the scope of the principle in question. Under Article 33 1) of the 1951 Geneva Convention, on the other hand, the only persons who can benefit from *non-refoulement* are those who find themselves already in the host country's territory. In effect, in the words of T. Clark, the principle of *non-refoulement* contained in Article 33 of the 1951 Geneva Convention '[i]s not absolute'.[48] As such, the 1969 African Convention extends this protection further to include persons waiting at the frontier. However, in spite of the theoretical innovations that the African legislator has introduced concerning the conception of the principle of *non-refoulement* in Africa – innovations which should exclusively benefit refugees and asylum-seekers; and episodes of *refoulement* in Sub-Saharan Africa – often carried out on the grounds of 'national security', have multiplied in recent decades. Such a situation has created a new challenge for the UNHCR and other international actors working on the field: to try to mediate the conflict between local governments and the individuals in need of protection. This is an effort to prevent vulnerable people from being returned to a country where they may fear persecution and also to assure authorities in the country of destination that the presence of aliens on their soil will not have any negative consequences for its national security or its socio-economic fabric. Moreover, in the same section, we will also wonder whether the principle of *non-refoulement*, which several scholars consider a *jus cogens*[49] could really be seen as such in the Sub-Saharan African context, or if it would be rather regarded as belonging to the category of *jus dispositivum*, considering the inconsistency of the elements that would effectively render it a peremptory norm of international law.

48 Clark, T., 'Rights based refuge, the potential of the 1951 Convention and the need for authoritative interpretation', in *International Journal of Refugee Law*, vol. 16, 2004, p. 588. At idem, the author explained: 'Its [of article 33] effect in the Convention text is to allow refuge which is temporary pending the adjudication of status of individuals or of groups who may be refugees. The person's refugee status is recognized by the state applying the [1951 Geneva] Convention definition.'

49 For instance, see Allain, J., 'The *jus cogens* nature of *non-refoulement*', in *International Journal of Refugee Law*, vol. 13, 2001, pp. 533–58.

In Chapter 2, the study will focus its attention on the concept of 'asylum', and how it is conceived in Sub-Saharan Africa. In this sense, Article II of the 1969 African Convention undoubtedly creates one the most important improvements introduced by the African refugee protection because it deals with the essential requirement that enables persons to seek legal recognition of their refugee status. However, the possibility for an individual fleeing his/her country of origin to enjoy asylum in Sub-Saharan Africa, above all in these last decades, is becoming increasingly difficult, as the examples will demonstrate in the text. Apart from this concept, we will also focus our analysis on temporary protection generally used in the case of mass-influx[50] and whose composing elements seem to be constituted by the following: 'admission or extension of the stay, *non-refoulement*, basic humanitarian standards, and eventual return.'[51] The 'expanded definition' of refugee provided in the 1969 African Convention[52] supports the implementation of a provision concerning temporary protection, contained in its Article II5, which has been regarded as a source of transitory protection also outside Africa. This type of protection assures secluded persons, that is, those with temporary protection, more or less the same set of benefits prescribed to ordinary refugees, although these benefits can be reduced depending on the dimension and nature of influx of persons in search of protection. In this regard, we can observe how the novel concept of 'temporary protection' represents a 'transformation' of the time-conception of protection in Sub-Saharan Africa: in several cases, 'temporary' protection has practically become 'permanent' with conflicts postponing self-reliance solutions for decades. Another challenge faced by international and regional organizations, as well as by national governments, is the need to address the root causes of the refugee situations in the region in order to try to reduce the time these aliens are required to stay in camps. Temporary protection, seen as an element of a comprehensive approach to the refugee problem, should pre-

50 UNGA, Third report on the expulsion of aliens, International Law Commission, 19 April 2007, document No. A/CN.4/581, paragraph 72, p. 25.

51 Rutinwa, B., 'Temporary protection and its expression under the "reformulation of refugee law" model', in Handmaker, J., De La Hunt, L.A. and Klaaren, J. (eds), *Perspectives on Refugee Protection in South Africa*, Pretoria: Lawyers for Human Rights, 2001, p. 77.

52 Ortiz Miranda, C., 'Toward a broader definition of refugee: 20th century development trends', in *California Western International Law Journal*, vol. 20, 1989–1990, p. 323. In detail, Article 1 2) of the 1969 OAU Convention provides as follows: '2) The term "refugee" shall also apply to every person who, owing to external aggression, occupation, foreign domination or events seriously disturbing public order in either part or the whole of his country of origin or nationality, is compelled to leave his place of habitual residence in order to seek refuge in another place outside his country of origin or nationality.' As also J. Hyndman and B.V. Nylund contended: 'The original definition of refugee, as outlined in the 1951 Convention, is becoming increasingly irrelevant, particularly in cases of large-scale flows of refugees resulting from ethnic conflicts or other internal disturbances. Put another way, the moral if not legal responsibility for wider categories of persons in need of protection by the international community is becoming increasingly expected.' See Hyndman, J. and Nylund, B.V., 'UNHCR and the status of *prima facie* refugees in Kenya', in *International Journal of Refugee Law*, vol. 10, 1998, p. 34.

lude repatriation – although the repatriation must not necessarily be voluntary in this case. The relevance of temporary protection is intensified in Sub-Saharan Africa due to the phenomenon of mass-influx which is typical in the region, and which is also accompanied by hopes for successful agreements for burden-sharing as resources are often already stretched in this context.[53]

In Part I of this work, we will also take into account four more aspects of the life of a persecuted man in Sub-Saharan Africa, that are distinctive features of refugee and asylum-seeker protection in this region, and that pose several challenges to local governments and/or organizations working there, as well as the international community all together.

The first aspect arises in the situation, all too common, of mass-influx of persecuted individuals fleeing persecution (Chapter 3). In the camps, *bona fide* refugees are increasingly intermingling with individuals who do not deserve this status. The phenomenon of mass-influx is also linked with the burden-sharing of the plight of asylum-seekers and refugees, this latter concept finding its legal consecration in Article II4 of the 1969 OAU Convention.

The UNHCR Executive Committee, hereinafter referred to as the ExCom has tried, rather vaguely we would say, to define the elements which constitute a mass-influx. They are the following: 'i) considerable numbers of people arriving over an international border; ii) a rapid rate of arrival; iii) inadequate absorption or response capacity in host States, particularly during the emergency; and iv) individual asylum procedures, where they exist, which are unable to deal with the assessment of such large numbers.'[54]

Situations of mass-influx have raised an interesting debate in academia regarding the role that *prima facie* ('at first sight') recognition of refugee status plays for the future of these persons in search of protection. We will explore this issue, although the main international legal instruments, which apply to Sub-Saharan Africa, do not provide standards for refugee recognition on a *prima facie* basis. Thus, such a situation has obliged and continues to oblige African countries to accept the challenge to develop their own procedures under national legislation and state practice to try to deal with mass-influx within their borders. The aim is to assess the existent conditions in the country of origin and to determine whether individuals who are part of the influx are entitled to refugee status or not. This is not a simple task, and often drives the host country authorities to a 'trade-off': being too magnanimous would run the risk of also sheltering individuals

53 Rutinwa, B., 'Temporary protection and its expression under the "reformulation of refugee law" model', op. cit. note 51, pp. 88–9.

54 ExCom, conclusion No. 100 (LV), 'International cooperation and burden and responsibility sharing in mass-influx situations', 2004, paragraph a). With regard to the question of borders we would like to remind the reader that: '[M]any borders in Africa were drawn with European interests rather than indigenous settlement patterns, class relations, or pre-colonial politics in mind. Conflict over the Kenyan-Somali border, in particular, can be traced back to colonial occupation at the turn of the [twentieth] century, when Britain exerted control over the semiarid region now known as the Northeast Province of Kenya.' See Hyndman, J., *Managing Displacement: Refugees and the Politics of Humanitarianism*, Minneapolis, MN: University of Minnesota Press, note iii, p. 44.

who do not deserve the status of refugees; while being quite strict, would mean excluding individuals who, in contrast, would deserve this protection. However, host countries sometimes also face other kinds of situations such as the existence of 'organized individualized groups' of asylum-seekers who arrive completely unnoticed. One example of this was the April 2005 entry of Sudanese asylum-seekers into Ghana, whose presence was not noted at any Ghanaian borders until the Sudanese went to declare themselves at a police station in order to legalize their stay.[55] At that point, it was clearly already too late for the Ghanaian authorities to make an effective screening of the Sudanese asylum-seekers, considering that these latter had had enough time to appear together in front of the Ghanaian authorities as genuine individuals fleeing persecution. Therefore, border control often constitutes a limit in terms of putting a correct policy into practice for keeping track of the massive flows of disadvantaged people.

This ulterior challenge evidently bears upon the shoulders of the African countries and international actors, which should set up a viable solution that would be a fair compromise between the two above-mentioned tendencies. It is not easy but it is feasible, above all if the mechanisms of RSD would be strengthened, for instance, in order to better operate the screening to distinguish between civilians and former combatants. We are, however, aware of how difficult it sometimes can be to train the field personnel responsible for carrying out such a procedure. Moreover, an agreement between African countries on more detailed standards than the ones provided by the UNHCR regarding what can be considered a real 'mass-influx' would be quite a challenging but necessary endeavour, filling the gaps in the vague definition provided by the UN agency.

In this section, we will also deal with another previously mentioned and distinctive aspect of refugee and asylum-seeker protection in Sub-Saharan Africa, which is also linked with mass-influx: the call by the African legislator to share the burden caused by the mass-influx of people fleeing persecution which is consecrated in Article II4 of the 1969 OAU Convention. However, in Sub-Saharan Africa we generally observe a hugely disproportionate number of countries calling for burden-sharing, generally almost all destination countries on the continent, while the number of the countries which declare themselves available to alleviate the plight of the other African states afflicted by the flow of people in search of protection, are only a minority of the continent. In this regard, the international organizations' – such as the UN – call for burden-sharing has not yet brought about the outcome they had hoped for at this juncture.[56] In effect, as we will see,

55 Mansa Sosuh, M., 'Border security in Ghana: challenges and prospects', KAIPTC occasional paper No. 32, March 2011, p. 17.

56 See, for instance, UNGA, Assistance to refugees, returnees and displaced persons in Africa, 21 December 2010, No. A/RES/65/193, paragraph 16: '[The UNGA] also affirms that respect by states for their protection responsibilities towards refugees is strengthened by international solidarity involving all members of the international community and that the *refugee protection regime is enhanced through committed international cooperation in a spirit of solidarity and burden – and responsibility – sharing among all states.*' Emphasis added.

the lack of the application of significant burden-sharing, coupled with the rising xenophobia – such as the one that gave rise to numerous attacks in several townships in South Africa in 2015[57] – is at the foundation of an increase in restrictive policies by many African states, and this undoubtedly represents a limit to the application of measures in favour of people fleeing persecution in this area of the world. Also in this case, the contribution brought by African protection hides in itself a challenge: to persuade African governments to implement a norm which they have accepted through their adoption of a convention.

Another issue that we will study in this part of the book is constituted by the problem posed by the presence of camps (Chapter 4), of which the largest and most famous – Dadaab, in north-eastern Kenya – a couple of years ago turned 20 years old. This particular camp hosts 10,000 third-generation refugees born there and has a population of approximately 450,000 refugees – mostly Somalis – while it was originally conceived to shelter no more than 90,000 persons.[58] As a consequence, the huge number of refugees in that camp has also created tensions between them and the locals.[59]

This chapter will present the many-sided aspects of the protection of the asylum-seekers/refugees in camps where we observe a melding of refugee and humanitarian law – inevitable in the Sub-Saharan African context for several reasons. The most important of these reasons is the fact that armed conflicts constitute the major factor which has compelled individuals to flee across the region over the last 50 years. In this case:

> As long as they do not actively participate in the hostilities, refugees are protected as civilians by international humanitarian law. They enjoy a general protection against the dangers of war and must be humanely treated at all times.[60]

Moreover, both the Office of the United Nations High Commissioner for Refugees (UNHCR) and the International Committee of the Red Cross (ICRC) address the protection of 'unprotected' people, serving as 'custodians' of the international

57 See, for instance, SABC, 'Zuma promises to curb xenophobic attacks', 6 February 2015, available at: www.sabc.co.za/news/a/42e9b70047358716baacbe686e648436/Zuma-promises-to-curb-xenophobic-attacks-20150602, accessed 15 February 2015; SABC, 'The human cost of xenophobia', 29 January 2015, available at: www.sabc.co.za/news/a/15f91300471c61da8c85ac686e648436/The-Human-Cost-of-Xenophobia-20152901, accessed 15 February 2015.

58 See UNHCR, 'Dadaab: World's biggest refugee camp 20 years old', 21 February 2012, available at: www.unhcr.org/4f439dbb9.html, accessed 10 October 2014. The same news is also available at: http://reliefweb.int/node/478075, accessed 10 October 2014. In the early 2000s Somalia was simply considered: 'The most dangerous country in the world.' See Webber, F., *Borderline Justice: The Fight for Refugee and Migrant Rights*, London: Pluto Press, 2012, p. 166.

59 IRIN, 'Kenya: Dadaab – locals v refugees', 2 September 2011, available at: www.refworld.org/docid/4e65ba032.html, accessed 1 February 2015.

60 Jacques, M., *Armed Conflict and Displacement: The Protection of Refugees and Displaced Persons under International Humanitarian Law*, Cambridge: Cambridge University Press, 2012, pp. 158–9. In the words of S.S. Juss: 'A situation of armed conflict or endemic violence almost always involves

refugee law and international humanitarian law respectively. These two organizations often face analogous limitations and difficulties in their work, and act on the basis of parallel codes of conduct.[61] For instance, both organizations seek to endorse policies respecting the equal dignity of asylum-seekers and refugees in comparison with other nationals, at the same time recognizing that relief plays a very important role in the protection of 'vulnerable individuals', such as, for instance, children, women or elderly people.[62] In addition, the humanitarian agencies should also keep in mind not to build camps too close to the place of origin of refugees fleeing violence. That said, different circumstances do not always allow for the building of camps far from dangerous zones, as the example of the camp in Yida, South Sudan and hosting Sudanese refugees, sadly shows.[63]

On a similar note, our analysis in Chapter 5, will scrutinize the expanding and evolving role of the UNHCR on the African continent. It will be very important to assess the challenges that it has faced until the dawn of this twenty-first century

unpredictability, ambiguity and conjecture, on how it is truly to be analyzed and then classified, precisely because it is so capricious, indeterminate and inconclusive, making any decision on it a most imprecise art. Moreover, one thing that all large-scale and small-scale exoduses of people have in common, in an era of the massification of influx from countries in a state of armed conflict or endemic violence, is the inescapable fact of random violence and moving frontlines, all of which make any assessment of present and future risk complex and baffling.' See Juss, S.S., 'Problematizing the protection of 'war refugees': a rejoinder to Hugo Storey and Jean-François Durieux', in *Refugee Survey Quarterly*, vol. 32, 2013, p. 146.

61 Jaquemet, S., 'The cross-fertilization of international humanitarian law and international refugee law', in *International Review of the Red Cross*, vol. 83, 2001, p. 672. For the role played by ICRC in helping refugees, see, for instance, Krill, F., 'ICRC action in aid of refugees', in *International Review of the Red Cross*, vol. 28, 1988, pp. 328–50.

62 Forsythe, D.P., 'Humanitarian protection: the International Committee of the Red Cross and the United Nations High Commissioner for Refugees', in *International Review of the Red Cross*, vol. 83, 2001, p. 682.

63 See the news: 'UNHCR chief visits South Sudan to spotlight "forgotten refugee crisis"', 23 November 2012: '[T]he High Commissioner was particularly concerned about the welfare of the 60,000 civilians living in Yida and he urged the refugees there to move to sites deeper inside South Sudan and located in a safer, healthier and easier to access environment. "This is the most threatening situation I have ever seen in a refugee camp. Not only because it is close to a war zone, but because of access – all things have to be brought in by plane", he said during his visit. Yida is located in wetland in South Sudan's Unity state just 12 kilometers from the border. "The proximity of refugees in Yida to a volatile conflict zone raises grave concerns about the security of refugees", said UNHCR Representative in South Sudan Mireille Girard, echoing the concerns of Guterres. "This is the most dangerous refugee site in South Sudan."' Document available at: www.unhcr.org/50af7a789.html, accessed 25 November 2014. In this regard, see also the previous news: 'UNHCR takes preparatory steps to relocate refugees from South Sudan's Yida settlement'; 2 November 2012: 'Yida's close proximity to the border has made it a high risk protection environment for refugees, with the recurrent presence of armed personnel in and around the settlement. "Right now, the safety of the refugees and the civilian character of the settlement cannot be guaranteed. We report incidents of armed elements being seen to the South Sudan authorities", Edwards said [UNHCR spokesman Adrian Edwards]. Safety of refugees is always a concern to UNHCR, but what makes the situation in Yida particularly worrying is that nearly 70 per cent of refugees there are below the age of 18 years.' Document available at: www.unhcr.org/5093a3126.html, accessed 5 November 2014.

in order to understand how this UN agency could move forward in its protection of peoples of concern in the region. One of the most typical characteristics of the work of the UNHCR in Sub-Saharan Africa remains its action in undertaking the applicants' RSD, often in shortage of really effective mechanisms put into place by local authorities in those countries. The UNHCR has derogated from its initial mandate in the region, not only by starting to take care also of the IDPs but, in addition, its action in favour of refugees has begun not to be limited to protection but, for instance, also often helping to reintegrate returnees within their home countries. This last task was previously and traditionally entrusted to the administration of the countries receiving back their own citizens. Furthermore, it is also true that in several humanitarian crises affecting the Sub-Sahara in the past decades, the UNHCR has often found itself at a crossroads.

If this agency has the idea to close a camp, it will undoubtedly fail to comply with its duty to assist and protect needy people. That is why the UNHCR is continuously studying alternatives to camps that should be viable and profitable, allowing refugees to have sustainable occupations and to achieve an economic independence.[64]

On the other hand, keeping the camps open often runs the risk of giving assistance to individuals who have violated human rights, and doing so compromises the non-combatants' protection, the major objective of the camps. Aside from this dilemma, the agency's decision cannot be judged *a posteriori* because at the time it was well intentioned.[65] Maintaining the civilian and humanitarian character of a refugee camp – particularly when armed elements migrate alongside refugees – remains a big challenge for the UNHCR,[66] one illustrated by the Tabarebarey camp in Niger hosting in 2012 more than 11,000 people fleeing from Mali.[67]

Another particular aspect of refugee protection in Sub-Saharan Africa that we will take into consideration is the ban of refugees' involvement in subversive activities (Chapter 6).[68] This ban is, however, often more hypothetical than real, considering that in Sub-Saharan Africa refugees can be potentially used – as they have been – by host countries as a means to subvert the governments in power

64 UNHCR, Alternatives to Camps, 2014, pp. 9–11.

65 Weiner, M., 'The clashes of norms: dilemmas in refugee policies', in *Journal of Refugee Studies*, vol. 11, 1998, p. 437.

66 Opaye, C., 'Refugee camp security in West Africa: an ECOWAS priority?', KAIPTIC occasional paper No. 11, 2005, p. 3.

67 See UNHCR, 'UNHCR and IOM start moving Malian refugees to new camp in Niger', 1 June 2012, available at: www.unhcr.org/4fc8dfa26.html, accessed 10 October 2014.

68 In this regard, C. Beyani affirmed that: '[T]he term "subversive activities" has a wider general criminal law content aimed at prohibiting the commission of hostile acts from the territory of a state against other states in a way which endangers peaceful relations between states. The prohibition applies in particular to attempts to disturb the internal political order or security of a foreign state by slander, malicious propaganda, or violence.' See Beyani, C., 'International legal criteria for the separation of members of armed forces, armed bands, and militia from refugees in the territories of host states', in *International Journal of Refugee Law*, vol. 12, 2000, p. 259.

in their country of origin.[69] The interdiction of the subversive activities, one of the most typical aspects of African 'refugeeism',[70] was consecrated in Article III of the 1969 OAU Convention, a commendable contribution accomplished by the African legislator to regulate this phenomenon through its translation into legal norms. It is clear that, also in this case, African organs are confronted with a difficult challenge because local authorities must be convinced not to use asylum-seekers and refugees as political instruments to run their international relations. In this sense, the Ugandan government was widely lauded by other African countries when, in 2006, it expelled eight refugees and asylum-seekers from the DRC, on the accusation of having practised 'subversive activities' (without any further explanation) against their home country in violation of the 1969 African Convention. They were not returned, however, to the DRC where they may have run the risk of being executed.[71] Additionally, section 22 of the 2002 Tanzanian Prevention of Terrorism Act exemplifies legislative practice intended to prevent the territory of a state from being used as a sanctuary to launch 'attacks' against other states; this section is addressed to 'any person', an expression which evidently includes refugees.[72]

Finally, this part of the work concludes with an analysis of a situation that is working against refugees: individual and mass expulsion (Chapter 7), a situation which, while not exclusively practised in Sub-Saharan Africa, remains all too frequent there. Expulsion has occurred several times in the past – and has always been condemned by the international organizations if it has been carried out unlawfully,[73] sometimes due to questionable decisions made by governments'

69 For a first approach on this issue see, for instance, Stedman, S.J. and Tanner, F., 'Refugees as resources in war', in Stedman, S.J. and Tanner, F. (eds), *Refugee Manipulation: War, Politics and the Abuse of Human Suffering*, Washington DC: Brookings Institution Press, 2003, p. 14: 'It is essential [. . .] to recognize the limits of legalistic approaches to the problem of refugee manipulation and to accept the need for political decisions that restrain those who seek to undermine the humanitarian nature of the refugee regime. [. . .] [S]ome within UNHCR and the refugee assistance committee are reluctant to adopt political solutions that label warring parties and states as offenders of the regime for fear of tarnishing their reputation for neutrality and impartiality.'

70 Among other authors, this word – a sort of 'neologism'– has been used by R.M. Anand in Chapter 4 of his work, entitled: 'Alternatives to Refugeeism'. See Anand, R.M., *African Refugees: An Overview*, New Delhi: Khama, 1993, pp. 53–87. See also Kuruk, P., 'Refugeeism: a dilemma in international human rights: problems in the legal protection of refugees in West Africa', in *Temple International and Comparative Law Journal*, vol. 1, 1987. This term is an alternative to the other term, commonly used, of 'refugehood' to define the entire set of refugee issues.

71 United States Committee for Refugees and Immigrants, US Committee for Refugees and Immigrants World Refugee Survey 2007 – Uganda, 11 July 2007, available at: www.unhcr.org/refworld/docid/4696388e1e.html, accessed 10 October 2014.

72 Tanzania, The Prevention of Terrorism Act, 2002, section 22: '*Every person* who, in the United Republic a) knowingly promotes or facilitates the doing of any act in a facilitation foreign state for the purpose of achieving any of the following objectives, whether or not the objective is achieved [. . .] commits of an offence and shall on conviction, be liable to imprisonment for a period of term not less than twenty years and not more than thirty years.' Emphasis added.

73 See, for instance, UNGA, Assistance to refugees, returnees and displaced persons in Africa, 19 December 2011, No. A/RES/66/135, paragraph 18: '[The UNGA] condemns all acts that pose

actors. Governments often take advantage of a sometimes unclear interpretation provided by the two concepts of 'national security' and 'public order', along with 'terrorism' which could be subsumed under both notions but particularly the first one.[74] These are the two non-cumulative[75] grounds in which Article 32 of the 1951 Geneva Convention permits the expulsion of a refugee lawfully present in the territory of an African country party to the convention. In contrast, the 1969 OAU Convention is less detailed on this feature, limiting itself to forbid expulsion of a 'person'; and therefore, it seems to explicitly include an asylum-seeker in the provision, enlarging its protection beyond 'refugees'. It is forbidden to expel this 'person' to a country 'where his/her life, physical integrity or liberty would be threatened for the reasons set out in article I, paragraphs 1 and 2 [of the same Convention].'[76] In this regard, in the above-mentioned example, Ugandan authorities also respected the provision contained in this article, considering that they refrained from returning the expelled asylum-seekers to the DRC. However, it is clear that expulsion should remain an exception and not the rule, considered acceptable on limited grounds.[77]

Part II of this book will focus on the durable solutions allowed for the refugees in the region, with a particular spotlight on the question of 'voluntary repatriation' (Chapter 8), which represents another specific feature of refugee protection in the region. This can be attested by the fact that the 1969 OAU Convention, in its Article 5, was the first legal instrument to explicitly provide for this possibility as the preferred solution invoked by African states to terminate the refugee status of both individuals and groups of persons. In this section, we will underline several characteristics specific to voluntary repatriation in Sub-Saharan Africa as undertaken with the UNHCR, in which a timeline for return has been often created, ensuring the constant protection of the refugee, commencing with individual voluntary repatriation, and concluding with the cessation of refugee status.[78] Many challenges arise from this solution in Sub-Saharan Africa, such as the reintegration of returnees, which probably represents the most difficult one. Several initiatives have been adopted towards this aim, for instance the adoption of micro-finance schemes to allow returnees to become self-reliant[79] after receiving the initial aid provided by both governmental organizations and NGOs, which

a threat to the personal security and well-being of refugees and asylum-seekers, such as *refoulement*, unlawful expulsion and physical attacks [. . .].'

74 UNGA, General Assembly, Third report on the expulsion of aliens, International Law Commission, 19 April 2007, document No. A/CN.4/581, paragraph 76, p. 26.

75 Ibid., paragraph 64, p. 23.

76 Article II3 of the 1969 OAU Convention.

77 UNGA, General Assembly, Third report on the expulsion of aliens, International Law Commission, 19 April 2007, document No. A/CN.4/581, paragraph 68, p. 24.

78 Cwik, M.E., 'Forced to flee and forced to repatriate? How the cessation clause of article 1C(5) and (6) of the 1951 Refugee Convention operates in international law and practice', in *Vanderbilt Journal of Transnational Law*, vol. 44, 2011, p. 742.

79 Ramcharan, R., 'The African refugee crisis: contemporary challenges to the protection of refugees and displaced persons in Africa', in *African Yearbook of International Law*, vol. 8, 2000, p. 138.

also requires the integrity of the returnees' reintegration programmes to be verified.[80]

We will also inquire whether repatriation in Sub-Saharan Africa is genuinely 'voluntary' in most cases, and whether this represents the best solution for the present well-being as well as for the future well-being of the refugees. To both of these questions the response will be mostly negative, considering that in many circumstances, African refugees did not wish to repatriate, albeit that they had the possibility to do so. Sometimes, however, refugees in this situation have also rejected local integration in the first country of asylum, preferring resettlement in a third country in North America or Europe, as also happened, for instance, with the Liberian refugees in Ghana.[81] Incidentally, we are doubtful about the effort made by international and regional organizations to convince refugees to repatriate. Repatriation is 'not for everyone',[82] and considering that our research is more human-oriented than state-oriented, we do not find it to be worth the organizations' efforts to find solutions which are, in several cases, not deemed acceptable by the asylum-seekers and refugees themselves.

In this Part II, we will finally focus on the other two typical 'durable solutions' indicated for refugees: their local integration – seen above all as a 'legal process'[83] – in the first country of asylum, and their resettlement in a third country either

80 Gorman, R.F., 'Private voluntary organizations in refugee relief', in Ferris, E.G. (ed.), *Refugee and World Politics*, New York/Philadelphia: Praeger, 1985, p. 94.

81 In this regard, see, for instance, Johnson, A.E., 'When refugees don't go home: the situation of Liberian refugees in Ghana', in *Journal of Immigrant and Refugee Studies*, vol. 9, 2011, pp. 105–26. However, in the same regard, see also UNHCR, 'UNHCR completes repatriation of 155,000 Liberians', 4 January 2013, available at: www.unhcr.org/50e6af089.html, accessed 10 January 2015: 'The UN refugee agency has completed its successful repatriation of more than 155,000 Liberians, 23 years after the start of the civil war in their homeland that made them into refugees. [. . .] The LRRRC is assisting returnees by referring them to job opportunities, providing scholarships, collaborating with government ministries to absorb returnees with specific skills, and assisting each refugee family to acquire a plot of land for building. [. . .] UNHCR and LRRRC officials say Liberian refugees who decided to locally integrate in countries of asylum are being provided legal and social assistance, such as income-generating activities for self-reliance and the issuance of Liberian passports in collaboration with Liberia's Ministry of Foreign Affairs.' In this regard, S.J. Nawyn has recently pointed out that: '[R]esettlement is the transfer of refugees from the country in which they have first sought asylum [. . .] to another country for permanent settlement. [. . .] Asylum-seekers differ from refugees in that they arrive in a country of (potentially) permanent settlement and then request asylum, which is different from refugees who request permanent settlement before arriving in the resettlement country. However, both groups may flee their home country for similar reasons, and asylum-seekers who are granted asylum are generally given the same rights [. . .] as refugees.' See Nawyn, S.J., 'Refugee resettlement policies and pathways to integration', in Gold, S.J. and Nawyn, S.J. (eds), *Routledge International Handbook of Migration Studies*, London/New York: Routledge, 2013, p. 107.

82 In this regard, see Omata, N., 'Repatriation is not for everyone: the life and livelihoods of former refugees in Liberia', in UNHCR, *New Issues in Refugee Research*, research paper No. 150, 2007, p. 29.

83 UNHCR, Global Consultations on international protection/third track: local integration, 25 April 2002, document No. EC/GC/02/6.

if the first country of asylum is unable to guarantee them a minimum standard for a decent life, or because of a wish expressed by refugees to be resettled elsewhere (Chapter 9). Although these two solutions are not strictly specific to the African context, it is very interesting to assess the various dynamics allowing African refugees to choose one rather than the other solution. That said, the term 'choice' should not be accompanied by the adjective 'free' in every circumstance, considering that, while local integration generally does not require any formal act by the host state, resettlement in a third country in Sub-Saharan Africa is often imposed upon refugees by states through an agreement between them and not necessarily in agreement with the UNHCR. This UN agency plays a role of mediator between host states with divergent opinions. For instance, at present, many countries in Sub-Saharan Africa are very reluctant to accept local integration of new refugees; and the country of origin is not always available to take back its own citizens. Refugees are frequently inclined to integrate into the country of asylum or else wish to be resettled in another country, preferably in the 'developed world', considering also Sub-Saharan African countries' disinclination to accept becoming 'countries of resettlement'. This happens despite the UNHCR's periodic calls for an increased number of resettlement places, and for greater support for resettled people, on the African continent as well as in the rest of the world.[84] Persuading Sub-Saharan African countries to become more generous with regards to resettlement undoubtedly constitutes another challenge for the continent, although this could not be done without the assurance of a structured plan of integration and material aid provided by organizations and states. And, as we will see, even when there are resettlement plans in Sub-Saharan Africa, they have failed until now because of a shortage of concrete prospects for creating a better life, inducing refugees to refuse them.

Having given a general view of what this study will consist of, we will now proceed, beginning with the analysis of the concept of *non-refoulement* applicable to the 'persecuted man', the fictitious protagonist of this study.

84 See UNHCR, 'UNHCR calls for more resettlement places and better support for resettled refugees', 4 July 2011, available at: www.unhcr.org/4e11ad1d6.html, accessed 10 October 2014. In this regard, as pointed out by M. Piper and others: 'In a regional context, resettlement can help balance the burdens and responsibilities of receiving countries, open dialogue about ways to strengthen refugee protection and reduce the influence of people smuggling and trafficking. It can also contribute to reducing the influence of some of the push-pull factors involved in refugee movements. Resettlement programs have also been demonstrated to benefit the receiving countries in many ways. Those who come, bring with them many skills and attributes that contribute not only to the economy but also to the social and cultural fabric of the country. Furthermore, the support programs put in place for resettling refugees contribute to fostering positive attitudes towards refugees and have flow on effects in terms of supporting asylum seekers.' See Piper, M., Power, P. and Thom, G., 'Refugee resettlement: 2012 and beyond', in UNHCR, *New Issues in Refugee Research*, research paper No. 253, 2013, p. 3.

PART I

The peregrination of a persecuted human being, first stage

Seeking asylum in Sub-Saharan Africa

1 Fleeing persecution and the risk of unjust rejection, return or expulsion

Non-refoulement in Sub-Saharan Africa

1.1 A critical assessment of the legal framework of *non-refoulement*

Non-refoulement is a concept which prohibits countries from returning an asylum-seeker or a refugee to a territory where there is a risk that his/her freedom or even life would be threatened on account of several reasons, such as membership of a particular social group, nationality, political opinion, race and religion.[1] It should be emphasized that *non-refoulement* is not about returning refugees to intermediate countries nor is *non-refoulement* about the failure to provide durable solutions. The central question in *non-refoulement* is about the risk posed to refugees.[2] J. Pirjola noted that from the perspective of an individual seeking protection, the situation is not ideal as one might believe, because the principle of *non-refoulement* would have a paradox. Since no common definition exists, national and international authorities and courts have extensive power of discretion to give content to terms such as 'persecution', 'degrading' or 'cruel treatment'.[3]

The concept of *non-refoulement* is relevant in a number of contexts, mainly, though not exclusively, of a treaty nature. The important role the UNHCR

1 Lauterpacht, E. and Bethlehem, D., 'The scope and content of the principle of *non-refoulement*: opinion', in Feller, E., Türk, V. and Nicholson, F. (eds), *Refugee Protection in International Law: UNHCR's Global Consultations on International Protection*, Cambridge/New York/Geneva: Cambridge University Press & UNHCR, 2003, p. 89.

2 Goodwin-Gill, G., '*Non-refoulement* and the new asylum seekers', in *Virginia Journal of International Law*, vol. 26, 1985–1986, pp. 897–918. See also Goodwin-Gill, G., '*Non-refoulement* and the new asylum seekers', in Martin, D. (ed.), *The New Asylum Seekers: Refugee Law in the 1980s*, Dordrecht/Boston/London: Martinus Nijhoff, 1988, pp. 103–4.

3 Pirjola, J., 'Shadows in Paradise: exploring *non-refoulement* as an open concept', in *International Journal of Refugee Law*, vol. 19, 2007, pp. 639–40. In this regard, as H. Storey noted about the concept of 'persecution': '[W]e should set about the work of refining a systematic definition of the term persecution that builds on the remarkable progress that has been made in the past sixty years towards giving it content.' See Storey, H., 'What constitutes persecution? Towards a working definition', in *International Journal of Refugee Law*, vol. 26, 2014, p. 285.

played in its evolution is also worth mentioning.[4] Refugee protection's best-known expression is in Article 33 of the 1951 Geneva Convention.[5] Yet it also appears in various forms in a number of later instruments which are applicable to Sub-Saharan Africa: Article 3 of the 1967 DTA (Declaration on Territorial Asylum), Article II3 of the 1969 OAU Convention,[6] and Article 3 1) of the 2001 AALCO Principles on status and treatment of refugees.[7]

4 Lewis, C. 'UNHCR's contribution to the development of international refugee law: its foundations and evolution', in *International Journal of Refugee Law*, vol. 17, 2005, pp. 86–8: 'UNHCR's work relating to *non-refoulement* occurs in several domains. From a practical standpoint, UNHCR voices to states' representatives [. . .] its objections to occurrences of *refoulement* and has expressed its general objections and concern in numerous Annual Reports submitted to General Assembly. [. . .] UNHCR has been instrumental in ensuring that a provision on *non-refoulement* is included in a General Assembly resolution annual basis. [. . .] Although General Assembly resolutions are not binding from a legal standpoint, they may be pronouncements of customary law principles, may help to influence state practice, and may serve as evidence of *opinio juris*. Additionally, from a political standpoint they raise expectations that states will act in conformity with the principle.'

5 Article 33 (prohibition of expulsion or return ('*refoulement*')) of the 1951 Geneva Convention reads: '1) No Contracting State shall expel or return ("*refouler*") a refugee in any manner whatsoever to the frontiers of territories where his/her life or freedom would be threatened on account of his/her race, religion, nationality, membership of a particular social group or political opinion. 2) The benefit of the present provision may not, however, be claimed by a refugee whom there are reasonable grounds for regarding as a danger to the security of the country in which he/she is, or who, having been convicted by a final judgment of a particularly serious crime, constitutes a danger to the community of that country.' In this regard, we note that at the time when the 1951 Geneva Convention was drafted, the principle of *non-refoulement* was quite new in itself, and there was uncertainty about the precise territorial reach of the obligation. The drafters left the language of the article vague probably in order to reach some agreement on the treatment of refugees. In this regard, see Newmark, R.L., '*Non-Refoulement* run afoul: the questionable legality of extraterritorial repatriation programs', in *Washington University Law Quarterly*, vol. 71, 1993, p. 835. The author, at p. 861, explained: 'Article 33 inescapably provides that *non-refoulement* applies to contracting states extraterritorially.' Referring to Article 33, J.C. Hathaway and C.J. Harvey identified two main tests that are applicable in assessing whether the asylum-seeker or refugee is a danger to the national security of the asylum state. The first test requires a high level of proof for the determination that the individual is a danger to the security of the asylum state, in that there must be 'reasonable grounds' for this conclusion. The asylum state must demonstrate that the refugee's continued presence in the state constitutes a threat to the security of the state. Second, the refugee may be excluded if 'having been convicted by a final judgment of a particular serious crime', he/she constitutes a danger to the community in the asylum state. In the 'Preparatory works' of the 1951 Geneva Convention, the drafters underlined that only serious crime, 'for example, rape, homicide, armed robbery, and arson' are considered as leading to exemptions in *non-refoulement* protection. See Hathaway, J.C. and Harvey, C.J., 'Framing refugee protection in the new world disorder', in *Cornell International Law Journal*, vol. 34, 2001, pp. 290–2. Further, in this same article: '[T]he Refugee's Convention peremptory exclusion rules and its limitations on the duty of *non-refoulement* embrace the notion of "deserving" and "undeserving" persons. Those found undeserving, even though at risk of serious harm, are not granted refugee status.' See ibid., p. 314.

6 Article II3 of the 1969 OAU Convention reads: 'No person shall be subjected by a Member State to measures such as rejection at the frontier, return or expulsion, which would compel him to return to or remain in a territory where his life, physical integrity or liberty would be threatened for the reasons set out in Article I, paragraphs 1 and 2.'

7 Article 3 1) of the 2001 Revised AALCO 1966 Bangkok Principles on status and treatment of refugees reads: 'No one seeking asylum in accordance with these Principles shall be subjected

Two questions are particularly relevant for the study at hand: whether Article 33 applies extra-territorially and whether 'indirect *refoulement*'[8] is prohibited under the 1951 Refugee Convention. As far as its geographical scope is concerned, the wording of Article 33 of the 1951 Geneva Convention makes it clear that return is forbidden to any territory where a risk exists regardless of whether that territory is the country of origin or another state. In addition, whether Article 33 excludes both 'direct' and 'indirect' *refoulement* is not controversial. This may be directly deduced from the wording of Article 33, which explains that *refoulement* includes return of any kind whatsoever to a territory where the life or liberty of the refugee is in danger. The probability of 'indirect' *refoulement* is obviously higher in the case of removal to a country that is not party to the 1951 Refugee Convention such as, for instance, Eritrea.[9] But we have also seen cases in which the country 'protagonist' of the removal was part of the 1951 Geneva Convention, such as the case of Guinea in 2004.[10]

J.C. Hathaway argued that the ban of *refoulement* allows states to give at least temporary protection to persons fleeing their countries, while proper determination of their refugee status is pending.[11] In effect, Article II3 of the 1969 OAU

to measures such as rejection at the frontier, return or expulsion which would result in his life or freedom being threatened on account of his race, religion, nationality, ethnic origin, membership of a particular social group or political opinion. The provision as outlined above may not however be claimed by a person when there are reasonable grounds to believe the person's presence is a danger to the national security or public order of the country in which he is, or who, having been convicted by a final judgment of a particularly serious crime, constitutes a danger to the community of that country.'

8 For an indication of 'indirect' *refoulement* see, for instance, UNGA, Executive Committee of the High Commissioner's Programme, 49th session, Note on international protection, document No. A/AC.96/898, 3 July 1998, p. 4, paragraph 14: 'In some cases, the *refoulement* was indirect, for example, the asylum-seeker was removed to a third country from where that person was further removed to his or her country of origin, and was the unfortunate result of the inappropriate application of the so-called "safe third country" notion.'

9 Hurwitz, A., *The Collective Responsibility of States to Protect Refugees*, Oxford: Oxford University Press, 2009, pp. 176–81.

10 ACHPR, *African Institute for Human Rights and Development (on behalf of Sierra Leonean refugees in Guinea) v Republic of Guinea*, Communication No. 249/02, 2004, paragraphs 72–4: 72. '72) As such, the Government of Guinea is entitled to prosecute persons that they believe pose a security threat to the State. However, the massive violations of the human rights of refugees as are outlined in this communication constitute a flagrant violation of the provisions of the African Charter. 73) Although the African Commission was not provided with a transcript of the speech of the President, submissions before the Commission led it to believe that the evidence and testimonies of eye witnesses reveal that these events took place immediately after the speech of the President of the Republic of Guinea on 9 September 2000. 74) The African Commission finds that the situation prevailing in Guinea during the period under consideration led to certain human rights violations.'

11 In this regard, J.C. Hathaway contended: '[R]efugees are to be afforded protection against *refoulement*. States are required only to avoid returning refugees to an ongoing risk of persecution. If and when the risk of serious harm ends, so too does refugee status. In this sense, refugee law is clearly based upon a theory of temporary protection.' See Hathaway, J.C., 'Can international refugee law be made relevant again?', in Hathaway J.C. (ed.), *Reconceiving International Refugee Law*,

Convention has broadened the scope of the principle of *non-refoulement* in international law because under Article 33 1) of the 1951 Geneva Convention, it is only those who are already within the country of refuge's territory that can benefit from this proviso.[12] The 1969 OAU Convention, on the other hand, extends the protection also to persons waiting at the border,[13] although state practice since 1951 seems not to strongly distinguish this difference.[14]

The Hague/Boston/London: Martinus Nijhoff, 1997, p. xviii. But, on the contrary, there is also a suggestion that the principle of *non-refoulement* can be limited if the individual acts contrary to the principles of the 1969 African Convention. See Murray, R., *Human Rights in Africa: from the OAU to the African Union*, Cambridge: Cambridge University Press, 2004, p. 189. In this regard, the author quoted Article 1 4) g) of the 1951 Geneva Convention that reads: '[This Convention shall cease to apply to any refugee if]: g) he/she has seriously infringed the purposes and objectives of this Convention.'

12 This concept has been strongly reaffirmed by Aga Khan, S., in 'Legal problems relating to refugees and displaced persons', in *Collected Courses of The Hague Academy of International Law*, vol. 149, 1976 (I), p. 318. In this regard, P. Hyndman clearly stated: 'article 33 contains no reference to an obligation not to reject at the frontier.' See Hyndman, P., 'An appraisal of the development of the protection afforded to refugees under international law', in *Lawasia*, vol. 1, 1981, p. 262. Further, in the same work: 'If *non-refoulement* does not include non-rejection at the frontier, rejection would be legally possible when the border is manned, but return would not be possible if the border, not being manned, had already been crossed.' See ibid., p. 269. However, the author, one year later affirmed: 'Thus, common sense at least would seem to be on the side of the inclusion of non-rejection within the concept of *non-refoulement*.' See Hyndman, P., 'Asylum and *non-refoulement*: are these obligations owed to refugees under international law?', in *Philippine Law Journal*, vol. 57, 1982, p. 51.

13 Okogbule, N., 'The legal dimension of refugee problem in Africa', in *East African Journal of Peace and Human Rights*, vol. 10, 2004, pp. 183–4; Newmark, R.L., op. cit. note 56, p. 844. Article II3 of the 1969 OAU Convention reads: '3) No person shall be subjected by a Member State to *measures such as rejection at the frontier*, return or expulsion, which would compel him/her to return to or remain in a territory where his/her life, physical integrity or liberty would be threatened for the reasons set out in Article I, paragraphs 1 and 2.' Emphasis added. And, in this regard, P. Kourula affirmed: 'Its [of the principle of *non-refoulement* contained in the 1951 Geneva Convention] application has also gradually been considered to cover such measures as rejection at the frontiers.' See Kourula, P., *Broadening the Edges: Refugee Definitions and International Protection Revisited*, The Hague/Boston/London: Martinus Nijhoff, 1997, p. 275. In addition, J.C. Hathaway had no doubts that: '[S]ince *non-refoulement* as defined in article 33 [of the 1951 Geneva Convention] *has always included both ejection from a state and non-admission at the frontier*.' Emphasis added. See Hathaway, J.C., *The Rights of Refugees Under International Law*, Cambridge: Cambridge University Press, 2005, p. 363.

14 Goodwin-Gill, G. and McAdam J., *The Refugee in International Law*, 3rd edition, Oxford: Oxford University Press, 2007, p. 208: '[b]y and large, States in their practice and in their recorded views, have recognized that *non-refoulement* applies to the moment at which asylum-seekers present themselves for entry, either within a State or at its border.' In this regard, see also Chetail, V., 'Are refugee rights human rights? An unorthodox questioning of the relations between refugee law and human rights law', 'Are refugee rights human rights? An unorthodox questioning of the relations between refugee law and human rights law' (September 17, 2012), in Rubio-Marin, R. (ed.), *Human Rights and Immigration, Collected Courses of the Academy of European Law*, Oxford: Oxford University Press, 2014, p. 13: '[T]he principle of *non-refoulement* covers equally both asylum-seekers and recognized refugees, provided that they are under the jurisdiction of a state party. Contrary to many other provisions of the Geneva Convention, article 33 is not dependent on the presence – whether lawful or unlawful – of asylum-seekers within the territory of a state party. It thus applies whether they enter the territory legally or illegally.'

In addition, W.J.E.M. Van Hövell noted that in the 1969 OAU Convention, *non-refoulement* applies to 'persons', while in the 1951 Convention the same principle applies exclusively to 'refugees'.[15] In the 1951 Geneva Convention, however, the principle of *non-refoulement* similarly applies to asylum-seekers, at least initially and in apposite conditions for where no protection will otherwise be provided.[16] Nevertheless, after such initial period or if these apposite conditions fail to be fulfilled, the 1969 African Convention protects a wider category of individuals from *refoulement* than the 1951 Geneva Convention.[17]

Furthermore, a refugee *refouled* back to a place where his/her life and/or freedom is threatened, because no other state will grant him/her refuge, should be entitled to 1951 Geneva Convention Article 31's protection,[18] even if his/her home-country does not border the place of refuge. Protection definitely should not depend on the proximity of the place of origin to the place of *refoulement.* However, and this undoubtedly represents a breach for the complete protection of refugees, P. Kuruk noted that under a literal reading of Article 33 of the 1951 Geneva Convention, as long as the rejecting state does not take the refugee back to the border of the prohibited place, it has not violated the terms of the convention occasioning serious injustice.[19]

The principle of *non-refoulement* is also applied as a component part of the prohibition of torture or cruel, inhuman or degrading treatment or punishment, as it is clearly stated in Article 3 of the 1984 CAT (Convention Against Torture).[20]

15 Van Hövell tot Westerflier, W.J.E.M., 'Africa and refugees: the OAU Refugee Convention in theory and practice', in *Netherlands Quarterly of Human Rights*, vol. 7, 1989, p. 176.

16 Goodwin-Gill, G. and McAdam J., op. cit. note 14, p. 232.

17 Boubakri, A., Lenaola, I. and Sharpe, M., 'A report on the African asylum systems', 2011, p. 4, pdf document, available at: www.iarlj.org/general/images/stories/BLED_conference/papers/WP_African_asylum_systems_-_A_Boubakri.pdf, accessed 10 April 2014.

18 Article 31 ('Refugees unlawfully in the country of refuge') reads as follows: '1) The Contracting States shall not impose penalties, on account of their illegal entry or presence, on refugees who, coming directly from a territory where their life or freedom was threatened in the sense of article 1, enter or are present in their territory without authorization, provided they present themselves without delay to the authorities and show good cause for their illegal entry or presence. 2) The Contracting States shall not apply to the movements of such refugees restrictions other than those which are necessary and such restrictions shall only be applied until their status in the country is regularized or they obtain admission into another country. The Contracting States shall allow such refugees a reasonable period and all the necessary facilities to obtain admission into another country.'

19 Kuruk, P., 'Asylum and the *non-refoulement* of refugees: the case of the missing shipload of Liberian refugees', in *Stanford Journal of International Law*, vol. 35, 1999, p. 328. See also Hathaway, J.C., 'Can international refugee law be made relevant again?', op. cit. note 11. At p. xviii the author explained that: 'States are required only to avoid returning refugees to an ongoing risk of persecution.'

20 Article 3 of the 1984 CAT reads: '1) No State Party shall expel, return ("*refouler*") or extradite a person to another State where there are substantial grounds for believing that he would be in danger of being subjected to torture. 2) For the purpose of determining whether there are such grounds, the competent authorities shall take into account all relevant considerations including, where applicable, the existence in the State concerned of a consistent pattern of gross, flagrant or mass violations of human rights.' See Convention against Torture and other Cruel, Inhuman

It is clear that, under this article, nationals of many Sub-Saharan African countries should not be *refouled* back in case they apply for asylum. In detail, in 2013, the Committee against Torture expressed its deep concern for the current situation in Gabon,[21] Senegal,[22] Togo,[23] Kenya[24] and Mauritania.[25]

Likewise, Article 7 of the 1966 ICCPR[26] provides that '[n]o one shall be subjected to torture or to cruel, inhuman or degrading treatment or punishment.' This obligation has been read by the Human Rights Council (HRC), in its General Comment No. 20 to include a *non-refoulement* component.[27]

As of 10 October 2014, with reference to the 1951 Geneva Convention, the 1969 OAU Convention, the 1984 CAT and the 1966 ICCPR, all the Sub-Saharan African countries are part of at least one of these legally binding instruments providing for the prohibition of *non-refoulement*.

However, one of the major differences between refugee instruments and human rights instruments is that the implementation and the application of relevant human rights instruments, such as the 1966 ICCPR and the 1984 CAT, are

or Degrading Treatment or Punishment. Adopted by the General Assembly of the United Nations on 10 December 1984, *United Nations Treaty Series*, vol. 1465, No. 24841, p. 85. The 1984 CAT entered into force on 26 June 1987, in accordance with its article 27 1). As of 1 July 2012, several important African countries facing the plight of refugees are not part of this convention, yet. They are: Angola, CAR, Eritrea, Tanzania and Zimbabwe. On the other hand, two countries such as Botswana and Ghana made two reservations to the 1984 CAT, with the clear intention of leaving a wider margin to the action of national authorities in the protection of refugees. In effect, adopting the 1984 CAT, Botswana made the following reservation: 'The Government of the Republic of Botswana considers itself bound by article 1 of the Convention to the extent that "torture" means the torture and the inhuman or degrading punishment or other treatment prohibited by section 7 of the Constitution of the Republic of Botswana.' Acceding the 1984 CAT, Ghana made the following reservation: '[The Government of Ghana declares] in accordance with article 30 2) of the said Convention that the submission under article 30 1) to arbitration or the International Court of Justice of disputes between states parties relating to the interpretation or application of the said Convention shall be the consent of all the Parties concerned and not by one or more of the Parties concerned.'

21 Committee against Torture, Report of the Committee against Torture – Forty-ninth session (29 October–23 November 2012) – Fiftieth session (6–31 May 2013), document No. A 68/44, 6 August 2013, pp. 12–22.

22 Ibid., pp. 68–75.

23 Ibid., pp. 85–93.

24 Ibid., pp. 132–43.

25 Ibid., pp. 143–54.

26 International Covenant on Civil and Political Rights. Adopted by the General Assembly of the United Nations on 19 December 1966, *United Nations Treaty Series*, vol. 999, No. 14668, p. 171. The 1966 ICCPR entered into force on 23 March 1976, in accordance with its Article 49. As of 1 December 2012, most of the Sub-Saharan African countries have ratified this Covenant. Exceptions are constituted by Comoros and Sao Tome and Principe, which have signed the treaty (on 2008 and 1995 respectively) but not ratified yet, and by Eritrea, which is not bound to the treaty in any way whatsoever.

27 Human Rights Committee, General Comment No. 20, Article 7, 3 April 1992, document No. HRI/GEN/1/Rev.1 at 30. Paragraph 9 of the document reads: 'States parties must not expose individuals to the danger of torture or cruel, inhuman or degrading treatment or punishment upon return to another country by way of their extradition, expulsion or refoulement.'

monitored by quasi-judicial bodies.[28] Under these instruments, states are bound not to transfer any person to another country if it would result in exposing that person to serious human rights violations including arbitrary deprivation of life, torture, or other cruel, inhuman and degrading treatment for the 1966 ICCPR, and torture for 1984 CAT. Provided such risk of abuse is established, there are no acceptable grounds for exclusion, such as those provided in Article 33 2) and Article 1F of the 1951 Refugee Convention.[29]

Non-refoulement, in the terms provided by the main international instruments, has been also confirmed in other documents concerning the African continent, such as the 1994 Addis Ababa Document on Refugees and Forced Population Displacements in Africa. In this document, recommendation No. 6 affirms that the symposium highlights the 'provisions on the non-projection[30] of refugees at borders and the prohibition of *refoulement* of refugees'.[31] Such a recommendation draws direct inspiration from the proviso of the 1969 OAU Convention that presents serious questions for some host countries, questions regarding how to face the influx of asylum-seekers.[32] Recognizing these difficulties, the drafters of the 1969 African Convention envisioned that other nations would come to the aid of first-asylum countries saddled with heavy refugee burdens.[33]

28 According to *Black's Law Dictionary* 'quasi-judicial' is '[a] term applied to the action, discretion [. . .] of public administrative officers or bodies, who are required to investigate facts, or ascertain the existence of facts, hold hearings, and draw conclusions from them, as a basis for their official action, and to exercise discretion of a judicial nature.' See *Black's Law Dictionary*, 5th edn, Saint Paul, MN: West Publishing Company, 1979, p. 1121. For instance, in South Africa, the Refugee Appeal Board is considered as a quasi-judicial body being 'an independent body established to give effect to relevant international legal instruments relating to refugees and asylum-seekers [. . .] According to its mandate, the appeal board must: a) hear and determine any question of law referred to it in terms of the Act; b) hear and determine any appeal lodged in terms of the Act; c) advise the Minister or Standing Committee regarding any matter which the Minister or Standing Committee refers to the appeal board.' See AA.VV., *The Law of South Africa*, 2nd edn, volume 11, Durban: LexisNexis, 2008, p. 479.

29 Hurwitz, A., op. cit. note 9, p. 188. See also Art. 1 F of the 1951 Geneva Convention: 'F. The provisions of this Convention shall not apply to any person with respect to whom there are serious reasons for considering that: a) He has committed a crime against peace, a war crime, or a crime against humanity, as defined in the international instruments drawn up to make provision in respect of such crimes; b) He has committed a serious non-political crime outside the country of refuge prior to his admission to that country as a refugee; c) He has been guilty of acts contrary to the purposes and principles of the United Nations.'

30 As strange as this may appear, the document uses exactly this expression. Available at: www1.umn.edu/humanrts/africa/REFUGEE2.htm, accessed 23 August 2014.

31 See also, previously, recommendation 1, paragraph 4 of the 1979 Arusha Conference on the Refugee Problems in Africa: '[The Conference] stresses the importance of the scrupulous observance of the principle of *non-refoulement* expressed in various international instruments [. . .]', in Eriksson, L.G., Melander, G. and Nobel, P. (eds), *An Analysis Account of the Conference on the African Refugee Problem, Arusha, May 1979*, Uppsala: Scandinavian Institute of African Studies, 1981, p. 47.

32 Barkley, D.W., 'Hope for the hopeless: international cooperation and the refugee', in *Columbia Human Rights Law Review*, vol. 21, 1989–1990, pp. 331–2.

33 Bakwesegha, C.J., 'Forced migration in Africa and the OAU Convention', in Adelman, H. and Sorenson, J. (eds), *African Refugees: Development Aid and Repatriation*, North York: York Lane Press, 1994, pp. 3 and 9.

Finally, we should also mention the fact that the principle of non-admission in a given country can be considered a form of *non-refoulement*. In effect, the right of a state to oppose a foreigner's admission to its territory, a right that was proclaimed by the Institute of International Law as early as 1892,[34] is also valid for foreigners who have applied for refugee status.[35] For refugees, a refusal of admission generally consists of an express decision by the competent authorities of the host state. In 2006, the UNGA noted that, often, in Sub-Saharan Africa, the decision not to admit an asylum-seeker has been adopted by an organ of the administration without a court decision or the possibility for the non-admitted asylum-seeker to appeal the decision.[36] Conversely, appeals should be always used in order to justify the fact that the decision adopted in the first instance contains a high grade of certainty, testing the legality of a state action against the will and integrity of an individual.[37]

However, the times in which the UNGA explicitly praised African states for receiving asylum-seekers in increasing numbers seem to be in the rather distant past.[38]

1.2 The contradictory practice of the application of *non-refoulement*

In recent decades, we have come across a phenomenon which demonstrates that international refugee protection has increasingly come to be dictated by security considerations.[39] A clear example of this situation is shown, for instance, by the 1997 round-up of Burundians living outside camps undertaken by the Tanzanian

34 AA.VV., *Annuaire de l'Institut de droit international*, édition nouvelle, Paris: A. Pedone éditeur, vol. III, 1928, p. 127: 'Considérant que le droit d'admettre ou de ne pas admettre sur son territoire, ou de n'y admettre que conditionnellement, ou d'en expulser des étrangers, est, *pour chaque Etat, une conséquence logique et nécessaire de sa souveraineté et de son independance* [. . .].' Emphasis added.

35 Turpin, D., 'L'expulsion des réfugiés', in *Revue française de droit administratif*, vol. 2, 1986, p. 142.

36 UNGA, Second report on the expulsion of aliens, International Law Commission, 20 July 2006, document No. A/CN.4/573, paragraph 173, p. 55. In full, the paragraph in question reads as follows: '173) Refusal of admission may consist in an express decision by the competent authorities of the State to which the request for admission is made, or in the refusal to grant a visa, a necessary but not sufficient condition for access to the territory of most States. In general, diplomatic and consular authorities have the discretionary power to refuse or grant a visa to an alien who requests it. The decision to refuse entry to the alien may be executed *ex officio* by the administration, in other words without the need for a court decision. This lies outside the scope of expulsion even in the broad sense. Non-admission therefore does not fall within the scope of the definition of expulsion for the purposes of this topic.'

37 Popovic, A., 'Evidentiary assessment and *non-refoulement*: insights from criminal procedure', in Noll, G. (ed.), *Proof, Evidentiary, Assessment and Credibility in Asylum Procedures*, Leiden/Boston: Martinus Nijhoff, 2005, p. 52.

38 UNGA, Assistance to refugees in Africa, 7 December 1965, No. 1840 (XX), preamble: '[the UNGA] noting with satisfaction that the African States are showing a continuing interest in the problems of refugees by generously receiving refugees in a truly humanitarian spirit and by acceding in increasing numbers to the 1951 Convention relating to the Status of Refugees.'

39 In this regard, see, for instance, Mogire, E., *Victims as Security Threats: Refugees Impact on Host State Security in Africa*, Farnham: Ashgate Publishing Company, 2011. Talking about the legislations

authorities who claimed that this was a necessary move to protect nationals residing in the border regions. This gradually securitized vision of refugees inspired the passing of more deterring legislation on refugees in 1998.[40]

In this regard, we need to highlight that the 1969 OAU Convention does not include an exception on national security that we can find in the 1951 Geneva Convention. And if an African state is part of both the 1951 Geneva and the 1969 African conventions, then G. Abi-Saab clearly affirmed that if a state accepted to comply with the '[m]ore strict obligations by virtue of the subsequent 1969 [African] Convention, [it] cannot escape [. . .] them by falling back on the less exacting provisions of the prior conventions'.[41]

This situation is well illustrated in situations in which international, regional or national security and the security of asylum-seekers collide, giving rise to an increasing number of cases of *refoulement* of asylum-seekers in Sub-Saharan Africa,[42] although J.C. Hathaway and C.J. Harvey argued that the option of indefinite incarceration in the asylum state as an alternative to *refoulement* should also be taken into consideration.[43] Building an image of the refugee as an existential threat constitutes a political technique to prevent integration. In constructing an issue as a threat to security, the social boundaries in which the threat is to be perceived are at the same time established.[44]

of Kenya and Tanzania, the author contended at p. 144: 'A closer look at these legislations reveals that their central concern is the control and regulation of refugees, hence security with refugee protection taking a secondary concern. This is because the refugee rights enshrined in these laws can be, and have been, suspended when in conflict to national security. Indeed, in practice Kenya and Tanzania often appear to amplify those elements that protect state security when there is a conflict between security and refugee protection.'

40 Milner, J., 'Two steps forward, one step back: understanding the shifting politics of refugee policy in Tanzania', in UNHCR, *New Issues in Refugee Research*, research paper No. 255, 2013, p. 7.

41 Abi-Saab, G., 'The admission and expulsion of refugees with special reference to Africa', in *African Yearbook of International Law*, vol. 8, 2000, p. 90.

42 In this regard, T. Maluwa affirmed: '[R]efugee movements can both create and exacerbate conflict between the sending and the receiving states, and perhaps even challenge the integrity of both states. Moreover, refugees [. . .] will often be perceived by both the sending and the receiving states as a threat to national stability and security. [. . .] Where the refugees pose a threat to the security or economic and social fabric of the receiving state, they will lead to tension and conflict. Unwanted [. . .] refugees may cause tension not only at the bilateral or regional levels between the states involved but [. . .] inter-communal tension within the receiving state.' See Maluwa, T., 'The refugee problem and the quest for peace and security in Southern Africa', in *International Journal of Refugee Law*, special issue, vol. 7, 1995, pp. 671–2. P. Hyndman openly affirmed it: 'However, when faced with a mass-influx of refugees, some countries have seized upon the idea of a threat to national security as ample justification for rejection at the border.' See Hyndman, P., 'An appraisal of the development of the protection afforded to refugees under international law', op. cit. note 5, p. 263.

43 Hathaway, J.C. and Harvey, C.J., op. cit. note 5, p. 293. However, at footnote 177 of their work, the authors affirmed that: 'The Convention drafters [of the 1951 Geneva Convention], however, assumed this option was no better than *refoulement.*' In this regard, see also the news: 'Spurned refugee ship returns to Liberia', 19 June 1996, available at: www.nytimes.com/1996/06/19/world/spurned-refugee-ship-returns-to-liberia.html, accessed 10 August 2014.

44 Haddad, E., *The Refugee in International Society: Between Sovereigns*, Cambridge: Cambridge University Press, 2008, p. 193.

One of the most tragic examples that best illustrates the importance of the national security aspect in protecting refugees was the 1996 case involving Liberian asylum-seekers who had embarked on the freighters *Bulk Challenge* and *Zolotitsa*[45] and escaped the ravages of the civil war. Their claims would have been legally recognized because they were comprised in the reasons mentioned in Article I2 of the 1969 OAU Convention. In actual fact, many of the claimants did not escape the country for fear of personal persecution but just because of the outbreak of war. The 1969 OAU Convention dispenses with the need to demonstrate 'well-founded fear of persecution'. If country A is subjected to events resulting in serious public disorder, this is sufficient reason for country B not to reject those nationals from country A seeking asylum.[46] But the states which denied the ships' dockage[47] did so mainly on the basis of fear for their national security[48] although, and this is very important to highlight, there are no exceptions to the 1969 OAU Convention's *non-refoulement* principle and states may not justify their actions by referring to perceived threats to national security or community safety.[49] Therefore, under the terms of the 1969 African Convention, the West African countries had no choice but to provide at least temporary refuge to asylum-seekers, and then seek assistance from other states if they found the burden disproportionate to their own possibilities.[50] This opinion is reinforced by the fact that at that time

45 For a description of the related events see Kuruk, P., 'Asylum and the *non-refoulement* of refugees: the case of the missing shipload of Liberian refugees', 'Asylum and the non-refoulement of refugees: the case of the missing shipload of Liberian refugees', in *Stanford Journal of International Law*, vol. 35, 1999, pp. 316–19.

46 Rwelamira, M.R.K., 'Two decades of the 1969 OAU Convention Governing the Specific Aspects of the Refugee Problem in Africa', in *International Journal of Refugee Law*, vol. 1, 1989, pp. 558–9.

47 Finally Ghana was obliged, under international pressures, to accept one of the two freighters to dock to its harbour.

48 For instance, see Article 4 of the Beninese Ordonnance No. 75–41 du 16 juillet 1975 portant statut des réfugiés, and Article 4 of the Senegalese Loi No. 68–27 du 24 juillet 1968 modifiée portant statut des réfugiés, 17 August 1968. Other states which expelled the ship from their territorial waters were Togo, whose national legislation on refugees dates from 2000, and Ghana, whose 1992 Refugee Law excludes that the prohibition of expulsion or return of refugees –*ex* Article 1 of the law – would apply to a refugee who '[i]s a danger to the security of Ghana.' Evidently, the Liberian asylum-seekers were considered as such. However, as we may note, all these legislations explicitly mention these kinds of provisions in their sections dedicated to the 'expulsion of refugees', while the Liberians taken into consideration in this example were not recognized as refugees, yet.

49 Kaelin, W., Caroni, M. and Heim, L., 'Article 33, paragraph 1', in Zimmermann, A. (ed.), *The 1951 Convention Relating to the Status of Refugees and its 1967 Protocol: A Commentary*, Oxford: Oxford University Press, 2011, p. 1347.

50 Kuruk, P., 'Asylum and the *non-refoulement* of refugees: the case of the missing shipload of Liberian refugees', op. cit. note 45, p. 332. See also Rifaat, A.M., 'Refugees and the right of asylum: an African perspective', in *Revue Egyptienne de droit international*, vol. 40, 1984, p. 106, where the author contended: '[According to the provisions contained in article II3 of the 1969 OAU Convention] the refugee, on the one hand, will not be forced to remain in his/her home state where he/she fears persecution on his/her own safety and, on the other, that he/she will not be forcibly returned to his/her native country. However, he/she may find him/herself passed on to some third state.' At the time of the episode of the Liberian asylum-seekers, only the Côte

all the countries concerned were parties to the 1969 OAU Convention (Benin since 1973, Ghana since 1975, Senegal since 1971 and Togo since 1970).

In the same years, another case that explains the reality in Sub-Saharan Africa was the situation of Rwandan and Burundian refugees in the DRC in August 1995. The government of Kinshasa decided to force expulsions, being equivalent to *refoulement*.[51] The government justified its action by the wording of the derogation clause of the 1967 DTA, according to which expulsion or compulsory return of refugees may be justified '[o]nly for overriding reasons of national security or in order to safeguard the population, as in the case of a mass-influx of persons',[52] as such persons had invaded the Kivu area. It is interesting to note that the DRC officials chose to justify their action without reference either to the 1951 Geneva Convention or to the 1969 OAU Convention but to a simple, non-legally binding instrument.[53] And, of course, the DRC authorities did not refer to any legal instrument when they decided to expel some 50,000 Angolans in early November 2009, most of them already possessing a refugee status in the DRC.[54]

d'Ivoire could be legally justified for having turned away the two ships considering that it had not ratified yet the 1969 OAU Convention – it did so just in 1998 – and as of 1 July 2012 it does not have any specific domestic legislation on the protection of refugees, yet but having adopted, however, an Arrêté No. 46 MAE/AGH/SDAH/SAARA du 1 février 2007 portant création, organisation et fonctionnement de la Commission nationale d'éligibilité au statut de réfugié [Côte d'Ivoire], No. 46 MAE/AGH/SDAH/SAARA, 1 February 2007 and an Arrêté No. 47 MAE/AGH/SDAH/SAARA du 1 février 2007 portant création, organisation et fonctionnement de la Commission de recours au statut de réfugié [Côte d'Ivoire], No. 47 MAE/AGH/SDAH/SAARA, 1 February 2007.

51 In this regard, R. Marx contended that: '[T]he principle of *non-refoulement* is not limited to prohibiting only forcible return to the alleged country of persecution. Rather, a customary rule has evolved extending the scope of this principle such that expulsion to any other country is strictly prohibited if after arrival *refoulement* is likely from that country.' See Marx, R., '*Non-refoulement*, access to procedures, and responsibilities for determining refugee claims', in *International Journal of Refugee Law*, special issue, vol. 7, 1995, p. 394.

52 Article 3 2) of the 1967 DTA.

53 Kourula, P., op. cit. note 13, pp. 277–9. In this regard, see also Emizet, K., 'The massacre of refugees in Congo: a case of UN peacekeeping failure and international law', in *Journal of Modern African Studies*, vol. 38, 2000, p. 184: '[T]he government of Congo [. . .] forced more than 14,000 refugees to return to Rwanda in August 1995 following a decision by the UNSC (Resolution 1011) to suspend its arms embargo against Rwanda, a move opposed by Congo. The Congolese government justified its action by security considerations. Article 3 2) of the General Assembly Declaration on Territorial Asylum provides a clause, according to which the compulsory return of refugees may be justified "only for overriding reasons of national security or in order to safeguard the population, as in the case of mass-influx of persons" (UNGA 1967). The Congo case indicates how political issues tend to overshadow humanitarian concerns. The SC responded wisely and concurred with the Congolese government by requesting it to stand by its humanitarian obligations to refugees.'

54 See the news 'UNHCR airlifts emergency relief items for expelled refugees in Angola', 3 November 2009, available at: www.unhcr.org/4af04ee49.html, accessed 17 September 2014. Already in January 2004, the UNHCR clearly expressed its concern for the Angolan rejected asylum-seekers from DRC, most of them returned to Angola in spite of the fact that their situation *vis-à-vis* a possible persecution they could suffer once back home was not assessed by Congolese authorities. See UNHCR, UNHCR's position on return of rejected asylum-seekers to Angola, 10 January 2004, p. 3.

In any case, as E. Lauterpacht and D. Bethlehem have maintained,[55] even in situations when a state rejects an asylum-seeker or a refugee, it must consider the possibility of sending him/her to a safe third country rather than to a country where he/she could risk persecution. We were unable to witness any concern from officials in Kinshasa to respect even this rule of common sense towards the Rwandan, Burundian and Angolan asylum-seekers.

Thus, we are sceptical in considering 'legal' the attitude held by the DRC officials in the episode described. At this point, we just question the concrete value of Article 30 of the 2002 Congolese law on refugees, which explicitly forbids *refoulement* of asylum-seekers. Is it a real attempt to delete the recent past? The answer would be 'yes' if we adhered to some of the latest reports[56] but, given the situation of political instability in the country,[57] we cannot be as optimistic about the future of asylum-seekers there.

Generally, Sub-Saharan African national legislations on refugees, with several exceptions and above all, among the French-inspired legislations, contain some provision on the ban of *refoulement*: for instance, Angola,[58] Cameroon,[59] Ethiopia,[60]

55 See, for instance, Lauterpacht, E. and Bethlehem, D., op. cit. note 1, p. 131. However, as stressed by R. Hofmann and T. Lohr: 'The concept [of "safe third country"] is still the subject of ongoing discussions as to its general legitimacy. Nevertheless the concept as such has been widely accepted, and the discussion mainly focuses on what conditions must be met in order to avoid breaches of international law.' See Hofmann, R., Lohr, T., 'Introduction to Chapter V: requirements for refugee determination procedure', in Zimmermann, A. (ed.), *The 1951 Convention Relating to the Status of Refugees and its 1967 Protocol: A Commentary*, Oxford: Oxford University Press, 2011, p. 1111.

56 For instance, see the 2006 Survey by the US Committee for Refugees and Immigrants – Congo-Kinshasa: 'In 2005, there were no reports of *refoulement* from the *Democratic Republic of Congo* (Congo-Kinshasa)': 'The Government continued to honor its 2002 Refugee Law, which codified the right to asylum guaranteed in the 1951 Convention Relating to the Status of Refugees and the 1969 Convention Governing the Specific Aspects of Refugee Problems in Africa [. . .]', available at: www.unhcr.org/cgi-bin/texis/vtx/refworld/rwmain?page=search&docid=4496ad0912&skip=0&query=refoulement%20democratic%20republic%20congo, accessed 30 September 2014.

57 For instance, see the analysis: DRC Instability: Kabila's Gamble, 24 July 2013, available at: www.chathamhouse.org/media/comment/view/193462, accessed 10 September 2014: 'The parameters of the conflict in Eastern DRC are depressingly familiar. An endless series of false dawns has flickered across the Kivu provinces. The most recent resumption of hostilities may be no more than the opening steps of the macabre dance of violence, suffering, hand-wringing and dissembling that is so familiar to long-term observers of Eastern DRC, and which will end in a few months in humiliation for an outclassed Congolese military (FARDC), a surge of international outrage, and another sticking-plaster deal.'

58 Angola, Article 4 1) of the Law No. 8/1990, 26 May 1990, Law on refugee status reads: '[a]n alien in the conditions specified in article 1 who applies for protection at the frontier may not be turned back, returned, expelled or subjected to other measures which oblige him/her to remain in or return to the territory where the threat to his/her security has occurred.'

59 Cameroon, Article 7 1) of the Loi No. 2005/006, portant statut des réfugiés au Cameroun, 27 July 2005 reads: '1) Aucune personne ne peut être refoulée à la frontière, ni faire l'objet d'autres mesures quelconques qui la contraindraient à retourner ou à demeurer dans un territoire où sa vie, son intégrité corporelle ou sa liberté seraient menacées pour l'une des raisons indiquées à l'article 2 de la présente loi.'

60 Ethiopia, Article 9 1) of the 2004 Refugee Proclamation No. 409 starts reading: 'No person shall be refused entry into Ethiopia or expelled or returned from Ethiopia to any other country or to

Ghana,[61] Guinea[62] and Kenya.[63] Kenya, in fact, has *refouled* back no less than 400 Somalis in 2007 – according to other sources it was a mass-influx of more than a thousand[64] – some months after the adoption of the 2006 Refugee Act.[65] The *refoulement* took place notwithstanding the fact that for the most part, elements of the doctrine regarding this subject are inclined to support the idea that the principle of *non-refoulement* is applicable also in the situation of mass-influx[66] as the ExCom has confirmed.[67] The ExCom stresses that application of *refoulement* does not depend on international assistance and/or on burden or responsibility-

be subject to similar measure if as a result of such refusal, expulsion or return or any other measure, such person is compelled to return or to remain in a country [. . .].'

61 Section 1 of the 1992 Ghanaian Refugee Law explicitly prohibits the *refoulement* of asylum-seekers: '1) Notwithstanding any other law to the contrary but subject to the provisions of this Law, no person who is refugee within a meaning of this Law shall be refused entry into Ghana, expelled or extradited from Ghana, or returned to the frontiers on any territory if as a result of such refusal, expulsion or return the person is compelled to return or to remain in a country [. . .].'

62 In Guinea, Article 5 b) of the 2000 Loi L/2000/012/AN adoptant et promulguant le statut des réfugiés en République de Guinée reads: 'Aucun demandeur d'asile [. . .] ne sera refoulé à la frontière ou exposé à toute mesure qui le contraindrait à retourner ou à demeurer sur un territoire où sa vie [. . .] seront menacées [. . .].'

63 Section 18 of the 2006 Kenyan Refugee Act reads: 'No person shall be refused entry into Kenya, or expelled, extradited from Kenya or returned to any other country or to be subjected to any similar measure if, as a result of such refusal, expulsion, return or other measure, such person is compelled to return to or remain in a country where the person may be subject to persecution [. . .].'

64 See the news 'Thousands of Somali refugees and asylum-seekers denied refuge', 2 May 2007, available at: www.liberationafrique.org/imprimersans.php3?id_article=1764&nom_site=Lib%C3%A9ration, accessed 15 September 2014.

65 AI, Kenya – *Denied Refuge: The Effect of the Closure of the Kenya/Somalia Border on Thousands of Somali Asylum-Seekers and Refugees*, London: Amnesty International, p. 3.

66 Among others, see Wouters, K., *International Legal Standards for the Protection from Refoulement*, Antwerp/Oxford/Portland: Intersentia, 2009, p. 156; Durieux, J.-F. and McAdam, J., '*Non-refoulement* through time: the case for a derogation clause to the refugee convention in mass-influx emergencies', in *International Journal of Refugee Law*, vol. 16, 2004, pp. 23–4. In the same regard, A.V. Eggli affirmed that it would be '[s]quarely incompatible with a literal and teleological interpretation to conclude that the reference in the article [33 of the 1951 Geneva Convention] to a "refugee" should, by means of an antithetic interpretation, exclude those on the move in larger groups or *en masse*.' See Eggli, A.V., *Mass Refugee Influx and the Limits of Public International Law*, The Hague/London/New York: Martinus Nijhoff, 2001, p. 71; and, ibid., at p. 172, the author clarified: '[t]he wording [of the article] clearly suggests that the danger must emanate from activities by an individual [. . .] dangers stemming from the sheer number or scale of a refugee influx do not fall logically within the formulation chosen in article 33 2).' See also Lauterpacht, E. and Bethlehem, D., op. cit. note 1, p. 119: 'Although by reference to passing comments in the *Travaux Préparatoires* of the 1951 Convention, it has on occasion been argued that the principle [of *non-refoulement*] does not apply to such situations [of mass-influx], this is not a view that has any merit. It is neither supported by the text as adopted nor by subsequent practice'; Goodwin-Gill, G. and McAdam J., op. cit. note 14, p. 339: 'Despite concerns about providing protection to large numbers of refugees, most states faced with a mass-influx will respect the principle of *non-refoulement*, if nothing else.'

67 ExCom, conclusion No. 22 (XXXII), 'Protection of asylum-seekers in situations of large-scale influx', 1981, paragraph II A): '1) In situations of large-scale influx, asylum seekers should be admitted to the State in which they first seek refuge and if that State is unable to admit them

sharing.[68] Moreover, the 2011 Kenyan Refugees Bill confirmed the importance of the principle of *non-refoulement*, although mitigated by the exception of persons who can be considered dangerous for Kenyan security in light of the ambiguous expression 'reasonable grounds'.[69] The country is not new to *refoulement*: we remember the 1987 statements made by the former Head of State, D. Arap Moi who, proclaiming the motto 'Kenya to Kenyans', encouraged the rejection of large numbers of Ugandans and Rwandans who lived in the country as refugees or were having their situation examined by competent authorities.[70] And in the early 1990s, he similarly wanted Somali refugees in certain regions of his country to be moved to camps inside Somalia.[71]

If all African national legislations on refugees, usually in the preamble, claim to draw inspiration from principles contained either in the 1951 Geneva Convention and/or in the 1969 OAU Convention, we nevertheless think that all African legislators should make a major effort. The effort would consist in confirming unequivocally, through the introduction of a proper provision, their opposition to a practice such as *refoulement* of asylum-seekers in the wake of Burundian authorities' incorporation of the principle of *non-refoulement* into their recent national legislation in a straightforward manner.[72] A firm reiteration of the

on a durable basis, it should always admit them at least on a temporary basis and provide them with protection according to the principles set out below. They should be admitted without any discrimination as to race, religion, political opinion, nationality, country of origin or physical incapacity. 2) In all cases the fundamental principle of *non-refoulement* – including non-rejection at the frontier – must be scrupulously observed.'

68 Kaelin, W., Caroni, M. and Heim, L., op. cit. note 49, p. 1379.

69 Kenya, The Refugees Bill 2011, 15 July 2011 section 15 2): 'The benefit of the provision of this section may not be available to a refugee or an asylum seeker where there are reasonable grounds for regarding such a refugee or asylum seeker as a danger to the security of Kenya.'

70 Verdirame, G. and Harrell-Bond, B., *Rights in Exile: Janus-Faced Humanitarianism*, New York/Oxford: Berghahn Books, 2005, p. 32. As explained also by J. Hyndman: 'The program of the Kenyan government in the late 1980s made life grim for Somalis from either side of the border (in Kenya and Somalia). State of emergency laws in the area allowed for up to fifty-six days' detention without trial, and harassment, beatings, and torture of Somalis were reported.' See Hyndman, J., *Managing Displacement: Refugees and the Politics of Humanitarianism*, Minneapolis, MN: University of Minnesota Press, 2000, p. 50. Mr. Arap-Moi was the President of Kenya from 1978 to 2002.

71 Chimni, B.S., 'The meaning of words and the role of the UNHCR in voluntary repatriation', in *International Journal of Refugee Law*, vol. 5, 1993, p. 446.

72 Articles 19 and 20 of the Loi No. 1/32 du 13 novembre 2008 sur l'asile et la protection des réfugiés au Burundi, No. 1/32, 13 Novembre 2008: '19) Un demandeur d'asile se trouvant régulièrement sur le territoire burundais ne peut être refoulé que pour des raisons de sécurité nationale ou d'ordre public. Le refoulement prévu à l'alinéa précédent n'a lieu qu'en exécution d'une décision rendue conformément à la procédure prévue par la présente loi. Sauf si des raisons impérieuses de sécurité nationale s'y opposent, le demandeur d'asile est admis à fournir des preuves tendant à le disculper, à présenter un recours et à se faire représenter à cet effet devant le comité de recours ». Aucune mesure de refoulement contre un demandeur d'asile ne peut être mise en exécution avant que n'aient été épuisées les voies de recours. 20) Aucun demandeur d'asile ne peut être refoulé, de quelque manière que ce soit, sur les frontières des territoires où sa vie ou sa liberté serait menacée en raison de sa race, de sa religion, de sa nationalité, de son appartenance à un certain groupe social ou de ses opinions politiques.'

provisions already contained in the international instruments regarding the acquisition of the status of refugees as well as the rights and duties of refugees is sought in their domestic legislations. Nonetheless, until now, we assumed that perhaps some national officials preferred to remain vague in the formulation of the principle of *non-refoulement* within their national legislation simply to keep a greater margin for manoeuvre when influxes of asylum-seekers occurred in their country. Therefore, the first experience of many refugees upon arrival to a new country is a traumatic experience of interrogation and detention rather than a welcoming one, sometimes preceding *refoulement*, as happened in late December 2011 to 20 Ethiopian asylum-seekers detained by Somaliland authorities and returned to Ethiopian frontier police on 28 December.[73] States want to retain their total sovereignty over their territories and this consists of strict border controls, so the first response to large influxes of refugees is *refoulement*.[74]

The examples provided have been preceded and followed by many others showing that the phenomenon of *refoulement* has been, at least in the last decades, quite common in Sub-Saharan Africa.[75] In this regard, Human Rights Watch (HRW), in 2002 witnessed the rejection of Liberian refugees from the transition

73 See the news: '*Refoulement* of refugees from Somaliland to Ethiopia', 29 December 2011, available at: http://gadaa.com/oduu/12082/2011/12/29/refoulement-of-refugees-from-somaliland-to-ethiopia/, accessed 10 September 2014.

74 Westra, L. *Environmental Justice and the Rights of Ecological Refugees*, London: Earthscan, 2009, p. 49. At idem, the author pointed out: 'Perhaps the rejection is neither explicit at the start nor eventually irrevocable; but the sort of reception that is offered speaks volumes regarding their resistance to invited "guests".'

75 For other recent examples: on 1994 Tanzania closed their borders to refugees attempting to flee the conflict in Rwanda without having a good reason to believe that internal security could be threatened by the entry of refugees. Namibia and Zimbabwe imitated this attitude throughout the 1990s, with Namibia, in 2001, imposing a dusk-to-dawn curfew along the 450 km stretch of the Kavango river, preventing Angolan asylum-seekers entry to the country. In the same period Guinea's Head of State, L. Comté, encouraged his citizens to form militia groups to force refugees from Liberia and Sierra Leone to go home. In 1999 Zambia ordered the immediate deportation without court review of all nationals of DRC, including many refugees, because those peoples were 'not budgeted for'. All these examples can be found in different sections of: Hathaway, J.C., *The Rights of Refugees Under International Law*, op. cit. note 13. R.L. Newmark cited the case of the Ethiopians in Djibouti in the early 1990s when Djibouti had forcibly repatriated asylum-seekers: 'Djibouti authorities, anxious that the Ethiopians – especially the soldiers – leave reportedly did not fully provide the Ethiopians an opportunity to apply for asylum.' See Newmark, R.L., op. cit. note 5, footnote 118, p. 852. T. Maluwa talked about '[t]he largely unpublicized expulsion from Botswana, in 1988, of a number of South African refugees who had previously been granted asylum and residence status in the country [. . .].' This happened in spite of the statements made by Botswana officials in the same period claiming that the country was open to offer asylum to refugees because this was a matter of international obligation – Botswana is part of the 1951 Geneva Convention since 1969 and of the 1969 OAU Convention since 1995 – and in keeping with an age-old tradition rooted in Botswana's culture. These statements have been, however, corrected by the former President Q.K.J. Masire who, in 1984, affirmed: 'In Botswana the granting of refugee status is carefully circumscribed, and has been so for many years.' See Maluwa, T., 'The concept of asylum and the protection of refugees in Botswana: some legal and political aspects', in *International Journal of Refugee Law*, vol. 2, 1990, pp. 593–4 and 607.

camp of Ouet-Kama and Tekoulo in Guinea,[76] and also saw the treatment of Zimbabweans, who, in a border area with South Africa called Musina, were subject to 'serious violations of their rights including arbitrary arrest, detention, and unlawful deportation constituting *refoulement*'.[77] The latter episode occurred notwithstanding that Article 2 of the 1998 South African Refugees Act No. 130 explicitly provides for the protection of an asylum-seeker against *refoulement*.[78] The *refoulement* of Zimbabweans is, however, unfortunately still of topical interest. The High Court of South Africa ruled in the 2006 case *Tafira and Others v Ngozwane and Others* that the measures adopted by the refugee reception office in Johannesburg preventing asylum claimants from exercising their rights in terms of the 1998 South African Refugees Act constituted a breach of their rights guaranteed under the South African constitution.[79]

Sometimes Sub-Saharan African countries contrive more astute behaviours for adopting *refoulement*: for example by denying essentials like water and food to refugees with the purpose of persuading them to repatriate, as happened in Tanzania – homeland of the so-called '*quasi non-refoulement*',[80] – as well as Rwanda and Uganda in the 1990s.[81] And what about the Mozambican refugees who, to gain entry into South Africa, had mainly two options: cross Kruger National Park or try to pass the electric fence South Africa had constructed in 1986 along that

76 HRW, Liberian refugees in Guinea: *refoulement*, militarization of camps, and other protection concerns, 25 November 2002, available at: www.unhcr.org/cgi-bin/texis/vtx/refworld/rwmain?page=search&docid=3e3141700&skip=0&query=refoulement%20guinea, accessed 18 September 2014.

77 HRW, *South Africa: Neighbors in Need: Zimbabweans Seeking Refuge in South Africa*, 2008, p. 85. In this regard, A.C. Helton clearly affirmed: 'Measures like "push backs", "interdictions", and border closures are breaches of a nation's obligations to admit refugees. [. . .] Measures such as prolonged, harsh, and arbitrary detention are inconsistent with a nation's obligation to receive genuine refugees.' See Helton, A.C., 'Refugee protection and repatriation: a critical view', in Stein, B.N., Cuny, F.C. and Reed, P. (eds), *Refugee Repatriation During Conflict: A New Conventional Wisdom*, Dallas: The Center for the Study of Societies in Crisis, 1995, p. 33.

78 Section 2 of the South African Refugee Act No. 130 starts by stipulating: 'Notwithstanding any provision of this Act or any other law to the contrary, no person may be refused entry into the Republic, expelled, extradited or returned to any other country or be subject to any similar measure [. . .].'

79 High Court of South Africa (Transvaal Provincial Division), *Tafira and Others v Ngozwane and Others*, Case No. 12960/06, 12 December 2006, paragraph 4, p. 46 of the judgment: 'It is declared that the current practice and policy of receiving applications for asylum at the Marabastad and Rosettenville Refugee Reception Offices are unconstitutional and unlawful in respect of the manner of scheduling appointments and in respect of the prescreening method adopted.'

80 Quoting from Kamanga, K., 'The (Tanzania) Refugees Act of 1998: some legal and policy implications', in *Journal of Refugee Studies*, vol. 18, 2005, p. 112, where the author explained: 'The non-refoulement provision in the Act effectively recognizes only two grounds (*ex* article 28 2) of the Act): the "political character of the offence" for which upon return, the asylum seeker will be tried; and the likelihood of the asylum seeker being subjected to "physical attack." Evidently, these fall short of the provisions of the UN Convention of 1951 and the OAU Convention of 1969. Contrast with section 10 ("Prohibition of expulsion on return of refugees") of the (Malawi) Refugee Act 1989 which more fully reflects the prevalent understandings of the rule.'

81 Hathaway, J.C., *The Rights of Refugees Under International Law*, note 13, p. 318.

part of the border which was not 'protected' by the park?[82] In truth, South African authorities did not consider Mozambicans crossing the border at that time as refugees but as illegal immigrants instead, whose presence was tolerated only if they could reach the so-called 'homelands' of Bophuthatswana and Lebowa, among others. Refugees who were found outside the 'homelands' were imprisoned or deported.[83]

Worse, the attitude of South African authorities has not changed towards a less restrictive admission policy. To this day, the South African asylum system seems to remain exclusively as an instrument of 'immigration control'. In the words of a South African researcher:

> The fact that they (Department of Home Affairs (DHA) officials) are routinely getting the law wrong, and are issuing rote rejections that ignore stories of rape, torture and other human rights violations, raises serious questions about the ability of DHA to perform its mandated functions. These failures mean that South Africa may be returning people to their deaths or to situations of serious human rights violations. [. . .] Refugee status determination officers incorrectly deployed refugee law and failed to consider the details of individual claims as required in a properly administered status determination process. The result is a bureaucracy that mass-produces rejection letters without any evidence of a reasoned decision-making process.[84]

82 Wilson, K.B. and Nunes, J., 'Repatriation to Mozambique', in Allen, T. and Morsink, H. (eds), *When Refugees Go Home*, London: James Currey, Trenton, NJ: Africa World Press, 1994, p. 170. A.M. Da Silva reported that almost 1,000 persons fleeing Mozambique have died in six years. See Da Silva, A.M., 'Mozambican refugees: from a historical overview of conflict to today's refugee camps and repatriation process', paper for 'First Country of Asylum and Development Aid' conference, June 1992, Lilongwe, Malawi, p. 24. See also Andersson, H., *Mozambique: A War against the People*, Basingstoke/London: Macmillan Press Ltd., 1992, p. 119: 'More people have been killed on the electrified fence running along the South African/Mozambican border in three short years than have been killed on the Berlin Wall since it was constructed.'

83 Zieck, M., *UNHCR and Voluntary Repatriation of Refugees*, The Hague/Boston/London: Martinus Nijhoff, 1997, pp. 338–9. In this regard, see also Andersson, H., op. cit. note 82, p. 121: 'The Homeland system and the way it relates to the Mozambican refugee issue is an area in which political wrangling gets in the way of human need in more ways than one. The Homelands are, usually, fairly barren areas of South Africa which have been set aside for blacks to govern themselves in. The implication of the Homelands policy, which threw blacks who wanted to govern themselves into the most barren parts of South Africa with no infrastructure [. . .] was that it was a form of imprisonment for the rebellious. It was a snub, and a very cruel one which caused great domestic and international uproar. The Homelands became semi-autonomous parts of South Africa in which the leaders have total responsibility for all the problems of their land but not for its productivity, nor for the areas of policy, especially foreign policy, which affect South Africa. The issue of the status for refugees is, in some people's eyes, a matter of foreign affairs and thus a South African matter.'

84 Declaration by Dr. Ron Amit in the news: '"Meaningless" system for asylum-seekers at mercy of poor rulings', 19 June 2012, available at: www.iol.co.za/the-star/meaningless-system-for-asylum-seekers-at-mercy-of-poor-rulings-1.1321974#.UIqqM2–6dMA, accessed 25 September 2012.

At other times, *refoulement* is simply a question of bureaucracy and compromise: for example, the UNHCR branch office in Kampala rejected the application for assistance of 60 Rwandan asylum-seekers, mostly students, on the grounds that, after contact with Rwandan authorities, it concluded that none of them deserved the status of refugee. As Z. Lomo further noted, the UNHCR did not give the students a possibility to substantiate and confirm the authenticity of the information it had received from Rwanda, and the UNHCR was suspected of endorsing the Rwandan government at the expense of the Rwandan students.[85] In 2010 for example, Uganda returned 1,700 Rwandan asylum-seekers under duress, an act that elicited condemnation from major NGOs present in the country.[86]

The entire range of these examples seems to confirm the predominance given to national security and the fact that the evolving relationship between national and human security has been incorporated into national refugee legislations and policies, often privileging national security over respect of group and individual human rights, as in the case of Tanzania, where the 1994 Rwandan genocide and the consequent influx of asylum-seekers into the country pushed the Tanzanian government to use the phrase 'new caseload' in official documents to define a shift in the change of policy. In December 1996, B.W. Mkapa's government issued an ultimatum to the half million refugees to return home by the end of the month, in contravention of international refugee law.[87] *Refoulement* of Rwandan refugees by the Tanzanian army took place in 1997, 1999 and 2001, encompassing even some refugees who were settlers from the 1960s and waiting for Tanzanian citizenship.[88] We might well ask, furthermore, about the 13 young Eritrean footballers to whom asylum had been denied by Tanzanian authorities in 2011, despite the UNHCR's contrary opinion in merit.[89]

Thus, it is not by chance that one of the declared objectives of the 1998 Tanzanian Refugee Act was to signal disengagement from the 'open door' policy

85 Lomo, Z., 'The struggle for protection of the rights of refugees and IDPs in Africa: making the existing international legal regime work', in *Berkeley Journal of International Law*, vol. 18, 2000, p. 279.

86 AI, 'Uganda forcibly returns 1,700 Rwandan asylum-seekers', 16 July 2010, available at: www.amnesty.org/en/news-and-updates/uganda-forcibly-returns-1700-rwandan-asylum-seekers-2010–07–16, accessed 10 September 2014.

87 The same President B. Mkapa told a meeting of foreign diplomats in 2001 that Tanzania's '[s]ympathy in assisting refugees should be supported by the international community because it was its responsibility.' Quoted in Loescher, G. and Milner, J.H.S., 'Understanding the problem of protracted refugee situations', in Loescher, G. (*et al.*) (ed.), *Protracted Refugee Situations: Political, Human Rights and Security Implications*, New York: United Nations University Press, 2008, p. 29. Mr. Mkapa was the *third President* of *Tanzania* (1995–2005) and former Chairman for the TRSP.

88 Chaulia, S.S., 'The politics of refugee hosting in Tanzania: from open door to unsustainability, insecurity and receding receptivity', in *Journal of Refugee Studies*, vol. 16, 2003, p. 161. The situation in Uganda is similar, where in the last few decades conditions for asylum-seekers have ostensibly worsened with the 'chasing' of Rwanda refugees from Western Uganda in 1982–1983 emblematic of the difficult situation which asylum-seekers are going through in the country. In this regard, see Khiddu-Makubuya, E., 'The legal condition of refugees in Uganda', in *Journal of Refugee Studies*, vol. 7, 1994, pp. 407–8.

89 See the news: 'Tanzania rejects Eritrean footballers' asylum bid', available at: www.bbc.co.uk/news/world-africa-15293132, accessed 10 September 2014.

of the former M.J. Nyerere administration, with the intent to make Tanzania a less attractive destination for asylum-seekers, and to send a deterrent message to authorities in refugee-generating countries. On the other hand, the Tanzanian Refugee Act aimed to assure the population that the government was determined to address the problem of seemingly endless refugee influxes that were considered a cause of insecurity, environmental degradation and electoral tensions.[90]

Therefore, in light of the situation analyzed, we disagree with the opinion voiced more than 20 years ago expressing that African countries comply with their relevant duties regarding the application of *non-refoulement* under international law.[91]

The practice examined is quite paradoxical if we think that the principle of *non-refoulement* seems to be considered almost unanimously by the doctrine as a rule of customary international law,[92] although with limitations.[93]

Providing a general framework of this issue, custom, also considered a 'matter of taste',[94] is composed of a subjective element (*opinio juris*) and of an objective element (state practice).[95] If we agree on the fact that the *opinio juris* in the case of

90 Kamanga, K., 'The (Tanzania) Refugees Act of 1998: some legal and policy implications', op. cit. note 80, pp. 104–5. Mr. Nyerere served as the first President of Tanzania from the country's founding in 1961 until his retirement in 1985.

91 Hofmann, R., 'Refugee law in the African context', in *Zeitschrift für Ausländisches Öffentliches Recht und Völkerrecht*, vol. 52, 1992, p. 328.

92 Kaelin, W., Caroni, M. and Heim, L., op. cit. note 49, p. 1345. As an example of scholars supporting this view, see, for example: Mushkat, R., 'Human rights under temporary refuge', in *Revue de droit international, sciences diplomatiques et politiques*, vol. 62, 1984, p. 172: 'International action thus appears to provide ample support for the view that *non-refoulement* has matured into a norm of customary international law binding on states even in the absence of treaty obligations to behave accordingly.' See also Westra, L., op. cit. note 74, p. 159; D'Angelo, E.F., '*Non-refoulement*: the search for a consistent interpretation of article 33', in *Vanderbilt Journal of Transnational Law*, vol. 42, 2009, p. 282, where, quoting the 2005 US case *Zaoui v Attorney-General*, affirmed: 'The prohibition on *refoulement*, contained in art. 33 1) of the Refugee Convention, is generally thought to be part of customary international law, the (unwritten) rules of international law binding on all states, which arise when states follow certain practices generally and consistently out of a sense of legal obligation.'

93 In this regard, P. Hyndman affirmed: 'Nevertheless, the often-repeated provisions for exception to safeguard national security cannot be ignored and may be indicative that if *non-refoulement* has become a binding principle it has become so with these limitations.' See Hyndman, P., 'Asylum and *non-refoulement*: are these obligations owed to refugees under international law?', in *Philippine Law Journal*, vol. 57, 1982, p. 69.

94 Kelly, J.P., 'The twilight of customary international law', in *Virginia Journal of International Law*, vol. 40, 1999–2000, p. 451, where the author continued: 'As such, it [customary international law] cannot function as a legitimate source of substantive legal norms in a decentralized world of nations without a broad base of shared values.'

95 In this regard, see Schachter, O., 'New custom: power, *opinio juris* and contrary practice', in AA.VV., *Theory of International Law at the Threshold of the 21st Century – Essays in Honor of Krzysztof Skubiszewski*, The Hague/London/Boston: Kluwer Law International, 1996, p. 531: 'In the words of the International Court of Justice judgment: "Not only must the acts concerned amount to a settled practice, they must also be such, or be carried out in such a way as to be evidence of a belief that this practice is rendered obligatory by the existence of a rule of law requiring it." As this passage indicates it, custom begins with "acts" that become a "settled practice"; that practice may then give rise to the belief that it had become obligatory.' The quotation from the ICJ is in ICJ, *North Sea Continental Shelf Cases (Federal Republic of Germany v Denmark; Federal Republic*

granting *non-refoulement* in Sub-Saharan Africa is certain,[96] we are very sceptical about the element of a coherent state practice, which tends to affirm the principle of *non-refoulement* as a custom.[97] Practice should be 'general and consistent'. If agreement exists on the term 'general', it is because it does not need to be interpreted strictly, as 'certain universality is not required'.[98] Although practice should be 'representative' of all major political and socio-economic systems',[99] the term 'consistent' leaves more than a doubt on the application of the 'would-be' custom of *non-refoulement* in Sub-Saharan Africa. Under this basis, we can ascertain that custom of *non-refoulement* is still too incoherent to contend with the conviction that its application can be considered a local custom in Sub-Saharan African countries. However, we must note that, by contrast, A.E. Roberts affirmed that 'modern' custom would be more derived from a deductive process which starts with general statements of rules rather than specific instances of practice. Evidently, this approach will emphasize more *opinio juris* than state practice because it relies mainly on statements rather than actions. Such an opinion has been reinforced by arguing that, as the frequency and consistency of state practice decline, and stronger evidence of *opinio juris* is required,[100] the trade-off between *opinio juris* and state practice will depend on the importance of the activity in question and the fairness of the rule involved.[101] According to this theory, *non-refoulement* could

of Germany v Netherlands), judgment of 20 February, 1969, in *ICJ Reports*, 1969, paragraph 77, p. 44. However, later in his work, the author, referring to the judgment of the ICJ in the 1986 *Nicaragua Case* pointed out that 'it is fair to say that it [the passage of the ICJ] reflected a widespread professional opinion that law-declaring resolutions particularly when adopted by a unanimous decision of the General Assembly could have a creative role in the formation of custom.' See ibid., p. 532.

96 We have some difficulties in finding scholarly opinions affirming that applying *non-refoulement* can be 'illegal'.

97 As indicated by several authors: 'For a practice of states to become a rule of customary international law it must appear that the states follow the practice from a sense of legal obligation [. . .]; a practice that is generally followed but which states feel legally free to disregard does not contribute to customary international law.' See Carter, B.E., Trimble, P.R. and Wiener, A.S., *International Law*, 5th edn, New York: Aspen, 2007, p. 124.

98 Brownlie, I., *Principles of Public International Law*, 7th edn, Oxford/New York: Oxford University Press, 2008, p. 8.

99 Villiger, M.E., *Customary International Law and Treaties: A Manual of Theory and Practice of the Interrelation of Sources*, fully revised 2nd edn, The Hague/London/Boston: Kluwer Law International, 1997, p. 29.

100 Roberts, A.E., 'Traditional and modern approaches to customary international law: a reconciliation', in *American Journal of International Law*, vol. 95, 2001, pp. 758–60. The author does not explain in detail when 'modern customs' began but she took an example of the ICJ in the *Nicaragua Case*, affirming at pp. 758–9: 'The Court paid lip service to the traditional test for custom but derived customs of non-use of force and non-intervention from statements such as UNGA resolutions. The Court did not make a serious inquiry into state practice, holding that it was sufficient for conduct to be generally consistent with statements of rules, provided that instances of inconsistent practice had been treated as breaches of the rule concerned rather than as generating a new rule.'

101 Kirgis, F.L. Jr., 'Custom on a sliding door', in *American Journal of International Law*, vol. 81, 1987, p. 149 where the author at idem further explained: 'The more destabilizing or morally distasteful

therefore be considered a veritable 'modern' custom without a general state practice. In effect, it is true that state practice is less important in forming 'modern' customs because these latter would set down more ideal standards of conduct than illustrate the existing practice.[102] And if we admit that *non-refoulement* is an important principle, which has been recognized by sovereign states for centuries, we can consistently affirm that *non-refoulement* is part of these 'modern' customs. However, these days the principle of *non-refoulement* is illustrated through the practice of granting it by Sub-Saharan African countries, which is far from usual. That is why we are still sceptical about considering *non-refoulement* to be a real, 'traditional' – as opposed to 'modern' – custom for Sub-Saharan Africa.

In this sense, and endorsing our scepticism, E. Odhiambo-Abuya contended that:

> However, the claim that by the 1980s the principle of *non-refoulement* had attained customary international law status is questionable, as it is not supported by any evidence of 'widespread authoritative' state practice.[103]

The hypothesis has even been advanced by N. Coleman that the principle of *non-refoulement*, if not universally accepted, is becoming at least a regional international customary law in Africa, although the same scholar admitted bafflement about the fulfilment of the requirement of generality of practice that a custom would necessitate. He concluded his study by arguing that he was not completely sure that serious breaches of the principle in question could be signalled, none would have sufficient weight to question the customary nature of the principle of *non-refoulement* on the continent.[104] To support this hypothesis, G. Stenberg argued that if states act contrary to a principle, they do so with a certain attempt at justification, which indicates that they feel they are infringing upon a rule of law.[105]

Although the majority of scholars do not discuss the customary nature of current *non-refoulement*, we note that African states, at least in their attitudes, clearly do not feel they are acting against an *opinio juris* in *refouling* asylum-seekers. No clear attitudes from the 'guilty states' have shown us an indication to the contrary;

the activity – for example, the offensive use of force or the deprivation of fundamental human rights – the more readily international decision makers will substitute one element for the other, provided that the asserted restrictive rule seems reasonable.'

102 Roberts, A.E., op. cit. note 100, p. 764.

103 Odhiambo-Abuya, E., 'Past reflections, future insights: African asylum law and policy in historical perspective', in *International Journal of Refugee Law*, vol. 19, 2007, p. 83.

104 Coleman, N., '*Non-refoulement* revised: renewed review of the status of the principle of *non-refoulement* as customary international law', in *European Journal of Migration and Law*, vol. 5, 2003, pp. 46–7.

105 For example, see Stenberg, G., *Non-Expulsion and Non-Refoulement: The Prohibition Against Removal of Refugees with Special Reference to Articles 32 and 33 of the 1951 Convention Relating to the Status of Refugees*, Uppsala: Iustus Forlag, 1989, p. 47; Fitzpatrick, J., 'Revitalizing the 1951 Refugee Convention', in *Harvard Human Rights Journal*, vol. 9, 1996, p. 237.

no official excuses or regretted actions have shown this either: only justifications that do not have any strong legal basis.

In this sense, J.C. Hathaway clearly rejected the hypothesis that *non-refoulement* has attained the status of customary law. He argued that:

> [T]here is no basis to assert that just because most countries have accepted some kind of *non-refoulement* obligation, applying to at least some kinds of cases, and in at least some contexts [. . .], it can now be concluded that there is a universally applicable duty of *non-refoulement* owed to refugees by all states-including the forty-five or so which have opted not to accede to either the Refugee Convention or Protocol.

Affirming that the nature of the different duties of *non-refoulement* relied upon is extremely erratic, he continues to argue that it does not give the foundations for even a common *opinio juris*, much less for universal respect of that provision in practice. In this way, although almost all states owe individuals a duty of *non-refoulement* as a minimum, the author concluded there was no reason to think that the content of the customary nature of *non-refoulement* in the case of refugee protection matches the interpretation of Article 33 of the 1951 Geneva Convention. Moreover, the fact of overstating determinedly the reached custom does not constitute *per se* a real assimilation of new standards into a clearly possible framework of enforceable duties.

He concluded his analysis by arguing that:

> Not only are courts disinclined to accept policy claims simply because they are advanced as customary legal claims, but there is a real risk that wishful legal thinking about the scope of the duty of *non-refoulement* may send the signal that customary law as a whole is essentially rhetorical, with a resultant dilution of emphasis on the real value of those norms which really have been accepted as binding by a substantial majority of states. [. . .] [I]t is simply disingenuous to assert that there is presently a universal duty of *non-refoulement* that is substantively in line with provisions of article 33 and which is owed to all refugees, by all states.[106]

106 Hathaway, J.C., *The Rights of Refugees Under International Law*, op. cit. note 13, pp. 365–7. Several years later, the author did not change his opinion contending: 'To be clear, I recognize that when a treaty-based norm stimulates a broadly embraced sense of obligation (in particular, among non-party states), *opinio juris* in support of a cognate customary international legal obligation may emerge. But there is no basis to conclude that just because most countries have accepted something that may broadly be termed a *non-refoulement* obligation – applying to at least some kinds of cases and some contexts – that there is a universally applicable duty of *non-refoulement* owed to the combined class of all refugees and other persons at risk of significant human rights abuse. Much less can *opinio juris* be located in General Assembly resolutions considered in isolation from the broader context of state attitudes towards the putative norm, particularly the attitudes of states especially affected by refugee flows.' See Hathaway, J.C., 'Leveraging asylum', in *Texas International Law Journal*, vol. 45, 2010, pp. 514–15.

If, historically, the sense of hospitality of African countries could have contributed to the establishment of a custom regarding the principle of *non-refoulement*, in the last decades we can affirm that we have come across a custom falling into disuse, a reality where rejection is becoming the rule. Cases such as Malawi, where Mozambican refugees were shown hospitality in the 1980s, seem to now constitute a real exception in a country that could be paradoxically defined as opposing the 'custom' of *refoulement*. In the last particular episode it is, however, interesting to note that the terminology employed in the Malawian statement when referring to Mozambican asylum-seekers was that of 'displaced persons' rather than that of 'refugees'.[107] In Sub-Saharan Africa, the situation in question is made more complicated because the almost totality of the countries has ratified at least one of the binding international instruments in which the principle of *non-refoulement* is codified.

In this regard, we therefore prefer the analysis carried out by R.L. Newmark, who has been less assertive in his statements affirming that:

> State practice, which is one of the best indications of what has become customary law, is inconsistent at best in this field [of *non-refoulement*].[108]

K. Hailbronner noted how the drafting of the 1967 DTA, as well as the statements made during the 1977 Draft Convention,[109] showed that Sub-Saharan African countries had a:

> [r]eluctance to enter into legally binding obligations to admit a large number of refugees even on a basis of a temporary stay.[110]

107 Maluwa, T., 'Human rights and refugees in Southern Africa: some perspectives on recent legislative developments in Malawi', in *Zeitschrift für Ausländisches Öffentliches Recht und Völkerrecht*, vol. 53, 1993, p. 102. The author, at idem, footnote 41, noted that in the Malawian context a distinction seemed to be drawn between 'refugees', namely those individuals confined to camps, and 'displaced persons', being either that group of individuals who leave their country of origin and integrate into the local population or those who come for brief spells and return to their country of origin thereafter.

108 Newmark, R.L., op. cit. note 5, p. 845. However, related to the last decades, this author continued affirming that: 'Regardless of where they are found, asylum-seekers in Africa are generally protected from *non-refoulement*.' In effect, the author cited the case of the Mozambican refugees in Malawi in the late 1970s. See ibid., pp. 851–2.

109 United Nations Conference on Territorial Asylum, document No. A/CONF./78/12, 4 February 1977. This conference considered, but finally rejected, the codification of a new convention that would set a clear right to enduring protection for refugees. It reached agreement in theory to require states parties to facilitate the admission of a refugee's wife and dependent children, and clearly to interpret the duty of *non-refoulement* to include the 'rejection at the frontier'. In this regard, see Hathaway, J.C., *The Rights of Refugees Under International Law*, op. cit. note 13, p. 112.

110 Hailbronner, K., '*Non-refoulement* and "humanitarian" refugees: customary international law or wishful legal thinking?', in Martin, D. (ed.), *The New Asylum Seekers: Refugee Law in the 1980s*, Dordrecht/Boston/London: Martinus Nijhoff, 1988, p. 129.

To support their conviction on customary law, scholars often quote a particular paragraph of the 1986 *Nicaragua Case* in which the judges of the ICJ argued:

> In order to deduce the existence of customary rule, the Court deems sufficient that the conduct of States should, in general, be consistent with such rules, and that instances of State conduct inconsistent with a given rule should generally have been treated as breaches of that rule, not as indications of the recognition of a new rule.[111]

Again, R. Mushkat affirmed that, in her opinion, under no circumstances could governments deny the binding nature of the principle of *non-refoulement*. Rather, she continued, they have instead tried to justify the measures adopted, stressing the inapplicability of the rule to the specific occasions.[112]

However, what if *refoulement* seems to constitute the rule in many situations in Sub-Saharan Africa? What about if the inapplicability of the norm, as has happened in many situations, has not been stressed? What about if the conducts inconsistent with a given rule constitute, *de facto*, the normal attitude by a given state and breaches to the norm are not justified in any way by the state that committed them? And what about if, in front of these violations, no other state in the region denounces the breaches to the norm, in so doing implicitly affirming its non-existence?

We hope to have clearly demonstrated that *refoulement* in Sub-Saharan Africa does not constitute the exception but instead it can be considered, particularly over the last decades, as a general rule of conduct. In our opinion, when it comes to a given group of states, there appears to be no intention of creating a new customary rule. Rather we observe a continuous breach of a customary rule *(non-refoulement)*, claimed to exist and whose violation has not, in any case, been denounced by any other important African governmental actors, through a sort of latent pact of mutual desistance among African states.

To reinforce our idea we are supported by Z. Lomo's analysis suggesting that relations of states on the continent show that granting refugee status has even been interpreted as '[a]n unfriendly act and refugees have paid heavily for conflicting state interests.'[113]

The entire situation on the continent is even more paradoxical if we accept the theory that *non-refoulement* has attained the normative status of *jus cogens*,[114] with

111 ICJ, Case concerning military and paramilitary activities in and against Nicaragua (*Nicaragua v United States of America*), judgment of 27 June 1986, in ICJ Reports, 1986, paragraph 186, p. 98.

112 Mushkat, R., 'Mandatory repatriation of asylum seekers: is the legal norm of *non-refoulement* "dead"?', in *Hong Kong Law Journal*, vol. 25, 1995, p. 46. Emphasis added.

113 Lomo, Z., op. cit. note 85, p. 280.

114 See, for instance, what is clearly affirmed by D. Kennedy: '*Non-refoulement* has become binding as a matter of both treaty and customary law if not also as a so-called peremptory norm of *jus cogens*.' See Kennedy, D., 'International refugee protection', in *Human Rights Quarterly*, vol. 8, 1986, pp. 60–1. For an 'alternative' opinion on the concept of *jus cogens*, see Glennon, M.J., 'Peremptory

states which at that point should be precluded from any derogation to it.[115] Regrettably, we think that *non-refoulement*, at least as it is conceived and applied in Sub-Saharan Africa, continues to be part of the so-called *jus dispositivum*, namely laws from which states may derogate, situations in which states, although violating an international obligation, may claim circumstances which preclude wrongfulness.[116] The particularity of domestic African legislations allowing states to expel refugees for reasons of national security and public order, such as interference with national policy and/or conviction for serious crimes, could be interpreted to support our opinion.[117] This conviction can be derived mainly because the two expressions 'national security' and 'public order' are used in Sub-Saharan Africa in an arbitrary way by local authorities to reject asylum-seekers.[118] However, although not homogeneous and constant in its application in Sub-Saharan Africa, *non-refoulement* seems to remain at the foundations at least of the legal relations between states and international organizations on the continent.

nonsense', in Breitenmomser, S., Ehrenzeller, B. *et al.* (eds), *Human Rights, Democracy and the Rule of Law: Liber Amicorum Luzius Wildhaber*, Zurich/St.Gallen: Dike Verlag AG, p. 1272: 'International Law, like other law, consists of multifarious norms that inevitably conflict and that survive, if at all, only through a continuous state of reconciliation. Attempting to ice up the dynamic of change with confused inventions like *jus cogens* advances neither the rule of law nor human dignity.'

115 Articles 53 and 64 of the 1969 Vienna Convention of the Law of the Treaties read respectively: '53) A treaty is void if, at the time of its conclusion, it conflicts with a peremptory norm of general international law. For the purposes of the present Convention, a peremptory norm of general international law is a norm accepted and recognized by the international community of States as a whole as a norm from which no derogation is permitted and which can be modified only by a subsequent norm of general international law having the same character'; '64) If a new peremptory norm of general international law emerges, any existing treaty which is in conflict with that norm becomes void and terminates.'

116 Allain, J., 'The *jus cogens* nature of non-refoulement', in *International Journal of Refugee Law*, vol. 13, 2001, pp. 534–5. We agree with A. Duffy when he clarified: 'Unfortunately, the arguments [. . .] that *non-refoulement* have acquired a *jus cogens* status, are less than convincing. That this principle was elevated to a peremptory place would suggest that no exceptions would be considered under any circumstance. This, sadly, is not the case.' See Duffy, A., 'Expulsion to face torture? *Non-refoulement* in international law', in *International Journal of Refugee Law*, vol. 20, 2008, p. 390.

117 For instance, Article 20 of the Angolan Law No. 8/1990, 26 May 1990, Law on refugee status reads: 'A person who has been granted asylum or refugee status may not be expelled, except for reasons of public order [. . .].' See also, for Benin Ordonnance No. 75–41 du 16 juillet 1975 portant statut des réfugiés, 16 July 1975; for Senegal: Décret No. 76–014 du 9 janvier 1976 modifie relatif à la commission prévue à l'article 3 de la Loi no. 1968–27 du 5 août 1968 portant sur le statut des réfugiés, 31 janvier 1976, article 4. Article 15 1) of the 1983 Zimbabwean Refugee Act also reads similarly: '1) Subject to the provisions of this section and of section thirteen, the Minister, after consultation with the Minister to whom the administration of the Immigration Act, 1979 (No. 18 of 1979), has been assigned, may order the expulsion from Zimbabwe of any recognized refugee or protected person if he/she considers the expulsion to be necessary or desirable on the grounds of national security or public order.'

118 For instance, 'In South Africa, section 28 of the Refugee Act also refers to a refugee being removed from South Africa on grounds of national security and public order. However, there is no guidance in the Act as to the meaning of public order. Moreover, the other limited areas of South Africa law that refer to public order, such as municipal or policing laws, do not offer

The first attempt to mention the principle of *non-refoulement* as part of *jus cogens* has been made by ExCom conclusion No. 25 of 1982, in which state members determined that the principle of *non-refoulement* 'was progressively acquiring the character of a peremptory rule of international law'.[119] Finally in 1996, the ExCom concluded that *non-refoulement* had gained a level of peremptory norm when it determined that the 'principle of *non-refoulement* is not subject to derogation'.[120] And, in Sub-Saharan Africa, several legislations have admitted the non-derogability of this principle as with, for example, South Africa,[121] where in the 2011 *Abdi Case* it was clearly affirmed that the

> [a]ppellants would face a real risk of suffering physical harm if they were forced to return to Somalia. [. . .] Deportation to another state that would result in the imposition of a cruel, unusual or degrading punishment is in conflict with the fundamental values of the Constitution [. . .]; [r]efusing a refugee entry to this country, and thereby exposing her or him to the risk of persecution or physical violence in his home country is in conflict with the fundamental values of the Constitution [. . .] [and] South Africa is clearly a sovereign and independent state. The appellants are within this country and are entitled to the protection of its laws, even if they happen to have arrived here in the course of being deported from another sovereign and independent state.[122]

One could also argue that violations of the norm may strengthen the principle of *non-refoulement*, as the ICJ explained in the 1986 *Nicaragua Case*:

> If a State acts in a way *prima facie* incompatible with a recognized rule, but defends its conduct by appealing to exceptions or justifications contained within the rule itself, then whether or not the State's conduct is in fact justifiable on that basis, the significance of that attitude is to confirm rather than to weaken the rule.[123]

a relevant or precise meaning of the term.' See Schreier, T., 'The expanded refugee definition', in Khan, F. and Schreier, T., *Refugee Law in South Africa*, Cape Town: Juta & Co. Ltd., 2014, p. 82.

119 ExCom, conclusion No. 25 (XXXIII), 'General conclusion on international protection', 1982, letter b).

120 ExCom, conclusion No. 79 (XLVII) 'General conclusion on international protection', 1996, letter i).

121 'South Africa is bound by the principle [of *non-refoulement*] in terms of its domestic laws that have been ratified and in terms of international laws and no derogation is permissible.' See Khan, F., 'The principle *of non-refoulement*', op. cit. note 118, p. 19.

122 *Mahamad Arwah Abdi and Another v Minister of Home Affairs and others*, Case No: 734/2010, South Africa: Supreme Court of Appeal, 15 February 2011, paragraphs 26–7, 29, available at: www.refworld.org/docid/50239bb62.html, accessed 3 October 2014.

123 ICJ, Case concerning military and paramilitary activities in and against Nicaragua (*Nicaragua v United States of America*), judgment of 27 June 1986, in ICJ Reports, paragraph 186, p. 98.

However, if we accept the fact that the principle of *non-refoulement*, as for the 1969 OAU Convention, provides for no justification or exception contained in itself, and if we consider that almost all Sub-Saharan African countries have accessed the treaty and consider it the cornerstone of refugee protection on the continent, we should simply concede that states do not comply with the international norm that they have adopted.

Therefore, Sub-Saharan African countries not only do not consider the principle of *non-refoulement* as a peremptory norm of international law but, as we have mentioned above, they also contravene a norm that they have accepted, by adopting specific conventions on the subject. In the scope of our analysis, it is relevant to consider that on no occasion have any Sub-Saharan African governments clearly denied the binding nature of the principle of *non-refoulement* in official statements. They have rather tried to justify several measures adopted, underlining the inapplicability of the rule to specific circumstances, often relying upon domestic legislation in considering exceptions.[124] In 2003, in the case *Tesfaye Shiferwa Awala (Applicant) v Attorney General (Respondent)*, the High Court in Kampala rejected the applicant's claim for refugee status although the lawyers of the applicant maintained that his deportation was equivalent to *non-refoulement.*[125]

Moreover, we note that, formally, domestic legislations in Sub-Saharan Africa do not present any provision contrary to the norms established in the main international instruments. And in any case, as we have seen, given that the principle of *non-refoulement* in the 1969 African Convention does not provide for any exceptions, albeit that the African national legislations present some provision contrary to the international instruments ratified, on the basis of Article 27 of the 1969 Vienna Convention on the Law of the Treaties,[126] Sub-Saharan African states should act accordingly, and respect the international norm.

The entire situation described is also of great concern if we think that, from a normative point of view, the country where the refugee arrives after having fled

124 Mushkat, R., 'Mandatory repatriation of asylum seekers: is the legal norm of *non-refoulement* "dead"?', op. cit. note 112, p. 46.

125 High Court of Uganda: *Tesfaye Shiferwa Awala (Applicant) v Attorney General (Respondent)*, No. 688 of 2003, 8 February 2005, available at: www.unhcr.org/refworld/country,LEGAL,UGA_HC,,UGA,,447bfa194,0.html, accessed 10 October 2014. The lawyers of Mr. Awala claimed that: 'A deportation to Kenya would be contrary to the principle of *non-refoulement* of the 1951 Convention, partly due to his problems in Kenya and because a deportation to Kenya effectively is the same as deportation to Ethiopia, where there is a strong likelihood that he will be detained, tortured and potentially killed.' See ibid., p. 15.

126 Article 27 of the 1969 Vienna Convention reads: 'A party may not invoke the provisions of its internal law as justification for its failure to perform a treaty. This rule is without prejudice to article 46' where Article 46 regards the form of the consent given by the state to be bound to a treaty but not substance of its domestic legislation: '1) A State may not invoke the fact that its consent to be bound by a treaty has been expressed in violation of a provision of its internal law regarding competence to conclude treaties as invalidating its consent unless that violation was manifest and concerned a rule of its internal law of fundamental importance. 2) A violation is manifest if it would be objectively evident to any State conducting itself in the matter in accordance with normal practice and in good faith.'

his/her country of origin should be responsible for respecting his/her human rights by adherence to the principle of *non-refoulement*. According to a common opinion, the host state should therefore be acting on behalf of the international community which, by developing refugee instruments and customary rules, has determined that the lack of national protection for the refugee should be substituted by adequate international protection.[127] As V. Chetail affirmed:

> Le principe de *non-refoulement* demeure l'ultime rempart contre l'oppression, le dernier des droits de l'homme lorsque tous les autres ont été bafoués. (The principle of non-refoulement remains the last stronghold against oppression, the last human right when all the others have been ridiculed.)[128]

Nevertheless, finally, after analyzing such a negative panorama of *non-refoulement* in Sub-Saharan Africa, we cannot refrain from agreeing with those who once wrote, 'Refugee law remains the unwanted child of states.'[129]

127 Marx, R., op. cit. note 51, p. 388.

128 Chetail, V., 'Le principe de *non-refoulement* et le statut de réfugié en droit international', in Chetail, V. and Flauss, J.F. (eds), *La Convention de Genève du 28 juillet 1951 relative au statut des réfugiés 50 ans après : bilan et perspectives*, Bruxelles: Etablissement Emile Bruylant, 2001, p. 61; and follows: Il assure à tout réfugié qu'il ne sera pas remis à ses bourreaux. [. . .] [Le principe de *non-refoulement*] demeure le point de départ incontournable de toute réflexion sur la protection internationale des réfugiés, et interpelle la communauté internationale toute entière dans sa capacité à répondre aux nouvelles réalités internationales à travers la recherche de solutions durables au problème des réfugiés.

129 Byrne, R. and Shacknove, A., 'The safe country notion in European asylum law', in *Harvard Human Rights Journal*, vol. 9, 1996, p. 187.

2 Individual admission in the host country, 'a peaceful and humanitarian act'

The pivotal concept of asylum as it is viewed in Sub-Saharan Africa

2.1 The conception of 'asylum'

The importance of asylum is that it represents an institution through which human values on ethics can be protected. At the same time, however, it must not be forgotten that asylum often has broad implications on international relations and can disturb interstate relations.[1]

The right to seek and enjoy asylum from persecution in other countries does not find an expression in the two main universal binding instruments applicable to the continent, the 1951 Geneva Convention or the 1967 New York Protocol, nor is it mentioned in the 1950 UNHCR Statute. An exception to this is in the preamble of the 1951 Geneva Convention, where the granting of asylum is mentioned as a burden placed 'on certain countries'.[2] In the Final Act of the conference where the 1951 Geneva Convention was adopted, it was, however, recommended that:

> Governments continue to receive refugees in their territories and that they act in concert in a true spirit of international cooperation in order that these refugees may find asylum and the possibility of resettlement.[3]

In Sub-Saharan Africa, the idea regarding African hospitality allowed one to believe that in the past refugees were generally welcomed by their co-ethnics across

1 Kaladrahan Nayar, M.G., 'The rights of asylum in international law: its status and prospects', in *Saint Louis University Law Journal*, vol. 17, 1972–1973, p. 18.

2 1951 Geneva Convention, preamble, paragraph 4: 'Considering that the grant of asylum may place unduly heavy burdens *on certain countries*, and that a satisfactory solution of a problem of which the United Nations has recognized the international scope and nature cannot therefore be achieved without international co-operation.' Emphasis added.

3 Takkenberg, A. and Tahbaz, C.C., *The Collected Travaux Préparatoires of the 1951 Geneva Convention Relating to the Status of Refugees*, 2nd edition, Amsterdam: Dutch Refugee Council, 1989, vol. III: The Conference of Plenipotentiaries on the Status of Refugees and Stateless Persons, 2–25 July 1951, p. 696.

the border and that they were provided with the necessary means to earn their living.[4] This stereotype, however, has been doubted by contemporary scholars,[5] who have affirmed that sometimes the governments of the refugee-generating countries feel that 'whoever gives asylum to my enemy is also my enemy'.[6] The official sources, however, have been more diplomatic on the issue, only partially admitting the real situation. In effect, the OAU and the UNHCR jointly asserted:

> Throughout the continent, countries are generous towards refugees and many practice liberal asylum policies.[7]

Nonetheless, they continued:

> [t]he institution of asylum and the system of refugee protection are under tremendous stress in Africa. The large number of refugees seeking asylum in countries already themselves experiencing tremendous social and economic hardships, has brought into question the very capacity of nations to come with refugees.[8]

The late 1980s saw a noticeable shift in refugee policies in Sub-Saharan Africa: Côte d'Ivoire and Guinea Conakry attempted to force refugees away through severe reductions in the rations of food provided. Benin, for its part, has housed refugees from Chad, the Central African Republic (CAR) and Congo Brazzaville behind camps fenced in with barbed wire.[9]

4 B. Rutinwa described the attitude adopted by many African states between the early 1960s and 1990 as an 'open door policy' towards refugees. See Rutinwa, B., 'The end of asylum? The changing nature of refugee policies in Africa', in UNHCR, *New Issues in Refugee Research*, research paper No. 5, 1999, p. 4.

5 For instance, see the affirmations in Kibreab, G., *African Refugees: Reflections on the African Refugee Problem*, Trenton, NJ: Africa World Press, 1985, pp. 68–9 and the examples of the disturbing trends developed in Africa in the 1980s at ibid., p. 80. In addition, P. Kagwanja and M. Juma, talking about the Somalis in Kenya, clearly affirmed that: 'Somali refugees have received little "African hospitality".' See Kagwanja, P. and Juma, M., 'Somali refugees: protracted exile and shifting security frontiers', in Loescher, G. *et al.* (eds), *Protracted Refugee Situations: Political, Human Rights and Security Implications*, New York: United Nations University Press, 2008, p. 223.

6 Bakwesegha, 'Forced migration in Africa and the OAU Convention', in Adelman, H.; Sorenson, J. (eds), *African Refugees: Development Aid and Repatriation*, North York: York Lane Press, 1994, p. 9.

7 OAU/UNHCR, Refugees and forced population displacement in Africa, 8–10 September 1994, document adopted in occasion of the symposium held in Addis Ababa by OAU/UNHCR, paragraph 12.

8 Ibid., paragraph 13, which points out as follows: 'In a number of countries, the basic principles of refugee protection are not being upheld. Refugees have been arrested and detained without charge. Others have been resumed against their will to places where their lives may be in danger. Yet others have been restricted to refugee camps or to remote, inaccessible locations where they are sometimes exposed to banditry, rape and other forms of criminality. Many have not been able to enjoy social, economic and civil rights.'

9 Vas Dev, S., 'Asylum in Africa: the emergence of the "reluctant host"', in *Development*, vol. 46, 2003, p. 114.

One could argue that the historical hospitality of Sub-Saharan African countries in admitting aliens went to show that at one point asylum could have been guaranteed to individuals and groups who were seeking it. However, as pointed out in Article II of the 1969 OAU Convention, granting asylum in Africa, in some way codifying a historical practice into a legal framework, should be considered as more of a 'humanitarian act'[10] than an action undertaken by the local authorities in an effort to adhere to a legally recognized 'right'. This concept was also confirmed several times by regional African organizations who, when discussing 'asylum', tended to define it as an 'institution' more than as a 'right'. This happened, for instance, in the document adopted on the occasion of the 1994 Symposium held in Addis Ababa.[11] In addition, we also agree with the very pragmatic opinion that a supposed 'open-door' policy – that, for instance, in places like Tanzania has been over since the mid-1990s[12] – in a general state of poverty cannot alleviate the plight of refugees. This is also because:

> The influx of a large number of refugees in the world's poorest nations brings with it a variety of difficulties and places great strains on the countries' inadequate national resources and this naturally erodes the hospitality demonstrated at the time of arrival. Consequently, unless there is an active

10 According to an author, by the provision of Article II1 the country concerned would be required to exercise this 'peaceful and humanitarian act' – asylum – merely in consideration of the African tradition. See Okogbule, N.S., 'The legal dimension of refugee problem in Africa', in *East African Journal of Peace and Human Rights*, vol. 10, 2004, p. 183.

11 OAU/UNHCR, Refugees and forced population displacement in Africa, 8–10 September 1994, document adopted in occasion of the symposium held in Addis Ababa by OAU/UNHCR, recommendation 8 iii). In 1979 the Arusha Conference on the African refugee noted that, although some progress had been made in the direction of strengthening the position of the individual in relation to asylum, '[a]sylum is still a right of the State'. See UNHCR, The recommendations from the Arusha Conference on the African Refugee Problem, Uppsala: Scandinavian Institute of African Studies, 1981, recommendation No. 1, p. 8.

12 See, for instance, Morel, M., 'The lack of refugee burden-sharing in Tanzania: tragic effects', in *Afrika Focus*, vol. 22, 2009, p. 112: '[I]n March 1995, the Tanzanian government closed its border with Burundi to prevent any further refugee influx. [. . .] This decision has been correctly characterized as being unfortunate but understandable. [. . .] Secondly, in December 1996, the Tanzanian government declared that all Rwandese refugees in Tanzania were expected to return home by the end of the year. [. . .] This announcement of the government is said to have been endorsed and co-signed by the UNHCR. [. . .] Patience seemed to have run out and the doctrine of imposed return arose. Lastly, change of practice leads to change in law: the Refugees Act 1998 does not refer explicitly any more to local integration or naturalization as a viable durable solution, but has confined itself to acknowledging only repatriation and resettlement [. . .].' In this regard, see also Ongpin, P., 'Refugees in Tanzania – asset or burden?', in *Journal of Development and Social Transformation*, vol. 5, 2008, pp. 13–14: 'President Nyerere's retirement from office in 1985 brought the entrance of leaders who were not as supportive of the refugees as their predecessor, and thus enacted legislations that inhibited on the freedom of refugees. This resulted in the "Refugee Act" of 1998 which instigated the end of the "Open Door Policy" and was a means of assuring the Tanzanian public that the government was addressing the refugee presence and influx. This new legislation also placed greater emphasis on voluntary repatriation and provided less support to the refugees than was given in the past.'

> intervention on the part of the international refugee assisting organizations, the plight of the refugees will continue unabated.[13]

Article II of the 1969 OAU Convention can be considered one of the most important innovations introduced by the regional instrument, dealing with refugees' fundamental need of legal recognition.[14] The term 'asylum' has generally been interpreted as protection tied to integration into a new society, touching strongly upon the issue of state sovereignty. If understood in this sense, there is no proof of any emerging right to asylum.[15] Furthermore, the issue of an existing right to be granted asylum by individuals who apply for it was also discussed by the ILC at its first session in 1949 in connection with a draft declaration on the rights and duties of states. On this occasion, a proposal was submitted to include an additional article in the draft declaration relating to the right of asylum:

> Every State has the right to accord asylum to persons of any nationality who request it in consequence of persecutions for offences which the State according asylum deems to have a political character. The State of which the refugee is a national has the duty to respect the asylum accorded and may not consider it an unfriendly act.[16]

During the debates surrounding this proposal, the first sentence was amended by erasing the words 'which the state according asylum deems to have'. The second sentence was rejected and it was finally decided not to include an article on asylum in the draft declaration, although one of the members of the committee in charge of writing the declaration pointed out:

> The right of asylum was one of the noblest creations of customary international law. It would be inconceivable not to include it in a general declaration on the rights and duties of States, and the proposed additional article should therefore be included in the declaration which the Commission was preparing.[17]

On the latter affirmation, we could certainly focus our attention specifically on the expression regarding the customary nature of the right to enjoy asylum.

13 Kibreab, G., *African Refugees: Reflections on the African Refugee Problem*, op. cit. note 5, p. 69.

14 Rifaat, A.M., 'Refugees and the right of asylum: an African perspective', in *Revue Egyptienne de droit international*, vol. 40, 1984, pp. 104–6.

15 Kourula, P., *Broadening the Edges: Refugee Definitions and International Protection Revisited*, The Hague/Boston/London: Martinus Nijhoff, 1997, pp. 273–4.

16 ILC, Yearbook of the International Law Commission, 1949, paragraph 67, p. 125, pdf document, available at: http://untreaty.un.org/ilc/publications/yearbooks/Ybkvolumes(e)/ILC_1949_v1_e.pdf, accessed 20 October 2014. Twenty years later, the latter sentence has been translated into the 1969 OAU Convention which at Article II2 argues that '[a]sylum [. . .] shall not be regarded as an unfriendly act by any Member State.'

17 Ibid., declaration made by J.M. Yepes, paragraph 74, p. 126.

In effect, while a state is not obliged to grant asylum, an individual, once admitted to the territory, should be entitled 'to enjoy' it.[18]

According to the general doctrine, 'the right to asylum' consists of several elements: to admit a person onto state territory; to allow him/her to remain there; to refuse to expel or extradite; and finally, not to prosecute, punish or otherwise restrict the individual's liberty.[19] Articles 31, 32 and 33 of the 1951 Geneva Convention seem to implicitly cover various aspects of this concept of asylum.[20] Therefore, the right to enjoy asylum cannot be considered an 'empty phrase',[21] but rather an expression of a historically-based custom, which had already been implicitly codified in Africa prior to 1951. While the right to flee the source of persecution is acknowledged, the right to offer protection from persecution remains a state prerogative. In other words, the most significant right for refugees – one that would reinstall the individual in the state–citizen–territory hierarchy – is not included. Consequently, the 1951 Geneva Convention appears to be one example of the way the refugee brings the clash between sovereign rights and human rights to the fore.[22]

18 According to the analysis of his entire report, we are able to affirm that J.M. Yepes with the expression 'right of asylum' meant the most correct expression 'right to enjoy asylum'. In this regard, see also ECOSOC, Promotion, protection and restoration of human rights at national, regional and international level: the right of everyone to leave any country, including his own, and to return to his country: analysis of the current trends and developments regarding the right to leave any country including one's own, and to return to one's own country, and some other rights or considerations arising therefrom. Final report prepared by Mr. C.L.C. Mubanga-Chipoya, 20 June 1988, Document No. E/CN. 4/Sub. 2/1988/35, paragraph 479, p. 103: 'The right of the State to grant asylum is limited only by treaties to which the State is party. Such limitations exist in the extradition treaties and other treaties on co-operation in criminal matters, in international conventions punishing crimes against humanity, genocide, grave breaches of humanitarian law, treaties for the suppression of terrorism, the International Convention on the Suppression and Punishment of the Crime of *Apartheid*, etc.'

19 Ibid., paragraph 478. At paragraph 477, it is explained that: 'The right to asylum is traditionally understood as the right of a State to grant asylum. Such a right of an individual may be laid down in provisions of municipal law. At the international level, such an individual right may issue from international conventions, but so far there are only rudimentary provisions to this effect.'

20 Edwards, A., 'Human rights, refugees and the right "to enjoy" asylum', in *International Journal of Refugee Law*, vol. 17, 2005, pp. 302–3. While articles 32 ('Expulsion') and 33 ('Prohibition of expulsion or return ("*refoulement*")') of the 1951 Geneva Convention will be further 'protagonists' in this work through two more specific chapters on these topics, Article 31 will be referred to in several, different points of the manuscript. In full, Article 31 ('Refugees unlawfully in the country of refuge') reads: '1) The Contracting States shall not impose penalties, on account of their illegal entry or presence, on refugees who, coming directly from a territory where their life or freedom was threatened in the sense of Article 1, enter or are present in their territory without authorization, provided they present themselves without delay to the authorities and show good cause for their illegal entry or presence. 2) The Contracting States shall not apply to the movements of such refugees restrictions other than those which are necessary and such restrictions shall only be applied until their status in the country is regularized or they obtain admission into another country. The Contracting States shall allow such refugees a reasonable period and all the necessary facilities to obtain admission into another country.'

21 Plender, R. and Mole, N., 'Beyond the Geneva Convention: constructing a *de facto* right of asylum from international human rights instruments', in Nicholson, F. and Twomey, P. (eds), *Refugees: Rights and Realities – Evolving International Concepts and Regimes*, Cambridge: Cambridge University Press, 1999, p. 82.

22 Haddad, E., *The Refugee in International Society: Between Sovereigns*, Cambridge: Cambridge University Press, 2008, p. 95.

character of asylum, as the UNHCR ExCom also frequently does,[33] by referring to asylum as an institution and adopting the formula regionally codified in Article II2 of the 1969 OAU Convention without going too much further.[34]

As an alternative, the UNGA sometimes recalls Article 14 of the 1948 UDHR to provide states with general guidelines:

> [The General Assembly] reaffirms that, as set out in article 14 of the Universal Declaration of Human Rights, everyone has the right to seek and enjoy in other countries asylum from persecution, and calls upon all States to refrain from taking measures that jeopardize the institution of asylum, in particular by returning or expelling refugees or asylum-seekers contrary to international standards.[35]

The ExCom, on the contrary, has been more generous in dealing with asylum, serving the purpose of providing a structured framework for protection and assistance to persons in need of international protection, while ensuring that proper durable solutions can be achieved.[36] This is mostly done by urging governments to follow 'liberal practices' in granting asylum to refugees who enter their territory, and calling on the governments to cooperate with the High Commissioner in the performance of his/her tasks – particularly with respect to asylum.[37] The ExCom reaffirmed in 1997:

> [t]hat the institution of asylum, which derives directly from the right to seek and enjoy asylum set out in Article 14 1) of the 1948 Universal Declaration of Human Rights, is among the most basic mechanisms for the international protection of refugees.[38]

Second International Conference on Assistance to Refugees in Africa, 7 December 1987, resolution No. A/RES/42/107, in particular paragraph 4.

33 For instance, see ExCom, conclusion No. 50 (XXXIX), 'General conclusion on international protection', 1998, paragraph c): '[The ExCom] stressed that States must continue to be guided, in their treatment of refugees, by existing international law and humanitarian principles and practice [. . .]', conclusion No. 82 (XLVIII), 'Safeguarding asylum', 1997, paragraph e): '[The ExCom] calls upon all concerned parties to respect and comply with the precepts on which the institution of asylum is based, and to implement their obligations in a spirit of true humanitarianism [. . .].'

34 For instance, see Assistance to refugees, returnees and displaced persons in Africa, 18 December 2007, resolution No. A/RES/ 62/125, paragraph 16; Assistance to refugees, returnees and displaced persons in Africa, 19 December 2006, resolution No. A/RES/61/139, paragraph 14; Assistance to refugees, returnees and displaced persons in Africa, 13 December 2005, resolution No. A/RES/60/128, paragraph 13.

35 UNGA, Office of the UNHCR, 17 December 1999, resolution No. A/RES/54/146, paragraph 6.

36 ExCom, conclusion No. 85 (XLIX) 'General conclusion on international protection', 1998, paragraph n).

37 ExCom, conclusion No. 5 (XXVIII), 'Asylum', 1977, paragraphs d) and e).

38 ExCom, conclusion No. 82 (XLVIII), 'Safeguarding asylum', 1997, paragraph b) but paragraph c) noticed that the: '[g]rowing complexity of refugee crises poses serious and novel challenges to the institution of asylum.' See also conclusion No. 85 (XLIX) 'General conclusion on

But, aware that there is no universally recognized legally binding instrument which promotes the enforcement of asylum, in 1977 the ExCom could not go beyond requesting the High Commissioner '*to draw the attention*'[39] of governments to the different international instruments existing in this field. At the regional level, the 2001 AALCO Principles indirectly weakened the concept of asylum by solemnly affirming that: '[a] State has the sovereign right to grant or to refuse asylum in its territory to a refugee [. . .].'[40]

In addition, the ExCom, which obviously welcomed the development of asylum legislation as well as the establishment of processes for status determination and admission of refugees in a number of countries,[41] provided rules to identify the country responsible for examining an asylum request by the adoption of common criteria, following several principles. In its work to determine the '[g]eneral policies, under which the High Commissioner shall plan, develop and administer the programs',[42] the ExCom limited itself to drawing sometimes very broad guidelines for the identification of such a country, so as not to go beyond its mandate.

Lastly, the ExCom stressed that it is considered fair for a state to try to call upon another state to grant asylum to an individual, if this second state has a closer connection with the individual than the state where he/she asked for asylum.[43] Furthermore, the ExCom confirmed several other important principles such as:

> While asylum-seekers may be required to submit their asylum request within a certain time limit, failure to do so, or the non-fulfillment of other formal requirements, should not lead to an asylum request being excluded from consideration.[44]

international protection', 1998, paragraph f): '[The Excom] notes that the 50th anniversary of the Universal Declaration of Human Rights is being commemorated this year and reaffirms that the institution of asylum, which derives directly from the right to seek and enjoy asylum from persecution set out in Article 14 of the Declaration, is among the most basic mechanisms for the protection of refugees.' Slightly different is the formulation of other conclusions, for instance, conclusion No. 65 (XLII), 'General conclusion on international protection', 1991, paragraph c): '[The ExCom] emphasizes the primary importance of *non-refoulement* and asylum as cardinal principles of refugee protection [. . .]'; conclusion No. 68 (XLIII), 'General conclusion on international protection', 1992, paragraph f): '[The ExCom] reaffirms the primary importance of the principles of *non-refoulement* and asylum as basic to refugee protection.'

39 Emphasis added.

40 Final text of the revised Asian-African Legal Consultative Organization 1966 Bangkok principles on status and treatment of refugees, AALCO's 40th session, New Delhi, 24 June 2001, Article II2. It is worth noting that the formulation of this paragraph has been accepted without any reservations by the African government, reservations on the contrary coming from four Asian governments.

41 ExCom, conclusion No. 99 (LV), 'General conclusion on international protection', 2004.

42 ECOSOC, Creation of the Executive Committee of the Program of the United Nations High Commissioner for Refugees, 30 April 1958, resolution No. 672 (XXV), letter a).

43 ExCom, conclusion No. 15 (XXX), 'Refugees without an asylum country', 1979, paragraph g) iv).

44 Ibid., paragraph i).

The verb 'should' used in the conditional terms could lead the reader to imagine that countries do not always follow this kind of instruction. As far as we know, however, usually Sub-Saharan African internal legislation on refugees contains no norms punishing the asylum-seeker if he/she does not fulfil the formal requirements requested by law.[45] In the 2005 case *The Republic of Malawi v Abdul Rahman and Others (Somalians)*, the Lilongwe Magistrate Court, made use of its flexibility to recognize the special situation occurring in Somalia, in some way justifying the illegal entry and stay of several Somali asylum-seekers to whom the right of seeking asylum was not denied. The court confirmed:

> Illegal entry of any person for purpose of seeking asylum does not disqualify the applicant to become a refugee. However, any person who illegally enters in Malawi as an asylum seeker is supposed to present him/herself within 20 hours of his/her entry before a competent officer but should not be detained, imprisoned, declared prohibited immigrant or otherwise penalized by reason only of his/her illegal entry or presence in Malawi until the committee makes a decision on his/her application.[46]

This judgment can be considered as a sort of turning point in Malawi's policy because this country, unlike other countries in the area, was rather cautious for a long time in formulating a clear refugee policy during the first decades of its independence. The explanation, in some measure, lies in the paradox and ambivalence that inspired Malawi's regional politics. It is consequently generally believed that legislative developments were prompted by a late realization that the growing refugee problem in the country could no longer be managed and contained without an accurately defined legislative framework. This change was also a response to external pressure engendered by rising international sympathy towards the plight of Mozambican asylum-seekers seeking refuge *en masse* in

45 For instance, Article 5 1) of the 1990 Angolan Law on Refugee Status reads: 'A refugee who is unlawfully present in the country shall not be punished for the act of unlawful entry or presence provided that he/she presents him/herself to the authorities and justifies his/her situation.' Section 9 1) of the 1999 Refugee Act (1998) of Tanzania clearly reads: 'Any person entering or who is within Tanzania, whether lawfully or otherwise and who wishes to remain in Tanzania as a refugee within the meaning of section 4 shall immediately and not later than seven days after entry, unless he/she can show reasonable cause for delay, present him/herself or report to the nearest authorized officer, village Executive Officer, or a justice of peace and apply for recognition as a refugee.' As a reader may note, nothing is said in the case of the asylum-seeker present him/herself after seven days and without showing a reasonable cause for his or her delay. An exception is constituted by the Law No. 021/2002, portant statut des réfugiés en République Démocratique du Congo, 16 October 2002. Article 29 2) of this latter law stipulates that if an asylum-seeker fails to present him/herself to the competent authority within 30 days of his/her entry in the country, he/she '[p]eut etre interpellé par les services compétents qui le déféreront devant la Commission Nationale pour les Réfugiés.' As a reader may easily observe, the formula used here in any case is not really severe towards an asylum-seeker.

46 Lilongwe Magistrate Court, *The Republic of Malawi v Abdul Rahman and Others (Somalians)*, judgment, Case No. 26 of 2005, 9 May 2005, available at: www.unhcr.org/cgi-bin/texis/vtx/refworld/rwmain?page=country&docid=4289d1664&skip=&category=LEGAL&publisher=MWI_RMCL&coi=MWI, accessed 22 September 2014.

neighbouring countries. This approach sharply contrasted with that taken by other countries in the region, which had placed refugees on their political and legislative agendas immediately following the attainment of their independence.[47]

In the example of the Malawian court, a South African High Court underlined that the rights contained in the 1998 National Refugee Act were applicable to asylum-seekers irrespective of whether they came to be in South Africa legally or not, and if they strictly complied with the formal terms to submit their application to claim refugee status.[48]

Despite these official statements, several African governments' reluctance to enforce the protection of crucial rights, such as the right to seek and enjoy asylum, significantly undermine the goals of refugee laws. A typical example of this is seen in several studies that show how many gross abuses of human rights have occurred on a daily basis in refugee camps and other settlements where asylum-seekers often wait for their destiny to be decided.[49]

In various circumstances, the ExCom has expressed its regret for the restrictive asylum practices, which have continued in Sub-Saharan Africa, above all in the early 1980s when countries closed their borders to aliens in search of asylum.[50] In response, the ExCom strongly confirmed several times throughout the entire 1990s and 2000s the 'right' granted to an alien to seek and enjoy asylum.[51]

47 Maluwa, T., 'The domestic implementation of international refugee law: a brief note on Malawi's Refugee Act of 1989', in *International Journal of Refugee Law*, vol. 3, 1991, pp. 506–7.

48 High Court of South Africa (Transvaal Provincial Division), *Judgment on the Lawfulness of Processes at the Refugee Reception Offices in Johannesburg and Pretoria*, Case No. 12960/06, 12 December 2006, available at: www.unhcr.org/cgi-bin/texis/vtx/refworld/rwmain?page=search&docid=45b4c8242&skip=&query=kiliko, accessed 10 October 2014. In South African legislation, Article 21 4) a) of the 1998 South African Refugee Act clearly reads: 'Notwithstanding any law to the contrary, no proceedings may be instituted or continued against any person in respect of his or her unlawful entry into or presence within the Republic [. . .].' However, see Section 23.1 (Asylum transit visa) of the Immigration Amendment Act 3 of 2007 – Government Notice 656 in Government Gazette 30095 dated 18 July 2007. Commencement date: 26 May 2014 and the Immigration Amendment Act 13 of 2011 – Government Notice 690 in Government Gazette 34561 dated 26 August 2011. Commencement date: 26 May 2014 [Proc. Nos. R32 and R33, Gazette No. 37679]. Document available at: www.saflii.org/za/legis/consol_act/ia2002138.pdf, accessed 30 May 2015.

49 For instance, see the description contained in Olsen, O.E. and Scharffscher, K.S., 'Rape in refugee camps as an organizational failure', in *The International Journal of Human Rights*, vol. 8, 2004, pp. 377–97.

50 For instance see conclusion No. 11 (XXIX), 'General conclusion on international protection', 1978, paragraph d): '[The ExCom] recalled the conclusions adopted at the twenty-eighth session regarding asylum and expressed concern that refugees still encountered difficulties in obtaining permanent or even temporary asylum in certain areas'; conclusion No. 25 (XXXIII), 'General conclusion on international protection', 1982, paragraph d); conclusion No. 29 (XXXIV), 'General conclusion on international protection', 1983, paragraph e); conclusion No. 33 (XXXV), 'General conclusion on international protection', 1984, paragraph d).

51 The first time was however in 1988 when the ExCom: '[i]nvited all States to continue actively to support the protection functions of the High Commissioner through all appropriate means, both bilateral and multilateral, as well as to abide by their own humanitarian responsibilities towards refugees, including, particularly, to safeguard the right to seek and enjoy asylum from persecution [. . .].' See ExCom, conclusion No. 52 (XXXIX) 'International solidarity and refugee protection', 1988, paragraph 5). For other more recent examples, see conclusion No. 75 (XLV)

Nevertheless, it appears as though Kenyan authorities did not have the same opinion, having denied these rights to 23 Somalis in November 2007,[52] as well as earlier that same year.[53] In this regard, we observe that Kenya, since gaining its independence, has been one of the few African states involved in the search for a real regional solution for the hundreds of thousands of refugees dispersed across Africa, in spite of the fact that Kenyan authorities delegated RSD to the UNHCR.[54] However, veritable negotiations between governments to make the burden-sharing more effective could provide a real regional solution, as opposed to closing borders to potential asylum-seekers. The Kenyan government's decision to establish a buffer zone within southern Somalia in 2011, where humanitarian aid was provided in order to prevent new asylum-seekers from arriving in Kenya, and to assist with repatriation represents another solution to this issue, although not a regional one.[55]

Somali refugees have also been, however, victims of repressive legislation, introduced in the aftermath of the terror attacks of 11 September 2001 as curbs against terrorist incursions. These anti-terrorist laws have failed to strike a balance between the security imperatives of combating terrorism and the need to protect the values of human rights. This made Somali refugees in Kenya easy targets for illegal arrests and prolonged detention on suspicion grounds, in violation of both universal and regional refugee conventions. Refugees also became targets of a special counter-terrorist unit that Kenya formed in early 2003.[56] But, for instance, the mass-influx of displaced persons from Somalia to Kenya in the last years did

'Internally displaced persons', 1994, paragraph l); conclusion No. 85 (XLIX) 'General conclusion on international protection', 1998, paragraph f); conclusion No. 94 (LIII), 'conclusion on the civilian and humanitarian character of asylum', 2002, paragraph c) i); conclusion No. 97 (LIV) 'conclusion on protection safeguards in interception measures', 2003, paragraph a) iii).

52 The dispatch by the JRS No. 227, 30 November 2007 reads as follows: 'According to the Consortium, the deported Somalis were denied the right to seek asylum and access to humanitarian organizations or the UN refugee agency (UNHCR). They have been returned to Mogadishu where their safety is uncertain.'

53 AI, Kenya – Denied refuge: the effect of the closure of the Kenya/Somalia border on thousands of Somali asylum-seekers and refugees, London: Amnesty International, 2007, p. 14.

54 For instance, see what E. Odhiambo-Abuya affirmed in this regard in Odhiambo-Abuya, E., 'Past reflections, future insights: African asylum law and policy in historical perspective', in *International Journal of Refugee Law*, vol. 19, 2007, p. 54: '[A]s the legislative history of the OAU Refugee Convention suggests, Kenya was one of the few states involved in the search for a regional solution for the hundreds of thousands of refugees then scattered over Africa after the wars of independence, which occurred mostly between 1955 and 1965. In addition, the country has had a long experience of refugees and asylum seekers dating back to the 1960s. Furthermore, owing to political stability and relative calm, Kenya has over the years hosted forced migrants from other African states. As of 2 June 2006, it was host to some 270,000 persons of concern from at least eight neighboring states. Lastly, UNHCR, the international guardian of refugees, has maintained a field presence in Kenya since 1969.'

55 Lindley, A., 'Between a protracted and a crisis situation: policy responses to Somali refugees in Kenya', in *Refugee Survey Quarterly*, vol. 30, 2011, p. 25.

56 Kagwanja, P.; Juma, M., op. cit. note 5, p. 225.

not stop because of the action of the counter-terrorism unit,[57] although Somalia is believed to host terroristic organizations on its territory.[58]

This restrictive attitude by the Kenyan authorities has also been shared by Ugandan authorities in recent years,[59] as Rwandan asylum-seekers were denied the right to seek asylum in 2005.[60] In 2001, Congolese individuals of Rwandan origin were denied the right to seek asylum in Rwanda because they were considered Congolese, then they were expelled from Congo because of their Rwandan origin.[61]

As a clear example of how difficult it is to take advantage of a practically presumptive right to enjoy asylum in Uganda, S.B. Tindifa contended:

> Many of these rights [provided in the 1951 Geneva and 1969 OAU Conventions] are violated [in Uganda] and include the following: the right to life; the right to equal treatment, education and naturalization; freedom

57 Lindley, A., op. cit. note 55, p. 22.

58 See, for instance, US Department of State, Country Reports on Terrorism 2013 – Somalia, 30 April 2014, available at: www.refworld.org/docid/536229be5.html, accessed 7 October 2014: 'Compared with previous years, the terrorist group Al-Shabaab executed a wider spectrum of attacks in Mogadishu and throughout Somalia, including more sophisticated, asymmetrical attacks and assassinations; and destruction of property. Several larger and more deadly Al-Shabaab attacks in Mogadishu involved two-part operations, where attackers targeted first responders and onlookers, producing higher casualties. Al-Shabaab also executed attacks on harder targets in Mogadishu, including international compounds and convoys.'

59 In this regard, S.B. Tindifa explained: '[I]ntegrating refugees into local communities has never been considered by the Ugandan authorities as a viable option. [. . .] This perception of the refugee question has led the Uganda Government to adopt measures aimed at tight control, segregation, "pacification" and the depoliticization of refugees. [. . .] This practice marginalizes refugees.' See Tindifa, S.B., 'Refugees and human rights in Uganda: a critical assessment of the law, policy and practice', in *East African Journal of Peace and Human Rights*, vol. 5, 1998, p. 59. And K.J. Kelley added: 'Kenya and Tanzania are violating the rights of refugees seeking asylum in the two countries. [. . .] Xenophobia and anti-refugee sentiment among East Africans have notably hardened. [. . .] Conditions for refugees are said to be significantly better in Uganda. But their treatment may worsen as Uganda negotiates with Kenya and Tanzania to standardize the refugee policies of all three nations.' Quoted in Katalikawe, J., 'Helping refugees to help themselves: Uganda's response to the refugee crisis in the Great Lake region', in *East African Journal of Peace and Human Rights*, vol. 8, 2002, pp. 212–13.

60 The dispatch by the JRS No. 175, 15 July 2005 reads as follows: 'According to a statement on 3 July from the Uganda Office of the Prime Minister (OPM), 90 per cent of Rwandan refugees have been rejected and will soon be asked to leave the country. This follows an influx of between 1,300–1,500 refugees from Rwanda into Uganda in April and May 2005, most of whom were confined to living in the Nakivale settlement in Western Uganda without a decent place to stay, or food to eat. The Ugandan government alleges that by confining refugees to this one site, it would prevent double registration.'

61 According to the dispatch by the JRS No. 86, 3 February 2001: 'JRS Grands Lacs reports that 146 Congolese people of Rwandan ethnic origin arrived in Kiziba camp, western Rwanda, after they were sent out of Congo and later rejected as Rwandans in Kigali. In June last year, some 800 Congolese people of Rwandan ethnic origin living in Kinshasa were placed in a camp for security reasons. In September, the government allegedly sent 146 of them to Rwanda. The people arrived in Kigali, where they were told they are not Rwandan and rejected.'

of expression, association and worship; freedom of movement; the right to gainful employment; the right against *refoulement*.[62]

This refers to a country with a long tradition of hosting refugees that dates back to the end of the Second World War, when the country hosted Polish refugees at Mpumude in the current Mukono district.[63]

We are far from the times in which African officials declaimed that the granting of asylum was a 'moral duty', in the words of the former President of Botswana, Q.K.J. Masire,[64] although the right of asylum-seekers to enter and remain in the country has never been explicitly indicated or assured.[65]

If the right to seek and enjoy asylum is often contradicted in Sub-Saharan Africa, we cannot be surprised in ascertaining that there is no practical evidence of the existence of such a right to be granted on the continent. The 50 Ethiopians who did not receive asylum from South Africa in 2000, without any convincing explanations, can easily testify to this, for example.[66] It is also evident from the only 500 Zimbabweans, out of the over 35,000 who applied for it, who received asylum in South Africa in the two-year period 2006–2007.[67]

Thus, not surprisingly, the ExCom finally stressed that the credibility of the institution of asylum can be seriously affected by the lack of prompt return of those who are found not to be in need of international protection.[68]

62 Tindifa, S.B., op. cit. note 59, p. 60.

63 Information available at: http://reliefweb.int/report/burundi/uganda-launches-progressive-refugee-act-world, accessed 10 September 2014. In this regard, see also http://ugandaradionetwork.com/a/story.php?s=22488, accessed 10 January 2014: 'Uganda's history with refugees began after World War II when over 4,000 Polish refugees were hosted in Uganda in Mpumude in Mukono District in Central Uganda. The country now hosts refugees from Democratic Republic of Congo, Rwanda, Burundi, Sudan and Kenya. Refugees also come to Uganda from as far as Somali, Eritrea, Malawi, Pakistan, Tanzania, Central African Republic, Chad, Iraq, Iran, Kuwait, Sierra Leone, Liberia, Ivory Cost and Guinea. Uganda's long history with refugees has led to a unique refugee experience where refugees live in settlements and not camps, like many other African countries. On arrival in Uganda, refugees are given plots of land for cultivation, settlement and other livelihood activities such as agriculture. As a result the refugees do not rely forever on relief aid but are encouraged to attain self-reliance.'

64 Maluwa, T., 'The concept of asylum and the protection of refugees in Botswana: some legal and political aspects', in *International Journal of Refugee Law*, vol. 2, 1990, p. 594. Q.K.J. Masire was the second *President* of *Botswana* for the BDP from 1980 to 1998.

65 Macharia-Makobi, E. and Pfumorodze, J., 'Advancing refugee protection in Botswana through improved refugee status determination', in *African Human Rights Law Journal*, vol. 13, 2013, p. 167.

66 JRS, Southern Africa Annual Report, 2000, p. 43.

67 See the news: 'Zimbabweans face uphill struggle in search for asylum in South Africa', 11 July 2008, available at: www.unhcr.org/48776e934.html, accessed 20 September 2014. Many of the Zimbabweans entering South Africa in that period were fleeing '[O]peration Murambatsvina, an urban demolitions campaign that forcibly displaced hundreds of thousands of people, virtually all supporters of the opposition. As a result, some 3.5 million people fled abroad. [. . .] And at least 2 million refugees remain in South Africa.' See Weiss, T.G., *Humanitarian Intervention: Ideas in Action*, 2nd edn, Cambridge/Malden, MA: Polity Press, 2012, p. 59.

68 ExCom, conclusion No. 96 (LIV) 'conclusion on the return of persons found not to be in need of international protection', 2003, paragraph b).

Nevertheless, as we have seen above, in Sub-Saharan Africa the problem starts before the possible repatriation of the individuals who do not deserve protection, and lies at the very roots of the concept of asylum: it derives from the lack of a set of unanimously recognized standards, which allow all aliens who seek asylum to be in an effective position to do so. As the UNHCR stressed in 2012:

> Asylum fatigue, once considered a defining feature of industrialized countries, is increasingly evident in Sub-Saharan Africa. Restrictive asylum policies in countries of transit and destination, as well as efforts to create 'refugee-free' zones at the national and/or sub-regional level, is evidence of a growing reluctance to provide protection and to keep borders open. Security concerns contribute to more restrictive asylum policies and to undermining support for asylum.[69]

2.2 'Temporary protection' as an increasingly frequent means of providing protection to refugees

As the implications of asylum sometimes present too much of a commitment for states to comply with, a more recent concept has been introduced: 'temporary protection',[70] a concept codified in Africa in the 1969 OAU Convention.[71]

It prohibits a state from repatriating by force foreign nationals who find themselves on its territory.[72] In Sub-Saharan Africa, the most common form of temporary protection programme arises when a host country consents to the UNHCR setting up and running a refugee camp.[73]

69 UNHCR, 2012 Regional Operations Profile: Africa, available at: www.unhcr.org/pages/4a02d7fd6.html, accessed 3 October 2014.

70 In this regard, D. Kennedy pointed out: 'The debate about what has been termed "temporary refuge" frankly acknowledges what it sees as an inevitable disjuncture between the international legal exhortations of international institutions and the practice of national politics.' See Kennedy, D., 'International refugee protection', in *Human Rights Quarterly*, vol. 8, 1986, p. 65.

71 Fitzpatrick, J., 'Temporary protection of refugees: elements of a formalized regime', in *American Journal of International Law*, vol. 94, 2000, p. 279.

72 Mandal, R., 'Protection mechanism outside of the 1951 Convention ("complementary protection")', in *UNHCR, Legal and Protection Policy Research Series*, No. 9, 2005, p. 3. Foreign nationals '[w]ho find themselves in its territory after having fled generalized violence and other threats to their lives and security caused by internal armed conflict within their own state. The prohibition on forced repatriation continues until the violence ceases and the alien's own state can assure the security and protection of its nationals. The refuge state may seek in the interim to resettle the aliens in a third country willing to accept them and to protect their lives and safety.' See Perluss, D. and Hartmann, J.F., 'Temporary refuge: emergence of a customary norm', in *Virginia Journal of International Law*, vol. 26, 1985–1986, p. 554.

73 Fouda, L., 'Compulsory voluntary repatriation: why temporary protection for Sudanese asylum-seekers in Cairo amounts to *refoulement*', in *Georgetown Journal on Poverty Law & Policy*, vol. XIV, 2007, p. 516. In this regard, at pp. 516–17, the author pointed out: 'Temporary protection in refugee camps is a costly and imperfect method of protecting those who claim a need for international help.'

Before continuing with this paragraph, I think it is necessary to provide the reader with a semantic explanation about my choice. In effect, after having read several works where the commentators interchangeably used expressions such as 'temporary asylum', 'temporary refuge' and 'temporary protection', to make things easier and clearer, the author of this work consulted a very renowned, terminological source for expressions concerning refugee issues: the UNHCR Thesaurus. The thesaurus only provides for the definition of 'temporary protection', defined as:

> Protection granted for a limited, though not necessarily defined, time by the country of refuge, usually in situations of large-scale influx. Temporary refuge is premised on the *non-refoulement* principle through time, and on the enjoyment of basic rights pending a lasting solution.[74]

Conversely, if the reader looks up the expression 'temporary refuge' and/or 'temporary asylum' in the same thesaurus, he/she will always be returned to the expression 'temporary protection' that is, the definition that we will privilege in this work along with the homologous expression 'temporary refuge'. This latter expression is also used by the UNHCR in the definition provided above as a synonym of the former.[75]

The concept of temporary protection has emerged to fill the gap between a decline in the willingness of states to grant asylum and a trend towards protection in the country of origin. The thinking behind this seems to be that refugees are given protection in host countries on the specific understanding that it is for a limited amount of time, and that once conditions in the country of origin return to normal they will be required to return home. Moving away from a universal refugee protection regime, temporary protection has the propensity to assist on an *ad hoc* basis to specific groups of refugees. In addition, since temporary protection status means that the individual will return home, it provides a useful

74 Definition available at: www.refugeethesaurus.org/hms/refugee_obj.php?type=terms&id=2077, accessed 25 September 2014.

75 In this regard, D. Luca wondered if the two expressions were really synonyms or they mean something different. The author, in her work, provided a bibliography through which everyone could draw appropriate conclusions. She concluded: 'The need for protection is the inherent condition of a refugee who has crossed an international border and starts at the very moment the State of origin is no longer providing it and lasts as long as persecution persists, should that be for a few weeks, or for many months or years. The way protection is implemented can range from *non-refoulement* to asylum and from one end to the other protection remains and is the foundation stone for the system. But the level is quite different.' See Luca, D., 'Questioning temporary protection', in *International Journal of Refugee Law*, vol. 6, 1994, p. 536. And, ibid., at p. 537, she complained that: 'It is also worrying that scholars have nearly ignored the existing literature on temporary refuge, when analyzing the issue of temporary protection. Any researcher who undertakes to discuss a topic must consider what has already been written on it, either to use it as a basis for his or her theory, or to criticize it and build up new reasoning. It is a simple question of methodology and at the same time a mistake to forget past developments.'

link between *non-refoulement* and coming to a durable solution.[76] As the ExCom affirmed in 1980, in its first conclusion explicitly dedicated to the phenomenon, the institution of 'temporary refuge' is considered particularly important in the event of mass-influx situations,[77] mainly in developing countries.[78] Having stressed the essential need for individuals to whom temporary protection has been granted to enjoy basic humanitarian standards of treatment,[79] this view was also highlighted in the following year. In effect, in 1981, in its conclusion No. 22 the ExCom provided a list of standards of protection to grant to individuals who are 'temporarily'[80] protected when a country faces an influx of vast proportions to

76 Haddad, E., op. cit. note 22, pp. 206–8. At p. 207 the author noted: '[S]upporters of temporary protection point out that the whole spirit of the 1951 Convention itself is temporary, since it is clearly spelt out in the cessation clauses that refugee status should end when the conditions that forced an individual to flee have come to an end. Refugee law reformulated would therefore look like a generalized temporary protection system, and would regain its relevance by acting "to reconcile the need for a secure and dignified refugee protection system to the legitimate interests of the countries in which refugees are sheltered."' The quotation in E. Haddad is from: Hathaway, J.C., 'Can international refugee law be made relevant again?', 'Making international refugee law relevant again: a proposal for collectivized and solution-oriented protection', in *Harvard Human Rights Journal*, vol. 10, 1997, p. xxvi.

77 In the words of J. Fitzpatrick: '[t]emporary protection serves as an interim response to mass-influx, providing safety while a durable solution is sought.' See Fitzpatrick, J., 'Temporary protection of refugees: elements of a formalized regime', op. cit. note 71, p. 287. At ibid., p. 289, the author raised a topical debate on the concept of temporary protection. In effect: '[t]emporary protection is often linked to mass-influx, but whether temporary protection should be so restricted is not clearly agreed. Admission to safety and protection against unsafe forced return are commonly assumed to be the guarantees most vital to mass arrivals, while other aspects of their treatment may have to be compromised, at least in the short term, to avoid placing an unrealistic burden on the state of refuge.' And, later at p. 295, she pointed out that: 'Thus, one pivotal question is whether temporary protection should be limited to situations of mass-influx, and, if so, what the triggering criteria should be. Potential elements might include, in addition to sheer numbers, the solidity and resiliency of the refuge state's status determination system, its economic vibrancy, its absorptive capacity, and its social/cultural links to arriving migrants.'

78 Pirjola, J., 'Temporary protection as a future model for asylum?', in *Nordic Journal of International Law*, vol. 64, 1995, pp. 424–5.

79 ExCom, conclusion No. 19 (XXXI), 'Temporary refugee', 1980, paragraphs a), c) and e) while paragraph g) explains: 'Considered that the practice of temporary refuge had not been sufficiently examined and should be further studied, particularly in regard to (i) procedures for the admission of refugees, (ii) their status pending a durable solution, (iii) the implications of temporary refuge for international solidarity, including burden sharing.'

80 ExCom, conclusion No. 22 (XXXII), 'Protection of asylum-seekers in situations of large-scale influx', 1981, paragraph II A 1): 'In situations of large-scale influx, asylum-seekers should be admitted to the State in which they first seek refuge and if that State is unable to admit them on a durable basis, it should always admit them at least on a temporary basis and provide them with protection according to the principles set out below. They should be admitted without any discrimination as to race, religion, political opinion, nationality, country of origin or physical incapacity.' The principles mentioned here are listed in paragraph IIB 2), letters a) to p): 'a) they should not be penalized or exposed to any unfavorable treatment solely on the ground that their presence in the country is considered unlawful; they should not be subjected to restrictions on their movements other than those which are necessary in the interest of public health and public order; b) they should enjoy the fundamental civil rights internationally recognized, in particular those set out in the Universal Declaration of Human Rights; c) they should receive all necessary

which it is not able, in the short term, to respect its 1951 Geneva Convention obligations. These documents make clear however, that after a transitory period of crisis management, host countries are to guarantee the rights of individuals under protection, according to the standards of the 1951 Geneva Convention.[81]

In early 2010, a South African High Court confirmed the importance of the concept of 'temporary protection', allowing an asylum-seeker to have his temporary asylum-seeker permit renewed because of the still unsafe situation reigning in Burundi. This can be contextualized by looking at a case where the respondents claimed for the imprisonment of the applicant because the situation in Burundi was, in their opinion, stabilized, and therefore the former asylum-seeker had become an irregular migrant once his/her previous temporary permit had expired.[82]

assistance and be provided with the basic necessities of life including food, shelter and basic sanitary and health facilities; in this respect the international community should conform with the principles of international solidarity and burden-sharing; d) they should be treated as persons whose tragic plight requires special understanding and sympathy. They should not be subjected to cruel, inhuman or degrading treatment; e) there should be no discrimination on the grounds of race, religion, political opinion, nationality, country of origin or physical incapacity; f) they are to be considered as persons before the law, enjoying free access to courts of law and other competent administrative authorities; g) the location of asylum-seekers should be determined by their safety and well-being as well as by the security needs of the receiving State. Asylum-seekers should, as far as possible, be located at a reasonable distance from the frontier of their country of origin. They should not become involved in subversive activities against their country of origin or any other State; h) family unity should be respected; i) all possible assistance should be given for the tracing of relatives; j) adequate provision should be made for the protection of minors and unaccompanied children; k) the sending and receiving of mail should be allowed; l) material assistance from friends or relatives should be permitted; m) appropriate arrangements should be made, where possible, for the registration of births, deaths and marriages; n) they should be granted all the necessary facilities to enable them to obtain a satisfactory durable solution; o) they should be permitted to transfer assets which they have brought into a territory to the country where the durable solution is obtained; and p) all steps should be taken to facilitate voluntary repatriation.' In this regard, F. Crépeau and L. Holland affirmed: 'It must be noticed that the level of protection offered by Conclusion 22 is lesser than that guaranteed by the Convention of 1951. This is explained by the *interim* nature of temporary protection meant as a tool to facilitate admission of asylees and a guideline as to the minimum standards applicable in a crisis situation where the host state simply does not possess the necessary resources to implement all facets of the protection guaranteed by the Convention. Because of this, the refugee, under a system of temporary protection, enjoys a lesser protection than the refugee whose status is based on the Convention of 1951.' See Crépeau, F. and Holland, L., 'Temporary protection, continuing insecurity: a regime replacing convention protection of refugees in violation of international law', in *Canadian Journal of Law and Society*, vol. 12, 1997, p. 244. At idem, the authors also explained: 'The legal nature of Conclusion 22 also differs from the Convention of 1951. Whereas the ratification of the Convention imposes obligations upon the state, Conclusion 22 is "soft law" which is made by *consensus* at ExCom. It does, however, contain some elements of customary law.'

81 Ibid., p. 242.

82 High Court of South Africa (South Gauteng, Johannesburg), *Kanyo Aruforse v Minister of Home Affairs and others*, Case No. 2010/1189, 25 January 2010, paragraph 11, p. 7: 'It is common cause

The expression 'temporary protection', mainly assured to individuals having fled generalized violence and other threats to their lives and insecurity caused by internal armed conflict within their own state,[83] seems in our opinion to have been enlarged to encompass other situations, such as natural disasters, a very common situation in Sub-Saharan Africa.[84]

This norm is currently growing to preside over the circumstances of civilians escaping into an unknown territory and into an unfamiliar legal scene, and presents an illuminating case study in developing customary international law.[85]

In addition, 'temporary protection' has been created '[a]t the intersection of refugee law, humanitarian law, and human rights law'[86] and assumes a particular interest in Sub-Saharan Africa. In effect, although there is nothing intrinsic preventing its application to individuals, it is generally used to describe a short-term emergency response to an influx of asylum-seekers,[87] a phenomenon that has sadly become common on the continent.[88]

It is not by chance that the 'expanded definition' of refugee provided in the 1969 OAU Convention, which seems to support the implementation of a norm

that the applicant was arrested and detained at Lindela since 15 July 2009. He was, on the respondents' version, arrested as an illegal foreigner and he is being detained pending his deportation. From 15 July 2009 until 12 August 2009, the applicant was detained without in terms of section 34 1). On 12 August 2009, the Magistrate's Court, in terms of section 34 1) d), extended the applicant's detention for a period of ninety calendar days. This period expired during November 2009 and was not extended again. It is to be noted that "court", in terms of section 1, means a Magistrate's Court.' The sections considered in the judgment referred to the South African Immigration Act, Act No. 13 of 2002.

83 In this regard, M. Jacques pointed out that: 'It should [. . .] be reminded that an asylum state's duties towards its refugees, as well as its general obligations under international humanitarian law, do not cease in time of armed conflict, whether international or non-international. Consequently, the principle of *non-refoulement* remains applicable in situations of armed conflict. However, for refugees caught up in an internal armed conflict, particularly if they find themselves in rebel-controlled territory, international humanitarian law clearly constitutes the first line of protection against abuse, not only due to its *lex specialis* character, but also because, unlike human rights and refugee law, it is widely regarded as binding upon states and non-state actors alike.' See Jacques, M., *Armed Conflict and Displacement: The Protection of Refugees and Displaced Persons under International Humanitarian Law*, Cambridge: Cambridge University Press, 2012, p. 184.

84 R. Black talked about '[t]hree sub-categories of environmental refugee, namely temporary displacement due to temporary environmental stress; permanent displacement due to permanent environmental change; and temporary or permanent displacement due to progressive degradation of the resource base.' See Black, R., 'Environmental refugees: myth or reality?', in *UNHCR, New Issues in Refugee Research*, research paper No. 34, 2001, pp. 1–2.

85 Perluss, D.; Hartmann, J.F., op. cit. note 72, p. 553.

86 McAdam, J., *Complementary Protection in International Refugee Law*, Oxford: Oxford University Press, 2007, p. 42.

87 Mandal, R., 'Protection mechanism outside of the 1951 Convention ("complementary protection")', op. cit. note 72, p. 3. However, J. Fitzpatrick was doubtful about the formalization of the temporary protection because, if it fills important legal lacunae, on the other hand it could appear to support questionable interpretations of existing treaty obligations. See Fitzpatrick, J., 'Temporary protection of refugees: elements of a formalized regime', op. cit. note 77, p. 296.

88 Ibid., p. 283.

explicitly regarding temporary protection,[89] has been considered as a fundamental basis for the transitory protection also outside the African continent. The UNHCR has even been of the opinion that 'an OAU refugee Convention writ large' was the most attractive option to internationally codify a complementary protection, and the concept of 'temporary protection' constituted its pivot.[90]

On the other hand, the 1969 OAU Convention has already served as a legal basis for a number of African states to provide temporary refuge to nationals of neighbouring countries who had fled violence or civil strife. There are, however, some exceptions such as Ghana and Nigeria which, as yet, have not commonly granted an individual the right to rely on the extended refugee definition provided in the 1969 OAU Convention.[91]

Temporary protection is often associated with effective burden-sharing, possibly involving the physical transfer of asylum-seekers and organized schemes for economic assistance to states of refuge.[92] This objective may be resisted by African states seeking to avoid legal commitment, as well as by refugee advocates who fear the commoditization of refugee protection. In any case, it often occurs that 'temporary' protection can be transformed into 'permanent', above all when the stay of the refugee in the country of asylum lasts for decades and it is difficult to control his/her every movement.[93] The Angolans, who were provided temporary protection by DRC officials since 1975, during the period of Angola's civil conflict, and were never repatriated, constitute a typical example of this situation.[94]

There are, however, exceptions to this general attitude, as in the case of Rwandans returning in the mid-1990s from Uganda where they were 'temporarily' protected since 1959.[95] On the contrary, for instance, even in recent years, South

89 Hailbronner, K., '*Non-refoulement* and "humanitarian" refugees: customary international law or wishful legal thinking?', in *Virginia Journal of International Law*, vol. 26, 1985–6, p. 135. In this regard, A.M. Rifaat contended that: 'Signatory states [of the 1969 OAU Convention] were also urged to grant temporary asylum to refugees even when they feel that they cannot grant them permanent asylum.' The author based his affirmations upon Article II5 of the 1969 OAU Convention. See A.M. Rifaat, op. cit. note 14, p. 106.

90 McAdam, J., Complementary Protection in International Refugee Law, op. cit. note 86, pp. 45–7.

91 Hailbronner, K., '*Non-refoulement* and "humanitarian" refugees: customary international law or wishful legal thinking?', op. cit. note 89, p. 135.

92 Fitzpatrick, J., 'Temporary protection of refugees: elements of a formalized regime', op. cit. note 71, p. 287.

93 In this regard, N.S. Okogbule observed: 'The problem [. . .] is that the longer a refugee stays in country of asylum, the more he/she acquires rights and interests which are at variance with the continuing grant of the temporary status of a refugee. For instance, a refugee may get married to a national of the asylum-granting country [. . .] and yet by law remain a refugee. The question then arises, under those circumstances, when can it be said that his or her refugee status has ended?' See Okogbule, N.S., op. cit. note 10, p. 188.

94 Perluss, D. and Hartmann, J.F., op. cit. note 72, p. 561.

95 Fitzpatrick, J., 'Temporary protection of refugees: elements of a formalized regime', op. cit. note 77, pp. 287 and 293. We need to point out that, historically, refugees were perceived as a temporary problem in Uganda, which considered itself just a transit point for them. See Tindifa,

African authorities, and also in spite of the presence of Article 22 in the domestic legislation on refugees,[96] denied temporary protection to asylum-seekers from Zimbabwe.[97] In the latter episode, the inconsistency of attitude, a recurrent trait regarding the application of refugee law in Sub-Saharan Africa, was also clearly shown by the following affirmations made at the same time:

> South Africa's very recent inclination to provide a special temporary residence permit to Zimbabweans (one that will legalize their stay for a short period of time and allow them to work in the interim) will hopefully fill the gap in South Africa's law. [. . .] [S]uch a permit would not only promote the legal entry of Zimbabweans into South Africa at a port of entry, but at the same time it will serve a much greater purpose – formulating a policy for socio-economic migrants who are facing a humanitarian crisis which will ensure that refugee protection is not being eroded.[98]

We would like to note that the 1997 South African Draft Green Paper on International Migration contained various recommendations pertaining to a separate and self-standing piece of refugee legislation in South Africa, which should:

> [b]e based on a model of refugee protection that is rights-based, solution-oriented, with the sharing of the burden across all SADC member states.

S.B., op. cit. note 59, p. 56. However, H.R. Garry warned: '[R]efugees should not be seen as only requiring temporary protection [in Uganda]. [. . .] [R]ather, refugees should be seen as persons entitled to durable and permanent solutions to their problem of protection.' See Garry, H.R., 'Applying the "plumb line" of Uganda's Bill of Rights: human rights and the draft bill of refugees', in *East African Journal of Peace and Human Rights*, vol. 5, 1998, p. 71.

96 See South Africa: Act No. 33 of 2008, Refugees Amendment Act, 26 November 2008: 'Amendment of section 22 of Act 130 of 1998. Section 22 of the principal Act is hereby amended by – a) the substitution for subsections 1), 2), 3) and 4) of the following Subsections, respectively: "(I) The [Refugee Reception Officer] Refugee Status Determination Officer must, pending the outcome of an application in terms of section 21 1), [issue to] refer the applicant to the officers contemplated in section 8 3) to be issued with an asylum seeker permit in the prescribed form allowing the applicant to sojourn in the Republic temporarily, subject to any conditions[,] determined and endorsed by the [Standing Committee] Director-General, which are not in conflict with the Constitution or international law [and are endorsed by the Refugee Reception Officer on the permit).'

97 The dispatch by the JRS, No. 222, 14 September 2007 reads as follows: '[I]inconsistencies have clouded what could be new thinking in the department. Home affairs director-general Mavuso Msimang said assisting Zimbabwean asylum seekers was not among his department's priorities.'

98 Khan, F. *Patterns and policies of migration in South Africa: Changing Patterns and the need for a comprehensive approach.* Paper presented for conference on Patterns on Policies of Migration in Loreto, Italy, 3 October 2007, p. 10, in Schreier, T.H., *A Critical Examination of South Africa's Application of the Expanded OAU Refugee Definition: Is Adequate Protection Being Offered Within the Meaning of the 1969 OAU Refugee Convention?*, Cape Town: University of Cape Town, Faculty of Law, LL.M. Thesis, 2008, pp. 59–60. We note that, in South Africa, in 2008 '[t]here were [also] about 18,900 *de facto* refugees [. . .] – legitimate refugees who did not apply for refugee status – about 11,800 of whom were Zimbabweans.' See Kriger, N., 'The politics of legal status for Zimbabweans in South Africa', in McGregor, J. and Primorac, R. (eds), *Zimbabwe's New Diaspora: Displacement and the Cultural Politics of Survival*, New York/Oxford: Berghahn Books, 2010, p. 84.

> The objective of the model is to provide temporary protection to persons whose basic human rights are at risk in their country of origin [. . .].[99]

Finally, a cessation of temporary protection presents two elements. First, temporary protection *may* be ended, and its recipients repatriated, when the situation in the country of origin allows a return in safety and with dignity. Second, temporary protection *should* be ended, and a solution not relating to repatriation delivered, when a dangerous situation persists in the state of origin and recipients of temporary protection can no longer acceptably be maintained in uncertainty and/or under standards of treatment falling short of the 1951 Geneva Convention.[100]

As a matter of fact, it remains doubtful whether the 1969 OAU Convention really does lend support to the supposition that a right of temporary refuge can be considered a regional customary international law. The practice of contracting states in cases of mass-influx is far from certain.[101] In addition, opponents of temporary refuge have argued that if it is to be pragmatic or grounded in the host state's particular capability to comply, it menaces the obligation of *non-refoulement*. Likewise, D. Kennedy contended that if temporary refuge would be binding, it would threaten the discretionary character of asylum and admission, mainly if the link with international burden-sharing cannot be established with equivalent normative and practical force. These kinds of criticism rely alternatively upon their claim to be different from both asylum and refugee law, as deems true for the defences of temporary refuge as well. As such, the debate about the validity of a notion of temporary refuge repeats the seemingly endless debate that has been taking place within the discussion on right to asylum and *non-refoulement*.[102] However, in this regard F. Crépeau and L. Holland have clearly explained that temporary protection needs to be considered as constituting provisional protection based on the different binding instruments on refugee protection and not as a discretionary act of moral choice. This can be done also through the lenses of the framework put in place by the UNHCR with a vision of expanding on ExCom conclusion No. 22,[103] because, lacking exacting guidelines on length and qualification to implement a regime of temporary protection renders this conclusion insufficient if seeking to protect asylum-seekers.[104] The problem arises

99 Schreier, T.H., op. cit. note 98, pp. 32–3.

100 Fitzpatrick, J., 'Temporary protection of refugees: elements of a formalized regime', op. cit. note 77, p. 300. Emphasis added. For an analysis of the voluntary repatriation, as a durable solution, see *infra*, Chapter 8.

101 Hailbronner, K., '*Non-refoulement* and "humanitarian" refugees: customary international law or wishful legal thinking?', op. cit. note 89, p. 135.

102 Kennedy, D., op. cit. note 70, p. 67.

103 Crépeau, F. and Holland, L., op. cit. note 80, p. 259.

104 In this regard, J. Fitzpatrick clarified that: 'As long as temporary protection is not harmonized, states may be tempted to treat temporary protection as a mere act of grace whose termination is essentially discretionary and standardless. In practice, states appear to assess the occurrence of changed conditions in the state of origin prior to withdrawal of temporary protection, in a

when, as it seems to happen often in the region, the UNHCR has implemented temporary protection in a way that weakens the 1951 Geneva Convention, rather than complementing it, with temporary protection being effective and ethical only whether the UNHCR limits its application.[105]

As a way of conclusion, we emphasize that the most evident trait in the affirmation of both concepts of 'temporary protection' and 'asylum' *tout court* on the African continent is the presence of an obvious inconsistency between the writing and application of these norms. To be clear, we think that African legislators and officials reveal themselves to be incoherent when writing norms which do not really take into consideration the situation 'on the field'. Alternatively, more often, they show their incoherence in the *de facto* non-application of both the international and national provisions contained in these legal instruments, unwillingly promoting the 'legal emptiness of the norm'.[106] An example of this attitude was involuntarily provided by Egypt in 2005, where Sudanese asylum-seekers called for the ending of the 'temporary protection' guaranteed by authorities in Cairo, described as a 'compelled voluntary repatriation',[107] because it afforded these refugees with very few rights in Egypt and no possibility to be resettled elsewhere.[108]

manner that suggests acceptance of familiar cessation criteria. However, empirical judgments concerning prevailing conditions may vary unless a collective assessment process is established.' See Fitzpatrick, J., 'Temporary protection of refugees: elements of a formalized regime', op. cit. note 77, p. 302. And ibid., at pp. 305–6: 'The duration of temporary protection is a crucial issue. A process and a set of substantive benchmarks for the withdrawal of protection must be agreed upon and consensus reached concerning a transition to more secure residence after several years of interim protection. Uniform standards of treatment for temporary protection beneficiaries can be articulated, taking into consideration both the economic, social, and cultural guarantees of the 1951 Refugee Convention and provisions of general international human rights law, in particular the norm against discrimination.'

105 Fouda, L., op. cit. note 73, pp. 512 and 537.

106 In our opinion M.H. Shapiro, although he was referring to a different domain of law, correctly argued: 'One claim may be that defending certain interests and even discussing certain topics reflect moral indifference and cause harm, at least if outrage is not expressed by the discussants. [. . .] The "emptiness" of law is reflected in its unthinking and offensive detachment.' Is the reality so different with legal matters implying the refugee protection in Africa? In this regard, see Shapiro, M.H., 'Lawyers, judges and bioethics', in *Southern California Interdisciplinary Law Journal*, vol. 5, 1996–1997, p. 155.

107 In this regard, J. Fitzpatrick affirmed: 'Temporary protection, with its overwhelming focus on repatriation, presents itself as an attractive option to prioritize migration control objectives while maintaining a credible commitment to humanitarianism.' See Fitzpatrick, J., 'Temporary protection of refugees: elements of a formalized regime', op. cit. note 77, p. 291.

108 Fouda, L., op. cit. note 73, pp. 511–12. About the non-hospitality of Egyptian authorities facing refugees from Sub-Saharan Africa, see also Kolmannskog, V., 'Gaps in Geneva, gaps on the ground: case studies of Somalis displaced to Kenya and Egypt during the 2011 drought', in UNHCR, *New Issues in Refugee Research*, research paper No. 248, 2012, pp. 13–14: 'The interviewees in Cairo reported that they had little interaction with Egyptians – although some worked for them. All interviewees lived in Somali areas of Nasr city. They did not speak Egyptian Arabic. Some reported that Egyptians made fun of their accent or that there had been instances of racism. They did not see any future in Egypt. [. . .] Most interviewees in Egypt were

At minimum, human dignity of the asylum-seekers should be respected at all times because, as the South African Supreme Court of Appeal once stated:

> Human dignity has no nationality. It is inherent in all people – citizens and non-citizens alike – simply because they are human.[109]

also hoping for resettlement. With a higher proportion of Somalis being resettled, that may be a reason why many come, according to a UNHCR interviewee. With the current anti-immigration sentiments in developing countries, there is less will to resettle, however. This does not stop people from trying to make it onwards on their own. As mentioned before, Ahmed felt that their current situation, being "in the middle", was part of the reason for their depression: "We are not sure if we will be resettled. We cannot continue living in Egypt. A friend of mine tried crossing from Libya over to Italy and died in the Mediterranean. If we try to go to Europe, we die in the Mediterranean. In Somalia we die of conflict and drought. The solution is in the hands of God."'

109 Supreme Court of Appeal of South Africa, *Minister of Home Affairs and Others v Watchenuka and Another*. No. 10/2003, 28 November 2003, paragraph 24, available at: www.unhcr.org/refworld/country,LEGAL,SASCA,,ZAF,,47fdfb093a7,0.html, accessed 21 September 2014. In this regard, see also Purkey, A.L., 'Questioning governance in protracted refugee situations: the fiduciary nature of the State-refugee relationship', in *International Journal of Refugee Law*, vol. 25, 2014, p. 703: 'Human dignity is the cornerstone on which human rights rest and is also the justification for why the fiduciary must act in the beneficiary's interests. [. . .] Human dignity is intimately linked to equality, human autonomy and moral agency.'

3 Groups of individuals on the run

Examining the Sub-Saharan African phenomena of mass-influx and burden-sharing

3.1 Tracing a legal framework of the mass-influx situation and of its relative principle of *prima facie* recognition

One of the predominant characteristics of the refugee situation in Sub-Saharan Africa is the phenomenon of mass-influx of asylum-seekers. A 'mass-influx', or 'large-scale influx' as it is also called, has been described by the UNHCR as referring to an exceptional situation in which rapid arrival of a large number of asylum-seekers may overwhelm the country's capacities, in particular for the individual administration of their claims.[1]

One of the main mechanisms,[2] which was developed to respond to the mass-influx of asylum-seekers is group determination of status on a *prima facie* basis.[3]

1 Rutinwa, B., '*Prima facie* status and refugee protection', in UNHCR, *New Issues in Refugee Research*, research paper No. 69, 2002, p. 1.

2 According to several scholars another mechanism is constituted by the 'temporary protection'. In this regard, J. Fitzpatrick asserted: 'In terms of the element of temporary protection, one can discern different emphases in the precedents that emerged in Africa. [. . .] Under the 1969 OAU Convention [. . .] the definition of refugee was expanded to embrace victims and other groups, without any suggestion that the quality or durability of their protection should be diminished as compared to that enjoyed by persons meeting the definition in the 1951 Convention. [. . .] Some African refugees, especially those in urban areas, resettle permanently in the state of refuge.' Citing the example of the Rwandese returning from Uganda in the mid-1990s after having fled in 1959 the author concluded that: 'Thus, refugee protection in Africa cannot be regarded as necessarily temporary, despite the adoption of broader criteria of eligibility.' See Fitzpatrick, J., 'Temporary protection of refugees: elements of a formalized regime', op. cit. note 705, p. 296.

3 Paragraph 9 of the UNHCR Guidelines on the application in mass-influx situations of the exclusion clauses of Article 1F of the 1951 Convention relating to the Status of Refugees, Geneva: UNHCR, 2006 clearly contends: '*Prima facie* recognition is appropriate where there are grounds for considering that the large majority of those in the group would meet the eligibility criteria set out in the applicable refugee definition.' In addition the UNHCR also pointed out that: 'The 1969 OAU Convention Governing the Specific Aspects of Refugee Problems in Africa explicitly applies not only to persons fleeing persecution but also to those fleeing situations of armed conflict and generalized violence. In African countries, refugee status is widely provided, often on a *prima*

F. Schnyder, former High Commissioner for Refugees, formally explained the essential difference between individual and *prima facie* group determination, stressing that *prima facie* group determination is not purely equivalent to the sum of eligibilities of the members of the group pronounced on an individual basis. The former Commissioner clarified that the mass of people seeking the status of refugee are fleeing the consequences of political situations, though for instance, this may also include economic[4] and environmental situations[5] in which they have not been active protagonists.[6]

In Sub-Saharan Africa, the High Commissioner for Refugees was invited by the UNGA to assist refugees for the first time in 1961: Angolan refugees in Congo had been granted refugee status *en masse*, which was not disputed.[7] Therefore, since the 1960s, *prima facie* determination has become common practice for large-scale

facie basis, for persons fleeing such situations.' See UNHCR, Providing international protection including through complementary forms of protection, 2 June 2005, document No. EC/55/SC, paragraph 9, p. 3.

4 In this regard, for instance, M. Bulcha observed that: 'A variety of economic problems caused refugee flows from Ethiopia. Factors such as the loss of property, heavy taxation and poverty due to the loss of family breadwinners, contributed to economic problems which led to flight.' See Bulcha, M., 'Historical, political and social causes of mass-flight from Ethiopia', in Nobel, P. (ed.), *Refugees and Development in Africa*, Uppsala: Scandinavian Institute of African Studies, 1987, p. 19. F. Schnyder served as the *United Nations High Commissioner for Refugees* from 1960 until 1965.

5 Talking about the 'refugee' definition included in the 1969 OAU Convention, also G.J. Naldi, like several other authors mentioned in other various sections of this work, clearly affirmed that the so-called 'environmental' refugees constitute a category to be taken into serious consideration analyzing the refugee problem in Sub-Saharan Africa. For the latter author: '[The 1951 Geneva Convention definition of "refugee"] was not deemed applicable to mass exoduses but the OAU considered that such a narrow definition failed to take account of the particular difficulties facing Africa, such as wars of national liberation *and environmental catastrophes such as drought and famine which had given rise to flight en masse* and displaced whole populations.' Emphasis added. See Naldi, G.J., *The Organization of African Unity: An Analysis of its Role*, 2nd edn, London/New York: Mansell, 1999, p. 79.

6 Schnyder, F., 'Les aspects juridiques actuels du problème des réfugiés', in *Recueil des Cours de l'Académie de La Haye*, vol. 114, 1965 (I), p. 440.

7 Aga Khan, S., 'Legal problems relating to refugees and displaced persons', in *Collected Courses of The Hague Academy of International Law*, vol. 149, 1976 (I), p. 340; UNGA, Problem raised by the situation of the Angolan refugees in the Congo, 10 December 1961, resolution No. 1671 (XVI). In this resolution the UNGA requested 'the High Commissioner to continue to lend his/her good offices in sending appropriate solutions to the problems arising from the presence of the Angolan refugees in the Republic of Congo [. . .].' In this regard, J. Hyndman and B.V. Nylund explained: 'The concept of "good offices" was developed in conjunction with *prima facie* determination. Both were pragmatic and strategic, as opposed to legalistic, approaches to the problem of mass human displacement which was becoming increasingly common. Good offices provided a framework for flexible and convenient action. The intent of "good offices" action was clearly to both broaden the legal scope of the refugee definition and to provide assistance to displaced populations.' See Hyndman, J. and Nylund, B.V., 'UNHCR and the status of prima facie refugees in Kenya', in *International Journal of Refugee Law*, vol. 10, 1998, p. 33. For the attribution of 'good offices' to UNHCR, see UNGA, Report of the High Commissioner for Refugees, 18 December 1961, resolution No. 1673 (XVI), paragraph 1: '[The UNGA] requests the United Nations High Commissioner for Refugees to pursue his activities on behalf of the refugees within his mandate *or those for whom he extends his good offices*, and to continue to report to

movements in Africa. Nevertheless, because of the discretionary application of the *prima facie* status, this move has sometimes allowed for a politicization of refugee determination processes and the gradual institutionalization of weaker standards for granting refugee status.[8]

It is clear that, procedurally, all asylum-seekers arriving in large numbers should be admitted into the country of asylum and should not be subjected to *refoulement*. Individuals considered *prima facie* refugees are presumably refugees within the meaning of the main relevant international instruments. The presumption is conclusive unless it is dislodged by evidence that either a person was wrongly recognized as a refugee or was legally subject to exclusion under the provisions of refugee law. It is also clear that, as a logical consequence, *prima facie* refugees are entitled to enjoy the entire range of rights granted to refugees under any instrument applicable to their situation.[9]

According to the host African countries, the most sought solution for refugees in a situation of large-scale influx is repatriation. However, this should not be a

the Executive Committee of the High Commissioner's Program and to abide by directions which that Committee might give him in regard to situations concerning refugees.' Emphasis added. In this regard, J. Hyndman noted that: '[This] resolution provided a basis for action that aimed to be flexible, responsive, and meaningful in emerging refugee situations, and it allowed the High Commissioner to define groups as *prima facie* refugees without normal determination procedures. *Prima facie* refugees were a new category of displaced persons, a category subordinated to the convention definition and more likely to be applicable to crises outside of Europe.' See Hyndman, J., *Managing Displacement: Refugees and the Politics of Humanitarianism*, Minneapolis, MN: University of Minnesota Press, 2000, p. 10. We hope that Republic of Congo will behave in the same way with the over 100,000 Congolese [from DRC] refugees who have crossed the Oubangui River and found refuge in the Republic of the Congo since inter-ethnic violence erupted in Equateur province in late 2009. See the news: 'Number of Congolese refugees in Republic of Congo passes 100,000 mark', 12 January 2010, available at: www.unhcr.org/4b4ca3439.html, accessed 15 October 2014.

8 Hyndman, J. and Nylund, B.V., op. cit. note 7, p. 32.

9 Rutinwa, B., '*Prima facie* status and refugee protection', op. cit. note 1, pp. 1–2. T. Maluwa confirmed this situation applied to Malawians' experience, although '[o]n an official level, Malawi's preferred solution [rather remains] that of voluntary repatriation of the Mozambican refugees as and when conditions permit [instead of an integration of the Mozambican *prima facie* refugees].' See Maluwa, T., 'Human rights and refugees in Southern Africa: some perspectives on recent legislative developments in Malawi', in *Zeitschrift für Ausländisches Öffentliches Recht und Völkerrecht*, vol. 53, 1993, p. 107. About the presence of Mozambican refugees in Malawi, L.D. Mvula explained: 'Malawi had taken a large share of Mozambican refugees. It is reported that over one million Mozambicans were in Malawi between 1989 and 1991, resulting in a situation where one of every six people in Malawi was a Mozambican refugee. This resulted in pressure over land and other resources. To minimize the pressure from its own people, the government placed restrictions on freedoms including on movement and economic activities.' See Mvula, L.D., 'Refugee status determination and rights in Malawi', paper presented at the Refugee Studies Centre Workshop Discussion on RSD and rights in Southern and East Africa', no date available, p. 9, pdf document, available at: www.google.ch/url?sa=t&rct=j&q=&esrc=s&source=web&cd=1&ved=0CDQQFjAA&url=http%3A%2F%2Fwww.rsc.ox.ac.uk%2Fevents%2Frefugee-status-determination-and-rights%2FRefugee%2520Rights%2520in%2520Malawi_MS.pdf&ei=RMMsUaTnIar54QSQy4GgDw&usg=AFQjCNG-wbEs1rbg0K6xXnDiO706HDRliA&bvm=bv.42965579,d.Yms, accessed 1 February 2014.

reason for adopting policies that limit refugees' rights with a view to encouraging them to repatriate. In addition, local integration and resettlement should remain available to those refugees for whom these are the most appropriate solutions.

Historically, recourse has been made to the *prima facie* mechanism in situations of mass-influx with factors that generate the application of this kind of approach that have been implicitly affirmed by the UNHCR:

> When refugee status must normally be determined on an individual basis, situations have also arisen in which entire groups have been under circumstances indicating that members of the group could be considered individually as refugees. In such situations, the need to provide assistance is extremely urgent and it may not be possible for purely practical reasons to carry out an individual determination of refugee status for each member of the group. Therefore, recourse has been had to so-called 'group determination' of refugee status, whereby each member of the group is regarded *prima facie* [. . .] as a refugee.[10]

Thus, the main factors for the application of the *prima facie* mechanism are the objective circumstances that led to the mass displacement, the numbers of asylum-seekers involved and the urgency to provide assistance which makes it costly and not viable to govern individual status determination. ExCom conclusion No. 100, entitled 'International cooperation and burden and responsibility sharing in mass-influx situations', although it does not provide standards of recognition of refugees on a *prima facie* basis, and does not give any formal definition of 'mass-influx', provides nevertheless a set of features which should connote the phenomenon. Among these characteristics are:

> i) considerable numbers of people arriving over an international border; ii) a rapid rate of arrival; iii) inadequate absorption or response capacity in host States, particularly during the emergency; iv) individual asylum procedures, where they exist, which are unable to deal with the assessment of such large numbers.[11]

10 UNHCR, Handbook on procedures and criteria for determining refugee status under the 1951 Convention and the 1967 Protocol relating to the status of refugees, 2nd edn, Geneva: UNHCR, 1992, paragraph 44.

11 Standing Committee, Ensuring international protection and enhancing international cooperation in mass-influx situations: Advance summary findings of the study commissioned by UNHCR, 7 June 2004, document No. EC/54/SC/CRP.11, paragraph 3, p. 1; ExCom, conclusion No. 100 (LV), 'International cooperation and burden and responsibility sharing in mass-influx situations', 2004, paragraph a). About the last element quoted in the list, J.-F. Durieux and A. Hurwitz affirmed: 'This last element adds an important qualitative dimension to the definition, making it impossible – and indeed undesirable – to establish in precise quantitative terms how large, or sudden, a refugee flow must be in order to be characterized as a "mass-influx".' See Durieux, J.-F. and Hurwitz, A., 'How many is too many? African and European legal responses to mass-influxes and refugees', in *German Yearbook of International Law*, vol. 47, 2004, pp. 106–7.

On this basis, officials in Benin, Cameroon and Liberia have several years ago accorded *prima facie* status to Togolese, Chadian and Ivorian asylum-seekers respectively,[12] while Ugandan authorities have done the same with Sudanese asylum-seekers in the last decade.[13]

In Sub-Saharan Africa, the question as to whether or not refugees recognized on a *prima facie* basis acquire refugee status under the legal international instruments applicable to the region in the same way and to the same extent as those whose status is individually considered has been subject to controversy. In this regard, it has been contended that the notion of *prima facie* denotes the circumstance of provisionally considering an individual to be a refugee without the necessity of going through the typical RSD procedures to ascertain once and for all the qualification of each person. A *prima facie* mechanism is fundamentally the way to make a preliminary decision regarding refugee status. Refugee status accorded on a *prima facie* basis would remain presumptive although such an assumption will be enjoyed until there is an unambiguous pronouncement to the contrary. This would entail that in situations where individuals are granted asylum after a group status determination, they are not automatically determined to be refugees under any of the legal definitions that apply to the African continent. In effect, according to this school of thought, the notion of *prima facie* would not contribute anything in terms of how to proceed in finally determining the refugee status of the applicants. As such, it does not add to any of the main refugee protection instruments, which remain silent on the issue.[14]

The second school of thought contends that the determination of a *prima facie* refugee group raises the presumption that the individual members of the group

12 United States Committee for Refugees and Immigrants, *World Refugee Survey 2008 – Benin*, 19 June 2009, available at: www.unhcr.org/cgi-bin/texis/vtx/refworld/rwmain?page=search&docid=485f50c31b&skip=0&query=prima%20facie, accessed 25 September 2012; United States Committee for Refugees and Immigrants, World Refugee Survey 2008 – Cameroon, available at: www.unhcr.org/cgi-bin/texis/vtx/refworld/rwmain?page=search&docid=485f50c66c&skip=0&query=prima%20facie, accessed 25 September 2012; United States Committee for Refugees and Immigrants, *World Refugee Survey 2008 – Liberia*, available at: www.unhcr.org/cgi-bin/texis/vtx/refworld/rwmain?page=search&docid=485f50c17b&skip=0&query=prima%20facie, accessed 25 September 2014.

13 Kaiser, T., 'Sudanese refugees in Uganda and Kenya', in Loescher, G. *et al.* (eds), *Protracted Refugee Situations: Political, Human Rights and Security Implications*, New York: United Nations University Press, 2008, p. 255.

14 Okoth-Obbo, G., 'Thirty years on: a legal review of the 1969 OAU Refugee Convention Governing the Specific Aspects of Refugee Problems in Africa', in *Refugee Survey Quarterly*, vol. 20, 2001, pp. 79–138. Also in *African Yearbook of International Law*, vol. 8, 2000, pp. 118–22. At p. 119, the author explained the device of *prima facie*: 'In particular, it enables an urgent decision to be made in favor of dealing with claimants for protection and assistance under refugee obligations without this being decisive of the question of their refugee status as such.' In addition, the author found that Zimbabwean legislation on refugees endorsed his theory. In effect, section 5 3) 2) of the 1983 Zimbabwean Refugee Act reads: '2) Subject to the provisions of subsection 3), if the Minister considers that any class of persons are refugees as defined in paragraph a), b), c) or d) of subsection 1), [in the Act] he/she may declare *such class of persons to be refugees* [. . .].' Emphasis added.

are refugees and can thus benefit from international protection and assistance provided by the UNHCR, on behalf of the international community. According to this theory, the concept of *prima facie* refugees was developed not as a separate juridical concept but within the framework of the definitions of 'refugee' under the 1950 UNHCR Statute and the 1951 Geneva Convention.[15] To this, it has also been added that in most contemporary large-scale influxes in Sub-Saharan Africa, the reference point to determine whether or not the asylum-seekers involved were refugees was not only the definition of the term under the 1950 UNHCR Statute but also that under the 1951 Geneva Refugee Convention.[16] Therefore, it is quite clear that, for this school of thought, *prima facie* recognition is presumptive, but conclusive in that individuals recognized as such are refugees under applicable definitions unless that presumption is explicitly removed. If the circumstances that triggered the application are those comprised under the definitions provided in Article 1A 2) of the 1951 Geneva Refugee Convention and in Article I1 of the 1969 OAU Convention, then the individuals recognized to be *prima facie* refugees are refugees within the framework of those definitions. If the circumstances referred to are those under Article I2 of the 1969 African Convention, then the individuals in question will probably be presumed to be refugees under that article. The increasing importance assumed by the regional instrument in determining the *prima facie* nature of the asylum-seekers in Sub-Saharan Africa is also confirmed by the fact that in the most recent, above-mentioned cases, Beninese authorities accorded *prima facie* status to Togolese asylum-seekers on the basis of the provisions of the 1969 OAU Convention.[17]

15 Jackson, I.C., *The Refugee Concept in Group Situations*, The Hague/London/Boston: Martinus Nijhoff, 1999, p. 4. J.-F. Durieux and J. McAdam reinforced this concept affirming that: '[t]he [1951 Geneva] Convention itself contains nothing to suggest its inapplicability in cases of mass-influx. [. . .] To assert that the Convention does not apply in cases of mass-influxes is tantamount to saying that the individual does not exist in a group. Similarly, the *travaux préparatoires* do not reveal any intention to exclude collective persecution from the ambit of the Convention. Rather, discussion at the drafting stage centered on "categories of refugees", with the implication that refugeehood was not an individualized concept but one that depended on belonging to a category or group.' See Durieux, J.-F. and McAdam, J., 'Non-refoulement through time: the case for a derogation clause to the refugee convention in mass-influx emergencies', in *International Journal of Refugee Law*, vol. 16, 2004, pp. 9–10.

16 In his work, the author took into consideration several cases of mass-influxes of refugees which occurred in Sub-Saharan Africa during the 1960s and 1970s, quoting official documents from the UNHCR, which would support his theory. Among these documents, several reports by the 1965 UNHCR Representative in Leopoldville – present-day Kinshasa – who clearly affirmed the *bona fide* nature of the Mozambique refugees in Zambia at that time. The author stressed that the groups of asylum-seekers under the aegis of the UNHCR in Sub-Saharan Africa in the period from 1961 to 1975 showed that they were either clearly determined to be refugees according to the 1950 UNHCR Statute or 1951 Geneva Refugee Convention definitions or they were considered in the framework of the 'good offices' of the UNHCR with the host countries. This last concept of 'good offices' was based on *prima facie* group refugee character established under the light of the two above-mentioned definitions. See Jackson, I.C., *The Refugee Concept in Group Situations*, op. cit. note 15, pp. 143–77, particularly pp. 154–8, and 176.

17 Such an affirmation is confirmed *a contrario* by J.-F. Durieux and J. McAdam who advanced that: 'The second misperception is the converse of the first: that the OAU Convention applies

As under the general rules of evidence, the burden of proving a refugee's claim lies with the individual who submits that claim and cases of fraudulent claims are not so unusual among African asylum-seekers.[18] But, due to the particular circumstances in which asylum-seekers find themselves, the duty to establish and assess the relevant fact is, under refugee law, shared between the examiner and the claimant.[19] Such an affirmation means that the evidential burden in the first instance should rest with the applicant. When the applicant discharges that duty, then he/she is presumed to be a refugee within the meaning of any applicable definition and the burden to refute this provisionally shifts to any individual who opposes this view. If for any reason, no such evidence is adduced, the evidence by, or in favour of, the claimant becomes conclusive. Therefore, the view that *prima facie* recognition is presumptive but conclusive more accurately reflects the law, unless the presumption is refuted. In Sub-Saharan Africa, this analysis is often in accordance with state practice.

Under the solicitations provided by the 1979 Arusha Conference on the African Refugee Problems, where it was contended that 'special arrangements for identifying refugees'[20] had to be adopted in case of large-scale influxes, the ExCom consequently adopted conclusion No. 22 'Protection of asylum-seekers in situations of large-scale influx' in 1981. This conclusion gave provisions for entrance and non-rejection although it remained silent on procedural standards including which procedures should be followed in granting *prima facie* status, and how persons who do not deserve international protection can be excluded from receiving it. The ExCom conclusion is relevant because it appears to concede that not all rights stipulated under the 1951 Refugee Convention may be afforded in situations of mass-influx. The recommendations included in the conclusion cover almost all civil and political rights as well as other issues specific to refugees. They do not include, however, certain rights found under the 1951 Geneva Convention such as the right to education and/or the right to be given identity papers or travel documents. This absence remains in conclusion No. 100 as well, which was conceived in 2004, although its paragraph j), recommendation v) vaguely affirms that relevant national and international actors could promote:

only to groups, not to individuals.' See Durieux, J.-F. and McAdam, J., op. cit. note 15, p. 10. In this regard, see also what the Lawyers' Committee for Human Rights argued on the fact that there is nothing in the 1969 OAU Convention to confirm the statement that a '[p]referable practice of group eligibility [is] provided for under' this instrument. See Lawyers' Committee for Human Rights, African Exodus: Refugee Crisis, Human Rights and the 1969 OAU Convention, New York: Lawyers' Committee for Human Rights Editions, 1995, 228 p., note 613, p. 22.

18 Kingsley-Nyinah, M.R., 'Need for an international presence: the return of refugees and immunity from prosecution for political offences in South Africa', in *International Journal of Refugee Law*, vol. 3, 1991, p. 302.

19 UNHCR, Handbook on procedures and criteria for determining refugee status under the 1951 Convention and the 1967 Protocol relating to the status of refugees, 2nd edn, Geneva: UNHCR, 1992, paragraph 196.

20 UNHCR, The recommendations from the Arusha Conference on the African Refugee Problem, Uppsala: Scandinavian Institute of African Studies, 1981, recommendation No. 2, p. 10.

> [t]he provision of support to host countries, especially developing countries, to assist the early and *effective registration and documentation* of refugees and asylum-seekers.[21]

In the absence of international legal instruments providing standards for refugee recognition on a *prima facie* basis, African states have developed their own procedures under national legislation and state practice.[22] States have developed two main mechanisms for granting group status: status determination by a specified body and ministerial declaration. Kenya and Gambia explicitly utilize the expression *prima facie* – but not the term 'influx' – in recognition of refugees, and provide for this type of large-scale situation in their national legislations, linking the meaning of *prima facie* solely to protection under the 1969 OAU Convention.[23] In Kenya, in the 2006 Refugee Act, the Minister responsible for refugee affairs was competent to declare arriving individuals as a group as refugees,[24] while in Gambia it is the Secretary of State.[25] Unfortunately, the 2011 Kenyan Refugee Bill does not present any provision regarding the treatment of the *prima facie* refugees.

African refugee protection has a long tradition of entrusting a single member of the national government with the responsibility of granting refuge to a group of individuals. This responsibility dates back to the 1970s, to the Zambian legislation, which was then followed by the Sudanese[26] legislation that introduced this practice in its mention of a 'class of persons' rather than 'individuals',[27] in

21 ExCom, conclusion No. 100 (LV), 'International cooperation and burden and responsibility sharing in mass-influx situations', 2004. Emphasis added.

22 Durieux, J.-F., 'The many faces of '*prima facie*': group-based evidence in refugee status determination', in *Refuge*, vol. 25, 2008, p. 154.

23 Albert, M., '*Prima facie* determination of refugee status: an overview and its legal foundation', *Oxford: Refugee Studies Centre*, working paper No. 55, 2010, p. 27.

24 Article 3 2) of the 2006 Kenyan Act clearly affirms that: '[a] person shall be a *prima facie* refugee for purposes of this Act if [. . .].' And section 3 explains: 'If the Minister considers that any class of persons is *prima facie* refugees [. . .] the Minister may declare such class of persons to be *prima facie* refugees and may at any time amend or revoke such declaration.' In this regard, E. Aukot asserted: '[The definition of *prima facie* refugees] fits the majority of refugees resident in Kenya, the consequence of which is the government's policy of encampment. Hence, no formal recognition of conventional refugees. This was the case of the 223,600 refugees in Kenya in 1998, when very few underwent status determination because they were granted status on a group basis.' See Aukot, E., 'Refugee protection in Africa: a developing country's dilemmas towards effective protection', in *East African Journal of Peace and Human Rights*, vol. 9, 2003, p. 223.

25 Section 31 of the Gambian Refugee Act, 2008, 17 November 2008.

26 In the 1974 Regulation of Asylum Act, the Minister of Interior in the last instance was responsible for granting asylum to everyone who sought it. Section 5 of the Act reads: 'The Minister shall have the power to grant asylum in the Sudan, and he/she may delegate such power.'

27 In Zambia, the entire section 3 1) of the 1970 Refugee (Control) Act reads: '1) Subject to the provisions of subsection 2), the Minister [the member of the Cabinet responsible for matters relating to refugees] may declare, by order, any class of persons who are, or prior to their entry into Zambia were, ordinarily resident outside Zambia to be refugees for the purposes of this Act.' Section 3 1) of the 1978 Swaziland Refugees Control Act contains exactly the same

response to the large-scale influx of Eritreans in the country.[28] There was even a precedent in the late 1960s in Botswana, though in that case, the national legislator simply dealt with the asylum-seeker claiming the status of refugee for political reasons and no allusion was made about groups of asylum-seekers.[29] M. Albert nonetheless affirmed that the Ministerial declaration under the Botswana Act could lead to *prima facie* RSD, while the status is legally founded more in domestic than in international law.[30] To some extent, Mali constitutes an exception to the rule of this determination being entrusted to a single organ because, in that country, it is an act of the entire government that accords the status of refugee to an applicant.[31]

On the other hand, in many other countries, above all, countries with very recent legislation on refugees, specific bodies are in charge of assessing the claims of asylum-seekers, although the procedures indicated sometimes seem too complicated to be applied in group situations. Such is the case in Angola, where the COREDA (Committee for the Recognition of Asylum Rights) put in place a mechanism evidently studied for individuals' claims.[32] Benin,[33] Burkina Faso,[34]

formulation while also the 1991 Mozambique Refugee Act provides that the Minister of Interior is the person ultimately responsible to rule upon asylum in the country: read Article 3 of the Act entitled 'Competence to rule upon asylum.'

28 Nobel, P., 'Refugee, law and development in Africa', in *Michigan Yearbook of International Legal Studies*, vol. 3, 1982, p. 270, where the author affirmed: 'The text (of the Sudanese Act) evidently has an experiential foundation – namely, the regular flow into Sudan of refugees from the relentless and cruel war in neighboring Eritrea.'

29 Botswana, Refugees (Recognition and Control) Act, Cap. 25:03, 1968, section 8. In full, section 8 ('Recognition of immigrant as political refugee') reads as follows: '1) When the Minister receives the report of an inquiry held under section 4 he may – a) *subject to paragraph b), if he is of the opinion that the person who has been the subject of the inquiry is a political refugee, declare that he recognizes such person as a political refugee;* b) if he is of the opinion that the person who has been the subject of the inquiry is not a political refugee or if he considers that there is no or insufficient reason to treat him as a political refugee, declare that he does not recognize such person as a political refugee; or c) direct the Committee to reopen the inquiry or to make further report in the matter. 2) Where, under subsection 1), the Minister declares that he does not recognize a person as a political refugee such person shall, if liable to be removed from Botswana under the Immigration Act, be so removed and shall, whether so liable or not, be subject in all respects to the provisions of that Act. 3) Save where this Act otherwise provides, a person who is recognized as a political refugee shall be subject to the provisions of the Immigration Act in all respects as if the declaration of recognition had not been made.' Emphasis added.

30 Albert, M., op. cit. note 23, p. 26.

31 Mali, Loi No. 1998–40 portant sur le statut des réfugiés, 20 July 1998, Article 3: 'Tout demandeur d'asile sur le territoire national peut bénéficier du statut de réfugié s'il relève du mandat du Haut Commissariat des Nations Unies pour les Réfugiés (HCR) et reconnu comme tel par un acte du Gouvernement de la République du Mali.'

32 Angola, Law on Refugee Status, 1990, Articles 10 through 17.

33 Benin, Ordonnance No. 75–41 du 16 juillet 1975 portant statut des réfugiés, 16 July 1975, Article 3; Décret No. 1984–303 du 30 juillet 1984, portant sur la création, composition, attributions et fonctionnement de la Commission nationale chargée des réfugiés, 30 July 1984.

34 Burkina Faso, Décret No. 1994–055/PRES/REX portant application du statut des réfugiés, 1997, Articles 2 to 9.

Djibouti,[35] Lesotho,[36] Liberia[37] and Nigeria,[38] among other countries, follow the same model. In effect, even though it may be more risky because the level of discretional assessments can be higher, the procedure of *prima facie* recognition by way of ministerial declaration is undoubtedly better for the asylum-seeker because in this particular case, the status of refugee is given by the Minister without an interview with the asylum-seeker. In a way, therefore, it is quicker and responds better to the type of emergency generated by a situation of mass-influx.[39] By contrast, in the procedure directed by a designate body, asylum-seekers commonly must appear before a body of examiners, which made the procedure heavier and at times too bureaucratic for the requirements and their cultural background. Often, people fleeing *en masse* from their country of origin in Sub-Saharan Africa also belong to its lowest socio-economic classes. In determining whether the persons of a group are entitled to refugee protection, however, both the minister and the designated body of examiners use the same criterion, consisting of the objective circumstances in the country of origin.[40]

A very simple procedure, a mix of the two mentioned above, was followed in Guinea before the mass-influx of Sierra Leoneans in early 1998. Asylum-seekers arriving in Guinea were not subjected to any controls at the border. Once in the country, the staff of the Bureau National de Coordination pour les Réfugiés (BNCR), located in the prefectures, registered asylum-seekers. They were granted *prima facie* recognition on a group basis and their list was then given to the local agency of the UNHCR for registration and assistance. Liberian officials in the same situation adopted an analogous procedure towards Sierra Leonean asylum-seekers.[41]

35 Djibouti, Ordonnance n. 77053/PR/AE portent statut des réfugiés sur le sol de la République de Djibouti, 9 novembre 1977, Article 3; Décret No. 2001–0101/PR/MI modifiant le décret n. 77–054/PR/AE du 9 novembre 1977 portant création de la Commission nationale d'éligibilité au statut des réfugiés, 28 May 2001.

36 Lesotho, Refugee Act, 1983, section 7. About the recognition of the refugee status, we note that the Lesotho legislation takes into consideration, *ex* subsection 1, exclusively '[a] person who has lawfully entered or is lawfully present in Lesotho'.

37 Liberia, Refugee Act, 1993, 19 January 1994, section 7 ('Recognition of refugees').

38 Nigeria, Decree, National Commission for Refugees, 29 December 1989, parts II to V.

39 For instance, section 7 3) of the Malawi Refugee Act stipulates: 'The Minister may, by notice published in the Gazette, direct that, with respect to any group of foreign nationals specified in the notice, seeking refugee status in Malawi, the committee shall apply such group determination procedure as may be prescribed.' In this regard, as T. Maluwa noted: 'This is, to be sure, a commendable provision which does not appear in most of the statutes dealing with refugee matters in other African countries. It is, of course, a provision specifically tailored to meet the special circumstances in which the Malawian legislation was conceived. The only problem which may arise here is to decide when the situation which created the refugee influx is over and, therefore, when to change to individual status determination. This would particularly be the case where large-scale arrivals continue while some of the parties involved begin to perceive the emergency as having come to an end.' See Maluwa, T., 'Human rights and refugees in Southern Africa: some perspectives on recent legislative developments in Malawi', op. cit. note 9, p. 107.

40 Rutinwa, B., '*Prima facie* status and refugee protection', op. cit. note 1, p. 10.

41 O'Neill, W., 'Conflict in West Africa: dealing with exclusion and separation', in *International Journal of Refugee Law*, special supplementary issue, vol. 12, 2000, pp. 178–87 for the Sierra Leonean caseloads in Guinea and pp. 187–94 for the Sierra Leonean caseloads in Liberia.

In Kenya, the mass-influx of Somali and Sudanese in the early 1990s put huge pressure on local officials who decided to suspend the status determination carried on by the Kenyan Eligibility Committee and handed this exercise over to the UNHCR.[42] Therefore, the UNHCR granted group recognition to these asylum-seekers on a *prima facie* basis, and assigned them to camps on the basis of refugee nationality. The camp at Kakuma, for example, was designated principally for Somali and Sudanese *prima facie* refugees. In 1998, however, the Kenyan government announced that it was terminating the UNHCR's mandate to grant refugee status in Kenya.[43] The UNHCR then showed concern about the strictness of policies in recognizing asylum-seekers in Kenya and elsewhere in Sub-Saharan Africa, proving that discretionary measures were sometimes adopted by officials of the host countries.[44]

In particular, most recent legislations had the phenomenon of large-scale influx in mind when they were conceived, for example the 2006 Ugandan Refugee Act and the 2007 Refugee Protection Act by Sierra Leone.[45] Both of these acts, much like, for instance, the 1998 South African Refugee Act,[46] contain specific

42 For example, see the article: 'Refugee status determination: justice delayed is . . . typical?', in *Kakuma News Reflector*, vol. 1, 2009, available at: http://kanere.org/2009/02/28/refugee-status-determination-justice-delayed-istypical/, accessed 10 September 2014.

43 O'Neill, W., Rutinwa, B. and Verdirame, G., 'The Great Lakes: a survey of the application of the exclusion clause in the Central African Republic, Kenya and Tanzania', in *International Journal of Refugee Law*, special supplementary issue, vol. 12, 2000, pp. 153–4. In the same regard, see Hyndman, J. and Nylund, B.V., op. cit. note 7, pp. 29–30. In addition, at p. 35, the authors gave an important specification on the *prima facie* status in Africa: 'It should be pointed out, however, that *prima facie* status is a means to avoid recognition under the OAU Convention, which would trigger other obligations from which recognized refugees may benefit under that Convention. *Prima facie* determination is generally utilized as a temporary designation in Africa because *prima facie* refugees must reside in refugee camps, and there is normally no access to individual status determination that would grant them the basic rights of a Convention refugee.'

44 For instance, see the news of 11 July 2008: 'Zimbabweans face uphill struggle in search for asylum in South Africa', where we may read: 'In the last 40 days alone, South Africa has sent back some 17,000 Zimbabweans through the Beit Bridge border post, despite earlier calls from UNHCR to suspend all deportations. UNHCR, refugee advocacy groups and rights organizations say Zimbabweans who come to South Africa face an uphill struggle in their bid to obtain asylum. "The government should do more to help them, in line with its international legal commitments", said Sanda Kimbimbi, UNHCR's regional representative. Of the 35,000 Zimbabweans who applied for asylum in South Africa in 2006 and 2007, only 500 were granted refugee status, according to official figures.' News available at: www.unhcr.org/news/NEWS/48776e934.html, accessed 25 September 2014.

45 However, for a relevant precedent, see section 3 2) of the 1983 Zimbabwean Refugee Act where the legislator talks about 'class of persons'. In this regard, see Hofmann, R., 'Refugee law in Africa', in *Law and State*, vol. 39, 1989, p. 87.

46 Article 35 ('Reception and accommodation of asylum seekers in event of mass-influx') of the 1998 South African Refugee Act reads as follows: '1) The Minister may if he or she considers that any group or category of persons qualify for refugee status as is contemplated in section 3, by notice in the Gazette, declare such group or category of persons to be refugees either unconditionally or subject to such conditions as the Minister may impose in conformity with

provisos concerning mass-influx and group recognition. In the 2006 Ugandan Act, the power of recognition of the group is delegated to the Minister responsible for refugees, who is able to 'issue an order permitting the asylum-seekers inside Uganda without requiring their individual status to be determined [. . .].'[47] Also the Sierra Leonean Act permits refugee status to be declared. However, such a declaration is made through the Authority of two Ministers and by UNHCR representatives. This act defines the declaration of the authority as being one that relates to 'large scale influxes', *ex* Article 4 2) c) and '*prima facie* declaration of refugee status', *ex* Article 6 2) a), although the concept of 'large scale influxes' is not defined. In addition, section 22 of the Sierra Leonean Act includes measures adopted by Sierra Leonean authorities in the event of large-scale influx such as the designation of reception areas, the provision of adequate and appropriate facilities necessary for the group, and ensuring the civilian and humanitarian character of areas designated for refugees. The Sierra Leonean Act, however, codifies *prima facie* RSD practice under international law in that it links the *prima facie* determination with a large-scale influx and results in a unique status.[48]

3.2 Past abuse and limitations of group recognition

In spite of its advantages, group recognition of refugee status has a number of limitations, the greatest being the difficulty of excluding certain elements that do not deserve international protection from the group. This is particularly important considering the end of colonial domination and *apartheid*, seeing that the group recognition approach to status determination is currently applied almost entirely to persons fleeing civil wars and/or natural catastrophes.[49]

the Constitution and international law and may revoke any such declaration by notice in the Gazette. 2) The Minister may, after consultation with the UNHCR representative and the Premier of the province concerned, designate areas, centers or places for the temporary reception and accommodation of asylum seekers or refugees or any specific category or group of asylum seekers or refugees who entered the Republic on a large scale, pending the regularization of their status in the Republic. 3) The Minister may appoint any person as a manager of an area, center or place designated under subsection 2). 4) The Minister may at any time withdraw the designation of an area, centre or place contemplated in subsection 2).'

47 Uganda, section 25 3) of the 2006 Refugee Act.

48 Albert, M., op. cit. note 23, p. 27. At p. 28, the author explained how also the Loi No. 1/32 sur l'asile et la protection des réfugiés au Burundi, No. 1/32, 13 November 2008 expressly provides for the grant of *prima facie* refugee status however not necessarily involving the UNHCR in the process.

49 In addition, we have several situations in which states often omit to declare their intention to treat arriving groups as refugees, or they do not record such a determination in an official document. J.-F. Durieux and J. McAdam brought the example of Ghana where some *prima facie* refugees were given ration cards evidencing their *de facto* status. However, once food rations were withdrawn, so also was their documentation. See Durieux, J.-F. and McAdam, J., op. cit. note 15, footnote 35 of the article, p. 11. J.-F. Durieux and A. Hurwitz, found in the Zambia a good example of screening asylum-seekers through identification, through the Joint Operation

The difficulty in excluding those not deserving international protection has serious implications for international refugee protection. There have been situations in which these excludable individuals managed to get through as a result of group determination, and then went on to create security problems in camps, as happened in the camps in the Eastern DRC after the genocide in Rwanda in 1994.[50] It is almost superfluous to say that the presence of individuals who have committed criminal acts as hideous as genocide in the camps, poses a moral dilemma for humanitarian organizations when providing aid to such camps.[51] The moral dilemma should be solved to benefit those who deserve protection. It should not sacrifice hundreds – or thousands – of innocent human lives for the sake of a few handfuls of criminals. Various measures can be adopted in order to try to avoid the consequences of hosting criminals: it must be admitted that the measures adopted by African governments until now have often implied sacrificing the well-being of genuine asylum-seekers. This occurred in the CAR, a country that at present does not have any specific legislation on the protection of refugees but possesses legislation for a Commission nationale pour les réfugiés, which specifies its composition and function. This act presents a paradoxical situation because it is similar to admitting implicitly an issue without having the courage to openly face the problem.[52] In 1997, hundreds of Rwandan refugees, fleeing

Committees, of those persons who should be separated from the mainstream refugee population because they are combatants or individuals benefiting from past amnesties. See Durieux, J.-F. and Hurwitz, A., op. cit. note 11, p. 122.

50 Durieux, J.-F., 'The many faces of "*prima facie*": group-based evidence in refugee status determination', op. cit. note 22, p. 159, where the author affirmed: 'The tragic experience of the Rwandan exodus following the 1994 genocide brought to light the very real possibility that refugee flows might be "contaminated" by the presence of serious offenders, war criminals or *genocidaires*.'

51 Rutinwa, B., '*Prima facie* status and refugee protection', op. cit. note 1, p. 11.

52 Among other acts, see, for instance, Arrêté de la Commission nationale pour les réfugiés, 22 August 1990; Décret No. 1983.278 portant organisation et fonctionnement de la Commission Nationale pour les Réfugiés en République Centrafricaine, 1983 ; Ordonnance No. 1983.042 portant création d'une Commission nationale pour les réfugiés en République Centrafricaine, 1 juin 1983. Another country with similar legislation is the Côte d'Ivoire, where no specific legislation exists on the legal protection of the refugees but, for instance, exists an Arrêté No. 11/PG/DAG, portant sur la création d'une Commission départementale chargée de se prononcer sur les demandes de statut de réfugiés, 11/PG/DAG, 11 May 1991. For the present situation in CAR, see, for instance, the news: 'UNHCR seeks immediate access to refugees and displaced civilians in Central African Republic', 11 January 2013, available at: www.unhcr.org/50eff2279.html, accessed 15 January 2013: 'The Central African Republic hosts some 17,000 refugees and 2,500 asylum-seekers. "We call on all sides to respect the human rights of all civilians and to allow humanitarian access to them", [a] UNHCR spokesman said. He added that UNHCR was particularly worried about some 2,000 Sudanese refugees in the Bambari camp, in the central part of the country – an area under rebel control. UNHCR is trying to re-establish contact with this refugee population. There were confirmed reports that the UNHCR office there was looted on December 28 after the staff were evacuated. Another UNHCR office, in Kaga-Bandoro, has also been looted.' In this regard, see also the update: 'UNHCR finds looting, empty

persecution in DRC, tried to enter the CAR. But the authorities there would not let them in because they did not have sufficient means of properly screening the *bona fide* refugees from criminals, resulting in the rejection of hundreds of genuine asylum-seekers.[53]

The abuse of the *prima facie* approach is also clear when it is given recognition by way of pretence, as happened in Lukole camp, Tanzania, in 1997 when Rwandan asylum-seekers pretended to be Burundians in order to receive refugee status *en masse* instead of going through an individual determination process;[54] this situation also caused clashes between the two communities despite the fact that both belonged to the Hutu ethnic group.[55]

The lack of serious enquiries into the background of asylum-seekers also contributes to the phenomenon of multiple refugee registrations at one or several camps in order to multiply the supplies they can obtain from the UNHCR.[56] In the aforementioned situation, Tanzanian authorities showed an evident lack of organization and coordination, and in effect left the control of the process of eligibility for refugee status to the same asylum-seekers through an informal system of co-operation.[57]

villages on mission to Bambari in Central African Republic', available at: www.unhcr.org/511a27e19.html, accessed 14 February 2013: 'A joint UNHCR-Mercy Corps assessment mission last week to Bambari in Central African Republic, some 400 kilometres north east of the capital Bangui, found wide displacement on the approach to Bambari. Villages along a 100 kilometre stretch of road between Grimari and Bambari were almost completely deserted, with most residents hiding in the bush. [. . .] Camp Pladama Ouaka, located 10 kilometres from the town of Bambari, where some 2,000 Sudanese refugees live, has not been spared. According to our colleagues, community facilities, the distribution center, and the warehouse of an NGO partner, have all been looted. Solar lamps, that were used to light the camp, have also been taken away.'

53 O'Neill, W., Rutinwa, B. and Verdirame, G., 'The Great Lakes: a survey of the application of the exclusion clause in the Central African Republic, Kenya and Tanzania', op. cit. note 43, p. 141. In the late 1990s, similar situations occurred in Guinea, where for a long time there was no control mechanism in place at its border with Sierra Leone and in Tanzania, where the potential existence of elements who did not deserve international protection prompted the Government to require as from 1997 all asylum-seekers from Rwanda to be screened individually.

54 In Sub-Saharan Africa this kind of situation occurs often also because the same ethnic groups, speaking the same language live in different countries. The case of some ethnic groups in Angola pretending to be Congolese thanks to the presence of the same ethnic groups in DRC, just in order to receive refugee status in the host countries, is perhaps the most famous example: the Yakas live in south-western DRC and Angola. Another example of this kind of pretence is represented by the Gur and Malinkés from other states that pretended to have Ivorian nationality just in order to apply for asylum. Information obtained directly by the author of this work at the UNHCR during his permanence there in 2006.

55 In his book, S. Turner dealt with these clashes in a very detailed way. See Turner, S., *Politics of Innocence: Hutu Identity, Conflict and Camp Life*, New York/Oxford: Berghahn Books, 2010, particularly pp. 79–81 ('Mixing as loss and as resource').

56 Rutinwa, B., '*Prima facie* status and refugee protection', op. cit. note 1, p. 14.

57 Durieux, J.-F., 'The many faces of "*prima facie*": group-based evidence in refugee status determination', op. cit. note 22, pp. 158–9.

Although *prima facie* group determination makes no room for the simultaneous assessment of possible exclusion grounds,[58] it does not preclude the screening of individual members of the group at a later stage. Until the point when an individual may be screened, individuals covered by a *prima facie* determination of a group character should be regarded as refugees according to the 1951 Geneva Refugee Convention.[59] *Prima facie* recognition of refugee status does not require subsequent 'confirmation', although individual eligibility determination becomes feasible at a later stage. It remains valid and may be terminated only if it is established, in accordance with applicable standards and following proper procedures, that the circumstances justify its cessation, cancellation or revocation.[60]

Refugees who have been admitted under *prima facie* status determination are nonetheless still liable to be excluded from refugee status if they come within the provisos of Article 1D, E and F of the 1951 Geneva Refugee Convention and also, particularly in Sub-Saharan Africa, Article I5 of the 1969 OAU Convention. Specifically, in the case of *prima facie* recognition, exclusion can only come after inclusion, insofar as it entails admission of all persons arriving in mass-influx and conclusively regarding them as refugees. Therefore, exclusion considerations, when appropriate, should follow later.[61] However, there can be exceptions to this particular situation, for instance, when an asylum-seeker coming as a part of mass-influx is discovered at the stage of reception and registration to be one of those already indicted by an international tribunal for having committed offences which would also make a person excludable from refugee law under relevant refugee law instruments. Given the individual and personal nature of the grounds on which an individual may be excluded from refugee status and the seriousness of the consequences of the exclusion, due process requires that excludable cases should be analyzed separately.[62] Whether, after such an assessment, it is found that a person who had been granted refugee status did not qualify for it, his/her exclusion should take place through a process of cancellation.[63] The UNHCR recently confirmed this, declaring:

58 Durieux, J.-F. and Hurwitz, A., op. cit. note 17, p. 123.

59 Jackson, I.C., *The Refugee Concept in Group Situations*, op. cit. note 15, p. 108.

60 UNHCR, Guidelines on the application in mass-influx situations of the exclusion clauses of Article 1F of the 1951 Convention relating to the Status of Refugees, Geneva: UNHCR, 2006, paragraph 13.

61 Durieux, J.-F., 'The many faces of "*prima facie*": group-based evidence in refugee status determination', op. cit. note 15, p. 159.

62 Durieux, J.-F. and Hurwitz, A., op. cit. note 11, pp. 123–4.

63 In this regard, S. Kapferer affirmed: '[c]ancellation may only be decided on an individual basis. This also applies where the original status determination was made as part of an expedited process, during which the circumstances of the individual case may not have been fully examined, or where members of a particular group were recognized as refugees on a *prima facie* basis. The existence of grounds which would render cancellation lawful and appropriate, for example in cases where a person is later found not to have met the criteria on which a *prima facie* recognition was based, must be established for each individual case.' See Kapferer, S., 'Cancellation of refugee status', in UNHCR, *Legal and Protection Policy Research Series*, 2003, paragraph 101, p. 32.

> In mass-influx situations, exclusion will often be examined in the context of cancellation proceedings. The onus to show that refugee status should be cancelled normally rests on the authority which reviews the initial decision.[64]

The 1992 Handbook states that obtaining refugee status by misrepresentation of material facts, or possession of another nationality or the fact that exclusion clauses are applicable once all the relevant facts are known, will comport cancellation of the refugee status.[65]

A more comprehensive list of grounds for cancellation of *prima facie* status is found in Article 36 of the 1998 South African Refugees Act No. 130, which includes:

> [a] person [who] has been recognized as a refugee erroneously on an application which contains any materially incorrect or false information, or was so recognized due to fraud, forgery, a false or misleading representation of a material or substantial nature in relation to the application.[66]

The 2007 Sierra Leonean Refugee Protection Act also adds to the list a situation in which new evidence becomes available that a person was wrongfully recognized as a refugee.[67]

It would be obvious to say that, as with exclusion, the process of cancellation should follow individualized procedures and that every refugee whose status is considered for cancellation should – at least in theory – have a genuine opportunity to refute the arguments and information against him/her. And, in any case:

> Despite being unable to access international refugee protection, however, an excluded individual is still entitled to be treated in a manner compatible with international law and, in particular, relevant human rights obligations. This also applies in the context of a mass-influx.[68]

64 UNHCR, Guidelines on the application in mass-influx situations of the exclusion clauses of Article 1F of the 1951 Convention relating to the Status of Refugees, Geneva: UNHCR, 2006, paragraph 27.

65 UNHCR, Handbook on procedures and criteria for determining refugee status under the 1951 Convention and the 1967 Protocol relating to the status of refugees, 2nd edn, Geneva: UNHCR, 1992, paragraph 117.

66 Article 1 1) a) of the 2007 Sierra Leonean Refugees Protection Act uses a similar expression, as well. On the contrary, the 1999 Namibian Act is quite vague comprising, in the category of individuals who deserve to have the status of refugee withdrawn, also a very discretionary category of person, such as: '[c]ategory of persons declared by the Minister by notice in the Gazette to be persons who are not entitled to refugee status in terms of this Act.'

67 Article 1 1) b) of the 2007 Sierra Leonean Refugees Protection Act.

68 UNHCR, Guidelines on the application in mass-influx situations of the exclusion clauses of Article 1F of the 1951 Convention relating to the Status of Refugees, Geneva: UNHCR, 2006, paragraph 34.

As for cessation, if individuals enjoying *prima facie* status are conclusively presumed to be refugees within the meaning of one or several relevant instruments, then cessation of their status should happen only when the grounds established within those instruments have been fulfilled, and the modalities laid down in refugee law and jurisprudence must be followed. The grounds that may lead to the cessation of refugee status, as spelt out in Article 1C, clauses 1 through 6 of the 1951 Geneva Convention, are considered applicable for *prima facie* refugees.[69]

In applying cessation clauses, relevant authorities should be guided by ExCom conclusion No. 69 on cessation of status of refugees, especially with regards to a group situation. In particular, where cessation is sought to be applied to refugees who are recognized as a part of a group situation:

> [the d]ecision to apply these cessation clauses must have the possibility, upon request, to have such application in their cases reconsidered on grounds relevant to their individual case.[70]

This is so because even when fundamental changes have taken place in the country of origin and, as a result, most of the refugees no longer need international protection, some refugees may still have legally valid reasons for not wanting to return to their country of origin. Hence, individual determination upon request ensures that no individual can be returned in violation of the 1951 Geneva Convention or any other relevant legal instrument.[71] In addition to individuals who may still be refugees at the time that cessation clauses are invoked, other individuals who should be heard individually are those who may invoke:

> [c]ompelling reasons arising out of previous persecution for refusing to re-avail themselves of the protection of their country. [The ExCom] recommends, so as to avoid hardship cases, that States seriously consider an appropriate status, preserving previously acquired rights, for persons who have compelling reasons arising out of previous persecution for refusing to re-avail themselves of the protection of their country, and recommends also that appropriate arrangements, which would not put into jeopardy their established situation, be similarly considered by relevant authorities for those persons who cannot be expected to leave the country of asylum, due to a long stay in that country resulting in strong family, social and economic links there.[72]

69 Rutinwa, B., '*Prima facie* status and refugee protection', op. cit. note 1, p. 22.

70 ExCom, conclusion No. 69 (XLIII), 'Cessation of status', 1992, paragraph d).

71 Fitzpatrick, J., 'Temporary protection of refugees: elements of a formalized regime', op. cit. note 2, p. 304.

72 ExCom, conclusion No. 69 (XLIII), 'Cessation of status', 1992, paragraph e).

in the 1984 Second International Conference on Assistance to Refugees in Africa (ICARA II) where, considering refugees as a burden on their economies, Sub-Saharan African host countries argued for financial aid from the developed countries: financial assistance to countries of first refuge; and financial assistance and, where necessary, provision of resettlement opportunities for the achievement of durable solutions.[93] But the African plea for this kind of burden-sharing met limited responses.[94] We easily see in this case that African governments went beyond the wording of the 1969 OAU Convention, invoking aid from countries other than 'member states' of the OAU.

In the UN, African states and the 'international community' followed a similar path. There, mainly the African countries[95] were appealed to:

> [R]espond positively, in the spirit of solidarity and burden [. . .] sharing, to the third-country resettlement needs of African refugees [. . .].[96]

In Sub-Saharan Africa, this should occur through assistance programmes that facilitate the temporary stay of refugees in the country of first asylum. Aid agencies from donor countries would thus tend to focus on emergency assistance measures at the expense of long-term, durable solutions, such as sponsoring development projects.[97]

asylum will be further advanced by the strengthening and development of institutional arrangements for "burden sharing" adopted within the framework of African solidarity and international cooperation [. . .].' In this regard, P. Nobel asserted: 'The conference found a vital need for an in-depth study of the various problems of burden-sharing. There is also a need for a continuous follow-up and collection of information concerning the refugees so that prompt action can be taken in cases of emergency and so that efforts on behalf of refugees can be properly coordinated.' See Nobel, P., 'Refugee, law, and development in Africa', op. cit. note 28, p. 271.

93 Martin, G., op. cit. note 73, p. 253.

94 Hans, A. and Suhrke, A., 'Responsibility sharing', in Hathaway J.C. (ed.), *Reconceiving International Refugee Law*, The Hague/Boston/London: Martinus Nijhoff, 1997, p. 91.

95 Tuitt, P., *False Images: Law's Construction of the Refugee*, London/East Haven, CT: Pluto Press, 1996, p. 22.

96 UNGA, Assistance to refugees, returnees and displaced persons in Africa, 18 December 2013, resolution No. A/RES/68/143, paragraph 24. In this regard, see also UNGA, Report of the United Nations High Commissioner for Refugees, questions relating to refugees, returnees and displaced persons and humanitarian questions, Report of the Third Committee, 1 December 2006, document No. A/61/436, Draft resolution IV, paragraph 22. In this regard, see also UNGA, Assistance to refugees, returnees and displaced persons in Africa, 21 December 2010, document No. A/RES/65/193, paragraph 25; UNGA, Assistance to refugees, returnees and displaced persons in Africa, 19 December 2011, document No. A/RES/66/135, paragraph 25; paragraph 14 of the Sudan draft resolution proposed in UNGA, Report of the United Nations High Commissioner for Refugees, questions relating to refugees, returnees and displaced persons and humanitarian questions, Report of the Third Committee, 11 November 2003, document No. A/C.3/58/L.37/Rev.: 'The General Assembly [. . .] expresses its appreciation and strong support for those African Governments and local population that, in spite of the general deterioration of socio-economic and environmental conditions and overstretched national resources, continue to accept the additional burden imposed upon them by increasing numbers of refugees [. . .] in compliance with the relevant principle of asylum.'

97 In this regard, G. Martin also noted that: '[s]ome legal experts have even proposed that the right of a country of asylum to claim compensation from the state of origin of the refugees be recognized, based

In spite of these proposals, the situation is not always favourable for refugees in Sub-Saharan Africa. For instance, South Africa, one of the richest countries in this area of the world, often countered the principle of burden-sharing, finding it more convenient for its government, but not for the refugees, to practise burden shifting, which allowed admitting almost no refugee on the South African territory[98] although in 2006, in the *Union of Refugee Women Case*, a domestic judicial body expressed a different opinion.[99] If the will to implement the principle is not always strong, it is then difficult to put into practice. In this regard, P. Nobel openly affirmed that there is an urgent need to construct and implement the legal and administrative mechanisms for burden-sharing.[100] In the end, however, much depends on the will of local governments in the area. But if this will is lacking, everything becomes more difficult and countries like Tanzania find their claims of burden-sharing unattended.[101]

In light of the example involving South Africa, international solidarity is called for in essentially three contexts. The first would consist of measures of cooperation and assistance which, while conceived and delivered within a refugee context, are

on the economic, social and other burdens due to the presence of large numbers of refugees on its territory.' See Martin, G., op. cit. note 73, p. 255. In effect, as J. Hyndman pointed out: 'Governments prefer interventions that provide assistance before potential refugees cross a border, as migrants increasingly pose an economic, if not political, threat to traditional refugee resettlement countries.' See Hyndman, J., *Managing Displacement: Refugees and the Politics of Humanitarianism*, op. cit. note 18, p. 3. At ibid., p. 187, the author, pragmatically, needed to conclude that: 'There is little, if any, constituency overlap between donors and refugees. UNHCR solicits funds and provides humanitarian assistance and protection with full accountability to its donors but with fewer such links to refugees and other recipients. This slippage allows for discretionary decision making regarding refugee status and camp operations. [. . .] Despite UNHCR's sustained efforts to enact relevant policies, hire experienced staff, and take concrete steps to make the organization more responsive to donors and refugee alike, there is no formal mechanism that links refugee recipient needs or demands to UNHCR operations. Government donors are UNHCR's main clients; refugees and displaced people are its recipients.'

98 The dispatch by the JRS No. 92, 2 May 2001 reads: 'According to J. Van Garderen of LHR, the South African Department of Home Affairs issued in these instructions in a Policy Circular sent around its border posts. "LHR will be challenging the circular in court very soon," said JRS advocacy officer in Johannesburg, Rampe Hlobo: "Sadly, South Africa, like many western states, is embracing the policy of burden shifting and not burden sharing. If the Policy Circular is followed to the letter and is not challenged, South Africa will have very few or no refugees from the rest of Africa, as the vast majority would never be able to afford a plane ticket to South Africa. Most of the refugees in South Africa walked or came down south by road and they had to pass through these 'safe neighboring States' mentioned in the policy circular." '

99 In the case *Union of Refugee Women and Others v Private Security Industry Regulatory Authority and Others*, Case No. CCT/39/06, Judgment Date: 12 December 2006, paragraph 140, the Constitutional Court of South Africa, recalling a precedent case declared: '[T]his has meant that South Africa has had to put into practice the concept of international solidarity and burden sharing, allowing the victims of international conflicts and human violations to seek a safe haven within our borders.'

100 Nobel, P., 'Refugee, law, and development in Africa', op. cit. note 28, p. 280.

101 In this regard see, among other authors: Morel, M., 'The lack of refugee burden-sharing in Tanzania: tragic effects', in *Afrika Focus*, vol. 22, 2009, especially the paragraph entitled: 'Durable solutions in Tanzania: the lack of international burden-sharing', p. 110–14.

designed to improve the overall social and economic conditions for refugees and nationals alike. The second aspect would refer to the financial, material and technical assistance that should be made available to the asylum countries directly within the refugee context, reinforcing the capacity and abilities of governments to protect and assist refugees.[102] The third aspect of international solidarity has a more direct objective tied closely to the state of international protection either within or outside the continent. Regional and universal levels of protection can be considered as two sides of the same coin.[103] There are legal issues involved in this context, as well: where there are clear standards for legal protection, it is not obvious which principles and obligations are applicable in the case of material assistance. If some exist, they are not being applied uniformly. But it is clear that the general framework should ensure that refugees receive the protection to which, for instance, human rights law already entitles them.[104] We should however pay attention to cases in which the host states, under the cover of protecting asylum-seekers, use their flight to discredit or destabilize the regime in the source country, as for instance, the former Zaire's policy towards Rwanda.[105]

102 Paragraph j) i) of the ExCom conclusion No. 100 (LV), 'International cooperation and burden and responsibility sharing in mass-influx situations', 2004 mentions, among the burden-sharing arrangements necessary and appropriate to the situation: '[t]he provision of emergency financial and technical assistance and other forms of support where necessary [. . .].'

103 Recommendation 10 of the OAU/UNHCR document on Refugees and forced population displacement in Africa, 8–10 September 1994 reads: 'The refugee crisis cannot be addressed effectively through rigid and regionalized approaches. The Symposium recommends that this problem be addressed in a global and comprehensive manner, as it will ultimately affect every region of the world. Likewise, countries should strive for effective cooperation and mutual assistance on refugee, displacement and migratory issues, the same way they collaborate on security, economic and environmental matters.' Therefore, international solidarity specifically geared to encouraging a genuinely refugee-protection oriented system should be fashioned as Recommendation 11 observes: 'The Symposium appeals for genuine international solidarity and burden-sharing to be brought back to the centre of the refugee problem, the international system of protection and of solutions for refugees. In particular, a truly international system embracing global standards and principles on prevention, refugee protection, assistance and solutions should be reinvigorated. The steady slide towards restrictive, deterrent laws, policies and practices at a global level must be halted and reversed.' In this regard, see also Office of the United Nations High Commissioner for Refugees, 'Issues and challenges in international protection in Africa', in *International Journal of Refugee Law*, vol. 7, Special Issue, 1995, pp. 69–70: '[I]n this relationship between African refugee law, policy and practice on the one hand, and global trends on the other lies the most serious likelihood of a further lowering of the thresholds of refugee protection in Africa. As has often been remarked [. . .] the political and ideological value attaching to refugees has waned. The attachment to upholding refugees' rights which may have previously characterized the approach to asylum is in fierce competition with tendencies towards the most restrictive and minimalist legal regimes, policies and practices. [. . .] It is difficult to expect that these trends will not be observed in Africa, where the underlying social and economic constraints are even more compelling. Indeed, the tendency to emulate these trends is said by some already to be in evidence.' Finally, see also Rogge, J.R., 'The challenges of changing dimensions among the South's refugees: illustrations from Somalia', in *International Journal of Refugee Law*, vol. 5, 1993, p. 26.

104 Schuck, P.H., op. cit. note 78, p. 271.

105 Ibid., p. 273.

Better management of mass refugee flows, for purposes of relief but also for longer term response,[106] would serve the interest of states, strengthen international order and stability, and at the same time protect the rights of refugees. Above all, better management means non-rejection of refugees if the host country has the possibility to grant a minimal set of rights to individuals in a difficult situation. Better management also means the real application of what has been described as 'proportional burden-sharing' according to the possibilities of every state but always through its consent, by which no state should be obliged to participate in the burden-sharing scheme unless it voluntarily undertakes to do so.[107] In effect, the possibility of African states accepting to be bound in advance by any precise formula going beyond a general duty to participate in good faith in any resettlement scheme devised in response to an existing refugee problem appears extremely remote. Any attempt in imposing predetermined burden-sharing quotas is expected to be basically counter-productive. It could increase the risk that widespread consensus existing in relation to international solidarity as a principle of collective responsibility may quickly crumble as states, in their determination to resist the 'distribution' of pre-allocated, individual quotas of resettlement liabilities, may be driven to calling into question the essential general principle of international solidarity itself.[108]

Whenever possible, the refugee-producing and refugee-receiving countries, through negotiated settlement, should share the burden equitably, to the satisfaction of all parties. In absence of that, the asylum state or the refugees may claim compensation from the country of origin, in accordance with the principles of state responsibility under international law.[109] It is clear, however, that as also proposed in practically all the conferences on refugees in Africa, burden-sharing can also be solved through link relief, recovery and development assistance, to facilitate the promotion of self-sufficiency and reduce the burden imposed on host countries and countries of origin, supporting regional peace processes for projects designated to integrate refugees and returnees into national development schemes.[110]

106 In this regard, see UN High Commissioner for Refugees, Persons covered by the OAU Convention Governing the Specific Aspects of Refugee Problems in Africa and by the Cartagena Declaration on Refugees (Submitted by the African Group and the Latin American Group), 6 April 1992, document No. EC/1992/SCP/CRP.6, paragraph 18: 'International *burden-sharing* is most needed for both relief and long term response. In recent years, however, international response has been falling behind the actual needs of refugees, and as a result, many programs have been adversely affected to barely meet life-saving and life-sustaining requirements.'

107 Schuck, P.H., op. cit. note 78, p. 276 and p. 297. At p. 297 the author argued: '[T]he refugee burden-sharing scheme by proposing a regionally-based, consensual arrangement combining a quota system that distributes refugee burdens among the wealthier states with a market option that can redistribute protection resources to other states that can more effectively use them to harbor more refugees – promises to increase the overall level and quality of protection.'

108 Fonteyne, J.-P.L., op. cit. note 74, p. 187.

109 Chhangani, R.C., *African Refugee Law: Problems and Prospects*, Maiduguri, Nigeria: University of Maiduguri Press, 1992, p. 22.

110 Martin, G., op. cit. note 73, p. 256.

Refugees need to be considered as a matter of international humanitarian concern, and it is therefore, in the end, the responsibility of the world community to ensure that they can be provided with the protection to which they are entitled,[111] burden-sharing and international cooperation being the solution considered by P. Hyndman as the most 'realistic' to avert the flow of refugees on the continent.[112]

We have, however, many doubts as to burden-sharing being effectively put in place in Sub-Saharan Africa when needed. We wonder if the notorious problems of poverty which afflict almost all countries in that continent, to be taken into consideration for a serious analysis of the specific situation there, are not used as a mere excuse not to fulfil moral obligations that, in any case, should go beyond every international legal norm.[113]

Numerous reports have pointed out the significance of the absence of meaningful burden-sharing and the growing xenophobia in many African states as the key factors motivating restrictive asylum policies.[114] Rather ironically, xenophobic feelings among African populations against refugees have emerged at a time when most of the continent is democratizing and governments are obliged to take into account public opinion in formulating various policies. The result has been the adoption of anti-refugee platforms by political parties that result in anti-refugee policies by the governments.[115] In Sub-Saharan Africa, however, the truth of the issue is that refugees from less-developed countries are being aided by less-developed countries. The situation has prompted the suggestion that while the international community completely supports the principle of burden-sharing, individual countries tend more and more to practise some form of burden-shifting instead,[116] also because they often need to face the case of irregular movement[117] of refugees and/or asylum-seekers, in this way triggering an involuntary sharing

111 Fonteyne, J.-P.L., op. cit. note 74, p. 188.

112 Hyndman, P., 'Refugees under international law with a reference to concept of asylum', in *The Australian Law Journal*, vol. 60, 1986, pp. 154–5.

113 For a different opinion see, for instance, the paragraph: 'Hospitality in a state of poverty is inconceivable', in Kibreab, G., *African Refugees: Reflections on the African Refugee Problem*, Trenton, NJ: Africa World Press, 1985, pp. 69–73. At p. 72 the author wondered whether: 'Can one speak of traditional hospitality when social interaction is determined by economic benefits? Or when the host population itself is in a state of abject poverty?'

114 Loescher, G. and Milner, J.H.S., *Protracted Refugee Situations: Domestic and International Security Implication*, Adelphi Papers, No. 375, Oxford: Routledge, 2005, p. 38.

115 Rutinwa, B., 'The end of asylum? The changing nature of refugee policies in Africa', in *UNHCR, New Issues in Refugee Research*, research paper No. 5, 1999, p. 2.

116 Martin, G., op. cit. note 73, p. 256.

117 The concept of 'irregular movements' is not dissimilar to the phenomenon of 'secondary movements' of refugees. In effect: '[i]n UNHCR's vocabulary, "secondary movements" describe the movements of refugees who have already been granted refugee status in a first country of asylum. The reasons for their movements can be of two sorts: either the refugee wants to improve his economic situation through migration, or he is forced to flee a second time due to lack of effective protection and security in the first country of asylum. In both cases, some governments in the sub-region interpret this kind of mobility simply as looking for economic opportunity and deny their refugee status.' See UNHCR, West Africa as a migration and protection area, November 2008, p. 48.

of burden which evidently will be not well appreciated by the new countries of destination of the refugees/asylum-seekers. However, to ensure that 'burden-sharing' does not change into 'burden-shifting', cooperative arrangements relating to redistribution of people would necessitate providing for a fair sharing of accountabilities between participating States.[118]

The phenomenon of the irregular movement, as the ExCom has underlined, is basically composed of persons who, although having received protection in a given country, feel the necessity to leave it, seeing no good education and/or work prospects[119] and, in any case, no satisfactory, durable solution to their situation there.[120] This is quite typical in Sub-Saharan Africa, having involved many communities of refugees in different regions of the continent, such as the Congolese, the Rwandans and Burundians who, hosted in Malawi, Mozambique, Zambia or Zimbabwe, were finally aiming to head to South Africa – also the preferred final destination of the Angolans, hosted for long periods in Namibia.[121]

Of course, in these circumstances, local authorities of the new country of destination should carefully assess the situation of these irregular movers, because there could be some among them who really are fleeing their first country of asylum because of the fear of being persecuted.[122] And in this latter case the

118 UNHCR, International Cooperation to Share Burden and Responsibilities, Expert Meeting in Amman, Jordan, 27 and 28 June 2011, discussion paper, paragraph 25, p. 10. The paragraph continued maintaining that: 'Factors which could be taken into account in this respect include demographics, absorption capacity and the presence of existing refugee communities. Regardless of how responsibility between States is allocated, it is important that relevant international refugee law standards are respected and persons in need of international protection are properly identified and protected against *refoulement*, their material needs are met, and durable solutions are found.'

119 Legomsky, S.H., 'Secondary refugee movements and the return of asylum seekers to third countries: the meaning of effective protection', in *International Journal of Refugee Law*, vol. 15, 2003, p. 596: 'In Africa generally, a majority of first countries of asylum provide no education at all to refugee children'.

120 ExCom, conclusion No. 58 (XL), 'Problem of refugees and asylum-seekers who move in an irregular manner from a country in which they had already found protection', 1989, paragraph b): 'Irregular movements of refugees and asylum-seekers who have already found protection in a country are, to a large extent, composed of persons who feel impelled to leave, due to the absence of educational and employment possibilities and the non-availability of long-term durable solutions by way of voluntary repatriation, local integration and resettlement.' In this regard, see also the definition provided in Kingsley-Nyinah, M.R., 'Reflections on the institution of asylum, refugee criteria, and irregular movements in Southern Africa', in *International Journal of Refugee Law*, special issue, vol. 7, 1995, pp. 307–8: irregular movers are '[t]hose refugees and/or asylum seekers who have already found protection (i.e. have been granted refugee status), or could reasonably be expected to seek protection, in the country or one of the countries which they transited through prior to seeking asylum in their current host country.'

121 Legomsky, S.H., op. cit. note 119, p. 589.

122 ExCom, conclusion No. 58 (XL), 'Problem of refugees and asylum-seekers who move in an irregular manner from a country in which they had already found protection', 1989, paragraph g): 'It is recognized that there may be exceptional cases in which a refugee or asylum-seeker may justifiably claim that he has reason to fear persecution or that his physical safety or freedom are endangered in a country where he previously found protection. Such cases should be given favorable consideration by the authorities of the State where he requests asylum.'

authorities of the new country should take into the highest consideration the situation of the new arrivals.

The authorities of the third country should, however, be paying a lot of attention to the phenomenon of the false documentation that movers could prepare – or the originals that they could destroy – in order to obtain the protection of a new country,[123] a similar situation to what happened with different caseloads in Malawi in the mid-1990s.[124] However, it seems clear that under the circumstances of the irregular movements, national governments, in cooperation with the UNHCR, should prevent refugees from leaving the first country of asylum without any authorization, instead supporting and providing them either with effective protection or with a regular, durable solution there.[125] The problem in Sub-Saharan Africa – although marginally if compared with other territories but just because the border control in Africa is very problematic – is that the first countries of asylum on the continent often refuse to take the irregular refugees back,[126] creating

123 Ibid., paragraphs h) to j): 'h) The problem of irregular movements is compounded by the use, by a growing number of refugees and asylum-seekers, of fraudulent documentation and their practice of willfully destroying or disposing of travel and/or other documents in order to mislead the authorities of their country of arrival. These practices complicate the personal identification of the person concerned and the determination of the country where he stayed prior to arrival, and the nature and duration of his stay in such a country. Practices of this kind are fraudulent and may weaken the case of the person concerned; i) It is recognized that circumstances may compel a refugee or asylum-seeker to have recourse to fraudulent documentation when leaving a country in which his physical safety or freedom are endangered. Where no such compelling circumstances exist, the use of fraudulent documentation is unjustified; j) The willful destruction or disposal of travel or other documents by refugees and asylum-seekers upon arrival in their country of destination, in order to mislead the national authorities as to their previous stay in another country where they have protection, is unacceptable. Appropriate arrangements should be made by States, either individually or in co-operation with other States, to deal with this growing phenomenon.' In this regard, see also UNHCR, Study of irregular movements of asylum-seekers and refugees, 1 August 1985, document No. WG/M/2, paragraph 37, p. 21.

124 Kingsley-Nyinah, M.R., 'Reflections on the institution of asylum, refugee criteria, and irregular movements in Southern Africa', op. cit. note 120, pp. 301–3.

125 ExCom, conclusion No. 58 (XL), 'Problem of refugees and asylum-seekers who move in an irregular manner from a country in which they had already found protection', 1989, paragraph d): 'Within this framework, governments, in close co-operation with UNHCR, should i) seek to promote the establishment of appropriate measures for the care and support of refugees and asylum-seekers in countries where they have found protection pending the identification of a durable solution and ii) promote appropriate durable solutions with particular emphasis firstly on voluntary repatriation and, when this is not possible, local integration and the provision of adequate resettlement opportunities.' See also Convention Plus: issues paper submitted by the UNHCR on addressing irregular secondary movements of refugees and asylum-seekers, 11 March 2004, Forum/SM/03, paragraph 40, p. 10: 'A special agreement to address the irregular secondary movements of refugees and asylum-seekers will call for three complementary types of efforts: 1) to ensure that effective protection is available in countries of asylum where people arrive; 2) to find durable solutions for refugees at an early stage; and 3) to develop strategies to ensure better control of irregular secondary movements in a protection sensitive manner.'

126 Legomsky, S.H., op. cit. note 119, p. 593. In this regard, see also UNHCR, Convention Plus: issues paper submitted by the UNHCR on addressing irregular secondary movements of refugees

a controversy with the new country of destination, a dispute where the UNHCR needs, not always with success, to play a role of intermediation between the two countries concerned. This role is played through, for instance, the facilitation of agreements between the two states for a form of responsibility-sharing,[127] or in readmission agreements – where readmission has been considered by UNHCR as 'necessarily part and parcel of any comprehensive response to irregular secondary movement'[128] – between the two states. Readmission agreements, which should take place with the unambiguous or at least as a minimum, the implied accord of the state to which an asylum-seeker is returned,[129] are believed to reduce the scale of irregular movements, because a refugee is less motivated to leave a country whether he/she knows that return is probable.[130] However, M.R. Kingsley-Nyinah

and asylum-seekers, 11 March 2004, Forum/SM/03, paragraph 19, p. 5: 'From the perspective of the first country of asylum, secondary movements may appear as the unintended consequence of its limited capacity to host refugees and provide effective protection for protracted periods of time. There is little doubt that the passing of time, without an improvement in the quality of protection and/or without prospects for durable solutions, is a factor in the increase of irregular secondary movements.'

127 UNHCR, Convention Plus: issues paper submitted by the UNHCR on addressing irregular secondary movements of refugees and asylum-seekers, 11 March 2004, Forum/SM/03, paragraphs 24 to 25, pp. 6–7: '24) It is equally important to note that an effective and fair system of responsibility sharing must recognize and address the wide disparity which currently prevails among State capacities to protect refugees, as well as the uneven distribution of the refugee burden among States, both of which have a serious impact on levels of protection world-wide. 25) UNHCR stands ready to play its role, as a multilateral organization, to facilitate agreements among States that will enhance refugee protection world-wide in conformity with the letter and spirit of international refugee law, and result in more effective and reliable burden-sharing. The responsibility of UNHCR for monitoring the adoption and implementation of inter-State agreements that have an impact on the protection of refugees must be seen as flowing directly from its Statute.'

128 UNHCR, Convention Plus core group on addressing irregular secondary movements of refugees and asylum-seekers: joint statement by the co-chairs, 8 November 2005, Forum 2005/7, p. 5. In this regard, see also Legomsky, S.H., op. cit. note 119, p. 577: 'UNHCR generally prefers readmission agreements over the unilateral application of safe third country notions that fail to guarantee readmission and access to an asylum procedure in a third country. Properly drafted and implemented, readmission agreements make for a more orderly return process, thus adding at least some assurance that the person being returned to the third country will in fact be readmitted there.'

129 UNHCR, UNHCR Position on Readmission Agreements, 'Protection Elsewhere' and Asylum Policy, 1 August 1994, 3 European Series 2, available at: www.refworld.org/docid/3ae6b31cb8.html, accessed 15 October 2014.

130 Legomsky, S.H., op. cit. note 119, p. 578. In this see also UNHCR, UNHCR Position on Readmission Agreements, 'Protection Elsewhere' and Asylum Policy, 1 August 1994, 3 European Series 2, available at: www.refworld.org/docid/3ae6b31cb8.html, accessed 15 October 2014. The document clarified that: 'In order to avoid the risk of so-called orbit situations, with the attendant hardships for asylum-seekers as well as the possibility of *refoulement*, it is recommended that the consent of the third country be obtained before an asylum applicant is sent to that country. Where such consent cannot be obtained, there must, in any event, be full assurance that the asylum-seeker will be admitted and his or her asylum application examined in fair procedures. To ensure that this in fact occurs, it is suggested that in all cases the authorities of

claimed that an irregular refugee, who has obtained protection from a new asylum-state through abusive or fraudulent conduct, should have assistance and protection to him/her clearly terminated, instead of simply sending him/her back to the first country of asylum.[131]

the third country be informed in advance of the return of any asylum-seeker whose application has not yet been substantively examined so that appropriate notification can be given to the border officials and the necessary protection guaranteed.'

131 Kingsley-Nyinah, M.R., 'Reflections on the institution of asylum, refugee criteria, and irregular movements in Southern Africa', op. cit. note 120, p. 311: 'That some dishonest conduct may be sufficiently grave to justify the withdrawal of assistance and protection from an irregular mover, is a position which may be vigorously defended. Where such an "irregular mover" is conclusively proved to have obtained international assistance through the deliberate presentation of misleading or false information to the UNHCR, a compelling case could be made for the outright termination of assistance and protection, rather than the mere return of the "offender" to the country of first asylum.' At idem the author also explained: 'There is no reason why refugees and asylum seekers should be exempt from such fundamental principles of basic legality, or why an "irregular mover" whose action is intentionally fraudulent should continue to receive assistance and protection.'

4 Refugee camps in Sub-Saharan Africa

Perpetuating the plight of refugees? Restrictions on free settlement and movement

4.1 Encamped refugees: an overview

Temporary asylum camps – probably the most visible manifestation of refugee problems – constitute a powerful line of defense for refugees in emergency situations. Compelled to lift normal alien entry requirements in the face of humanitarian emergencies, asylum states, however, try to control security and stability concerns by making entry conditional at the time of encampment.[1]

In Sub-Saharan Africa today these camps have become almost synonymous with the refugee experience. This is shown by Gambian legislation which, while constituting an exception in the African legal panorama, provides the possibility to set up camps in areas directly designated by the Secretary of State.[2]

One of the most essential features of the camps is the authoritarian character of their administration. They are total institutions, places where everything is highly organized, and the inhabitants are depersonalized,[3] a situation which also often represents 'an ongoing criminal disregard for human rights'.[4]

However, before moving on with our analysis, we would like to explain that in this study we will talk about 'camps', although in Sub-Saharan Africa the UNHCR categorizes refugee built-up areas as either 'camps', 'settlements' or 'centres'. The definition of 'centre' represents this agglomeration as a very temporary shelter being constituted by '[l]ocations where refugees are gathered in order to receive the necessary material assistance which meets their needs'.[5]

1 Jamal, A., 'A realistic, segmented and reinvigorated UNHCR approach to resolving protracted refugee situations', in Loescher, G. *et al.* (eds), *Protracted Refugee Situations: Political, Human Rights and Security Implications*, New York: United Nations University Press, 2008, p. 146.

2 Article 42 ('Designation of refugee camps') of the Gambian Refugee Act, 2008, 17 November 2008.

3 Harrell-Bond, B., 'Are refugee camps good for children?', in UNHCR, *New Issues in Refugee Research*, research paper No. 29, 2000, p. 1.

4 Westra, L., *Environmental Justice and the Rights of Ecological Refugees*, London: Earthscan, 2009, p. 140.

5 UNHCR, International Thesaurus of Refugee Terminology. Definition available at: www.refugeethesaurus.org/content.php/home?expand=2, accessed 10 September 2014.

A typical example of a centre of this kind is represented by the one in Johannesburg, South Africa, which closed on 1 June 2011 and whose re-opening has been recently requested by several NGOs present there.[6]

Conversely, a different discourse merits highlighting the distinction between the 'camp' and the 'settlement'. In this regard, Schmidt listed the most important characteristics of camps: the separation from the population of the host country, the necessity to share public services, a lack of privacy, overcrowding – even if 'camps of over 20,000 people should be avoided',[7] and restrictions to areas where the refugee conducts his/her private life. The parameters allowing us to distinguish camps from settlements were therefore the following: freedom of movement, with less freedom the more a settlement is considered to be a camp, and a level of self-sufficiency. In addition, in camps there is little possibility for refugees to engage in subsistence agricultural activities and/or other economic activities. Modes of governance of camps are, after all, distinguished from settlements by the stricter parameters of control over their population (i.e., restrictions on socio-economic, cultural and political freedoms placed on their inhabitants over and above those existing for the local residents). Although no real explanation is provided about the length of time a camp should remain open, we also have the issue of time management to consider, with the opening of temporary locations/shelters being a question of discretion on the part of authorities, knowing that a camp should not, in theory, be open for long. Finally, to determine the classification of the grouping, we should also look at that area's population size and/or density, with camps, in principle, being more overcrowded than settlements.[8]

Having established these premises, we note that at the end of 2012, in Sub-Saharan Africa 109 refugee camps were open, along with 142 refugee settlements, and 26 refugee centres – making a total of 277 places hosting refugees, with a higher number of settlements over camps and therefore, at least hypothetically, with more stable places where refugees can shelter and perhaps establish

6 HRW, 'South Africa: open new Johannesburg refugee center', 2 June 2011, available at: www.unhcr.org/refworld/docid/4dedf0fc2.html, accessed 15 October 2014. In this regard, see also the two cases brought in front of the High Court in Cape Town in 2012, regarding the closing of the Scalabrini reception centre for refugees: High Court of South Africa (Western Cape, Cape Town), *Scalabrini Centre, Cape Town and Others v Minister of Home Affairs and Others*, No. 11681/12, 19 March 2013, where, at paragraph 122, p. 50, it was explained that: 'a) The second respondent's decision, taken by not later than 30 May 2012, to close the Cape Town Refugee Reception Office to new applicants for asylum after 29 June 2012 is declared unlawful and is set aside. b) The first to third respondents are directed to ensure that by Monday 1 July 2013 a Refugee Reception Office is open and fully functional within the Cape Town Metropolitan Municipality at which new applicants for asylum can make applications for asylum in terms of s 21 of the Refugees Act 130 of 1998 and be issued with permits in terms of s 22 of the said Act.'

7 UNHCR, Handbook for Emergencies, 2nd edn, Geneva: UNHCR, 1999, p. 137.

8 Schmidt, A., FMO thematic guide: camps versus settlements, no data available, pp. 4–5, pdf document, available at: www.forcedmigration.org/research-resources/expert-guides/camps-versus-settlements/fmo021.pdf, accessed 10 October 2014.

themselves. A huge number of African countries hosted at least one of these places where foreign nationals could find refuge. If Chad was the country hosting the highest number of camps, 20 (due to the ongoing situations occurring in Sudan, South Sudan and Libya), several countries hosted only one refugee camp on their territory, often the legacy of past turmoil in bordering states, such as for instance, Botswana (Dukwi), Cameroon (Langui), CAR (Batalimo), Gambia (Bambali), Guinea Bissau (Jolmete), Guinea Conakry (Kouankan), Malawi (Dzaleka),[9] Mauritania (M'Bera), Mozambique (Marratane), Namibia (Osire) and Nigeria (Oru).

As for settlements, Uganda by far held the primacy for their number with 76 – more than half of the total amount – due to the strategic position of the country, bordering with several massive 'refugee-generating' countries, such as DRC, Ethiopia, Rwanda and South Sudan. In detail, Uganda's history with the south of Sudan is very long, considering that since the independence of Sudan, in 1956, people from the south of the country started crossing the border into Uganda.[10]

9 In regards to the Dzaleka camp, J. Crisp and E. Kiragu observed: 'A key location on the long route to South Africa is Dzaleka refugee camp in Malawi, which accommodates both a long-term group of residents, mainly from the Great Lakes region, and a transitory population, primarily from the Horn of Africa. All new arrivals at the camp receive basic food and other assistance and are expected to stay in the camp's transit area for three months before they are registered and allocated a plot of land in which to construct a more permanent shelter. Within this period, interviews are undertaken and documentation prepared for Refugee Status Determination.' See Crisp, J. and Kiragu, E., 'Refugee protection and international migration: A review of UNHCR's role in Malawi, Mozambique and South Africa', paper for UNHCR/Policy Development Evaluation Service (PDES), August 2010, paragraph 33, p. 8, available at: www.unhcr.org/4c629c4d9.html, accessed 12 October 2014. In this regard, see also Mvula, L.D., 'Refugee status determination and rights in Malawi', paper presented at the Refugee Studies Centre Workshop Discussion on RSD and rights in Southern and East Africa, no date available, p. 5, pdf document available at: www.rsc.ox.ac.uk/files/publications/other/dp-rsd-malawi-2010.pdf/@@download, accessed 1 June 2015:: 'It is worth pointing out that Malawi initially had two refugee camps, namely Dzaleka and Luwani. However, the latter was closed down in May 2007 without warning, citing security concerns triggered by asylum seekers from the horn of Africa who were suspected of involvement in human trafficking. The camp held 300 refugees at the time of its closure and the refugees were transferred to Dzaleka camp. Notably, Dzaleka was already holding 5,000 refugees and the addition of the new refugees put a huge strain on the already limited resources at the camp. For example, the primary school at the camp, which also catered for locals, had its enrolment increase sharply from 1,200 to 1,900, prompting the authorities to introduce learning in shifts and to hold classes in tents. Expectedly, the transfer also sapped medical resources at Dzaleka.' For an update of the present situation in Dzaleka, see the news: 'Reaching out brings results for UNHCR in Malawi refugee camp', 8 November 2012, available at: www.unhcr.org/509bd6839.html, accessed 10 November 2014. About the Langui camp in Cameroon, instead, we observe that: 'After the anticipated repatriation of the majority of Chadian refugees from Langui camp, UNHCR will focus on the local integration of the residual population and rehabilitate the basic infrastructure of the camp.' See UNHCR, Global Appeal 2013, Update, Geneva: UNHCR, December 2012, p. 13. At ibid., p. 17, concerning the Batalimo camp in CAR, UNHCR affirmed that: 'Voluntary return will be pursued for some 6,000 Congolese refugees from the DRC's Equateur Province who are currently staying in Batalimo camp, and for whom local integration opportunities are limited. For those who do not opt for voluntary return, UNHCR will provide protection and multi-sectoral assistance, with an emphasis on self-reliance.'

10 Kaiser, T., 'The experience and consequences of insecurity in a refugee populated area in Northern Uganda, 1996–1997', in *Refugee Survey Quarterly*, vol. 19, 2000, p. 41. Ibid., at p. 45,

Other countries, as regards the camps, hosted only one settlement. These countries included, for example, Swaziland (Malindza) and Zimbabwe (Tongogara). In the case of centres, the DRC hosted 12 of them – almost half of the entire number of centres functioning in Sub-Saharan Africa.[11]

Unfortunately, it was not possible for us to know exactly who runs all these places. Either because the relevant information was not in possession of the UNHCR offices in Geneva – their representative, when asked, said '[I] would say that most are organized by the UNHCR and the local government'[12] – or because of changes in the *de facto* status of the camps. We do not know, for example, who decides in favour of the creation of a camp rather than a settlement, and we must suppose that also this choice represents the result of consultations between the UNHCR and local authorities considering, among other aspects, the funds available. However, in several cases, other organizations apart from the UNHCR contribute in helping the encampment of refugees, like the International Organization for Migration (IOM) that, for instance, relocated Sudanese refugees in a new camp in Ethiopia.[13]

Camps help allay security concerns[14] represented by those perceived, rightly or wrongly, as potentially volatile and disruptive. They also ease the burden that huge influxes of asylum-seekers place on host populations. As traditional African hospitality towards refugees gives way to 'host fatigue', camps strengthen asylum by encouraging hosts to accept the presence of refugees.[15]

Camps generally consign refugees to a situation in limbo, with no legal status and no opportunity to integrate. In recent years, in Kenya, even the possibilities of repatriation for Somali refugees were, and remain, slight due to the insecurity of their country of origin.[16] This in spite of the Tripartite

the author explained: 'The language used by [Ugandan] officials of central government in relation to refugees in Uganda is one of solidarity and brotherhood. [. . .] Government policy towards refugees is described by UNHCR as "progressive and liberal" and is generally accepted to be generous and sympathetic.'

11 The entire list of camps, settlements and centres was provided directly by the UNHCR and it is on file with author.

12 Email received on 29 October 2012 by Mr. Yvon Orand working at the UNHCR Department for Population and Geographic Data in Geneva, on file with author.

13 See the news: 'IOM starts relocation of Sudanese refugees to new camp in Ethiopia', 15 June 2012, available at: www.iom.int/cms/en/sites/iom/home/news-and-views/press-briefing-notes/pbn-2012/pbn-listing/iom-starts-relocation-of-sudanese-refuge.html, accessed 25 September 2014.

14 M.-F. Cuellar, however, explained: '[T]he [. . .] neglect of security by refugee advocates contributes to episodes of refugee assistance plainly at odds with the law, as with the continued flows of resources reaching tightly militarized camps in the Goma region of Eastern Congo in the mid-1990s and in Southern Africa in the early 1980s.' See Cuellar, M.-F., 'Refugee security and the organizational logic of legal mandates', in *Georgetown Journal of International Law*, vol. 37, 2005–2006, pp. 720–1.

15 Jamal, A., 'Camps and freedoms: long-term refugee situation in Africa', in *Forced Migration Review*, No. 16, 2003, p. 4.

16 Kagwanja, P. and Juma, M., 'Somali refugees: protracted exile and shifting security frontiers', in Loescher, G. (*et al.*) (eds), *Protracted Refugee Situations: Political, Human Rights and Security Implications*, New York: United Nations University Press, 2008, p. 221. C. Horst described in a very detailed

Agreement[17] stipulated on 10 November 2013 and having as an objective '[t]o provide for a legal framework for the safe and dignified voluntary repatriation of Somali refugees from the Republic of Kenya and their reintegration in the Federal Republic of Somalia.'[18]

No one chooses freely to move into a refugee camp to stay. Those who can, leave as quickly as possible. This is why there are often more refugees living within host countries, yet outside the camps with, of course, several exceptions.[19] However, it happens sometimes that refugees are forced to return to camps as, for instance, was ruled by the Malawian High Court in the 2008 case *Nsabimana and Others; S v the Department of Poverty and Disaster Management Affairs and Another*. In this specific case, despite the court ruling that the refugees did not constitute a danger to national security and/or the public order of the country, this was effectively irrelevant because the body who issued the order to refugees to settle outside the camps was simply considered to be 'a non-existent entity'.[20] What

way the life of Somali refugees in Kenyan camps in her work. See Horst, C., *Transnational Nomads: How Somalis Cope With Refugee Life in the Dadaab Camps of Kenya*, New York/Oxford: Berghahn Books, 2006, p. 226. At p. 20 of her work, the author is quite critical with UNHCR policy in Kenya, noting that: 'The shift in responsibility for the care of the refugees from the government to the international community had the positive effect of attracting external funds. The negative consequence was, however, that the *laissez-faire* policy before 1991 had provided few obstacles to the local integration of refugees, except maybe that the overall situation of poverty in the country was a complicating factor. The refugees had the right to employment, education, and freedom of movement. When the UNHCR took over, none of these positive aspects were preserved. It was not very efficient for the UNHCR to operate a large number of smaller refugee camps, and the government of Kenya was also not happy with the dispersal of refugees across a large number of camp sites throughout the country.'

17 For an analysis of Tripartite Agreements, see *infra*, Chapter 8.

18 UNHCR, Tripartite Agreement between the Government of the Republic of Kenya, the Government of the Federal Republic of Somalia and the United Nations High Commissioner for Refugees governing the voluntary repatriation of Somali refugees living in Kenya, 2013, 10 November 2013, Article 2. Just thirteen days after, on 26 November, the UNHCR reaffirmed that the 'UNHCR does not support forced returns'. See the news: 'UNHCR stresses that repatriation of Somalis from Kenya must be voluntary', 26 November 2013, available at: www.unhcr.org/5294819e9.html, accessed 10 October 2014.

19 For instance, see Schmiechen, M.M., 'Parallel lives, uneven justice: an analysis of rights, protection and redress for refugee and internally displaced women in camps', in *Saint Louis University Public Law Review*, vol. 22, 2003, p. 478: 'In some places, such as Kenya, refugees are allowed outside the camp, while in others, such as Guinea, refugees are kept in the camps by camp security.'

20 High Court of Malawi, *Nsabimana and Others; S v the Department of Poverty and Disaster Management Affairs and Another*, 17 April 2008, Misc. Civil Application No. 19 of 2006, paragraph 24, where the judge affirmed: 'Of particular importance is the fact that there is no provision which empowers the Refugee Committee to delegate its functions and powers to a subcommittee or other body. Therefore it was/is unlawful for a subcommittee to busy itself to grant permits to refugees/asylum seekers authorizing them to reside outside camps. Because the purported subcommittee was/is a nonexistent entity. If the subcommittee was a mere internal administrative arrangement for purposes of efficiency in the discharge of the Refugee Committee's duties, that was in order, but only the name of the Refugee Committee has to stand out', available at: www.unhcr.org/refworld/docid/4c9872c22.html, accessed 18 September 2014.

occurred in Kenya was very different, where, on 26 March 2014, the government ordered all refugees living in urban areas to return to camps as part of the measures adopted by the government in order to address the growing menace of terrorism in the country.[21] This decision was thus appealed by refugees.[22]

Wherever possible, in Sub-Saharan Africa refugees have become integrated into the host society. Refugees who are able to obtain some land, are not restricted in movement and/or are able to find employment, are better off than those living in camps. They are not merely using the resources of the host institutions, but also contributing to their host's economy.

The camp situation in Sub-Saharan Africa is often dehumanizing and deprives the inhabitants of most of their fundamental rights. Sometimes, as in the case of the Sudanese in Uganda, due to the UNHCR's inability to support refugee settlement programmes, government authorities considered scrapping the settlement system in favour of encampment.[23]

4.2 The law applicable to refugee camps and the problem of their security

4.2.1 Refugee camps and the application of the International Humanitarian Law

International humanitarian law directly provides for at least two articles which benefit refugees.[24] Article 44 of the 1949 Fourth Geneva Convention establishes

21 Allafrica, 'Kenya: Government orders refugees back to the camps', 26 March 2014, available at: http://allafrica.com/stories/201403260798.html, accessed 10 September 2014.

22 AI, 'Kenya: Refugees appeal against forced relocation to camps', 11 July 2014, available at: www.amnesty.org/en/news/kenya-refugees-appeal-against-forced-relocation-camps-2014-07-11, accessed 10 September 2014: 'The Somali refugees are appealing against a 30 June ruling made by High Court Judge Justice Majanja that stated that the relocation of refugees from urban centers is constitutional. This High Court decision directly contradicts the previous ruling by Justice Majanja of July 2013. Then, he found that forcibly relocating refugees to camps would violate their human rights, dignity and freedom of movement, and would risk indirectly forcing them back to Somalia.'

23 Kaiser, T., 'Sudanese refugees in Uganda and Kenya', in Loescher, G. (et al.) (eds), *Protracted Refugee Situations: Political, Human Rights and Security Implications*, New York: United Nations University Press, 2008, p. 260.

24 As reminded by M. Jacques: '[T]he two bodies of law [international humanitarian law and international refugee law] do not operate in isolation from each other and are, in fact, interconnected. International humanitarian law and international refugee law may indeed apply successively, when violations of the laws of war force individuals to flee and seek refuge in a neighboring or third country. [. . .] When assessing persecutory harm in situations of armed conflict, reference should be made to the relevant norms of international humanitarian law, particularly the rules governing the conduct of hostilities and the principle of civilian immunity. [. . .] International humanitarian law and international refugee law will also apply concurrently, when refugees find themselves in the hands of a party to an armed conflict. As civilian refugees in a situation of armed conflict they may claim protection under both branches of international law. Indeed, as refugees, they benefit from the continuing protection of international

non-discrimination of aliens of an enemy state on the sole basis of their nationality. In effect, potential refugees may also be among the detained aliens.[25] For this purpose, Fernandez-Sanchez underlined that, as there is no definition of 'refugee' present in this convention, the concept of 'refugee' in the 1951 Geneva Convention should be taken into consideration, although this latter instrument was posterior to the 1949 Fourth Geneva Convention.[26] Another provision concerning refugees is Article 45 of the same convention, which deals with protected individuals who may not be transferred to a power that is not a party to the convention, adding that in no case should a protected person be transferred to a country where he/she

refugee law, which applies at all times, even in times of armed conflict.' See Jacques, M., *Armed Conflict and Displacement: The Protection of Refugees and Displaced Persons under International Humanitarian Law*, Cambridge: Cambridge University Press, 2012, pp. 156–8.

25 1949 Fourth Geneva Convention, Article 44: 'In applying the measures of control mentioned in the present Convention, the Detaining Power shall not treat as enemy aliens exclusively on the basis of their nationality *de jure* of an enemy State, refugees who do not, in fact, enjoy the protection of any government.' In this regard, it has been added: 'Article 44 of the Fourth Convention, which applies to aliens in the territory of a party to the conflict [. . .] provides that the state of refuge or the state of residence, when it takes measure of control as laid down in the Convention, must not treat refugees as enemy aliens exclusively on the ground that their nationality *de jure* is that of an enemy state.' See Sandoz, Y., Swinarski, C. and Zimmermann, B. (eds), *Commentary on the Additional Protocols of 8 June 1977 to the Geneva Conventions of 12 August 1949*, Geneva: International Committee of the Red Cross/Martinus Nijhoff, 1987, paragraph 2945, p. 848. In addition, M. Jacques explained: 'Article 44 does not make any distinction between refugees recognized as such before the beginning of hostilities and those recognized during the hostilities. Consequently, Article 44 is the only provision of international humanitarian law which protects refugees displaced by war from arbitrary treatment. *Article 44 [. . .] served as a precedent for a related provision in the 1951 Geneva Convention, on account that if this rule was to be applied in time of war, a similar rule should a fortiori be applied in time of peace.*' Emphasis added. See Jacques, M., op. cit. note 24, p. 169. And further, at p. 176, the author explained: 'Article 70 2) [of the 1949 Fourth Geneva Convention] and article 44 are complementary: article 44 deals with the refugees' relations with the authorities of the country of asylum. Article 70 2) governs their position *vis-à-vis* their country of origin when it becomes the occupying power. Like article 44, which is restricted to measures of control towards refugees, article 70 2) does not cover all situations affecting refugees in occupied territory. In fact, it offers an even more limited protection, as it deals with arrest, prosecution, conviction and deportation. No reference is made to other measures which may be taken against refugees, such as the confiscation of property or denial of religious freedom.' In full, Article 70 of the 1949 Fourth Geneva Convention reads: '1) Protected persons shall not be arrested, prosecuted or convicted by the Occupying Power for acts committed or for opinions expressed before the occupation, or during a temporary interruption thereof, with the exception of breaches of the laws and customs of war. 2) Nationals of the occupying Power who, before the outbreak of hostilities, have sought refuge in the territory of the occupied State, shall not be arrested, prosecuted, convicted or deported from the occupied territory, except for offences committed after the outbreak of hostilities, or for offences under common law committed before the outbreak of hostilities which, according to the law of the occupied State, would have justified extradition in time of peace.'

26 Fernandez-Sanchez, P.A., 'The interplay between international humanitarian law and refugee law', in *Journal of International Humanitarian Legal Studies*, vol. 1, 2010, p. 344. But, as the ICRC noted: 'The article [44] does not give refugees an absolute right to exemption from security measures. It is only an urgent recommendation to belligerents. The status of refugees does not of itself give anyone a right to immunity. It does not prevent the adoption of security measures, internment for example.' See ICRC, Convention (IV) relative to the Protection of Civilian Persons in Time of War, Geneva, 12 August 1949, Commentary to Article 44, available at: www.icrc.org/ihl.nsf/COM/380-600050?OpenDocument, accessed 10 September 2014.

may fear persecution because of his/her religion and/or political opinions.[27] We can easily see the importance of these two articles with regards to the existence of camps on the continent, although they are obviously applicable exclusively on a territory where there is an armed conflict. In detail, as M. Jacques highlighted:

> Article 45 4) prohibits *refoulement* only when the protected person has reason to fear political or religious persecution. [. . .] However, Article 45 4) is complemented by Article 45 3) [. . .] that [. . .] not only prohibits the transfer of a protected person to a state that is not party to the Fourth Geneva Convention, but also to one that is unwilling or unable to apply and respect all the protections in the Convention. Accordingly, [. . .] [the] transfer [of aliens in the territory of an international armed conflict] will be prohibited if they [fear] persecution or if [. . .] any of the rights and protections in the Fourth Geneva Convention cannot be assured in the country of transfer.[28]

27 1949 Fourth Geneva Convention, Article 45, reads: 'Protected persons shall not be transferred to a Power which is not a party to the Convention. This provision shall in no way constitute an obstacle to the repatriation of protected persons or to their return to their country of residence after the cessation of hostilities. Protected persons may be transferred by the Detaining Power only to a Power which is a party to the present Convention and after the Detaining Power has satisfied itself of the willingness and ability of such transferee Power to apply the present Convention. If protected persons are transferred under such circumstances, responsibility for the application of the present Convention rests on the Power accepting them, while they are in its custody. Nevertheless, if that Power fails to carry out the provisions of the present Convention in any important respect, the Power by which the protected persons were transferred shall, upon being so notified by the Protecting Power, take effective measures to correct the situation or shall request the return of the protected persons. Such request must be complied with. In no circumstances shall a protected person be transferred to a country where he or she may have reason to fear persecution for his or her political opinions or religious beliefs. The provisions of this Article do not constitute an obstacle to the extradition, in pursuance of extradition treaties concluded before the outbreak of hostilities, of protected persons accused of offences against ordinary criminal law.' In this regard, as noted by ICRC: 'The prohibition in this paragraph [paragraph 4] is absolute, covering all cases of transfer, whatever the country of destination may be and whatever the date. It is already implicit in the previous paragraphs which only permit transfers if the receiving State is a Party to the Convention and willing and able to apply it in practice. Since one of the fundamental principles proclaimed by the Convention is the prohibition of discrimination (Article 27, paragraph 3), it follows that the Detaining Power cannot transfer protected persons unless it is absolutely certain that they will not be subject to discriminatory treatment or, worse still, persecution. This clause, which was inserted in the Convention by the 27th International Red Cross Conference, should be compared with the preceding Article on refugees.' See ICRC, Convention (IV) relative to the Protection of Civilian Persons in Time of War, Geneva, 12 August 1949, Commentary to Article 45, available at: www.icrc.org/ihl.nsf/COM/380–600051?OpenDocument, accessed 11 September 2014.

28 Jacques, M., op. cit. note 24, p. 181. In converse, ibid., p. 183, the author pointed out that: 'International humanitarian law does not specifically address the issue of refugees in non-international armed conflicts and there is no equivalent to article 45 3) in common article 3 or Protocol II. Yet [. . .] refugees are in urgent need of protection from multiple displacements and forced repatriation to their country of origin by government forces or rebel armed groups.'

The separation[29] of armed elements presents another important issue which concerns the application of the humanitarian law to the camps, in order to preserve their civilian character. The ICRC has underlined that international humanitarian law provides for these individuals to have their weapons removed and to be interned.[30] In the case of members of the armed forces involved in a conflict, these operations should be the duty of the host state to which the potential refugees have fled.[31] In effect, as a UNHCR protection officer has declared:

> The responsibility for security is vested in the sovereign state. The presumption is that refugee protection in terms of physical security must be the responsibility of the host state.[32]

29 For a definition of 'separation', see Beyani, C., 'International legal criteria for the separation of members of armed forces, armed bands, and militia from refugees in the territories of host states', in *International Journal of Refugee Law*, vol. 12, 2000, p. 255: 'In refugee situations, separation may be defined as an act or process by which the protection of refugees necessitates the isolation and removal, from the civilian and *bona fide* refugees, of armed elements and others incompatible with the protection of the status of refugees on grounds of public safety and public, or national, security. As an act, separation is a factual and physical phenomenon of dividing, isolating, secluding or removing, armed elements from ordinary civilian and *bona fide* refugees. As a process, separation involves the identification of these elements and their seclusion from refugees according to the application of relevant legal criteria or principles on which the decision to separate out can be made.'

30 In this regard, P.A. Fernandez-Sanchez asserted: 'The principle of internment is a way of restricting movement and freedom and is applied in various contexts as a protection measure for interned combatants and prisoners of war in international conflict.' See Fernandez Sanchez, P.A., 'The interplay between international humanitarian law and refugee law', in *Journal of International Humanitarian Legal Studies*, vol. 1, 2010, p. 365. About the role played in Africa in peace enforcement situations by the ICRC, C. Ewumbue-Monono listed, among others, the following agreements: '[T]he Lancaster House talks of 1979, which led to the ceasefire in the conflict in Zimbabwe and gave the ICRC a role in providing postwar humanitarian assistance there; the 13 May 1991 Bicesse Agreement, which called on the ICRC as a neutral intermediary to supervise the release of prisoners in the hands of the warring parties; the ceasefire agreement of 15 May 1991 between the government of Angola and the rebel UNITA, which contained the provision that verification for the release of prisoners of war "[w]ill be performed by the International Committee of the Red Cross"; the Kinihira agreement of 30 May 1993 between the government of Rwanda and the rebel RPF, which stipulated that in matters related to aid distribution "[t]he ICRC position on each individual shall be final"; the 4 August 1993 Arusha Peace Agreement on Rwanda, providing for the mandatory protection of the expatriate community and the security of contributors of humanitarian assistance such as the ICRC.' See Ewumbue-Monono, C., 'Respect for international humanitarian law by armed non-state actors in Africa', in *International Review of the Red Cross*, vol. 88, 2006, p. 916.

31 ICRC, statement on 'The civilian character of asylum' for the UNHCR Global Consultations on International Protection, 8–9 March 2001, Geneva, available at: http://reliefweb.int/node/83922, accessed 22 September 2014. Later in the same document we read: 'As stated in UNHCR's background paper, the situation is addressed by the Fifth Hague Convention of 1907 respecting the Rights and Duties of Neutral Powers and Persons in Case of War on Land, whose provisions can be considered to have attained customary status. The first point that must be made is that this convention relates to the duties of neutral states in situations of international armed conflict. It is the ICRC's view that it can also be applied by analogy in situations of non-international conflicts, in which combatants either from the government side or from armed opposition groups have fled into a neutral state.'

32 Quotation from: Cuellar, M.-F., op. cit. note 14, p. 700.

In addition, the ICRC, on the basis of the 1949 Third Geneva Convention, as well as the right of humanitarian initiative granted to it by the 1986 ICRC Statutes, has the task to visit the detained persons and carry out on their behalf its traditional activities of protection for individuals dispossessed of their freedom through causes rising from armed conflict.[33] In this regard, we note that the ICRC, in several of its documents, uses the term 'internee' when referring to 'detention'.[34]

Furthermore, the ICRC is also concerned that former combatants in camps be excluded from the protection provided by the 1951 Geneva Convention, although the convention lacks a real definition of 'combatant'.[35] However, every

33 ICRC, statement on 'The civilian character of asylum' for the UNHCR Global Consultations on International Protection, 8–9 March 2001, Geneva, available at: http://reliefweb.int/node/83922, accessed 22 September 2012. Further, in the same paragraph, we may read: '*The activities of the ICRC with respect to such internees aim to ascertain the treatment accorded to them and their conditions of detention.*' In detail, paragraphs 2–4 of Article 126 of the 1949 Third Geneva Convention read: '2) Representatives and delegates of the Protecting Powers shall have full liberty to select the places they wish to visit. The duration and frequency of these visits shall not be restricted. Visits may not be prohibited except for reasons of imperative military necessity, and then only as an exceptional and temporary measure. 3) The Detaining Power and the Power on which the said prisoners of war depend may agree, if necessary, that compatriots of these prisoners of war be permitted to participate in the visits. 4) The delegates of the International Committee of the Red Cross shall enjoy the same prerogatives. The appointment of such delegates shall be submitted to the approval of the Power detaining the prisoners of war to be visited.' In addition, Article 4 2) of the Statutes of the International Red Cross and Red Crescent Movement, adopted by the 25th International Conference of the Red Cross at Geneva in October 1986 and amended by the 26th International Conference of the Red Cross and Red Crescent at Geneva in December 1995 and by the 29th International Conference of the Red Cross and Red Crescent at Geneva in June 2006 reads: '2) The ICRC may take any humanitarian initiative which comes within its role as a specifically neutral and independent institution and intermediary, and may consider any question requiring examination by such an institution.'

34 *Supra*, previous note. See the highlighted section.

35 Fernandez-Sanchez, P.A., op. cit. note 30, p. 360. To reinforce this idea, at ibid., the author quoted Article 43 2) of the Protocol additional to the Geneva Conventions of 12 August 1949, and relating to the protection of victims of international armed conflicts (Protocol I), in *Official Records of the Diplomatic Conference on the Reaffirmation and Development of International Humanitarian Law Applicable in Armed Conflicts, Geneva (1974–1977)*, Berne: Federal Political Department, 1978, vol. I, pp. 115–83. In full, Article 43 reads: '1) The armed forces of a Party to a conflict consist of all organized armed forces, groups and units which are under a command responsible to that Party for the conduct of its subordinates, even if that Party is represented by a government or an authority not recognized by an adverse Party. Such armed forces shall be subject to an internal disciplinary system which, inter alia, shall enforce compliance with the rules of international law applicable in armed conflict. 2) Members of the armed forces of a Party to a conflict (other than medical personnel and chaplains covered by Article 33 of the Third Convention) are combatants, that is to say, they have the right to participate directly in hostilities. 3) Whenever a Party to a conflict incorporates a paramilitary or armed law enforcement agency into its armed forces it shall so notify the other Parties to the conflict.' And Article 44 1) of the same protocol stipulates: 'Any combatant, as defined in article 43, who falls into the power of an adverse party shall be a prisoner of war.'

former combatant should have his/her situation individually assessed,[36] and Article 1F of the 1951 Refugee Convention should be interpreted in a restrictive way.[37] Having carried weapons onto the camp premises should not be reason in itself for exclusion from refugee status, although, evidently we would say, participation in military activities constitutes a reason for non-inclusion. Only former combatants who categorically reject weapons can claim asylum and deserve, once their individual situation is assessed, the title of 'refugee'.[38] However, as separation and disarmament can be very difficult when undertaken exclusively by the host state, the ICRC and other states parties to the 1949 Geneva Conventions bear a responsibility to assure assistance to the host state with respect to these operations.[39] But, it has often happened in the history of encampment in Sub-Saharan Africa that, even if regular camps were liberated by the presence of genuine combatants, these men could establish themselves in so-called 'shadow camps', created near the regular camps whose infrastructures, such as hospitals, would still have been used by combatants, who can take advantage of the lack of security in the regular camps.[40]

In addition, another issue which can be discussed in relation to refugee camps in Sub-Saharan Africa is the concept of detention, which the UNHCR considers to be effective in the case of closed refugee camps, as it confirmed in 1999[41] and, more recently, in 2012.[42]

36 Fernandez-Sanchez, P.A., op. cit. note 30, p. 364.

37 For this kind of approach, see UNHCR, Global Consultations on International Protection, Expert Roundtable, Lisbon, 3–4 May 2001, Cessation, Exclusion, document No. EC/GC/01/2Track/1, 30 May 2001. See, in detail, paragraphs 4 and 14: '4) Exclusion clauses are of an exceptional nature and should be applied scrupulously and restrictively because of the potentially serious consequences of exclusion from refugee status for the individual concerned. [. . .] 14) In view of its vague and imprecise language, it should be interpreted restrictively and with caution. It should be limited to acts contrary to the purposes and principles of the United Nations, as defined by the UN.'

38 Fernandez-Sanchez, P.A., op. cit. note 30, p. 365. This author stressed at ibid., p. 373: '[T]he 1951 Convention contemplates grounds for exclusion which would have prevented an ex-combatant from obtaining asylum-seeker status, but the mere fact of being an ex-combatant is not sufficient for the application to be rejected.'

39 Brett, R. and Lester, E., 'Refugee law and international humanitarian law: parallels, lessons and looking ahead: a nongovernmental organization's view', in *International Review of the Red Cross*, vol. 83, 2001, p. 718.

40 Jacobsen, K., 'A framework for exploring the political and security context of refugee populated areas', in *Refugee Survey Quarterly*, vol. 19, 2000, p. 9.

41 UNHCR, UNHCR's Revised Guidelines on Applicable Criteria and Standards relating to the Detention of Asylum-Seekers, Geneva: UNHCR, 26 February 1999, p. 3: 'For the purpose of these guidelines, UNHCR consider detention as: confinement within a narrowly bounded or restricted location, including prisons, closed camps [. . .] where freedom of movement is substantially curtailed, and where the only opportunity to leave this limited area is to leave the territory.'

42 UNHCR, Detention Guidelines: guidelines on the applicable criteria and standards relating to the detention of asylum-seekers and alternatives to detention, Geneva: UNHCR, September

Detention consists in a

> [r]estriction on freedom of movement, usually through enforced confinement, of persons prior to court appearance, after conviction and sentence, pending sentence, pending a decision on refugee status, admission to or removal from the state, or for purposes of internment, for example, in times of national emergency.[43]

Detention may be resorted to exclusively in the following circumstances: during verification of identity; while determining the elements at the basis of the claim for refugee status; to protect public order and national security; or when the asylum-seekers have destroyed their identity documents – or used fraudulent ones – in order to mislead the authorities of the state where they wish to claim asylum.[44]

As we have seen in the definition provided above, detention could occur also for purposes of 'internment', this last term defined as the '[d]eprivation of liberty ordered by the executive authorities when no specific charge is made against the individual concerned'.[45] Internment constitutes an exceptional instrument of control which may be ordered for reasons of security during armed conflict, or for protecting the security of a state or public order during non-conflict situations.[46] In this sense, we see that it applies to former combatants confined

2012, p. 9: 'Detention can take place in a range of locations, including at land and sea borders, in the "international zones" at airports, on islands, on boats, *as well as in closed refugee camps*.' Emphasis added.

43 UNHCR, International Thesaurus of Refugee Terminology, available at: www.unhcr.org/pages/4a30ba786.html, accessed 25 September 2014. In this regard, see also the definition provided in UNHCR, Operational protection in camps and settlements, Geneva: UNHCR, 2006, p. 52: '[Detention is the] confinement within a narrowly bounded or restricted location, including prisons, closed camps, detention facilities or airport transit zones where freedom of movement is substantially curtailed, and the only opportunity to leave this limited area is to leave the territory. It is a serious restriction on freedom of movement, usually through enforced confinement, which, in UNHCR's view, should not normally be used as a measure to control asylum-seekers.'

44 UNHCR, UNHCR's Revised Guidelines on Applicable Criteria and Standards relating to the Detention of Asylum-Seekers, Geneva: UNHCR, 26 February 1999, pp. 4–5.

45 Sandoz, Y., Swinarski, C. and Zimmermann, B. (eds), op. cit. note 25, paragraph 3063, p. 875.

46 Pejic, J., 'Procedural principles and safeguards for internment/administrative detention in armed conflict and other situations of violence', in *International Review of the Red Cross*, vol. 87, 2005, p. 375. In this regard, see also Olson, L.M., 'Practical challenges of implementing the complementarity between international humanitarian and human rights law: demonstrated by the procedural regulation of internment in non-international armed conflict', in *Case Western Reserve Journal of International Law*, vol. 40, 2007–2009, p. 437, by which internment is defined as: '[t]he deprivation of liberty of a person without criminal charge as a preventative security measure' [and usually happening during armed conflicts]. At idem, the author pointed out: 'Such deprivation of a person's liberty is one of the most extreme measures that can be taken and hence requires adherence to safeguards.'

in African camps,[47] as happened in Sierra Leone, with former combatants from Liberia.[48]

International humanitarian law provides grounds for internment in the case where an international armed conflict establishes the conditions for particular categories of protected individuals. For instance, the 1949 Third Geneva Convention stipulates that '[t]he Detaining Power may subject prisoners of war to internment'.[49] Concerning civilians, the 1949 Fourth Geneva Convention provides that – referring to aliens in the territory of a party to the conflict – '[t]he internment or placing in assigned residence of protected persons may be ordered only if the security of the Detaining Power makes it absolutely necessary.'[50] And, for occupied territories, '[i]f the Occupying Power considers it necessary, for imperative reasons of security, to take safety measures concerning protected persons, it may, at the most subject them to assigned residence or to internment'.[51] Conversely, the international humanitarian treaty law applicable to non-international armed conflict presents no particular basis for internment.[52] However, international humanitarian treaty law recognizes that internment occurs also in non-international armed conflict, as shown by the indications to internment found in Articles 5 and 6 of the 1977 Second Protocol to the 1949 Geneva

47 UNHCR, Refugees in Africa: the challenges of protection and solutions, outcome of the June 2004 regional parliamentary conference co-organized by the African Parliamentary Union and the UNHCR, in association with the Inter-Parliamentary Union and the ICRC, Cotonou 1–3 June 2004, p. 21, 53–54.

48 UNHCR, Operational protection in camps and settlements, Geneva: UNHCR, 2006, pp. B1, B10.

49 In full, Article 21 1) of 1949 Third Geneva Convention reads: '1) The Detaining Power may subject prisoners of war to internment. It may impose on them the obligation of not leaving, beyond certain limits, the camp where they are interned, or if the said camp is fenced in, of not going outside its perimeter. Subject to the provisions of the present Convention relative to penal and disciplinary sanctions, prisoners of war may not be held in close confinement except where necessary to safeguard their health and then only during the continuation of the circumstances which make such confinement necessary.'

50 1949 Fourth Geneva Convention, Article 42 1). In full, Article 42 reads: 'The internment or placing in assigned residence of protected persons may be ordered only if the security of the Detaining Power makes it absolutely necessary. 2) If any person, acting through the representatives of the Protecting Power, voluntarily demands internment, and if his situation renders this step necessary, he shall be interned by the Power in whose hands he may be.'

51 Ibid., Article 78 1). In full, Article 78 reads: '1) If the Occupying Power considers it necessary, for imperative reasons of security, to take safety measures concerning protected persons, it may, at the most, subject them to assigned residence or to internment. 2) Decisions regarding such assigned residence or internment shall be made according to a regular procedure to be prescribed by the Occupying Power in accordance with the provisions of the present Convention. This procedure shall include the right of appeal for the parties concerned. Appeals shall be decided with the least possible delay. In the event of the decision being upheld, it shall be subject to periodical review, if possible every six months, by a competent body set up by the said Power. 3) Protected persons made subject to assigned residence and thus required to leave their homes shall enjoy the full benefit of Article 39 of the present Convention.'

52 Olson, L.M., op. cit. note 46, p. 440.

Conventions.[53] In contrast, Article 3 common to the four 1949 Geneva Conventions establishing the fundamental principle of humanity, in both international and non-international conflicts,[54] makes no reference to internment.

Although the prohibition of arbitrary detention is not considered a non-derogable right according to Article 4 of the 1966 ICCPR,[55] the conditions which permit derogation are limited. Since derogation is allowed merely in urgent situations that threaten the existence of the nation, it is probable that, in the context of asylum, measures of derogation are allowed, conflicting with other obligations of the state under international law.[56]

53 Protocol additional to the Geneva Conventions of 12 August 1949, and relating to the protection of victims of non-international armed conflicts (Protocol II), in *Official Records of the Diplomatic Conference on the Reaffirmation and Development of International Humanitarian Law Applicable in Armed Conflicts, Geneva (1974–1977)*, Berne: Federal Political Department, 1978, vol. 1, pp. 185–98, Article 5 1): '1) In addition to the provisions of Article 4 the following provisions shall be respected as a minimum with regard to persons deprived of their liberty for reasons related to the armed conflict, whether they are interned or detained [. . .]' and following sub-paragraphs; Article 6 5): '5) At the end of hostilities, the authorities in power shall endeavor to grant the broadest possible amnesty to persons who have participated in the armed conflict, or those deprived of their liberty for reasons related to the armed conflict, whether they are interned or detained.'

54 For the full text of Article 3, common to the four 1949 Geneva Conventions, see *supra*, footnote 772.

55 Article 4, paragraphs 1 and 2 of the 1966 ICCPR reads: '1) In time of public emergency which threatens the life of the nation and the existence of which is officially proclaimed, the States Parties to the present Covenant may take measures derogating from their obligations under the present Covenant to the extent strictly required by the exigencies of the situation, provided that such measures are not inconsistent with their other obligations under international law and do not involve discrimination solely on the ground of race, color, sex, language, religion or social origin. 2) No derogation from articles 6, 7, 8 (paragraphs 1 and 2), 11, 15, 16 and 18 may be made under this provision.'

56 Brett, R. and Lester, E., op. cit. note 39, p. 720. Considering also the conditions about detention in the refugee instruments see, for instance, UNHCR, UNHCR's guidelines on applicable criteria and standards relating to the detention of asylum-seekers, February 1999, pp. 1–2, paragraphs 2 through 4: '2) Of key significance to the issue of detention is Article 31 of the 1951 Convention. Article 31 exempts refugees coming directly from a country of persecution from being punished on account of their illegal entry or presence, provided they present themselves without delay to the authorities and show good cause for their illegal entry or presence. The article also provides that Contracting States shall not apply to the movements of such refugees' restrictions other than those which are necessary, and that any restrictions shall only be applied until such time as their status is regularized, or they obtain admission into another country. 3) Consistent with this Article, detention should only be resorted to in cases of necessity. The detention of asylum-seekers who come "directly" in an irregular manner should, therefore, not be automatic, or unduly prolonged. This provision applies not only to recognized refugees but also to asylum-seekers pending determination of their status, as recognition of refugee status does not make an individual a refugee but declares him to be one. Conclusion No. 44 (XXXVII) of the Executive Committee on the Detention of Refugees and Asylum-Seekers examines more concretely what is meant by the term "necessary". This Conclusion also provides guidelines to States on the use of detention and recommendations as to certain procedural guarantees to which detainees should be entitled. 4) The expression "coming directly" in Article 31(1), covers the situation of a person who enters the country in which asylum is sought directly from the country

Moreover, the 1949 Fourth Geneva Convention contains regulations concerning the treatment of internees. Article 79[57] clearly stipulates that the parties

of origin, or from another country where his protection, safety and security could not be assured. It is understood that this term also covers a person who transits an intermediate country for a short period of time without having applied for, or received, asylum there. No strict time limit can be applied to the concept "coming directly" and each case must be judged on its merits. Similarly, given the special situation of asylum-seekers, in particular the effects of trauma, language problems, lack of information, previous experiences which often result in a suspicion of those in authority, feelings of insecurity, and the fact that these and other circumstances may vary enormously from one asylum-seeker to another, there is no time limit which can be mechanically applied or associated with the expression "without delay". The expression "good cause", requires a consideration of the circumstances under which the asylum-seeker fled. The term "asylum-seeker" in these guidelines applies to those whose claims are being considered under an admissibility or pre-screening procedure as well as those who are being considered under refugee status determination procedures. It also includes those exercising their right to seek judicial and/or administrative review of their asylum request.' Article 31 ('Refugees unlawfully in the country of refugee') of the 1951 Geneva Convention reads: '1) The Contracting States shall not impose penalties, on account of their illegal entry or presence, on refugees who, coming directly from a territory where their life or freedom was threatened in the sense of article 1, enter or are present in their territory without authorization, provided they present themselves without delay to the authorities and show good cause for their illegal entry or presence. 2) The Contracting States shall not apply to the movements of such refugees restrictions other than those which are necessary and such restrictions shall only be applied until their status in the country is regularized or they obtain admission into another country. The Contracting States shall allow such refugees a reasonable period and all the necessary facilities to obtain admission into another country.' In this regard, see also ExCom, conclusion No. 44 (XXXVII), 'Detention of refugees and asylum-seekers', 1986, particularly its paragraph b): '[The ExCom] *expressed the opinion that in view of the hardship which it involves, detention should normally be avoided.* If necessary, detention may be resorted to only on grounds prescribed by law to verify identity; to determine the elements on which the claim to refugee status or asylum is based; to deal with cases where refugees or asylum-seekers have destroyed their travel and/or identity documents or have used fraudulent documents in order to mislead the authorities of the State in which they intend to claim asylum; or to protect national security or public order.' Emphasis added.

57 In detail, Article 79 reads: 'The parties to the conflict shall not intern protected persons, except in accordance with the provisions of Articles 41, 42, 43, 68, and 78.' Article 41 stipulates: 'Should the Power, in whose hands protected persons may be, consider the measures of control mentioned in the present Convention to be inadequate, it may not have recourse to any other measure of control more severe than that of assigned residence or internment, in accordance with the provisions of Articles 42 and 43. In applying the provisions of Article 39, second paragraph, to the cases of persons required to leave their usual places of residence by virtue of a decision placing them in assigned residence elsewhere, the Detaining Power shall be guided as closely as possible by the standards of welfare set forth in Part III, Section IV of this Convention.' Article 42 stipulates: 'The internment or placing in assigned residence of protected persons may be ordered only if the security of the Detaining Power makes it absolutely necessary. If any person, acting through the representatives of the Protecting Power, voluntarily demands internment, and if his situation renders this step necessary, he shall be interned by the Power in whose hands he may be.' Article 43 stipulates: 'Any protected person who has been interned or placed in assigned residence shall be entitled to have such action reconsidered as soon as possible by an appropriate court or administrative board designated by the Detaining Power for that purpose. If the internment or placing in assigned residence is maintained, the court or administrative board shall periodically, and at least twice yearly, give consideration to his or her case, with a view to

to a conflict do not have to intern protected persons[58] with the exception of what is stated in Articles 41, 42, 43, 68 and 78. These exceptions limit the measures of control to an assigned residence or internment, imposing further requirements such as, for instance, limiting internment or placing internees in residences designated for protected persons exclusively, depending on whether the security of the detaining state makes it completely necessary – Article 42. Another requirement is the fact that any protected person who has been interned is entitled to have his/her case reconsidered as soon as possible by a court or administrative board designated by the detaining state – Article 43. Finally, according to Article 68, the specification that the period of internment imposed within a camp, in the

the favorable amendment of the initial decision, if circumstances permit. Unless the protected persons concerned object, the Detaining Power shall, as rapidly as possible, give the Protecting Power the names of any protected persons who have been interned or subjected to assigned residence, or who have been released from internment or assigned residence. The decisions of the courts or boards mentioned in the first paragraph of the present Article shall also, subject to the same conditions, be notified as rapidly as possible to the Protecting Power.' Article 68 stipulates: 'Protected persons who commit an offence which is solely intended to harm the Occupying Power, but which does not constitute an attempt on the life or limb of members of the occupying forces or administration, nor a grave collective danger, nor seriously damage the property of the occupying forces or administration or the installations used by them, shall be liable to internment or simple imprisonment, provided the duration of such internment or imprisonment is proportionate to the offence committed. Furthermore, internment or imprisonment shall, for such offences, be the only measure adopted for depriving protected persons of liberty. The courts provided for under Article 66 of the present Convention may at their discretion convert a sentence of imprisonment to one of internment for the same period. The penal provisions promulgated by the Occupying Power in accordance with Articles 64 and 65 may impose the death penalty against a protected person only in cases where the person is guilty of espionage, of serious acts of sabotage against the military installations of the Occupying Power or of intentional offences which have caused the death of one or more persons, provided that such offences were punishable by death under the law of the occupied territory in force before the occupation began. The death penalty may not be pronounced against a protected person unless the attention of the court has been particularly called to the fact that since the accused is not a national of the Occupying Power, he is not bound to it by any duty of allegiance. In any case, the death penalty may not be pronounced on a protected person who was under eighteen years of age at the time of the offence.' Article 78 stipulates: 'If the Occupying Power considers it necessary, for imperative reasons of security, to take safety measures concerning protected persons, it may, at the most, subject them to assigned residence or to internment. Decisions regarding such assigned residence or internment shall be made according to a regular procedure to be prescribed by the Occupying Power in accordance with the provisions of the present Convention. This procedure shall include the right of appeal for the parties concerned. Appeals shall be decided with the least possible delay. In the event of the decision being upheld, it shall be subject to periodical review, if possible every six months, by a competent body set up by the said Power. Protected persons made subject to assigned residence and thus required to leave their homes shall enjoy the full benefit of Article 39 of the present Convention.'

58 In this regard, Article 4 of the same convention defines '[p]ersons protected by the Convention are those who, at a given moment and in any manner whatsoever, find themselves, in case of a conflict or occupation, in the hands of a Party to the conflict or Occupying Power of which they are not nationals. Nationals of a State which is not bound by the Convention are not protected by it. Nationals of a neutral State, who find themselves in the territory of a belligerent State, and nationals of a co-belligerent State, shall not be regarded as protected persons while the

event that the individual has committed an offence, should be proportionate to the offence committed, requiring that the decision to place the individual in an internment is made in accordance with a regular procedure and the provisions of the same convention – Article 78.

In conclusion, we would like to highlight how both the ICRC and the UNHCR have mandates to protect and assist populations in need.[59] However, J. Baloro noted that the definition of 'refugee' has not been provided within the various humanitarian legal instruments, and the lack of a clear definition of this term has repercussions on the mandate of the ICRC, whose mandate is, incidentally, considered as more flexible and ample compared to the UNHCR's.[60] On the other

State of which they are nationals has normal diplomatic representation in the State in whose hands they are. The provisions of Part II are, however, wider in application, as defined in Article 13. Persons protected by the Geneva Convention for the Amelioration of the Condition of the Wounded and Sick in Armed Forces in the Field of 12 August 1949, or by the Geneva Convention for the Amelioration of the Condition of Wounded, Sick and Shipwrecked Members of Armed Forces at Sea of 12 August 1949, or by the Geneva Convention relative to the Treatment of Prisoners of War of 12 August 1949, shall not be considered as protected persons within the meaning of the present Convention.'

59 Article 4 1) d) of the 1986 ICRC Statutes clearly read: 'The role of the ICRC shall be in particular: [. . .] d) to endeavor at all times – as a neutral institution whose humanitarian work is carried out particularly in time of international and other armed conflicts or internal strife – to ensure the protection of and assistance to military and civilian victims of such events and of their direct results.' Moreover, see also Articles 73 and 81 of the 1977 First Protocol. Article 73 reads: 'Persons who, before the beginning of hostilities, were considered as stateless persons or refugees under the relevant international instruments accepted by the parties concerned or under the national legislation of the State of refuge or State of residence shall be protected persons within the meaning of parts I and III of the Fourth Convention, in all circumstances and without any adverse distinction.' In addition, Article 81 1) clarifies: 'The parties to the conflict shall grant to the International Committee of the Red Cross, all facilities within their power so as to enable it to carry out the humanitarian functions assigned to it by the Conventions and this Protocol in order to ensure protection and assistance to the victims of conflicts; the International Committee of the Red Cross may also carry out any other humanitarian activities in favor of these victims, subject to the consent of the Parties to the conflict concerned.' In this regard, as M. Jacques pointed out: 'International humanitarian law and international refugee law share a similar goal: the protection of persons in the hands of a state of which they are not nationals.' See Jacques, M., op. cit. note 24, p. 156. At ibid., p. 161 the author also explained: 'The extension of the protection offered by article 73 [. . .] only applies to refugees who have fled from persecution or threat of persecution, rather than persons displaced by the conflict itself.' And, ibid., pp. 176–7: '[I]n accordance with article 73 of the First Protocol, refugees in occupied territory now benefit from the protection of the whole of the Fourth Geneva Convention. [. . .] Additionally, by virtue of article 73, refugees may not be subjected to acts of violence, torture, collective penalties or reprisals against their person or their property. They may be entitled to receive individual relief consignments and they may not be forcibly displaced or deported from the occupied territory. This provision is an important safeguard for refugees against deportation in the case of the occupying power being an ally of their country of origin. [. . .] Article 73 of the First Protocol significantly improves the protection of refugees in occupied territory. Provided that they sought refugee status before the beginning of the hostilities, refugees should be considered as "protected persons" and treated as such, irrespective of their nationality.'

60 Baloro, J., 'International humanitarian law and situations of internal armed conflicts in Africa', in *African Journal of International and Comparative Law*, vol. 4, 1992, p. 470.

hand, the UNHCR increasingly finds itself facing difficult decisions as to how far it should raise the subject of rights violations of refugees in camps with governments without putting its own staff into danger or obliging them to leave the country.[61]

And, briefly returning to our analysis to refugee law, we note that the 1969 OAU Convention unfortunately does not make any reference to the matter of camps although O.S. Oyelade suggested that this is a specific problem the 1969 OAU Convention should address. In addition, although the 1969 OAU Convention contains some provisions relating to the security of refugees, the problem in much of Sub-Saharan Africa consists in the implementation of such provisions relating to the security of refugees in camps, and the lack of political will from African governments to recognize the applicability of the law and the obligation to abide by it.[62]

4.2.2 Armed attacks and the security of camps

The question of armed attacks[63] constitutes one of the main aspects concerning the legal aspects of camps, although a refugee camp should not be considered a military target as noted in Article 48 of the 1977 First Protocol to the 1949 Geneva Conventions.[64] Within the meaning of Article 50 2)[65] of the 1977 First Protocol, refugee camps constitute 'civilian populations' and, therefore, need to be protected against attack.[66] Furthermore, because refugees are considered as civilians they are therefore entitled to the general protection of international humanitarian law against the effects of hostilities.[67]

Article 48, governed by the fundamental rule that parties to a conflict do not have an unrestricted option of means of combat,[68] urges the distinction between

61 Brett, R. and Lester, E., op. cit. note 39, p. 723. Often UNHCR staff also suffer from insecurity in camps. In this regard J. Crisp affirmed: '[I]t is clear that the insecurity experienced by UNHCR staff and other aid agency employees in Kakuma and Dadaab imposes an additional constraint on the ability of such organizations to address the problem of violence.' See Crisp, J., 'A state of insecurity: the political economy of violence in Kenya's refugee camps', in *African Affairs*, vol. 99, 2000, p. 59.

62 Oyelade, O.S., 'A critique of the rights of refugees under the OAU Convention governing the specific aspects of refugee problems in Africa', in *East African Journal of Peace and Human Rights*, vol. 12, 2006, pp. 178–80.

63 For the term 'attacks', see Article 49 1) of the 1977 First Protocol: '1) "Attacks" means acts of violence against the adversary, whether in offence or in defense.'

64 For the text of Article 48, see, *infra*: footnote 69.

65 Article 50 2) of the 1977 First Protocol reads: '2) The civilian population comprises all persons who are civilians.'

66 Jacques, M., op. cit. note 24, p. 221.

67 In this regard, Article 50 1) of the 1977 First Protocol reads: '1) A civilian is any person who does not belong to one of the categories of persons referred to in Article 4 A) 1), 2), 3) and 6) of the Third Convention and in Article 43 of this Protocol. In case of doubt whether a person is a civilian, that person shall be considered to be a civilian.'

68 Jacques, M., op. cit. note 24, p. 214. In this regard, see 1977 First Protocol, Article 35: '1) In any armed conflict, the right of the Parties to the conflict to choose methods or means of warfare is not unlimited. 2) It is prohibited to employ weapons, projectiles and material and methods of

combatants and the civilian population, and between military and civilian objectives, further stating that military operations should be directed exclusively at the former.[69] Also identified as the principle of distinction, this customary rule of international humanitarian law is relevant in both international and non-international armed conflicts.[70] It is complemented by two basic principles of international humanitarian law: a ban on indiscriminate attacks[71] and the proscription from direct attack on civilians and civilian targets.[72] Therefore,

warfare of a nature to cause superfluous injury or unnecessary suffering. 3) It is prohibited to employ methods or means of warfare which are intended, or may be expected, to cause widespread, long-term and severe damage to the natural environment.'

69 Article 48 of the 1977 First Protocol reads: 'In order to ensure respect for and protection of the civilian population and civilian objects, the Parties to the conflict shall at all times distinguish between the civilian population and combatants and between civilian objects and military objectives and accordingly shall direct their operations only against military objectives.'

70 Henckaerts, J.-M. and Doswald-Beck, L., *Customary International Humanitarian Law*, vol. I: Rules, Cambridge. UK: Cambridge University Press, 2005, rules 1 and 7, pp. 3 and 25. In detail, see p. 4, where the authors affirmed that: '[a]rticle 51 2) [is] a valuable reaffirmation of an existing rule of customary international law.' Article 51 2) reads: '2) The civilian population as such, as well as individual civilians, shall not be the object of attack. Acts or threats of violence the primary purpose of which is to spread terror among the civilian population are prohibited.' See, also p. 25, where the author argued that: 'State practice establishes this rule [the distinction between civilian objects and military objects] as a norm of customary international law applicable in both international and non-international armed conflicts.'

71 In this regard, Article 51 of the 1977 First Protocol, especially its paragraph 5), reads: '5) Among others, the following types of attacks are to be considered as indiscriminate: a) an attack by bombardment by any methods or means which treats as a single military objective a number of clearly separated and distinct military objectives located in a city, town, village or other area containing a similar concentration of civilians or civilian objects; and b) an attack which may be expected to cause incidental loss of civilian life, injury to civilians, damage to civilian objects, or a combination thereof, which would be excessive in relation to the concrete and direct military advantage anticipated.' See, also Article 57 2) a) iii) of the 1977 First Protocol: '2) a) With respect to attacks, the following precautions shall be taken: a) those who plan or decide upon an attack shall: iii) refrain from deciding to launch any attack which may be expected to cause incidental loss of civilian life, injury to civilians, damage to civilian objects, or a combination thereof, which would be excessive in relation to the concrete and direct military advantage anticipated.' In this regard, see also 1977 First Protocol, Article 85 3) b): '3) In addition to the grave breaches defined in Article 11, the following acts shall be regarded as grave breaches of this Protocol, when committed willfully, in violation of the relevant provisions of this Protocol, and causing death or serious injury to body or health: [. . .] b) launching an indiscriminate attack affecting the civilian population or civilian objects in the knowledge that such attack will cause excessive loss of life, injury to civilians or damage to civilian objects, as defined in Article 57, paragraph 2 a) iii).' In this regard, M. Jacques argued that: 'Furthermore, in application of the customary principle of proportionality, an attack on a refugee [. . .] camp composed of a mixed population of armed elements and civilians will be considered indiscriminate and therefore unlawful if the incidental killings and injuries to the displaced civilians outweigh the military advantage anticipated.' See Jacques, M., op. cit. note 24, p. 225.

72 Ibid., p. 214. In this regard see, also Article 52 1) and 2) of the 1977 First Protocol: '1) Civilian objects shall not be the object of attack or of reprisals. Civilian objects are all objects which are not military objectives as defined in paragraph 2. 2) Attacks shall be limited strictly to military objectives. In so far as objects are concerned, military objectives are limited to those objects which

refugee camps as they constitute residences used by civilians are entitled to civilian immunity. This immunity is not, however irreversible and can be nullified if the camps are used for military goals.[73] More specifically, camps may be targeted if there is a direct participation of civilians in hostilities[74] and in case of the presence of combatants within the civilian populations of camps. This was the case, for instance, of the Rwandan camps in Eastern DRC in the mid-1990s.[75]

In order to respect the rules outlined in Article 48, it is necessary to adopt several measures to prevent possible attacks. For instance, the parties to the conflict or bordering states should exclude all camps in the surrounding areas from military objectives.[76] Moreover, Articles 51, 57 and 58 of the 1977 First Protocol prescribe the protection of the civilian population,[77] the precautions to adopt during attacks, and the precautions to adopt to protect against the consequences of an attack, respectively.[78] Article 85 of the protocol defines a serious violation to this same instrument as the act of deliberately making the civilian population or individual civilians the target of attacks if the attacks cause death or serious

by their nature, location, purpose or use make an effective contribution to military action and whose total or partial destruction, capture or neutralization, in the circumstances ruling at the time, offers a definite military advantage.'

73 Jacques, M., op. cit. note 24, p. 220. In this regard, Article 52 3) of the 1977 First Protocol stipulates: '3) In case of doubt whether an object which is normally dedicated to civilian purposes, such as a place of worship, a house or other dwelling or a school, is being used to make an effective contribution to military action, it shall be presumed not to be so used.'

74 In this regard, see 1977 First Protocol, Article 51 3); 1977 Second Protocol, Article 13 3), both reading as follows: '3) Civilians shall enjoy the protection afforded by this section, unless and for such time as they take a direct part in hostilities.'

75 Jacques, M., op. cit. note 24, pp. 221–5. In this regard, Article 50 3) of the 1977 First Protocol reads: '3) The presence within the civilian population of individuals who do not come within the definition of civilians does not deprive the population of its civilian character.' However, as noted by M. Jacques at p. 225: 'The application of article 50 3) is limited to situations where *small numbers* of combatants mingle with the civilian population.' No further explanation provided on what figure the concept of 'small numbers' amounts to. Emphasis added.

76 Fernandez-Sanchez, P.A., op. cit. note 30, p. 376.

77 In detail, Article 51 4) of the 1977 First Protocol prescribes that: '4) Indiscriminate attacks are prohibited. Indiscriminate attacks are: a) those which are not directed at a specific military objective; b) those which employ a method or means of combat which cannot be directed at a specific military objective; or c) those which employ a method or means of combat the effects of which cannot be limited as required by this Protocol.'

78 In detail, Article 57 of the 1977 First Protocol prescribes that: '1) In the conduct of military operations, constant care shall be taken to spare the civilian population, civilians and civilian objects [. . .]; 5) No provision of this article may be construed as authorizing any attacks against the civilian population, civilians or civilian objects.' In addition, Article 58 reads: 'The Parties to the conflict shall, to the maximum extent feasible: a) without prejudice to Article 49 of the 1949 Fourth Convention, endeavor to remove the civilian population, individual civilians and civilian objects under their control from the vicinity of military objectives; b) avoid locating military objectives within or near densely populated areas; c) take the other necessary precautions to protect the civilian population, individual civilians and civilian objects under their control against the dangers resulting from military operations.'

health problems for the victims.[79] Finally, the 1977 First Protocol also prohibits attacks against civilians through reprisals in international armed conflicts.[80] This happens while Article 33 3) of the 1949 Fourth Geneva Convention bans reprisals against protected civilians, specifically civilians in the hands of a state party of which they are not nationals, while civilians under the control of their own state, IDPs included, are not protected against reprisals under the 1949 Geneva Conventions.[81]

The situation of attacks on camps has raised concern not only within the UNHCR statutory bodies, but also at the UNGA and UNSC level. UNGA resolution No. 41/124, of 4 December 1984 is noteworthy in this regard, as it condemns:

> [A]ll violations of the rights and safety of refugees and asylum seekers, in particular those perpetrated by military or armed attacks against refugee camps and settlements and other forms of brutality.[82]

The UNSC, more than ten years later, confirmed the primary responsibility of host countries.[83] It noted that a range of measures by the international community were needed to support efforts made by African countries to ensure the security and the civilian and humanitarian character of refugee camps and settlements,[84]

79 Article 85 of the 1977 First Protocol whose first two paragraphs read: '1) The provisions of the Conventions relating to the repression of breaches and grave breaches, supplemented by this Section, shall apply to the repression of breaches and grave breaches of this Protocol. 2) Acts described as grave breaches in the Conventions are grave breaches of this Protocol if committed against persons in the power of an adverse Party protected by Articles 44, 45 and 73 of this Protocol, or against the wounded, sick and shipwrecked of the adverse Party who are protected by this Protocol, or against those medical or religious personnel, medical units or medical transports which are under the control of the adverse Party and are protected by this Protocol.'

80 Article 51 6) of the 1977 First Protocol reads: '6) Attacks against the civilian population or civilians by way of reprisals are prohibited.'

81 Article 33 3) of the 1949 Fourth Convention reads: '3) Reprisals against protected persons and their property are prohibited.'

82 UNGA, Office of the United Nations High Commissioner for Refugees, 4 December 1986, resolution No. A/RES/41/124, paragraph 4.

83 UNSC, On the situation in Africa, refugee camps, 19 November 1998, resolution No. 1208, S/RES/1208, paragraph 3.

84 In this regard see UNSC, Protection of civilians in armed conflicts, resolution No. 1296, S/RES/1296, paragraph 14: '[The UNSC] invites the Secretary-General to bring to its attention situations where refugees and internally displaced persons are vulnerable to the threat of harassment or where their camps are vulnerable to infiltration by armed elements and where such situations may constitute a threat to international peace and security, expresses in this regard, its willingness to consider such situations and, where necessary, adopt appropriate steps to help create a secure environment for civilians endangered by conflicts, including by providing support to States concerned in this regard, and recalls in this regard, its resolution 1208 (1998) of 19 November 1998.' See also ExCom, Conclusion No. 87 (L), 'General conclusion on international protection', 1999, paragraph q): '[The ExCom] remains gravely preoccupied with the continuing occurrence of military or armed attacks and other threats to the security of refugees, including

including in the areas of law enforcement, disarmament of armed elements,[85] reduction of the flow of arms into camps, and separation of refugees from other persons who are not eligible for international protection.[86]

In effect, as F. Cuellar pointed out, the discussion on the security of a refugee in a camp should be understood to include interconnected notions such as the protection of the physical integrity of refugees from menaces coming from both other refugees and the neighbouring population, the lessening of the degree to which criminals manipulate refugees and the reduction in the possibility that the presence of refugees in camps will intensify regional conflicts.[87]

The intervention of the international community has also been judged as being of great importance for guaranteeing the police security of a camp, considering that the level of criminality and violence there[88] – sometimes used for

the infiltration of armed elements in refugee camps and settlements; re-emphasizes the responsibility of States, working, where appropriate, with UNHCR in collaboration with each other and with other parts of the UN system, to uphold the civilian and humanitarian character and to ensure the security of refugee camps and settlements, *inter-alia*, by identifying and separating armed elements from refugee populations and settling refugees in secure locations; and encourages States and UNHCR, in collaboration with each other and with other parts of the UN system, to continue their efforts to enhance the security and civilian nature of refugee camps and settlements.'

85 For a definition of 'armed elements', see UNHCR, Global Consultations on International Protection/third track: the civilian character of asylum: separating armed elements from refugees, 19 February 2001, document No. EC/GC/01/5, paragraph 11: '[T]he term "armed element" is applied to any person who is "a member of an armed or military organization or establishment, whether regular or irregular, or has been participating actively in military activities and hostilities, or has undertaken activities to recruit or train military personnel, or has been in a command or decision-making position in an armed organization or establishment, or has arrived in the receiving country carrying arms or in military uniform, or having presented himself in the receiving country as a civilian, assumes or shows the intention to assume any of the above attributes."'

86 UNSC, On the situation in Africa, refugee camps, 19 November 1998, resolution No. 1208, S/RES/1208, paragraph 6. And paragraph 7 explains: '[The UNSC] notes also that the range of measures referred to in paragraph 6 above could include training, logistical and technical advice and assistance, financial support, the enhancement of national law enforcement mechanisms, the provision or supervision of security guards and the deployment in accordance with the Charter of the United Nations of international police and military forces.' Paragraph 11 concludes: '[The UNSC] expresses its support for the inclusion in the United Nations Stand-by Arrangements of military and police units and personnel trained for humanitarian operations, as well as related equipment, which relevant United Nations bodies and organizations could draw on in providing advice, supervision, training and technical or other assistance related to the maintenance of the security and civilian and humanitarian character of refugee camps and settlements, in coordination as appropriate with the African States hosting refugees.'

87 Cuellar, M.-F., op. cit. note 14, pp. 599–600. At p. 601, the author explained: '[R]efugee security is properly understood to encompass both the welfare of the refugees directly, and the regional implications of refugee flows – implications that [. . .] can turn sharply negative when the "civilian and humanitarian character of refugee protection" turns into farce.'

88 Regarding violence broken out in the African camps read, for instance, Lefing, D., 'Exchanging rapists: the rape of Sudanese women in Chadian refugee camps: who should be held responsible under international law?', in *Gonzaga Journal of International Law*, 2011, p. 17, available at: www.gonzagajil.org/content/view/190/26/, accessed 10 September 2014.

political purposes as in the case of the camps in Goma in the 1990s[89] – may threaten refugees, the local population and also humanitarian workers.[90]

Moreover, the humanitarian personnel should be assured that arms confiscated in the camp will not be used again and, obviously, not returned to the people who carried them, preserving the civilian and humanitarian nature of the camps, as stressed, with reference to Sub-Saharan Africa, by both the UNSG[91] and the AU.[92]

89 Jacobsen, K., 'A framework for exploring the political and security context of refugee populated areas', op. cit. note 40, p. 5: 'Violence and intimidation in camps are also used for political purposes: to pressure refugees to leave the camps, or to enter them; to repatriate, or not to repatriate. The latter was widely believed to be the case of Goma camps, where camp leaders intimidated and threatened refugees who sought to return to Rwanda.'

90 UNHCR, Standing Committee, The security, civilian and humanitarian character of refugee camps and settlements: operationalizing the 'ladder of options', 27 June 2000, document No. EC/50/SC/INF.4, point 1: 'The international community's current focus on the issue of security in refugee-populated areas can be ascribed to a number of related developments: The changing nature of conflict, with internal and regional wars generating cross-border movements of mixed groups, including military elements; A recognition that the militarization of refugee camps, armed attacks on such settlements and other forms of insecurity in refugee-populated areas are likely to undermine public and political support for the institution of asylum and the principles of refugee protection; The proven danger that the militarization of refugee-populated areas can create or aggravate tensions between States, thereby posing a threat to regional peace and security; and The prevalence of lawlessness in some refugee-populated areas, manifested in levels of crime, banditry and violence which pose a serious threat to the security of refugees, local populations and humanitarian personnel.'

91 UNSC, Report of the Secretary-General on security in the Rwandese refugee camps, 18 November 1994, No. S/1994/1308, paragraph 19, p. 5: '[t]wo well-trained and well-equipped mechanized battalions would spearhead the operation in the camps north of Lake Kivu. Each battalion would establish secure areas within large camp sites, providing safe conditions for the refugees in those areas. The force would establish screening procedures to keep weapons out of the secure areas. Humanitarian assistance operations would be intensified within these secure areas.'

92 OAU, The Khartoum Declaration of the OAU Ministerial Meeting on refugees, returnees and internally displaced persons in Africa, Khartoum 13–14 December 1998, paragraph 12: '[We, the Ministers representing the Member States of the Organization of African Unity] urge Member States and all other actors, in consultation with the OAU and UNHCR, to separate armed elements from civilian refugee population to ensure the civilian and humanitarian character of refugee camps and settlements.' Further, in the recommendations adopted by the meeting, paragraph 9: 'The presence of armed elements among civilian refugee population is a major concern. Member States are urged to take necessary measures, in consultation with the OAU and the UNHCR, to preserve the civilian and humanitarian character of refugee camps and settlements by separating armed elements from the civilian population.' In this regard, see also Article 56 2) of the 1977 First Protocol prescribing that: 'The special protection against attack provided by paragraph 1 shall cease: a) for a dam or a dyke only if it is used for other than its normal function and in regular, significant and direct support of military operations and if such attack is the only feasible way to terminate such support; b) for a nuclear electrical generating station only if it provides electric power in regular, significant and direct support of military operations and if such attack is the only feasible way to terminate such support; c) for other military objectives located at or in the vicinity of these works or installations only if they are used in regular, significant and direct support of military operations and if such attack is the only feasible way to terminate such support.'

The Second Report of the UNSG on Security in the Rwandan Refugee Camps in 1995 gives a clear idea of the situation in the camps of the Great Lakes region, through its description of the total lack of security, above all in the camps north of Lake Kivu in the DRC where Rwandan refugees were intimidated into not publicly expressing their desire to return to Rwanda.[93] There were significant threats posed by civil disturbances in the camps as well. These threats became particularly acute when refugees gathered for the distribution of relief supplies with the endorsement of the camp leaders who, while called upon to facilitate the delivery of relief assistance, misused this responsibility by using the delivery of assistance to persuade refugees to behave according to their interests and by selling such assistance rather than distributing it.[94] It is important to underline the fact that long-term interests of refugees could have been fulfilled simply by their return to Rwanda, according to the opinion given by the UNSG.[95]

In order to handle this situation, the UNSC requested that the UNSG assessed the possibility of launching a peacekeeping operation to enhance security in the camps, with the goals of providing security for international relief workers, protection for the storage and delivery of humanitarian assistance,[96] and safe

93 For an interesting chronology of the events of those years, see, for example: Emizet, K., 'The massacre of refugees in Congo: a case of UN peacekeeping failure and international law', in *Journal of Modern African Studies*, vol. 38, 2000, pp. 163–202. At ibid., p. 178 the author noted that: '[T]he number of refugees reaching each new refugee camp was smaller than at the preceding camp. This is an indication of systematic and deliberate killing. But Médecins sans Frontières also reported that twenty to thirty refugees died every day in refugee camps from severe malnutrition, dehydration, exhaustion, malaria, yellow fever and other diseases.' In this regard, see also Jacques, M., op. cit. note 24, pp. 217–20.

94 Jacobsen, K., 'A framework for exploring the political and security context of refugee populated areas', op. cit. note 40, p. 5.

95 UNSC, Second report of the Secretary-General on security in the Rwandese refugee camps, 25 January 1995, document No. S/1995/65, paragraph 20, p. 4.

96 In this regard, C. Rottensteiner explained: 'The denial of humanitarian assistance may have various aims. In a conflict where civilians are targeted, the displacement of part of the population or their starvation is such an aim; this could, for example, further a policy of "ethnic cleansing". The aim of sieges or blockades is to bring hostilities to a quicker end with fewer casualties for the besieging forces by obliging the besieged forces to surrender. Furthermore, belligerents may confiscate aid in order to fortify their troops, instead of "[f]eeding useless mouths". Also, bandits or criminal gangs may loot humanitarian assistance for the sole purpose of making profits. However, drawing the line between criminal gangs and forces directly involved in the conflict is not always easy. The consequence of denying humanitarian assistance is a deterioration in the living conditions of the civilians affected. This may in turn lead to malnutrition, the spread of diseases, or even death. Lack of resources may also aggravate inter-community tension, especially between displaced persons and the resident population. Those who prevent assistance from reaching people in need will not normally disclose their real intentions. The reasons given may be of a legalistic nature, for example the claim that such assistance constitutes interference in the conflict, or insistence on the right of supervision. The urgency of the need for outside aid may not be acknowledged. Reprisals, although generally considered illegal when committed against civilians, might also serve as a justification. Military considerations are often put forward to justify starvation, on the ground that only such rigorous measures can bring the hostilities to a speedy close. The civilian nature of a population may also be questioned, with the suggestion that its members belong in reality to rebel forces.' See Rottensteiner, C., 'The denial of humanitarian assistance as a crime under international law', in *International Review of the Red Cross*, vol. 39, 1999, pp. 561–2.

passage to the Rwandan border for those refugees who wished to return to Rwanda.[97] Peacekeeping operations, however, essentially constitute an instrument for conflict management and resolution, although they have also sometimes been used to ensure security in refugee camps.[98] Nevertheless, as mentioned above, it has traditionally been the responsibility of host countries to provide security to the refugees located on their territory,[99] albeit with an appropriate level of support from the international community.[100] If strengthening security in camps is considered necessary for the well-being of the people settled there, this action should always be accompanied by parallel steps with the aim of promoting durable solutions for refugees, considering that, in theory, their presence in camps should be temporary, so as to prepare the path for a durable solution.[101] However in Sub-Saharan Africa, the only preoccupation, at times, is with closing the camps without providing a decent alternative to the people settled there. In this regard,

97 UNSC, Second report of the Secretary-General on security in the Rwandese refugee camps, 25 January 1995, document No. S/1995/65, paragraphs 21–5, pp. 5–6.

98 Fernandez-Sanchez, P.A., op. cit. note 30, p. 366.

99 For instance, see OAU, Council of Ministers, resolution on the regional conference on assistance to refugees, returnees and displaced persons in the Great Lakes Region, resolution No. CM/Res. 1589 (LXII), 21–23 June 1995, paragraph 7: '[The Council of Ministers] commends the asylum countries and the UNHCR for putting in place security arrangements to enhance security in refugee camps.' In this regard, see also Corliss, S., 'Asylum state responsibility for the hostile acts of foreign exiles', in *International Journal of Refugee Law*, vol. 2, 1990, p. 208: 'A movement is evident in international law towards broader asylum state responsibility for the hostile acts of foreign exiles. Activities having a purely humanitarian focus or those involving political expression provide no legitimate cause for complaint.'

100 UNSC, Second report of the Secretary-General on security in the Rwandese refugee camps, 25 January 1995, document No. S/1995/65, p. 9. See also ExCom, conclusion No. 99 (LV), 'General conclusion on international protection', 2004, paragraph m): '[The ExCom] [. . .] emphasizes the importance of host States taking appropriate measures to protect refugee camps and settlements including whenever possible through ensuring, in consultation with UNHCR, their location at a reasonable distance from the border; and also emphasizes the importance of protecting refugees from other forms of threat and harassment from any groups or individuals.'

101 But, for instance, a detailed description of a transitory camp finally becoming a real city is present in Perouse de Montclos, M.-A. and Kagwanja, P.M., 'Refugee camps or cities? The socio-economic dynamics of the Dadaab and Kakuma camps in Northern Kenya', in *Journal of Refugee Studies*, vol. 13, 2000, pp. 205–22. At p. 205, the authors clearly contended: 'Refugee camps are often perceived as transient settlements, reflecting the temporary nature of the refugee phenomenon. Yet some camps have been in existence for years and can be likened to virtual cities in view of their population and demographic density. With approximately 85,000 refugees in the mid-1980s, the four camps of Jalalaqsi, for instance, formed the third largest human concentration in Somalia after Mogadishu and Hargeisa.' To underline the living conditions that should be assured in the camps A.M. Da Silva contended: 'Inside the camps too, refugees should be able to carry out farming or other productive activities since this will become part of the process of rebuilding their livelihoods, self-esteem and will contribute to alleviate their dependency on external aid thus enabling them to become self-sufficient.' See Da Silva, A.M., 'Mozambican refugees: from a historical overview of conflict to today's refugee camps and repatriation process', paper for 'First Country of Asylum and Development Aid' conference, June 1992, Lilongwe, Malawi, p. 26.

for instance, in 2000, the Council of Ministers of the AU asked the government of Burundi to dismantle the 'regroupment camps' by the end of the month of July of that year, but gave no further indication of what should be done with their inhabitants.[102]

Armed attacks on refugee camps sometimes took huge proportions as in the attack on Namibian refugees by the South African Defence Forces (SADF) in Kassinga, southern Angola, on 4 May 1978, which resulted in the death of 600 refugees and injuries to another 400,[103] or the 100 refugees who died in 1996, in the Ugandan Achol-Pii camp after an attack by the Lord's Resistance Army (LRA) opposing Y. Museveni's power in the country.[104] It is not rare, however, to also witness attacks from people already living in the camp.[105]

The 1979 ExCom conclusion No. 14, among the first condemnations of armed attacks on refugee camps, was inspired by the events in Kassinga. This conclusion

102 OAU, Council of Ministers, Decision on Burundi (CM/2164 (LXXII)-b), Decision No. CM/Dec.522 (LXXII) Rev.1, 6–8 July 2000, paragraph 7. We note that in 1997 the Council made a similar request to the Burundi government that found no practical response in Bujumbura. OAU, Council of Ministers, Report of the Secretary-General on the conflict situations in Africa: (Doc.Cm/2004 (LXVI)), Decision No. CM/Dec.353 (LXVI), 28–31 May 1997, paragraph e).

103 Othman-Chande, M., 'International law and armed attack in refugee camps', in *Nordic Journal of International Law*, vol. 59, 1990, p. 154. In this regard, see also Jacques, M., op. cit. note 24, p. 209. E.-E. Mtango in his work has added other examples of assaults occurring in African refugee camps: 'At the height of the Zimbabwe liberation war, in August 1976 and November and December 1977, Rhodesian forces repeatedly attacked Zimbabwean refugee camps in Manica Province, Mozambique, killing over 3,600 refugees. [. . .] Raids by South African armed forces on refugee camps in Angola, Mozambique, and Zambia and commando-style attacks on refugee homes and places of residence in Botswana, Lesotho, Swaziland, and Zimbabwe have been increasing since 1974, thus making the security of refugees in Southern Africa a priority problem for the region and for the international community.' See Mtango, E-E., 'Military and armed attacks on refugee camps', in Loescher, G. and Monahan, L. (eds), *Refugees and International Relations*, New York: Oxford University Press, 1989, p. 93. As explained by M. Janmyr: 'SADF justified their attack on the ground that the refugees were actively engaged in an armed struggle against South African control over Namibia.' See Janmyr, M., *Protecting Civilians in Refugee Camps: Unable and Unwilling States, UNHCR and International Responsibility*, Leiden: Martinus Nijhoff, 2014, p. 9.

104 Moro, L.N., Refugee Camps in Northern Uganda: Sanctuaries or Battlegrounds?, p. 1, paper available at: www.sudanstudies.org/leben03.pdf, accessed 10 July 2014. In this regard, see also what is contended by Janmyr, M., op. cit. note 103, pp. 19–20: '[I]n Uganda, any real attempts to provide physical security for the Sudanese refugees on the part of UNHCR were to a great extent smothered by the arguably unjustified focus on UNHCR's flagship project aiming to make the refugees self-reliant through farming. [. . .] The case of Uganda is [. . .] a reminder that securing the basic rights of refugees [. . .] remains a prerequisite to safeguarding all other human rights standards.'

105 For instance, talking about some armed attacks in the Kenyan Dadaab camp a refugee living there told: 'The bandits live in Dadaab and in the blocks, so they know which refugees are working and where everybody goes to and comes from. The bandits have associates standing near the bus station to be able to recognize exactly who is leaving and who is coming to Dadaab and what those coming to the camps are carrying. If a refugee comes with bus from Garissa or Nairobi carrying something that might be of interest, he/she can generally expect "visitors" the same night. If someone receives money from the remittances the bandits will soon be at his or her doorstep.' Story quoted in Horst, C., op. cit. note 16, p. 90.

severely condemned the inhuman attacks on refugee camps in Southern Africa.[106] Two years later the ExCom reiterated its grave concern, about the:

> [i]nhuman military attacks on refugee camps in Southern Africa and elsewhere, involving extreme and indescribable hardships to refugees and called upon the High Commissioner to examine the serious humanitarian problems resulting from military attacks on refugee camps and settlements which are of UNHCR concern, and the need for special measures to protect and ensure the safety of such refugees, and to report thereon at the earliest possible date to the ExCom.[107]

This situation seemed to improve the following year, when the ExCom expressed hopes of adopting measures to make refugee camps safe from military attacks[108] with the competences of the UNHCR to be defined in more detail. International protection, one of the basic and most important statutory functions of the agency,[109] did not involve providing actual physical protection to the refugees since this was the primary responsibility of the authorities of the country of asylum. The UNHCR, in carrying out its purely humanitarian and non-political mandate, however, played a role in promoting conditions ensuring that refugees in camps were not exposed to the dangers of an attack. The actions undertaken towards these aims included the settling of refugees away from state borders, allowing the High Commissioner's representatives full and regular access to the camps, and maintaining regular contact with the countries concerned. As an intermediary, the High Commissioner would support governments in finding appropriate durable solutions to the problem.[110]

106 ExCom, conclusion No. 14 (XXX), 'General conclusion on international protection', 1979, paragraph e).

107 ExCom, conclusion No. 21 (XXXII), 'General conclusion on international protection', 1981, paragraph h).

108 ExCom, conclusion No. 27 (XXXIII), 'Military attacks on refugee camps and settlements in Southern Africa and elsewhere', 1982, paragraph d): '[The ExCom] welcomed the appointment by the High Commissioner of Ambassador Schnyder to carry out a survey of the various aspects of the problem of military attacks on refugee camps and settlements of concern to UNHCR and, in taking note with appreciation of his preliminary report on the matter (EC/SCP/23) expressed the hope that this survey would lead to the adoption of measures which would make refugee camps and settlements safer from military attacks than they have so far been.'

109 In this regard, A. Edwards noted: 'Nowhere in the [1950 UNHCR] Statute is the term [of international protection] explicitly defined, although nine paragraphs of article 8 are dedicated to identifying the activities that UNHCR is expected to engage in. The list appears to be exhaustive, although the provisions are particularly broad to be able to include a whole range of activities not initially foreseen.' See Edwards, A., 'Crossing legal borders: the interface between refugee law, human rights law and humanitarian law in the "international protection" of refugees', in Arnold, R. and Quénivet, N. (eds), *International Humanitarian Law and Human Rights Law: Towards a New Merger in International Law*, Leiden/Boston: Martinus Nijhoff, 2008, pp. 434–5.

110 Othman-Chande, M., 'International law and armed attack in refugee camps', op. cit. note 103, p. 155.

The UNHCR has often argued, however, that governments are responsible for the policy of forcing refugees to stay in camps. The agency contended that governments want refugees in camps because of their concerns about 'security', as it was confirmed by a Kenyan court in 2013.[111] Given that the majority of refugees in Sub-Saharan Africa live outside of the camps, however, justifying camps on the grounds of security is an argument that, if strictly examined, cannot be sustained in certain situations. In effect, it is well known that congregating refugees in camps can create insecurity for refugees themselves,[112] above all where there is a severe failure to respect the civilian and humanitarian character of asylum, as occurred in Rwanda in the aftermath of the genocide.[113]

Until now, the UNHCR has accepted and promoted the building of camps, in spite of its patently negative impact on refugee protection, for several reasons. First, the great visibility of the encamped refugees makes it easier for the organization to raise funds from donors. Second, refugees can be more easily controlled in camps. This control serves to ease the process of humanitarian assistance, whose denial may be considered as a crime under international law.[114] Third, the UNHCR's way of operating has remained unchanged over decades: institutional inaction is responsible for the perpetuation of camp policy, and experience or knowledge of other ways of assisting refugees is almost entirely lacking in many countries on the continent. Fourth, encampment is promoted by the UNHCR's approach to durable solutions: with repatriation being considered

111 Kenya: High Court, *Kituo Cha Sheria and others v The Attorney General*, 26 July 2013, paragraph 68: 'The petitioners and other refugees have established roots in the country and are productive residents and if the policy is implemented they will be uprooted from their homes and neighborhoods in what is intended to be a security operation.'

112 Harrell-Bond, B., op. cit. note 3, p. 5. In the same regard, C.R. Veney noted: 'Asylum countries such as Kenya bear the responsibility for the physical safety of refugees, which was more endangered when camps were located near border areas. Oftentimes, because of their close proximity to border areas, refugees were unwillingly drawn into the conflicts from which they fled by forced recruitment and cross-border attacks. [. . .] Following the stabilization of the Somali refugee crisis, the UNHCR attempted to ensure adequate security by advising the government on how to establish and improve security in and around camps.' See Veney, C.R., *Forced Migration in Eastern Africa: Democratization, Structural Adjustment, and Refugees*, Basingstoke: Palgrave MacMillan, 2007, p. 171.

113 UNHCR, Standing Committee, The security, and civilian and humanitarian character of refugee camps and settlements, 14 January 1999, document No. EC/49/SC/INF.2, paragraph 2: '[t]he presence among refugees of former combatants and persons involved in grave crimes against humanity has been a tragic illustration of the failure of states hosting refugees and of the international community to ensure the neutrality of camps. Insecurity can also arise as a result of several other factors, such as conflict amongst different groups within the refugee population, common crime and banditry, and, in certain cases, the deployment of undisciplined police and security forces.'

114 Rottensteiner, C., op. cit. note 96, p. 582: 'It is undoubtedly essential to show caution when declaring a certain conduct a crime under international law, in particular where crimes against humanity or genocide are concerned. However, it should not be forgotten that – although not always as obvious or as easy to prove in the reality of armed conflicts – the impact of the denial of humanitarian assistance can be just as strong as massacres "committed with knives".'

by the agency the most acceptable solution for refugees, camps in themselves become tolerable as intermediate holding grounds until repatriation takes effect.[115]

The questions of the physical safety of refugees and national security were likewise main subjects of discussion at the 1983 Round Table organized in Sanremo, Italy.[116] The conclusions of that conference recognized the serious problems of physical safety, including armed attacks on refugee camps and settlements, bombardments and the location of refugee populations close to the borders with countries of origin.[117] And, as reality in Sub-Saharan Africa has shown that this has often been the case,[118]included the example of the Sudanese refugees in northern Uganda, who live in constant fear not only because their camps are close to the border with Sudan, the country they fled, but also because their camps are located within particularly dangerous conflict zones.[119]

115 Verdirame, G. and Harrell-Bond, B., *Rights in Exile: Janus-Faced Humanitarianism*, New York/Oxford: Berghahn Books, 2005, p. 288.

116 The promoter of the conference was the International Institute of Humanitarian Law, based there.

117 Othman-Chande, M., 'International law and armed attack in refugee camps', op. cit. note 103, p. 156. In effect, as Article II6 of the 1969 OAU Convention reads, it should occur that: 'For reasons of security, countries of asylum shall, as far as possible, settle refugees at a reasonable distance from the frontier of their country of origin.' This has been confirmed also in recommendation 6, paragraph 7 of the 1979 Arusha Conference on the African Refugee Problem: '[The Conference] further notes the obligation of Member States [. . .] defined in article II paragraph 6 of the same convention [1969 OAU Convention], as far as possible to settle refugees at a reasonable distance from the frontier of their country of origin.'

118 See, for instance, Milner, J.H.S. and Christoffersen-Deb, A., 'The militarization and demilitarization of refugee camps and settlements in Guinea, 1999–2004', in Muggah, R. (ed.), *No Refuge: the Crisis of Refugee Militarization in Africa*, London/New York: Zed Books, 2006, pp. 51–87. At p. 80 the authors concluded their analysis: 'Guinea's refugee population [. . .] was affected by the 2000/2001 cross-border attacks and the Liberian civil war. Not only did both sides target refugees during the fighting, but the infiltration of armed groups in the refugee camps caused suspicion and led to further harassment and displacement of refugees. [. . .] In addition, as the boundaries of refugee camps are not enforced, insecurity and small-arms proliferation outside the refugee camps can have a direct impact on refugees inside the camps.' In the same regard, see also Mogire, E., 'Preventing or abetting: refugee militarization in Tanzania', in Muggah, R. (ed.), *No Refuge: The Crisis of Refugee Militarization in Africa*, London/New York: Zed Books, 2006, pp. 137–78. At p. 148 the author contended: '[T]anzania has indirectly supported refugee militarization. [. . .] The location of refugee camps close to international frontiers has allowed groups of defeated or stranded Hutu insurgents to retreat into the refugee camps at regular intervals and use the camps to prepare for subsequent raids.'

119 Jacques, M., op. cit. note 24, p. 227. Further, at idem the author explained: 'Neighbor countries Liberia and Côte d'Ivoire [. . .] have been torn by regional conflicts and civil wars for years, with Liberian and Ivorian refugees shifting between borders depending on the state of the conflict within these countries. This constant flow of refugees crossing and recrossing the border threatens to further destabilize the region and the camps situated close to the border are frequently subjected to attacks by rebel fighters.' In this regard, Article 58 of the 1977 First Protocol reads: '58) The Parties to the conflict shall, to the maximum extent feasible: a) without prejudice to Article 49 of the 1949 Fourth Convention, endeavor to remove the civilian population, individual civilians and civilian objects under their control from the vicinity of military objectives; b) avoid locating military objectives within or near densely populated areas; c) take the other necessary precautions to protect the civilian population, individual civilians and civilian objects under their

In effect, there is not always a direct link between the proximity of a camp to a border and the highest possibility for that camp to become target of attacks, as the example of Mozambican camps in Malawi has shown. Conversely, host governments often place camps near the origin country of these refugees in order to prevent them from integrating into the local community.[120] In order to favour a better location of the camps where asylum-seekers and refugees can live safely, M.F. Cuellar suggested that the UNHCR, through a more clearly expressed 'financing mechanism', can compensate African states available to offer more favourable locations to set up camps.[121]

In this sense, the 1969 OAU Convention under Article III establishes a categorical obligation on the part of refugees to abstain from any subversive activities against any OAU member state, and for the countries of asylum to forbid refugees residing in their territories from any activity expected to cause tensions between member states.[122] For this purpose, the DRC government was not too far-sighted, or maybe it was simply an accomplice, in settling the Rwandan refugee camps too close to the border with Rwanda, often within walking distance. But in Sub-Saharan Africa, refugee resettlement close to borders is the rule rather than the exception, as we note has happened in the past in several countries such

control against the dangers resulting from military operations.' See also, Article 51 7) of the same protocol that reads: '7) The presence or movements of the civilian population or individual civilians shall not be used to render certain points or areas immune from military operations, in particular in attempts to shield military objectives from attacks or to shield, favor or impede military operations. The Parties to the conflict shall not direct the movement of the civilian population or individual civilians in order to attempt to shield military objectives from attacks or to shield military operations.' In the same regard, see also the news: 'UNHCR moves Malian refugees to safer areas of Burkina Faso', 21 December 2012, available at: www.unhcr.org/50d443e46.html, accessed 24 December 2014: 'Mariam, her two daughters and her blind father were among the first to be moved by UNHCR to the Goudebou camp, 150 kilometres from the border, under a programme to relocate people away from the Fererio and Gandafabou camps, which respectively housed some 7,675 and 2,974 refugees when the exercise began in late October. Security is a concern at both sites, while Gandafabou suffers from water supply problems. [. . .] [T]he refugees at Fereiro have not felt safe there because of its proximity to the border at a time when the north of Mali has come under the strict control of Islamic militants, causing more people to flee. [. . .] At Goudebou, the security is much better and it is easier to provide protection, shelter, general assistance and access to basic services than the isolated camp near the border. The new camp is located on the outskirts of Dori, capital of Burkina Faso's Sahel region.'

120 Jacobsen, K., 'A framework for exploring the political and security context of refugee populated areas', op. cit. note 40, pp. 10–11.

121 Cuellar, M.-F., op. cit. note 14, pp. 712–13.

122 See also ExCom, conclusion No. 94 (LIII), 'Conclusion on the civilian and humanitarian character of asylum', 2002, paragraph a): '[The ExCom] acknowledges that host States have the primary responsibility to ensure the civilian and humanitarian character of asylum by, *inter alia*, making all efforts to locate refugee camps and settlements at a reasonable distance from the border, maintaining law and order, curtailing the flow of arms into refugee camps and settlements, preventing their use for the internment of prisoners of war, as well as through the disarmament of armed elements and the identification, separation and internment of combatants.'

as in Guinea, Liberia, Kenya and Tanzania.[123] And this occurs in spite of the UNHCR recommendations to the contrary, relative to the African situation[124] and in spite of the fact that the location of refugee camps at a 'sufficient distance from the border and the area of conflict creates a disincentive to use them as a base for military activities'.[125] Nonetheless, should camps be kept close to the border, a 'reasonable distance' of at least 50 km should be respected.[126] This should be a deliberate choice by the host country, as part of a specific strategy aiming to limit possible problems derived by the presence of refugees only to the peripheral areas of the host country, as happened in Tanzania in the mid-1990s – even though in this case the local government was politically sympathetic towards the refugees opposing the Tutsi government in Burundi.[127]

Consequently, refugees organized to destabilize the government in Kigali from camps in DRC. Cross-border attacks against Rwanda occurred throughout 1995 and 1996, with Hutu attackers targeting genocide survivors and abducting local men to participate in militias across the border.[128] The conflict escalated brusquely in late 1996, when the government in Kigali and Congolese rebels attacked the refugee camps, dispersing nearly a million people.[129]

123 Lomo, Z., 'The struggle for protection of the rights of refugees and IDPs in Africa: making the existing international legal regime work', in *Berkeley Journal of International Law*, vol. 18, 2000, p. 282.

124 See, for instance, UNHCR, Global Consultations on International Protection, UNHCR Regional Symposium on maintaining the civilian and humanitarian character of asylum refugee status, camps and other locations, 26–27 February 2001, Pretoria, South Africa, 30 May 2001, document No. EC/GC/01/9, conclusion 4 b): 'Refugee camps should be located at a significant distance from the border in situations arising from protracted political polarization and conflict. [. . .] There should be visible and effective government presence, including of law enforcement authorities, in and around the area of camps and settlements, as well as a proper management of these locations. [. . .] There should be adequate UNHCR presence in and monitoring of the refugee camps and settlements.'

125 UNHCR, Global Consultations on International Protection/third track: the civilian character of asylum: separating armed elements from refugees, 19 February 2001, document No. EC/GC/01/5, paragraph 13, p. 4.

126 Crisp, J., 'A state of insecurity: the political economy of violence in Kenya's refugee camps', op. cit. note 61, p. 66.

127 Jacobsen, K., 'A framework for exploring the political and security context of refugee populated areas', op. cit. note 40, p. 15.

128 Unfortunately, in this situation: '[t]he UNSC could only note its concern through reports of military preparations and incursions into Rwanda by elements of the former regime. [. . .] Instead of taking action, however, it [. . .] chose to merely observe.' See Adelman, H., 'The use and abuse of refugees in Zaire', in Stedman, S.J. and Tanner, F. (eds): *Refugee Manipulation: War, Politics and the Abuse of Human Suffering*, Washington DC: Brookings Institution Press, 2003, p. 108.

129 Lischer, S.K., *Dangerous Sanctuaries: Refugee Camps, Civil War, and the Dilemmas of Humanitarian Aid*, Ithaca/London: Cornell University Press, 2005, pp. 76 and 94. At p. 79 the author clarified: 'In the first few months of the refugee crisis, chaos and violence ruled the camps in eastern Zaire. [. . .] Human rights observers noted that men walking around the camps wearing uniforms and "armed with every conceivable type of weapon". [. . .] Numerous refugees were killed after merely obtaining information about repatriation. Militants set up roadblocks within the camps and instituted neighborhood security patrols to monitor refugee activity.' At p. 81 the author observed

In 1995, the ExCom also summarized its ideas on the character and location of refugee camps, as follows:

> [The ExCom] reaffirms its conclusion No. 48 (XXXVIII) on Military or Armed Attacks on Refugee Camps and Settlements[130] and reiterates that, the grant of asylum or refuge being a peaceful and humanitarian act, refugee camps and settlements must maintain their exclusively civilian and humanitarian character,[131] and all parties are obliged to abstain from any activity likely to undermine this; condemns all acts which pose a threat to the personal security of refugees and asylum-seekers, and also those which may

that OAU estimated that around 10 per cent of the refugees in DRC eastern camps in that period – over 100,000 people – were militants and war criminals. At p. 94 the author argued: '[B]order camps exist because they meet political goals of receiving states and, often, the refugee themselves. Thus it is not possible to consider camp location as a purely logistic issue. Even if border camps prove a necessary – if not sufficient – condition for cross-border violence, one cannot separate the demographic from the political aspects of camp location decisions.' This episode is mentioned also in Lomo, Z., op. cit. note 123, p. 280.

130 Among other instruments, paragraph 4) of the ExCom's conclusion No. 48 (XXXVIII), 'Military or armed attacks on refugee camps and settlements', 1987 reads: '[The ExCom] urges States and other parties to be guided by the following considerations in promoting measures to enhance the protection of refugee camps and settlements; a) refugees in camps and settlements have, together with the basic rights they enjoy, duties deriving from the refuge and protection granted or afforded to them by the country of refuge. In particular, they have duties to conform to the laws and regulations of the State of refuge including lawful measures taken for the maintenance of public order and to abstain from any activity likely to detract from the exclusively civilian and humanitarian character of the camps and settlements; b) it is essential that States of refuge do all within their capacity to ensure that the civilian and humanitarian character of such camps and settlements is maintained. All other States are called upon to assist them in this regard. To this end relevant organs of the United Nations, within their respective terms of reference, are also called upon to co-operate with all States in providing assistance whenever necessary; c) UNHCR and other concerned organs of the United Nations should make every effort, within their respective terms of reference and in keeping with the principles of the United Nations Charter, to promote conditions which ensure the safety of refugees in camps and settlements. For UNHCR this may include maintaining close contact with the Secretary-General of the United Nations and providing liaison, as appropriate, with all the parties concerned. It may also involve making appropriate arrangements with States of refuge on methods of protecting such refugee camps and settlements including, whenever possible, their location at a reasonable distance from the frontier of the country of origin; d) states have a duty to cooperate with the High Commissioner in the performance of his/her humanitarian protection and assistance functions, which can only be effectively accomplished if he/she has access to camps and settlements of his/her concern.'

131 In this regard, see also '[The ExCom] reiterating that refugee camps and settlements should have an exclusively civilian and humanitarian character, that the grant of asylum is a peaceful and humanitarian act which should not be regarded as unfriendly by another State, as stated in the 1969 OAU Convention Governing the Specific Aspects of Refugee Problems in Africa and a number of Executive Committee conclusions, and that all actors, including refugees themselves, have the obligation to cooperate in ensuring the peaceful and humanitarian character of refugee camps and settlements.' See ExCom, conclusion No. 94 (LIII), 'conclusion on the civilian and humanitarian character of asylum', 2002, preamble.

> endanger the safety and stability of States; calls on States of refuge to take all necessary measures to ensure that the civilian and humanitarian character of refugee camps and settlements is maintained and, in this regard, calls on all other States to assist them; and further calls on States of refuge to take effective measures to prevent the infiltration of armed elements, to provide effective physical protection to refugees and asylum-seekers, and to afford UNHCR and other appropriate organizations prompt and unhindered access to them.[132]

It is clear that attacks on camps find no support in international law. The validity of this view can be traced to Article 2 4) of the 1945 UN Charter,[133] the UNGA Declaration on the admissibility of intervention in the domestic affairs of states, and the protection of their independence and sovereignty,[134] the UNGA resolution No. 1815 (XVII) of 18 December 1962,[135] and UNGA resolution No. 3314 (XXIX) of 14 December 1974 on the definition of aggression.[136] As established through these documents, international law regards all attacks on refugee camps

132 ExCom, conclusion No. 77 (XLVI), 'General conclusion on international protection', 1995, paragraph q). In effect in South Africa authorities had a different opinion on the subject: 'On 15 October [2008], in the southern Cape province, the authorities announced that Harmony Park would be closed within two days. Civil society groups expect chaos and homelessness to follow for the 250 asylum seekers currently residing in the camp. The authorities added that two more camps, Youngsfield and Bluewaters, will close by the end of the month. Approximately 2,000 individuals will be affected [by] the closures.' See JRS, Briefings of the 17 October 2008. Some months before: 'On 26 August, an unofficial refugee camp established by a church in Musina near the Zimbabwe border has been brought down on the orders of the municipality. "Situations like this continue to happen in Musina because the authorities do not necessarily take care of Zimbabweans. While some officials do a lot of good work, it totally depends on the person in charge", said Thandi Hadebe, JRS South Africa Project Director in the northernmost province of Limpopo, told dispatches on 27 August.' See JRS, dispatch No. 243, 29 August 2008.

133 Article 2 4) of the 1945 UN Charter reads: 'All Members shall refrain in their international relations from the threat or use of force against the territorial integrity or political independence of any state, or in any other manner inconsistent with the Purposes of the United Nations.'

134 UNGA, Declaration on the inadmissibility of intervention in the domestic affairs of states and the protection of their independence and sovereignty, 21 December 1965, No. 2131 (XX). In detail, paragraph 2 of the Declaration reads: '[A]lso no State shall organize, assist, foment, finance, incite or tolerate subversive, terrorist or armed activities directed towards the violent overthrow of the regime of another State or interfere in civil strife in another State.'

135 UNGA, Consideration of principles of international law concerning friendly relations and cooperation among states in accordance with the Charter of the United Nations, 18 December 1962, resolution No. 1815 (XVII). In detail, its paragraph 1 reads: '[The UNGA recognizes the importance of those principles]: a) the principle that States shall refrain in their international relations from the threat or use of force against the territorial integrity or political independence of any State, or in any other manner inconsistent with the purposes of the United Nations.'

136 UNGA, Definition of aggression, 14 December 1974, No. 3314 (XXIX). In detail, see Article 3, which enumerates practical examples of what can be considered as an act of aggression and Article 4 which reads: 'The acts enumerated above are not exhaustive and the Security Council may determine that other acts constitute aggression under the provisions of the Charter.'

inside a state's territory as evidence of an act of aggression, and thus to be condemned by the international community.[137]

In addition, the principle of refraining from attack on refugee camps is in line with Article 51 of the 1977 First Protocol[138] and Article 13 1) and 2) of the 1977 Second Protocol.[139] A further elaboration of this principle may clarify the right of the country of asylum and of refugees themselves to demand compensation for damages caused, as well as to demand punishment of the individual criminals.[140]

4.3 Final reflections on the problem of camps

To a certain extent, it is the international assistance agencies, and especially the UNHCR, that have borne the brunt of criticism about the establishment of camps. These agencies are seen as favouring a policy that either helps them to carry out their mandate to assist refugees, or alternatively, strengthens their control of camp populations and accountability to donors, depending on one's point of view.[141] But, in several camps, for example in Dadaab,[142] refugees have explicitly declared that the UNHCR treated the refugee staff working there in a harsh and discriminatory way compared to the treatment reserved to national and international staff,[143] and that:

> Taken together, the agencies make significant efforts to hide the truth of the situation of refugees in the camps of Dadaab when visitors arrive.[144]

137 Othman-Chande, M., 'International law and armed attack in refugee camps', op. cit. note 103, p. 166.

138 Article 51 1) of the 1977 First Protocol, clearly reads: '1) The civilian population and individual civilians shall enjoy general protection against dangers arising from military operations. To give effect to this protection, the following rules, which are additional to other applicable rules of international law, shall be observed in circumstances.'

139 Article 13, paragraphs 1) and 2) of the 1977 Second Protocol, stipulate: '1) The civilian population and individual civilians shall enjoy general protection against the dangers arising from military operations. To give effect to this protection, the following rules shall be observed in all circumstances. 2) The civilian population as such, as well as individual civilians, shall not be the object of attack. Acts or threats of violence the primary purpose of which is to spread terror among the civilian population are prohibited.'

140 Mtango, E-E., op. cit. note 103, p. 116.

141 Black, R., 'Putting refugees in camps', in *Forced Migration Review*, vol. 2, 1998, p. 5.

142 In this regard, A. Lindley and A. Haslie noted: 'By the end of July 2011, the camp, originally established to host 90,000 people, had a population of 386,229, the vast majority Somalis.' See Lindley, A. and Haslie, A., 'Unlocking protracted displacement: Somali case study', *Oxford: Refugee Studies Centre*, working paper No. 79, 2011, pp. 27–8.

143 Refugee Silent Welfare Committee, A voice from the voiceless: Dadaab Refugee Camps Kenya, 7 July 2011, on file with author, p. 2. At p. 43 is added: 'The incentive system is often claimed to be necessary because of limited budgetary resources and because refugee staff members are not allowed to officially work under Kenyan law. However, in actuality, these supposed justifications serve only as mere excuses for the agencies to hide behind so that they can continue to exploit refugee labor.'

144 Ibid., p. 7.

Sometimes, however, reality is better than what one imagines. Let us take the example of the Kakuma camp in Kenya, a camp that, in 2012, counted more than 100,000 refugees sheltered there.[145] With high levels of violence (in various forms: domestic and communal violence, sexual abuse, armed robbery, violence within national refugee groups, violence between national refugee groups, violence between refugees and local populations),[146] temporary shelters and tense refugee-local relations, the Kaluma camp is often seen as an example of a camp in which the UNHCR has not been able to maintain even minimum standards. Yet a 2000 study revealed that, broadly speaking, not only had minimum standards been attained, but, in some cases, the conditions in the camps were better than those prevailing in either the refugees' home countries or elsewhere in Kenya. However, distress and apathy remain palpable to a visitor to Kakuma, making it clear that the minimum standards paradigm is still incomplete, for even attaining such standards fails to address larger questions of needs and freedoms.[147] In addition, indirect security threats resulting from the presence of protracted refugees in Kenya – but not only there[148] – include tensions and conflict between refugees and host populations, as well as violence within the refugee communities themselves. In this regard, T. Kaiser noted that in the case of the Kakuma camp, situated in a very poor and semi-arid area of Kenya, refugees outnumber the local Turkana population, who feel they have to compete with them for employment and natural resources, causing political instability in the region.[149] In addition, another plight afflicting refugee camps in Sub-Saharan Africa is the growing practice of forced military recruitment there, such as the forced recruitment of Liberian refugees by the Ivorian governmental authorities in 2003[150] or the forced recruitment of Sudanese operated by Chadian

145 See the news: 'Kakuma camp in Kenya surpasses its 100,000 capacity', 6 August 2012, available at: www.unhcr.org/501fdb419.html, accessed 10 August 2014.

146 Crisp, J., 'A state of insecurity: the political economy of violence in Kenya's refugee camps', op. cit. note 61, pp. 54–9.

147 Jamal, A., 'Camps and freedoms: the long-term refugee situation in Africa', op. cit. note 15, p. 4.

148 In this regard, see Kirui, P. and Mwaruvie, J., 'The dilemma of hosting refugees: a focus on the insecurity in north-eastern Kenya', in *International Journal of Business and Social Science*, vol. 3, 2012, pp. 164–5: '[I]n Chad and Darfur, "where there are large congregations of displaced persons in an arid environment, there are huge demands on the scarce local water resources and this gives rise to friction with the local communities". In Ghana, Liberian refugees are widely cited by Ghanaians as the cause of recent armed robberies and wife stealing. In addition, the Ghanaian population says that Liberians engage in illegal activities such as prostitution, drugs robbery, and gambling.'

149 Kaiser, T., 'Sudanese refugees in Uganda and Kenya', op. cit. note 23, p. 265. In this regard, see also Crisp, J., 'A state of insecurity: the political economy of violence in Kenya's refugee camps', op. cit. note 61, p. 64: 'There is a general recognition in Kakuma and Dadaab that the refugees enjoy a standard of living which is equal to if not better than many local people. According to aid agency workers, the level of malnutrition amongst the Turkana is higher than it is the refugees in Kakuma.'

150 AI, Côte d'Ivoire: No escape: Liberian refugees in Côte d'Ivoire, 23 June 2003, p. 15: '[L]iberian refugees, including children under 18, have been recruited, often forcibly, by armed opposition

authorities in 2006.[151] Forced recruitment of refugees threatens the civilian character of the camps, and critically compromises the security of their inhabitants. This practice happens despite the fact that NGOs regularly denounce forced recruitment, like the mentioned one that occurred among the Sudanese encamped in eastern Chad in 2006[152] and despite the fact that the UNGA has also denounced this kind of practice in its 1991 resolution No. 46/106.[153]

It is clear that camps may provide security from persecution, but if refugees are to prosper, and prove to be less of a burden, they must also be given the freedom to make their own choices and to lead productive lives.[154] This is not always obvious, such as in Bukavu camps in DRC, and especially at Kinshushu and Inera camps also in DRC, which had a high proportion of former military and militia who took over complete and exclusive control of the camps.[155]

groups and by the government forces of President Gbagbo. With regard to the recruitment carried out by armed opposition groups, some refugees seem to have been forced to fight after being threatened with violence, while others have joined up voluntarily, hoping to use this as a form of self-protection. In addition, in March 2003, Amnesty International gathered a significant number of statements on the recruitment organized by members of the security forces, especially in the Nicla camp and in the Abidjan transit centers. A Liberian refugee said that members of the Côte d'Ivoire security forces threatened refugees who hesitated when asked to join up', available at: www.amnesty.org/en/library/asset/AFR31/012/2003/en/93ada32b-d6f3–11dd-b0cc-1f0860013475/afr310122003en.pdf, accessed 8 October 2014. In this regard, we point out that both the 1977 Protocols ban the recruitment of children under 15. See 1977 First Protocol, Article 77 2) that reads: '2) The Parties to the conflict shall take all feasible measures in order that children who have not attained the age of fifteen years do not take a direct part in hostilities and, in particular, they shall refrain from recruiting them into their armed forces. In recruiting among those persons who have attained the age of fifteen years but who have not attained the age of eighteen years the Parties to the conflict shall endeavor to give priority to those who are oldest'; 1977 Second Protocol, Article 4 3) c): 'Children shall be provided with the care and aid they require, and in particular: [. . .] children who have not attained the age of fifteen years shall neither be recruited in the armed forces or groups nor allowed to take part in hostilities.'

151 See the news: UNHCR expresses alarm over continuing reports of forced recruitment in Chad refugee camps, 16 May 2006, available at: www.unhcr.org/4469eba94.html, accessed 18 September 2014.

152 Jacques, M., op. cit. note 24, p. 230.

153 UNGA, Office of the United Nations High Commissioner for Refugees, 16 December 1991, resolution No. A/RES/46/106, paragraph 5: '[The UNGA] condemns all violations of the rights and safety of refugees and asylum-seekers; in particular those perpetrated by military or armed attacks against refugee camps and settlements and *forced recruitment into armed forces*.' Emphasis added. But, on the other hand, there are also individuals who manage to flee to another country fearing forced recruitment in their own country of origin. In this regard, see for instance the news: 'Young Congolese men fear forced recruitment, flee to Uganda', 24 December 2012, available at: www.unhcr.org/50d85a046.html, accessed 2 September 2014: 'Marc, Philippe and Georges are all young, fit and male – ideal material for forced military recruitment. That's why the 20-year-olds fled their homes, like thousands of other young men living in fear of being forced to fight in eastern Democratic Republic of the Congo's (DRC) endless conflict.'

154 Jamal, A., 'Camps and freedoms: long-term refugee situation in Africa', op. cit. note 15, p. 6.

155 Lischer, S.K., op. cit. note 129, p. 80.

Another camp where former military and militia combatants were numerous is the Mwisa camp in Tanzania. It was a 'closed' camp, administered by a nearby prison and inhabited by several Rwandan army officers, immigration and security officers, and five high profile town mayors who were implicated in the genocide. In the camp, movement was restricted to a two-kilometre radius around the camp and guarded by several prison guards, conditions which were shared by other camps, like Dadaab in Kenya, where the restricted movement of refugees has been one of the main causes of the deterioration of their conditions, as well as their underdevelopment. In any event, in April 2015, the Kenyan government, after the brutal Al-Shabaab attack in Garissa, has formally demanded the UN to close the camp.[156]

The screening of the Mwisa case-load took place in early 1997 and both Articles 1F a) of the 1951 Geneva Convention and Article I5 of the 1969 OAU Convention were applied. Finally, eight individuals were granted refugee status and transferred to Mkugwa camp while the others were rejected.[157]

156 Refugee Silent Welfare Committee, op. cit. note 143, p. 1. In this regard, the Committee added: 'Many people have died from simple disease because they could not move to get treatment in Glarissa (a town only 90 km from Dadaab). [. . .] Many people have been forced into greater poverty by being denied the chance to work and by having to pay three times the price of goods in other regions because they cannot move to get cheaper goods for consumption or business.' See also the news: 'Kenya orders Somali refugees to go to Dadaab', 18 December 2012, available at: www.bbc.co.uk/news/world-africa-20768955, accessed 18 September 2014: '"The government of Kenya has decided to stop reception, registration and close down all registration centres in the urban areas with immediate effect", read a statement from Badu Katelo, Kenya's Acting Commissioner for Refugee Affairs. "The refugees, particularly those living in urban centres, are contributing to insecurity in the country." He also said aid agencies, including the UNHCR, should stop giving assistance to asylum seekers and refugees in Kenya's towns and cities and only provide help in camps.' For the latter, refer CNN, '147 dead, Islamist gunmen killed after attack at Kenya college', 2 April 2015, available at: http://edition.cnn.com/2015/04/02/africa/kenya-university-attack/, accessed 3 April 2015; and further, BBC, 'Kenya tells UN to close Dadaab camp after Garissa attack', 11 April 2015, available at: www.bbc.com/news/world-africa-32269944, accessed 12 April 2015: 'Kenya's Deputy President William Ruto has called on the United Nations to close the Dadaab refugee camp and relocate more than 500,000 Somalis. Dadaab, near the border with Somalia, is the largest refugee camp in Africa. On 2 April, Somali militants from the al-Shabab Islamist movement attacked a college in the Kenyan town of Garissa, killing 148 students. But the head of the UN refugee agency UNHCR in Kenya told the BBC they had not been asked to close the camp. Mr Ruto said UNHCR had three months to close Dadaab and make alternative arrangements for its residents – otherwise, Kenya would "relocate them ourselves", he said.'

157 O'Neill, W., Rutinwa, B. and Verdirame, G., 'The Great Lakes: a survey of the application of the exclusion clause in the Central African Republic, Kenya and Tanzania', in *International Journal of Refugee Law*, special supplementary issue, vol. 12, 2000, pp. 165 and 168. We note that since the adoption of the 1998 national law on refugees, Tanzania has adopted a policy of forced encampment that requires all refugees to reside in camps. In this regard, C.R. Veney observed: '[T]he government [of Tanzania] enacted an exclusion zone around the camps' and other restrictive measures '[i]n violation of international law that guarantees refugees freedom of movement in countries of asylum without discrimination.' See Veney, C.R., op. cit. note 112, p. 89. This right is found in Article 26 of the 1951 Geneva Convention and Article 12 of the 1966 International Covenant on Civil and Political Rights as well as in section 15 1) of the Tanzanian Constitution which reads: 'Every person has the right to freedom and to live as a free person.'

In addition, international humanitarian law also plays an important role in the framework of refugee protection in the camps, above all guarding against armed attacks, with the separation between civilians and armed elements of the utmost importance in guaranteeing better immunity for the genuine civilians under the principle of humanitarian law and encouraging, at the same time, belligerents to find an accord for the creation of 'safe zones' free from attacks.[158]

If a temporary camp becoming a 'quasi-permanent settlement' is not generally sought as a solution by host governments, we wonder what they should do with these refugees, who often remain without any concrete hope of returning to their countries of origin, and without any solid perspective to be resettled anywhere else. Therefore, camps cannot constitute the best solution for refugees, though, if they are run in a more efficient manner and provided with better facilities, they can nevertheless constitute a good solution for refugees, forming a sort of 'enclave' in the host state justifiable on the basis of the current conditions in their country of origin. Perhaps camps would work better if more responsibilities would be given to the women, who are often the majority of the population in the camps, and are usually relegated to a very marginal role in Sub-Saharan Africa, but whose importance no one can deny. In a sense, camps could constitute a 'laboratory' for the continent where women could take effective power and show their capabilities.[159] This should occur within the framework of 'controlled' autonomy of camps, in our view not being contrary to the fact that, with time, camps could develop into new cities of the host countries, and therefore administered by the central administrative power of the host country. Until now, however, reality has taken a different path. The case of South Africa is indicative, where Zimbabweans move for the purpose of work rather than protection. A refugee-type camp would

158 Jacques, M., op. cit. note 24, pp. 231–2. In this sense, see also Henckaerts, J.-M.; Doswald-Beck, L., op. cit. note 70, rule 22, p. 68: 'The parties to the conflict must take all feasible precautions to protect the civilian population and civilian objects under their control against the effects of attacks.'

159 For a general panorama of women's life in camps, see, for instance, Maravanyika, E., 'Some issues of protection and participation of refugee women: the case of Mozambican refugee women in Zimbabwean camps', in Musalo, K., Moore, J. and Boswell, R.A., *Refugee Law and Policy: Cases and Materials*, Durham, NC: Carolina Academic Press, 1997, pp. 611–15. The author concluding her work: '[E]fforts need to be taken to facilitate the participation of women refugees in decisions and implementation of policies relevant to their survival in host countries, such as Zimbabwe. The best way this can be done is to have a participatory role through consultation and sharing of views and information on policies affecting the refugee population, particularly women refugees.' However, as J. Hyndman generally noted: '[T]hese camps, which are intended to provide asylum and uphold certain human rights, suspend other basic entitlements such as the right to work, to move freely, and to establish an independent livelihood. The discrepancy between a language of rights and the conditions of the camps is clear. Nor does this language fully address the current conditions of displacement generated by civil conflict, often occurring within state borders. The camps represent contradictory segregated spaces of ongoing displacement and assistance at once, what might also be thought of as displaced assistance.' See Hyndman, J., *Managing Displacement: Refugees and the Politics of Humanitarianism*, Minneapolis, MN: University of Minnesota Press, 2000, p. 183.

thus be unsuitable, since its occupants would be unlikely to remain there. Moreover, the UNHCR and the South African government have a mutual interest in avoiding the escalation of a mixed-migration challenge into a refugee problem.[160]

In effect, in recent decades, the tragedy has been that camps that once sustained refugees' lives are becoming the first vehicle for denying basic rights to those same refugees, such as the right to liberty and the right to security of person. The price for extending this short-term measure year by year causes frustration over non-obtainment of rights, capabilities deprived and expectations not met. A. Jamal contended that these camps have come to embody the refugee experience; to represent the content of international refugee protection, to demonstrate how badly needed new approaches for responding to refugee issues are, and the magnitude of the difficulties and challenges faced by both the organizations and governments dealing with the encamped African asylum-seekers and refugees.[161]

160 Crisp, J. and Kiragu, E., op. cit. note 9, paragraph 134, p. 24.

161 Jamal, A., 'A realistic, segmented and reinvigorated UNHCR approach to resolving protracted refugee situations', op. cit. note 1, p. 146.

5 Alleviating the plight of refugees in Sub-Saharan Africa

The role and mandate of the UNHCR

5.1 The original mandate and its further expansion

The UNHCR is a human rights agency with a specific mandate[1] and it was intentionally conceived as a non-operational UN agency.[2] As underlined in Chapter I of its Statute, the UNHCR was established to act under the authority of the UNGA in order to serve two precise functions: to protect refugees and to find a permanent solution to their plight, notably through voluntary repatriation or, alternatively, through assimilation into the host community.[3] While the UNHCR has reserved an actual control over the protection of refugees, the protection of other displaced populations is efficiently coordinated and joined with other organizations.[4]

1 Feller, E., 'Where principle and pragmatic meet: the world of UNHCR's protection work', in *Durham Law Review*, 2013 volume, 2013, p. 170.

2 Zieck, M., *The UNHCR's Worldwide Presence in the Field*, Nijmegen: Wolf Legal, 2006, p. 17. In this regard, R. Zetter noted: '[U]NHCR is not an operational agency; it coordinates and monitors relief programs, which are delivered and implemented by its operational partners, primarily NGOs and the host government, but also other intergovernmental agencies such as the WFP and the UNDP. See Zetter, R., 'International perspective on refugee assistance', in Ager, A. (ed.), *Refugees: Perspectives on the Experience of Forced Migration*, London/New York: Continuum, 1999, p. 58.

3 Chapter I, paragraph 1 of the 1950 UNHCR Statute reads: 'The United Nations High Commissioner for Refugees, acting under the authority of the General Assembly, shall assume the function of providing international protection, under the auspices of the United Nations, to refugees who fall within the scope of the present Statute and of seeking permanent solutions for the problem of refugees by assisting Governments and, subject to the approval of the Governments concerned, private organizations to facilitate the voluntary repatriation of such refugees, or their assimilation within new national communities.' In this regard, A. Suhrke and K. Newland noted: '[b]y its Statute and *raison d'être*, UNHCR is committed to defend the institution of asylum.' See Suhrke, A. and Newland, K., 'UNHCR: uphill into the future', in *International Migration Review*, vol. 35, 2001, p. 292. And, about durable solutions, M. Gottwald noted that: '[T]he ultimate aim of international protection and the UNHCR's mandate is the pursuit of durable solutions.' See Gottwald, M., 'Back to the future: the concept of "comprehensive solutions"', in *Refugee Survey Quarterly*, vol. 31, 2012, p. 101.

4 Betts, A., 'Regime complexity and international organizations: UNHCR as a challenged institution', in *Global Governance*, vol. 19, 2013, p. 74. At idem, the author clarified: 'Some

The protection provided by the UNHCR is primarily formulated in Article 8 of the 1950 UNHCR Statute, which mainly provides for non-operational measures,[5] although scholars do not unanimously agree on this point.[6] In addition, Article 8 g) disposes for the agency to be in touch with the governments of the countries concerned with the plight of refugees, while Article 16 establishes a physical presence of the agency within the border of the states as another means of protection of the refugees.[7] This latter article does not take into consideration, however, the question of how the UNHCR and the host state must proceed in order to establish an agency's representation there. In general, this is done through a Cooperation Agreement between the UNHCR and the competent authorities of the host state, which generally sets the terms and conditions under which the UNHCR shall operate as an office in the host country.[8] Nevertheless, unlike the cooperation envisaged in Article VIII of the 1969 OAU Convention,[9] the term 'cooperation' considered in the Cooperation Agreement is related to a particular place and is more specific because it determines the instruments establishing its content to be either *ratione personae* or *ratione materiae*.[10] In any case, the adoption

commentators have expressed concern that UNHCR's expanded role in protecting other displaced populations may divert resources, political attention and capacity away from refugee protection.'

5 Article 8 of the 1950 UNHCR Statute reads in full: 'The High Commissioner shall provide for the protection of refugees falling under the competence of his Office by: a) Promoting the conclusion and ratification of international conventions for the protection of refugees, supervising their application and proposing amendments thereto; b) Promoting through special agreements with Governments the execution of any measures calculated to improve the situation of refugees and to reduce the number requiring protection; c) Assisting governmental and private efforts to promote voluntary repatriation or assimilation within new national communities; d) Promoting the admission of refugees, not excluding those in the most destitute categories, to the territories of States; e) Endeavoring to obtain permission for refugees to transfer their assets and especially those necessary for their resettlement; f) Obtaining from Governments information concerning the number and conditions of refugees in their territories and the laws and regulations concerning them; g) Keeping in close touch with the Governments and inter-governmental organizations concerned; h) Establishing contact in such manner as he may think best with private organizations dealing with refugee questions; i) Facilitating the co-ordination of the efforts of private organizations concerned with the welfare of refugees.'

6 For an opposite opinion, see, for instance, Lewis, C., 'UNHCR's contribution to the development of international refugee law: its foundations and evolution', in *International Journal of Refugee Law*, vol. 17, 2005, p. 69: '[T]he General Assembly assigned the office of the UNHCR, an organization with operational responsibilities for refugees. [. . .]'

7 Article 16 of the 1950 Statute reads: 'The High Commissioner shall consult the Government of the countries of residence of refugees as to the need for appointing representatives therein. In any country recognizing such need, there may be appointed a representative approved by the Government of that country. Subject to the foregoing, the same representative may serve in more than one country.'

8 Zieck, M., *UNHCR's Worldwide Presence in the Field*, op. cit. note 2, p. 53.

9 In detail, Article VIII of the 1969 OAU Convention reads: '1) Member States shall co-operate with the Office of the United Nations High Commissioner for Refugees. 2) The present Convention shall be the effective regional complement in Africa of the 1951 United Nations Convention on the Status of Refugees.'

10 Zieck, M., *UNHCR's Worldwide Presence in the Field*, op. cit. note 2, p. 248.

of the 1969 OAU Convention allowed the UNHCR to take a huge step forward in order to undertake group-based determination of refugee status.[11]

While the UNHCR took the initiative to establish an office in several Sub-Saharan African countries, such as Djibouti, DRC, Gabon, and Togo, in other cases, for instance in South Africa, it has been the host state itself which has extended an invitation to the UNHCR to open an office in that country.[12]

It has also occurred that the UNHCR has needed to open additional offices in a host country in Sub-Saharan Africa, and the establishment of these offices was regulated in special agreements in cooperation with the local authorities concerned, these last agreements distinct from the Cooperation Agreement, which facilitated the opening of the first UNHCR office. One typical example of this kind of special agreement was the Memorandum of Understanding (MoU) between the UNHCR and the Zambian government in Lusaka, which was stipulated for the repatriation and reintegration[13] of the Angolan refugees in June 1995. In effect, Article 13 of the MoU read:

> In order to fulfill more effectively its responsibilities under this MoU, the UNHCR may, whenever necessary, and after exchanging ideas with the Government open Field Offices in the border posts or near the same, the reception centers, transit centers or final destination places.[14]

As we have partially mentioned above, in our opinion, another significant remark to make regarding the activities of the UNHCR is that, originally, its mandate did not include the provision of material assistance to refugees, nor did it include IDPs as subjects to be protected.[15] It was through the terms of the UNGA resolution No. 1672 (XVI) of 1961 that the mandate *rationae materiae* of the

11 Cuellar, M.-F., 'Refugee security, and the organizational logic of legal mandates', in *Georgetown Journal of International Law*, vol. 37, 2005–6, p. 665.

12 Zieck, M., *UNHCR's Worldwide Presence in the Field*, op. cit. note 2, pp. 162–3. Specifically about the situation in South Africa, the author noted that: 'Specific needs [for the refugees in that country] are [. . .] mentioned in the agreements which were concluded with South Africa in 1991 and 1993: initially the reason for a UNHCR presence was related to the voluntary repatriation of South African returnees, and subsequently extended, in 1993, to comprise improving the situation of asylum-seekers and refugees in South Africa.'

13 In this regard, E. Feller contended: 'Rights are a very important barometer when it comes to UNHCR's work in countries of origin particularly in the context of return and reintegration. It is the extent to which individuals are able to exercise their rights upon return that determines the viability and sustainability of return. With this in mind UNHCR carries out protection monitoring in countries of return and regularly partners in this regard with national human rights institutions.' See Feller, E., 'Where principle and pragmatic meet: the world of UNHCR's protection work', op. cit. note 1, p. 205.

14 UNHCR, Government of Angola, MoU between the Government of the Republic of Angola and the United Nations High Commissioner for Refugees for the voluntary repatriation and reintegration of Angolan Refugees, 14 June 1995.

15 Loescher, G., Betts, A. and Milner, J.H.S., *The United Nations High Commissioner for Refugees (UNHCR): The Politics and Practice of Refugee Protection into the Twenty-First Century*, London/New York: Routledge, 2008, p. 13.

UNHCR was expanded to also include the possibility of facilitating the practical re-establishment of the refugees in their own country,[16] although the 1950 UNHCR Statute already contemplated this opportunity as an 'additional' activity of the UNHCR, in its Article 9.[17]

Finally, it was only in 2003 that UNGA confirmed the UNHCR as a programme of the UN 'until the refugee problem is solved',[18] while for more than 50 years, UNGA had only granted limited extensions to the UNHCR's mandate since its creation in 1949.[19]

5.2 A historical analysis of the role of the UNHCR

The history of the UNHCR on the African continent is quite long and complex if we imagine that, for instance, in the 1960s the UNHCR believed that in order to give effect to the refugee assistance programmes in the region, it needed to be part of a larger development programme there.[20] The following decade saw the UNHCR's role in Sub-Saharan Africa shift from an agency mostly focusing on the promotion of international refugee instruments and legal protection to an

16 UNGA, Refugees in Morocco and Tunisia, 18 December 1961, resolution No. 1672 (XVI), paragraph b): '[The UNGA] requests to the United Nations High Commissioner for Refugees to: use the means at his disposal to assist in the orderly return of those refugees to their homes and consider the possibility, when necessary, of facilitating their resettlement in their homeland as soon as circumstances permit.'

17 Article 9 of the 1950 Statute read: 'The High Commissioner shall engage in [. . .] additional activities, including repatriation and resettlement, as the General Assembly may determine, within the limits of the resources placed at his disposal.'

18 UNGA, Implementing actions proposed by the United Nations High Commissioner for Refugees to strengthen the capacity of his office to carry his mandate, 22 December 2003, resolution No. A/RES/58/153, paragraph 9: '[The UNGA] decides to remove the temporal limitation on the continuation of the Office of the High Commissioner contained in its resolution 57/186 and to continue the Office until the refugee problem is solved.' See, therefore, UNGA, Continuation of the office of the United Nations High Commissioner for Refugees, 18 December 2002, resolution No. A/RES/57/184, paragraphs 1–3: '1) decides to continue the Office of the United Nations High Commissioner for Refugees for a further period of five years from 1 January 2004; 2) also decides to review, not later than at its sixty-second session, the arrangements for the Office of the High Commissioner with a view to determining whether the Office should be continued beyond 31 December 2008; 3) Further decides to consider at its fifty-eighth session proposals of the High Commissioner on the basis of his report, prepared in consultation with the Executive Committee of the Program of the United Nations High Commissioner for Refugees and the Secretary-General, regarding the strengthening of the capacity of the Office to carry out its mandate.'

19 UNGA, Refugees and stateless persons, 3 December 1949, No. 319 (IV), paragraphs 1, 5: '1) [The UNGA] decides to establish, as of 1 January 1951, a High Commissioner's Office for Refugees in accordance with the provisions of the annex to the present resolution to discharge the functions enumerated therein and such other functions as the General Assembly may from time to time confer upon it [. . .]; 5) decides to review, not later than at its eighth regular session, the arrangements for the High Commissioner's Office for Refugees with a view of determining whether the office should be continued beyond 31 December 1953.'

20 Loescher, G., Betts, A. and Milner, J.H.S., op. cit. note 15, p. 27.

agency devoted to humanitarian assistance.[21] Over the last few decades, the UNHCR has therefore evolved into a major field-based organization in Sub-Saharan Africa.[22] In effect, as it happened with the repatriation of Sudanese in 1973 where the High Commissioner intervened personally,[23] the UNGA requested that the UNHCR not only handle the return of refugees to the countries of origin, but also contribute to their resettlement and reintegration in the socio-economic fabric.[24] This expansion of the UNHCR's functions soon became common practice and was used also in the repatriation of Mozambicans and Angolans in 1975–1976, with the UNHCR acting as the agency that coordinated the UN-wide humanitarian programmes at that time.[25] On this occasion, the role of the UNHCR was even more important if we consider that South Africa, where the majority of returnees lived before repatriation, was not part of any international or regional legal instrument dealing with the protection of refugees during that period, nor was there a municipal law specifically regulating the position and the treatment of refugees in the country.[26] The reader can now begin to fathom how terrible the persecution suffered by Angolans and Mozambicans during the colonial period must have been for those who were compelled to seek refuge in South Africa, which was under an *apartheid* regime at the time.

The situation of refugees across Sub-Saharan Africa was protracted and seemed to become insoluble during the 1980s, when the majority of refugees were fleeing from regional conflicts and were accommodated in camps. The failure of the

21 Aga Khan, S., 'Legal problems relating to refugees and displaced persons', in *Collected Courses of The Hague Academy of International Law*, vol. 149, 1976 (I), p. 304: 'In providing assistance to these various groups [from Ethiopia and Burundi in the early 1970s], largely of rural background – the UNHCR has been concerned both with immediate needs and with longer term solutions. [. . .] Rural settlements projects have been elaborated to enable the refugees to attain self-sufficiency within their countries of asylum.' In this regard, E. Feller clearly affirmed that: 'Action in support of refugees is essentially humanitarian, and has to be able to rely on confidence-building and neutrality, which can make the difference when it comes to access to beneficiaries, success or failure of interventions on their behalf, and the security of agency staff.' See Feller, E., 'Where principle and pragmatic meet: the world of UNHCR's protection work', op. cit. note 1, p. 213.

22 Vernon, A., 'UNHCR and the current security environment', in *Refugee Survey Quarterly*, vol. 24, 2004, p. 148. As M. Zieck noted, partially quoting a 1994 UNHCR Note on International Protection: 'The importance of field offices for the work of UNHCR is still worded in terms of an "indispensable complement to protection activities in the legal and political domains" and, in strikingly similar terms to those used by the first High Commissioner with respect to the UNHCR's branch offices, are characterized as a "tool of crucial importance".' See Zieck, M., *UNHCR's Worldwide Presence in the Field*, op. cit. note 2, p. 41.

23 Cuellar, M.-F., op. cit. note 11, p. 667.

24 UNGA, Assistance to Sudanese refugees returning from abroad, 12 December 1972, resolution No. A/RES/2958 (XXVII), paragraph 2: '[The UNGA] commends the United Nations High Commissioner for Refugees for his efficient role in the coordination of relief and resettlement operations of refugees and other displaced persons.'

25 Loescher, G., Betts, A. and Milner, J.H.S., op. cit. note 15, p. 31.

26 Faris, J.A., 'The Angolan refugees and South Africa', in *South African Yearbook of International Law*, vol. 2, 1976, p. 177.

international community to formulate long-term solutions to this dilemma was further exacerbated by armed groups establishing themselves in the camps throughout the entire region. In effect, N. Bwakira openly explained that, in his opinion, during that period there was a strategic interest by African countries in granting asylum, but no interest in looking for durable solutions for African refugees. This strong affirmation, however, has not further been explained by the author.[27]

Also the possibility of resettling refugees in other African countries, a solution in vogue in the 1970s, lost a lot of its momentum a decade later due to its non-sustainability, having reached too large a dimension to meet the basic needs of the refugees concerned.[28]

However, taking advantage of its growing influence in the UNGA, the UNHCR was able to push for additional resources for host states in Africa in the early 1980s. In November 1980 the UNGA passed a resolution recognizing the heavy burden placed on African countries as a consequence of the increased number of refugees hosted on the continent. This resolution, calling for the International Conference on Assistance to Refugees in Africa (ICARA) I to be held in the following year, also requested that the UNHCR keep the refugee situation on the continent under observation in order to ensure the necessary assistance was available.[29]

Unfortunately, the three main objectives of the ICARA I – to focus world attention on Africa's refugee problems, to mobilize additional resources towards the refugees' plight as well as to assist host countries through the application of these additional resources[30] – fell short of meeting the expectations of the organizers. This could have been predicted, considering, for instance, the very little money pledged by donors to host states considered most in need, such as those in the Horn of Africa.[31] This was perceived as a loss for the UNHCR, considering the great focus the conference put on burden-sharing as a veritable pivot of refugee protection in Sub-Saharan Africa.[32]

27 Bwakira, N., 'From Nansen to Ogata: the UNHCR's role in a changing world', in *International Migration Review*, vol. 35, 2001, p. 279.

28 Loescher, G., Betts, A. and Milner, J.H.S., op. cit. note 15, pp. 35–9.

29 UNGA, International Conference on Assistance to Refugees in Africa, 25 November 1980, No. A/RES/35/42. See, in detail: paragraphs 1, 3, 10: '1) [The UNGA] notes with profound regret that the international community has not given sufficient attention to the plight of refugees in Africa [. . .]; 3) approves the report of the Secretary-General calling for an international conference to mobilize assistance for refugees in Africa [. . .]; 10) requests the High Commissioner [. . .] to keep under constant review the situation of refugees in Africa in order to ensure maximum international assistance on a global basis.'

30 UNGA, International Conference on Assistance to Refugees in Africa, 25 November 1980, No. A/RES/35/42.

31 Loescher, G., Betts, A. and Milner, J.H.S., op. cit. note 15, p. 40.

32 Betts, A., *Protection by Persuasion: International Cooperation in the Refugee Regime*, Ithaca, NY/London: Cornell University Press, 2009, p. 56. At idem, the author explained: 'The African states were invited by UNHCR to compile project proposals with the technical assistance of UNHCR, which would then be submitted to the conference. The intention was that the projects would focus on supporting long-term infrastructural development that could simultaneously compensate host

The lack of results of ICARA I and the persistent, unsatisfactory situation of refugees in the region, gave the organization the impetus to have ICARA II, in order to provide the national economies of African countries with the necessary assistance to face the increasing number of refugees on the continent.[33] However, this conference – which focused mostly on durable solutions for the plight of African refugees[34] – similarly had little success because, as the UNHCR conceived both ICARA I and ICARA II as one-off pledging conferences rather than as a political process, it was quite impossible for the agency to meet the different expectancies of African states. African states were inclined to focus on burden-sharing and compensation for host states, while donor states were more inclined to focus on durable solutions for refugees.[35]

Until the end of the 1980s, Cold War politics paralyzed initiatives to break the deadlock arrived at in regional conflicts in Sub-Saharan Africa and, therefore, most refugees remained in the camps for the entire decade. The obvious consequence of this situation was that the UNHCR's major efforts were concentrated in allocating funds to take care of the protracted refugee situations on the continent as well as funding new emergencies, such as the ones in Mozambique and Somalia – the latter having hosted approximately two million refugees in the early 1980s[36] – along with cases of mass returns, such as the ones

communities while improving refugee protection and the prospects for durable solutions. Bearing in mind the neglect of the increasingly protracted rural and border settlements, much of the focus was on meeting basic needs such as food provisions.'

33 UNGA, International Conference on Assistance to Refugees in Africa, 18 December 1982, No. A/RES/37/197. See, in particular, preamble and paragraph 5 c): '[The UNGA] noting that the Conference [ICARA I] succeeded in raising world consciousness with regard to the plight of refugees and returnees in Africa, as well as the problems of asylum countries, the overall results of the Conference in terms of financial and material assistance have fallen short of the expectations of African countries' [. . .]; '5 c) [The UNGA] requests the Secretary-General [. . .] to convene at Geneva in 1984 a second International Conference on Assistance to Refugees in Africa to consider the impact imposed on the national economies of the African countries concerned and to provide them with the required assistance to strengthen their social and economic infrastructure to cope with the burden of dealing with large numbers of refugees and returnees.'

34 Betts, A., *Protection by Persuasion: International Cooperation in the Refugee Regime*, op. cit. note 32, p. 61.

35 Loescher, G., Betts, A. and Milner, J.H.S., op. cit. note 15, p. 41. In this regard, A. Betts noted: 'Most donors had regarded ICARA I as a major commitment and were highly suspicious of African motives for convening a second conference. Donors were therefore no longer prepared to commit to providing significant funding unless the projects were clearly linked to durable solutions.' See Betts, A., *Protection by Persuasion: International Cooperation in the Refugee Regime*, op. cit. note 32, p. 64. In this regard, see also Betts, A., Loescher, G. and Milner, J., *UNHCR: The Politics and Practice of Refugee Protection*, 2nd edn, London/New York: Routledge, 2012, p. 43: 'ICARA II ultimately had little lasting practical legacy and the additional financial contributions it raised were insignificant relative to the growing needs of African host countries. As with the previous conference, the cause of failure was primarily a North-South polarization in expectations and interests, and a North-South division in the understanding of the purpose of the conference.'

36 Cuellar, M.-F., op. cit. note 11, p. 670.

having occurred in Namibia.[37] Nevertheless, eventually, the amount of funds allocated in these African protracted refugee situations was relatively little compared to the necessities.[38]

These situations ended up bringing the agency to a serious deficit and showed how dependent it was on voluntary contributions in order to carry out the programmes it had established.[39]

At the end of the Cold War, the agency's approach in Sub-Saharan Africa experienced a sharp change: at that point, 'repatriation' – a concept that we will explore more in detail in Chapter 8 of this work – became the new rallying cry in the region. Namibia, Ethiopia and Mozambique were the main sites of these repatriations. However, as the UNHCR also needed to face new emergencies, in Liberia, Rwanda and Sierra Leone, for example, the agency started to consider less demanding standards for repatriation. During this period, repatriations took place under an assessment made almost exclusively by the UNHCR, which ascertained whether the conditions for repatriation were favourable or not.[40] Moreover, as a good number of refugees were still repatriating under the conditions of instability of the country to where they were being repatriated, the UNHCR facilitated their reintegration into their countries of origin, which could have been easier if the agency could also contribute to the development of those countries, often completely devastated by years of civil or international wars. That is why the UNHCR started to imbue its work in the region with development aims, first promoting a reintegration that, at a second stage, should also be supported by international development agencies. In this manoeuvre, the UNHCR reoriented itself, ceasing to be a 'refugee-specific' agency, and becoming more 'homeland-oriented'.[41]

37 In this regard, R. Zetter noted: 'The second [major] activity [of the UNHCR] is [. . .] fundraising. UNHCR has only modest permanent funding and what is available is used for its general programs and administrative activities; but even the budget for this sector substantially comprises pledges and donations rather than core funding from the UN regular budget.' See Zetter, R., 'International perspective on refugee assistance', op. cit. note 2, p. 58.

38 Crisp, J. and Slaughter, A., 'A surrogate state? The role of UNHCR in protracted refugee situations', in UNHCR, *New Issues in Refugee Research*, research paper No. 168, 2009, p. 6.

39 Crisp, J., 'Mind the gap! The UNHCR, humanitarian assistance and the development process', in *International Migration Review*, vol. 35, 2001, pp. 171–2.

40 Barnett, M., 'Humanitarianism with a sovereign face: UNHCR in the global undertow', in *International Migration Review*, vol. 35, 2001, p. 261.

41 Crisp, J., 'Mind the gap! UNHCR, humanitarian assistance and the development process', op. cit. note 39, p. 175. In this period it is worth noting also the new policy undertaken by the UNHCR and defined as 'preventive protection'. As quoted by J. Hyndman: 'UNHCR originally defined "preventive protection" as the establishment or undertaking of specific activities inside the country of origin so that people no longer feel compelled to cross borders in search of protection and assistance. In this sense, for instance, action on behalf of the internally displaced can be defined as preventive protection, although the primary motive may be to addressing a genuine gap in protection rather than to avert outflow. Preventive protection in this sense may also include the establishment of "safety zones" or "safe areas" inside the country of origin where protection may be sought. It relates therefore to the protection of nationals in their own country.' See UNHCR,

However, the refugee plight having involved too many individuals, it became a domestic security concern for African countries, and the UNHCR had the possibility to change its role in Sub-Saharan Africa again, to one more frequently involved in intra-state conflicts, and cooperating with the UN in providing assistance to displaced populations within their own home countries. In addition, the UNHCR also showed a greater interest in preventing refugee flows, finding solutions to the political problems that result in mass flight. By emphasizing the responsibility of refugees' countries of origin, and by considering the mass-influx of refugees as a threat to regional peace and security, the UNHCR legitimized both its own action in order to make repatriation easier and UN and state interventions that sought to solve the causes of flight within the refugees' region of origin.[42]

During the same period, in the 1980s and early 1990s, the emergence of a new international security environment changed the way the UNHCR operated in Sub-Saharan Africa. The UNHCR started working more in refugees' countries of origin, in order to reduce the likelihood of massive refugee flows across borders. Furthermore, the UNHCR was also frequently asked to take part in integrated peacekeeping operations, like in Namibia or Mozambique, involving cooperation with political and military actors.[43] As a consequence, the UNHCR became a veritable humanitarian agency, securing more generous funding for its operations, although the accent was always put on the prevention of flight-causing factors more than on their reparation.[44]

Nonetheless the situation in Sub-Saharan Africa rapidly changed again, and the agency needed to face situations in which Africa felt let down by the

Report of the UNHCR working group on international protection, 6 July 1992, quoted in Hyndman, J., *Managing Displacement: Refugees and the Politics of Humanitarianism*, Minneapolis, MN: University of Minnesota Press, 2000, pp. 17–18. In this regard, at ibid., p. 28, the author concluded: 'Preventive protection is an expression of the more powerful states' desire to avoid the legal obligations of refugees and to save non refugee taxpayers' money in their home territories. It speaks to a desire for a multilateral, or UN, solution to displacement in order to avoid incurring the perceived expense of refugees, both economically and politically, within the precarious and declining welfare states of donor governments.' For the definition of 'safe area', see also *supra*, Chapter 2.

42 Loescher, G., Betts, A. and Milner, J.H.S., op. cit. note 15, pp. 53–4.

43 Zieck, M., *UNHCR's Worldwide Presence in the Field*, op. cit. note 2, pp. 310–11, where the author noted: 'UNHCR may also itself form a constituent part of a peace-keeping operation as its repatriation or humanitarian component either to discharge its usual statutory tasks or additional ones when it is called upon to act as the lead agency in the provision of humanitarian assistance to those, such as internally displaced persons, who would otherwise be considered to fall outside its mandate.'

44 UNGA, Report of the Secretary-General on the work of the Organization, 31 August 1999, document No. A/54/1, supplement No. 1, paragraph 21: 'Taking prevention more seriously will help to ensure that there are fewer wars and less consequential disasters to cope with in the first place. There is a clear financial incentive for doing so. [. . .] The Carnegie researchers argued that most of these costs could have been saved if greater attention had been paid to prevention.' For a general vision of the role of UNHCR as a humanitarian actor see UNHCR, *The State of the World's Refugees 1997: A Humanitarian Agenda*, Oxford: Oxford University Press, 1997.

international community, such as the Rwandan genocide or the militarization of the refugee camps in DRC in the mid-1990s. The UNHCR confronted these situations practically alone, although the plight of the refugees on the continent needed significant involvement of the international community as well, in order to ameliorate their condition. However, the UNHCR recognized that in situations of mass-influx, as occurred in the camps of DRC at that time, '[b]lanket protection was preferable to *refoulement*'.[45] But such an approach made it clear that, in order to better protect refugees, it was necessary to complete an accurate RSD, preferably with the aid of other actors, like the local authorities. Unfortunately, such aid seemed to be completely lacking at that time.[46] At the same time, the management of the Great Lakes crisis was perceived as a fiasco both within the UNHCR and by observers from without, with most criticism centring around the fact that the UN agency seemed to focus more attention on disaster relief and material assistance than on the security of the refugees in the camps.[47] However, and in spite of its weaknesses, the UNHCR constitutes one of the few viable ways through which refugee security issues in Sub-Saharan Africa can be alleviated – even if only partially – and obtain larger world attention.[48]

It was in that period in Sub-Saharan Africa, that the name of the UNHCR started to be coupled with 'human security'. It was particularly difficult for the UNHCR to impose this new idea, which lacks any veritable definition,[49] in the region. According to this concept, the UNHCR began to place the individual, rather than the state, at the centre of its attention, stressing the fact that the sovereignty of states, not absolute like before, should be respected on the condition that human beings have access to basic human rights and development. Through the use of the notion of 'human security', the UNHCR wanted to show that the

45 Fitzpatrick, J., 'Flight from asylum: trends toward temporary "refuge" and local responses to forced migration', in *Virginia Journal of International Law*, vol. 35, 1994–1995, p. 42.

46 Wagner, K., 'UNHCR's involvement in the Great Lakes refugee crisis', in *Pace International Law Review*, vol. 21, 2009, p. 378.

47 Cuellar, M.-F., op. cit. note 11, pp. 674 and 688. In this regard, the author explained at ibid., pp. 695–6: '[T]he agency's strategic choice to focus on material assistance might seem less troubling if it simply served as a temporary response to ephemeral political constraints, thereby allowing future agency leaders the chance to forcefully advocate for refugee security while continuing to provide material assistance through increasingly large contributions from, for example, domestic publics rather than governments.'

48 Ibid., p. 708.

49 Edwards, A., 'Human security and the rights of refugees: transcending territorial and disciplinary borders', in *Michigan Journal of International Law*, vol. 30, 2009, p. 778. In this regard, A. Suhrke noted that: 'As the concept "human security" has evolved in the last decade, it has at least two distinct meanings: 1) A broad, nearly encompassing concept that links a wide range of developmental and physical security dimensions [. . .] 2) A specific policy agenda promoted by a network of states or international organizations. [. . .] The idea of "human security" was extracted from a stock of ideas that had become increasingly salient towards the end of the twentieth century.' See Suhrke, A., 'Human security and the protection of refugees', in Newman, E. and Van Selm, J. (eds), *Refugees and Forced Displacement: International Security, Human Vulnerability, and the State*, Tokyo/New York/Paris: United Nations University Press, 2003, p. 99.

real security of states and the international community could only be achieved by providing security for people.[50] Legally speaking, and apart from the lack of a real specific definition, the other problem linked to this concept is that its non-binding nature may weaken pre-existent legal guarantees, particularly concerning human rights provisions.[51] However, the concept of human security has been pushed too far in Sub-Saharan Africa, given that it generally underestimates the consequences of hosting a huge number of refugees. In addition, if this concept considers that refugees are a product of conflicts, it also ignores that conflicts can break out because of refugees.[52]

At the dawn of the twenty-first century, under the sign of 'Convention Plus', the UNHCR tried to formulate a CPA to find a solution to certain longstanding refugee situations in Sub-Saharan Africa. The 'Convention Plus' initiative was launched and coordinated by the UNHCR, and its objective was the promotion of refugees' rights through the UNHCR's negotiation with states and other international partners in order to reach stricter commitments on several features, such as: reinstallation as an instrument of protection; an increase in development aid; as well as to make clarifications on state responsibility in case of irregular secondary movement.[53]

The pilot case for the launching of the 'Convention Plus' initiative concerned the Somali refugees in Djibouti, Ethiopia and Kenya and their access to durable

50 Loescher, G., Betts, A. and Milner, J.H.S., op. cit. note 15, pp. 56–7.

51 Edwards, A., 'Human security and the rights of refugees: transcending territorial and disciplinary borders', op. cit. note 49, p. 782. At ibid., the author clarified: 'This is tied to the vagueness of the concept, which is said to provide scope to states to avoid any legal imperatives to act. [. . .] This concern over legality should be taken seriously. However, it can be overstated by those who assume that it is a legal character of human rights that brings about their implementation and ensures the protection and security of individuals.'

52 Adelman, H., 'From refugee to forced migration: the UNHCR and human security', in *International Migration Review*, vol. 35, 2001, p. 17.

53 In this regard, see UNHCR, Convention Plus at a glance, 1 June 2005, pp. 1–2: 'UNHCR will pursue generic multilateral agreements to tackle three priority challenges: The strategic use of resettlement as a tool of protection, a durable solution and a tangible form of burden-sharing; More effective targeting of development assistance to support durable solutions for refugees, whether in countries of asylum or upon return home; and clarification of the responsibilities of States in the event of irregular secondary movements of refugees and asylum-seekers, that is, when refugees and asylum-seekers move, in an irregular manner, from an initial country of refuge to another country. These generic agreements will set out shared understandings and commitments which can be relied upon and incorporated into situation-specific multilateral agreements designed to resolve a particular refugee situation. The Convention Plus effort will also promote and support the development of these agreements.' In addition, A. Betts noted: 'Convention Plus explicitly attempted to address areas of refugee protection that were inadequately dealt with in the 1951 Convention and its 1967 Protocol. In particular, it attempted to develop a normative framework for a range of old and new problems.' See Betts, A., *Protection by Persuasion: International Cooperation in the Refugee Regime*, op. cit. note 32, p. 146. The problems were identified by A. Betts: '[t]o increase the quantity and predictability of burden sharing [. . .] [t]o channel this commitment into new approaches to addressing protracted refugee situations.' See ibid., pp. 146–7.

solutions in those countries. Somalis were chosen particularly because the project donors – mostly European – at the beginning feared an increasing number of Somali refugees moving to Europe. However, the plan was ultimately never launched, because of the little interest shown by donors, although the UNHCR tried to raise their interest by highlighting its commitment to protection and durable solutions in the place of origin.[54]

In effect, the entire initiative was of no significant success and this was due mainly to a number of reasons deriving from the dynamic between the developed north and the developing – or underdeveloped – south.[55]

In the first years of the twenty-first century, however, the role of the UNHCR in Sub-Saharan Africa has also been characterized by encouraging self-reliance as an alternative scheme of protection, pending durable solutions. While the UNHCR supported these kinds of projects, notably in Uganda and Zambia, most states in the region were sceptical about this solution, considering it an indirect attempt to locally integrate refugees.[56] This situation should be considered in light of the extension of the mandate of the agency to also deal with IDPs. The extension was formally adopted by the Inter-Agency Standing Committee (IASC)[57] in 2005, and attributed to the UNHCR the role of protecting IDPs as well,[58]

54 Loescher, G., Betts, A. and Milner, J.H.S., op. cit. note 54, pp. 64–5.

55 These reasons, among others, were: 'First, the initiative took place in a low-trust environment in which, based on past experiences, North and South were mutually suspicious. [. . .] Second, the suspicions of the South were exacerbated by the feeling that it was being marginalized within the debate. [. . .] Third, the Convention Plus was perceived by Southern states as a vehicle of Northern hegemony. [. . .] [S]outhern requests were largely ignored. For example, the request by African states for a framework of basic principles of burden-sharing was sidelined.' See Betts, A., *Protection by Persuasion: International Cooperation in the Refugee Regime*, op. cit. note 32, pp. 152–4.

56 Loescher, G., Betts, A. and Milner, J.H.S., op. cit. note 15, p. 66.

57 'The Inter-Agency Standing Committee is a unique inter-agency forum for coordination, policy development and decision-making involving the key UN and non-UN humanitarian partners. The IASC was established in June 1992 in response to UNGA resolution No. 46/182 on the strengthening of humanitarian assistance. UNGA resolution No. 48/57 affirmed its role as the primary mechanism for inter-agency coordination of humanitarian assistance.' Information available at: www.humanitarianinfo.org/iasc/pageloader.aspx?page=content-about-default, accessed 30 September 2014.

58 UNHCR, UNHCR's Role in IASC humanitarian reform initiatives and in the strengthening of the inter-agency collaborative response to Internally Displaced Persons situations, 20 September 2005, pp. 2, 5: 'At the 2005 March Standing Committee, the Assistant High Commissioner addressed the IDP issue and delivery gaps, commenting that UNHCR had a "predisposition" to deal with IDPs provided it is at the request of and in collaboration with our UN and other humanitarian partners. Given UNHCR's unique expertise in the protection sphere as well as with issues related to shelter and camp management/coordination matters, the AHC stressed that UNHCR had a contribution to make. [. . .] UNHCR is likely to be the agreed lead agency in the three areas in which it has already chaired the preparatory working groups over the summer, i.e. protection, camp coordination and management, and emergency shelter. Like other prospective "lead agencies", UNHCR is carefully considering the resource and staffing implications; it furthermore intends to consult with its governing body on the optimal and most practical arrangements through which it can deliver. UNHCR is acutely aware of the size of the challenge offered to it and to its sister agencies by the ERC, and of the fact that this challenge involves a

although the UNHCR occasionally already had the responsibility of protecting IDPs in the region, for instance, in Sudan in 1972[59] or in Angola, Guinea Bissau and Mozambique in 1974.[60] Since the early 1990s, the UNGA also encouraged the UNHCR to become involved in IDP issues more broadly.[61] In effect, in several situations like Angola and Mozambique, where IDPs outnumbered repatriating refugees, it would have appeared a bit contradictory to launch a reintegration programme for returnees if the IDPs still remained without roots.[62] The extended mandate found an application in Sub-Saharan Africa more or less immediately, considering the eruption of violence in Darfur in early 2003, with more than 200,000 people asking for asylum in Chad and over 1.6 million IDPs remaining in Sudan.[63]

In any event, also at the dawn of the twenty-first century, the UNHCR faced other typical protection-related challenges, which sometimes required also taking the security of its own staff into consideration, as happened in Liberia in 2003, where the UNHCR had been working in very difficult conditions because it not only needed to provide support for emergency repatriation of Sierra Leonean refugees from Liberia, but the UNHCR personnel who were to undertake this task were compelled to flee Monrovia, which had been taken over by rebels. However, the security of the UNHCR staff in the field in this instance should have been assured under the responsibility of the host state, as it did not happen in Guinea in September 2000, where national authorities fomented the discontent of the local population against refugees and UNHCR personnel, this latter 'guilty' of favouring the well-being of the refugees who ended up having a higher quality of life than the nationals. Hostilities against UNHCR staff obliged the headquarters of the agency to constitute a task force on staff security.[64]

category of beneficiaries whose needs could compete with UNHCR's priority focus on refugees and other persons in need of international protection. Although the proposed new responsibilities would be within the letter and the spirit of previous policy directives and guidelines from the General Assembly and ExCom on involvement in IDP situations, for the first time UNHCR, like other agencies, would be held accountable, for specific sectors and within the humanitarian coordination system, for delivery on a permanent and global basis (albeit one which would be reached in incremental steps).'

59 UNGA, Assistance to Sudanese refugees returning from abroad, 12 December 1972, No. A/RES/2958 (XXVII), paragraph 2: '[The UNGA] commends the United Nations High Commissioner for Refugees for his efficient role in the coordination of relief and resettlement operations of refugees and *other displaced persons*.' Emphasis added.

60 Loescher, G., Betts, A. and Milner, J.H.S., op. cit. note 15, p. 106.

61 UNGA, Office of the United Nations High Commissioner for Refugees, 20 December 1993, No. A/RES/48/116, paragraph 12: '[The UNGA] reaffirms its support for the High Commissioner's efforts, on the basis of specific requests from the Secretary-General or the competent principal organs of the United Nations and with the consent of the concerned State, and taking into account the complementarities of the mandates and expertise of other relevant organizations, to provide humanitarian assistance and protection to persons displaced within their own country in specific situations calling for the Office's particular expertise, especially where such efforts could contribute to the prevention or solution of refugee problems.'

62 Bwakira, N., op. cit. note 27, p. 281.

63 Loescher, G., Betts, A. and Milner, J.H.S., op. cit. note 15, p. 68.

64 Zieck, M., *UNHCR's Worldwide Presence in the Field*, op. cit. note 2, pp. 233–7.

The UNHCR *in loco* has not always been 100 per cent sympathetic towards refugees. For instance, on 1 June 1994 Somali refugees, 'accused' by nationals of benefiting from preferential treatment by the UNHCR,[65] were removed from the UNHCR headquarters in Lilongwe, Malawi, with the consent of the agency's authorities there, who had given permission to local police to enter the seat of the agency.[66] It is interesting to note how in Malawi the UNHCR has been given a free hand to local authorities to oversee the practical administration of the local refugee act since 2005[67] through the establishment of a Refugee Status Determination Unit, acting under direct supervision of agency authorities within the country.[68] However, people arriving from the Horn of Africa are usually not interested in seeking asylum in Malawi, considering it not to represent their ideal, final destination – South Africa.[69]

In effect, national authorities in several countries in the Sub-Saharan Africa have delegated the task of undertaking RSD of asylum-seekers to the UNHCR. In these cases the UNHCR sometimes works via national institutions while in others it acts alone.

In many more cases the protection provided by the UNHCR was also physically provided to refugees in their own compounds, in the event that the country of asylum was found to be unsafe. In 2003, almost 200 Sudanese, fleeing a wave of violence in an Ethiopian camp, found refuge in the UNHCR staff compounds. That year, the same thing happened to several Sierra Leonean refugees, escaping violence in a camp in Liberia and seeking 'refuge' in the UNHCR building, and to the 1,000 Liberians in the Ivory Coast that the local population had accused of backing Ivorian rebels.[70]

65 Nkhoma, T.S., 'The institution of asylum in Malawi and international refugee law: a review of the 1989 Refugee Act', in *Malawi Law Journal*, vol. 4, 2010, p. 100: 'However, with the advent of the new refugees from other countries [among them: Somalia] [we assisted to a] growing public resentment in Malawi that UNHCR was giving such support to refugees that they were accused of sustaining lifestyles unattainable by many local Malawians.'

66 Zieck, M., *UNHCR's Worldwide Presence in the Field*, op. cit. note 2, p. 171.

67 Malawi, Refugee Act, 8 May 1989. Quoting B. Rutinwa, T.S. Nkhoma noted that the Malawian Refugee Act: '[i]s perhaps more notable for what it did not contain than what it provided for.' See Nkhoma, T.S., op. cit. note 65, p. 109. In this regard, as also L.D. Mvula noted: '[I]t is clear that the main challenge for refugee rights in Malawi is the unfavorable legal framework for the implementation of the rights of refugees in the country. The Refugee Act, while providing a broad definition of a refugee, does not address the basic rights that refugees have under international law. According to the UNHCR, it is outdated and insufficient to cater for the refugee population in Malawi. Secondly, the reservations entered to the 1951 Convention have also impeded efforts to implement local integration activities for refugees including wage earning employment and freedom of movement.' See Mvula, L.D., 'Refugee status determination and rights in Malawi', paper presented at the Refugee Studies Centre Workshop Discussion on RSD and rights in Southern and East Africa, no date available, p. 14, pdf document available at: www.rsc.ox.ac.uk/files/publications/other/dp-rsd-malawi-2010.pdf/@@download, accessed 1 June 2015.

68 Nkhoma, T.S., op. cit. note 65, p. 116.

69 Crisp, J. and Kiragu, E., 'Refugee protection and international migration: A review of UNHCR's role in Malawi, Mozambique and South Africa', paper for: UNHCR/Policy Development Evaluation Service (PDES), August 2010, paragraph 34, p. 8, pdf document, available at: www.unhcr.org/4c629c4d9.html, accessed 5 April 2015, paragraph 34, p. 8.

70 Zieck, M., *UNHCR's Worldwide Presence in the Field*, op. cit. note 2, pp. 275–6.

Nonetheless, the UNHCR field offices in Sub-Saharan Africa, despite having the capacity to protect refugees, cannot, for instance, become a place of asylum in every circumstance. In this regard, we can clearly read in the agreement adopted between the UNHCR and the government of Burkina Faso in relation to the headquarters of the agency in Ouagadougou, that:

> 5) Sans préjudice des dispositions du présent Accord, le HCR empêchera que le bureau ne devienne le refuge de personnes qui tentent d'échapper à une arrestation ordonnée en exécution d'une loi du Burkina Faso ou qui sont réclamées par le Gouvernement pour être extradées dans un autre état ou encore qui cherchent à se dérober à l'exécution d'un acte de procédure.[71]

Finally, it also has occurred that, under the pretext of protecting the UNHCR's staff in host countries, national authorities deny the UNHCR personnel entrance into given areas of the country. But, considering that the mandate of the agency provides for work in increasingly dangerous areas, this permits the UNHCR to also bypass bans by national authorities and to operate in areas considered inaccessible by the local government.[72]

5.3 Conclusion: assessing the changing role of the UNHCR

Many scholars hold the view that it would be quite superfluous to enlarge the mandate of the UNHCR in Sub-Saharan Africa, the core of its tasks being to ensure refugee protection and to find a durable solution to their plight,[73] if it does not first respond to the primary tasks which have been assigned to it.[74] However, among scholars there is not a general agreement on this point:

71 UNHCR/Burkina Faso, Headquarters Agreement of the Office of the High Commissioner for Refugees in Ouagadougou. Signed at Geneva on 19 February 1996, *United Nations Treaty Series*, vol. 1991, No. 32589, p. 317, Article 8 5).

72 Zieck, M., *UNHCR's Worldwide Presence in the Field*, op. cit. note 2, p. 285.

73 However, as A. Betts noted in this regard: 'Meanwhile, many of the most relevant decisions regarding the viability of durable solutions – especially the prospects for repatriation and local integration – are indirectly determined in regimes such as the security regime and the development regime, rather than in the principal multilateral forums of the refugee regime such as its Executive Committee (ExCom) of the High Commissioner's Dialogue. This means that UNHCR is faced with the imperative of engaging with an ever wider and growing set of venues and contexts within which the substance of refugee politics is actually taking place.' See Betts, A., 'Regime complexity and international organizations: UNHCR as a challenged institution', op. cit. note 4, p. 75.

74 Barutciski, M., 'A critical view of UNHCR's mandate dilemmas', in *International Journal of Refugee Law*, vol. 14, 2002, p. 380: 'A large transformed agency engaging primarily in vague humanitarian relief is not necessarily in the best interests of the world's refugees who need dedicated specialists who can tackle the specific problems of asylum-seeking. If UNHCR is not focusing seriously on difficult issues such as a mandate repatriation and regional burden-sharing, then who will?' A. Betts also noted that: 'A risk of [the] expanded activity [of the UNHCR], however, has been that UNHCR may undermine its ability to fulfill its core mandate of refugee protection. [. . .] [But i]n a changing world, UNHCR has recognized that it cannot remain static in how it

> While some have applauded and encouraged UNHCR for addressing humanitarian needs on a more 'comprehensive' basis, others have accused UNHCR of undermining the institution of asylum without being able to ensure effective protection within borders.[75]

In effect, the expansion of the UNHCR's activities – interesting to note, the UNHCR has always expanded its work in new areas of interest exclusively due to its own decision[76] – can also, as history has shown, come to be contradictory, with genuinely negative consequences for refugee protection in the region. For instance, the involvement of the UNHCR in the humanitarian operation in DRC in the 1990s allowed the agency to provide assistance also to those responsible for persecution.

In this regard, K. Wagner noted that:

> The UNHCR failed its obligations in the refugee camps of the Great Lakes region by not making early, formal assessments on the refugee caseload.[77]

In addition, also refugee law has played an important role in determining the UNHCR's evolution. In the UNHCR's history for example, refugee law has provided authoritative texts to set up the features of refugee protection, which constituted the background to the agency's evolution and, by providing a set of legal norms, justified several of its specific actions.[78]

Finally, the role of the UNHCR in Sub-Saharan Africa has been patently transformed in the course of these last decades, since the organization has tried to act in the name of the well-being of the refugees in the region. Nevertheless, the UNHCR has, for instance, also turned into a dynamic contributor in meetings concerning the management of situations overlapping with the protection of refugees. The agency frequently is involved for the best interests of its protected populations in meetings inherent, for instance, the development, humanitarian and security regimes, given that the most recent and significant policies for the

interprets its mandate and role.' See Betts, A., 'Regime complexity and international organizations: UNHCR as a challenged institution', op. cit. note 4, p. 77.

75 Bwakira, N., op. cit. note 27, p. 281.

76 Betts, A., 'Regime complexity and international organizations: UNHCR as a challenged institution', op. cit. note 4, p. 77: '[The UNHCR] has not been asked explicitly by states to expand its work, and the original problem for which the organization was created has not disappeared since it has taken on this range of new tasks.'

77 Wagner, K., op. cit. note 46, p. 381. In this regard, see also Loescher, G., Betts, A. and Milner, J.H.S., op. cit. note 15, pp. 122–3. On the same purpose J. Hyndman concluded: 'The crisis of Rwanda and its aftermath highlight [a] dimension [of the work carried out by the UNHCR in the field]: humanitarian operations demand a framework of consent and political solutions as well as resources to ensure protection and assistance to people at risk.' See Hyndman, J., *Managing Displacement: Refugees and the Politics of Humanitarianism*, op. cit. note 41, p. 190. The same author, at ibid., p. 181, reflected however on the fact that: 'At the end of the twentieth century, the formal mandate of UNHCR appears sorely outdated, and its role in relation to OCHA, UNICEF, and other operational UN agencies remains ill defined. Yet the agency is well equipped to deal with an array of humanitarian emergencies on an *ad hoc* basis.'

78 Cuellar, M.-F., op. cit. note 11, p. 703.

defence of refugees' rights has moved to these areas.[79] Today, legal involvements, advocacy and capacity building represent an essential part of the UNHCR's work in protecting refugees.[80]

By its actions, the UNHCR has met many constraints and perhaps been overly dispersed across many different fields. Likewise, in several cases – such as the case of Zimbabwean asylum-seekers in South Africa in the 1980s and in the 1990s – the UNHCR has been compelled to interpret its mandate in a flexible way and to become more involved in migration issues. To take the aforementioned example:

> [I]n South Africa, an involvement with refugees and asylum seekers inevitably means an involvement with migrants, because such large numbers of migrants have entered the asylum system and because the UNHCR cannot only provide protection to refugees when xenophobic violence takes place: it has to be concerned with the situation of all foreigners.[81]

In this case the UNHCR's effort may not have produced the outcome expected. It would therefore, be quite easy to affirm that the UNHCR's concentration on solely refugee protection would have been possibly more fitted to their mission of

79 Betts, A., 'Regime complexity and international organizations: UNHCR as a challenged institution', op. cit. note 4, p. 76. At ibid., p. 77, the author explained: 'Consequently, [the UNHCR] has tried to use its engagement in other regimes as an opportunity to demonstrate how those wider state interests can be met through contributing to protection or durable solutions for refugees and other displaced populations.'

80 Feller, E., 'Where principle and pragmatic meet: the world of UNHCR's protection work', op. cit. note 1, p. 202.

81 Crisp, J. and Kiragu, E., quoting a UNHCR staff member in South Africa, op. cit. note 69, paragraph 114, p. 21. In this regard, see ibid., paragraphs 155–7, p. 28: '155) Xenophobia has taken two recent forms in South Africa. First, and despite the generous provisions of the South African Constitution, practical access to public services such as education and health is often very difficult for foreign nationals. Non-South Africans are also subject to abuse, exploitation and discrimination by employers (sometimes migrants find that they are dismissed or arrested just before pay-day), as well as the police, government officials and members of the local community. 156) Second, and in addition to such day-to-day discrimination, refugees, asylum seekers and migrants in South Africa live in constant fear that large-scale violence of the type witnessed in May 2008 will erupt once again. Indeed, attacks have continued to take place since that time and were being reported at the time of writing. The Somali refugee communities in South Africa, who have a reputation for being successful entrepreneurs and retailers, buying in bulk and selling cheaply, who often keep their money in cash rather than in bank accounts, have been amongst the most prominent targets of such attacks. 157) Xenophobic violence in South Africa is often interpreted as a popular and spontaneous reaction to the government's perceived failures in relation to service delivery, a lack of jobs and mounting income inequality, not to mention the influx of foreign nationals in the past few years. According to some commentators, however, xenophobic violence is more deeply rooted in the South African state and society, is a great deal more organized than it appears, does not necessarily take place in the very poorest neighborhoods and is often provoked by powerful actors who have an economic or political interest in large-scale looting, the displacement of people and the administration of mob justice.'

promoting the genuine well-being of refugees. However, we think that the agency needs to be praised for the work it has done, and continues to do in the region, because it has always tried to do its best in the field, as episodes occurred in the last years clearly demonstrate,[82] with the research of new funds, representing an important task of the agency, recently seeking US$34 million for the over 75,000 people fleeing the turmoil in Nigeria.[83] In effect, the funds at the UNHCR's disposal seem currently insufficient to cope with the entire world crisis, some of them, like in DRC and Somalia, still far from being resolved.[84] To this, we need to add that, in several countries, such as in Malawi and Namibia, the effectiveness of the existing refugee protection policies and systems in place, such as the RSD Unit, is entirely and heavily reliant on constant UNHCR funding and sponsorship.[85]

82 See, for instance, the following news: 'Innovation: UNHCR and Vodafone bring tablet-based learning to 18,000 Somali refugees', 9 October 2014, available at: www.unhcr.org/5436a6cf6.html, accessed 10 October 2014; 'UNHCR's governing ExCom renews commitment to Africa's refugees', 30 September 2014, available at: www.unhcr.org/542aaceb6.html, accessed 10 October 2014; 'UNHCR helps first group of Ivorian refugees return home from Liberia', 25 October 2011, available at: www.the UNHCR.org/4ea6d4499.html, accessed 5 October 2014. See also the news: 'UNHCR moves Sudanese refugees away from volatile border area', 20 October 2011, available at: www.the UNHCR.org/4ea040419.html, accessed 5 October 2014; 'As tens of thousands flee, UNHCR ups assistance to Malian refugees', 20 March 2012, available at: www.the UNHCR.org/4f6882586.html, accessed 21 October 2014.

83 'UNHCR and partners seek US$34 million for Nigeria refugees', 14 September 2014, available at: www.unhcr.org/541831e19.html, 15 October 2014: 'UNHCR and its 16 partners need the funding to provide protection and life-saving aid to the more than 75,000 people who have to date fled from the escalating violence in north-east Nigeria's Adamawa, Borno and Yobe states, and to help thousands more expected to arrive in Cameroon, Chad and Niger by year's end.'

84 UNHCR, Opening remarks at the 65th session of the Executive Committee of the High Commissioner's Programme. António Guterres, United Nations High Commissioner for Refugees, Geneva, 30 September 2014, available at: www.unhcr.org/542a6e6e9.html, accessed 15 October 2014: 'In addition to the on-going Syria crisis, new conflicts in the Central African Republic, South Sudan, Ukraine and most recently in Iraq have caused terrible human suffering and massive displacement. The international humanitarian community has scrambled to respond to these needs. But with every new crisis, we get closer to the limits of how much we can do, and we are clearly no longer able to do enough. At the same time, drawn-out emergencies – Afghanistan, the Democratic Republic of Congo, Mali, Somalia – and the many more "forgotten" conflicts all over the world, continue to require significant attention and resources. But we all know they are not getting sufficient amounts of either.'

85 Nkhoma, T.S., 'The institution of asylum in Malawi and international refugee law: a review of the 1989 Refugee Act, University of Cape Town: Refugee Rights Unit', Working Paper Series, paper No. 2, 2012, p. 51; De Jager, J., Working paper on Namibia's refugee legislation, University of Cape Town: Refugee Rights Unit, Working Paper Series, paper No. 1, 2012, p. 18.

In the end, quoting A. Betts:

> It is important that the whole UN system is aware that refugees are not exclusively a UNHCR issue, but that they are a UN-wide responsibility. If complementary overlaps can be identified and used as the basis for partnership, UNHCR may be able to do more by doing less.[86]

For this reason, the UNHCR is also increasingly making efforts to build up its ties with other UN human rights and regional bodies,[87] because, while most departments within these bodies allow complaints to be lodged, contending abuse of their rights by a state party, no analogous mechanism exists with reference to the rights of refugees. Hence, this gap has led to a growth in asylum-seekers and refugees bringing claims before the human rights mechanisms.[88]

86 Betts, A., 'Regime complexity and international organizations: UNHCR as a challenged institution', op. cit. note 4, p. 78.

87 Feller, E., 'Where principle and pragmatic meet: the world of UNHCR's protection work', op. cit. note 1, p. 184 where the author explained: 'From information-sharing to contributions to the preparation of the General Comments on [1951 Geneva] Convention articles by the treaty-based committees, the Office tries constructively to feed into their knowledge and understanding about the links between particular rights and refugee protection and to become a more predictable resource generally on refugee issues.'

88 Ibid., p. 186.

6 Managing the subversive activities of refugees and their ban

Responding to abuses of refugee status

6.1 The legal framework on the ban of subversive activities of asylum-seekers and refugees

Should 'subversion' result in recognizing that state security '[r]equires that political freedom ought not to seek reform of the sovereign, a limitation on liberty'? Or, rather, should the concept of subversion '[s]uggest[s] that political freedom ought not to obstruct government policy, which while also a limitation, is so drastic that it implies a radical transformation of liberty'?[1] In (supposed?) free democracies one of the most difficult problems is to maintain a balance between the preservation of good order, which protects freedoms of individuals, and the non-encroachment by the government on their freedoms.[2]

Even before the OAU was established in 1963,[3] recent independent African countries were already concerned about the question of 'subversive activities' within the state of refuge.

1 Spjut, R.J., 'Defining subversion', in *British Journal of Law & Society*, vol. 6, 1979, p. 261.

2 Hoar, R.S., 'Subversive activities against government: two conflicting doctrines', in *Marquette Law Review*, vol. 27, 1942–1943, p. 72.

3 Charter of the Organization of African Unity. Done at Addis Ababa, on 25 May 1963, *United Nations Treaty Series*, vol. 479, No. 6947, p. 40. In this regard, R.M. D'Sa asserted: 'The Organization is clearly concerned with the humanitarian aspects of the refugee problem since they affect the goal, in Article II1 b) of the Charter, of seeking a 'better life for the peoples of Africa'. It also engages by virtue of its status as a political organization composed of African States, in some diplomatic activity aimed at the conciliation and discussion between countries of origin and asylum.' See D'Sa, R.M., 'The African refugee problem: relevant international conventions and recent activities of the Organization of African Unity', in *Netherlands International Law Review*, vol. 31, 1984, pp. 378–9. We note that the goal quoted above does not have any homologue in the Constitutive Act of the African Union, this latest document preferring to refer more specifically, in Article 3 c) to the achievement of a 'greater unity and solidarity between the African countries and the peoples of Africa' and Article 3 d) adds that one of the goals of the Union is to: 'Promote and defend African common positions on issues of interest to the continent and its peoples.'

For instance, for M.R. Garcia-Mora, 'subversive activities' was a synonym of 'revolutionary propaganda', a concept that is suitable to the African panorama.[4] The concern was that activities carried out in the open by refugees and exiles were also causing worry among other countries of refuge in the region with the same problematic. Therefore it was no surprise that, once established, the keystone principles of the OAU also included 'unreserved condemnation of [. . .] subversive activities on the part of neighboring states or any other states.'[5]

When it was conceived, it was not easy for the drafters of the 1969 African Convention to establish exactly the meaning of the term 'subversion' which, in plain terms, means to undermine the power of an institution or state. Already in 1827, with regard to the effectiveness of 'subversive activities', H. Hallam that '[n]othing so much strengthens any government as an unsuccessful endeavor to subvert it'.[6] As a matter of fact, this demonstrates that a solid government should not fear attempts to overthrow it. History shows that this is not really the case of many Sub-Saharan African countries, whose democracy at the time of the adoption of the 1969 OAU Convention, but also now, in some cases, can be considered more fragile than solid.[7]

The principle of the condemnation of subversive activities has successively been translated into the 2000 AU Charter, in Article IV o) although the condemnation is no longer reinforced by the adjective 'unreserved', which strengthened the concept in the 1963 OAU Charter. In detail, Article iv o) of the 2000 AU Charter (Article iv listing the principles of the AU) provides that:

> The Union shall function in accordance with the following principles:
>
> [. . .]
>
> o) respect for the sanctity of human life, condemnation and rejection of impunity and political assassination, acts of terrorism and subversive activities.

Subversion was among the very first issues which the OAU Assembly tackled. In its second session, in 1965, four years before the adoption of the African Refugee Convention, the Assembly produced a declaration, therefore a non-binding measure, dealing with the question of subversion in the context of regional and

4 Garcia-Mora, M.R., 'International responsibility for subversive activities and hostile propaganda by private persons against foreign states', in *Indiana Law Journal*, vol. 35, 1959–1960, p. 306.

5 Article III5 of the 1963 OAU Charter.

6 Hallam, H., The Constitutional History of England, from the Accession of Henry VIII to the Death of George II, quoted in *The Oxford English Dictionary*, Oxford: Clarendon Press, volume X, 1978, Su-Sz, p. 73.

7 We note that, on 29 May 2009, AI still challenged the Zimbabwean new government's coalition to impose the rule of law. Information available at: www.zimbabwesituation.com/index.html#news, accessed 10 October 2014. In the same regard, see also The Africa Report: 'When Zimbabwe's power is no longer shared', 19 July 2012, available at: www.theafricareport.com/Soapbox/when-zimbabwes-power-is-no-longer-shared.html, accessed 10 October 2014.

international relations. Five paragraphs of this declaration concerning refugees deserve to be mentioned in full:

> [The Assembly solemnly undertakes]:
>
> [. . .]
>
> 3. To oppose collectively and firmly by every means at our disposal every form of subversion conceived, organized or financed by foreign powers against Africa, OAU of its Member States individually;
>
> 4. b) To refrain from conducting any press or radio campaign against any Member States of the Organization of African Unity, and to resort instead to the procedure laid down in the Charter and the Protocol of Mediation, Conciliation and Arbitration of the Organization of African Unity;
>
> [. . .]
>
> 6. To observe strictly the principles of international law with regard to all political refugees who are nationals of any Member States of the Organization of African Unity;
>
> 7. To endeavor to promote, through bilateral and multilateral consultations, the return of refugees to their countries of origin with the consent of both the refugees concerned and their governments;
>
> 8. To continue to guarantee the safety of political refugees from non-independent African territories, and to support them in their struggle to liberate their countries.[8]

In the same session, the OAU Assembly also adopted a resolution recalling the guarantee by member states '[t]o prevent refugees living on their territories from carrying out by any means whatsoever any acts harmful to the interests of other states members of the Organization of African Unity'[9] and called for '[a]ll member states never to allow the refugee question to become a source of dispute amongst them'.[10] By the time the Assembly met, the Council of Ministers of the OAU had previously established a commission on refugee issues which was later to be instructed to draft a convention covering the entire set of problems of refugees in the African continent.[11] Those instructions, however, did not clarify which specific matters should be covered in the drafting of the convention. Specific areas to be

8 OAU, Assembly of Heads of State and government, Declaration on the problem of subversion, resolution No. AHG/Res.27 (II), 21–25 October 1965.

9 OAU, Assembly of Heads of State and government, The problem of refugees in Africa, resolution No. AHG/Res.26 (II), 21–25 October 1965, paragraph 2.

10 Ibid., paragraph 3.

11 OAU, Council of Ministers, Commission on the problem of refugees in Africa, resolution No. CM/Res. 36 (III), 13–17 July 1964, paragraph 6.

addressed were to be indicated by the Assembly, which instructed the commission established the previous year to re-examine the draft 1969 OAU Convention on the Status of Refugees regarding the Assembly's views expressed at that session, which concerned the question of subversive activities, among other issues.[12]

The obligation to dissuade subversive activities among refugees in Sub-Saharan African countries would subsequently continue to be reiterated in several resolutions of the OAU, always along the lines of the 1965 documents mentioned.[13] Thus, it was no surprise that, when the African Refugee Convention was adopted in 1969, one of the organization's most serious concerns regarding the refugee situation was present in its provisions.

The provision dealing with subversive activities in the 1969 OAU Convention essentially requires refugees to recognize the sovereign rights of the state of refuge over all individuals and events taking place in its territory. It also emphasizes the obligation of present AU member states not to support or assist any individual engaged in subversive activities against other members of the organization. This represents clearly the AU's concern with the conservation of territorial integrity and existing political structures of its member states.[14]

As it stands in Article III of the 1969 OAU Convention, the prohibition of subversive activities is expressed as follows:

> 1) Every refugee has duties to the country in which he/she finds him/herself, which require in particular that he/she conforms with its laws and regulations as well as with measures taken for the maintenance of public order. He/she shall also abstain from any subversive activities against any member state of the OAU.
>
> 2) Signatory states undertake to prohibit refugees residing in their respective territories from attacking any state member of the OAU, by any activity likely to cause tension[15] between member states, and in particular by use of arms, through the press, or by radio.'

12 OAU, Assembly of Heads of State and government, The problem of refugees in Africa, resolution No. AHG/Res.26 (II), 21–25 October 1965, paragraph 6.

13 For instance, see Council of Ministers, Resolution on the problem of refugees in Africa, resolution No. CM/Res. 104 (IX), 4–10 September 1967, preamble: '[The Council of Ministers of the Organization of African Unity] anxious that, in accordance with resolutions AHG/Res. 26 and AHG/Res. 27 of October 1965, adopted by the Heads of State and Government, the refugee problem shall not become a source of friction between States.'

14 Okogbule, N.S., 'The legal dimension of refugee problem in Africa', in *East African Journal of Peace and Human Rights*, vol. 10, 2004, p. 184.

15 Specifically about this expression, it has been noted that: '[b]y calling on member states to prohibit any activities "likely to cause tension", the OAU Convention empowers host states to make highly discretionary political determinations about refugee activities, carrying with it the danger of suppression of basic political rights of refugees. Such suppression, in particular of the rights to political speech and association, would run counter to those provisions of the 1951 Convention requiring equal treatment of refugees who, after all, are defined in the convention as victims of political persecution.' See McGuinness, M.E., 'Legal and normative dimensions of the

Originally, Article III of the 1969 OAU Convention was substantively composed only of the following paragraph:

> Member States shall undertake to prohibit refugees residing in their respective territories, from attacking any member state of the Organization of African Unity either through press or radio, with arms or through any other activities which may cause tension between the Member States.[16]

The prohibition of subversive activities, mentioned also in the OAU Convention for the Elimination of Mercenarism in Africa,[17] and which refers only to acts against member states of the OAU/AU and not to activities in relation to non-member states, considering that the abolition of colonialism was one of the purposes of the OAU,[18] does not stand alone in the 1969 OAU Refugee Convention. Several other provisos, including a number in its preamble, strengthen directly and indirectly the prohibition in question. For instance, paragraph 2 of the preamble talks about the 'need for an essentially humanitarian approach towards solving the problems of refugees'. At the same time, in its paragraph 4, the convention seeks to make a distinction 'between a refugee who seeks a peaceful and normal life and a person fleeing his/her country for the sole purpose of fomenting subversion from outside' with the determination, set in paragraph 5, to discourage 'the activities of such subversive elements [. . .] in accordance with the Declaration on the Problem of Subversion and Resolution on the Problem of Refugees adopted at Accra in 1965'. Also the exclusion clause contained in Article I5 C) dealing with 'acts contrary to the purposes and principles of the Organization of African Unity' patently has a repercussion on the matter as well as Article II6, by which '[f]or reasons of security, countries of asylum shall, as far as possible, settle refugees at a reasonable distance from the frontier of their country of origin'. Incidentally, it is also useful to remind ourselves of the exclusion clause set in Article 1F c) of the 1951 UN Refugee Convention[19] which might have been

manipulation of refugees', in Stedman, S.J. and Tanner, F. (eds), *Refugee Manipulation: War, Politics and the Abuse of Human Suffering*, Washington DC: Brookings Institution Press, 2003, p. 160.

16 Draft Convention on the Status of Refugees in Africa as revised by the General Secretariat, in Gyeke-Dako, K., 'Some legal and social aspects of African refugee problems', paper written for the OAU Council of Ministry for its ninth ordinary session, September 1967, Kinshasa, p. 64.

17 OAU, OAU Convention for the Elimination of Mercenarism in Africa, 3 July 1977, CM/817 (XXIX) Annex II Rev.1, preamble: 'We, the Heads of State and Government of the Member States of the Organization of African Unity; [. . .] convinced that total solidarity and co-operation between Member States are indispensable for putting an end to the subversive activities of mercenaries in Africa [. . .].'

18 Weis, P., 'The Convention of the Organization of the African Unity Governing the Specific Aspects of Refugee Problems in Africa', in *Revue des Droits de l'homme*, vol. 3, 1970, p. 460. The eradication of colonialism is mentioned in Article II1 d) of the 1963 OAU Charter. In this regard, see also Goundiam, O., 'African refugee convention', in *Migration News*, vol. 3, 1970, p. 10.

19 Article 1F c) of the 1951 Geneva Convention reads as follows: 'The provisions of this Convention shall not apply to any person with respect to whom there are serious reasons for considering that: [. . .] c) he has been guilty of acts contrary to the purposes and principles of the United Nations.'

drafted – according to a view advanced by J.C. Hathaway – in a way that clause 1F c) would entail a duty to desist from subversive activities in the country of asylum. This would be in the case of whoever disempowers any major initiative undertaken by the UN.[20]

Following the provision set in the 1969 OAU Convention, attempts have been made to move settlements further inland, although this is not without complications of course. For instance, problems arose when the territory of host countries is considerably small, as in Swaziland, where 86 persons were given assistance in a refugee camp not far from the border with Mozambique in 2004, being difficult to establish their genuine intentions.[21] This was also the case in Gambia, where Article 29 of its 2008 legislation on refugee protection deals with the question of abstention from subversive activities, although the dimensions of the country do not allow for the shelter of refugees very far from the border with Senegal.[22] In addition, it is not rare that in several areas in Africa, such as in the Horn, countries of refuge have not only tolerated, but have even actively supported refugee involvement in subversive and armed activities directed against their country of origin.[23]

Broadly speaking, the prohibition of subversive activities and the obligations reflected in Article III of the 1969 OAU Convention are not unique in the African continent and they conform to the general principles of international law,

20 Hathaway, J.C., *The Law of Refugee Status*, pp. 227–8.

21 UNHCR, UNHCR projected global resettlement needs 2005, 15 June 2004, available at: www.unhcr.org/refworld/docid/41597821fa.html, accessed 25 August 2014, p. 50. At 50–51, UNHCR pointed out that: '[t]he caseload in Swaziland consists mainly of Burundian (18 per cent of the applications), Congolese (14 per cent of the applications), Angolan (14 per cent of the applications), Somali (11 per cent of the applications) and Rwandan nationals (10 per cent of the applications).' We note that in Swaziland there is still in force a 'Sedition and Subversive Activities Act' which dates back to 1938 when the country was still under the British protectorate. In particular, this act bans the publication of any criticism of the monarchy.

22 Article 29 of the Refugee Act, 2008, 17 November 2008, reads as follows: '1) A person seeking refugee status in The Gambia, or a person recognized as a refugee in The Gambia is under an obligation to conform with the laws and regulations in force in The Gambia and with measures taken for the maintenance of public order. 2) A person seeking refugee status in The Gambia, or a person recognized as a refugee in The Gambia shall abstain from any subversive activities, including through the use of arms, through the press or by radio, or otherwise, directed against The Gambia or any foreign State.'

23 Van Hövell tot Westerflier, W.J.E.M., 'Africa and refugees: the OAU Refugee Convention in theory and practice', in *Netherlands Quarterly of Human Rights*, vol. 7, p. 182. At idem, the author noted also that: 'The active and passive support of states is not only contrary to article III of the Convention, but also to the more general principle that refugee camps and settlements have a strictly civilian and humanitarian character and that it is essential for states of refuge to do all within their capacity to ensure the maintenance of this character.' Such assertion is also confirmed by the ExCom in its conclusion No. 48 (XXXVIII), 'Military or armed attacks on refugee camps and settlements', 1987. Paragraph 4 a) of the conclusion clearly asserts: 'Refugees in camps and settlements have, together with the basic rights they enjoy, duties deriving from the refuge and protection granted or afforded to them by the country of refuge. In particular, they have duties to conform to the laws and regulations of the State of refuge including lawful measures taken for the maintenance of public order *and to abstain from any activity likely to detract from the exclusively civilian and humanitarian character of the camps and settlements*.' Emphasis added.

as set out in the 1970 UNGA Declaration on Principles of International Law Concerning Friendly Relations and Cooperation among States, in accordance with the 1945 UN Charter.[24] In 1967, two years before the adoption of the 1969 OAU Convention, the 1967 DTA adopted by the UNGA in its Article 4 also stipulated that: 'States granting asylum shall not permit persons who have received asylum to engage in activities contrary to the purposes and principles of the United Nations.'[25]

However, the matter is by no means all that simple. In effect, international law also reflects the position that not every act by refugees, which may be considered hostile in their country of origin, is harmful to the sovereign interests of the host country. For example, exiled political organizations fundamentally constitute a manifestation of the exercise of basic human rights. In this regard, S. Corliss argued that international law gives a host state the discretion to restrain the political freedoms permitted to aliens. Yet, allowing the exercise of these rights does not grant the country of origin of refugees valid reason to protest.[26]

However, an organization of exiles, often designating itself a 'government in exile' – as that of the Republic of Cabinda based in Kinshasa, the Biafran Government based in Washington DC or the Republic of Ambazonia[27] – may

24 UNGA, Declaration on principles of international law concerning friendly relations and cooperation among states in accordance with the charter of the United Nations, 24 October 1970, resolution No. 2625 (XXV). In the section of the Declaration dedicated to 'The principle concerning the duty not to intervene in matters within the domestic jurisdiction of any State, in accordance with the Charter' the UNGA declares: 'Also, no State shall organize, assist, foment, finance, incite or tolerate subversive, terrorist or armed activities directed towards the violent overthrow of the regime of another State, or interfere in civil strife in another State.'

25 UNGA, Declaration on territorial asylum, 14 December 1967, No. 2312 (XXII).

26 Corliss, S., 'Asylum state responsibility for the hostile acts of foreign exiles', in *International Journal of Refugee Law*, vol. 2, 1990, p. 181, where the author continued: 'The provision of financial and material assistance, hostile propaganda and other forms of non-violent support to subversive groups active within the State of origin has a more complex legal character. As purely humanitarian assistance is unlikely to alter the course of a civil conflict, an asylum State may permit or even encourage such efforts. Asylum States ought not to support more openly hostile acts of non-violent subversion, but international law at present imposes no active obligation to prevent similar conduct by private persons.'

27 The states controlling their claimed territory are, respectively: Angola for Cabinda, Nigeria for Biafra and Cameroon for Ambazonia. Particularly concerning the question of Biafra under an international law light, see Okoronkwo, P.L., 'Self-determination and the legality of Biafra's secession under international law', in *Loyola Los Angeles International and Comparative Law Review*, vol. 25, 2002–2003, pp. 110–11: 'The proclamation of Biafra described that "defenseless men, women, and children were shot down or hacked to death [and] some were burnt alive. Women and young girls were ravished with unprecedented bestiality; unborn children were torn out of the wombs of their mothers and killed." Over 50,000 Biafrans lost their lives and over two million others became refugees as a consequence of these abuses. The federal government left the culprits unpunished, and the whole matter uninvestigated. Further, the federal government compounded Biafra's plight by imposing a blockade restricting all communication and other transactions with the Eastern region. The government also refused to give the Eastern region its share of statutory revenue months before Biafra declared its independence.' About Ambazonia, for instance, we may read: '*Communication No. 1134/2002, Gorji-Dinka v Cameroon*, Views of 17 March 2005,

well support the overthrow of the regime in the country of origin or in another third state. Nevertheless, when support consists exclusively in openly backing groups involved in an armed struggle, whether the host government is obligated to bear down on such an organization is unclear. The situation would probably be different if the organization was clearly promoting full-scale war between states, in which case the country of refuge would be obliged to prevent such views from being aired. Short of that, its activities must be tolerated, unless authorities can show that the group, in some manner, constitutes a threat to national security or public order in the country of refuge.[28]

Consequently, even among those who otherwise accept the grounds of the prohibitions, the expression contained in Article III2 of the 1969 OAU Convention has been qualified by eminent scholars as being 'too wide',[29] 'obscure',[30] or 'rather

(violation of Articles 9 1), 10 1) and 2) a), 12 1) and 25b)). The author of the communication claimed to be the head of the exile government of "Ambazonia". As a result of the process of decolonization, Ambazonia had become part of the Federal Republic of Cameroon. According to the author, this was contrary to the results of a United Nations plebiscite held in 1961, in which the population had voted in favor of a situation in which Southern Cameroon would join the Republic of Cameroon (the former French Cameroon), and where Ambazonia would preserve its nationhood and a considerable degree of sovereignty. According to the author, human rights violations of the Ambazonians led to riots. Subsequently, Parliament enacted a law, dissolving the union of the two countries. The author became the head of the Ambazonian Restoration Council. He published several articles, calling on the President of the Republic to comply with the law and to withdraw from Ambazonia. In May 1985, the author was arrested and detained, which led to riots. The author was charged with high treason before a military tribunal. He was acquitted of all charges and released. Subsequently, between 1986 and 1988 he was placed under house arrest. In 1988, the author went into exile in Nigeria, and in 1995 went to Great Britain where he was recognized as a refugee. The author claimed that many provisions of the Covenant had been violated. The State party has not responded to the Committee's requests for information.' See Boerefijn, I., 'Human Rights news: United Nations', in *Netherlands Quarterly of Human Rights*, vol. 23, 2005, pp. 442–3. For further information about the Cabinda government in exile, see the website: www.cabinda.org/, accessed 10 October 2014.

28 Mandal, R., 'Political rights of refugees', in UNHCR, *Legal and protection policy research series*, 2003, pp. 14–15.

29 Hofmann, R., 'Refugee law in Africa', in *Law and State*, vol. 39, 1989, p. 85. The author also noted that the general clause found in Article III2 '[w]hereby "any activity likely to cause tension between member states" is prohibited seems [. . .] problematic, because in fact it can make all political activity during exile impossible.' See idem. In this regard, see also Van Garderen, J. and Ebenstein, J., 'Regional developments: Africa', in Zimmermann, A. (ed.), *The 1951 Convention Relating the Status of Refugees and its 1967 Protocol: a Commentary*, Oxford: Oxford University Press, 2011, p. 193, where the two authors chose the adjective 'overbroad' to define the clause on prohibition on subversive activities provided in the 1969 OAU Convention.

30 Rwelamira, M.R.K., 'Some reflections on the OAU Convention on refugees: some pending issues', 'Some reflections on the OAU Convention on refugees: some pending issues', in *The Comparative and International Law Journal of Southern Africa*, vol. 16, 1983, p. 174, where the author noted: 'What remains obscure [. . .] is whether activities other than those mentioned in article III2 [. . .] would be regarded as sufficiently serious to warrant cessation of refugees status, in accordance with article I5 c) of the Convention. Our contention in this regard is that article I5 c) does not apply to circumstances under article III. The latter presupposes that the person has already been granted refugee status, in which case he/she can only be handled in accordance with rules governing *non-refoulement* and expulsion under the two [1951 Geneva and 1969 OAU] Conventions.'

vague in its wording',[31] while P. Nobel has argued that the prohibition of activities through the press and radio might infringe freedoms protected under the 1948 UDHR.[32] In 2001, the Global Consultations promoted by the UNHCR, premising that the prohibition of subversive activities represents a means of promoting the civilian character of asylum, included the broad categories of war propaganda, incitement to imminent violence and hate speech among the subversive activities. It also underlined that the denunciation of '[c]oncrete and demonstrable abuses of human rights should not be considered as subversive'.[33]

The ban on subversive activities present in the 1969 OAU Convention has attracted other kinds of criticism, with one in particular worth mentioning. E.-R. Mbaya noted that, for the 1969 OAU Convention, a subversive activity consists of any action which:

> [i]s such as to cause tension between the member states [of the AU] and particularly through the use of armed force, the press and broadcasts, we can more fully appreciate the extent of the danger such cases threaten a subversive refugee who is guilty of remaining interested in his/her country's political problems. To accept such a situation without reacting to it is tantamount to ensuring that the African refugee is considered what has been defined as a 'subhuman species'.[34]

The same view has been shared contending that while refugees have the permission to remain in exile, expecting that the circumstances which compelled them to flee their country of origin will change, they are not allowed to take it upon themselves to accelerate such a political change. In this sense, asylum offered to individuals in a Sub-Saharan African country would be subordinated to their passivity, even if – for instance – their search for freedom of expression denied in the home-country was the factor which propelled their flight.[35] This is a comparable passivity to which M. Issoufou, President of Niger, requested to S. Gaddafi in order to grant him asylum on 'humanitarian grounds' in

31 Weis, P., 'The Convention of the Organization of the African Unity Governing the Specific Aspects of Refugee Problems in Africa', op. cit. note 18, p. 459.

32 In this regard, P. Nobel affirmed: 'This prohibition [the one concerning the subversive activities], which includes attacks against member states through the press or by radio, is so strict that it seems to conflict with article 19 of the UDHR which affirms everyone's right to freedom of opinion and expression "and to seek, receive, and impart information and ideas through any media and regardless of frontiers".' See Nobel, P., 'Refugee, law, and development in Africa', in *Michigan Yearbook of International Legal Studies*, vol. 3, 1982, p. 267.

33 UNHCR, Global Consultations on International Protection, UNHCR Regional Symposium on maintaining the civilian and humanitarian character of asylum refugee status, camps and other locations, 26–27 February, 2001, Pretoria, South Africa, document No. EC/GC/01/9, section 4 a).

34 Mbaya, E.-R., quoted in Okoth-Obbo, G., 'Thirty years on: a legal review of the 1969 OAU Refugee Convention Governing the Specific Aspects of Refugees Problems in Africa', in *Refugee Survey Quarterly*, vol. 20, 2001, p. 132.

35 Bakwesegha, C.J., 'Forced migration in Africa and the OAU Convention', in Adelman, H. and Sorenson, J. (eds), *African Refugees: Development Aid and Repatriation*, North York: York Lane Press, 1994, p. 11.

November 2011. The respect of this passivity constitutes an entirely different issue.[36]

Most of the discussions around the provisos of Article III of the 1969 African Convention focus on what is specified in the prohibitions, as well as the imprecision of the language used by the drafters. What really constitutes a 'subversive act' is often a matter of considerable controversy in the doctrine. The practice has been either to look at the cause of the particular act, or the consequences of it. Neither of these approaches, however, has been said to resolve the subjective element of what constitutes a subversive act. In addition, the provision contained in Article III is meant to protect member states from the activities of refugees in neighbouring countries where they have sought asylum.[37]

In a pivotal study on the legal condition of refugees in the Sub-Saharan African countries, the Lawyers' Committee for Human Rights noted that the provisions of Article III of the 1969 OAU Convention are not in conflict with Articles 9 and 10 of the 1981 Banjul Charter. These articles concern, respectively, freedom of expression and of association. The Lawyers' Committee for Human Rights noted that since both of these articles are qualified by the contention that such rights may be enjoyed 'within the law',[38] there was no conflict with the 1969 OAU Convention. By contrast, the provisions contained in Article III of the 1969 OAU Convention would not comply with Article 2 of the 1981 Banjul Charter providing that 'every individual', and not 'every citizen':

> Shall be entitled to the enjoyment of the rights and freedoms recognized and guaranteed in the present Charter without distinction of any kind such as race, ethnic group, color, sex, language, religion, political or any other opinion, national and social origin, fortune, birth or other status.

In addition, the Lawyers' Committee for Human Rights claimed that provisions of Article III of the 1969 OAU Convention seem to be in violation of Articles 19 and 22 of the 1966 ICCPR, guaranteeing the rights of freedom of expression and

36 See the news: 'Niger President grants Gaddafi's son asylum', 12 November 2011, available at: http://vibeghana.com/2011/11/12/niger-president-grants-gaddafi-son-asylum/, accessed 5 November 2014.

37 Rwelamira, M.R.K., 'Some reflections on the OAU Convention on refugees: some pending issues', op. cit. note 30, p. 174.

38 Lawyers' Committee for Human Rights, *African Exodus: Refugee Crisis, Human Rights and the 1969 OAU Convention*, New York: Lawyers' Committee for Human Rights Editions, 1995, p. 93. Quoting the two Articles: Article 9: '1) Every individual shall have the right to receive information. 2) Every individual shall have the right to express and disseminate his/her opinions within the law'; Article 10: '1) Every individual shall have the right to free association provided that he/she abides by the law. 2) Subject to the obligation of solidarity provided for in 29 no one may be compelled to join an association.' For a different opinion, see Van Garderen, J. and Ebenstein, J., op. cit. note 29, p. 193: '[T]his provision [Article III of the 1969 OAU Convention] limits refugees' right to freedom of expression and contradicts the rights enshrined in the 1981 Banjul Charter.'

of association.[39] But, as can easily be understood from reading the latter articles, the permitted limitations on the stipulation of both these rights are considerations of national security and public order, rather than the quite broadly defined 'subversive activities' or 'attacking' through the media.

Finally, the principle of banning subversive activities has been reaffirmed in Article 23 2) of the 1981 Banjul Charter. This article has as its goal the strengthening of peace, solidarity and friendly relations between states. It also compels state parties to assure that an individual enjoying the right of asylum under the same charter will not engage in any subversive activities against his/her country of origin or any other state party. In addition, this article establishes that the territory of states parties will not be used as bases for subversive activities against the people of any other state party of the 1981 Banjul Charter. As a corollary of the ban of subversive activities we also note that there is a duty on refugees to obey the laws of the host country.[40] However, F. Ouguergouz has suggested to:

> [P]romote a stricter definition of the subversive activity thus prohibited, such as the one which only covers armed or terrorist actions; this is the only way

39 Lawyers' Committee for Human Rights, op. cit. note 38, p. 93. Article 19 stipulates: '1) Everyone shall have the right to hold opinions without interference. 2) Everyone shall have the right to freedom of expression; this right shall include freedom to seek, receive and impart information and ideas of all kinds, regardless of frontiers, either orally, in writing or in print, in the form of art, or through any other media of his/her choice. 3) The exercise of the rights provided for in paragraph 2 of this article carries with it special duties and responsibilities. It may therefore be subject to certain restrictions, but these shall only be such as are provided by law and are necessary: a) For respect of the rights or reputations of others; b) For the protection of national security or of public order (*ordre public*), or of public health or morals'; Article 22 stipulates: '1) Everyone shall have the right to freedom of association with others, including the right to form and join trade unions for the protection of his/her interests. 2) No restrictions may be placed on the exercise of this right other than those which are prescribed by law and which are necessary in a democratic society in the interests of national security or public safety, public order (*ordre public*), the protection of public health or morals or the protection of the rights and freedoms of others. This article shall not prevent the imposition of lawful restrictions on members of the armed forces and of the police in their exercise of this right. 3) Nothing in this article shall authorize States Parties to the International Labor Organization Convention of 1948 concerning freedom of association and protection of the right to organize to take legislative measures which would prejudice, or to apply the law in such a manner as to prejudice, the guarantees provided for in that Convention.'

40 Beyani, C., 'International legal criteria for the separation of members of armed forces, armed bands, and militia from refugees in the territories of host states', in *International Journal of Refugee Law*, vol. 12, 2000, p. 260. In full, Article 23 2) of the 1981 Banjul Charter reads: '2) For the purpose of strengthening peace, solidarity and friendly relations, States parties to the present Charter shall ensure that: a) any individual enjoying the right of asylum under 12 of the present Charter shall not engage in subversive activities against his country of origin or any other State party to the present Charter; b) their territories shall not be used as bases for subversive or terrorist activities against the people of any other State party to the present Charter.' As F. Ouguergouz explained: 'The exercise of the freedoms, and more particularly of the freedom of expression, of a person benefiting from asylum in a state party to the African Charter ought [. . .] logically to be subjected to the limits imposed by article 23 2) a) [of the 1981 Banjul Charter] in the light of article III of the OAU Convention of 1969.' See Ouguergouz, F., *The African Charter on Human and Peoples' Rights*, The Hague/London/New York: Martinus Nijhoff Publishers, 2003, pp. 351–2.

> to eliminate all risk of arbitrariness regarding the exercise by the refugee of his/her freedom of expression.[41]

C.R. Snyman does not share such an opinion, asserting that:

> Terrorism is a more serious offence than [. . .] subversion [. . .]. The death penalty may be imposed for terrorism, but not for subversion [. . .]. It would be an anomaly if the mental element of terrorism might be proved by *dolus eventualis* but not that of the less serious offences of subversion [. . .].[42]

6.2 Clarifying 'freedom of expression'

Democracy cannot abstract from freedom of expression, which is important for its function of supporting democracy, and its facilitation in searching for truth by society.[43]

To better understand what 'freedom of expression' means in Sub-Saharan Africa we start considering how major NGOs try to clarify the limits of restrictions upon freedom of expression, such as Article 19.[44] One of the major attempts at clarification came in October 1995, when were drafted the Johannesburg Principles.

41 Idem.

42 Snyman, C.R., '*Dolus eventualis* in the offences of terrorism, subversion and sabotage', in *South African Law Journal*, vol. 107, 1990, p. 375.

43 Nevondwe, L. and Matotoka, M., 'The right to freedom of expression, press and culture in South Africa: a survey of recent developments', in *International Human Rights Law Review*, vol. 2, 2013, p. 180.

44 Article 19 was established in 1987, deriving its name from Article 19 of the 1948 UDHR which reads: 'Everyone has the right to freedom of opinion and expression; this right includes freedom to hold opinions without interference and to seek, receive, and impart information and ideas through any media and regardless of frontiers.' For more information about the NGO Article 19, see the website: www.article19.org/, accessed 20 September 2014. In this regard, see also Articles 19 and 20 of the 1966 ICCPR. Article 19 reads: '1) Everyone shall have the right to hold opinions without interference. 2) Everyone shall have the right to freedom of expression; this right shall include freedom to seek, receive and impart information and ideas of all kinds, regardless of frontiers, either orally, in writing or in print, in the form of art, or through any other media of his choice. 3) The exercise of the rights provided for in paragraph 2 of this article carries with it special duties and responsibilities. It may therefore be subject to certain restrictions, but these shall only be such as are provided by law and are necessary: a) For respect of the rights or reputations of others; b) For the protection of national security or of public order (*ordre public*), or of public health or morals.' Article 20 reads: '1) Any propaganda for war shall be prohibited by law. 2) Any advocacy of national, racial or religious hatred that constitutes incitement to discrimination, hostility or violence shall be prohibited by law.' The 1966 International Convention on the Elimination of All Forms of Racial Discrimination also refers to freedom of opinion and expression in its Articles 4 and 5. Article 4 stipulates: 'States Parties condemn all propaganda and all organizations which are based on ideas or theories of superiority of one race or group of persons of one color or ethnic origin, or which attempt to justify or promote racial hatred and discrimination in any form, and undertake to adopt immediate and positive measures designed to eradicate all incitement to, or acts of, such discrimination and, to this end, with due

Quoting Principle 6 of the 1995 Johannesburg Principles, the way the words 'expression' 'intended' and 'likely' to incite imminent violence can threaten national security, are given as frameworks within which the legal and justifiable restriction of speech is seen.[45] In addition, freedom of expression 'can never be prohibited on the ground that it is in a particular language of a national minority'[46] – which can often be the case of refugees – and governments need to adopt 'reasonable measures to prevent private groups or individuals from interfering unlawfully with the peaceful exercise of freedom of expression'.[47] It seems obvious that the drafters of the 1995 Johannesburg Principles wished to create a large arena within which both freedom of expression and information would flourish.

Yet, it also seems that the 1995 Johannesburg Principles remain a sort of 'dead letter' in Sub-Saharan Africa, with many states of the region intolerant of criticism, and having severe limitations on freedom of expressions, as well as restrictions on media coverage.[48] Indeed, the independent organization Freedom House in 2014

regard to the principles embodied in the Universal Declaration of Human Rights and the rights expressly set forth in article 5 of this Convention, *inter alia*: a) Shall declare an offence punishable by law all dissemination of ideas based on racial superiority or hatred, incitement to racial discrimination, as well as all acts of violence or incitement to such acts against any race or group of persons of another color or ethnic origin, and also the provision of any assistance to racist activities, including the financing thereof; b) Shall declare illegal and prohibit organizations, and also organized and all other propaganda activities, which promote and incite racial discrimination, and shall recognize participation in such organizations or activities as an offence punishable by law; c) Shall not permit public authorities or public institutions, national or local, to promote or incite racial discrimination.' Article 5 d) viii) stipulates: 'In compliance with the fundamental obligations laid down in article 2 of this Convention, States Parties undertake to prohibit and to eliminate racial discrimination in all its forms and to guarantee the right of everyone, without distinction as to race, color, or national or ethnic origin, to equality before the law, notably in the enjoyment of the following rights: [. . .] d) Other civil rights, in particular: [. . .] iii) The right to freedom of opinion and expression.' No African state has made any declaration and/or reservation on Articles 4 and 5.

45 In full, principle 6 ('Expression that may threaten national security') reads: 'Subject to Principles 15 and 16, expression may be punished as a threat to national security only if a government can demonstrate that: a) the expression is intended to incite imminent violence; b) it is likely to incite such violence; and c) there is a direct and immediate connection between the expression and the likelihood or occurrence of such violence.'

46 In full, principle 9 ('Use of a minority or other language') reads: 'Expression, whether written or oral, can never be prohibited on the ground that it is in a particular language, especially the language of a national minority.'

47 In full, Principle 10 ('Unlawful interference with expression by third parties') reads: 'Governments are obliged to take reasonable measures to prevent private groups or individuals from interfering unlawfully with the peaceful exercise of freedom of expression, even where the expression is critical of the government or its policies. In particular, governments are obliged to condemn unlawful actions aimed at silencing freedom of expression, and to investigate and bring to justice those responsible.'

48 Freedom of expression is still far to be established to an acceptable level in Sub-Saharan Africa. See, for instance, the following news: 'The Gambia condemned again by ECOWAS Human Rights Court over crime against journalist', 13 June 2014, available at: www.article19.org/join-the-debate.php/150/view/, accessed 26 September 2014; 'Africa Court on Human and People's

listed only four countries in Sub-Saharan Africa (Cape Verde, Ghana, Mauritius, and Sao Tome and Principe) as 'free', relating to the freedom of the press,[49] while in other countries, such as Ethiopia and Swaziland, there are still perpetrated abuses again journalists and/or human rights activists, guilty of 'subversive activities' against the integrity of these two countries.[50] According to L. Nevondwe and M. Matotoka taking as a parameter the situation in South Africa, where the standing of the media is low, in most other Sub-Saharan African countries the situation is similar, if not worse, where the objectivity and the freedom of the media is considered unresponsive, discriminating and not respectful of the rights protected by the national constitution.[51]

The AU has also openly examined the guaranteeing of freedom of expression and freedom of the press, including access to the media, for all political actors.[52] Nevertheless, commentators – among which C.E. Jr. – have affirmed that the 1981 Banjul Charter contains an inadequate protection of freedom of expression. The ACHPR has given little attention to the freedom of expression within states that, in their turn, have used one of the principles placed at the very foundation of the AU, the non-interference in the domestic affairs of states,[53] to justify the inaction among African leaders, for whom protection of national sovereignty remains a leading value.[54]

Having been drafted in general terms,[55] the 1981 Banjul Charter provides for a weak formulation of the freedom of expression. However, under Articles 60 and 61,[56] the charter establishes that the ACHPR has the right to take into account

Rights reaffirms State's obligation to protect journalists', 11 April 2014, available at: www.article19.org/join-the-debate.php/141/view/, accessed 26 September 2014.

49 Information available at: www.freedomhouse.org/report/freedom-press-2014/press-freedom-rankings#.VE-2ESKUdDA, accessed 26 September 2014.

50 Reporters without Borders, 'Ethiopian government to bring criminal charges against six weeklies', 12 August 2014, available at: www.refworld.org/docid/53f44b794.html, accessed 20 October 2014; AI, 'Further information: Swaziland: Two men sentenced to two years in prison', 28 July 2014, AFR 55/004/2014, available at: www.refworld.org/docid/53df39cd4.html, accessed 29 October 2014. At the time of writing this (10 June 2015) Swazi prisons still host Mr Thulani Maseko, human rights lawyer and currently LLD candidate at the Centre for Human Rights, Faculty of Law, University of Pretoria, where I am working. Mr Maseko was jailed on the 18 March 2014 for disrespect of court after censuring the attitude of Swaziland's judicial system.

51 Nevondwe, L. and Matotoka, M., op. cit. note 43, p. 176.

52 Murray, R., 'Human Rights in Africa: from the OAU to the African Union', op. cit. note 344, p. 105.

53 Constitutive Act of the African Union. Lomé, 11 July 2000, *United Nations Treaty Series*, vol. 2158, No. 3733, p. 328, Article 4 ('Principles'), letter g).

54 Welch, C.E. Jr., 'The African Charter and freedom of expression in Africa', in *Buffalo Human Rights Law Review*, vol. 4, 1998, p. 111.

55 Ouguergouz, F., op. cit. note 40, p. 161.

56 In detail, Articles 60 and 61 of the 1981 Banjul Charter read: '60) The Commission shall draw inspiration from international law on human and peoples' rights, particularly from the provisions of various African instruments on human and peoples' rights, the Charter of the United Nations, the Charter of the Organization of African Unity, the Universal Declaration of Human Rights, other instruments adopted by the United Nations and by African countries in the field of human and peoples' rights as well as from the provisions of various instruments adopted within the Specialized Agencies of the United Nations of which the parties to the present Charter are

other relevant human rights instruments in order to implement its action. Therefore, the ACHPR has helped to address continent-wide freedom of expression through several channels. These channels include the adoption of a resolution on the right to freedom of expression,[57] a Declaration of Principles on freedom of expression,[58] the appointment of a *Special Rapporteur* on Freedom of Expression in Africa[59] as well as jurisprudence.[60] According to Article 9 of the 1981 Banjul Charter:

members'; '61) The Commission shall also take into consideration, as subsidiary measures to determine the principles of law, other general or special international conventions, laying down rules expressly recognized by member states of the Organization of African Unity, African practices consistent with international norms on human and people's rights, customs generally accepted as law, general principles of law recognized by African states as well as legal precedents and doctrine.'

57 ACHPR, Resolution on the right to freedom of association, resolution No. 5 (XI), 1992. This resolution reads: 'The ACHPR [. . .]; Taking into consideration all rights stipulated in the Universal Declaration of Human Rights, with special reference to articles 20, 23 guaranteeing the right to freedom of peaceful assembly and association; Recalling article 22 of the International Covenant on Civil and Political Rights, and article 8 of the International Covenant on Economic, Social and Cultural Rights assuring that everyone shall have the right to freedom of association with others; Highly evaluating the UN Sub-Commission on the Prevention of Discrimination, resolution No. 13 (XXXIII) on the 11th of September 1980 which adopted the right to freedom of association; Taking into consideration the provisions of the African Charter on Human and Peoples' Rights, in particular article 10.1, guaranteeing every individual the right to free association provided that he abides by the law; considers that: 1) The competent authorities should not override constitutional provisions or undermine fundamental rights guaranteed by the constitution and international standards; 2) In regulating the use of this right, the competent authorities should not enact provisions which would limit the exercise of this freedom; 3) The regulation of the exercise of the right to freedom of association should be consistent with State's obligations under the African Charter on Human and Peoples' Rights.'

58 ACHPR, Resolution on the adoption of the Declaration of Principles on freedom of expression in Africa, resolution No. 62 (XXXII), 2002, where section I ('The Guarantee of Freedom of Expression') reads: '1) Freedom of expression and information, including the right to seek, receive and impart information and ideas, either orally, in writing or in print, in the form of art, or through any other form of communication, including across frontiers, is a fundamental and inalienable human right and an indispensable component of democracy. 2) Everyone shall have an equal opportunity to exercise the right to freedom of expression and to access information without discrimination.'

59 ACHPR, Resolution on the mandate of the *Special Rapporteur* on refugees, asylum seekers and internally displaced persons in Africa, resolution No. 71 (XXXVI), 2004; Resolution on the expansion of the mandate and re-appointment of the *Special Rapporteur* on freedom of expression and access to information in Africa, resolution No. 122 (XXXXII), 2007. The mandate of the *Special Rapporteur* has been explained in the 2004 resolution, at paragraph I, and substantially renewed in 2007.

60 See, for instance, ACHPR, *John D. Ouko v Kenya*, communication No. 232/99, 2000, paragraph 28: 'The above provision [Article 9 of the 1951 Banjul Charter] guarantees to every individual the right to free expression, within the confines of the law. Implicit in this is that if such opinions are contrary to laid down laws, the affected individual or government has the right to seek redress in a court of law. Herein lays the essence of the law of defamation. This procedure has not been followed in this particular instance. Rather the government has opted to arrest and detain the Complainant without trial and to subject him to a series of inhuman and degrading treatments. The Commission finds this in violation of article 9 of the Charter.' See also ACHPR, *Dawda Jawara v The Gambia*, communications Nos. 147/95 and 149/96, 2000, paragraph 65:

> 1) Every individual shall have the right to receive information. 2) Every individual shall have the right to express and disseminate his opinions within the law.

Under Article 9 of the 1981 Banjul Charter, a person not only has the right to express himself/herself, but has also the right to receive information. Moreover, the article prescribes, without defining, the individual's right to express and circulate his/her opinions. Freedom of opinion is therefore implicitly recognized by the same definition.[61] Even if not obvious from the definition set out in Article 9, linguistic freedom constitutes another crucial element of freedom of expression. In this regard, the HRC affirmed in a communication from the year 2000, regarding *Diergaardt v Namibia* that: '[m]inority languages must be treated without discrimination'.[62] Indeed, the freedom to use the idiom of the individual's choice is very important in Sub-Saharan Africa, where multi-ethnicity – also among asylum-seekers and refugees – remains a dominant aspect of its society. It is in this way that the freedom to choose a language has been read into the definition of the rights protected by Article 9 of the 1981 Banjul Charter.[63]

Another feature of Article 9 of the 1981 Banjul Charter resides in the ambiguity of the clause provided in Article 9 2), which limits the rights proscribed in the entire article. Paragraph 2 seems to regard only personal freedom to express and disseminate opinions, while the individual's right to be informed would seem absolute. Nevertheless, the right of being informed – an extrapolation of the right to express and disseminate information also found in Article 9 1) – seems to be affected by the limitation placed on Article 9 2). This is despite the fact that the right of a person to be informed should be limited only by what is prescribed in Article 27 2) of the 1981 Banjul Charter – '[r]espect of the rights of others, collective security, morality and common interest'.[64]

'The government did not provide any defense to the allegations of arrests, detentions, expulsions and intimidation of journalists, made by the complainant. The intimidation and arrest or detention of journalists for articles published and questions asked deprives not only the journalists of their rights to freely express and disseminate their opinions, but also the public, of the right to information. This action is clearly a breach of the provisions of article 9 of the Charter.'

61 Ouguergouz, F., op. cit. note 40, p. 161.

62 Human Rights Committee, *J.G.A. Diergaardt (late Captain of the Rehoboth Baster Community) et al. (represented by Dr. Y.J.D. Peeters, their international legal counsel) v Namibia*, communication No. 760/1997, 6 September 2000, document No. CCPR/C/69/D/760/1997. Individual opinion by Abdalfattah Amor (dissenting), paragraph 4.

63 Ouguergouz, F., op. cit. note 40, p. 161.

64 Ibid., pp. 161–2. In full, Article 27 of the 1981 Banjul Charter reads as follows: '1) Every individual shall have duties towards his family and society, the State and other legally recognized communities and the international community. 2) The rights and freedoms of each individual shall be exercised with due regard to the rights of others, collective security, morality and common interest.'

To date,[65] the ACHPR has produced no documentation regarding Article 9 that explicitly refers to refugees and/or asylum-seekers. It is worth noting, however, that in a past communication the commission concluded that there had been a violation of Article 9 2) of the 1981 Banjul Charter because the victims could not express their freedom of conscience, as outlined in Article 8 of the same 1981 Banjul Charter.[66] In this way, the ACHPR contended the existence of a connection between freedoms of opinion and conscience.[67]

In effect, through the case law of the ACHPR, we see that action has always gone towards denouncing all violations of freedom of expression, taken through this jurisprudence to represent an indispensable element for the democratization of the region under study.[68]

Until now, the ACHPR has adopted an approach in its interpretation and application of Article 9 of the 1981 Banjul Charter in order to ensure that the control imposed on freedom of expression does not go beyond the limits necessary for the rationale behind Articles 9 2) and 27 2) of the 1981 Banjul Charter. This happened, for instance, in the 2003 case *The Law Offices of Ghazi Suleiman v Sudan*. In this case, the ACHPR, showing its hesitation to permit constraints on freedom of expression on the basis of national security and public order – as invoked by Sudan[69] – quoted the Inter-American Court and affirmed that:

> When an individual's freedom of expression is unlawfully restricted, it is not only the right of that individual that is being violated, but also the right of all others to 'receive information and ideas'. It is particularly grave when information that others are being denied concerns the human rights protected in the African Charter [. . .].[70]

65 1 October 2014. The last communication issued on freedom of expression by the ACHPR concerning a Sub-Saharan country dates back to 26 May 2010, *Kenneth Good v Republic of Botswana*, communication No. 313/05, 2010.

66 Article 8 of the 1981 Banjul Charter reads as follows: 'Freedom of conscience, the profession and free practice of religion shall be guaranteed. No one may, subject to law and order, be submitted to measures restricting the exercise of these freedoms.'

67 ACHPR, *Amnesty International v Zambia*, communication No. 212/98, 1999, paragraph 54: 'Both Banda and Chinula were leading politicians and businessmen. Both had lived in Zambia for decades. Even if deportation action had been initiated against them in 1974 and 1976, it can be safely assumed that the action had been advanced unless it is proved that that was due to unlawfulness, fraud or obstruction of the course of justice. None of this was alleged. Action was accelerated upon the assumption of office of MMD government in 1991; we are therefore persuaded that the deportations were politically motivated. *This provision of the Charter reflects the fact that freedom of expression is a fundamental human right, essential to an individual personal development, political consciousness and participation in the public affairs of his country. The Commission has to determine whether the 'deportations', being politically motivated violate the provisions of Article 9(2) of the African Charter as the two victims were denied the right to freedom of conscience as stipulated in Article 8 of the Charter.*' Emphasis added.

68 Ouguergouz, F., op. cit. note 40, p. 167.

69 Olaniyan, K., 'Civil and political rights in the African Charter: articles 8–14', in Evans, M.D. and Murray, R. (eds), *The African Charter on Human and Peoples' Rights: the System in Practice: 1986–2006*, Cambridge: Cambridge University Press, 2008, p. 223.

70 ACHPR, *The Law Offices of Ghazi Suleiman v Sudan*, communication No. 228/99, 2003, paragraph 50.

However it is also true that the last expression of Article 9 2) of the 1981 Banjul Charter ('within the law') appears to exclude any kind of justification for a state to reduce freedom of expression and information.[71] The ACHPR has instead interpreted this expression to mean that all constraints on freedom of expression need to be 'provided by law',[72] in effect making it a sort of 'claw-back' clause. For F. Viljoen, Article II1 of the 1969 OAU Convention,[73] limiting rights from the beginning, shares the same characteristic.[74]

However, as the ACHPR contended in 1999, the expression 'within the law' contained in Article 9 2) of the 1981 Banjul Charter does not mean that domestic law can leave behind the right to express and disseminate one's opinion assured at the international level, because this would make the protection of the freedom of expression ineffective.[75]

Unfortunately, the ACHPR declared in 2007 that it was a matter of concern that only very few countries in Africa had adopted legislation allowing the public access to information held by public institutions, or laws guaranteeing freedom of information.[76] On the other hand, the ACHPR should also try to challenge the kind of limits envisaged in the 'within the law' qualifications of the freedom enshrined in Article 9 of the 1981 Banjul Charter.[77] This is in order to facilitate

71 In this regard, see F. Ouguergouz, op. cit. note 40, p. 162: '[T]hese rights [freedom of expression and freedom of information] must [. . .] be exercised "within the law": what it means, in other words, is that their exercise must comply with the requirements of the law, whatever these are.'

72 ACHPR, Resolution on the adoption of the Declaration of Principles on freedom of expression in Africa, resolution No. 62 (XXXII), 2002, paragraph II ('Interference with Freedom of Expression'): '1) No one shall be subject to arbitrary interference with his or her freedom of expression. 2) Any restrictions on freedom of expression shall be provided by law, serve a legitimate interest and be necessary and in a democratic society.'

73 F. Viljoen affirmed: 'The duty of state under the OAU Refugee Convention is "[t]o use their best endeavors [. . .] to receive all refugees." The way in which this duty was phrased led Weis to conclude that the requirement is recommendatory, rather than binding. This happened also because these endeavors must "[b]e consistent with their respective legislations", states need merely to comply with internal laws, whatever their content. This provision may be viewed as a precursor to the inclusion of "claw-back" clauses in the African Charter.' See F. Viljoen, *International Human Rights Law in Africa*, Oxford/New York: Oxford University Press, 2007, p. 256.

74 In this regard, see Gittleman, R., 'The Banjul Charter on Human and Peoples' Rights: A Legal Analysis', in Welch, C.E. Jr. and Meltzer, R.I, *Human Rights and Development in Africa*, Albany: State University of New York Press, 1984, pp. 157–8: 'The African Charter contains no specific provision entitling a state to derogate from its obligations, i.e., to temporarily suspend a right guaranteed under the Charter. Many of the provisions, however, contain "claw-back clauses" that entitle a state to restrict the granted rights to the extent permitted by domestic law. [. . .] While derogation clauses permit the suspension of previously granted rights, claw-back clauses restrict rights *ab initio*. [. . .] Claw-back clauses do not provide the external control over state behavior that derogation provisions provide.'

75 ACHPR, *Constitutional Rights Project, Civil Liberties Organization and Media Rights Agenda v Nigeria*, communications Nos. 140/94, 141/94, 145/95, 1999, paragraph 40.

76 ACHPR, Resolution on the expansion of the mandate and re-appointment of the *Special Rapporteur* on freedom of expression and access to information in Africa, resolution No. 122 (XXXXII), 2007, preamble.

77 Nmehielle, V.O.O., *The African Human Rights System: Its Laws, Practice and Institutions*, The Hague/London/New York: Martinus Nijhoff, 2001, p. 109.

the life of asylum-seekers and refugees via the provision of more detailed statutes which can better define 'subversive' activities, going beyond questions of freedom of expression.

In effect, doctrinal opinions on Article 9 of the 1981 Banjul Charter remain, in the end, divided. Some scholars remain cautious on the validity of Article 9.The reason for this position derives from the concerns of its drafters, more worried in assuring and securing stability for the recently independent countries than with the real protection of human rights within member states.[78] In contrast, V.O.O. Nmehielle has affirmed that Article 9 of the 1981 Banjul Charter emphasizes that freedom of expression in Africa is linked '[i]n the same way as [with] other regional and international legal instruments'.[79]

In the end, and considering that publications founded and directed by refugees like the Kakuma News Reflector,[80] are growing in number and popularity in Sub-Saharan Africa, we like to quote what the first OAU Ministerial Conference on Human Rights, held in Grand Bay – Mauritius – declared in 1999:

> [t]he medias are important actors for building bridges between governments and peoples; it [the Ministerial Conference], therefore, urges States Parties [of the OAU] to guarantee a free and independent press within their national borders to enable it [to] play a role in the promotion of human rights in Africa.[81]

6.3 How countries in the region have acted towards the prohibition of 'subversive activities', and the breaches they have committed regarding this prohibition's regulatory elements

Restrictions on freedom of expression and information to protect national security are allowed in serious cases of political and military threat to the entire nation,[82] as happened in Zambia in 1999.[83] Many governments have a tendency to invoke

78 Welch, C.E. Jr., 'The African Charter and freedom of expression in Africa', op. cit. note 54, pp. 114–15.

79 Nmehielle, V.O.O., op. cit. note 77, p. 107.

80 'The *Kakuma News Reflector*, or *Kanere*, is an independent news magazine produced by Ethiopian, Congolese, Ugandan, Rwandan, Somali, Sudanese, and Kenyan journalists operating in Kakuma Refugee Camp, Kenya. It is the first fully independent refugee-run news source of its kind to emerge from a refugee camp, and has attracted considerable international attention.' Information available at: http://kanere.org/about-kanere/, accessed 10 September 2014.

81 OAU Ministerial Conference on Human Rights, Grand Bay declaration and Plan of Action, 12–16 April 1999, paragraph 21.

82 Kiss, A.C., 'Permissible limitations on rights', in Henkin, L. (ed.), *The International Bill of Rights: The Covenant on Civil and Political Rights*, New York: Columbia University Press, 1981, p. 296.

83 At that time the newspaper *Post* published an article warning of the Zambian army's vulnerability to a possible attack from Angola, raising critical issues of national security. The government cracked down, and the entire *Post* staff was charged with espionage and endangering national

protection of national security to justify far-reaching restrictions on freedom of expression of opposition groups, politicians and critical media,[84] as seen in Angola in 2011.[85]

Public order is used as a limitation on the right of expression and it has been disputed as to what extent it should be applied to Article 19 3) of the 1966 ICCPR.[86] However, it appears clearly from the preparatory works of this article that the licensing of broadcasting, cinema or television enterprises or import restrictions on printed works may be justified by this purpose for interference.[87] This term also covers the procurement and dissemination of confidential information and endangering the impartiality of the judiciary. Finally, certain limitations on freedom of expression by members of security forces or by officials, as well as on the freedom of information of prisoners, may be justified in terms of the protection of public order.[88]

The Lawyer's Committee for Human Rights said that the most restrictive provisions of the 1969 OAU Convention, rather than the more permissive ones of the 1981 Banjul Charter and of the 1966 ICCPR, correspond more closely to the thinking and practice of most African governments. Furthermore, whether or not a host government narrows the political activities of refugees depends almost entirely on its own positions and preferences. For instance, several generations of Ugandan refugees in Kenya have been allowed to engage in political activities, depending on whether they supported a party or faction favoured by the Kenyan government. Along the same lines, in the early 1990s, the Ivorian authorities allowed unconcealed activities by refugees supporting one Liberian political faction, yet detaining refugees on suspicion of supporting another.[89] By contrast, Ugandan authorities expelled eight refugees and asylum-seekers from the DRC

security. Example taken in Nyamnjoh F.B., *Africa's Media: Democracy and the Politics of Belonging*, London/New York: Zed Books, 2005, p. 67.

84 Nowak, M., *UN Covenant on Civil and Political Rights: CCPR Commentary*, 2nd edn, Kehl am Rhein/Strasbourg/Arlington: N.P. Engel Verlag, 2005, p. 464.

85 United States Department of State, 2011 Country Reports on Human Rights Practices – Angola, 24 May 2012, available at: www.unhcr.org/refworld/docid/4fc75ac041.html, accessed 14 October 2014: 'The government sometimes arbitrarily restricted the *activities* of associations it considered *subversive* by refusing to grant permits for organized *activities*.'

86 J. Humphrey termed this ground for restriction to be '[h]ighly dangerous (from the point of view of human rights) civil law concept [. . .] a concept which [. . .] covers at least as much ground as public policy in English-American law and perhaps much more.' See Humphrey J, 'Political and related rights', in Meron T. (ed.), *Human Rights in International Law: Legal and Policy Issues*, Oxford: Clarendon Press, 1984, p. 185. M.J. Bossuyt noted that during the preparatory works of the 1966 ICCPR that it had been proposed to substitute the term 'public order' with the expression: 'the prevention of disorder or crime', a proposal finally rejected. See Bossuyt, M.J., *Guide to the 'Travaux Préparatoires' of the International Covenant on Civil and Political Rights*, Dordrecht/London/Boston: Martinus Nijhoff, 1987, p. 390.

87 Ibid., references at pp. 384–9.

88 Guradze, H., 'Die Menschenrechtskonventionen der Vereinten Nationen vom 16 Dezember 1966', in *German Yearbook of International Law*, vol. 15, 1971, p. 259.

89 Lawyers' Committee for Human Rights, op. cit. note 38, p. 94.

in 2006, accusing them of vague 'subversive activities' although the refugees were not returned to Kinshasa's authorities.[90] In addition, in 1990, the Kenyan President, D. Arap Moi accused Rwandan refugees of using Kenya as a base for subversive activities and proceeded to the summary deportation of Rwandan refugees who had been residing in Kenya for many years.[91]

It appears to us that, generally, provisions of Article III of the 1969 OAU Convention do not achieve their purported goal of protecting states from hostile activities by their own nationals in neighbouring countries. They simply serve as restrictions on the rights of refugees, restrictions that are undoubtedly felt stronger by urban refugees, who have been granted individual asylum, since they are more likely to be political activists, rather than rural refugees who are usually not politically active and who, for the most part, flee from war and disorders in their country of origin.

Considering the Sub-Saharan African domestic legislations, section 15 of the 1983 Refugee Act from Zimbabwe[92] contains typical legal powers allowing the

90 US Committee for Refugees and Migrants, World Refugee Survey 2007, Uganda, 11 July 2007, p. 1, available at: www.unhcr.org/refworld/docid/4696388e1e.html, accessed 10 October 2014. Always in Kenya, the Islamic Party has been accused in the mid-1990s of training guerrillas, also among refugees, to take part in subversive activities against the government. See Immigration and Refugee Board of Canada, Kenya: Information on the IPK, its policies and methods for achieving them, 1995, available at: www.unhcr.org/refworld/docid/3ae6ab3374.html, accessed 10 October 2014.

91 Immigration and Refugee Board of Canada, Kenya: Information on the Rwandan Front/Movement and its activities in Kenya, 1 March 1991, available at: www.unhcr.org/refworld/docid/3ae6ad0e34.html, accessed 10 October 2014. In this regard, see also Immigration and Refugee Board of Canada, Kenya/Burundi: Situation of stateless Tutsis, 1 March 1991, available at: www.unhcr.org/refworld/docid/3ae6abd664.html, accessed 10 October 2014.

92 Section 15 of the 1983 Refugee Act of Zimbabwe stipulates: '1) Subject to the provisions of this section and of section thirteen, the Minister, after consultation with the Minister to whom the administration of the Immigration Act, 1979 (No. 18 of 1979), has been assigned, may order the expulsion from Zimbabwe of any recognized refugee or protected person if he/she considers the expulsion to be necessary or desirable on the grounds of national security or public order. 2) Before making an order in terms of subsection 1), the Minister shall cause a written notice to be served upon every recognized refugee or protected person whom he/she intends to expel, informing such recognized refugee or protected person – a) of the Minister's intention to expel him/her/, the grounds for expelling him/her and the country to which it is proposed to expel him/her; and b) of his/her right to make representations to the Minister in terms of subsection 3). 3) A recognized refugee or protected person upon whom a notice has been served in terms of subsection 2) may, either by him/herself or through a legal practitioner registered in terms of the Legal Practitioners Act, 1981 (No. 15 of 1981), within a period of fourteen days from the date of such service, make written representations to the Minister in respect of either or both of the following matters: a) the necessity or desirability, on the grounds of national security or public order, of expelling him/her from Zimbabwe; or b) the possibility of his/her being prosecuted or of his/her life or freedom being threatened in the country to which it is proposed to expel him/her on account of his/her race, religion, nationality, membership or a particular social group or political opinion, or on account of external aggression, occupation, foreign domination or events seriously disrupting public order in part or the whole of that country. 4) Before ordering the expulsion from Zimbabwe of any recognized refugee or protected person in terms of

expulsion of a refugee on grounds of 'national security or public order'. It is clear that it has been verified that there have been in the past a number of instances in which refugees were expelled for political activities judged as 'subversive'. In October 1989, for instance, E. Yapwantha, leader of the MAFREMO was expelled from Zimbabwe – but not returned to Malawian authorities – apparently for activities that breached the terms of asylum. The reason for the expulsion was probably a request from the government seated in Lilongwe: possibly the Zimbabwean government wanted no more Malawian political violence on its soil, making acceptance of the Malawian request timely and expedient.[93] However, the point of principle is that there is nothing in the 1969 African Convention to prevent a refugee from engaging in political activities in the host country unless, as seems to be the case of Zimbabwe in the above-mentioned episode, foreign politicians are considered a threat to national security.

Efforts in domestic law, other than in national refugee laws, have also been made. Section 22 of the 2002 Tanzanian Prevention of Terrorism Act exemplifies legislative practice intended to prevent the territory of a state from being used as a sanctuary to launch 'attacks' against other states; this section is addressed to 'any person', an expression that evidently also includes refugees.[94] Nevertheless, this section, as the entire act, is silent on the modalities of the attacks. In converse, section 54.2 of the 1982 South African Internal Security Act is very detailed and well-articulated and, in our opinion, could even serve as a model for a more thorough draft of normativity valid to a regional level. However, of course, in that case the norms should be addressed towards other states, given that, evidently, the Internal Security Act deals with subversion that is 'domestic' not taking account of subversion against other states.[95]

subsection 1), the Minister shall give due consideration to any representations made to him/her in terms of subsection 3). 5) The execution of any order for the expulsion of a recognized refugee or protected person made in terms of subsection 1) shall, if such recognized refugee or protected person so requests, be delayed for a reasonable period to enable such recognized refugee or protected person to seek admission to a country other than the country to which he/she is to be expelled.'

93 Lawyers' Committee for Human Rights, op. cit. note 38, pp. 94–5.

94 Tanzania, The Prevention of Terrorism Act, 2002, section 22: 'Every person who, in the United Republic – a) knowingly promotes or facilitates the doing of any act in a facilitation foreign state for the purpose of achieving any of the following objectives, whether or not the objective is achieved [. . .] commits of an offence and shall on conviction, be liable to imprisonment for a period of term not less than twenty years and not more than thirty years.'

95 South Africa, Act No. 74 of 1982, entered into force on 2 July 1982 in terms of Proclamation No. 119 of 1982, Article 54: '1) Any person who with intent to – a) overthrow or endanger the State authority in the Republic; b) achieve, bring about or promote any constitutional, political, industrial, social or economic aim or change in the Republic; c) induce the Government of the Republic to do or to abstain from doing any act or to adopt or to abandon a particular standpoint; or d) put in fear or demoralize the general public, a particular population group or the inhabitants of a particular area in the Republic, or to induce the said public or such population group or inhabitants to do or to abstain from doing any act [. . .] 2) Any person who with intent to achieve any of the objects specified in paragraphs a) to d), inclusive, of subsection

Other dissident members of Southern African liberation movements have been especially vulnerable in the past to abuses of this kind. The African National Congress (ANC) in South Africa and the South West African People's Organization (SWAPO) in Namibia enjoyed a collective status in which the movement itself assumed a 'quasi-governmental' role. Questions arose either because refugees did not desire to place themselves under the discipline of the liberation movements, or because individual members became disillusioned with the movement's leadership and wished to express dissenting views. Hence, the widespread human rights abuses against members of both ANC and SWAPO in Angola during the 1980s, at the time, were regarded as being largely an internal affair for these movements.[96]

Undoubtedly, both law and jurisprudence on the matter of 'subversive activities' should include a clearer and more ample definition of the activities that are understood as prohibited in the context of the institution of asylum. In this regard, the 1965 Ethiopia-Sudan memorandum of agreement on prevention of subversive activities was an effective attempt to clarify this, though it unfortunately was not repeated in later years. This agreement distinctly banned several activities, such as hostile propaganda – conducted by press, radio or any other media – within

1) – a) causes or promotes general dislocation or disorder at any place in the Republic, or attempts to do so; b) cripples, prejudices or interrupts at any place in the Republic any industry or undertaking, or industries or undertakings generally, or the production, supply or distribution of commodities or foodstuffs, or attempts to do so; c) interrupts, impedes or endangers at any place in the Republic the manufacture, storage, generation, distribution, rendering or supply of fuel, petroleum products, energy, light, power or water, or of sanitary, medical, health, educational, police, fire-fighting, ambulance, postal or telecommunication services or radio or television transmitting, broadcasting or receiving services or any other public service, or attempts to do so; d) endangers, damages, destroys, renders useless or unserviceable or puts out of action at any place in the Republic any installation for the rendering or supply of any service referred to in paragraph c), any prohibited place or any public building, or attempts to do so; e) prevents or hampers, or deters any person from assisting in, the maintenance of law and order at any place in the Republic, or attempts to do so; f) impedes or endangers at any place in the Republic the free movement of any traffic on land, at sea or in the air, or attempts to do so; g) causes, encourages or foments feelings of hostility between different population groups or parts of population groups of the Republic, or attempts to do so; h) destroys, pollutes or contaminates any water supply which is intended for public use in the Republic, or attempts to do so; i) in the Republic or elsewhere performs any act or attempts, consents or takes any steps to perform any act which results in or could have resulted in or promotes or could have promoted the commission of any of the acts or the bringing about of any of the results contemplated in paragraphs a) to h), inclusive; j) conspires with any other person to commit, bring about or perform any of the acts or results contemplated in paragraphs a) to h), inclusive, or any act contemplated in paragraph i), or to aid in the commission, bringing about or performance thereof; or k) incites, instigates, commands, aids, advises, encourages or procures any other person to commit, bring about or perform such act or result, shall be guilty of the offence of subversion [. . .].'

96 Lawyers' Committee for Human Rights, op. cit. Chapter 3, note 38, p. 95. In its turn, we note that on 26 December 1988, the Angolan government also announced an amnesty for all expatriates who had conducted 'subversive activities' against the government seated in Luanda. See Immigration and Refugee board of Canada, 'Angola: Angolan government response to its nationals returning after having left illegally', 1990, available at: www.unhcr.org/refworld/docid/3ae6ab4034.html, accessed 10 October 2014.

its jurisdiction and against the national interests of the other party; transfer of arms; and activities designed for use by secessionist movements, comprising the training of dissidents. This agreement has represented a first effort to provide a legal framework for a domain, which until then and until today as well, has remained substantially lacking in legal discipline.[97]

In our view, the fact that the provisos of the 1969 African Refugee Convention sought to deter subversive activities, yet did not establish a regime of sanctions for the contravention of Article III, must be pointed out as a weakness of the convention, and, therefore, for the protection of asylum-seekers and refugees in the region. It is also wondered whether, in law, individuals who engage in these kinds of activities could not and should not be dealt with at all. Under refugee obligations and facilities, any individual with a mind to pursue extra-constitutional competition for power with the government of his/her country of origin should not be granted the status and facilities of refuge in the first place. This constitutes a point of law, rather than a question of fairness of the pursued cause. The point being made here thus has a direct link with the argument for the necessity to make refugee status procedures more complex, especially those procedures that will ensure that individuals bent on political resistance must not be admitted into the refugee system.[98]

In effect, one of the problems raised by Article III of the 1969 OAU Convention is the so-called 'vicarious responsibility' of countries for acts of individuals within their jurisdiction.[99] The extent of this responsibility is, however, controversial. In this regard, P. Weis has contended that Sub-Saharan African countries have a duty as far as possible to prevent persons under their jurisdiction from perpetrating harmful acts against other states. From a legal point of view there is no difference

97 Memorandum of agreement between the governments of the Sudan and Ethiopia – on prevention of subversive activities – 28 July 1965, paragraphs 1 through 6.

98 Okoth-Obbo, G., 'Thirty years on: a legal review of the 1969 OAU Refugee Convention Governing the Specific Aspects of Refugee Problems in Africa', op. cit. note 34, pp. 134–5.

99 In this regard, see Jennings, R. and Watts, A. (eds), *Oppenheim's International Law*, pp. 501–2 quoted in Grant, J.P. and Barker, J.C., *Encyclopaedic Dictionary of International Law*, 3rd edn, Oxford/New York: Oxford University Press, 2009, p. 660: 'A distinction is sometimes made between the original and the so-called vicarious responsibilities of a state. 'Original' responsibility is borne by a state for acts which are directly imputable to it, such as acts of its government, or those of its officials or private individuals performed at the government's command or with its authorization. 'Vicarious' responsibility, on the other hand, arises out of certain international injurious acts of private individuals (whether nationals, or aliens in the state's territory), and of officials acting without authorization. It is apparent that the essential difference between original and vicarious responsibility in this sense is that whereas the former involves a state being in direct breach of legal obligations binding on it, and is accordingly a particularly serious matter, the latter of the state's responsibility is at one removed from the injurious conduct complained of: in such cases the state's responsibility calls for it to take certain preventive measures and requires it to secure that as far as possible the wrongdoer makes suitable reparation, and if necessary to punish him/her. But these preventive and remedial obligations of the state in cases of "vicarious" responsibility are themselves obligations for the breach of which (as by refusing to take the remedial action which is required) the state bears direct responsibility.'

in the responsibility of the state for the activities of refugees enjoying asylum within its territory and for the activities of other private persons within its jurisdiction.[100]

Yet, nothing written until now should be understood to signify that activities for purposes of resistance and, in this framework, the circumstance for states to conduct foreign policy endorsing resistance groups, should be wholly condemned. By contrast, no such activities should be allowed within the legal framework of the humanitarian institution of asylum. This is the response to those who claim to support the right of refugees to continue to fight against the government that induced them to flee.[101]

In effect, it may happen that refugees, who are primarily victims of domestic political conflict in their countries of origin, can be a source of international conflict as well. As the history of Sub-Saharan Africa has sufficiently demonstrated, offering protection and support to refugees, particularly those who may be involved in military and/or political campaigns against their country of origin, regularly incurs military retaliation and draws the country of asylum into tumult.[102]

To reinforce the prohibition of subversive activities in their own countries, several domestic legislations, other than the aforementioned case of Zimbabwe, have incorporated this concept, as have the Congolese (DRC) and the Congolese Brazzaville. Subversive activities in these countries are banned on grounds of national security in order not to spoil relations between DRC and Congo Brazzaville and the country of origin of the refugee and, in particular, between the former two.[103] It is, however, taken for granted that the refugee should not, in any case, be returned to the country where he/she fears persecution. At most, the country of asylum or temporary asylum can insist that the refugee be transferred to another country of asylum.[104]

It is also clear that several measures have been sought to prevent refugees from engaging in subversive activities and these measures find their background more in ethical common sense than in strictly legal measures. These measures generally consist in informing refugees of their obligations under refugee and national law;

100 Weis, P., 'The Convention of the Organization of the African Unity Governing the Specific Aspects of Refugee Problems in Africa', op. cit. note 18, p. 460.

101 Okoth-Obbo, G., 'Thirty years on: a legal review of the 1969 OAU Refugee Convention Governing the Specific Aspects of Refugee Problems in Africa', op. cit. note 34, p. 135.

102 Maluwa, T., *International Law in Post-Colonial Africa*, The Hague/London/Boston: Kluwer Law International, 1999, p. 192.

103 DRC, Article 36 1) of the Law No. 021/2002, portant statut des réfugiés en République Démocratique du Congo, 16 October 2002; Congo, Article 30 of the Arrêté No. 8041, Portant création, organisation, attribution et fonctionnement de la Commission d'éligibilité au statut de réfugié, 28 décembre 2001. By way of example, Article 30 of the law of the Republic of Congo stipulates: '30) Tout refugie et tout demandeur d'asile est tenu de s'abstenir d'entreprendre toute activité subversive de nature à compromettre la sécurité nationale ou les rapports qu'entretient le Congo avec son pays d'origine.' The text of the law of DRC is not dissimilar.

104 See, for example: Rwelamira, M.R.K., 'Some reflections on the OAU Convention on refugees: some pending issues', op. cit. note 30, p. 174.

working on a regional basis to reduce tensions and halting subversive influences from abroad; and, more generally, improving the climate for peace, democracy and respect of human rights.[105]

However, as the reader may easily observe, if peace, democracy and respect of human rights reigned on the continent, not only would subversive activities be non-existent, but the very phenomenon of 'refugeeism' would disappear: it is the best we can hope for the African continent but, for now, it remains purely wishful thinking.

105 UNHCR, Global Consultations on International Protection, UNHCR Regional Symposium on maintaining the civilian and humanitarian character of asylum refugee status, camps and other locations, 26–27 February, 2001, Pretoria, South Africa, document No. EC/GC/01/9, section 4 a).

7 Misusing the help received and its consequences

National governments and the expulsion of refugees

7.1 Legal framework for expulsion

The notion of state sovereignty grants states the right to freely decide about the admission and continuing presence of aliens on their territory, and this right implies the possibility to expel them. For a long time, the arbitrary power of governments to expel aliens was almost unlimited. Today, this is no longer entirely true.[1]

During several decades of the twentieth century, refugees in Sub-Saharan Africa who were allowed to enter an asylum state often found themselves exposed to expulsion because they had committed even minor criminal offences, or were deemed 'public charges' because they were unable to meet their own needs due to their indigence. The practice of expulsion caused great suffering to refugees, who were often pushed back and forth between countries and punished each time for illegal entry, causing also significant troubles for the countries to which the expelled person was sent in the first place. In so doing, the expulsion of refugees became an issue of preoccupation for the entire African community. And if the limitation of the use of expulsion in situations dictated by reasons of national security and public order is already a way to limit the arbitrariness of the decisions adopted by African governments, the same expulsion also should be carried out exclusively if a refugee could be lawfully admitted to another country.[2] However, this latter is not always the case in Sub-Saharan Africa, as was seen in 2006, when 150,000 Arab refugees from neighbouring countries were expelled by Niger for reason of national security. They were sent back to their countries of origin, primarily Chad, where they were persecuted for decades, as well as to other

1 Kaelin, W., 'Aliens, expulsion and deportation', in *Max Planck Encyclopedia of Public International Law on-line*, pdf document, available at: www.mpepil.com/subscriber_article?script=yes&id=/epil/entries/law-9780199231690-e745&recno=7&searchType=Quick&query=refugee, paragraph 4, accessed 30 October 2014. In this regard, see also Sanderson, M., 'Statelessness and mass expulsion in Sudan: a reassessment of the international law', in *Northwestern Journal of International Human Rights*, vol. 12, 2014, p. 108.

2 Grahl-Madsen, A., *Commentary on the Refugee Convention 1951: Articles 2–11, 13–37*, Geneva: UNHCR, 1997, pp. 185–6.

neighbouring countries, which had never expressed any wish to receive them.[3] A similar case occurred in Zambia in 2010, when dozens of refugees from DRC were expelled and forced to return to DRC after having protested against the removal of a corrupted Zambian registration official.[4]

As W. Kaelin argued, the expulsion of aliens may take place generally in three situations: either if the person concerned is lawfully in the territory of the country ordering the expulsion, for instance with a residence permit; if his/her stay in that territory is no longer lawful, for example because a visa or residence permit has expired; or if the alien's presence has never been lawful, for instance after an illegal border crossing. Domestic laws often use different terminology for each of these three situations, qualifying, for example, the last situation as non-admission to the territory.[5] In a practical situation, the tens of thousands of Angolans expelled from DRC in October 2009 seem to belong to the first of the categories mentioned.[6]

The particular worry is that if expelled, refugees normally have no safe place to go. This ethical concern often clashes with the will of several African countries that think that the presence of refugees in their territory is simply not compatible with their own interest.[7] Therefore, it is not by chance that, generally, doctrine considers the purpose of Article 32 ('Expulsion') of the 1951 Geneva Convention to be such that it should not be possible to put an end to the lawful presence of a refugee by any means, but only for specific, substantial reasons.[8] However, if a

3 See the news: 'Niger expels 150,000 Arab refugees', 25 October 2006, available at: http://208.43.71.196-static.reverse.softlayer.com/english/news/africa/432089, accessed 30 October 2014.

4 See the news: 'UN blasts Zambia over refugee expulsion', 13 April 2010, available at: http://mg.co.za/article/2010–04–13-un-blasts-zambia-over-refugee-expulsion, accessed 30 October 2014: 'The UNHCR noted that even though refugees are required to abide by the law of their host countries, they should not be expelled if they failed to do so. Rather, they should be prosecuted under national laws, stressed Fleming. "The UNHCR urges the government of Zambia to halt the expulsion of refugees and asylum-seekers and to uphold its refugee protection responsibilities under international law," she added.'

5 Kaelin, W., 'Aliens, expulsion and deportation', op. cit. note 1, paragraph 3.

6 See the news: 'Some 30,000 expelled Angolans in "dire" need of assistance', 20 October 2009, available at: www.unhcr.org/4adde3aa9.html, accessed 30 October 2014. In detail, see the following passage: 'Some of them claimed they had been rounded up and taken to the border, despite the fact they carried documents certifying their refugee status. Others said they were forced back without having had a chance to take their identification documents or any of their belongings. Most of them were deported from the Bas Congo province in southern DRC. These forced returns came in response to the waves of expulsions of large numbers of Congolese from Angola since December 2008. According to UN estimates, Angola forcibly returned 160,000 Congolese up to October this year. The Congolese claimed ill treatment while being expelled.'

7 Hathaway, J.C., *The Rights of Refugees Under International Law*, Cambridge: Cambridge University Press, p. 659.

8 Stenberg, G., *Non-Expulsion and Non-Refoulement: The Prohibition Against Removal of Refugees with Special Reference to Articles 32 and 33 of the 1951 Convention Relating to the Status of Refugees*, Uppsala: Iustus Forlag, 1989, p. 84. Article 32 of the 1951 Geneva Convention reads as follows: '1) The Contracting States shall not expel a refugee lawfully in their territory, save on grounds of national security or public order. 2) The expulsion of such a refugee shall be only in pursuance of a decision reached in accordance with due process of law. Except where compelling reasons of national

legal refugee in the host country does not have his/her permit of stay renewed by the local authorities, this measure by itself does not provide for an automatic expulsion of the person concerned. Rather, it makes the presence of the refugee illegal, and his/her expulsion will be therefore not subject to the provision contained in Article 32.[9]

When an asylum-seeker arrives looking for protection in a given country, he/she enjoys a limited right of non-repatriation. Under this circumstance, the safeguard which an unauthorized asylum-seeker may claim derives from the principle of *non-refoulement* set by Article 33 of the 1951 Geneva Convention,[10] and the right not to be arbitrarily detained for unlawful entry set in Article 31 ('Refugees unlawfully in the country of refuge') of the same instrument. This latter represents a new solution never previously adopted in international refugee law, with the necessity of 'legalizing' the illegal entry constituting the rationale of this norm.[11] These duties do not automatically prevent a country party to the 1951 Geneva Convention from expelling an asylum-seeker in the initial phases of his/her reception. Consequently, an asylum-seeker whose presence is not yet legal – for instance because he/she has not yet applied for refugee status – may be expelled to another country.[12]

In addition, there is a specific logic to the interpretation of Article 32 of the 1951 Geneva Convention, which intends to provide protection for asylum-seekers who are still awaiting the result of their application for refugee status. As these individuals are respecting the formal host state's legal obligation, permitting them to remain in the country pending the results of their application constitutes simply a question of fairness.[13] Nevertheless, this was not the case, for instance, for the Burundian and Rwandan asylum-seekers waiting for the response to their application for refugee status in the Kisangani transit refugee camp in 1997: it

security otherwise require, the refugee shall be allowed to submit evidence to clear himself, and to appeal to and be represented for the purpose before competent authority or a person or persons specially designated by the competent authority. 3) The Contracting States shall allow such a refugee a reasonable period within which to seek legal admission into another country. The Contracting States reserve the right to apply during that period such internal measures as they may deem necessary.'

9 Abi-Saab, G., 'The admission and expulsion of refugees with special reference to Africa', in *African Yearbook of International Law*, vol. 8, 2000, p. 83.

10 We note that '[a]lthough the principle of *non-refoulement* has been enunciated in article 33, its scope is not limited to convention refugees. In other words, its application is not tied to any formal determination of refugee status. It applies to both legally admitted as well as other refugees who invoke the principle.' See Henckaerts, J.-M., *Mass Expulsion in Modern International Law and Practice*, The Hague: Martinus Nijhoff, 1995, p. 102.

11 Abi-Saab, G., op. cit. note 9, p. 78. The author explained at idem and at p. 79: '1) The refugee has to come directly from a country of persecution [. . .]; 2) He must present himself without delay to the authorities [. . .]; 3) He must show good cause for the illegal entry or presence.'

12 Hathaway, J.C., *The Rights of Refugees Under International Law*, op. cit. note 7, pp. 663–4.

13 In this regard, G. Stenberg clearly observed that: '[a]n alien is generally allowed to stay in the territory of the expelling state pending the outcome of his/her request for determination of his/her refugee status. This stay is generally allowed whether or not his/her prior sojourn in the state has been lawful according to the rules set out for ordinary aliens. Third, there are situations

went against the fundamental norms of equality to deny *interim* protection to these individuals just because the formalities to validate their status had not yet been completed.[14]

It is important to remember that asylum states genuinely unable to cope with refugee arrivals always retain the option under Article 33 of the 1951 Geneva Convention, to initially redirect those refugees to other states where they could acquire rights able to be respected, and in which there is no direct or indirect risk of being persecuted. However, once the refugee has been allowed to enter an RSD procedure and has been acquitted of all responsibilities to contribute to the inquiry into his/her claim, it would be unnecessarily harsh to force him/her away before a final answer is given.

This duty to desist from expulsion is purely provisional since the refugee's lawful presence ends if and when a refugee status is denied. In the meantime, the legitimate concerns of the host state are adequately safeguarded by the right to expel a refugee on national security or public order grounds,[15] two concepts not always clear to define operationally because of a huge margin of subjectivity.[16] In this framework, we can understand the expulsion of Kenyans from Tanzania in 1990, some rejected by their 'extended family' present in the host country. The main reason for this expulsion of Kenyans was that, during their stay in

in which there is no right to provisional stay pending the examination of the request.' See Stenberg, G., op. cit. note 8, p. 119.

14 Hathaway, J.C., *The Rights of Refugees Under International Law*, op. cit. note 7, pp. 667–8. We note that the 2002 Congolese refugee law provides for two articles – 30 and 31 – that exclude expulsion and, if admitted – for reasons of national security or public order – provides for several guarantees for the refugee expelled such as the right for a hearing and even the possibility to be helped by Congolese authorities to find a new country of asylum for resettlement. A similar proviso is also present in the legislation of other countries such as, for instance, in Ethiopia, where section 10, subsection 4 of the 2004 Refugee Proclamation stipulates: '4) The execution of any expulsion order may, if the concerned refugee requests, be delayed for a reasonable period to enable such refugee, to seek admission to a country other than the country to which he/she is to be expelled.' In this regard, see also Henckaerts, J.-M., *Mass Expulsion in Modern International Law and Practice*, op. cit. note 10, p. 101. At idem, the author observed: 'According to Africa Watch, registered refugees had their documents destroyed by the police and the security forces were herded into courts en masse charged with illegal residence while no one had access to a lawyer. Such practices are obviously unlawful.'

15 A. Grahl-Madsen gave a plain explanation of the expression 'national security': 'The meaning of the words "national security" is rather clear. If a refugee is spying against his/her country of residence, he/she is threatening the national security of that country, and he/she may consequently be expelled. The same applies if he/she is engaged in activities, directed at the overthrow by force or other illegal means of the Government of his/her country of residence, or in activities which are directed against a foreign Government, which as a result threatens the Government of the country of residence with intervention of a serious nature. Generally speaking, the expression "national security" covers acts of a rather serious nature threatening directly or indirectly the Government, the integrity or the independence of the state on whose territory a refugee stays.' See Grahl-Madsen, A., 'Expulsion of refugees', in *Nordisk Tidsskrift International Ret*, vol. 33, 1963, p. 42. By contrast, this scholar observed that '[t]he expression "public order" [. . .] is open to a wide range of interpretations' and that 'the expression "public order" is being interpreted somewhat different in various countries which are Parties to the Refugee Convention.' See ibid., pp. 42 and 46.

16 Abi-Saab, G., op. cit. note 9, p. 84.

Tanzania, Tanzanian 'extended family' lands had been demarcated and subdivided among individual family members by the local authorities. Kenyans were then considered a threat to individual property. Other reasons for rejection included the importation of 'alien' cultural practice, such as witchcraft.[17]

More importantly, Article 32 of the 1951 Geneva Convention sets up a guarantee of due process compared to the standards established by Article 13 of the 1966 ICCPR,[18] in that it unambiguously gives refugees the possibility to appeal to competent authorities. This standard was clearly preferred in order to prevent the possibility that a simple police officer could expel a refugee, this latter constituting precisely the approach Kenya wanted to impose in the early 2000s on Ethiopian and Somali refugees, amassed in Nairobi with the intention to expel them.[19] In this regard, the 'due process of law' before the expulsion order, provided for in section 21 2) of the 2006 Kenyan Refugee Act might have had the goal to reduce the tendency to arbitrariness of Kenyan authorities. Unfortunately, however, this has not been the case; in spite of the intention of the 2006 Kenyan Refugee Act to reduce arbitrary expulsions, in October 2011, expulsions of refugees in Kenya were still practiced under various pretexts. Kenyan authorities threatened the expulsion of hundreds of thousands of Somalis under the pretext that the Kenyan troops sent into South Somalia shortly before, could guarantee conditions suitable for the return of Somali refugees at home.[20] This expulsion occurred in spite of the fact that, several times, the Somali government warned Kenyan authorities that the expulsion and return of Somali at home could have created a difficult situation in Somalia.[21]

17 Opondo, E.O., 'Refugee repatriation in the Horn of Africa', in Allen, T. (ed.), *In Search of Cool Ground: War, Flight and Homecoming in Northeast Africa*, London: James Currey; Trenton. NJ: Africa World Press, 1996, p. 30.

18 Article 13 of the 1966 ICCPR reads: '[A]n alien lawfully in the territory of a State Party to the present Covenant may be expelled therefrom only in pursuance of a decision reached in accordance with law and shall, except where compelling reasons of national security otherwise require, be allowed to submit the reasons against his/her expulsion and to have his/her case reviewed by, and be represented for the purpose before, the competent authority or a person or persons especially designated by the competent authority.' To date, 10 November 2012, no general comment of its implementation has been provided for.

19 Hathaway, J.C., *The Rights of Refugees Under International Law*, op. cit. note 7, p. 671.

20 See the news: 'Kenya threatens mass refugee expulsion', 28 October 2011, available at: www.sbs.com.au/news/article/1600485/kenya-threatens-mass-refugee-expulsion, accessed 30 October 2014.

21 For instance, see the news: 'Somalia warns Kenyan refugee expulsion will lead to "chaos and anarchy"', 27 May 2014. Available at: www.ipsnews.net/2014/05/somalia-says-kenyan-refugee-expulsion-will-lead-chaos-anarchy/, accessed 30 October 2014: 'Somalia's State Minister for Interior and Federalism Affairs Mohamud Moalim Yahye has told IPS that the hasty repatriation and mass deportation of its citizens by Kenya could compromise recent, critical security improvements made by regional governments against the Islamic extremist group, Al-Shabaab. "The unplanned and uncoordinated deportation of people, especially the youth, will create chaos and anarchy as there are no resources to support and create jobs for them," Yahye told IPS by phone from Mogadishu, Somalia's capital.'

In their action, however, Kenyan authorities were supported by Article 17 of the recently adopted Refugees Bill 2011, where, the expression 'due process of law' has been finally omitted in its treatment of the expulsion of refugees, attributing to Kenyan authorities a high level of discretion regarding when and how to expel refugees and/or asylum-seekers.[22]

The importance of granting refugees increased protection against erroneous or other unjustified expulsion is emphasized as well by the specificity of the 1951 Geneva Convention's procedural requirements. Like all aliens, refugees are presumptively entitled to claim the benefit of the 1966 ICCPR's right to submit reasons against their expulsion, and to be represented on the review of any decision to expel them.[23] Nonetheless, the more explicit language of the 1951 Geneva Convention Article 32 2) unequivocally affirms the right of a refugee to submit evidence in support of his/her case, not simply to state his/her reasons for resisting expulsion. In addition, the extent of relevant evidence includes any evidence that may assist the refugee to 'clear him/herself', not just evidence against expulsion.[24] Thus, there is no question that the organ considering a refugee's appeal against expulsion must consider evidence relevant to, for example, the reliability of a criminal conviction which was the basis for the expulsion order. However, the criminal conviction alone is not sufficient to return a refugee to a country of persecution.[25]

Another striking difference between the provisos of the 1966 ICCPR and the 1951 Geneva Convention is that the latter expressly requires that the decision to expel a refugee shall be exclusively in pursuance of a decision reached in accordance with due process of law.[26] The more general formulation in the 1966 ICCPR requires simply that the expulsion decision be reached in accordance with

22 Kenya, The Refugees Bill 2011, 15 July 2011, Article 17: '1) Subject to section 16 and subsection 2) of this section, where the Cabinet Secretary considers the revocation of the refugee status of any person and the expulsion from Kenya of that person to be necessary on grounds of national security and public order, the Cabinet Secretary may, after consultation with the Cabinet Secretary responsible for matters relating to internal security, order the revocation of the refugee status and proceed to expel such a person or member of his family from Kenya.'

23 In this regard, M. Nowak, in his 1993 work correctly observed: '[e]ven though the reasons against a pending expulsion should, as a rule, be asserted in oral hearing, article 13 does not [. . .] give rise to a right to a personal appearance', and later in the same study: '[a] person threatened with expulsion is not entitled to legal counsel or to the appointment of an attorney.' See Nowak, M., *UN Covenant on Civil and Political Rights: ICCPR Commentary*, 1st edn, Kehl am Rhein/Strasbourg/Arlington: N.P. Engel Verlag, 1993, pp. 228 and 231.

24 While M. Nowak may be right that the more constrained language of the 1966 ICCPR '[d]id not change the substance of the right' as conceived in the 1951 Refugee Convention, the greater precision of Article 32 of the 1951 Geneva Convention readily forecloses debate in this regard. For the opinion by M. Nowak, see ibid., p. 228.

25 Grahl-Madsen, A., 'Expulsion of refugees', op. cit. note 15, p. 49.

26 P. Weis observed that the due process of law also has a fundamental substantive dimension which '[m]eans that the [expulsion] decision must be based on law that it may not be unreasonable, arbitrary or capricious and must have a real and substantive relation to its object.' See Weis, P., *The Refugee Convention, 1951/The travaux préparatoires analyzed*, Cambridge International Document Series, vol. 7, Cambridge/New York: Cambridge University Press, 1995, p. 322.

the law.[27] The 1966 ICCPR's formulation was considered a decision decreeing expulsion, which must be made by a court or an administrative authority on the basis of a law affording protection against arbitrary expulsion through the establishment of corresponding procedural guarantees.[28] However, not even compelling reasons of national security would justify the expulsion of a refugee under a procedure considered to be arbitrary or unfair.[29] Whatever preoccupations Nigeria had about the Chadian refugees who supported attacks on their home country from its territory, or that Kenya feared concerning illegal activities of Rwandan and Ugandan refugees, they simply could not justify the elimination of the right of refugees to have a hearing before the measure of expulsion could be enacted.[30] Worse still, the Congolese, recognized as refugees, were expelled in 2004 from Angola with the clear pretext that they were illegal diamond workers, in an attempt to control the illegal trade. Under this pretext, Angolan authorities referred to Articles 6 and 20 of their domestic legislation in order to legally justify the expulsions.[31] However, those expelled cited cases of physical aggression, rape, robbery and destruction of documents by the Angolan police and army. Moreover, they had no access to any hearing at all.[32]

27 Article 13 of the 1966 ICCPR reads: 'An alien lawfully in the territory of a State Party to the present Covenant may be expelled therefrom only in pursuance of a decision reached in accordance with law and shall, except where compelling reasons of national security otherwise require, be allowed to submit the reasons against his expulsion and to have his case reviewed by, and be represented for the purpose before, the competent authority or a person or persons especially designated by the competent authority.'

28 Nowak, M., UN Covenant on Civil and Political Rights: CCPR Commentary, 1st edn, op. cit. note 23, p. 226.

29 Referring specifically to Kenya and Tanzania C.R. Veney observed that: '[T]he insecurity and crime posed by the refugees were used as an excuse to adopt new policies that included forced encampment, round-ups, sweeps, detentions, and forcible deportations [. . .].' See Veney, C.R., *Forced Migration in Eastern Africa: Democratization, Structural Adjustment, and Refugees*, Basingstoke: Palgrave MacMillan, 2007, p. 220.

30 Hathaway, J.C., *The Rights of Refugees Under International Law*, op. cit. note 7, p. 675. The situation is worse if we consider the so-called right of the 're-hearing' of a refugee. In this latest regard, the South African Refugee Appeal Board in 2001 pointed out that: '[a] re-hearing could be ordered if the findings of fact made by the Authority at the appeal hearing were erroneous by reason of being based on a fundamental misunderstanding of the Appellant's evidence [. . .] the authority stated that it could not re-hear a case on the basis that at the first hearing the Appellant's evidence was misunderstood [. . .].' See Refugee Appeal Board of South Africa (Ethiopia), South Africa: Refugee Appeal Board, *Application for the re-opening and/or re-hearing and reconsideration of an appeal heard by the Refugee Appeal Board* on 6 April 2001.

31 Article 6 of the 1990 Angolan refugee law stipulates: '1) Any person who is in the situation of a refugee shall respect the Angolan Constitution and laws, not interfere in Angolan politics and not engage in activities that may endanger or jeopardize national security or Angola's relations with other States. 2) Failure to comply with the law shall not absolve the refugee from the responsibility deriving from the obligations set forth in the preceding paragraph; non fulfillment of these obligations may constitute grounds for expulsion, in conformity with article 20.' Article 20 1) of the same law reads: 'A person who has been granted asylum or refugee status may not be expelled, except for reasons of public order [. . .].'

32 JRS, dispatch No. 150, 18 May 2004. The dispatch continued: 'Relations between the two governments have been tense. Officials on both sides of the borders have refused to cooperate

While respect for due process before deciding to expel a refugee is clearly important, the 1951 Refugee Convention does not limit itself – as does Article 13 of the 1966 ICCPR[33] – to purely procedural constraints on expulsion. Under some of the early proposals for Article 32, there were no substantive limits to either the power to expel refugees or to only tribunal-dependent substantive restrictions. But as finally adopted, the 1951 Geneva Convention establishes presumptive immunity from expulsion for refugees lawfully living in an asylum state.[34] As aforementioned, Article 32 includes certain substantive safeguards against arbitrary and discriminatory expulsion and, as a rule, these conditions must be satisfied prior to the execution of a decision to expel.[35]

7.2 'National security' and 'public order': the use and abuse of these reasons to justify the past expulsion of refugees

The expulsion of a refugee may be lawfully pursued in only two cases, specifically when either 'national security' or 'public order' grounds justify such action, as shown, for instance, in the 2008 Burundian legislation.[36]

The clearest situation in which a refugee may lawfully be expelled is when his/her presence in the state of asylum poses a risk to that country's 'national

with each other. The Angolan authorities have dumped thousands of so-called illegal immigrants, some recognized refugees, at the Congolese border post, while the Congolese authorities have in many cases refused to grant them access to the territory.'

33 In this regard, T. Clark argued: 'Limits or prohibitions on any form of expulsion or transfer of persons from one state to another stem from two sources. These would form the reasons in the required expulsion hearing under Covenant article 13. There are obligations under human rights treaties to anticipate violations of non-derogable rights as a consequence of return [. . .].' See Clark, T., 'Human rights and expulsion: giving content to the concept of asylum', in *International Journal of Refugee Law*, vol. 4, 1992, p. 196. Article 13 of the 1966 Pact on Civil and Political Rights reads: 'An alien lawfully in the territory of a State Party to the present Covenant may be expelled therefrom only in pursuance of a decision reached in accordance with law and shall, except where compelling reasons of national security otherwise require, be allowed to submit the reasons against his/her expulsion and to have his/her case reviewed by, and be represented for the purpose before, the competent authority or a person or persons especially designated by the competent authority.' The author also observed that an explicit obligation against return is found in Article 3 of the 1984 Convention against Torture and other Cruel, Inhuman or Degrading Treatment. See ibid., pp. 196–7.

34 With regard to the expression 'lawfully in their territory' used in Article 32 1) of the 1951 Geneva Convention, G. Stenberg noted that: '[I]t was the intention of the drafters of the Convention that a refugee should be considered as lawfully staying in the territory of a contracting State if his/her intended stay extended a period of three months after his/her entry and he/she possessed the necessary documents for such a stay. A refugee should be considered to be lawfully in the territory of a contracting State, however, as soon as he/she was present in the territory of the State, provided that he/she satisfied the criteria for lawfulness pertaining to aliens in general.' See Stenberg, G., op. cit. note 8, p. 92.

35 Eggli, A.V., *Mass Refugee Influx, and the Limits of Public International Law*, The Hague/London/New York: Martinus Nijhoff Publishers, 2001, p. 158.

36 Article 19 but also Articles 70 through 80 of the Loi No. 1/32 du 13 novembre 2008 sur l'asile et la protection des réfugiés au Burundi, No. 1/32, 13 novembre 2008.

security'. Because a threat to national security is also grounds for *refoulement* under Article 33 2) of the 1951 Geneva Convention,[37] a refugee expelled on national security grounds may be removed to his/her country of origin, if no alternative destination can be identified. Persons expelled as national security risks may or may not be prosecuted by the host state. When they are suspected of crimes such as terrorism or hostage taking, they can either be deported or formally rendered pursuant to a bilateral or multilateral extradition treaty.[38]

The cases most readily identified as justifying expulsion on grounds of national security are those involving a refugee who seeks directly to attack the political integrity of the host state.[39] Therefore, if Zimbabwean authorities had followed the mandatory procedures to expel CAR refugees who intended to assassinate political leaders in the country, expulsion on national security grounds would have been compatible with Article 32 of the 1951 Geneva Convention.[40] The decision of expulsion seemed to comply also with section 15 1) ('Expulsion of recognized refugees and protected persons') of the 1983 Zimbabwean Refugee Act, which provides for expulsion on grounds of national security albeit the procedure required by the same section 15 as well as by section 16 ('Detention or recognized refugees and protected persons pending expulsion') were not fully respected. In addition, indiscriminate expulsions in that country would contrast with section 22 1) of the Declaration of Rights, an integral part of the 1979 Zimbabwean Constitution, which clearly affirms several immunities from expulsion from Zimbabwe for *every person*.[41] The Harare Supreme Court in the 1994 case of *Rattigan and Others v Chief Immigration Officer of Zimbabwe* confirmed the validity of section 22 of the Declaration of Rights.[42]

However, under the current conception, the danger to national security would not need to be either direct or immediate. By contrast, a refugee is considered to

37 In this regard, A. Grahl-Madsen argued: 'The most interesting part of Article 33 is paragraph 2, containing the exceptions to the main rule. [. . .] Paragraph 2 states that the benefit of the present provision may not be claimed by a refugee whom there are reasonable grounds for regarding as a danger to the security of the country in which he/she is, or who, having been convicted by a final judgment of a particularly serious crime, constitutes a danger to the community of that country.' See Grahl-Madsen, A., 'Expulsion of refugees', op. cit. note 15, p. 49.

38 Fitzpatrick, J., 'The post-exclusion phase: extradition, prosecution and expulsion', in *International Journal of Refugee Law*, vol. 12, 2000, special supplementary issue, p. 288. Further, at idem, the author explained that: '[t]he application of article 33 2) is subject to abusively overbroad interpretation by some asylum states.'

39 In this regard, G. Abi-Saab argued that: '[National Security] covers basically all that touches the internal and external security of the state, and the safety of its leaders. National security is a very sensitive political area, hence largely subjective, and covered by secrecy.' See Abi-Saab, G., op. cit. note 9, p. 84.

40 Hathaway, J.C., *The Rights of Refugees Under International Law*, op. cit. note 7, pp. 678–9.

41 Emphasis added.

42 Supreme Court, Zimbabwe, *Rattigan and Others v Chief Immigration Officer of Zimbabwe*, Cases No 45/94; 92/94, 13 June 1994. Read the section of the judgment entitled: 'The alleged violation of section 22 1) of the Declaration of Rights'.

constitute a risk for the host state's national security if his/her actions or simple presence cause the real and reasonable possibility of inflicting damage to the host state's basic interests, including both the destruction of its democratic institutions and the threat of an armed attack on its territory.[43] There is no requirement stating that the refugee needs to have already been convicted or charged with a criminal offence. In this regard, Grahl-Madsen noted that a refugee may act against the national security though he/she is guilty of no crime in the host country.[44] A typical example often recalled by the doctrine in this regard is the *Taylor Case* decided by the Federal High Court in Abuja in 2004.[45] The court decided for the expulsion of the respondent, C. Taylor, former president of Liberia, not on the basis of section 1 2) a) of the Decree 1989, Nigerian National Commission for Refugee Act, as invoked by the applicant who thought that this article could not be applicable to him and that is relevant to refugees who constitute a threat for the Nigerian national security,[46] but on the basis of the 1949 Geneva Conventions through which Nigeria is:

> [o]bliged to either prosecute or hand over any person suspected of having committed grave breaches of the Conventions. This is perhaps the most decisive principle upon which the Court could compel the handing over of Taylor to the Special Court in Sierra Leone. In this case, the principle of universal jurisdiction will apply.[47]

43 Hathaway, J.C., *The Rights of Refugees Under International Law*, op. cit. note 7, p. 679. However, as W. Kaelin observed: 'This exception [set in Article 33 2)] is without effect [. . .] where prohibitions of *refoulement* under human rights law are applicable, since these provisions take precedence in cases where the Refugee Convention as such would permit *refoulement*.' See Kaelin, W., 'Aliens, expulsion and deportation', op. cit. note 1, p. 3.

44 Grahl-Madsen, A., *Commentary on the Refugee Convention 1951: Articles 2–11, 13–37*, op. cit. note 2, p. 203.

45 Federal High Court of Abuja, *Egbuna v Taylor*, SUIT NO: FHC/ABJ/M/216/2004; *Anyaele v Taylor*, SUIT NO: FHC/ABJ/M/217/2004. For a reference on the legal issues derived from the *Taylor Case* see, for instance, Miglin, J.L., 'From immunity to impunity: Charles Taylor and the Special Court for Sierra Leone', in *Dalhousie Journal of Legal Studies*, vol. 16, 2007, pp. 21–46. The author noted at p. 45 that: 'It is important to remember that Charles Taylor is before the Special Court today because of a political process that resulted in Liberia's request to Nigeria for Taylor's transfer. Nigeria, ever suspicious of the jurisdiction of the Special Court, was only willing to fly him back to Liberia where UNMIL arrested and transported him to the Special Court.'

46 Nigeria: Decree of 1989, National Commission for Refugees, 29 December 1989, Article 1 2) a): '2) The provisions of subsection 1) of this section (concerning the prohibition of expulsion of refugees) shall not apply to a refugee who: a) is a danger to the security of Nigeria.'

47 Commentary of the judgment of the *Taylor Case* in the Oxford Law Reports website at: www.oxfordlawreports.com/, accessed 30 October 2014, p. 3. At idem, we find it interesting to quote another section of the commentary referring to the application of the refugee conventions, both regional and universal, in the country: 'The Court could rely on the relevant treaties applicable to refugees to whom Nigeria is a party, namely, in this case, the 1951 UN Convention and the 1969 OAU Convention. However, suffice it to state in this regard that although Nigeria has ratified these Conventions, they are yet to be made part of Nigerian law. *As Nigeria operates on the basis of the "dualist" position regarding the relationship between international law and municipal law, Nigerian courts are not bound to apply these Conventions. At best, they can be cited as persuasive authority.*' Emphasis added.

In light of the strong influence exercised by *apartheid* on the international relations in Southern Africa during the 1970s and 1980s,[48] the same approach could be used to the South African government's threats to invade neighbouring states, which provided asylum to African National Congress (ANC)[49] members. In effect, the expulsion of the members of this organization in line with the guarantees of the due process would not have violated Article 32 of the 1951 Geneva Convention.[50] Of greater contemporary relevance, objection could also not be made to the expulsion of a refugee whose terrorist acts against other countries did not directly pose a likely threat to the security of the host state.

Luckily, times have changed; since the abolition of *apartheid* South Africa seems also to act upon higher recognized standards – for the continent – in the protection of asylum-seekers, as shown in the prevention of deportation of an asylum-seeker, in the 2002 *Katambayi Case*.

In this case, a South African High Court judge had issued a ruling against the DHA to prevent a Congolese, Mr. J. Katambayi, from being deported to the DRC by Australia via Johannesburg. Mr. Katambayi fled the DRC after he was forced to join the army. His application for asylum was rejected in Australia. Amnesty International (AI) had been following Mr. Katambayi's case in Australia and they

48 Until its formal abolition occurred on the 30 June 1991, *apartheid* was historically considered as one of the root causes of the flux of refugees in Southern Africa as it was underlined, among others, in the 1988 Oslo Declaration and Plan of Action on the Plight of Refugees and Displaced Persons in Southern Africa. See letter B), paragraph 3 of the Declaration in UNGA, Office of the United Nations High Commissioner for Refugees, Report of the Secretary-General, 19 October 1988, document No. A/43/717.

49 The ANC has been South Africa's governing party, supported by its tripartite alliance with the COSATU and the SACP, since the establishment of non-racial democracy in May 1994. It has been the ruling party of post-apartheid South Africa on the national level since 1994. It gained support in the 1999 elections, and further increased its majority in 2004. For an introductive history of the ANC, see its website at: www.anc.org.za/show.php?doc=ancdocs/about/umzabalazo.html&title=Mzabalazo, accessed 30 October 2014.

50 Regarding one such neighbouring country, Botswana, T. Maluwa observed: 'Botswana's commitment and *bona fide* with regard to the protection of refugees from other States in the region, and in particular those from South Africa, cannot be doubted. Nor, judging from its official pronouncements, can one charge Botswana with a failure to appreciate the duties and obligations incumbent upon it under international law with regard to the granting of asylum and protection to South Africa and other refugees. Responsibility for the breach of international law in this regard, therefore, must be placed squarely upon South Africa alone.' See Maluwa, T., 'The concept of asylum and the protection of refugees in Botswana: some legal and political aspects', in *International Journal of Refugee Law*, vol. 2, 1990, pp. 607–8. At ibid., p. 603, the author was clear in explaining: 'There can be no doubt that the purport of both the widely publicized Nkomati Accord and the less publicized Non-Aggression Pact between South Africa and Swaziland was to force Mozambique and Swaziland to desist from accepting any political refugees fleeing the *apartheid* regime, and to expel certain designated categories of refugees. Similarly, the South African cross-border military incursions into Botswana, allegedly aimed at forestalling infiltration into South Africa by national liberation movement fighters, were intended to frighten Botswana into changing its policy on South African refugees. In all these cases, the message was clear: any neighboring State which persisted in granting asylum to certain designated refugees would only have itself to blame in the event of reprisal attacks by South Africa.'

alerted the League for Human Rights (LHR). The DHA refused LHR access to consult with Mr. Katambayi and refused to allow him to apply for asylum in South Africa. While Mr. Katambayi was in the transit area of the Johannesburg International Airport, LHR approached the court to prevent Mr. Katambayi's deportation. A court interdiction was issued by the judge, preventing the deportation of Mr. Katambayi and ordering the DHA to allow him to apply for asylum in their office in Johannesburg. According to LHR, this is an important ruling as it recognizes the right of an asylum-seeker to apply for asylum while in the transit area of an international airport. Previously, South Africa had allowed its transit area at the Johannesburg International Airport to be used for deporting asylum-seekers from Australia to their home countries, despite concerns that some of the deportees might face persecution and even death upon return. This would appear to contravene Article 33 of the 1951 UN Refugee Convention, as well as the South African Refugee Act of 1988, both of which guard against the forcible repatriation of individuals if they are likely to face persecution or physical harm upon return.[51]

Refugees who have committed serious crimes or who have refused to abide by the law constitute the main objects of public order exclusion under Article 32.[52] Under the 1951 Geneva Convention, public order concerns are those which forerun a danger to the internal security of the country of refuge. Public order concerns are, for instance, those based on the fact that a refugee has committed a serious crime, or that he/she has engaged in activities that result in a serious threat to social norms or to public morality. Yet, social plights such as ill health or poverty cannot be considered grounds on which to expel a refugee because of the infringement of public order.[53] As a practical example, a public order has been

51 High Court of South Africa (Witwatersrand Local Division), *Katambayi and Lawyers for Human Rights v Minister of Home Affairs et al.*, Dec. No. 02/3512, 24 March 2002, also in JRS, dispatch No. 110, 16 April 2002. We would also like to note that the 1998 South African Refugee Act represents one of the most categorical legal attempts made in Sub-Saharan Africa to avoid the expulsion of refugees. Section 2 of the Act stipulates: '2) Notwithstanding any provision of this Act or any other law to the contrary, no person may be refused entry into the Republic, expelled, extradited or returned to any other country or be subject to any similar measure, if as a result of such refusal, expulsion, extradition, return or other measure, such person is compelled to return to or remain in a country where: a) he/she may be subjected to persecution on account of his or her race, religion, nationality, political opinion or membership of a particular social group; or b) his or her life, physical safety or freedom would be threatened on account of external aggression, occupation, foreign domination or other events seriously disturbing or disrupting public order in either part or the whole of that country.'

52 For a domestic example of what Article 32 provides for, see, for instance, section 16 1) number 2 of the 2007 Sierra Leonean Refugees Protection Act: 'Provided that nothing in subsection 1) shall prevent the expulsion, under the provisions of any law, of a refugee to any country whatsoever where, in the opinion of the Authority – for refugees – after consultation with other relevant authorities, such removal is necessary, on the grounds of national security or where the refugee has been convicted by a final judgment of a court of a particularly serious crime which, in the opinion of the Authority, indicates that the refugee constitutes a danger to the community.'

53 Hathaway, J.C., *The Rights of Refugees Under International Law*, op. cit. note 7, p. 695. This opinion has been shared by another commentator such as G. Stenberg: '[t]he fact that a refugee [has]

invoked for the right of states to expel a refugee who had trafficked in narcotics or committed robbery.[54] Only the commission of a 'serious' crime – not any crime – is grounds for public order expulsion, and other concerns – such as basic offences to public morality or social norms of the asylum country – are to be considered as grounds for expulsion only in very serious cases.[55]

In Sub-Saharan Africa, the expulsion of refugees is common and not very likely to be carried out under formal legal procedures. The UNGA is completely aware of this phenomenon.[56] Both the same UNGA[57] and African countries have condemned it several times in official meetings[58] although the AU until now

become indigent or suffered from illness, or that he/she [has] committed a minor offence [cannot] justify expulsion on the grounds of public order; on the other hand it must be stated that, apart from the general intention that the concept of "public order" in article 32 1) of the 1951 Convention should be interpreted restrictively, much has been left to the subsequent practice of the contracting states. It can thus be stated that the ultimate content of the concept of public order depends on how this concept has been treated by individual states.' See Stenberg, G., op. cit. note 8, pp. 146–7. In this regard, G. Abi-Saab explained: 'Public order [. . .] has a definite meaning, but this meaning changes from one legal system to the other and even from one branch of law to another [. . .] [its general meaning] can be approximately described as covering the basic foundations [. . .] of the social and political, hence legal order of the state.' See Abi-Saab, G., op. cit. note 9, p. 84.

54 Hathaway, J.C., *The Rights of Refugees Under International Law*, op. cit. note 7, p. 680.

55 In this regard, A. Grahl-Madsen contended: '[it] was obviously the intention of the drafters [of the 1951 Geneva Convention] that expulsion should only be resorted to where the continued presence of the refugee would to some extent upset the very equilibrium of society.' See Grahl-Madsen, A., *Commentary on the Refugee Convention 1951: Articles 2–11, 13–37*, op. cit. note 2, p. 209. In any case, as G. Abi-Saab noted: '[T]he condemnation of a refugee for a particularly serious crime could serve as a basis for expulsion on this ground, if the crime is considered in the country as a violation of public order. But it is important to note here that *it is not* the condemnation itself, however serious the crime, which justifies the expulsion; for expulsion should not be considered as an additional penalty for serious crime. *It is only the revelation* by the condemnation that the person is, and is liable to continue after purging his/her sentence to be, a threat to public order that justifies expulsion.' Emphasis added. See Abi-Saab, G., op. cit. note 9, p. 85.

56 For instance, see UNGA, Report of the United Nations High Commissioner for Refugees, questions relating to refugees, returnees and displaced persons and humanitarian questions, Report of the Third Committee, 11 November 2003, document No. A/C.3/58/L.37/Rev. 1, paragraph 16: '[The UNGA] expresses its concern about instances in which the fundamental principles of asylum are jeopardized by unlawful expulsion [. . .].' See also UNGA, Report of the United Nations High Commissioner for Refugees, questions relating to refugees, returnees and displaced persons and humanitarian questions, Report of the Third Committee, 29 November 2005, document No. A/60/499, paragraph 14 of the Draft resolution II, paragraph 18 of the Draft resolution III.

57 For instance, UNGA, Assistance to refugees, returnees and displaced persons in Africa, 18 December 2008, No. A/RES/63/149, paragraph 17: '[The UNGA] condemns all acts that pose a threat to the personal security and well-being of refugees and asylum-seekers, such as [. . .], unlawful expulsion.'

58 For instance, see recommendation 5, number ii) of the African Union's document: Refugees and forced population displacement in Africa, 8–10 September 1994, document adopted in occasion of the symposium held in Addis Ababa by OAU/UNHCR: 'The Symposium reaffirms its belief in the continuing validity of the 1969 OAU Convention as the cornerstone of refugee

never mentioned explicitly the indiscriminate expulsion of refugees as one of the problems to face regarding refugee issues.

Many refugees were among the thousands of Rwandans expelled by the Ugandan authorities in an outbreak of anti-Rwandan hostility in the early 1980s.[59] Ugandan officials instigated public antipathy accusing Rwandans of having displaced locals economically and of supporting anti-government guerrillas.[60]

Also a state that has made a reservation to Article 32 of the 1951 Geneva Convention cannot expel a refugee without considering the effects of that act.[61] As a result, while Uganda's reservation of its right to expel any refugee in its territory meant that it did not violate Article 32 of the 1951 Geneva Convention when the Ugandan government sent Rwandans back to their country of origin, its actions could be nonetheless considered in breach of Article 33 of the same convention.[62] In addition, it is also true that, after the adoption of the 2006 Ugandan National Refugee Act, of which section 40 is entirely dedicated to expulsion,[63] we have

protection and solutions in Africa. In this regard, and in order to implement the Convention more effectively, it is recommended that States: [. . .]: ii) should uphold the principles of the Convention on the humanitarian nature of asylum, prohibit activities inconsistent with refugee status, safeguard refugees against *refoulement* or expulsion, actively promote voluntary repatriation, respect the principle of voluntariness in repatriation, and practice burden-sharing and solidarity among States.'

59 Uganda has a long history of expulsion of aliens. R.J. Nogel observed as already in the early 1970s Major General Idi Amin Dada Oumee '[o]rdered all Ugandans of Asian descent out of the country within three months, accusing them of "sabotaging the economy".' See Nogel, R.J., 'Human rights and Ugandan expulsion of its Asian minority', in *Denver Journal of International Law and Policy*, vol. 3, 1973, p. 107. J.-M. Henckaerts taking rise from the same issue added: 'Just as the Ugandan Asians had to leave merely because they were Asians, so too do refugees of a particular group have to leave because of membership of that group. The only practical difference is that in the former case Uganda issued an official expulsion order while in the latter no such measure is taken. But both instances are identical in their effect, namely they force people to leave. [. . .] Such expulsion would be arbitrary by definition.' See Henckaerts, J.-M., *Mass Expulsion in Modern International Law and Practice*, op. cit. note 10, p. 110.

60 Hathaway, J.C., *The Rights of Refugees Under International Law*, op. cit. note 7, p. 661.

61 Ibid., p. 665.

62 This is acknowledged in the text of Uganda's reservation that provides that '[w]ithout recourse to legal process the Government of the Republic of Uganda shall, in the public interest, have the unfettered right to expel any refugee in his/her territory and may at any time apply such internal measures as the Government may deem necessary in the circumstances; so however that, any action taken by the Government of the Republic of Uganda in this regard shall not operate to the prejudice of the provisions of article 33 of this Convention.' Two commentators further argue that summary expulsion by Uganda violates Article 16 1) of the 1951 Geneva Convention requiring that refugees have access to the courts of law of all state parties. See Blay, S.K.N. and Tsamenyi, M.B., 'Reservations and declarations under the 1951 Convention and the 1967 Protocol relating to the status of refugees', in *International Journal of Refugee Law*, vol. 2, 1990, pp. 544–5.

63 Section 40 of the 2006 Ugandan Refugee Act reads: '1) The Minister may, after consultation with the Minister responsible for internal affairs, order the expulsion of any recognized refugee from Uganda, if the Minister considers the expulsion to be necessary or desirable in the interest of national security or public order. 2) Before ordering the expulsion of a recognized refugee under subsection 1) of this section, the Minister shall give due consideration to any representation made by the refugee concerned or his/her representative or the representative of the UNHCR.'

witnessed in 2013 the indiscriminate expulsion of over 60,000 Congolese, 'guilty' of having refused to be relocated in a camp far from the border with DRC.[64]

In 1990, Kenyan President D. Arap Moi ordered all refugees engaged in 'illegal activities' to leave the country. Without access to lawyers, trainloads of refugees were shipped to the Ugandan border and handed over to that country's security officials.[65] In 2002, Kenyan authorities threatened to summarily repatriate hundreds of Ethiopian and Somali refugees arrested in a police sweep in Nairobi.[66]

Rwandans also suffered from expulsion from Tanzania in 1995. Tanzania thereby effectively abandoned its previous and well-known 'open-door policy' with respect to refugees, deciding on forced repatriation of all Rwandan refugees by 1 January 1996. Thus Tanzania argued that national security concerns, apparently threatened by Rwandan refugees, had the highest priority and that these concerns would prevail over the interests of refugees. More recently, the same measure would have been adopted towards Burundian refugees who, by contrast, had signed up for repatriation just as a precautionary measure against sudden expulsion.[67] It is useless to say that several decades before, in 1972, hospitable Tanzania had welcomed a large number of refugees from Burundi who had been

64 See the news: 'Over 60,000 Congolese refugees "expelled" from Uganda', 9 November 2013, available at: www.africareview.com/News/Over-60000-Congolese-refugees-expelled-from-Uganda/-/979180/2066930/-/eg3117z/-/index.html, accessed 30 October 2014.

65 Veney, C.R., op. cit. note 29, p. 96. The author added: 'The insecurity in North Eastern Province [of Kenya] in and around refugee camps was evident [. . .] in 1993. [. . .] One incident resulted in the deaths of nine Kenyan security personnel who were escorting relief food. Unfortunately, insecurity remained a problem in this province even after the government closed most of the camps because of tensions between refugees and local communities and among Somali clans [that constituted a danger for the public order of Kenya].' See idem. In this regard, J.H.S. Milner pointed out: 'The first feature of Kenya's post-1991 approach was the abdication of responsibility for refugees from the government to UNHCR. Notwithstanding the principle that the primary responsibility for refugees lies with the host state, a deliberate choice was made by Kenyan government officials in the 1990s to largely cede refugee affairs to UNHCR.' See Milner, J.H.S., *Refugees, the State and the Politics of Asylum in Africa*, Basingstoke: Palgrave/Macmillan, 2009, p. 88.

66 HRW, 'Kenya: illegal expulsion of more than 1000 refugees', 11 December 1990, pp. 1–5. At p. 7 the document continued affirming that mass-expulsion of refugees from Kenya was striking, '[n]amely, total disregard for the correct legal process, police abuse and the law and lack of access to legal representation, confiscation and destruction of legitimate identity cards and documentation; and summary deportations of people without recourse to fair investigations.'

67 JRS, dispatch No. 185, 16 January 2006: 'Tanzania: government pressures reluctant refugees to return home: from its peak of 5,000 refugee returns from Tanzania to Burundi in August, the number had dropped to less than 500 a month by the end of December. According to UNHCR, the UN refugee agency, this is explained by cyclical factors as refugees are less willing to return home during the rainy season and wish to leave after they have harvested their crops to ensure they have enough food to last them until the next season. Continued military activity of the Front national de libération rebel group and rumors in the camp that each person wishing to do so must present a receipt proving financial contributions to the CNDD-FDD are also discouraging refugees from returning home. However, despite fears of persecution in Burundi, mounting pressure by Tanzanian officials is being placed on refugees to return. According to Radio Kwizera, a JRS-run refugee station, the Kibondo district commissioner in northeastern Tanzania, John Muzulikwao, told the refugees there on 5 December that he would close two of the three camps in the area in the next three months. Muzulikwao's visit was followed by

in the country following ethnic violence. This group of refugees was integrated into local communities on agricultural settlement sites and some were even allowed to serve in the military.[68] Finally, however, on 30 October 2009 the UNHCR sent home the final group of long-term Burundian refugees in Tanzania who wanted to return, a landmark operation ending one of the world's most recent,[69] most protracted refugee situations,[70] whose terms have been well described by the doctrine.[71]

Generally, the expulsion of all post-1994[72] refugees from Tanzania may be considered from at least two different angles. First, as mentioned, there is an

more restrictive measures such as stopping all refugees from working for relief organisations in the camp because, he said, jobs encouraged them to remain in Tanzania. He was acting in compliance with Tanzanian law banning all income-generating activities in the camps. In August, police destroyed all the shops in the camps. Afraid of returning home and of staying, many refugees feel trapped. Many refugees have signed up for repatriation as a precautionary measure against sudden expulsion, as happened with Rwandan refugees in 1996.'

68 Veney, C.R., op. cit. note 29, p. 138.

69 In this regard, E. Morris and S.J. Stedman asserted: 'If international and local actors succeed in implementing peace after the North-South war in the Sudan, and the war in Burundi, in addition to consolidating peace in Liberia, the number of protracted refugee situations in Africa will be reduced almost by half. This is how protracted refugee situations are ultimately resolved – bringing one war after another to an end.' See Morris, E. and Stedman, S.J., 'Protracted refugee situations, conflict and security: the need for better diagnosis and prescription', in Loescher, G. *et al.* (eds), *Protracted Refugee Situations: Political, Human Rights and Security Implications*, New York: United Nations University Press, 2008, p. 72.

70 In this regard, see the news: 'The repatriation of 400 Burundians closes a chapter in long-running refugee saga', 30 October 2009, available at: www.unhcr.org/4aeb050b9.html, accessed 30 October 2014. The news continued: 'With the gradual return of peace in Burundi, more than half-a-million Burundian refugees have returned home, including over 430,000 from camps in Tanzania. That now leaves just 36,000 Burundian refugees in one remaining camp in Tanzania, Mtabila, as well as another 21,500 in the DRC, Rwanda and Uganda.' In this regard see also HRW, 'Tanzania: expulsions put vulnerable people at risk', 9 May 2007, available at: www.hrw.org/news/2007/05/08/tanzania-expulsions-put-vulnerable-people-risk, accessed 30 October 2014.

71 In this regard, G. Loescher and J.H.S. Milner argued that: 'Protracted refugee situations involve large refugee populations that are long-standing, chronic or recurring, and for which there are no immediate prospects for a solution. They are not static populations, but many involve periods of increase and decrease in the total populations as well as changes within it. They are typically [. . .] concentrated in a specific geographical area, but may include camp-based and urban refugee populations, in addition to displaced populations currently not included in UNHCR's refugee statistics. The nature of a protracted refugee situation will be the result of both conditions in the country of origin of the refugees, and the responses and conditions in the host country.' See Loescher, G., Milner, J.H.S., 'Understanding the problem of protracted refugee situations', in Loescher, G. (*et al.*) (eds), *Protracted Refugee Situations: Political, Human Rights and Security Implications*, New York: United Nations University Press, 2008, p. 23. The authors gave an example of this kind of situation also mentioning the situation of Somali refugees in the Horn and Liberians in the neighbouring West African states. See ibid., pp. 27–8.

72 We would like to note that in 1994, over the course of approximately 100 days, from the assassination of the President J. Habyarimana on 6 April up until mid-July at least 500,000 people were killed in the Rwandan genocide. Most estimates indicate a death toll between 800,000 and 1,000,000, which could be as high as 20 per cent of the total Rwanda population. As we mentioned, after the genocide Tanzanian policy towards Rwandan asylum-seekers changed accordingly because Tanzania started fearing for its internal security.

argument to be advanced to the effect that legitimate national security grounds existed. National security risks emanated from Tanzania's nervous relations with neighbouring countries, especially Burundi. Focusing on the border, it was feared that ongoing conflicts in the region would spread out into Tanzania. Initially, it may be concluded that refugees who entered after 1994 were lawfully present in Tanzania within the meaning of Article 32 of the 1951 Geneva Convention as they all received refugee status. In line with the OAU framework and practice, this was provided in the form of temporary protection. The legality of the refugees' stay was therefore quite clear.[73] By contrast, no assessment of risk upon return was undertaken and due process was thus denied. Possibly, the induced return of all post-1994 Rwandan refugees from Tanzania in 1996 was not a measure of repatriation in less than ideal circumstances, but a measure of mass-expulsion[74] – episodes of arbitrary expulsions that, since then, seem to have decreased thanks to the adoption of a national law that is very detailed in providing for guarantees against the deportation of refugees.[75]

73 Eggli, A.V., op. cit. note 35, pp. 247 and 250.

74 Ibid., p. 251. At p. 252 the author explained: 'Another major concern [about the presence of Rwandan refugees in Tanzania] was, finally, that of environmental degradation in the broad sense of the word. This was evidenced, for example, by the occurrence of deforestation and serious strains on the already weak infrastructure in Tanzania. Although these adverse side-effects of hosting large numbers of displaced persons are both unpleasant and costly, they hardly qualify as threats to the security of a nation under major international and regional [. . .] refugee law conventions.' C.R. Veney also noted: 'Refugee's rights [in Tanzania] were again violated in October 1997 when approximately 5,000 Burundian refugees, mainly women and children were forcibly deported. [. . .] The government's actions violated international law pertaining to the protection of refugees – the principle of *non-refoulement* – that no one should be forcibly returned to a country where her life or freedom could possibly be threatened.' See Veney, C.R., op. cit. note 29, p. 88.

75 Article 28 ('Deportation of asylum seeker or refugee') of the Refugees Act (1998), Act No. 9, 15 April 1999 reads: '1) a) The Minister or as the case may be, competent authority appointed by the Minister on that behalf may at any time order in writing that – i) any asylum seeker who has not qualified to be granted refugee status under section 4 of this Act, or ii) a refugee who is dangerous to the security of the state or has ceased to be a refugee shall be deported from Tanzania by such means or route as he may direct; b) a refugee deported under subsection a) of this section shall be informed in writing about his deportation; c) a refugee who is issued with a deportation order under this section may appeal to, or may petition for review to the Minister or a competent authority within seven days from the date he is served with the deportation order. Where the petition or review has been filed to the competent authority such competent authority shall immediately transmit the same to the Minister; d) the Minister in consultation with the Director may consider the appeal or review and shall have power to confirm or revoke the deportation order provided that pending the determination of the appeal or review by the Minister the deportation order issued shall not be executed. 2) A court convicting any asylum seeker or refugee of an offence under the provisions of this section, shall order the deportation of such asylum seeker or refugee to the territory from which he entered Tanzania or any other country of his choice which shall take effect immediately after commission or after serving the sentence. 3) When any person is deported under sub-section 1) or 2) of this section he may be held in custody pending deportation. 4) No order shall be made under subsection 1) or 2) in respect of an asylum seeker or a refugee if the Minister, the competent authority or the court,

In Sub-Saharan Africa, the expulsion of refugees is often linked to the fear that their presence will involve the host state in an armed conflict. As mentioned above, the threat of military attacks from *apartheid*-era South Africa led some neighbouring countries, such as Mozambique,[76] Swaziland,[77] and Botswana,[78] to expel refugees from South Africa.[79] Since 1992, Nigerian officials have expelled Chadian refugees because they were using north-eastern Nigeria as a base from which to attack Chad. The Nigerian government adduced no evidence of rebel activity by the refugees, however, and denied refugees a public trial or access to legal representation, although several Nigerian courts gave them reason; as happened, for instance, in the 1993 *Allatchi Case*, in which the judge clearly affirmed that, under section 34 of the Nigerian Constitution,[80] the arrest of the applicants [Chadian

as the case may be, is of the opinion that such a person will be tried or punished for an offence of a political character after arrival in the territory from which he came or is likely to be the subject of physical attack in such territory. 5) Any asylum seeker or refugee who fails to comply with an order made under this section shall be guilty of an offence under this Act.'

76 In Mozambique expulsion of refugees is now regulated by Article 13 of the 1991 Refugee Act: 1) A refugee who is lawfully in the Republic of Mozambique shall not be expelled save on grounds of national security or public order. 2) A refugee shall be expelled only in pursuance of a decision of the Ministry of the Interior, and on condition that that decision conforms to the rules governing the legal process of expulsion. 3) The refugee shall be allowed to defend himself, by the means prescribed by law, against the facts that determined his expulsion, specifically by submitting evidence to clear him.'

77 In Swaziland, section 10 of the 1978 Refugee Control Order is dedicated to deportation of refugees. We note that subsection 2 of this section provides for the deportation of the refugee '[t]o the territory from which he/she enters Swaziland', without taking into consideration that that territory could just have been used as a transit. In the Swazi legislation we see, not present, many guarantees for the refugee that are instead present in successive legislations.

78 The legislation of Botswana does not present any proviso strictly related to expulsion and/or deportation.

79 Mtango, E-E., 'Military and armed attacks on refugee camps', in Loescher, G. and Monahan, L. (eds), *Refugees and International Relations*, New York: Oxford University Press, 1989, p. 95.

80 Section 34 of the Constitution in force in 1993 is the present section 35 1) of the 1999 Nigerian Constitution. It clearly stipulates: '1) Every person shall be entitled to his/her personal liberty and no person shall be deprived of such liberty save in the following cases and in accordance with a procedure permitted by law: a) in execution of the sentence or order of a court in respect of a criminal offence of which he/she has been found guilty; b) by reason of his/her failure to comply with the order of a court or in order to secure the fulfillment of any obligation imposed upon him/her by law; c) for the purpose of bringing him/her before a court in execution of the order of a court or upon reasonable suspicion of his/her having committed a criminal offence, or to such extent as may be reasonably necessary to prevent his/her committing a criminal offence; d) in the case of a person who has not attained the age of eighteen years for the purpose of his/her education or welfare; e) in the case of persons suffering from infectious or contagious disease, persons of unsound mind, persons addicted to drugs or alcohol or vagrants, for the purpose of their care or treatment or the protection of the community; or f) for the purpose of preventing the unlawful entry of any person into Nigeria or of effecting the expulsion, extradition or other lawful removal from Nigeria of any person or the taking of proceedings relating thereto: Provided that a person who is charged with an offence and who has been detained in lawful custody awaiting trial shall not continue to be kept in such detention for a period longer than the maximum period of imprisonment prescribed for the offence.' We note that the judge in the case found not applicable any of the exceptions provided for in letters a) through f).

refugees] was 'illegal, null and void' as well as their deportation to Chad.[81] In early 2001, Zimbabwean police ordered the expulsion of about 30 CAR refugees, who were suspected by the authorities in Harare of being rebels from DRC sent to kill R. Mugabe.[82]

As A. Grahl-Madsen observed, under Article 32 1) of the 1951 Geneva Convention:

> [e]xpulsion is not justified unless it will have a salutary effect with regard to [national security or public order]. It is not something to which one [resorts] lightly but rather [. . .] one must consider whether the measure will serve its end – in other words, that it is necessary.[83]

This interpretation is in line with the view of the UNHCR's ExCom that measures of expulsion against a refugee should be adopted exceptionally and exclusively after having taken into consideration all the circumstances.[84] This latter affirmation has been considered by J.-M. Henckaerts as a prohibition of mass-expulsions because expulsion represents an exceptional measure not to be generalized, while mass-expulsion does just that.[85] Mass-expulsion (or, as defined in this document, 'collective expulsions') are also prohibited under Article 10 of the Draft Articles on the Expulsion of Aliens, in its Ninth Report, dated to 2014,[86] while draft Article 11 bans 'disguised expulsions'[87] consisting in acts and/or omissions to indirectly force the expulsion of the alien.[88]

Specifically regarding mass-expulsions in Africa, Article 12 5) of the 1981 Banjul Charter[89] defines the prohibition of mass-expulsion for certain groups.[90] However,

81 High Court of Justice of Borno State of Nigeria, *Ahmed Allatchi & 243 others v Chief of Army Staff & 4 Others*, M/64m/92, 2 September 1993, paragraph 6 b).

82 Hathaway, J.C., *The Rights of Refugees Under International Law*, op. cit. note 7, pp. 662–3.

83 Grahl-Madsen, A., *Commentary on the Refugee Convention 1951: Articles 2–11, 13–37*, op. cit. note 2, p. 200.

84 ExCom, conclusion No. 7 (XXVIII), 'Expulsion', 1977, paragraph c).

85 Henckaerts, J.-M., *Mass Expulsion in Modern International Law and Practice*, op. cit. note 10, p. 106.

86 UNGA, Ninth Report on the Expulsion of Aliens, submitted by Mr. Maurice Kamto, Special Rapporteur, UN document A/CN.4/670, 25 March 2014, Article 10, paragraphs 39–40, pp. 15–16.

87 Ibid., Article 11, paragraphs 41–2, pp. 16–17.

88 Murphy, S.D., 'The expulsion of aliens and other topics: the sixty-fourth session of the International Law Commission', in *American Journal of International Law*, vol. 107, 2013, p. 167.

89 In full, Article 12 5) of the 1981 Banjul Charter reads: '5) The mass expulsion of non-nationals shall be prohibited. Mass expulsion shall be that which is aimed at national, racial, ethnic or religious groups.'

90 In this regard, M. Sanderson contended that: 'Bearing in mind the singular nature of the definition of "mass expulsion" in article 12 5), it might be argued that it is unnecessary to actually expel a large group of individuals to violate this article. Rather, and taken most strictly, this article might restrict any act of expulsion which is literally "aimed at" a particular national, racial, ethnic or religious group. On this meaning, any expulsion, even of only one person, might amount

this article appears to cover all aliens in a *de facto* manner because the original intent of the charter drafters appears to have been to prevent repetitions of the continent-wide expulsions, which took place in the 1960s and 1970s. An example of this latter kind of expulsion includes the mass-expulsion of Beninese citizens from Gabon in 1978 during which both refugees and migrant workers were thrown out of the country.[91] In effect, Article 12 5) of the 1981 Banjul Charter, more than just condemning the right of a state to expel non-nationals, also appears to condemn the method in which this right is put in practice, that is, the implementation of an expulsion without the safeguards generally associated with individual expulsions.[92] This position was confirmed by the ACHPR in its 1997 communication No. 159/96 *Union Inter Africaine des Droits de l'Homme, Fédération Internationale des Ligues des Droits de l'Homme and Others v Angola:*

> The Commission concedes that African States in general and the Republic of Angola in particular are faced with many challenges, mainly economic. In the face of such difficulties, States often resort to radical measures aimed at protecting their nationals and their economies from non-nationals. Whatever the circumstances may be, however, such measures should not be taken at the detriment of the enjoyment of human rights. Mass expulsion of any category of persons, whether on the basis of nationality, religion, ethnic, racial or other considerations 'constitutes a special violation of human rights'.[93]

The Commission continued:

> The Commission does not wish to call into question nor is it calling into question the right of any State to take legal action against illegal immigrants and deport them to their countries of origin, if the competent courts so decide. It is however of the view that it is unacceptable to deport individuals without giving them the possibility to plead their case before the competent national courts as this is contrary to the spirit and letter of the Charter and international law.[94]

to a violation of article 12 5) if the act of expulsion was "aimed at" [. . .] their particular national, racial, ethnic or religious association. In this case, such an expulsion would be "mass" only because of its concern with the larger group, regardless of the practicalities of expulsion on any given occasion.' See M. Sanderson, op. cit. note 1, p. 104.

91 Henckaerts, J.-M., *Mass Expulsion in Modern International Law and Practice*, op. cit. note 10, p. 16.

92 Ouguergouz, F., *The African Charter on Human and Peoples' Rights*, The Hague/London/New York: Martinus Nijhoff 2003, pp. 129–30.

93 ACHPR, *Union Inter Africaine des Droits de l'Homme, Fédération Internationale des Ligues des Droits de l'Homme and Others v Angola*, communication No. 159/96, 1997, paragraph 16.

94 Ibid., paragraph 20. In this sense, see also ACHPR, *Rencontre Africaine pour la Défense des Droits de l'Homme v Zambia*, communication No. 71/92, 1996, paragraph 31: 'The African Commission will not dispute that the Zambian state has the right to bring legal action against all persons illegally residing in Zambia, and to deport them if the results of such legal action justify it. However, the mass deportations of the individuals in question here, including their arbitrary

Similarly, in *African Institute for Human Rights and Development (on behalf of Sierra Leonean refugees in Guinea) v Republic of Guinea*, communication No. 249/02, 2004, the ACHPR affirmed that the Guinean President's ordering of the detention of Sierra Leonean refugees in refugee camps – obliging thousands to flee their homes or be forcibly repatriated to Sierra Leone by the Guinean authorities – violated, among other articles, Article 12 5) of the 1981 Banjul Charter.[95]

Finally, and while the object of the communication did not strictly concern refugees, in *Institute for Human Rights and Development in Africa (on behalf of Esmaila Connateh & 13 others) v Republic of Angola*, communication No. 292/04, 2008, the ACHPR, for the first time in its history, required a government, found to have violated the ban against mass expulsions, to adopt very specific actions remedying these violations. This happened because it was '[n]ot the first time in which [the ACHPR] found similar violations of the human rights of non-nationals in the context of mass expulsions/deportations by the Republic of Angola.'[96]

detention and deprivation of the right to have their cause heard, constitute a flagrant violation of the Charter.'

95 Paragraph 69 of the communication reads as follows: 'In *Rencontre Africaine pour la Défense des Droits de l'Homme v Zambia* [(2000) AHRLR 321 (ACHPR 1996)], the African Commission pointed out that: "[T]he drafters of the Charter believed that mass expulsion presented a special threat to human rights." In consequence, the action of a state targeting a specific national, racial, ethnic or religious group is generally qualified as discriminatory in this sense as it has no legal basis.' In paragraph 72 the ACHPR went on: '[T]he government of Guinea is entitled to prosecute persons that they believe pose a security threat to the state. However, the massive violations of the human rights of refugees as are outlined in this communication constitute a flagrant violation of the provisions of the African Charter.' Concerning refugees, another violation of Article 12 5) has been found in ACHPR, *Organisation mondiale contre la Torture and Others v Rwanda*, communications Nos. 27/89, 46/91, 49/91, 99/93, 1996, paragraph 23: 'There is ample evidence in this communication that groups of Burundian refugees have been expelled on the basis of their nationality. This constitutes a clear violation of Article 12 5) [of the 1981 Banjul Charter].'

96 ACHPR, *Institute for Human Rights and Development in Africa (on behalf of Esmaila Connateh & 13 others) v Republic of Angola*, communication No. 292/04, 2008, paragraph 69: '[T]he position of the African Commission regarding mass expulsions is clear. And as the Complainant avers, 'simply because the victims were a part of a larger group of non-nationals, not just Gambians, but also other West and Central Africans, does not negate discrimination on the part of the Respondent State', and that the fact that 'so many aliens received the same treatment is tantamount to an admission of a violation of Article 12 5).' Moreover, the fact that the deportees as a group were arrested over a period of several months at different places and may have been served with deportation orders on different dates does not qualify, for purposes of the African Commission, to be sufficient to negate the *en masse* element of the expulsions. The African Commission underscores that any expulsions or deportations must comply with the human rights obligations found in the African Charter. Accordingly, the African Commission finds the Respondent State in violation of Article 12 5) of the African Charter.' The recommendations could be found in paragraph 87 of the communication, paragraph that in full reads as follows: 'The African Commission notes that the present communication is not the first in which it found similar violations of the human rights of non-nationals in the context of mass expulsions/deportations by the Republic of Angola. It, therefore, recommends that the Republic of Angola should: 1) Ensure that its immigration policies, measures and legislations do not have the effect of

However and unfortunately, up to now this judgment could not find any concrete implementation.[97]

If reasons of national security or public order require a refugee's expulsion, it does not automatically follow that the host state must immediately proceed to the expulsion of refugees. In effect, safeguards against *refoulement* – which in Sub-Saharan Africa have been made possible also through so-called 'security agreements' which have permitted or facilitated forcible return[98] – continue to apply with an exception constituted by the more thorough standards of Article 33 2) of the 1951 Geneva Convention concerning the expulsion to a state where the refugee runs the risk of being persecuted. The joint effect of Articles 32 and 33 2) is that all expulsions, apart from those sprouting from the most evident forms of public order, are forbidden unless the expulsions can take place towards a

discriminating against persons on the basis of race, color, descent, national, ethnic origin, or any other status, and particularly take into account the vulnerability of women, children and asylum seekers; 2) Take measures to ensure that all persons in detention are provided with proper medical examination and medical treatment and care; 3) Ensure regular supervision or monitoring of places of detention by qualified and/or experienced persons or organizations; 4) Put in place mechanisms allowing all detained persons access to effective complaint procedures regarding their treatment with a view to curb, in particular, cases of physical and/or psychological abuse; 5) Put in place procedural safeguards or clear procedures/policies that guarantee for all persons deprived of their liberty (nationals and non-nationals alike) effective access to competent authorities such as administrative tribunals and courts responsible for prison/detention oversight and/or review; 6) Establish a Commission of Inquiry to investigate the circumstances under which the victims were expelled and ensure the payment of adequate compensation of all those whose rights were violated in the process; 7) Institute safeguards to ensure that individuals are not deported/expelled to countries where they might face torture or their lives could be at risk; 8) Allow representatives of the African Commission, relevant international organizations, ICRC, NGOs, concerned consulates and others access to detainees and places of detention, including to those where non-nationals are held; 9) Institute human rights training programs for law enforcement agencies and relevant civil servants dealing with matters involving non-nationals on non-discrimination, due process, and the rights of detainees, among others; 10) The African Commission further requests that the Republic of Angola report back to it, at a later stage, measures it has taken to implement the recommendations made in this communication.'

97 In this regard, see Bekker, G., 'Mass expulsion of foreign nationals: a "special violation of human rights" – Communication 292/2004 *Institute for Human Rights and Development in Africa v Republic of Angola*', in *African Human Rights Law Journal*, vol. 9, 2009, p. 273, where the author noted that: '[T]he absence of a formal mechanism to compliance means that any gains made by one of the most progressive judgments in relation to the treatment of non-nationals in Africa to date are likely to amount to naught.'

98 As explained by G. Stenberg the 'security agreements' have been entered into from time to time by states of a certain region. For instance, during the *apartheid* era, the agreements concluded between South Africa and its frontier states raised questions pertaining to forcible return of refugees, especially of members belonging to the ANC. Such an agreement has been, for instance, the Nkhomati Agreement, a non-aggression agreement concluded between Mozambique and South Africa in 1984, according to which Mozambique continued to grant unconditional support to South African refugees provided that they did not engage in subversive activities aimed against the country of origin. The agreement did not affect all refugees, but only those members of the ANC who were considered by South Africa as being combatants. See Stenberg, G., op. cit. note 8, pp. 249–50.

country that will not persecute the refugee.[99] It is clear that not being really possible to expel the refugee to his/her country of origin – where he/she supposedly suffers harm – the host country should always be sure that there is another country ready to accept the expelled, where he/she will not suffer any persecution.[100]

Second, Article 32 3) of the 1951 Geneva Convention explicitly requires the expelling state to grant the refugee a 'reasonable period' to allow him/her to organize his/her own admission to some other safe country. This paragraph, which in principle should prevent massive expulsion,[101] is doubly innovative. Distinct from prior instruments, it obliges states parties to delay expulsion allowing the refugee to pursue viable alternatives, rather than purely recognizing the logic of delay. Besides, Article 32 3), as adopted, has a broad scope intended to acknowledge that when the refugee has received the permission to enter another state, he/she can ask for an additional delay to leave the country because of serious compelling personal reasons, such as a sick child or a pregnancy. Article 32 3) has been conceived to be interpreted, however, in light of its primary rationale to allow a refugee to pursue non-coercive opportunities to leave.[102] When there is a delay in proceeding to an expulsion, an African state party to the 1951 Geneva Convention may apply '[s]uch internal measures, as they may deem necessary'.[103] In light of the interpretations given to this paragraph, such measures may also include detention,[104] which in the case of a refugee may be longer than in the case of other foreigners who can be immediately repatriated,[105] although this detention should not be 'unduly prolonged'.[106]

7.3 Final considerations on the expulsion of refugees

To recapitulate, Article 32 of the 1951 Geneva Convention is intended to supplement Article 33, which protects against *refoulement*. Article 32 limits the right of states parties to expel refugees to countries that will not persecute them on both

99 Hathaway, J.C., *The Rights of Refugees Under International Law*, op. cit. note 7, p. 692.

100 Weis, P., *The Refugee Convention, 1951/The travaux préparatoires analyzed*, op. cit. note 26, p. 323, where the author affirmed: 'No expulsion order may be carried out unless another country is willing to admit [the] refugee.'

101 Henckaerts, J.-M., *Mass Expulsion in Modern International Law and Practice*, op. cit. note 10, p. 101.

102 Hathaway, J.C., *The Rights of Refugees Under International Law*, op. cit. note 7, pp. 692–3.

103 Article 32 3) of the 1951 Geneva Convention.

104 In this regard, N. Robinson observed: 'The second sentence of paragraph 3 is less liberal than article 31, paragraph 2, first sentence: the former speaks of measures as "they may deem necessary" [. . .] while the latter mentions measures "which are necessary". [. . .] The difference is in the subjective appraisal of the measures: in the case of article 31, they must appear to be necessary to an objective observer. [. . .] [Under] article 32, it suffices if the competent authorities consider them to be required.' See Robinson, N., *Convention Relating to the Status of Refugees: Its History, Contents and Interpretation. A Commentary*, New York: Institute of Jewish Affairs, 1953, pp. 159–60.

105 UNHCR, Note on expulsion of refugees, 24 August 1977, document No. EC/SCP/3, paragraph 8.

106 Ibid., paragraph 10.

procedural and substantive grounds.[107] Procedurally, a refugee may be expelled by an administrative agency, but he/she must have the guarantee to appeal that decision to an authority, which has the power to consider all the circumstances of the case and to adopt an authoritative decision. But, for instance, in South Africa we would have been in the presence of such a situation '[e]xcept where compelling reasons of national security require otherwise.'[108]

The appeal should respect the norms of due process, including either the requisite of procedural impartiality or the protection against a result not based on law, or which is arbitrary or unreasonable. However, compelling reasons of national security may infringe upon several rights of the refugee: the submission of proof, and the right to appeal or to representation.[109]

As mentioned above, in practice, the expulsion of a refugee is lawful exclusively if it is based on reasons of public order or national security, as was also confirmed by South African authorities in a statement released on the 2014 World Refugee Day.[110]

The fact that Article 32 of the 1951 Geneva Convention imposes more than a nominal limitation on the power of expulsion is in the first place implied by the construction of the proviso: it does not reserve a right to expel refugees on the grounds of public interest; instead, it declares a prohibition against expulsion, to which there are exceptions.[111]

In the case of expulsion effected on the basis of national security, the state of refuge is required to show an objective, reasonable risk that the simple presence of a refugee, or his/her actions can put the host state under the danger of direct or indirect considerable harm to its basic interests. Basic interests can be concretely represented, for instance, when there is a reasonable possibility of an armed attack on the host state's territory, or when the essential democratic institutions of the states are threatened. Expulsion may be also based on 'public order', a notion that is not considered by doctrine to be contiguous with the traditional civil law term *ordre public*, an expression consisting of a broad variety of public policy concerns.[112] It appears that one single infraction committed by a refugee is not

107 Pellonpää, M., *Expulsion in International Law*, Helsinki: Suomalainen Tiedeakatemia, 1984, p. 297.

108 The White Paper for Refugee Affairs Task Team, Draft Refugee White Paper, no date available, paragraph 4.3, available at: www.polity.org.za/polity/govdocs/white_papers/refugees.html, accessed 10 October 2014.

109 Hathaway, J.C., *The Rights of Refugees Under International Law*, op. cit. note 7, p. 694.

110 Address by Home Affairs Director-General Mkuseli Apleni at the commemoration of World Refugee Day, Friday 20 June 2014, Pretoria, available at: www.dha.gov.za/index.php/statements-speeches/478-address-by-home-affairs-director-general-mkuseli-apleni-at-the-commemoration-of-world-refugee-day-friday-20-june-2014-pretoria, accessed 10 October 2014.

111 Pellonpää, M., op. cit. note 107, p. 299.

112 According to M. Sanderson, and a little different to what we have seen *supra* in this chapter: 'It should be noted that the concept of public order (*ordre public*) [. . .] is substantially broader than simply the prevention of civil disorder and may, in some circumstances, encompass expulsions conducted on economic, political or health grounds.' See Sanderson, M., op. cit. note 1, p. 100.

important enough to give a good reason for expulsion to maintain public order unless it is a question of common crime that, in the law and practice of the contracting state, is deemed so serious as to merit incarceration for at least two or three years.[113]

Yet, there is always a significant degree of discretion by the country of destination in deciding what represents a danger for its national security, as witnessed by the mass deportation of 300 Eritrean asylum-seekers from Sudan in late 2011. Sudanese authorities did not allow the majority of them to claim asylum even after they had remained in a camp at the border for some time. This occurred while other Eritreans who had already been granted asylum were handed over to Eritrean authorities who threatened to attack the Sudanese border.[114]

It is still not clear, however, whether a state is invariably obliged to allow the entry of a person forcibly expelled, albeit if the person is a national. If the receiving state is willing but unable to guarantee the most basic human rights of a returning national, that state's human rights obligations would be breached by receiving that person. According to C. Clark, there would therefore be a basis for denying entry. Looking at it in another way, if the sending country does not follow the principles and policies of the UN in expelling the individual, the receiving state has a basis for not allowing admission. Perhaps for these reasons, the same doctrine affirms that there is some evidence that the return of significant numbers of nationals requires a specific international agreement,[115] that, as will be seen in more detail in the next chapter, it sometimes takes the form of a 'tripartite agreement' in Sub-Saharan Africa to facilitate the readmission of the refugees to their countries of origin.

113 Pellonpää, M., op. cit. note 107, p. 306.

114 See the news: 'Sudan: End mass summary deportations of Eritreans', 25 October 2011, available at: www.hrw.org/news/2011/10/25/sudan-end-mass-summary-deportations-eritreans, accessed 30 October 2014.

115 Clark, T., 'Human rights and expulsion: giving content to the concept of asylum', op. cit. note 33, p. 195.

PART II

The peregrination of a persecuted human being, second stage

Durable solutions for refugees in Sub-Saharan Africa

Introduction to Part II

Long-term perspectives of recognized asylum-seekers: prospects and possibilities

The final goal of the UNHCR's mandate and of international protection is the quest for *durable* solutions,[1] although G.J. Cole affirmed that it was never considered in depth what the concept of solution means, clarifying that to define a solution it would be necessary first to '[d]efine the problem that requires solving'.[2] Therefore, this part of our work will take into consideration the fundamental issue regarding the prospects of durable solutions for refugees in Sub-Saharan Africa. First, we will consider the most common durable solutions sought, by host governments as well as by international organizations, for the repatriation of refugees. These examples, include the repatriation of 25,000 Congolese (DRC) returning home from Congo Brazzaville, between May and October 2012,[3] while in November 2012, the UNHCR called on governments not to return people to North and South Kivu regions in DRC by force, as improvements were pending in the human rights and security situations of these provinces.[4] In a similar way,

1 Gottwald, M., 'Back to the future: the concept of "comprehensive solutions"', in *Refugee Survey Quarterly*, vol. 31, 2012, p. 101.

2 Coles, G.J.L., 'The human rights approach to the solution of the refugee problem: a theoretical and practical enquiry', in Nash A.E. (ed.), *Human Rights and the Protection of Refugees Under International Law: Proceedings of a Conference held in Montreal, November 29–December 2, 1987*, Halifax: Institute for Research on Public Policy; Canadian Human Rights Foundation, 1988, pp. 195–7.

3 UNHCR, 'More than 25,000 refugees return home from Republic of Congo since May', 2 October 2012, available at: www.unhcr.org/506ab34a6.html, accessed 5 October 2014: 'The UN refugee agency has helped more than 25,000 Congolese return to their homes in northern Democratic Republic of the Congo (DRC) from neighboring Republic of Congo under a voluntary repatriation program launched in May this year.'

4 UNHCR, 'As fighting reaches Goma, UNHCR asking states not to return refugees', 20 November 2012, available at: www.unhcr.org/50ab67829.html, accessed 21 November 2014. For an update of the situation, UNHCR, 'DRC: Grave human rights abuses as thousands continue to flee in South Kivu', 7 December 2012, available at: www.unhcr.org/50c1d3779.html, accessed 8 December 2014: 'Government troops, M23 rebels and other armed groups have all been accused of the rights abuses in South Kivu, including the rebel FDLR and Mai Mai militia groups. UNHCR believes the abuses are unacceptable and again appeals to all armed groups involved in the conflict to refrain from threatening and abusing the civilian population and to take measures to prevent rights violations and to investigate cases when they occur and punish those found guilty.' See also the news: UNHCR, 'UNHCR still concerned about security situation in camps near

in early 2015, the UNHCR called on the governments of Niamey and Abuja to suspend the *repatriation* from Niger of hundreds of refugees who fled hostilities in Nigeria's north-eastern Borno state. According to the UN agency, the return of refugees cannot be carried out while the insecurity still reigns in that area of Nigeria.[5] Conversely, to show how multi-faceted this phenomenon can be, the repatriation of Ivorians from Liberia has been stopped in September 2014 for *force majeure*, because of the outbreak of Ebola in Liberia.[6]

Then, in Chapter 8 we will consider the legal basis of this solution and how it is conceived in the 1969 OAU Convention. This convention represents the first binding instrument ever to regulate such a 'movement back home' of refugees. We will also explore how regional repatriation is put into practice, focusing on the adoption of the so-called 'tripartite agreements' (that witness the involvement of both the country of origin and the country of asylum with the fundamental mediation of the UNHCR) and the adoption of amnesty laws by the countries of origin, amnesties used as instruments to convince refugees to return home. One of the most notorious Tripartite Agreements is the one stipulated in 2001 between Tanzania, Burundi and the UNHCR, envisaging the repatriation of Burundians. This accord followed the 2000 Arusha Peace and Reconciliation Agreement which created the CNRS (Commission nationale pour la réintegration des sinistrés), having the mandate of organizing and coordinating the return of Burundian refugees.[7] A more recent one has been stipulated on January 2015 between Burkina Faso, Mali and the UNHCR for the voluntary repatriation

Goma', 19 December 2012, available at: www.unhcr.org/50d049206.html, accessed 23 December 2014: 'The presence of armed men at Mugunga III and other [. . .] sites around [the North Kivu provincial capital of] Goma is a threat to the civilian character of the camps, something we have repeatedly urged all sides to respect [. . .]', said Adrian Edwards, a UNHCR spokesman.'

5 UN News Service, 'UN agency urges halt in Nigerian refugee repatriation amid mounting violence in country', 16 January 2015, available at: www.refworld.org/docid/54be146d4.html, accessed 9 February 2015.

6 IRIN, 'Côte d'Ivoire refugees stuck in Liberia due to Ebola crisis', 19 September 2014, available at: www.refworld.org/docid/542120e64.html, accessed 9 February 2015.

7 Arusha Peace and Reconciliation Agreement for Burundi, 28 August 2000, Annex IV, paragraph 1 4). In this regard, as we may read: 'Assistance to refugees and the reintegration of returnees was explicitly mentioned in many parts of the Arusha Agreement. Chapter 1 of Protocol IV (Reconstruction and Development) of the agreement focused specifically on the rehabilitation and resettlement of refugees and all others that were displaced, regrouped and dispersed. One of the aims was to establish a National Commission for the Rehabilitation of Sinistrés (CNRS), whose objectives included: b) To give all returning families, including female- and child-headed families, food aid, material support and assistance with health, education, agriculture and reconstruction until they become self-sufficient; d) To settle all those who believe that they cannot yet return on sites close to home, in order to enable them to go and till their fields initially and return to their land later on; h) To help returnees to recover the property and bank accounts left in Burundi before their exile and whose existence has been duly proven.' See Fransen, S. and Kuschminder, K., 'Back to the land: the long-term challenges of refugee return and reintegration in Burundi', in UNHCR, *New Issues in Refugee Research*, research paper No. 242, 2012, p. 8.

of Malians from Burkina Faso[8] with the commitment from the government of Burkina to readmit on its territory all Malians who could not find a favourable situation to repatriation,[9] and the UNHCR that will guarantee all Malians who would like to remain in Burkina for well founded reasons, to continue to be protected.[10]

Finally however, not all voluntary repatriations were successful. Instead, many of them have been forced, pushing refugees to return to dangerous environments where their lives were threatened. Despite this gloomy history, voluntary repatriation seems to have become the panacea of all problems afflicting Africa *vis-à-vis* refugees. Its importance has been reaffirmed in 2015 by the UNGA, which stated that repatriation '[s]hould not necessarily be conditioned on the accomplishment of political solutions in the country of origin in order not to impede the exercise of the refugees' right to return.'[11]

Finally, in Chapter 9, we will analyze the two other typical durable solutions historically adopted in Sub-Saharan Africa for refugees: local integration and resettlement in a third country of asylum. Both of them, however, are of decreasing relevance in the policies of African states reluctant to either practise local integration or accept becoming refugee resettlement countries. The case of local integration is still open to debate if refugees to be integrated are either urban refugees, or, alternatively if refugees in camps are intended to be considered as 'integrating' in the country of destination. In our opinion, apart from several exceptions constituted by camps becoming veritable towns, like Daadab in Kenya – where a university has been established[12] – the integration of refugees in a host country should be measured on the integration of the urban ones. We have numerous examples of urban refugees – often obliged to adopt strategies of 'invisibility' in order to avoid discrimination by locals[13] – still missing the basics

8 UNHCR, Accord Tripartite entre le Gouvernement du Burkina Faso, le Gouvernement de la République du Mali et le Haut-Commissariat des Nations Unies pour les Refugies pour le rapatriement volontaire des refugies Maliens vivant au Burkina Faso, 9 January 2015, available at: www.refworld.org/docid/54b360614.html, accessed 1 February 2015.

9 Ibid., Article 6 3).

10 Ibid., Article 8 6).

11 UNGA, Assistance to refugees, returnees and displaced persons in Africa, 22 January 2015, resolution No. A/RES/69/154, paragraph 22. On the same regard, see also UNGA, Assistance to refugees, returnees and displaced persons in Africa, 21 December 2010, resolution No. A/RES/65/193, paragraph 23; Assistance to refugees, returnees and displaced persons in Africa, 19 December 2011, resolution No. A/RES/66/135, paragraph 23.

12 UNHCR, 'UNHCR lauds establishment of university in Kenya's refugee camp', 10 October 2012, available at: http://news.xinhuanet.com/english/world/2012-10/10/c_131896291.htm, accessed 11 October 2014.

13 Anderson, J.L., 'Urban displacement and peacebuilding: an analysis of South African social cohesion interventions', in UNHCR, *New Issues in Refugee Research*, research paper No. 243, 2012, p. 4. At idem, the author pointed out that: 'Refugees and asylum-seekers often prefer to remain "hidden", which has implications for how they engage with the state and South African citizens, and certainly their willingness to participate in peacebuilding interventions.' Social-cohesion was

for a decent life in the country of destination, as happens, for instance, to Chadians and Central Africans living in Yaoundé and Douala.[14]

In these past decades, however, Sub-Saharan Africa has witnessed 'mixed-solutions', like the ones adopted in Tanzania facing the Burundian protracted refugee situation started in 1972. The solutions consist of a partial repatriation, conducted under the aegis of the UNHCR, accompanied by a campaign of naturalization for the most difficult caseloads to repatriate[15] and by a small percentage of refugees resettled in neighbour countries, although this last option often ended up in the encampment of Burundians in locations where they did not achieve self-reliance.[16] Or still in the region, we have also witnessed 'flexible solutions', as in the case of Liberian and Sierra Leonean refugees in West Africa: economically linked to their host countries because of having grown up there, these refugees did not want to undergo a process of naturalization because they did not

also very important in the case of the reintegration of Burundians returning home after the civil conflict that upset the country in 1972. In this regard, see Fransen, S. and Kuschminder, K., op. cit. note 7, pp. 21–2: 'Overall, however, the issue of greatest concern is community social cohesion and poverty. The research indicates that social cohesion in the communities in our sample is low, which is an issue of great concern in a "post-conflict" environment. Returnees and locals appear to maintain superficial relationships and substantive support is only provided from members of one's own group. The fundamental issue that divides the groups is poverty and land.'

14 In this regard, see Mattheisen, E., '"Because I am a stranger" Urban refugees in Yaoundé, Cameroon', in UNHCR, *New Issues in Refugee Research*, research paper No. 244, 2012, 13 p. In this regard, see also High Court of Kenya, Constitutional and Human Rights Division, *Kituo Cha Sheria v The Attorney General*, 23 January 2013, paragraph 1: '[It is hereby ordered]: that a conservatory order be and is hereby issued prohibiting any State officer, public Officer agent of the Government from implementing the decision evidenced by and/or contained in the Press Release dated 18th December, 2012 pending further orders of this court.' For the press release, see, for instance: 'Kenya orders all refugees back to camps', 18 December 2012, available at: http://reliefweb.int/report/kenya/kenya-orders-all-refugees-back-camps, accessed 5 January 2015. In this regard, see also UNHCR, UNHCR position on the directive by the Kenyan Government on the relocation of refugees from the urban centres to the refugee camps, 25 January 2013, available at: www.unhcr.org/refworld/docid/510681a82.html, accessed 28 January 2015: 'The Government [of Kenya] has since provided assurances that a round-up would not take place and reiterated its readiness to work with UNHCR to ensure that refugee protection principles would be respected. Meanwhile, on 22 January, in an application brought by two refugee rights NGOs, the High Court of Kenya issued an injunction temporarily halting any action to implement the relocation direction pending a full hearing on the matter. UNHCR is sustaining its efforts with the Government to ensure that in any implementation of the new directive, refugees and asylum-seekers would not be put in harm's way or their vital protection and human rights transgressed as unfortunately often happens in operations of this nature and scale.'

15 In this regard, J. Milner explained: 'The formulation of Tanzania's naturalization policy can largely be explained by the leadership role played by certain individuals in response to unexpected opportunities, characteristics of the refugee population, dynamics within Tanzania's ruling party, and a changing regional context.' See Milner, J., 'Can global refugee policy leverage durable solutions? Lessons from Tanzania's naturalization of Burundian refugees', in *Journal of Refugee Studies*, vol. 27, 2014, pp. 561–2.

16 Gottwald, M., op. cit. note 1, p. 122.

want to preclude the possibility of going back home one day. So, through an agreement signed by ECOWAS, the UNHCR, and the governments of Nigeria, Liberia and Sierra Leone, refugees were delivered a three-year residency permit in the country of asylum but were also issued with a passport from their country of nationality allowing them the right to return to their home countries.[17]

17 See: Multipartite Agreement for the Local Integration of Liberian and Sierra Leonean refugees in Nigeria between the Government of the Republic of Liberia, the Government of the Republic of Sierra Leone, the Government of the Federal Republic of Nigeria, the Economic Community of West African States (ECOWAS), and the Office of the United Nations High Commissioner for Refugees (UNHCR), June 2007, available at: www.unhcr.org/50aa09319.pdf, accessed 10 May 2015. In detail, see: paragraph 1, p. 3: '1) The Governments of Liberia and Sierra Leone agree to issue a passport of ordinary duration to those of their citizens who: are of eligible age to receive a passport (underage applicants being included on the passports issued to their parents), have been recognized as refugees by the Government of the Federal Republic of Nigeria (confirmed by UNHCR), have submitted a completed application form together with the required supporting documentation, are physically resident in Nigeria at the time of passport issuance'; paragraph 5, p. 3 '5) The Government of Nigeria agrees to place in the passports issued to integrating Sierra Leonean and Liberian refugees an ECOWAS residence permit valid for three years. Such permit shall be renewable'; paragraph 7, p. 4: '7) ECOWAS agrees to facilitate the issuance of three years residence permit for Sierra Leonean and Liberian refugees opting to integrate locally in Nigeria and to monitor compliance with the terms of such issuance for this period and the first period of renewal (i.e. four years)'; and paragraph 11, p. 4 '11) Liberian and Sierra Leonean refugees opting to locally integrate in Nigeria will acknowledge that by accepting passports issued to them by their respective countries of origin they are voluntarily re-availing themselves of the protection of those countries. Their status as refugees will thus cease in accordance with Article 1C (1) of the 1951 Convention and the corresponding provisions of Nigerian law'. In this regard, see also: Long, K., 'Extending protection? Labor migration and durable solutions for refugees', in UNHCR, *New Issues in Refugee Research*, research paper No. 176, 2009, pp. 10–11.

8 Voluntary, spontaneous, forced repatriations

Refugees and their way back home

8.1 Introduction

The uprooting of individuals and communities from their homeland is one of the clearest manifestations of the collapsing relationship between the citizen and his/her state, which occurs in situations of extensive human rights violations. The physical return of individuals to their territory of origin requires rebuilding ties between these individuals and their countries, ties that go beyond a simple geographical return but require also the re-establishment of civil, cultural, economic, political and social rights of the 'returnee'. A 'returnee' is a person whose status is not yet legally defined – distinct from a 'refugee' or an 'IDP'[1] – and who is on an equal basis with one who never suffered displacement.[2] As L. Hovil explained:

> [Repatriation] is not about crossing a border – although that may be part of the process – but about a gradual process of restoring the political contract between citizens and the state that was broken prior to exile. It is a process of re-securing of citizenship [. . .] that negotiates the reconnection of the polity to the individual.[3]

The expression 'voluntary repatriation of refugees' has been, however, maintained and seems to be a contradiction of terms, as refugees are by definition unwilling and/or unable to return home,[4] while the term 'voluntary' entails an informal

1 Kaun, A., 'When the displaced return: challenges to "reintegration" in Angola', in UNHCR, *New Issues in Refugee Research*, working paper No. 152, 2008, p. 6.

2 Tennant, V., 'Return and reintegration', in Chetail, V. (ed.), *Post-Conflict Peacebuilding: a Lexicon*, Oxford: Oxford University Press, 2009, pp. 308–9.

3 Hovil, L., 'Hoping for peace, afraid of war: the dilemmas of repatriation and belonging on the borders of Uganda and South Sudan', in UNHCR, *New Issues in Refugee Research*, research paper No. 196, 2010, p. 3.

4 Feitsma, J., 'Repatriation law and refugees', in *The Netherlands Quarterly of Human Rights*, vol. 7, 1989, p. 299. In this regard, see also Van Krieken, P.J., 'Repatriation of refugees under international law', in *Netherlands Yearbook of International Law*, vol. 1, 1982, p. 98.

decision regarding the conditions which permitted an unforced act or will to make a choice between returning and not returning home.[5]

Today's refugee questions in Sub-Saharan Africa have become more complex than in the past, and the disruptions caused by flight are more severe and long lasting than before. For a number of reasons, some refugees may not wish to return to their country of origin if and when the opportunity arises. Others have, in the process of becoming refugees, also undergone major cultural and social transformations, such as, for instance, becoming urbanized,[6] or joining insurgent movements and thereby exchanging their initial political passivity to one of militancy. These conditions will complicate any attempt to return to the traditional agrarian economies and societies from which the majority of refugees originate. In addition, we need to consider that if a government feels that the return of a large number of refugees unaccompanied by international assistance can destabilize the social or political order, the result will most likely be complete rejection.[7]

Therefore, while repatriation would constitute the 'ideal' and 'obvious'[8] solution to their dilemma as refugees, local integration and resettlement in a third country, where viable and suitable, also constitute workable alternatives to facing the condition of refugees in Sub-Saharan Africa.[9]

For many refugees, there is a large cloud of uncertainty surrounding the prospect of returning home.[10] Generally, the refugee's will to return home is taken for granted, so the question of motivation for repatriating often may not necessarily arise. Similarly, it is assumed that once the root causes that prompted population movements are eliminated, the affected populations will go back home in order to re-establish themselves in their former areas of origin or habitual residence.[11]

5 Othman-Chande, M., 'The emerging international law norms for refugee repatriation', in *Revue héllenique de droit international*, vol. 46, 1993, pp. 105–6.

6 About urban refugees, see, for instance, Karadawi, A., 'The problem of urban refugees in Sudan', in Rogge, J.R. (ed.), *Refugees: A Third World Dilemma*, Totowa, NJ: Rowman and Littlefield, 1987, pp. 115–29; Kibreab, G., 'Urban Eritrean refugees in Sudan: yearning for home of the diaspora?', in *Eritrean Studies Review*, vol. 4, 2005, pp. 115–41. M. Sommers described the life of the Burundian urbanized refugees in his work: *Fear in Bongoland: Burundi Refugees in Urban Tanzania*, New York/Oxford: Berghahn Books, 2001, p. 219, where the author stressed that the majority of the Burundian refugees in Dar-el-Salaam lived 'hidden' to the local populations.

7 Kibreab, G., 'Left in Limbo', in Allen, T. (ed.), *In Search of Cool Ground: War, Flight and Homecoming in Northeast Africa*, London: James Currey; Trenton, NJ: Africa World Press, 1996, pp. 56–7.

8 Bakewell, O., 'Refugee repatriation in Africa: towards a theoretical framework?', University of Bath: occasional paper, 1996, p. 12.

9 UNGA, Assistance to refugees, returnees and displaced persons in Africa, 18 December 2008, resolution No. A/RES/63/149, paragraph 21. For an analysis of local integration and resettlement in a third country, see *infra*, Chapter 9.

10 Rogge, J.R., 'Repatriation of refugees: a not-so-simple "optimum" solution', paper prepared for the Symposium on social and economic aspects of mass voluntary return of refugees from one African country to another, Winnipeg: University of Manitoba, 1991, p. 9.

11 Bakewell, O., 'Returning refugees or migrating villagers? Voluntary repatriation programs in Africa reconsidered', in UNHCR, *New Issues in Refugee Research*, research paper No. 15, 1999, p. 6.

When refugee law in Sub-Saharan Africa started to be analyzed in detail, voluntary repatriation seemed to arouse little interest among scholars, one of the reasons being perhaps its relative insignificance compared to the problem of the flight of millions of Africans from their home countries. Therefore, academics and other interested parties had at first the tendency to focus on the economic, legal, political and social problems arising from the phenomenon of refugees on the continent, rather than what is considered to be a tangential aspect due to its infrequency.[12]

The right of a person to return to his/her own country is implied in Article 9 of the 1948 UDHR which prohibits 'arbitrary arrest detention or exile', as well as the prohibition of expulsion of nationals.[13] In addition, Article 13 2) of the 1948 UDHR also expressly recognizes the right to return[14] with the exclusive restriction that beneficiaries of the right in question must be citizens[15] although, for instance, Article 12 4) of the 1966 ICCPR talks about 'no one' instead of 'citizen', and Article 12 2) of the 1981 Banjul Charter talks about the 'individual' having the right 'to return to his/her country'. In fact, K. Hailbronner wondered whether:

> One may ask whether public international law does not support a right of return for foreigners legally resident for a long time in the country. It is prohibited under public international law to organize mass deportations of people legally resident, regardless of their nationality.[16] A corresponding right of return seems to be a logical consequence.[17]

12 Baloro, J., 'The law and pattern of repatriation of Namibian and South African refugees: possible lessons for a program of repatriation of Mozambican refugees', paper for 'First Country of Asylum & Development Aid' conference, June 1992, Lilongwe: Malawi, pp. 7–8.

13 In this regard, see Anonymous, 'Governing Rule 11: expulsion or deportation of nationals', in *Studies in Transnational Legal Policy*, vol. 23, 1992, p. 85: 'It is a firmly established rule of international law that a State may not expel or deport its own nationals. This rule is a corollary of the principle that all nationals of a State have the right to enter and remain in the territory of that State. The obligation of a State to permit its nationals to reside within the State's territory is inherent in the concept of sovereignty and nationality. Indeed, a State owes a duty to other States to receive back into its territory any of its nationals expelled or deported from another State. For a State to expel or deport a national would be inconsistent with all these obligations. A State which expels its nationals destroys in effect the legal bond between a State and its nationals and renders them stateless.'

14 Article 13 2) of the 1948 UDHR reads as follows: '2) Everyone has the right to leave any country, including his/her own, and to return to his/her country.'

15 Goodwin-Gill, G., 'The right to leave, the right to return and the question of a right to remain', in Gowlland-Debbas, V. (ed.), *The Problem of Refugees in the Light of Contemporary International Law Issues*, The Hague/Boston/London: Martinus Nijhoff, 1996, p. 101.

16 In this regard, we note again that Article 12 5) of the 1981 Banjul Charter reads as follows: 'The mass expulsion of non-nationals shall be prohibited. Mass expulsion shall be that which is aimed at national, racial, ethnic or religious groups.' Article 12 4) of the 1966 ICCPR reads as follows: '4) No one shall be arbitrarily deprived of the right to enter his own country.'

17 Hailbronner, K., 'Comments on: the right to leave, the right to return and the question of a right to remain', in Gowlland-Debbas, V. (ed.), *The Problem of Refugees in the Light of Contemporary International Law Issues*, The Hague/Boston/London: Martinus Nijhoff, 1996, p. 116.

But state practices and state obligations to each other seem to require a limited interpretation of the application of the right to return. However, the human rights dimension of refugees is relevant for the premise of voluntary repatriation as the primary solution is based upon their fundamental human right to return to their own country under conditions of dignity and safety,[18] conditions that, for instance, according to the UNHCR, had still not been met by November 2012, in order to allow the return of refugees in North and South Kivu,[19] and considered as essential in the repatriation of Somalis from Kenya, which began in November 2013 and, given the situation is still quite unstable in several regions of the country, to which no deadline was fixed.[20]

8.2 An analysis of the legal basis of voluntary repatriation with a special mention of the practice of 'spontaneous repatriation'

Voluntary repatriation as a solution to refugee situations has its origins in the 1950 UNGA resolution, which adopted the 1950 UNHCR Statute. Resolution 428 (V) of 14 December 1950 calls upon governments to cooperate with the High Commissioner in the performance of their functions, among others, by assisting him/her in his/her efforts to promote voluntary repatriation of refugees.[21] UNHCR competence to be involved in the programmes of repatriation relies upon the provision of Article 8 c) of the agency's statute, which affirms:

> The High Commissioner shall provide for the protection of refugees falling under the competence of his/her Office by: c) Assisting governmental and private efforts to promote voluntary repatriation or assimilation within new national communities.

18 Goodwin-Gill, G., 'The right to leave, the right to return and the question of a right to remain', op. cit. note 15, p. 101.

19 UNHCR, UNHCR position on returns to North Kivu, South Kivu and adjacent areas in the Democratic Republic of Congo affected by on-going conflict and violence in the region, 15 November 2012, paragraph 5, p. 2.

20 See the news: 'Kenya: Repatriation process to Somalia starting, must be voluntary', 26 November 2013, available at: www.unhcr.org/52948a7d9.html, accessed 10 October 2014.

21 Leckie, S., 'New directions in housing and property restitution', in Leckie, S. (ed.), *Returning Home: Housing and Property Restitution Rights of Refugees and Displaced Persons*, Ardsley, NY: Transnational Inc., 2003, p. 27. M. Zieck explained that, in case of voluntary repatriation: 'UNHCR's responsibilities include monitoring the repatriation exercise and to that end the agreements [concluded by UNHCR with the countries interested] contain provisions which guarantee UNHCR free and unhindered access to refugees and returnees respectively.' See Zieck, M., 'Voluntary repatriation: paradigm, pitfalls, progress', in *Refugee Survey Quarterly*, vol. 23, 2004, p. 39. In the same regard, see also Loescher, G., Betts, A. and Milner, J.H.S., *The United Nations High Commissioner for Refugees (UNHCR): the Politics and Practice of Refugee Protection into the Twenty-First Century*, London/New York: Routledge, 2008, p. 13: '[U]NHCR was established to act under the authority of the General Assembly to serve two specific functions: to protect refugees and to find permanent solutions to their plight, either through voluntary repatriation or through their assimilation within new national communities.'

This interpretation could be criticized, given that, as provided in Article 9, which follows, an explicit mandate by the UNGA is indispensable, despite the article's use of the conditional '*may*'.[22] On the other hand, R. Hofmann emphasized that the conclusion of any agreement providing for an extensive decision-making function of the UNHCR hinges upon the unequivocal consent of the country of origin. In principle, no government should fear that the agency's supervision would meddle in the country's internal affairs, given the UNHCR's strictly humanitarian approach to refugee crises and the fact that its intervention occurs only in those exceptional cases where the provisions of a repatriation agreement would not be observed.[23] Nonetheless, the UNHCR's role is also to cooperate with the different national and international actors operating on African soil.[24] It is true, however, that because the majority of repatriations in Sub-Saharan Africa involve returns from one less developed country to another, poorer host states which lack resources to effectuate repatriation on their own have often turned to the UNHCR for support and/or to conduct the repatriation effort.[25] This was the case in the 2010 incident when 40,000 Congolese returning from Zambia were helped by the UNHCR through, among other programmes, micro-credit schemes.[26] The vast majority of scholars agree on the fact that, for the UNHCR, it is very important to 'facilitate'[27] or to 'promote'[28] return. This happened, in one of the most famous

22 Article 9 of the 1950 UNHCR Statute stipulates that: 'The High Commissioner shall engage in such additional activities, including repatriation and resettlement, as the General Assembly *may* determine, within the limits of the resources placed at his disposal.' Emphasis added. In this regard, see also Hathaway, J.C., 'The meaning of repatriation', in *International Journal of Refugee Law*, vol. 9, 1997, p. 552.

23 Hofmann, R., 'Voluntary repatriation and UNHCR', in *Zeitschrift für Ausländisches Öffentliches Recht und Völkerrecht*, vol. 44, 1984, pp. 334–5.

24 Loescher, G., Betts, A. and Milner, J.H.S., op. cit. note 21, pp. 85–91.

25 In this regard, J.C. Hathaway made an example involving Burundi and Tanzania that, in 2002, announced that they would send a delegation to the UNHCR headquarters in Geneva to petition for allowing repatriation to all areas in Burundi. See Hathaway, J.C., 'The right of states to repatriate former refugees', in *Ohio State Journal on Dispute Resolution*, vol. 20, 2005, note 56 of the Article, pp. 191–2.

26 See the news: 'Repatriation of Congolese from Zambia reaches 40,000; camps to close', 24 September 2010, available at: www.unhcr.org/4c9cc3146.html, accessed 29 October 2014.

27 For instance, see Chimni, B.S., 'The meaning of words and the role of the UNHCR in voluntary repatriation', in *International Journal of Refugee Law*, vol. 5, 1993, p. 448; Othman-Chande, M., 'The emerging international law norms for refugee repatriation', op. cit. note 5, p. 122.

28 See what the Africa Bureau of UNHCR affirmed in this sense: '*Facilitation of voluntary repatriation*: in this case UNHCR still considers that return movements are premature as conditions are not fulfilled for voluntary repatriation in safety and dignity. However, individual refugees directly approach the Office to request assistance towards return to their country of origin. Certain criteria need to be met in order for UNHCR to facilitate movements and provide assistance. These would include free access and ability to monitor returnees, minimum conditions of safety and security in the areas of return as well as security for humanitarian staff. *Promotion of voluntary repatriation*: this situation arises when UNHCR determines that voluntary repatriation in safety and dignity is feasible under the circumstances, and encourages it by informing refugees on conditions prevailing in the country of origin and providing comprehensive assistance packages and monitoring to ensure safe return and sustainable reintegration. Promotion of voluntary

examples, in the late 1970s–early 1980s in Zimbabwe:[29] the principal consideration was attributed to the refugee's interest and the protection of his/her rights, security and welfare[30] as was also confirmed in the ExCom conclusion No. 40 of 1985.[31] On the other hand, the UNHCR should not 'influence' repatriation, in accordance with respect for the knowledge and decisions of the refugees.[32] Also playing its general role of adviser, in 2009 the UNHCR counselled refugees in Burundi against returning to DRC, where their life could still be in danger.[33] As it also did with north-eastern Nigerians in 2013.[34]

But the UNHCR has often been unwilling or unable to participate in voluntary repatriations.[35] For instance, refugees who do not register with the UNHCR, or where the country of asylum does not officially recognize them as refugees – as with some 10,000 Rwandans and 100,000 Burundians in Tanzania in the late

repatriation is usually undertaken within the framework of a comprehensive political settlement which addressed the root causes of the refugee movement in the country of origin, and is normally based on amnesty laws or public assurances/guarantees issued by the government to encourage refugees to return.' Emphasis added. See UNHCR, Africa Bureau, Africa protection directions, 2004, p. 56. For a recent example of reiteration of these measures, see, for instance, UNSC, Burundi, 13 February 2013, resolution No. 2090, S/RES/2090, paragraph 10: '[The UNSC] further encourages the Government of Burundi, with the support of international partners as appropriate, to ensure the voluntary, safe and orderly return and sustainable reintegration of refugees to Burundi.'

29 In this regard, see Jackson, J., 'Repatriation and reconstruction in Zimbabwe during the 1980s', in Allen, T. and Morsink, H. (eds), *When Refugees Go Home*, London: James Currey; Trenton, NJ: Africa World Press, 1994, p. 129: 'The repatriation of Zimbabwean refugees from Mozambique, Zambia and Botswana at the end of the liberation war fits a classical model. Helped by the [UNHCR], refugees returned to their country of origin after cessation of conflict. However, the repatriation depended critically on refugees' own informal networks and on channels created independently of the UN effort. Together these alternative structures dealt with more returnees than did the UN system. Many refugees chose not to use formal channels.'

30 Goodwin-Gill, G.; McAdam J., *The Refugee in International Law*, 3rd edition, Oxford: Oxford University Press, 2007, p. 494.

31 In detail, paragraph l) of the conclusion affirms: 'The High Commissioner should be recognized as having a legitimate concern for the consequences of return, particularly where such return has been brought about as a result of an amnesty or other form of guarantee. The High Commissioner must be regarded as entitled to insist on his/her legitimate concern over the outcome of any return that he/she has assisted. Within the framework of close consultations with the State concerned, he/she should be given direct and unhindered access to returnees so that he/she is in a position to monitor fulfillment of the amnesties, guarantees or assurances on the basis of which the refugees have returned. *This should be considered as inherent in his/her mandate.*' Emphasis added.

32 Chimni, B.S., 'The meaning of words and the role of the UNHCR in voluntary repatriation', op. cit. note 27, p. 448.

33 See the news: 'UNHCR advises refugees in Burundi against returning to Eastern Congo', 6 October 2009, available at: www.unhcr.org/4acb4fcf9.html, accessed 20 October 2014.

34 UNHCR, International Protection Considerations with regard to people fleeing north-eastern Nigeria (the states of Borno, Yobe and Adamawa), 29 October 2013, p. 3, available at: www.refworld.org/docid/526fcea47.html, accessed 4 September 2014.

35 Makanya, S.T., 'Voluntary repatriation in Africa in the 1990s: issues and challenges', in *International Journal of Refugee Law*, special issue, vol. 7, 1995, p. 181.

1990s[36] – may not receive any assistance when they spontaneously return,[37] simply because the agency is not party to their movements or because there are no government requests that any assistance be provided.

This phenomenon of 'spontaneous repatriation' (or 'self-repatriation') takes place at the initiative of, and is managed by, the refugees themselves.[38] An example of spontaneous repatriation, happening between the mid-1980s and the early 1990s, occurred in Ethiopia and Somalia, involving Sudanese and Ethiopian refugees respectively.[39] Somalia was also the theatre of spontaneous repatriation in the 1990s. Self-repatriation began instantly after Somali government forces were defeated and expelled from northern Somalia in 1991. Immediately thereafter, many crossed the border into Somalia, some to assess conditions before returning and others to stay for good. Their quick response to the return of relative stability in northern Somalia was a function of many variables. First and most important, the Somalis have always viewed their exile in Ethiopia as temporary because of the suspicion they have always harboured against Ethiopia, their traditional enemy. Likewise, Ethiopia was apprehensive of their presence and maintained the strict control of camps and of movements outside of the camps. The self-repatriated Somali refugees behaved like typical migrants when they decided to return. Indeed there were obvious economic, political and social variables pushing

36 United States Committee for Refugees and Immigrants, US Committee for Refugees World Refugee Survey 1998 – Tanzania, 1 January 1998, available at: www.unhcr.org/refworld/docid/3ae6a8c5c.html, accessed 10 October 2014. In this regard, B. Rutinwa noted that the decision of the Tanzanian government to put an end to its traditional 'open door' policy towards refugees was 'unfortunate but understandable', considering the economic situation of the country. See Rutinwa, B., 'The Tanzanian government's response to the Rwandan emergency', in *Journal of Refugee Studies*, vol. 9, 1996, p. 300.

37 Chimni, B.S., 'The meaning of words and the role of the UNHCR in voluntary repatriation', op. cit. note 27, p. 447.

38 In this regard, the Africa Bureau of the UNHCR has clarified: 'In this situation, refugees return on their own to often less than ideal circumstances in the country of origin. UNHCR may or may not assist and monitor them depending on conditions prevailing in areas of return, particularly security conditions which affect the Office's ability to have access to returnees. Other factors such as avoiding creating a pull factor or a revolving door would also have to be considered in any decision on assistance to and monitoring of spontaneous returnees.' See UNHCR, Africa Bureau, Africa protection directions, 2004, p. 55. However, O. Bakewell correctly noted: 'The term 'spontaneous' repatriation suggests that refugees suddenly decide to return home, without forethought or planning. However, this is clearly not the case as refugees organize their own repatriation in the light of their resources information, expectations and the external pressures exerted on them. Many of those who return outside the UNHCR sponsored program may never have been recognized as refugees and may be "spontaneously" or "self" settled in the country of asylum.' See Bakewell, O., 'Refugee repatriation in Africa: towards a theoretical framework?', op. cit. note 8, p. 10.

39 The Sudanese repatriation dates back to the early 1990s, while the Ethiopian repatriation dates back to the mid-1980s. In this regard, A. Bariagaber argued that: 'We may refer to the Sudanese and Ethiopian Somali repatriation [. . .] as "spontaneous" because it is conceptually distinct from self-repatriation in terms [. . .] of the nature of the motivations. Simply put, "spontaneous" repatriation is "flight" to one's country of origin.' See Bariagaber, A., *Conflict and the Refugee Experience: Flight, Exile and Repatriation in the Horn of Africa*, Aldershot: Ashgate, 2006, p. 133.

them away from the refugee camps, including their residual suspicion of Ethiopia, their restricted movements and the government control of the camps.[40]

The UNHCR should not support refugee-induced spontaneous repatriation unless it is convinced through an overall assessment that it would be in the best interests of the refugees. Exercising caution better matches the UNHCR's protection function with regards to refugee repatriation.[41] In addition, unassisted repatriation should not be promoted unless all countries involved in the process can ensure the protection and respect of the refugees' fundamental human rights.[42] Proper human rights standards must be verified before organizing repatriation, in order to assess whether repatriation is a real option. Actions such as 'obtaining firm commitments' to abide by human rights standards should be a condition of repatriation, not something to be attempted after the refugees have all returned.[43]

When refugees choose to return spontaneously, they do so for a variety of reasons: they usually prefer to control their own lives and returnees often have different objectives for their future than official plans might assume; formal programmes have not always involved many refugees because they are implemented inadequately or too late. Also, formal programmes do not often attract many refugees because they offer too little assistance to make a real contribution to people's needs. In effect, to show how informal repatriations have been

40 Ibid., pp. 128–9. Another self-repatriation, although it has been contested as such, has occurred in late 1996 from Eastern DRC, to Rwanda. In detail, J. Pottier wondered if the repatriation from Mugunga camp, in Eastern DRC was really voluntary or if the refugees there were in some way 'solicited' to return home by false promises and false information received. The author concluded his analysis affirming: 'Even the term "complex repatriation", although an improvement on voluntary-involuntary dichotomy, cannot adequately describe the unique mixture of elements found in the repatriation that followed the seizure of Mugunga.' See Pottier, J., 'The "self" in self-repatriation: closing down Mugunga camp, Eastern Zaire', in Black, R. and Koser, K. (eds), *The End of the Refugee Cycle? Refugee Repatriation and Reconstruction*, Oxford: Berghahn Books, 1999, p. 169. For a more recent case of a 'spontaneous repatriation', although this involved more IDPs than refugees, see the one that took place in Mali, in early 2013. In this regard, see the news: 'UNHCR gearing up to support possible spontaneous returns in Mali', 29 January 2013, available at: www.unhcr.org/5107b3899.html, accessed 10 February 2014: 'With the fast-evolving situation in Mali, UNHCR is readying itself to assist in the possible spontaneous return of thousands of conflict-displaced people in the north of the country. We aim to open new presences in Gao and other cities in the north as soon as it becomes feasible. So far, insecurity has hampered humanitarian access to the north. From interviews over the past few days in Bamako with internally displaced people, it appears that many are hoping to return soon to areas including Gao, Timbuktu and Kidal. Returns are not yet a wide trend, but they are already being seen in some instances. In the central Mali town of Konna, for example, a UN security evaluation mission has confirmed that people are coming back. Up to half the town's population of 10,000 was earlier reported as having fled into the surrounding countryside when Konna was overrun by rebel fighters on 10 January, prompting the French military intervention.'

41 Chimni, B.S., 'The meaning of words and the role of the UNHCR in voluntary repatriation', op. cit. note 27, p. 453.

42 Helton, A.C., 'Refugee protection and repatriation: a critical view', in Stein, B.N., Cuny, F.C. and Reed, P. (eds), *Refugee Repatriation During Conflict: A New Conventional Wisdom*, Dallas: The Centre for the Study of Societies in Crisis, 1995, p. 41.

43 Takahashi, S., 'The UNHCR Handbook on voluntary repatriation', in *International Journal of Refugee Law*, vol. 9, 1997, p. 607.

sometimes preferred to formal ones, in the late 1980s and early 1990s, of the tens of thousands of Mozambican refugees who returned home before and immediately after the end of the civil war, not a single one was formally repatriated. This example illustrates the extent to which self-repatriation has sometimes been preferred to formal programmes. The apparent lack of relevance of such formal arrangements for return leads one to question if the efforts of governments and aid agencies might not be better applied to assisting self-return movements.[44] Alternatively, when a country of origin identifies returnees as members of an insurgent movement, as for instance, the Eritrean Islamic Jihad Movement (ERIJM) – a small, Sudan-based insurgent group that has continually made attacks in the north and west of Eritrea since 1993[45] – and does not, in consequence, sanction their return, the UNHCR is evidently unable to assist with their return.[46]

8.3 The principle of voluntary repatriation as it was conceived in the 1969 OAU Convention

Distinct from the 1951 Geneva Convention, in which this solution was not formulated as a legal obligation because individuals could conceivably refuse to repatriate although able to return home safely after a short period in exile,[47] the 1969 African Convention in its Article V, gave the strongest guidance regarding voluntary repatriation.[48] In full, the article stipulates as follows:

> 1) The essentially voluntary character of repatriation shall be respected in all cases and no refugee shall be repatriated against his/her will. 2) The country

44 Makanya, S.T., 'Voluntary repatriation in Africa in the 1990s: issues and challenges', op. cit. note 35, pp. 179–80. The author also explained that, in her opinion: '[t]hree main constraints limit the provision of adequate assistance to refugees under repatriation programs. First, donor funding is usually inadequate for the size of the task in hand. [. . .] Secondly, most assistance programs lack the policy instruments (power and knowledge) to provide refugees with what they need on the ground. [. . .] Third, repatriation programs usually operate in specific types of situations, such as marginal border areas with war-destroyed economies and infrastructure, or in circumstances of great political and military instability. All activities prove extremely difficult and slow, and even good plans often have to be aborted owing to concerns for the safety of international staff or the refugees themselves.' See ibid., pp. 180–1.

45 See, for instance, the document: United States Department of State, US Department of State Country Report on Human Rights Practices 2004: Eritrea, 28 February 2005, available at: www.unhcr.org/refworld/docid/4226d96a2f.html, accessed 20 October 2014.

46 Rogge, J.R., 'Repatriation of refugees: a not-so-simple "optimum" solution', op. cit. note 10, p. 21.

47 Barutciski, M., 'Involuntary repatriation when refugee protection is no longer necessary: moving forward after the 48th session of the Executive Committee', in *International Journal of Refugee Law*, vol. 10, 1998, p. 248. Nevertheless, J.C. Hathaway noted that: 'Under article 1C 4) [of the 1951 Geneva Convention] it is only if and when the refugee is re-established in the country of origin that refugee status comes to an end.' See Hathaway, J.C., 'The right of states to repatriate former refugees', op. cit. note 25, p. 176.

48 Takahashi, S., op. cit. note 43, p. 599.

> of asylum, in collaboration with the country of origin, shall make adequate arrangements for the safe return of refugees who request repatriation. 3) The country of origin, on receiving back refugees, shall facilitate their resettlement and grant them the full rights and privileges of nationals of the country, and subject them to the same obligations. 4) Refugees who voluntarily return to their country shall in no way be penalized for having left it for any of the reasons giving rise to refugee situations. Whenever necessary, an appeal shall be made through national information media and through the Administrative Secretary-General of the OAU, inviting refugees to return home and giving assurance that the new circumstances prevailing in their country of origin will enable them to return without risk and to take up a normal and peaceful life without fear of being disturbed or punished, and that the text of such appeal should be given to refugees and clearly explained to them by their country of asylum. 5) Refugees who freely decide to return to their homeland, as a result of such assurances or on their own initiative, shall be given every possible assistance by the country of asylum, the country of origin, voluntary agencies and international and intergovernmental organizations, to facilitate their return.

This article is intended to guarantee that countries of asylum, international organizations, and NGOs will facilitate voluntary repatriation of refugees. In addition, the article is also intended to ensure that the country of origin will not impose any sanctions or discriminate in any way against refugees who freely return home.[49] The implementation of this article requires a clear collaboration between the country of origin and the host country during repatriation, and prohibits the punishment of refugees who return to their country of origin.[50] This article begins with the following statement: 'The essentially[51] voluntary character of repatriation shall be respected in all cases and no refugee shall be repatriated against his/her will.' According to P.J. Van Krieken, however, the voluntary character of repatriation can be overruled if the refugee cannot argue validly against his/her return.[52]

If the two phrases of the above-mentioned sentence (separated by the conjunction 'and') are meant to be read independently, the first phrase seems to ignore the possibility of involuntary repatriation when an individual is no longer

49 Othman-Chande, M., 'The emerging international law norms for refugee repatriation', op. cit. note 5, pp. 110–11.

50 Baloro, J., 'The law and pattern of repatriation of Namibian and South African refugees: possible lessons for a program of repatriation of Mozambican refugees', op. cit. note 12, p. 18.

51 Inclusion of the adverb 'essentially' is noteworthy. It is used in a similar way in the ExCom conclusion No. 18 (XXXI), 'Voluntary repatriation', 1980, paragraph b) that affirms: '[The ExCom] stressed that the essentially voluntary character of repatriation should always be respected.'

52 Van Krieken, P.J., 'Repatriation of refugees under international law', op. cit. note 4, p. 101.

a refugee according to the cessation clause set out in Article I4 e) of the 1969 OAU convention and concerning the change of circumstances in the country of origin.[53] *A contrario*, the second phrase may suggest that refugees can be voluntarily repatriated, which is visibly not the case given the inclusion of the term 'refugee' applying exclusively to persons fearing persecution and who are protected under Article II3 of the 1969 African Convention.[54] If the drafters of the 1969 OAU Convention intended that the two phrases of the sentence be read jointly in order to establish a unique standard that relates to individuals who satisfy the refugee definition, then the above-mentioned contradiction still applies and a consistent proviso would have stated that 'no refugees shall be repatriated', not considering whether it is against his/her will.[55]

The 1969 OAU Convention, however, does not clarify how the provision in Article V1 relates to the cessation clause. In this regard, M. Zieck affirmed:

> [I]t is submitted that voluntary repatriation actually draws on those cessation clauses. Apart from the fact that voluntary repatriation allows States to justify invoking the fourth cessation clause, the fifth and the sixth cessation clauses would seem to be crucial for benchmarking purposes such as those UNHCR implicitly recognizes when it identifies the timing of its promoting voluntary repatriation in terms of a threshold that it derives from the pertinent cessation clauses.[56]

On the one hand, the mention of the obligation to respect the deliberate character of repatriation at all times could be seen to limit the right of countries to return even one individual who is not a refugee because of the cessation of his/her status. On the other hand, the clause of Article V1 of the 1969 OAU Convention

53 Article I4 e) of the 1969 OAU Convention stipulates: 'This Convention shall cease to apply to any refugee if: [. . .] e) he can no longer, because the circumstances in connection with which he was recognized as a refugee have ceased to exist, continue to refuse to avail himself of the protection of the country of his nationality [. . .].' To make a practical example, in interviews carried out with Sudanese refugees in Uganda and Kenya in 2006, refugees argued that before they were ready to go back to their country of origin they wanted to see substantial developments in their home areas. Mention was made of a need for clearance landmines, reconstruction of roads and infrastructure, the reestablishment of social services including schools and health facilities and the maintenance of a level of security to enable ordinary living to take place there. See Kaiser, T., 'Sudanese refugees in Uganda and Kenya', in Loescher, G. (*et al.*) (ed.), *Protracted Refugee Situations: Political, Human Rights and Security Implications*, New York: United Nations University Press, 2008, p. 267. In this regard, at ibid., p. 268, the author noted that: '[I]n 2005 [. . .] UNHCR assisted in the resettlement of 4,600 Somali and Sudanese refugees from Kenya and a further 600 from Uganda, demonstrating that even in the presence of a [. . .] peace agreement there were Sudanese refugees for whom a return to the country of origin was not considered a viable option.'

54 Article II3 of the 1969 OAU Convention stipulates: 'No person shall be subjected by a Member State to measures such as rejection at the frontier, return or expulsion, which would compel him/her to return or to remain in a territory where his/her life, physical integrity or liberty would be threatened [. . .].'

55 Barutciski, M., 'Involuntary repatriation when refugee protection is no longer necessary: moving forward after the 48th session of the Executive Committee', op. cit. note 47, p. 250.

56 Zieck, M., 'Voluntary repatriation: paradigm, pitfalls, progress', op. cit. note 21, p. 51.

'no refugee shall be repatriated against his/her will' stipulates that the requisite of voluntarism may be raised exclusively by an individual who is a refugee, thus not considering a former refugee whose status has been terminated.[57]

The explicit stipulation in a legally binding instrument that repatriation might be a voluntary act represents a valuable corroboration of the principle of *non-refoulement.* At present, voluntary repatriation is considered by eminent scholars, such as R. Degni-Segui, as a custom, although its inclusion in the 1969 OAU Convention represented an early attempt to codify the concept in a legally binding instrument.[58]

As aforementioned, the 'right to return' to one's country of origin, evidently in connection with the will of refugees to repatriate, constitutes a basic human right, confirmed in other international legal instruments which are not strictly related to the protection of refugees.[59] However, S. Takahashi noted that the 'right to return' whether it is a human right *per se* or simply the corollary of an obligation between states:

> [i]s largely irrelevant to refugee protection, for refugees are by definition people who for the time being at least cannot return. They have been driven from their homes by persecution, by conflict, by mass violations of human rights. Most of them may wish to return to their country, but the point is they are unable to do so.[60]

The 1969 OAU Convention explains in detail the duties of both the country of asylum and the country of origin regarding registration of returnees. These stipulations are intended to guarantee that states of asylum, international organizations, and NGOs support the voluntary repatriation of refugees. Additionally, the country of origin shall not impose any sanctions nor discriminate in any way against refugees who voluntarily return home.[61] The 1969 African Convention seems to envisage only organized repatriation, meaning repatriations that require

57 Hathaway, J.C., 'The right of states to repatriate former refugees', op. cit. note 25, footnote 10 of the Article, p. 178. At idem, the author affirmed: 'If read to apply only to present refugees, then the OAU provision cannot only be reconciled to its own cessation clauses, but also be applied in consonance with article 1C 4) of the Refugee Convention, which does require voluntary re-establishment by a person otherwise entitled to refugee status before the duty to protect him or her comes to an end.'

58 Degni-Segui, R., 'L'action des institutions africaines en matière de réfugiés', in *Colloque de Caen: droit d'asile et des réfugiés, Société française pour le droit international*, Paris: Éditions A. Pedone, 1997, p. 233.

59 For instance, see Article 13 2) of the 1948 UDHR, Article 12 4) of the 1966 ICCPR, Article 12 2) of the 1981 Banjul Charter which, however, allows for the following restriction: '[p]rovided for by law for the protection of national security, law and order, public health or morality.'

60 Takahashi, S., op. cit. note 43, p. 610.

61 Weis, P., 'The Convention of the Organization of the African Unity Governing the Specific Aspects of Refugee Problems in Africa', in *Revue des Droits de l'homme*, vol. 3, 1970, pp. 460–1.

formal written agreements, as opposed to the phenomenon of spontaneous repatriations previously mentioned.[62]

Within the OAU, the decision-making organization's developments regarding voluntary repatriation have been narrowed, with the exception of a 1975 resolution of the Council of Ministers. This document touches upon a number of legal and practical matters not otherwise covered in the 1969 African Convention itself. These include modalities for the implementation of repatriation, the right to return in the case of mixed marriages and the facilitation of refugees' ability to return home with their property and savings.[63] This resolution was conceived with the objective of incorporating the participation of liberation movements, whose nationals the OAU had been recognized for repatriating at that time.[64] In 1987, the OAU reiterated the same concept, confirming the fundamental right of an individual refugee to return to his/her country of origin in peace and dignity, calling upon the member states of the OAU to observe this right completely by creating conditions conducive to voluntary repatriation by ensuring full integration into the social and economic fabric of their national society.[65]

Nevertheless, already in 1979 the Arusha Conference on the Situation of the Refugees in Africa noted that there have been circumstances in which African refugees have been subjected to persecution once returned home. Thus the conference recommended that:

> [a]n earnest appeal is addressed to Governments of countries of origin to respect any guarantees of safety given to refugees with a view to encouraging their return.[66]

62 Okoth-Obbo, G., 'Thirty years on: a legal review of the 1969 OAU Refugee Convention Governing the Specific Aspects of Refugee Problems in Africa', in *Refugee Survey Quarterly*, vol. 20, 2001, pp. 123–6. In this regard, see also Van Garderen, J. and Ebenstein, J., 'Regional developments: Africa', in Zimmermann, A. (ed.), *The 1951 Convention Relating the Status of Refugees and its 1967 Protocol: a Commentary*, Oxford: Oxford University Press, 2011, p. 195: 'Together with the conclusions reached by the UNHCR ExCom, this provision [the 1975 resolution] has created the framework for several successful voluntary repatriation agreements in Southern Africa during the early 1990s.' Apart from the examples already made, another example of huge, spontaneous repatriation was the one that took place in Guinea after the death of President S. Touré in 1984. This example is mentioned in Van Hövell tot Westerflier, W.J.E.M., 'Africa and refugees: the OAU Refugee Convention in theory and practice', in *Netherlands Quarterly of Human Rights*, vol. 7, 1989, p. 184.

63 OAU, Council of Ministers, Voluntary repatriation of African refugees, resolution No. CM/Res. 399 (XXIV), 13–21 February 1975 where letter a) states: '[Member States] accept and abide scrupulously by the international agreements and the OAU Convention on Refugees, particularly as regards the voluntary nature of repatriation.'

64 Okoth-Obbo, G., 'Thirty years on: a legal review of the 1969 OAU Refugee Convention Governing the Specific Aspects of Refugee Problems in Africa', op. cit. note 62, p. 123.

65 OAU, Council of Ministers, resolution on the situation of refugees in Africa, resolution No. CM/Res. 1117 (XLVI), 20–25 July 1987, paragraph 5).

66 Recommendations from the Pan-African Conference on the Situation of Refugees in Africa, Arusha (Tanzania), 17 May 1979, recommendation 7, available at: www.refworld.org/docid/3ae6b37214.html, accessed 6 July 2014. In this regard, see also Feitsma, J., op. cit. note 4, p. 302.

Voluntary repatriation seems to reflect the citizen's right to return and, in addition, on the ground of self-interest, most countries of refuge prefer to limit their obligations to refugees. Voluntary repatriation is also believed to be ideal when there is stability between the countries of origin and asylum.[67] In this regard, the attitude of the host government towards the refugee is essential in making the decision of repatriation.[68]

8.4 The spread of tripartite agreements and their actual utility until now

At the present time the concept of voluntary repatriation seems to denote more of an institutional policy than a group of norms accepted by states and other actors of the international community. The UNHCR has often assumed direct responsibility in encouraging both simple dialogue and negotiations between country of origin and country of asylum, often assisting repatriates with resettlement in their own country,[69] one of the first and most famous cases in Sub-Saharan Africa being the assisted return of South Sudanese in the mid-1970s.[70]

67 Karadawi, A., *Refugee Policy in Sudan: 1967–1984*, New York/Oxford: Berghahn Books, 1999, p. 203.

68 Stein, B.N. and Cuny, F.C., 'Voluntary repatriation during conflict: contemporary practice', in Stein, B.N., Cuny, F.C. and Reed, P. (eds), *Refugee Repatriation During Conflict: A New Conventional Wisdom*, Dallas: The Centre for the Study of Societies in Crisis, 1995, p. 5.

69 Over the years, the work of this kind made by the UNHCR in the African continent has been outstanding. It suffices to cite the coordination of the repatriation of some 200,000 Sudanese from Ethiopia in 1972/1973 as far as the 250,000 Zimbabweans repatriated in 1980/1981 or the 250,000 Chadian repatriated from Cameroon and Central African Republic in 1982, because of the temporary cessation of hostilities in N'Djamena. As A. Adepoju noted, Cameroon at that time was still trying to relieve of its caseload of refugees after a large number of refugees voluntarily repatriated themselves to Guinea Bissau. See Adepoju, A., 'The dimension of the refugee problem in Africa', in *African Affairs*, vol. 81, 1982, p. 27.

70 In this regard, see Mohamed Salih, M.A., 'Responding to situations of mass voluntary return', in Allen, T. (ed.), *In Search of Cool Ground: War, Flight and Homecoming in Northeast Africa*, London: James Currey; Trenton, NJ: Africa World Press, 1996, pp. 165–8. At p. 168, the author described the situation at the end of the repatriation as follows: 'In 1975 [. . .] the South (Sudan) was still very poor. Communications remained impossible in many places during the wet season [. . .] an acute shortage of skilled staff in the public sector combined with a lack of employment opportunities for uneducated people, and the informal economy benefited very few. Nevertheless, infrastructure was in better condition than it had ever been. Even more significantly, according to observers from the ILO, for nearly all food crops, the area under cultivation was higher in the 1973/4 season than before the start of hostilities. Independent commentators at the time agreed that things looked promising.' For a more recent repatriation of South Sudanese, see the news: 'Returnees build their own village back in South Sudan', 11 December 2012, available at: www.unhcr.org/50c722839.html, accessed 14 December 2014: 'After two decades in exile, 1,600 particularly vulnerable people returning to independent South Sudan no longer had a place they could call home. The solution has been to help them build their own village. [. . .] In a week-long operation, UNHCR and partner organizations relocated the group from the transit center to their new home, 35 kilometers north of Juba. Land for the village and agriculture was allocated by the government and a welcoming host community.'

In this regard, numerous agreements have been signed over the years between the African states and the UNHCR. These agreements generally concern the more significant voluntary repatriation operations and set out the respective roles and responsibilities of the countries concerned and the UNHCR, the rights of refugees and returnees, as well as certain operational modalities. These kinds of agreements – usually denominated 'tripartite' because they involve the presence of three actors: country of origin, country of refuge and the UNHCR – are very common on the continent, reinforcing the legal keystones of voluntary repatriation. It is through these agreements that many of the 'legal safety' issues[71] have been addressed,[72] although not exclusively.

The tripartite agreement, signed in late 1988 between Malawi, Mozambique and the UNHCR, contains in the preamble an observation pertaining to the 'adverse effects that the policy of destabilization in Southern Africa has on the countries of the region',[73] followed by a reference to the alleged aspiration of refugees to return, and the rather optimistic allegation that improvement of material conditions in Mozambique would be important for a return in safety.[74] This agreement constitutes a framework rather than a firm set of detailed rules on voluntary repatriation,[75] for the substance of the agreement revolved around the establishment of a tripartite commission and an outline of its functions:

71 For several examples on what is intended for 'legal safety' in Sub-Saharan Africa see, for instance, Article 4 6) of the tripartite agreement on the voluntary repatriation of Burundian refugees from Tanzania, concluded between the UNHCR, Burundi and Tanzania on 8 May 2001: 'The Government of the Republic of Burundi guarantees the reintegration of all returnees into the country's socio-economic life. It also guarantees to all returnees equal enjoyment with all Burundians, of all the socio-economic, civil and political rights of the nation as recognized in domestic and international law.' The same proviso has been included also in Article 4 6) of the tripartite agreement on voluntary repatriation of Rwandan refugees in Uganda, concluded between the UNHCR, Rwanda and Uganda on 23 July 2003. A comparable Article is also Article 4 6) of the tripartite agreement on voluntary repatriation of Rwandan refugees in Malawi, concluded between the UNHCR, Rwanda and Malawi on 4 November 2003.

72 UNHCR, Standing Committee, Legal safety issues in the context of voluntary repatriation, 7 June 2004, document No. EC/54/SC/CRP.12, paragraph 5, p. 2: 'Numerous agreements on voluntary repatriation have been signed over the years between States (as countries of asylum or countries of origin) and UNHCR. These agreements generally concern the more significant voluntary repatriation operations and set out the respective roles and responsibilities of the States concerned and UNHCR, the rights of refugees and returnees as well as certain operational modalities. Such agreements reinforce the legal underpinnings of voluntary repatriation, and it is through these agreements that many of the legal safety issues have been addressed, as arising in specific situations.'

73 In the original Portuguese version we may read: '[UNHCR, Mozambique and Malawi] Estandos cientes dos efeitos que a politica de desestabilizacao na Africa Austral tem sobre os paises da regiao'. See Acordo entre o Governo da Repûblica Popular de Moçambique e o Governo da Repûblica do Malawi e o Alto Comissariado das Naçôes Unidas para os Refugiados sobre o repatriamento dos refugiados Moçambicanos no Malawi, 21 December 1988, available at: www.unhcr.org/refworld/docid/3ee09fe24.html, accessed 15 October 2014.

74 Zieck, M., *UNHCR and Voluntary Repatriation of Refugees*, The Hague/Boston/London: Martinus Nijhoff, 1997, p. 347.

75 About the role of this tripartite agreement, it has been affirmed that: 'Furthermore, when the fighting ended, Malawi, Mozambique, and the UNHCR cooperated in voluntary repatriation

> The principal role of the Commission shall be to facilitate the attainment of a durable solution to the plight of the Mozambican refugees in Malawi through the voluntary repatriation to Mozambique.[76]

However, as we have seen above, the role played by the UNHCR during the repatriation process is essential. That is why Article 9 of the 1993 Tripartite Agreement for the repatriation of the Mozambicans from Zimbabwe highlights the importance for the agency to come in contact with both Mozambican refugees in Zimbabwe and the Mozambican returnees.[77]

In the 1996 Tripartite Agreement to promote the repatriation of Rwandans, the government of Tanzania limited itself to only facilitating the departure of the refugees and '[s]implifying the formalities for the exportation of their property and personal effects.'[78]

In 2002, Zambia signed a tripartite agreement with Angola for the repatriation of refugees from that country in which were once again confirmed the conditions of the voluntary character of repatriation that were required to be made in safety and dignity.[79] It needs to be noted that the government of Zambia, also because of the existence of a community of several ethnic groups shared with Angola,[80] has been historically benevolent towards Angolan refugees although they were

efforts that are considered to be a model in the field of refugee protection. *Thus it is possible for receiving countries to provide humanitarian access and manage potential security risks.*' Emphasis added. See Salehyan, I. and Gleditsch, K.S., 'Refugees and the spread of civil war', in *International Organization*, vol. 60, 2006, p. 361.

76 Article 3 1) of the Tripartite Agreement. This kind of situation occurred also because, quoting the UNHCR: '[T]he formal legal criteria for repatriation do not always coincide with the regime of obligations necessary to ensure the optimal conditions to realize a right to return to one's country, and to do so in conditions of both physical and material security. Put differently, these gaps point to the necessity to link refugee (solutions) law much more closely to the body of human rights law in particular and international law in general.' See UNHCR, 'Issues and challenges in international protection in Africa', in *International Journal of Refugee Law*, vol. 7, 1995, special issue, p. 68.

77 UNHCR, Tripartite Agreement Between the Government of the Republic of Mozambique, the Government of Zimbabwe and the United Nations High Commissioner for Refugees for the Voluntary Repatriation of Mozambican Refugees from Zimbabwe, 22 March 1993, Article 9, available at: www.refworld.org/docid/3ee884a74.html, accessed 13 November 2014.

78 UNHCR, Tripartite Agreement on the Voluntary Repatriation of Rwandese Refugees from Tanzania, 12 April 1995, Article 5, available at: www.refworld.org/docid/3ee712db4.html, accessed 13 November 2014.

79 UNHCR, Agreement on the establishment of a Tripartite Commission for the voluntary repatriation of Angolan refugees between the Government of the Republic of Angola, the Government of the Republic of Zambia and the United Nations High Commissioner for Refugees, 28 November 2002 Articles 6 and 7, available at: www.refworld.org/docid/447d6a4c4.html, accessed 13 November 2014.

80 In this regard, O. Bakewell noted: 'Particularly in rural Africa where borders cut across ethnic groups and the reach of the state may be limited, distinguishing people by such bureaucratic means as identity papers is likely to be impossible. The result will be a costly way of targeting aid to anyone, refugee or not, who chooses to jump through the bureaucratic hoops. Perhaps more importantly, where a local solution to the refugee problem has been found, reintroducing

often concentrated in camps where, while supplied with food and shelter, they remained at the same time under government observation and control.[81]

In order to assure security for the repatriating refugees, Article 4, section 4 of the 2005 Tripartite Agreement for the repatriation of Burundians in Rwanda, attributes to the Burundian government the responsibility 'of ensuring the safety and security of refugees', not only during the repatriation but also during the transport and in the transit areas.[82] To underline the role of the UNHCR, from one short article contained in the aforementioned 1993 Tripartite Agreement, we now come to an article (Article 5) that includes five sections. Thus, the role of the UNHCR in this case is multiple: 'to ascertain voluntariness' (section 1), 'to facilitate return and reintegration in safety and dignity' (section 2), 'to address special protection needs' (section 3), 'ongoing protection of refugees' (section 4), 'coordinating and funding the voluntary repatriation reintegration operation' (section 5).[83]

We also find a similar article in the 2006 Tripartite Agreement to repatriate Sudanese refugees from the Central African Republic (Article 9).[84] This agreement,

the concept of refugees as a special group in need of aid runs the danger of undermining the local solution.' See Bakewell, O., 'Refugee repatriation in Africa: towards a theoretical framework?', op. cit. note 8, p. 23.

81 Ibid., p. 16.

82 UNHCR, Tripartite Agreement on the Voluntary Repatriation of Burundian Refugees in Rwanda, 18 August 2005, available at: www.refworld.org/docid/44ae612dc6.html, accessed 13 November 2014.

83 In full, Article 5 reads as follows: '5) Responsibilities of UNHCR: Section 1) (To Ascertain Voluntariness) UNHCR shall verify the voluntary character of the decision to return through free access to refugees. Section 2) (To Facilitate Return and Reintegration in Safety and Dignity) UNHCR shall facilitate the voluntary repatriation of the refugees in conditions of safety and dignity and contribute to the implementation of reintegration measures. In this respect, UNHCR will provide its assistance, if necessary in cooperation with other United Nations agencies and non-governmental organizations. Section 3): (To Address Special Protection Needs) UNHCR shall ensure that the special protection needs of single women, unaccompanied minors and other vulnerable groups among the refugees are taken into full account. UNHCR will also be charged with ensuring, *vis-a-vis* the other Contracting Parties to this Agreement, that the refugees' fundamental rights, in particular the principle of family unity, are safeguarded. Section 4): (Ongoing Protection of Refugees) UNHCR shall, in accordance with its Mandate, continue to provide international protection to those Burundian refugees who do not opt to repatriate. UNHCR will cooperate closely with the Government of the Republic of Rwanda to ensure that those refugees who meet the relevant criteria of the 1951 Convention and the 1969 OAU Convention, continue to enjoy asylum in Rwanda. Section 5): (Coordinating and Funding the Voluntary Repatriation and Reintegration Operation) UNHCR will take the lead role with regard to all operational aspects. UNHCR will use its best efforts to mobilize the necessary resources for carrying out and funding the voluntary repatriation and reintegration operation.'

84 UNHCR, Tripartite Agreement between the Government of the Central African Republic and the Government of the Republic of the Sudan and the United Nations High Commissioner for Refugees for the Voluntary Repatriation of Sudanese Refugees in the Central African Republic Back to the Sudan, 1 February 2006, available at: www.refworld.org/docid/44044a274.html, accessed 13 November 2014.

different to the precedent, takes into consideration, in Article 5 3), the phenomenon of spontaneous repatriations with spontaneous returnees who will need to be provided support to the 'extent feasible'[85] and with a clause specifically dedicated to explaining how to fund repatriation.[86]

Spontaneous repatriations are also the object of Article 11 of the 2011 Tripartite Agreement for the return of Ivorian refugees from Liberia.[87] This agreement provided for the protection of the returnees also under the provision of the 2007 amnesty ordinance in force in the country.[88] In addition, this agreement introduces a provision explicitly targeting the needs of the 'vulnerable groups', broadly defined as 'groups with specific needs'[89] and another concerning the transfer of the detainees, including the refugees having committed 'non-serious political crimes' in Liberia who had the possibility of being transferred to the Ivory Coast, if they so wished.[90]

85 In full, Article 5 3) reads as follows: 'Nothing in this Agreement shall affect the right of any Sudanese refugee in the Central African Republic to return to his country of origin on his or her own at any time and/or outside the framework of this Agreement. Sudanese refugees who thus repatriate spontaneously, or to areas not deemed by the Contracting Parties to be conducive for secure and sustainable returns, shall nevertheless be provided support to the extent feasible, and UNHCR shall have the right to monitor their physical, legal and material safety as provided for in Clause 4 of this Article.'

86 Article 9 6) reads as follows: 'UNHCR shall mobilise the funds for implementing the voluntary repatriation provided for in this Agreement, both by itself and in co-ordination with the other stakeholders, including United Nations agencies, intergovernmental and non-governmental organisations. The Governments of Central African Republic and Sudan shall, respectively, work closely with and support UNHCR in its fund-raising efforts, including, particularly, in advocating with representatives of the international donor community and development partners.'

87 UNHCR, Tripartite Agreement Between the Government of the Republic of Liberia, the Republic of Côte d'Ivoire and the Office of the United Nations High Commissioner for Refugees for the Voluntary Repatriation of Refugees from Côte d'Ivoire Living in Liberia, 11 August 2011, available at: www.refworld.org/docid/4f21501f2.html, accessed 13 November 2014.

88 For the importance of amnesty laws in the decision to repatriate, see *infra*, paragraph 8 5), Article 8 2) of the agreement reads as follows: '2) Those repatriated will benefit from pertinent arrangements of the law No. 2003–309 of August 8, 2003 bearing amnesty, modified by ordinance 2007 457 of April 12, 2007 bearing amnesty currently in force in Côte d'Ivoire.' Article 1 of the 2007 Amnesty ordinance stipulates as follows: '1) Sont amnistiées de plein droit quels que soient leurs auteurs, coauteurs ou complices, militaires ou civils, et quelles que soient leurs natures et les peines qu'elles ont entraînées ou sont susceptibles d'entraîner, les infractions contre la sûreté de l'Etat et la Défense nationale ainsi que les infractions connexes commises par les nationaux ivoiriens se trouvant sur le territoire national ou en exil, entre le 17 septembre 2000 et la date de signature de la présente ordonnance.' This ordinance is available at: www.geneva-academy.ch/RULAC/pdf_state/Order-N-2007–457-of-12-April-2007-on-Amnesty.pdf, accessed 10 July 2014.

89 Article 15 of the Tripartite Agreement.

90 In full, Article 16 of the Tripartite Agreement stipulates as follows: 'The Governments accept according to the Extradition Treaty between the Republic of Liberia and the Republic of Côte d'Ivoire of August 24, 1972 and the Organization of African Unity (OAU) Convention of September 10, 1969 Governing the Specific Aspects of Refugee Problems in Africa, that the refugees from Côte d'Ivoire who committed non serious political crimes in Liberia and who have

The 'vulnerable groups' also have their place in the 2013 Tripartite Agreement for the repatriation of Somali from Kenya. In this regard, Article 18 addresses the fact that special measures will be adopted in order to guarantee the protection of 'children, women, the elderly and other vulnerable groups'.[91] However, to underline how sometimes these kinds of agreements express more (utopic?) wishful thinking than factual realities, Article 24 (on responsibilities of Somalia), paragraph vii) of the agreement provides for a commitment of the Somali government in promoting peace and reconciliation within the country. Such a condition seems still a long way from being reached given that, for instance, in 2014 Somalia still holds the negative record of being the worst-ranked country in the annual African governance index.[92] But the Global Initiative on Somali Refugees launched earlier in 2013 by the High Commissioner of the UNHCR, A. Gutierres, has tried to pave the way to a safe return of Somalis to their homeland. In particular, the meeting convened in August 2014 (held in Addis Ababa between the UNHCR and ministers from Djibouti, Ethiopia, Kenya, Somalia, Uganda and Yemen, as well as representatives of the UN Mission in Somalia, the AU, the Inter-Governmental Authority on Development and the UN Economic Commission for Africa). The meeting approved the proposal to consider an approach that highlighted the autonomy of refugees, and to preserve space for asylum on condition that circumstances in Somalia were not favourable for repatriation.[93]

The tripartite agreements design a category of 'special agreements' that Article 8 b) of the 1950 UNHCR Statute authorizes the agency to conclude[94] with a view to improving the situation of refugees and reducing the number of refugees in

been judged and sanctioned, be transferred to Côte d'Ivoire if they wish. The parties will cooperate to assure that the appropriate arrangements will be established to transport and transfer them.'

91 UNHCR, Tripartite Agreement Between the Government of the Republic of Kenya, the Government of the Federal Republic of Somalia and the United Nations High Commissioner for Refugees Governing the Voluntary Repatriation of Somali Refugees Living in Kenya, 2013, 10 November 2013, available at: www.refworld.org/docid/5285e0294.html, accessed 5 December 2014. In full, Article 18 reads as follows: '1) The Parties shall take special measures, to ensure that children, women, the elderly and other vulnerable groups receive adequate protection, assistance and care throughout the repatriation and reintegration process. 2) Parties shall take necessary measures to ensure that unaccompanied minors and or separated children are returned after a successful tracing of family members or others who by law or custom are responsible for the child. For those cases where tracing was not successful adequate reception and care arrangements shall be put in place by the Federal Government of Somalia.'

92 Reuters: 'Somalia: worst ranking in African rule of law index', 29 September 2014, available at: www.theafricareport.com/East-Horn-Africa/somalia-worst-ranking-in-african-rule-of-law-index.html, accessed 5 November 2014.

93 UNHCR, Addis Ababa Commitment towards Somali Refugees. Adopted at the Ministerial meeting of the UNHCR Global Initiative for Somali Refugees (GISR), 20 August 2014, Addis Ababa, paragraph ii), available at: www.unhcr.org/540dac2c6.html, accessed 6 December 2014.

94 Article 8 b) of the 1950 UNHCR Statute stipulates: 'The High Commissioner shall provide for the protection of refugees falling under the competence of his/her Office by: b) Promoting through special agreements with Governments the execution of any measures calculated to improve the situation of refugees and to reduce the number requiring protection.'

need of protection. The 'special agreements' are international agreements governed by international law and they are therefore legally binding.[95] In this regard, as M. Zieck has put it:

> Those [special] agreements [concerning repatriation] may be distinguished on the basis of their contents into agreements which comprise both the legal principles governing voluntary repatriation as such and the practical measures required to implement this solution and agreements which likewise comprise the governing legal principles but confine the requisite practical measures to the establishment of a functional commission.[96]

The role played by the UNHCR in the tripartite agreements should be one of supervising the return and, when possible, the first phase of reinstallation. In addition, R. Hofmann suggested that the UNHCR has the right to challenge the agreement before competent international bodies, such as the UNSG or the UNGA, if, after a careful analysis of the situation of the country of origin, conditions remain unfavourable for the reinstallation of the refugees.[97] In the repatriation process, the determination of when a refugee ceases to be one can probably assist in identifying where the jurisdiction of the UNHCR ends. The logic behind this view would be that as the agency is concerned essentially with refugees, it will not offer assistance programmes for those who have ceased to be refugees, handing their case over to other agencies and bodies in charge of the execution of development programmes in Sub-Saharan Africa. In this regard, former High Commissioner for Refugees, S. Ogata, clearly affirmed that the UNHCR was not a development agency.[98]

95 Zieck, M., 'Voluntary repatriation: paradigm, pitfalls, progress', op. cit. note 21, pp. 37–8. In this regard, the author more extensively argued that: 'In view of the two different purposes the special agreements may serve, the agreements may be distinguished accordingly as focusing on measures which either improve the situation of refugees or seek to reduce the number of refugees requiring protection, although they may occasionally serve both ends simultaneously.' See Zieck, M., *UNHCR's Worldwide Presence in the Field*, Nijmegen: Wolf Legal, 2006, p. 62.

96 Ibid., p. 68. In the first category of agreements the author mentioned, among others: the agreement between Malawi, Mozambique and UNHCR of 1988; the protocol between SWAPO, Angola and UNHCR of 1989; the protocol between SWAPO, Zambia and UNHCR of 1989; the tripartite agreement between DRC, Rwanda and UNHCR of 1994; the agreement between Eritrea, Sudan and UNHCR of 2000; the tripartite agreement between Namibia, Botswana and UNHCR of 2002. In the second category of agreements the author mentioned, among others: the tripartite agreement between Burundi, Tanzania and UNHCR of 1991; the agreement between DRC, Angola and UNHCR of 1992; the tripartite agreement between Mozambique, South Africa and UNHCR of 1993; the tripartite agreement between Burundi, Tanzania and UNHCR of 2001; the agreement between Angola, Namibia and UNHCR of 2002; the agreement between Angola, Zambia and UNHCR of 2002. See ibid., footnotes 27–28.

97 Hofmann, R., 'Voluntary repatriation and UNHCR', op. cit. note 23, p. 334.

98 Opondo, E.O., 'Refugee repatriation in the Horn of Africa', in Allen, T. (ed.), *In Search of Cool Ground: War, Flight and Homecoming in Northeast Africa*, London: James Currey; Trenton, NJ: Africa World Press, 1996, p. 29. S. Ogata served as the *United Nations High Commissioner for Refugees* from 1991 until 2001.

8.5 The importance of amnesty laws and how the choice of the refugee to repatriate has been influenced by amnesties

Several years ago J. Crisp listed a series of reasons why repatriation is preferred to other durable solutions in Sub-Saharan Africa. These reasons were as follows: because the efforts to promote earlier local settlement and self-reliance in rural settlements had achieved very limited results;[99] because refugees were gradually considered as an economic and environmental burden on host countries;[100] because the countries in Sub-Saharan Africa with huge refugee populations felt that the burden they had accepted was not being sufficiently shared by the world's wealthier countries; because many refugee-hosting countries in Sub-Saharan Africa had growing populations, decreasing economies, and were themselves affected by instability; and because refugees came to be considered – particularly after the Great Lakes crisis – as a menace to security at the local, national and regional level, mostly in the circumstances whereby they were mixed with armed and criminal people.[101] This view was held because the post-Cold War development towards democratization in several states in the area meant that politicians were interested in activating electoral support on the basis of xenophobic and anti-refugee sentiments.[102] Nevertheless, sometimes the refugees simply did not feel at ease in the host countries, because of the different customs and habits. This was, for instance, the case with Ethiopian refugees in Sudan, who were mostly coming from the heartland of the conservative Ethiopian Orthodox Christian tradition and had to live in a Muslim host environment. On this occasion, Ethiopian repatriation was understood through the so-called 'pull-push'

99 A similar situation occurred, for instance, in Zimbabwe. See Jackson, J., op. cit. note 29, p. 130.

100 In this regard, S.T. Makanya pointed out: 'The hospitality of the receiving populations has been stretched to the limit. The hosting of large numbers of refugees by poor areas has meant competition for the use of limited resources. This has resulted in more and more resentment by host populations who see no prospect of the refugees returning to their home country.' See Makanya, S.T., 'Voluntary repatriation in Africa in the 1990s: issues and challenges', op. cit. note 35, p. 174.

101 In this regard it has been affirmed that: 'Although it is possible that the presence of refugees in general raises the probability of conflict, we believe the most important factor in raising the risk of conflict is the presence of refugees from neighboring countries. Refugees from distant countries are less likely to have ethnic kin in the host country. They are also less likely to mobilize militarily, bring in arms, and concentrate in large numbers in particular areas. Accordingly, [. . .] Somali refugees could increase the risk of civil conflict in Ethiopia. To recapitulate a point made earlier, although we use the term "refugee" out of convenience, we realize that it is only a small subset of the refugee population who may engage in political violence – most refugees are civilians and retain their civilian status.' See Salehyan, I. and Gleditsch, K.S., op. cit. note 75, p. 350.

102 Crisp, J., 'No solution in sight: the problem of protracted refugee situations in Africa', in UNHCR, *New Issues in Refugee Research*, research paper No. 75, 2003, pp. 19–20. The above-mentioned list of reasons is present in ibid., pp. 3–4.

migration model, the main 'push' factor being the different religion while the 'pull' factors included political stability at home.[103]

On the other hand, the choice to remain in the country of asylum can be dictated by several factors: because 'residual caseloads'[104] of refugees have an enduring and genuine fear of persecution in their own place of origin; or because they originate from minority groups at risk of forms of discrimination. It could also be because the degree of devastation of the refugees' country of origin is so vast that the people concerned do not feel able to survive there;[105] or because the conditions forcing people to become refugees are so upsetting that they cannot return home, even though they would not be at risk if they did repatriate. In addition, refugees may not wish to return home because they do not have the necessary amount of money to make the journey back and to start their reintegration; or because they are too old, too young or too sick to undertake a repatriation and reintegration process that will inevitably be too arduous for them. Perhaps refugees have also close economic, ethnic, linguistic, and/or social bonds with the local population;[106] and/or refugees who remain in the asylum

103 Bariagaber, A., op. cit. note 39, pp. 125–6. In the same regard, O. Bakewell noted that: 'In addition to measures to push refugees out, the "pull" factor of aid packages to entice them home is another instrument available to influence their decision. The fact that so many refugees return without receiving any aid suggests that the effectiveness of such measures may be limited.' See Bakewell, O., 'Refugee repatriation in Africa: towards a theoretical framework?', op. cit. note 8, p. 9.

104 The expression 'residual caseloads' defines the refugees who do not join an organized voluntary repatriation and will be further subjected to status re-determination procedures upon completion of the voluntary repatriation movement. To quote the UNHCR: 'In other words, a refugee may continue to refuse to avail him or herself of the protection of his/her country of origin so long as the circumstances in connection with which he/she has become a refugee have not ceased to exist. This should be determined on a case by case basis through interviews with a view to ascertaining whether the individual not wishing to return is still in need of international protection. In particular where refugee status has been granted on the basis of *prima facie* (group) determination or under temporary protection arrangements, the *individual determination of status* following a mass voluntary repatriation should be explicitly negotiated with the government of the country of asylum. Persons determined in this procedure as still requiring international protection continue to be treated as refugees. Unless the country of asylum grants them permission to stay as a group, persons no longer in need of international protection should be treated according to the applicable aliens/immigration laws of the country of asylum, with due consideration given to granting residence permits or naturalization to compelling humanitarian cases.' Emphasis added. See UNHCR, Handbook on voluntary repatriation: international protection, Geneva: UNHCR, 1996, paragraph 3 8).

105 See, for instance, the case of Somalis in Bariagaber, A., op. cit. note 39, pp. 129–30. At p. 129 the author contended that: '[T]hey [the Somalis] now have a new kind of fear – that of going back to a ruined homeland and starting over again with very little.'

106 A. Adepoju gave an example of this kind of situation: 'Refugees living close to borders which to them arbitrarily divide ethnically homogeneous groups, as in the case with the Uganda/Tanzania border where people sometimes literally have to cross borders in order to visit their relations. This situation also has been observed in Somalia, where the colonialists' boundary arbitrarily divided the Somali nomads into both Somalia and Ethiopia.' See Adepoju, A., 'The dimension of the refugee problem in Africa', op. cit. note 69, p. 28.

states may enjoy an easier access to education facilities, health services and resettlement opportunities[107] than those who return at home, above all when refugees have become self-reliant in their countries of asylum. But sometimes they decide to abandon their improved economic circumstances and risk having to start all over again on return to their home areas, as happened to Angolans returning from DRC in the late 1970s or the Southern Sudanese who repatriated from DRC in the same period.[108] Finally, certain groups of refugees may choose to remain in exile and pursue their political objectives from the country of asylum[109] (refugees are often regarded as being hostile to the government in power in the home country and, consequently, may not be welcomed for fear of the opposition they may generate).[110] Another reason why refugees may not decide to return is that the longer they have been in exile, the greater is their degree of acculturation to their host society.[111]

As aforementioned, many refugees rapidly become fully integrated in the host-societies mainly when they find refuge among ethnically similar societies but not exclusively, as witnessed by Eritreans in Eastern Sudan in the 1970s and 1980s and by the Southern Sudanese in the early 1970s in Uganda, where refugees generally underwent considerable transformation in attitudes due to their high level of interaction with locals.[112] However, in the wave of refugees from Sudan generated in the last decade, the Ugandan government – and the Kenyan, as well – have made it clear that their eventual preference is the repatriation of refugees to their country of origin. This is clearly reflected in the host country arrangements emphasizing the containment and control of refugees in camps and settlements and declining to support the permanent, or even the temporary, integration of refugees in any noteworthy way.[113]

107 E.O. Opondo cited the case of Ethiopians in Somalia in 1983 with the Somali government favouring this integration. See Opondo, E.O., op. cit. note 98, p. 30.

108 But J.R. Rogge and J.O. Akol underlined that the knowledge that refugees risk losing accumulated wealth may well 'act as a strong deterrent to repatriation. This is especially the case when the asylum country is not particularly insistent about whether or not the refugees return.' See Rogge, J.R. and Akol J.O., 'Repatriation: its role in resolving African's refugee dilemma', in *International Migration Review*, vol. 23, 1989, pp. 194–5.

109 Crisp, J., 'No solution in sight: the problem of protracted refugee situations in Africa', op. cit. note 102, p. 21.

110 Rogge, J.R. and Akol J.O., op. cit. note 108, p. 196. At idem, the authors explained: 'This is especially the case where refugees have been associated with [. . .] past or present insurgencies.'

111 Crisp, J., 'No solution in sight: the problem of protracted refugee situations in Africa', op. cit. note 102, pp. 4–5.

112 Rogge, J.R. and Akol J.O., op. cit. note 108, p. 194. In this regard, T. Kaiser observed: 'Sudanese refugee communities in Uganda have had a positive impact on the local economies in areas where they have been permitted to make a contribution via agricultural activity or business.' See Kaiser, T., 'Sudanese refugees in Uganda and Kenya', op. cit. note 1350, p. 256. See also Hovil, L., 'Hoping for peace, afraid of war: the dilemmas of repatriation and belonging on the borders of Uganda and South Sudan', in *UNHCR, New Issues in Refugee Research*, research paper No. 196, 2010, pp. 6–7: '[F]or sure, many [among the Sudanese refugees] reached a strong degree of integration at a local level. [. . .] However, local belonging has always been vulnerable without Ugandan nationality to validate it.'

113 Kaiser, T., 'Sudanese refugees in Uganda and Kenya', op. cit. note 53, p. 254. In this regard, see also Hyndman, J., *Managing Displacement: Refugees and the Politics of Humanitarianism*, Minneapolis,

Legally, in Sub-Saharan Africa, the destiny of those who do not wish to return is often indicated as follows in the tripartite agreements:

> The status of those refugees who decide not to avail themselves of the voluntary repatriation program under this Agreement shall continue to be governed by the relevant international protection principles and standards.[114]

But, for instance, such a proviso totally lacks in the 2013 Tripartite Agreement for the return of Somali from Kenya.[115]

Once favourable changes towards repatriation have taken place, a programme of voluntary repatriation could be set up although its success relies upon several factors, including the clearly expressed wish by the country of origin that refugees return.

A typical example of one of these factors is represented by the concession of amnesty by the country of origin,[116] which should be accompanied by an express

MN: University of Minnesota Press, 2000, p. 23: 'Refugee camps constitute [a] strategy of containment with assistance. Though camps are arguably a useful and acceptable short-term emergency measure, the second-rate status accorded to refugees in these "temporary cities" is problematic.'

114 See, for instance, Article 6 of the Agreement on the establishment of a Tripartite Commission for the voluntary repatriation of Angolan refugees between the Government of the Republic of Angola, the Government of the Republic of Zambia and the United Nations High Commissioner for Refugees, 28 November 2002; Article 6 of the Agreement on the establishment of a Tripartite Commission for the voluntary repatriation of Angolan refugees between the Government of the Republic of Angola, the Government of the Republic of Namibia and the United Nations High Commissioner for Refugees, 28 November 2002. For a different approach, see Article 15 of the Tipartite Agreement on the voluntary repatriation of Congolese refugees concluded between the UNHCR, Tanzania and DRC on 21 August 1997: UNHCR shall '[i]n accordance with its Mandate, endeavor to ensure that those Congolese refugees who do not opt to repatriate can continue to enjoy asylum in the United Republic of Tanzania in accordance with the 1951 Convention on the Status of Refugees and the 1969 OAU Convention until such time the cessation clauses are applied.' See also Article 17 of the tripartite agreement on the voluntary repatriation of Rwandan refugees concluded between UNHCR, Zambia and Rwanda on 15 January 2003: 'The [UNHCR] ensures that those Rwandan refugees who do not opt to repatriate, continue to enjoy asylum in Zambia in accordance with recognized international conventions on refugees.'

115 UNHCR, Tripartite Agreement Between the Government of the Republic of Kenya, the Government of the Federal Republic of Somalia and the United Nations High Commissioner for Refugees Governing the Voluntary Repatriation of Somali Refugees Living in Kenya, 2013, 10 November 2013, available at: www.refworld.org/docid/5285e0294.html, accessed 10 August 2014.

116 In this regard, it is worth noting that the 1979 Arusha 'Conference on the Situation on Refugees in Africa' called upon all African governments to take into consideration official proclamations of amnesty to their nationals in exile in order to boost their voluntary repatriation. In this circumstance, the Conference invited the OAU: '[t]o make a declaration to the effect that granting of amnesty should be held sacrosanct and inviolate.' In this recommendation, the Conference also called upon all African Governments: 'To consider making official public declarations of amnesty to their respective nationals currently in exile, so as to encourage their voluntary repatriation. Guarantees for safe return and machinery to supervise such guarantees to be considered and worked out both by the countries of origin and the countries of asylum in

desire of the refugee him/herself to be amnestied.[117] In detail, amnesty laws and their enforcement are most important at an early stage of a voluntary repatriation process. They enforce immunity from prosecution to encourage refugees to return home voluntarily and without fear of prosecution or punitive measures against them. Most amnesties exempt returnees from discrimination or punishment for the mere fact of having left the country of origin, while dealing also with matters of desertion, or armed service. In this circumstance, the role of the UNHCR should be to promote the adoption of amnesty laws and to monitor their enforcement. Amnesties should not, however, be extended to returnees charged with serious violations of international humanitarian law or serious common crimes committed prior to or during exile against the country of origin and not correctly detected by the country of refuge. This would include genocide, war crimes or crimes against humanity.[118]

co-operation with the OAU, the refugee-serving agencies and the refugees concerned or their representatives.' See UNHCR, Report of the Conference on the situation of refugees in Africa, Arusha, Tanzania, 7–17 May 1979, document No. REF/AR/CONF/Rpt.1, HCR/140/12/79, document No. A/AC.96/INF.158.

117 See what occurred in Ethiopia in the early 1980s or other similar examples such as Uganda (1964) and Zaire (1967), this latter cited in Van Krieken, P.J., 'Repatriation of refugees under international law', op. cit. note 4, p. 113. Writing about amnesties in Zaire (1978–1979) and Guinea (1971), A. Adepoju pointed out: 'However, amnesties themselves are not sufficient; countries of origin should create conditions conducive to the reception of returnees and ensure their integration in the country.' See Adepoju, A., 'Refugees in Africa: problems and prospects', paper presented at the symposium 'Assistance to Refugees: Alternative Viewpoints', 27–31 March 1984, Oxford: 'Refugees in Africa: problems and prospects', p. 12. J. Jackson mentioned a series of national amnesties in Zimbabwe in the early 1980s. See Jackson, J., op. cit. note 29, p. 147.

118 UNHCR, Standing Committee, Legal safety issues in the context of voluntary repatriation, 7 June 2004, document No. EC/54/SC/CRP.12, paragraph 12, p. 4: 'Amnesty laws and their enforcement are most important at an early stage of a voluntary repatriation process. They elaborate immunity from prosecution to encourage refugees to repatriate voluntarily and without fear of prosecution or punitive measures taken against them. Most amnesties exempt returnees from discrimination or punishment for the sole fact of having left the country, while dealing also with issues of draft evasion, desertion, or armed service, including in non-recognized armed forces. UNHCR's role is to promote the adoption of amnesties and to monitor their enforcement. Amnesties should not, however, be extended to returnees charged with serious violations of international humanitarian law or a serious common crime, committed prior to or during exile. This would include genocide, war crimes or crimes against humanity.' In this regard, see also Meisenberg, S., 'Legality of amnesties in international humanitarian law: the Lomé amnesty decision of the Special Court for Sierra Leone', in *International Review of the Red Cross*, vol. 84, 2004, p. 842: 'In its last argument the Appeals Chamber [of the Special Court for Sierra Leone] discusses the limits of amnesties in international law. Here the judges mainly drew on the doctrine of universal jurisdiction to establish their opinion. They determined that the grant of amnesties falls under the authority of the State exercising its sovereign powers. However, where a jurisdiction is universal, such a State could not deprive another State of its jurisdiction to prosecute perpetrators by granting amnesties. The Appeals Chamber opined: 'A State cannot bring into oblivion and forgetfulness a crime, such as a crime against international law, which other States are entitled to keep alive and remember. [. . .] Amnesties granted by Sierra Leone, therefore, cannot cover crimes under international law, as they are subject to universal jurisdiction

Amnesty laws have become quite common in African countries that have been the scene of cruel civil wars in the last few decades. It is worthwhile to note that the 1979 Arusha Conference on the Situation of Refugees in Africa already called upon all African governments to take into consideration official proclamations of amnesty for their nationals in exile in order to boost their voluntary repatriation. The conference invited the OAU to make a declaration where it was clear the intent was to consider amnesties as an important tool in order to end the refugee plight in the continent. In this recommendation, the conference also called upon all African governments:

> [T]o consider making official public declarations of amnesty to their respective nationals currently in exile, so as to encourage their voluntary repatriation. [with] [G]uarantees for safe return and machinery to supervise such guarantees to be considered and worked out both by the countries of origin and the countries of asylum within the OAU, the refugee-serving agencies and the refugees concerned or their representatives.[119]

and by reason of the fact that "the obligation to protect human dignity is a peremptory norm and has assumed the nature of obligation *erga omnes*." The grant of an amnesty for international crimes therefore is not only in breach of international law, "[b]ut is in breach of an obligation of a State towards the international community as a whole." However, the Appeals Chamber finds, too, that there is no customary rule prohibiting national amnesty laws, but only a development towards an exclusion of such laws in international law.'

119 UNHCR, The recommendations from the Arusha Conference on the African Refugee Problem, Uppsala: Scandinavian Institute of African Studies, 1981, recommendation No. 9, paragraphs 7 and 8, p. 22. No country has made any reservation on these paragraphs of the recommendation. To give an idea of the situation created by the adoption of an amnesty law by a state with nationals asking for refugee status abroad, we mention the Tripartite Commission launched in the framework of repatriations of the Ethiopians from Djibouti in 1982/1983. The UNHCR pushed back all the critics that maintained that Ethiopian refugees were forced to sign a declaration in which they agreed to be repatriated. In a way, it seems effectively very hard that there were a high percentage of volunteers for repatriation among the strictly Ethiopian political exiles in Djibouti. On the other hand, it should be highlighted that after the cessation of hostilities in the refugees' home country and the promulgation of the amnesty proclamation by the Government in Addis Ababa, Djiboutian authorities had the right to consider refugees no longer as such because, as for Article 1C 5) of the 1951 Geneva Convention and for Article I4 e) of the 1969 OAU Convention, the circumstances in connection with which they had been recognized as refugees had ceased to exist. For this example, see Hofmann, R., 'Voluntary repatriation and UNHCR', op. cit. note 23, pp. 329–32. To urge countries to adopt amnesty laws: UNGA, Office of the United Nations High Commissioner for Refugees, Report of the Secretary-General, 22 August 1984, document No. A/39/402, paragraph 8: 'Essential conditions should be established to facilitate the voluntary repatriation of refugees, which has been recognized as the best means of promoting permanent and durable solutions. This could be done by the promulgation of amnesty laws [. . .].' In this regard, we like to quote P. Clark who, about the situation in Uganda and the good results derived from an amnesty there, explained that: 'The Uganda case [. . .] poses a major challenge for opponents of amnesty, who often argue that the use of amnesty hampers a long-term transition toward democracy. Uganda represents an example of a democratic amnesty with wide-spread popular consultations conducted by Ugandan government and civil society indicating nationwide support for amnesty. [. . .] Arguably, international opposition to democratic amnesty may undermine democracy in the long term.' See Clark, P.,

Several countries have used this kind of instrument and it is obvious that the more unstable the internal political situation, the more national governments use amnesty laws as a means of allowing refugees to return. For instance, in the last decades Angola has promulgated amnesty laws in 1991,[120] 1994,[121] 1996,[122] 2000[123] and 2002;[124] the DRC adopted an amnesty law in 2003,[125] 2005,[126] and 2009;[127] Ivory Coast in 2003[128] and 2007;[129] Senegal in 1991;[130] Togo in 1994[131] and each time to favour the social integration of the previously convicted persons for the crimes listed in the laws.[132] Amnesty was also the object of an article of the statute of the Special Court for Sierra Leone,[133] an article which, as aforementioned, excluded a possible amnesty for individuals guilty of crimes against humanity and of serious violations of the international humanitarian law.[134]

'Creeks of justice: debating post-atrocity accountability and amnesty in Rwanda and Uganda', in Lessa, F. and Payne, L.A. (eds), *Amnesty in the Age of Human Rights Accountability: Comparative and International Perspectives*, Cambridge/New York, Cambridge University Press, 2012, p. 235.

120 Angola, Law No. 24/1991, 12 July 1991, Amnesty Law.

121 Angola, Law No. 18/1994, 10 November 1994, Amnesty Law.

122 Angola, Law No. 11/1996, 9 May 1996, Amnesty Law. On a different note, in 1996 the Amnesty Committee in South Africa started working, whose work brought the committee to accept '[e]very strategy adopted by a political organization or institution during the conflict as political irrespective of a repulsiveness of that strategy in moral terms. It refused to pass any kind of judgment on the objective itself and to treat certain objectives as insufficiently weighty to justify the use of some means in their pursuit.' See Du Bois-Pedain, A., 'Accountability through conditional amnesty: the case of South Africa', in Lessa, F. and Payne, L.A. (eds), *Amnesty in the Age of Human Rights Accountability: Comparative and International Perspectives*, Cambridge, UK/New York, Cambridge University Press, 2012, p. 251.

123 Angola, Law No. 7/2000, 15 December 2000, Amnesty Law.

124 Angola, Law No. 4/2002, 4 April 2002, Amnesty Law.

125 DRC, Décret-loi No. 03–001 portant amnistie pour faits de guerre, infractions politiques et d'opinion, 15 April 2003.

126 DRC, Loi No. 05/023 portant amnistie pour faits de guerre, infractions politiques et d'opinion, 19 December 2005.

127 DRC, Loi No. 09 portant amnistie pour faits de guerres et insurrectionnels commis dans les provinces du Nord-Kivu et du Sud-Kivu, 6 May 2009.

128 Ivory Coast, Loi portant amnistie, No. 2003–309, 6 August 2003.

129 Ivory Coast, Ordonnance No. 2007 457 du 12 avril 2007 portant amnistie.

130 Sénégal, Loi No. 91–40 du 10 juillet 1991 portant amnistie, 10 July 1991.

131 Togo, Loi de l'Etat sur l'amnistie, 22 December 1994.

132 For example, see the list of crimes that could be amnestied by the government in Article 1 2) of the 2000 Angolan Amnesty Law.

133 The Special Court for Sierra Leone is an independent judicial body set up to 'try those who bear greatest responsibility' for the war crimes and crimes against humanity committed in Sierra Leone after 30 November 1996 during the Sierra Leone Civil War. The court was established by: UNSC, The situation in Sierra Leone, 14 August 2000, resolution No. 1315, S/RES/1315. For the legal basis of the court, see Kanu, A.I. and Tortora, G., 'The legal basis of the Special Court for Sierra Leone', in *Chinese Journal of International Law*, vol. 3, 2004, pp. 515–52.

134 Article X of the Statute of the Special Court for Sierra Leone: 'An amnesty granted to any person falling within the jurisdiction of the Special Court in respect of the crimes referred to in articles 2 to 4 of the present Statute shall not be a bar to prosecution.' Article 2 provides for a list of the crimes against humanity while Article 4 provides for a list of the other 'serious violations

As R. O'Brien has pointed out:

> [T]he state [. . .] is disadvantaged by an amnesty. [. . .] It may [. . .] help to create a culture of impunity where perpetrators can anticipate immunity, and thus jeopardize the governing power of the state in the future. [. . .] Despite their obvious disadvantages, amnesties allow parties to concede military or political power, without the fear that such power will then be used against them. Not only states but also the individuals within them may be advantaged by the use of amnesties in bringing an end to conflict [*which is precisely the use made of an amnesty in the case of refugees.*][135]

And continuing on the same lines:

> [A]mnesties have greater advantage when they are carefully designed, usually as a part of a package of measures. In this case, the whole package may be aimed not only to bring about an end to conflict, but also to build a shared future.[136]

It is always possible that amnesties will be violated, in which case returnees would then have to experience flight into exile once again. That is one of the reasons why, at least until 1980, the UNHCR encouraged a policy of settlement in the country of asylum rather than favouring voluntary repatriation. In 1980, there was an important shift in UNHCR policy and voluntary repatriation became a major priority on the continent, particularly in the Horn and in Southern Africa. This shift was a bit strange because it occurred at a time in which there was no significant change in the circumstances that had generated the flight of refugees, as was the case, for instance, in Zimbabwe.[137] To justify this shift, however, the UNHCR issued a new interpretation of the refugee phenomenon under which the previous attempts to provide assistance to asylum-seekers in the host countries did not result in durable solutions. In practice, the UNHCR shifted to voluntary repatriation in order to prevent the country of origin from resorting to *refoulement* and did so under conditions that simply justified its facilitating voluntary return. In this regard, M. Zieck has affirmed that although voluntary repatriation can be

of the international humanitarian law.' For a point of view of the amnesty provided by the court, see Schabas, W.A., 'Amnesty, the Sierra Leone Truth and Reconciliation Commission and the Special Court for Sierra Leone', in *University of California Davis Journal of International Law and Politics*, vol. 11, 2004–2005, pp. 145–70.

135 Note by the author. Emphasis added.

136 O'Brien, R., 'Amnesty and international law', in *Nordic Journal of International Law*, vol. 74, 2005, pp. 275–6.

137 Makanya, S.T., 'The desire to return', in Allen, T. and Morsink, H. (eds), *When Refugees Go Home*, London: James Currey, Trenton, NJ: Africa World Press, 1994, p. 120 where the author clarified: 'However, the determination to return home, the hope that there would be a peaceful future and especially the desire to take part in the elections made the refugees courageous enough to face the repressive machinery again.'

used as a means to prevent *refoulement*, if the return occurs voluntarily, this return can be in conflict with the legal consequences of voluntary repatriation, considered as a durable solution.[138]

At this point, the reader can wonder whether these kinds of activities by the UNHCR have a legal basis, considering that Article V of the 1969 OAU Convention, which deals with voluntary repatriation, does not expressly mention the UNHCR, to which the 1969 African Convention attributes a role of 'cooperation' with the member states of the AU in order to implement the convention.[139] The same role of cooperation, for instance, has been attributed to the 2001 MoU between the UNHCR and ECOWAS, where its Article II.2 provides for the possibility of cooperation between the two institutions also in the framework of organized and spontaneous voluntary repatriation.[140]

In the case of the massive repatriation of Ethiopians from Sudan in the mid-1980s, repatriation was carried out by the Tigrayan People's Liberation Front.[141]

138 Zieck, M., 'Voluntary repatriation: paradigm, pitfalls, progress', op. cit. note 21, p. 40.

139 In this regard, Article 8 1) of the 1969 OAU Convention reads as follows: 'Member States shall cooperate with the Office of the United Nations High Commissioner for Refugees.'

140 Memorandum of Understanding between ECOWAS and UNHCR, UNTS, vol. 2165, II-1242, 19 November 2001, Article II.2, p. 175: 'The parties shall co-operate in the following areas: [. . .] 2) Organized and spontaneous repatriation, as well as related rehabilitation and reintegration activities; local settlement and resettlement with ECOWAS countries.' In the framework of ECOWAS, see also UNHCR, Protecting Refugees and Other Persons on the Move in the ECOWAS Space, January 2011, 1st edn, p. 35, available at: www.refworld.org/docid/4e54961d2.html, accessed 10 September 2014: 'The major forced displacements of the 1990s and early 2000s in West Africa, mainly from Sierra Leone, Liberia and Ivory Coast, have given way more recently to increased stability throughout the region. This has allowed for major voluntary repatriation movements to take place. In 2007, a tripartite agreement was signed between the Governments of Mauritania and Senegal and UNHCR, resulting in the ongoing repatriation of Mauritanian refugees from Senegal. After the situation had fundamentally improved in Sierra Leone, the "changed circumstances" cessation clause was invoked for Sierra Leonean refugees in 2008 and UNHCR facilitated voluntary repatriation for those wishing to return. Encouraging signs of peace and stability in Liberia have also allowed UNHCR to support voluntary repatriation to Liberia, preparing the ground for a possible invocation of the cessation clause for this refugee population in the near future. The current situation in Côte d'Ivoire is the exception to these positive trends in national peace building and peace consolidation. While there had been progress in the implementation of the 2007 Ouagadougou Political Agreement, which paved the way for the return of Ivorian refugees, the crisis triggered by the 2010 presidential elections has resulted in a new outflow of refugees and an increase in internal displacement.'

141 Okoth-Obbo, G., 'Thirty years on: a legal review of the 1969 OAU Refugee Convention Governing the Specific Aspects of Refugee Problems in Africa', op. cit. note 62, p. 128. Repatriation carried on by non-recognized entities has been quite usual in the 1990s, not only in Tigray but also in Eritrea, Western Sahara and Namibia. In this regard it is interesting to note that the UN has been of two minds on principles related to this issue: '[I]t has insisted on respect for the sovereignty of its member states and non-interference in their internal matters. At the same time, the UN has passed resolutions calling for humanitarian access to and protection for displaced persons and brought attention to the threat to international peace and security of certain internal actions.' See Stein, B.N. and Cuny, F.C., op. cit. note 68, p. 21. In this regard,

In detail, this repatriation – the influx of Tigrayans in Sudan believed to have been an indirect consequence of war and, more directly, a result of the politicization of humanitarian aid to the war zones[142] – was considered an excellent example of a case that falls outside existing protocols on voluntary repatriation. In effect, there is no authority for the UNHCR to cooperate with non-recognized entities in situations where the government of the country of origin does not also give its consent.[143] In the case of Ethiopians in Sudan, the Ethiopian government required that each refugee who wished to return would obtain a *laissez-passer* for his/her departure. As a consequence, the Tigrayans effectively fell between the cracks of a donor-assisted repatriation programme. In this context, the only alternative for the UNHCR to give institutional support would have been to play a highly informal role at the local level: to coordinate assistance provided through other entities and engage in secret lobbying and information sharing. This is exactly what happened in 1986 and 1987, with positive results.[144]

8.6 An appraisal of the characteristics of voluntary repatriation and of the UNHCR's policy

As mentioned above, voluntary repatriation has received increased attention from the international community since the beginning of the 1980s, although the OAU had already previously invoked it several times.[145] Since then, and contrary to all

see also Opondo, E.O., op. cit. note 98, p. 31. Again, in this regard B. Hendrie also pointed out that: '[T]igrayan refugees returned across the border without formal assistance from UNHCR; further, given UNHCR's central position as the coordinating body for refugee assistance, its failure to engage in the operational aspects of the return meant that no other major donors, and only those NGOs already working in camps along the border, were mobilized to provide assistance.' See Hendrie, B., 'Assisting refugees in the context of warfare', in Allen, T. (ed.), *In Search of Cool Ground: War, Flight and Homecoming in Northeast Africa*, London: James Currey; Trenton, NJ: Africa World Press, 1996, p. 38.

142 In this regard, see Hendrie, B., 'Assisting refugees in the context of warfare', op. cit. note 141, pp. 36–7.

143 Chimni, B.S., 'The meaning of words and the role of the UNHCR in voluntary repatriation', op. cit. note 27, p. 451. In this regard, quoting B. Hendrie, at idem B.S. Chimni added: 'Although other entities, such as NGOs and ICRC, can in some cases fill the gaps left by UNHCR, the need remains for strong multilateral institutions that are capable of acting transnationally in the interests of refugees without regard to the political contingencies involved.'

144 Hendrie, B., 'The Tigrayan refugee repatriation: 1985–1987', in Stein, B.N., Cuny, F.C. and Reed, P. (eds), *Refugee Repatriation During Conflict: A New Conventional Wisdom*, Dallas: The Centre for the Study of Societies in Crisis, 1995, pp. 115–16. This author, in 'Assisting refugees in the context of warfare', op. cit. note 141, p. 43 ended up her analysis explaining: '[T]he issue remains as to whether or not specific protocols are required to address circumstances such as the Tigrayan case, that will enable UNHCR to become involved. UNHCR's involvement [. . .] remains important in every repatriation process. In the absence of formal guidelines, however, UNHCR becomes vulnerable to the influence of member governments or its own major donors.'

145 In pursuance of the ideal solution to the refugee flow in the African continent, the OAU had urged countries of origin of refugees to encourage refugees to return home. The following

the indications that refugee movements were caused directly or indirectly by political conflict, the UNHCR started affirming that most African refugees were individuals who did not fall within the 'classic' definition provided by the 1950 UNHCR Statute, as in Eastern Sudan in the late 1980s.[146] This interpretation indicated an inclination to deny that the international community had some responsibility towards African refugees, in spite of the fact that, since 1957, the UNHCR had continuously provided assistance without applying the 1951 definition of refugee to the dynamic African situation.

In denying the majority of African refugees their legal status and, in so doing, material assistance, the UNHCR declared that most refugee movements from the country of origin had been prompted by programmes of assistance in the countries of asylum offering people an enticement to leave their homes. In addition, the concentration of assistance in the country of refuge discouraged repatriation. Subsequently, any attempt to encourage voluntary repatriation would unavoidably require restraining the material assistance provided to refugees in the countries of asylum.[147]

Since the 1980s, the UNHCR has been called upon by the UNSG to carry out different functions in connection with large-scale repatriation operations that resulted in an expansion of the original terms of its mandate, particularly concerning the provisions of assistance to countries of origin to facilitate the re-integration of returning refugees.[148] In effect, the original task of the UNHCR was to favour repatriation but its responsibility ended at the border of the country of origin of the refugees because, once repatriated, a refugee ceased to be a refugee.[149]

measures were recommended to such governments: '[T]o bring to an end those situations which led the refugees to leave their country; to assure refugees that they will be favorably received in their country of origin and can resume a normal and useful life there without fear of persecution or punishment [. . .] to help refugees who [. . .] wish to return to their home and to facilitate their resettlement and resumption of normal and peaceful life in their country of origin; to grant a general amnesty to those refugees whose fear of persecution on political grounds needs to be allayed and to assure them that they will be welcomed and genuinely reintegrated in their own environment, with full restoration of their rights and privileges.' See OAU, Africa and its Refugees (Africa Refugee Day), Addis Ababa, 1975, p. 53; cited in Adepoju, A., 'The dimension of the refugee problem in Africa', op. cit. note 69, p. 33.

146 Example provided in Karadawi, A., *Refugee Policy in Sudan – 1967–1984*, op. cit. note 67, p. 205.

147 Ibid., pp. 204–5.

148 In this regard, in 1965 the High Commissioner for Refugees F. Schnyder affirmed: 'Il convient de souligner aussi que, pour compléter le rôle du HCR à cet égard, les programmes d'assistance autorisent celui-ci à favoriser dans certains cas le rapatriement librement consenti des réfugiés en finançant leur transport du pays d'asile au pays d'origine. En outre, il existe des accords conclus avec certains gouvernements, qui prévoient la participation du HCR aux efforts tendant à encourager le rapatriement librement consenti des réfugiés.' See Schnyder, F., 'Les aspects juridiques actuels du problème des réfugiés', in *Recueil des Cours de l'Académie de La Haye*, vol. 114, 1965 (I), p. 411.

149 Zieck, M., UNHCR and Voluntary Repatriation of Refugees, op. cit. note 74, p. 96.

The extension of UNHCR responsibilities is evident in the 1994 UNGA resolution:

> [The UNGA] reiterates that voluntary repatriation, when it is feasible, is the ideal solution to refugee problems, calls upon countries of origin, countries of asylum, the Office of the High Commissioner and the international community as a whole to do everything possible to enable refugees to exercise freely their right to return home in safety and dignity, ensuring that international protection continues to be extended until that time, and assisting, where needed, the return and reintegration of repatriating refugees, and further calls upon the High Commissioner, in cooperation with States concerned, to promote, facilitate and coordinate the voluntary repatriation of refugees, including the monitoring of their safety and well-being on return.[150]

To stress the importance of voluntary repatriation, the UNGA has also clarified that:

> [T]he Assembly would further call upon the High Commissioner and others to intensify their support to African Governments through capacity-building activities. It would also reaffirm the right of return and the principle of voluntary repatriation, *as well as the fact that voluntary repatriation should not necessarily be conditioned on accomplishing political solutions in the country of origin.*[151] [. . .]

Over the last few decades, however, and deviating from what were its original tasks, the UNHCR actively creates conditions encouraging the return of refugees: the UNHCR takes charge of a '[l]egitimate interest in the consequences of return and should have access to returnees'.[152] This practice is still taking place in a 'legal vacuum',[153] considering that resolutions adopted by the UNGA following the 1950 UNHCR Statute only formulate guidelines of these responsibilities without really going too much into detail on their content. The ExCom tried to elaborate basic standards relative to the legal issue of voluntary repatriation[154] by examining this topic in detail back in 1980, and in the ensuing years

150 UNGA's resolution, Office of the United Nations High Commissioner for Refugees, 23 December 1994, resolution No. A/RES/49/169, paragraph 9.

151 Emphasis added. UNGA's resolution, Assistance to refugees, returnees and displaced persons in Africa, 19 December 2006, resolution No. A/RES/61/139, paragraph 20. The same expression has been, for instance, used also in UNGA, Assistance to refugees, returnees and displaced persons in Africa, 18 December 2008, resolution No. A/RES/63/149, paragraph 22.

152 ExCom, Note on international protection, 1987, document No. A/AC/96/693.

153 Chetail, V., 'Voluntary repatriation in public international law: concepts and contents', in *Refugee Survey Quarterly*, vol. 23, 2004, 2004, p. 12.

154 As we mentioned *supra*, Chapter 1.4, the ExCom conclusions cannot be in any event considered as binding, belonging more to that category of provisions sometimes called 'soft law'. About the legal content of the 'conclusions' elaborated upon by the ExCom, see also Sztucki, J., 'The conclusions on the international protection of refugees adopted by the Executive Committee of the UNHCR programme', in *International Journal of Refugees Law*, vol. 1, 1989, pp. 285–318.

until around 2004, during which time it emphasized the voluntary nature of repatriation as an essential prerequisite for dealing with refugees' crises. Thus the ExCom:

> a) Recognized that voluntary repatriation constitutes generally, and in particular when a country accedes to independence, the most appropriate solution for refugee problems; b) Stressed that the essentially voluntary character of repatriation should always be respected;[155] c) Recognized the desirability of appropriate arrangements to establish the voluntary character of repatriation, both as regards the repatriation of individual refugees and in the case of large-scale repatriation movements, and for UNHCR, whenever necessary, to be associated with such arrangements; d) Considered that when refugees express the wish to repatriate, both the government of their country of origin and the government of their country of asylum should, within the framework of their national legislation and, whenever necessary, in co-operation with UNHCR take all requisite steps to assist them to do so; e) Recognized the importance of refugees being provided with the necessary information regarding conditions in their country of origin in order to facilitate their decision to repatriate; recognized further that visits by individual refugees or refugee representatives to their country of origin to inform themselves of the situation there – without such visits automatically involving loss of refugee status – could also be of assistance in this regard.[156]

The same conclusion identifies two complementary principles that are in a position to implement the repatriation operation. The ExCom:

> f) Called upon governments of countries of origin to provide formal guarantees for the safety of returning refugees and stressed the importance of such guarantees being fully respected and of returning refugees not being penalized for having left their country of origin for reasons giving rise to refugee situations; [. . .] i) Called upon the governments concerned to provide repatriating refugees with the necessary travel documents, visas, entry permits and transportation facilities and, if refugees have lost their nationality, to arrange for such nationality to be restored in accordance with national legislation.[157]

Surprisingly, a change of circumstances in the country of origin is not mentioned explicitly albeit it constitutes a type of signal that often suffices to draw refugees

155 For instance, an example of repatriations where the will of refugees has been respected is provided by the '[m]ajority of repatriations in the Horn of Africa. [. . .] The only possible exception to this may be the repatriation of some 30,000 Ethiopians from Djibouti in 1983–1984.' See Bariagaber, A., op. cit. note 39, p. 123.

156 ExCom conclusion No. 18 (XXXI), 'Voluntary repatriation', 1980.

157 Idem.

back; this is particularly so when the new government is known to be sympathetic to the refugees although it is not always the case, as in Zaire during the Mobutu era.[158] Every effort made by the UNHCR to try to cause such changes would contravene its mandate. It should be up to the international community, on behalf of the UN, to attempt to achieve such a change.

Large-scale repatriation has occurred in the Sub-Saharan African region, where the intervention of the UNHCR and other aid organizations was only important as a *complement*[159] to the political changes which were taking place in the country of origin.[160]

The above-mentioned section of the ExCom's Conclusion No. 18 employs an indirect reference to the 'formal guarantees for the safety[161] of returning refugees' (point f), as a condition of the repatriation programme itself, rather than as a precondition for repatriation. The subjective element of voluntary repatriation overshadowed the objective element of the situation in the country of origin. These two elements are, however, complementary in identifying the legal precondition of voluntary repatriation.

The status of refugee requires that, in the absence of circumstances or events that would deserve the cessation of that status, it is exclusively the refugee who can choose and show that he/she is no longer reluctant to benefit from the protection of his/her country of origin. He/she may do so, *inter alia*, by willingly returning to his/her country of origin. In the context of voluntary repatriation,

158 Rogge, J.R., 'Repatriation of refugees: a not-so-simple "optimum" solution', op. cit. note 10, pp. 26–7. At p. 24 the author clarified: '[F]or example, Mobutu's many periodic amnesties to refugees have failed to bring many Zairians out of exile. In most such cases, refugees tend to adopt a "wait and see" attitude; a few courageous or desperate souls may return and the rest of the refugees wait to see how they fare. Again, this is where it is critical that an accurate flow of information to the remaining refugees is facilitated.' Several years before, J.R. Rogge along with J.O. Akol underlined that: 'Such reluctance to return for fear of personal security is common to many repatriation exercises, and there is clearly a need for the establishment of an effective and independent mechanism that can provide convincing assurances to refugees that a return to their home area is a truly safe option.' See Rogge, J.R. and Akol J.O., op. cit. note 108, p. 197.

159 Emphasis added.

160 In this regard, A. Karadawi mentioned the return of southern Sudanese refugees in 1972–1973; always in Sudan, the return of Ansars fighters in 1977 and 1980 (due to the reconciliation between the Khartoum central government and the Sudanese National Front). In addition, the return in Chad of the supporters of H. Habré (when he returned to power in 1982–1983) and the return in Uganda of the opponents of S. Amin, once he was overthrown in 1979. See Karadawi, A., *Refugee Policy in Sudan – 1967–1984*, op. cit. note 67, p. 203.

161 However, in this regard G. Goodwin-Gill and J. McAdam correctly observed: 'Who decides [that the return is safe]? International law provides no clear answers to situations involving large movements of people in flight from complex situations of risk. If the conditions that caused flight have fundamentally changed, the "refugee" is no longer a "refugee" and [. . .] can be required to return home like any other foreign national. That a "refugee" may voluntarily repatriate seems to imply a decision to return while the conditions for a well-founded fear of persecution continue to exist.' See Goodwin-Gill, G. and McAdam J., op. cit. note 30, p. 497.

refugee movement depends to a large degree on how this possibility is presented to refugees by the UNHCR.

In practice, the particular information presented to the refugees seems to vary according to the circumstances that bring the UNHCR to become involved in any particular repatriation. For example, the repatriation of South African dissidents in the early 1990s occurred in circumstances in the country of origin such that a return appeared feasible without involving risks for the repatriated. The Government Gazette Notice, published on 7 November 1990, dealt quite exhaustively with the return home of the South African refugees.[162] Hence, the UNHCR seemed to warrant promotion rather than facilitation of voluntary repatriation, as exemplified also by the case of the Mozambicans repatriated from Malawi in 1993–1995, where emphasis shifted from voluntary repatriation to 'return'. In this latter case, refugees were merely told it was time to return home. Although legitimate refusal to return was necessarily presupposed, it was never specifically mentioned as the corollary of refugee status, implied by voluntary repatriation, and to be observed by the UNHCR and the country of refuge by virtue of the prohibition of the rejection.[163]

Sometimes the role of the UNHCR was not as clear as, for instance, during negotiations with national authorities over the implementation of repatriations. There are doubts as to whether the agency has always remained fully aware of the perceptions and will of the refugees. Furthermore, there was widespread criticism levelled at the agency's role in the repatriation of Ethiopians from Djibouti.[164] In effect, the media reported that as many as one half of all repatriates from Djibouti subsequently sought refuge in other countries, confirming assertions that this repatriation was far from being fully voluntary.[165] In this specific circumstance, in 1982 and 1983, the UNHCR denied criticism, maintaining that Ethiopian refugees were not forced to sign a declaration in which they agreed to be repatriated. In a way, it seems effectively very hard to believe that there was a high percentage of volunteers for repatriation among the strictly Ethiopian political exiles in Djibouti. On the other hand, it should be highlighted that after the cessation of hostilities in the refugees' home country and the promulgation of the amnesty proclamation by the Government in Addis Ababa, Djiboutian authorities had the right to consider refugees no longer as such. This was so because, as for Article 1C 5) of the 1951 Geneva Convention and for Article I4 e) of the 1969

162 For an analysis of this document, see Kingsley-Nyinah, M.R., 'Need for an international presence: the return of refugees and immunity from prosecution for political offences in South Africa', in *International Journal of Refugee Law*, vol. 3, 1991, pp. 301–19.

163 Zieck, M., *UNHCR and Voluntary Repatriation of Refugees*, op. cit. note 74, pp. 435–8. In footnote 34, p. 437 of her work the author explained that: '[I]n the case of Mozambique [return] was pressed home by means of "consolidating" the distribution of food in the country of asylum [Malawi].'

164 Rogge, J.R., 'Repatriation of refugees: a not-so-simple "optimum" solution', op. cit. note 10, p. 22.

165 Rogge, J.R. and Akol J.O., op. cit. note 108, p. 196.

OAU Convention, the circumstances through which they had been recognized as refugees had ceased to exist.[166] And this poses the still unresolved dilemma in which, in the usual African practice, the country of refuge alone basically decides when the change of circumstances in the country of origin is sufficient to allow the repatriation of refugees hosted on its territory. In addition, it is common practice in Sub-Saharan Africa for not only the state of refuge to decide when a refugee can repatriate safely, but also whether it is necessary for him/her to return exactly to the place he/she was compelled to leave.[167]

Voluntariness of refugees to return home is justified given that the refugee is the best judge of whether to go back, because it allows for the particular experiences of the individual (such as severe persecution) to receive due weight, and also because there is value in individual choice. The voluntary character of repatriation is the necessary correlative to the subjective fear which compels the refugee to flee: willingness to return defeats that fear, nonetheless it necessitates an attentive verification.[168] A person's agreement to repatriate voluntarily would indicate that he/she no longer believes protection is required, and is thus no longer a refugee. If a refugee wishes to be repatriated, while there are no 'objective' indications that the circumstances in his/her country of origin have changed, and the wish to be repatriated appears to depend solely on the refugee's change of opinion, it is still compulsory to ensure that the repatriation is undeniably voluntary.[169] However, a person's refusal to repatriate voluntarily would not indicate that he/she is a genuine refugee, since the refusal could be motivated by reasons that are not related to international protection. In this kind of situation, the state would have to verify the individual's status before repatriating.[170]

Any different interpretation of the notion of voluntary repatriation would suggest that the 1950 UNHCR Statute permits the encouragement of refugees to return to unsafe territories, whereas this clearly does not represent the drafters' intentions. And this can also entail repatriated refugees who sometimes express their desire to return to the country of asylum, even if they are confined in camps. This happened to the Liberians who, at the end of 2008, given the incapacity to integrate back into their country of origin, openly expressed their wish to return to Buduburam camp, in Ghana, where they settled for years before trying to return

166 Hofmann, R., 'Voluntary repatriation and UNHCR', op. cit. note 23, pp. 329–32. In regard to this repatriation, E.O. Opondo simply affirmed: 'The repatriation of Ethiopian refugees in Djibouti in the 1980s is a further vivid illustration of how what starts off as persuading refugees to go back home can easily become forced repatriation. In response to pressure exerted on limited resources of Djibouti, the refugees were coerced to volunteer to repatriate using threats of imprisonment, cutting off of assistance and being bundled into a "human shield" refugee camp.' See Opondo, E.O., op. cit. note 98, p. 26.

167 Chimni, B.S., 'From resettlement to involuntary repatriation: towards a critical history of durable solutions to refugee problems', in *Refugee Survey Quarterly*, vol. 23, 2004, pp. 62–3.

168 Goodwin-Gill, G.; McAdam J., op. cit. note 30, p. 496.

169 Van Krieken, P.J., 'Repatriation of refugees under international law', op. cit. note 4, p. 103.

170 Barutciski, M., 'Involuntary repatriation when refugee protection is no longer necessary: moving forward after the 48th session of the Executive Committee', op. cit. note 47, p. 249.

to Liberia.[171] And those who decided to remain in Liberia mainly stayed in the capital, Monrovia, causing its clog.[172]

However, a question remains: how meaningful is the 'voluntariness' element when, for instance, Rwanda, Uganda or Djibouti withhold food, water and other essential goods from refugees in order to induce them to repatriate 'voluntarily'?[173] These kinds of actions have sometimes even been considered 'disgusting'.[174] In addition, we wonder how clear the connection is between the principle of voluntariness and cessation clauses regarding repatriation, a connection whose definition remains in a 'grey-zone'.[175]

In 1985, the ExCom repeated the voluntary character of repatriation as the central principle:

> a) The basic rights of persons to return voluntarily to the country of origin is reaffirmed and it is urged that international co-operation be aimed at achieving this solution and should be further developed; b) The repatriation of refugees should only take place at their freely expressed wish; the voluntary and individual character of repatriation of refugees and the need for it to be carried out under conditions of absolute safety, preferably to the place of residence of the refugee in his/her country of origin, should always be respected.[176]

Differing from the previous conclusion, the ExCom now explicitly mentions the situation of the country of origin that caused the refugee to want to escape. However, the key aspect of voluntary repatriation, in connection with the prevention of refugee flow and the responsibilities of countries towards their nationals, is formulated in vague terms. This conclusion affirms:

> c) The aspect of causes is critical to the issue of solution and international efforts should also be directed to the removal of the causes of refugee movements. Further attention should be given to the causes and prevention of such movements, including the co-ordination of efforts currently being pursued by the international community and in particular within the UN.

171 Omata, N., 'Repatriation is not for everyone: the life and livelihoods of former refugees in Liberia', in *UNHCR, New Issues in Refugee Research*, research paper No. 150, 2007, p. 20. At ibid., p. 21, the author, interviewing several Liberians returning to the camp in Ghana, received the following answer to the specific question why they decided to return to the camp: 'In the camp, at least I can find some helpers. They can give me small jobs and also some food. [. . .] I do not want to go back there [in Liberia]. I like to stay in the camp. I do not like this camp life but at least it is better than Liberia.'

172 Omata, N., 'Repatriation and integration of Liberian refugees from Ghana: the importance of personal networks in the country of origin', in *Journal of Refugee Studies*, vol. 26, 2012, p. 269.

173 The examples of Rwanda and Uganda are taken in Hathaway, J.C., *The Rights of Refugees Under International Law*, Cambridge: Cambridge University Press, 2005, p. 318. The example of Djibouti is taken in Crisp, J., 'Ugandan refugees in Sudan and Zaire: the problem of repatriation', in *African Affairs*, vol. 86, 1986, p. 179. At idem, the author clearly contended that: 'For refugees suffering in this way, anything was better than the prospect of indefinite exile.'

174 Feitsma, J., op. cit. note 4, p. 301.

175 Takahashi, S., op. cit. note 43, p. 601.

176 ExCom, conclusion No. 40 (XXXVI), 'Voluntary repatriation', 1985.

> An essential condition for the prevention of refugee flows is sufficient political will by the States directly concerned to address the causes, which are at the origin of refugee movements; d) The responsibilities of States towards their nationals and the obligations of other States to promote voluntary repatriation must be upheld by the international community. International action in favor of voluntary repatriation, whether at the universal or regional level, should receive the full support and co-operation of all States directly concerned. Promotion of voluntary repatriation as a solution to refugee problems similarly requires the political will of States directly concerned to create conditions conducive to this solution. This is the primary responsibility of States.[177]

The ExCom attempted to clarify the guidelines to repatriate in the 1996 Handbook. This document provides a theoretical framework by defining the crucial components of voluntary repatriation and stressing the interaction between its voluntary nature and the change of circumstances in the country of origin.

At first, the 1996 Handbook confirms how the principle of voluntariness:

> [v]iewed in relation to both: conditions in the country of origin (calling for an informed decision); and the situation in the country of asylum (permitting a free choice) [. . .] is the cornerstone of international protection with respect to the return of refugees.[178]

The 1996 UN High Commissioner for Refugees (UNHCR) Handbook continues to define the concept of voluntariness in terms that can be deemed as broad and negative:

> Voluntariness means not only the absence of measures which push the refugee to repatriate, but also means that he/she should not be prevented from returning, for example by dissemination of wrong information or false promises of continued assistance. In certain situations economic interests in the country of asylum may lead to interest groups trying to prevent refugees from repatriating.[179]

177 Idem. In this regard, see also Koehn, P.H., 'Refugee settlement and repatriation in Africa: development prospects and constraints', in Adelman, H. and Sorenson, J. (eds), *African Refugees: Development Aid and Repatriation*, North York: York Lane Press, 1994. At p. 109 the author pointed out: 'Although the international community has an important role to play in focusing attention on the underlying factors that promote refugee formation and in overseeing secure repatriation, "what governments do of their own accord or with their eye on the other governments will have the greatest effect in encouraging or obviating forced migration." In the end, "if states want their people to return, they must create conditions which are conducive."'

178 In the case of the repatriation of Mozambicans in the early 1990s, UNHCR confirmed that: 'The principle of voluntary repatriation *will be strictly observed*. [. . .] The voluntary character of repatriation *must be respected* by the country of asylum and the country of origin.' Emphasis added. Quoted in Zieck, M., *UNHCR and Voluntary Repatriation of Refugees*, op. cit. note 74, p. 376.

179 UNHCR, Handbook on voluntary repatriation: international protection, Geneva: UNHCR, 1996, paragraph 2 3). It is worth noting that paragraph 4 1) provides for three examples where

The free and well-informed choice, which forms the basis of voluntary repatriation, signifies that the refugee is informed about the possibility and the timing of repatriation. Likewise, it requires that the refugee is made aware of the fact that he/she can also choose not to opt for repatriation yet still remain entitled to his/her refugee status and sojourn in the country of asylum until this status ceases on account of the application of the cessation clauses relating to change of circumstances in the country of origin.[180] While the UNHCR has given several examples of what the change of circumstances in the country of origin should consist of,[181] its position has been not to wait for a fundamental change before actively promoting the voluntary repatriation of refugees, but only for 'general improvement'.[182] This was the case in the Ivory Coast in late 2011, where the repatriation of more than 500 refugees from Liberia was permitted.[183] Nonetheless, the UNHCR also admitted that in the last decades a good proportion of repatriations, including the ones in Sub-Saharan Africa, have occurred under 'some form of duress'.[184]

As a consequence, some refugees choose not to go home even when conditions in their country of origin superficially appear to have stabilized. For example, at the end of the 1990s, a sizeable number of Liberian refugees preferred to remain in a country of asylum such as Ghana and Guinea rather than to return home, where the situation could seem to have stabilized. But it had not and that is why the hypothesis to undertake a 'semi-organized' repatriation was taken into

the essential precondition of voluntariness is not considered as satisfied. These are: '1) host country authorities deprive refugees of any real freedom of choice through outright coercion or measures such as, for example, reducing essential services, relocating refugees to hostile areas, encouraging anti-refugee sentiment on the part of the local population; 2) factions among the refugee population or exiled political organizations influence the refugees' choice either directly by physically pressuring them to return, or indirectly by activities such as disinformation campaigns about the risk of remaining in the country of asylum or dangers related to returning home; 3) certain interest groups in the host country actively discourage voluntary repatriation by disseminating false information including incorrect promises of assistance, economic opportunities or improvement of the legal status.'

180 Zieck, M., 'Voluntary repatriation: paradigm, pitfalls, progress', op. cit. note 21, p. 42. In this regard, M. Barutciski observed: 'The promotion of involuntary repatriation if and when refugee protection ceases to be necessary is a pragmatic approach that represents an acceptable compromise between legitimate state concerns and the protection needs of refugees.' See Barutciski, M., 'Involuntary repatriation when refugee protection is no longer necessary: moving forward after the 48th session of the Executive Committee', op. cit. note 47, p. 254.

181 Takahashi, S., op. cit. note 43, p. 602. At idem, the author contended that: 'It seems to be taken for granted that the promotion of return must begin as soon as possible. Postponing repatriation pending a fundamental change in the home country appears to be incompatible with the objective of repatriation.'

182 UNHCR, Handbook on voluntary repatriation: international protection, Geneva: UNHCR, 1996, paragraph 3 1).

183 See the news: 'UNHCR steps up repatriation from Liberia to Côte d'Ivoire', 9 December 2011, available at: www.unhcr.org/4ee232296.html, accessed 10 October 2014.

184 UNHCR, The State of the World's Refugees 1997: a Humanitarian Agenda, Oxford: Oxford University Press, 1997, p. 147.

consideration, and while ensuring some material assistance, the protection of the returnees could not be guaranteed. In this specific circumstance, O. Abdi and C. Tinstman theorized that repatriation could be achieved in areas where political conflict was not yet resolved but where there was no military confrontation.[185] In a similar situation, it comes as no surprise to the author of this work that only a few Liberians accepted repatriation at that time.[186] However, S.T. Makanya clearly maintained that although refugees cannot obtain sufficient information to aid in their decision to repatriate, this was very rarely the main reason why the UNHCR halted repatriations in Sub-Saharan Africa.[187]

In substance, the two basic components of voluntary repatriation are reaffirmed throughout the 1996 Handbook. The improvement of conditions in the country of origin is considered, on the same level as voluntariness, as one 'essential precondition'[188] before the UNHCR will promote voluntary repatriation. The case of repatriation of Mozambicans from Malawi in the mid-1990s illustrates the tendency to limit the duration of voluntariness. When a voluntary repatriation movement reaches its conclusion, those who are still in the host country cannot rely on a protracted stay until the time when the application of the cessation clauses ends their status as refugees.[189] The 1996 Handbook clarifies in paragraph 3 1):

185 Abdi, O. and Tinstman, C., 'Voluntary repatriation to Liberia', in Stein, B.N., Cuny, F.C. and Reed, P. (eds), *Refugee Repatriation During Conflict: A New Conventional Wisdom*, Dallas: The Centre for the Study of Societies in Crisis, 1995, pp. 224–6.

186 In this regard, however, J.H.S. Milner pointed out: 'The end of conflict in [. . .] Liberia [. . .] had significant implications on the refugee populations in Guinea. Most specifically, it led to the repatriation of more than 130,000 refugees to [. . .] Liberia between 2003 and 2006.' See Milner, J.H.S., *Refugees, the State and the Politics of Asylum in Africa*, Basingstoke: Palgrave/Macmillan, 2009, p. 153. However, as J. Byrne noted: 'Local integration is one of the remaining durable solutions available to Liberian refugees in Ghana. While there is some promise for local integration to be an effective strategy in bringing this protracted refugee situation to an end, the data in this study suggests that conceptions of national identity influence support or opposition to this program. While living conditions in Ghana remain difficult for the refugees and their families, the composition of Liberian identity appears to play a prominent role in fostering opposition to local integration.' See Byrne, J., 'Should I stay or should I go? National identity and attitudes towards local integration among Liberian refugees in Ghana', in *Refugee Survey Quarterly*, vol. 32, 2013, p. 71.

187 Makanya, S.T., 'Voluntary repatriation in Africa in the 1990s: issues and challenges', op. cit. note 35, p. 175.

188 UNHCR, Handbook on voluntary repatriation: international protection, Geneva: UNHCR, 1996, paragraph 3 1): 'These are some of the essential preconditions to be met for UNHCR to promote voluntary repatriation movements: 1) There must be an overall, general improvement in the situation in the country of origin so that return in safety and with dignity becomes possible for the large majority of refugees. 2) All parties must be committed to fully respect its voluntary character. 3) The country of origin must have provided a formal guarantee, or adequate assurances for the safety of repatriating refugees, as appropriate. 4) UNHCR must have free and unhindered access to refugees and returnees. The basic terms and conditions of return must be incorporated in a formal repatriation agreement between UNHCR and the authorities concerned.'

189 Zieck, M., *UNHCR and Voluntary Repatriation of Refugees*, op. cit. note 74, p. 441.

> Promotion of repatriation can take place when a careful assessment of the situation shows that the conditions of 'safety and dignity' can be met: in other words, when it appears that objectively, it is safe for most refugees to return and that such returns have good prospects of being durable.

It also explains the difference between 'promotion' and 'facilitation' of repatriation, describing how in the latter case, respect for the refugees will require the passive involvement of the UNHCR if there is no change of circumstances in the country of origin.[190]

The 1996 Handbook also attempts to explain the expression, 'return in safety and *with*[191] dignity', which is considered an essential precondition for the issue in question although it is an extremely tricky expression with impossibly tangled legal, moral and psychological interpretations.[192] The phrase 'return in safety' seems easy to define – albeit some doctrine interpreted it differently[193] – and the 1996 Handbook provides specific examples of changes in the country of origin after which return is possible. State proponents of 'safe return' efficiently substitute 'objective' changes of circumstances for the refugee's subjective assessment, in that way crossing the refugee/non-refugee line.[194] For instance, in the case of the repatriation of Mozambicans from Malawi, returnees would, to the extent

190 UNHCR, Handbook on voluntary repatriation: international protection, Geneva: UNHCR, 1996, paragraph 3 1): 'Respecting the refugees' right to return to their country at any time, UNHCR may facilitate voluntary repatriation when refugees indicate a strong desire to return voluntarily and/or have begun to do so on their own initiative, even where UNHCR does not consider that, objectively, it is safe for most refugees to return. This term should be used only when UNHCR is satisfied that refugees' wish to return is indeed voluntary and not driven by coercion. [. . .] While the condition of fundamental change of circumstances in the country of origin will usually not be met in such situations, UNHCR may consider facilitating return in order to have a positive impact on the safety of refugees/returnees as well as to render assistance, which the refugees may require in order to return. Such assistance may have to be given in the absence of formal guarantees or assurances by the country of origin for the safety of repatriating refugees, and without any agreement or understanding having been concluded as to the basic terms and conditions of return. In designing and carrying out its protection and assistance functions, UNHCR, however, has to make it clear to the authorities and, most importantly, to the refugees, that UNHCR support for such repatriations is based on respect for the refugees' decision to repatriate and cannot be interpreted as an indication of adequate security.'

191 Emphasis added.

192 Bradley, M., 'Return in dignity: a neglected protection challenge', *Oxford: Refugee Studies Centre*, working paper No. 40, 2007, p. 2. At p. 3 the author noted that: '[F]rom 1978 to 2007 in 92 per cent of the total High Commissioners' speeches mentioned the return of refugees only the 25 per cent of speeches mentioned the return of refugees in condition of "safety and dignity".'

193 In this regard, for instance, M. Barutciski asserted: '[T]he standard of return to safety is not unproblematic especially in relation to the determination of what conditions are considered "safe". A norm appears to be evolving whereby return is possible to a place that is "relatively safe", the expression used by the UN High Commissioner for Refugees at the 48th session [he talked about the Rwandan context].' See Barutciski, M., 'Involuntary repatriation when refugee protection is no longer necessary: moving forward after the 48th session of the Executive Committee', op. cit. note 47, p. 251.

194 Goodwin-Gill, G. and McAdam J., op. cit. note 30, p. 497.

applicable, benefit from any amnesty, clemency or indemnity laws in force in the country of return, in addition to not being subject to any form of legal process, discrimination and persecution for any reason of any kind or for the sole fact that they have been refugees.[195] For the Rwandan returnees in 2010, the government in Kigali established a Ministry of Disaster Management and Refugee Affairs which explicitly dealt with them. In principle, this should represent a clear sign, at least on paper, of the elimination of the fear of persecution for the Rwandans who chose to repatriate.[196]

The 'return with dignity' concept is more difficult to explain.[197] We note that

195 Article 5 1) and 2), of the 1992 Memorandum of Understanding between the UNHCR and Mozambique on the repatriation of Mozambican refugees from the neighbour countries. In addition, Article 7 2) of the MoU deals with the physical safety of the returnees at the transit centre in Mozambique; the government will ensure '[t]hat the freedom, security and dignity of the returnees are maintained'. Regarding the physical safety of the returnees, the UNHCR clearly pointed out that: 'Safety considerations will be the most serious initial concern. The safety of returnees must be assured by the authorities, supported as necessary by the international community and monitored, wherever return takes place. This, clearly, can best take place after violence and intimidation have ended and meaningful steps have been taken towards the (re)establishment of enforcement agencies that are compliant with human rights, as well as of a functioning, independent judiciary. The presence of mines and unexploded ordnance is often a prevalent threat in repatriation operations. De-mining and mine-awareness training programs are therefore essential.' See UNHCR, Standing Committee, Legal safety issues in the context of voluntary repatriation, 7 June 2004, document No. EC/54/SC/CRP.12, paragraph 9, p. 3.

196 Information available in the official website of the ministry: www.midimar.gov.rw/, accessed 12 October 2014. Quoting from the website, the general mission of the ministry is the following: '1) To attain a highly proficient mechanism for preventing, mitigating, responding, recovering, securing, monitoring and timely acting positively in order to promote disaster awareness culture within a sector policy framework oriented to management of natural and man-made disasters risks such as volcanic activity, floods, earthquakes, landslides, mudslides, storms, fire, deforestation, landslides, drought 2) To have a really pro-active refugee policy and good mechanism for handling of Rwandan and Foreign Refugees affairs in respect of Rwandan law and international treaties signed for protection of refugees which permit to develop a comprehensive advance response strategy.'

197 UNHCR, Handbook on voluntary repatriation: international protection, Geneva: UNHCR, 1996, paragraph 2 4): '*Return in safety*: Return which takes place under conditions of legal safety (such as amnesties or public assurances of personal safety, integrity, non-discrimination and freedom from fear of persecution or punishment upon return), physical security (including protection from armed attacks, and mine-free routes and if not mine-free then at least demarcated settlement sites), and material security (access to land or means of livelihood). *Return with dignity*: The concept of dignity is less self-evident than that of safety. The dictionary definition of "dignity" contains elements of "serious, composed, worthy of honor and respect". Emphasis added. In practice, elements must include that refugees are not manhandled; that they can return unconditionally and that if they are returning spontaneously they can do so at their own pace; that they are not arbitrarily separated from family members; and that they are treated with respect and full acceptance by their national authorities, including the full restoration of their rights. Among the elements of "safety and dignity" to be considered are: – the refugees' physical safety at all stages during and after their return including en route, at reception points and at the destination, – the need for family unity, – attention to the needs of vulnerable groups, – the waiver or, if not possible, reduction to a minimum of border crossing formalities, – permission

the previous expression of 'return in dignity'[198] was replaced by the expression 'return with dignity' in 1996, although the two references do not appear to be of much consequence, with the UNHCR using the two phrases interchangeably. While several aspects of 'return in safety' and 'with dignity' refer to the movement phase itself, the greater part of it refers to the reintegration of the returnees into their communities of origin.[199] To this purpose, the 2004 Handbook for Repatriation and Reintegration Activities makes a strong connection between dignity and the refugees' ability to return to their original home environment, encouraging authorities in the country of origin to create conditions conducive to ensuring that refugees are able to effectively exercise their right to return, with safety and dignity, to their places of origin or former places of residence.[200]

The evolution of the concept of 'return in safety and with dignity' has stressed the role of the objective element to the detriment of the subjective one, as is evident in the 2002 UNHCR 'Background Note' on voluntary repatriation: the document mentions the voluntary nature of repatriation in elusive terms and considers safety in the country of origin as the most important condition.[201]

for refugees to bring their movable possessions when returning, – respect for school and planting seasons in the timing of such movements, and – freedom of movement.' However, as noted by M. Bradley: 'The subjectivity of dignity is evident when we consider the different experiences of people exposed to discrimination and political violence. For example, South Africa's *apartheid* policy was a clear affront to human dignity. [. . .] Despite the degrading treatment he/she endured, Nelson Mandela epitomized dignity, declaring that: "Any man or institution that tries to rob me of my dignity will lose because I will not part with it at any price or under any pressure." Equally, many survivors of *apartheid* say they lost their dignity under white rule, but regained it through the proceedings of the South African Truth and Reconciliation Commission. For others, the idea that the Commission could revive their trampled dignity was a farce.' See Bradley, M., op. cit. note 192, p. 8. At p. 11 the author concluded his analysis stating that: 'Repatriation and dignity alike are challenges that belie easy answers.'

198 But the expression 'return in dignity' still remains in some specific agreements. See, for instance, Article 6 of the Tripartite Agreement on the voluntary repatriation of Rwandese refugees from Tanzania, 12 April 1995.

199 Zieck, M., *UNHCR and Voluntary Repatriation of Refugees*, op. cit. note 74, p. 445. The UNHCR, however, tried to give the following definition for a return: 'In practice, elements must include that refugees are not manhandled; that they can return unconditionally and that if they are returning spontaneously they can do so at their own pace; that they are not arbitrarily separated from family members; and that they are treated with respect and full acceptance by their national authorities, including the full restoration of their rights.' See UNHCR, Handbook on voluntary repatriation: international protection, Geneva: UNHCR, 1996, paragraph 2 4).

200 UNHCR, Handbook for repatriation and reintegration activities, Geneva: UNHCR, 2004, p. 144.

201 UNHCR, Global Consultation in international protection, 'voluntary repatriation', document No. EC/GC/02/5, 25 April 2002, paragraphs 14 and 15: '14) The search for solutions has generally required UNHCR to promote measures, with governments and with other international bodies, to establish conditions that would permit refugees to make a free and informed choice and to return safely and with dignity to their homes. Creating the most conducive actual conditions for return remains, however, fundamentally a political process, going well beyond the role and capacity of UNHCR, and involving actors with different and not necessarily converging interests. 15) From UNHCR's perspective, the core of voluntary repatriation is return

It should be stressed that the concept of 'safety' applied to the 1969 OAU Convention is based on the hypothesis that the conditions for return in safety already subsist. Hence, the provisions focus mainly on the legal organization and on the conditions of the return itself.[202] It is also clear that, in this case, the judgment of states will replace the judgment of refugees in assessing the situation in the country of origin, therefore pushing for repatriation under coercion, and may be equivalent to violating the principle of *non-refoulement*. Once this has happened it will be difficult to stop other negative practices by the host state. Practices like, for instance, limiting freedom of movement and association.[203]

8.7 Final considerations on voluntary repatriation

A state can promote repatriation exclusively when an individual no longer fulfils the refugee definition, a condition addressed in the cessation clause. Evidently, if a situation is covered by a cessation clause, then the refugee can be repatriated and the involuntary or voluntary nature of return is irrelevant because we are no longer in a refugee protection context. If the situation is not covered by the cessation clause, then return cannot be promoted by the state of asylum.[204]

Over the years, there has been a reversal in terms of what is considered the core criteria for voluntary repatriation by the UNHCR. For decades, the main element of repatriation was the character of voluntariness, which today has been replaced by the criteria of the situation in the country of origin. This proves that the subject is not always well defined, and is sometimes influenced more strongly by political considerations than by strictly legal ones.[205]

The history of repatriations in Sub-Saharan Africa has however taught us that the UNHCR can barely be expected to promote political and socio-economic conditions for return in situations of instability or 'relative stability' that are implicit in the concept of 'safe return', when its resources are limited even in a peaceful environment. For instance, in the case of the early 1990s Namibian repatriation that took place under apparent stability, the country was nevertheless

in and to conditions of physical, legal and material safety, with full restoration of national protection the end product [. . .].'

202 Okoth-Obbo, G., 'Thirty years on: a legal review of the 1969 OAU Refugee Convention Governing the Specific Aspects of Refugee Problems in Africa', op. cit. note 62, p. 126.

203 Chimni, B.S., 'The meaning of words and the role of the UNHCR in voluntary repatriation', op. cit. note 27, pp. 454–5.

204 Barutciski, M., 'Involuntary repatriation when refugee protection is no longer necessary: moving forward after the 48th session of the Executive Committee', op. cit. note 47, pp. 248–9.

205 Chetail, V., 'Voluntary repatriation', op. cit. note 153, p. 18. In this regard, G. Goodwin-Gill and J. McAdam added: 'Independence, successful secession, an amnesty or other change of circumstance may indicate that the basis for a claim to refugee status has been removed, and the state of refuge must decide whether this is a sufficient or necessary reason for requiring the individual to quit national territory. This may be justified [. . .] where the period of refuge has been relatively short or where sheer numbers alone have meant that only temporary protection could be accorded.' See Goodwin-Gill, G. and McAdam J., op. cit. note 30, p. 496.

not ready to receive such a huge number of returnees: therefore a comprehensive peace does not always constitute an effective prerequisite for return.[206]

In 2003, however, the UNHCR along with the UNDP and the World Bank, launched the '4Rs' ('repatriation, reintegration, rehabilitation and reconstruction') programme, considered as indispensable in averting conflicts[207] on the continent, and was piloted in, among other places, Burundi, Eritrea and Sierra Leone.[208]

206 Chimni, B.S., 'The meaning of words and the role of the UNHCR in voluntary repatriation', op. cit. note 27, pp. 455–6. For an example of more recent repatriation in Namibia, see: UNHCR, 'Namibia: First voluntary repatriation from Botswana to Caprivi region since 2002', 15 April 2005, available at: www.unhcr.org/425f9bc332.html, accessed 10 May 2015: 'The refugees are returning under the terms of an agreement reached in 2002 between Namibia, Botswana and UNHCR which incorporates the internationally-recognised principles of refugee protection, including the establishment of a commission to promote repatriation, cross-border visits by refugee representatives, simplification of border procedures and access to returnees by UNHCR.'

207 Declaration by Mrs. Kusorgbor, Ghanaian delegate at the UN, in UNGA, Third Committee, Summary record of the 33rd meeting, 7 November 2003, document No. A/C.3/58/SR. 33, p. 8. In this regard, see also UNHCR, Framework for durable solutions for refugees and persons of concern, May 2003, p. 18: '4Rs is a program concept referring to the related repatriation, reintegration, rehabilitation and reconstruction processes of a given operation and which aims to ensure linkages between all four processes so as to promote durable solutions for refugees, ensure poverty reduction and help create good local governance. The concept provides an overarching framework for institutional collaboration in the implementation of reintegration operations allowing maximum flexibility for field operations to pursue country specific approaches. While development programs are in the process of maturing, UNHCR would focus on supporting activities that facilitate the initial reintegration/reinsertion of returnees. This means, amongst others, monitoring protection agreements, providing for the repair or reconstruction of family shelters, supporting small scale micro-credit schemes and other types of productive activities, and reviving, within the national/regional strategies, essential water, educational and health services in returnee communities. Such an approach should also serve as a framework for the coordinated phase out of UNHCR and phase in of development agencies. The guiding principles and critical success factors for this integrated approach are: a) ownership by host governments of the processes which the 4Rs concept embodies; b) integrated planning process at the country level by the UN Country Team; c) strong institutional cooperation and commitment to support punctually and at decisive moments, the needs and efforts of country teams to bridge essential gaps in transition strategies; and, d) participation of the plethora of actors who form part of the development community – UN agencies bilateral and multilateral institutions.'

208 In this regard, J.H.S. Milner pointed out: '[UNHCR facilitated] the return of refugees to Sierra Leone, either by boat from Conakry to Freetown or overland. [. . .] The IOM and UNHCR assumed the responsibility for the operation on 9 January 2001, and facilitated the return of some 4800 refugees by the end of the month.' See Milner, J.H.S., op. cit. note 186, p. 148. About Burundi we may also read: 'One of the solutions for the reintegration challenges as proposed by Burundi's National Strategy for Socio-Economic Reintegration is the accommodation of landless returnees and other vulnerable people in Burundi's VRIs. VRIs, designed by the Burundian government and UN agencies, were to provide a solution for the large population of landless returnees, which are mainly the 1972 refugees.' See Fransen, S. and Kuschminder, K., 'Back to the land: the long-term challenges of refugee return and reintegration in Burundi', in *UNHCR, New Issues in Refugee Research*, research paper No. 242, 2012, p. 12. At ibid., p. 13, the authors continued: 'The design of the VRIs is based on an integrated approach to assistance for vulnerable populations and therefore focuses not only on returnees: the village population consists of eighty percent returnees and twenty percent residents. Residents are households from the area that are considered vulnerable as well. This way the VRI is not only a tool to accommodate the landless returnees, but also to foster coexistence between the returnees

The goal of this approach was to provide a framework for institutional collaboration in the implementation of reintegration operations and to address the mainstreaming of reintegration – considered as a 'corollary' of repatriation[209] – of former refugees into national development programmes.[210] It is true, however, that all kinds of refugee programmes are dependent on financial assistance from international donors, and sometimes asylum-seekers become a heavy burden for these donors.[211] This was so in Zimbabwe in the late 1970s[212] or in Rwanda in

and residents and to stimulate development in general. On average each VRI hosts around 250 households. The opinions on the VRIs of the different actors are mixed. Some respondents called the VRIs an outright "failure" and a "disaster" due to the high levels of poverty, the shortage of land and the cooperation problems between different implementers. Others stressed that the VRIs have been successful in providing the returnees with "protection", "shelter" and other basic needs and that even though it is a work in progress there is no clear alternative.'

209 Van Krieken, P.J., 'Repatriation of refugees under international law', op. cit. note 4, p. 112.

210 Tennant, V., note 2, p. 317. See also Anonymous, 'Dialogue on voluntary repatriation in Africa', discussion paper, in *Refugee Survey Quarterly*, vol. 23, 2004, pp. 269–70. In this regard, M. Zieck in an illuminating way observed: 'Those 4Rs [. . .] signify a concept which aims to ensure linkages between all four processes so as to promote durable solutions for refugees, ensure poverty reduction and help create good local governance. In institutional terms it entails an overarching framework for institutional collaboration in the implementation of reintegration operations. [. . .] The envisaged institutional collaboration is set out by UNHCR in terms of a conglomerate of agencies and actors. [. . .] In short, an integrated approach with the participation of quite a number of actors with sufficient means to embark on the wholesale recovery of countries which have been ravaged and devastated by conflict. It cannot be considered other than in terms of a massive effort.' See Zieck, M., 'Voluntary repatriation: paradigm, pitfalls, progress', op. cit. note 21, pp. 46–7. See also UNHCR, Refugees in Africa – the challenges of protection and solutions – Cotonou, 1–3 June 2004, in *Collection of International Instruments and Other Legal Texts Concerning Refugees and Others of Concern to UNHCR*, vol. 3, Geneva: UNHCR, 2006, p. 955; as a separate document, 56 p. At p. 39 of the separate document we may read: 'The aim [of the 4Rs approach] is to ensure that more resources are allocated to create an environment inside the countries of origin conducive to facilitating sustainable repatriation while preventing the recurrence of mass outflows.' Previously, G. Kibreab, quoting the UNHCR, noted that: 'For solutions to last, assistance to refugees and returnees must aim at their participation, productivity and durable self-reliance; it should be development-orientated as soon as possible and, in least developed countries, it should take into account the needs of local people as well.' See Kibreab, G., 'Left in Limbo', op. cit. note 7, p. 55. Further, at idem, the author highlighted the three goals of a developmental approach to reintegration: '[t]o provide relief assistance for refugees and returnees in Africa; to help those refugees and returnees to find new lives for themselves and their families; and to help the countries that harbor the refugees or returnees.' In this regard, see also the declaration by Mr. Redai, Ethiopian delegate at the UN: 'Their reintegration [of the Ethiopian returnees] into the local community remained a daunting challenge in the face of endemic poverty and weak social institutions, however, and the difficulties were compounded by recurrent droughts. Repatriation should not be seen in isolation but should take place in the context of sustainable development.' See UNGA, Third Committee, Summary record of the 48th meeting, 3 December 2002, document No. A/C.3/57/SR. 48, p. 4. Emphasis added.

211 Karadawi, A., *Refugee Policy in Sudan – 1967–1984*, op. cit. note 67, p. 204. Quoting the UNHCR, the author affirmed in this regard: 'While being a refugee should be a temporary state of affairs, there is a real danger of refugee situations and the problems of refugees being institutionalized and of people remaining refugees forever. The foremost challenge facing the international community today is to reverse this trend.' See idem.

212 Makanya, S.T., 'The desire to return', op. cit. note 137, pp. 114–19.

the mid-1990s, where the UNSG clearly noted the lack of support for the local government, made apparent in the way that it could not develop the necessary projects to integrate the returnees.[213] Sometimes local governments call on their citizens to return home from asylum, although the means at their disposal are not sufficient to guarantee a decent standard of well-being for the returnees, as occurred with Mauritanian refugees returning from Senegal in 2007[214] and 2010.[215]

Finally, in Sub-Saharan Africa we have historically witnessed another form of repatriation, which can be called 'periodic repatriation'. There are several areas on the continent where refugees cross a border but remain close to it, anticipating a prompt return. In many cases, they remain in the same ethnic region or areas into which they may traditionally travel on a seasonal basis. Their sojourn can be considered as 'periodic': during outbreaks of conflict they cross the border, returning home when conditions permit only to shift back across the border during ulterior hostilities. People involved in these movements are unlikely to be accorded refugee status in the country of periodic asylum. Some of the movements occurring out of Chad during the Tombalbaye regime (1960–1975) constitute a good illustration of this, as were the movements of Beni Amer out of Ethiopia into Eastern Sudan during the 1960s. While the persons involved in 'periodic repatriations' are usually able to survive without external assistance, the nature of their existence reduces their access to basic services in both the home country and in the country of asylum, and, as such, their vulnerability increases.[216] Whether it is possible to provide assistance to such individuals and, if so, what type of assistance is most appropriate, are questions which are not completely resolved.

As L. Hammond noted, the idea that voluntary repatriation represents the ideal solution to refugee problems is based on the supposition, often proven to be false in Sub-Saharan Africa, that living in his/her own country after repatriation is undoubtedly better than a life spent in exile. And this idea has been considered helpful to legitimize measures obliging refugees to repatriate.[217]

213 UN, Report of the United Nations Secretary-General to the Security Council on the situation in Africa (The causes of conflict and the promotion of durable peace and sustainable development in Africa), document No. A/52/871-S/1998/318, 13 April 1998, p. 14.

214 See the news: 'Mauritania: Appeal for US$7 million for Mauritanian refugee return', 31 August 2007, available at: www.unhcr.org/46d7f3042.html, accessed 10 October 2014: 'UNHCR is launching a US$7 million appeal today to fund the voluntary repatriation of 24,000 Mauritanian refugees from Senegal and Mali – a return that will help resolve one of the most protracted refugee situations in the world. Some of the refugees have spent more than two decades in exile. The 17-month operation, which faces some major logistical challenges, is scheduled to start in October.'

215 See the news: 'UNHCR resumes repatriation of Mauritanian refugees in Senegal', 19 October 2010, available at: www.unhcr.org/4cbdbad36.html, accessed 10 October 2014.

216 Rogge, J.R., 'Repatriation of refugees: a not-so-simple "optimum" solution', op. cit. note 10, p. 24.

217 Hammond, L., 'Examining the discourse of repatriation: towards a more proactive theory of return migration', in Black, R. and Koser, K. (eds), *The End of the Refugee Cycle? Refugee Repatriation and Reconstruction*, Oxford: Berghahn Books, 1999, p. 230.

9 Local integration and resettlement in a third country

9.1 An analysis of the legal basis justifying local integration

Commonly referred to as one of the three durable solutions available for refugees,[1] local integration, considered at the beginning to be almost exclusively 'rural integration',[2] is based on the assumption that refugees will remain in their country of asylum permanently and find a solution to their plight in that country. It is an economic, legal and socio-cultural process related to, but also distinguished from, local settlement as well as self-reliance.[3]

1 However, commentators do not fully agree with this definition. For instance, see the NGO statement on Local Integration, Global Consultations on International Protection, 22–24 May 2002 quoted in Fielden, A., 'Local integration: an under-reported solution to protracted refugee situations', in UNHCR, *New Issues in Refugee Research*, research paper No. 158, 2008, p. 1: 'Although local integration is always listed among the three durable solutions, in fact it is rarely used in cases of mass-influx and has, in that context, almost become a "non-solution".'

2 For instance, see Anand, R.M., *African Refugees: an Overview*, New Delhi: Khama Publishers, 1993, pp. 64–72. At p. 64 the author asserted: 'Since most refugees are from a rural background, rural settlement is an appropriate solution [to the refugee problem].'

3 The concept of local integration is to be distinguished from the concepts of self-reliance and local settlement. The concept of '*self-reliance*' is defined in the Handbook for Self-Reliance, Geneva: UNHCR, 2005, p. 1 as follows: 'Self-reliance is the social and economic ability of an individual, a household or a community to meet essential needs (including protection, food, water, shelter, personal safety, health and education) in a sustainable manner and with dignity. Self-reliance, as a program approach, refers to developing and strengthening livelihoods of persons of concern, and reducing their vulnerability and long-term reliance on humanitarian/external assistance.' Self-Reliance does not presuppose that refugees will find a durable solution in the country of asylum, but should be considered as a part of a continuum, gradually to local integration. Self-reliance strategy was for instance applied in Uganda in the 1990s, conceptualized specifically for Sudanese refugees living in the West Nile districts of Arua, Adjumani and Moyo, recognizing the long-term nature of their situation. In this regard, see Dryden-Peterson, S. and Hovil, L., 'A remaining hope for durable solutions: local integration of refugees and their hosts in the case of Uganda', in *Refuge*, vol. 22, 2004, p. 29. These authors, at p. 39, concluded affirming that: 'Local integration need not to be conceived of as a fallback option, but instead as a positive step in securing long-term stability for both refugees and host communities.' For a further analysis, see also Dryden-Peterson, S. and Hovil, L., 'Local integration as a durable solution: refugees, host population and education in Uganda', 'Local integration as a durable solution: refugees, host population and education in Uganda', in *UNHCR, New Issues in Refugee Research*, research paper No. 93, 2003, particularly pp. 7–12. Concerning the same experience, A. Fielden noted: 'The

Local integration in the refugee context has been formally defined as:

> [t]he end product of a multi-faceted and on-going process, of which self-reliance is but one part. Integration requires preparedness on the part of refugees to adapt to the host society, without having to forego their own cultural identity. From the host society, it requires communities that are welcoming and responsive to refugees, and public institutions that are able to meet the needs of a diverse population. As a process leading to a durable solution for refugees in the country of asylum, local integration has three inter-related and quite specific dimensions.[4]

Conceived in this way, local integration is therefore not discernible from the main solution envisaged by the 1951 Geneva Convention, which simply consisted of the respect for refugee rights.[5] Paragraph 6 of the same document explains that local integration is above all a 'legal process':

> [w]hereby refugees are granted a progressively wider range of rights and entitlements by the host State that are broadly commensurate with those enjoyed by its citizens. These include freedom of movement, access to education and labor market, access to public relief and assistance, including

initial provision of land to refugees in the local settlement scheme enabled them to become self-reliant. Uganda allows refugees free access to the employment market, including the right to sell produce in local markets. Refugees in settlements were limited in their freedom of movement, however.' See Fielden, A., op. cit. note 1, p. 11. The relationship between the concepts of local integration and local settlements is more ambiguous, since the terms are sometimes used interchangeably by authors. '*Local settlement*' can be more correctly situated somewhere between self-reliance and local integration and is a practice most commonly found in mass-influx situations where host countries recognize refugees on a *prima facie* basis. While in some cases refugees might be allowed to remain and be gradually integrated in the host country, in other situations local settlement is just a temporary phase during which refugees are allowed to become self-reliant until they can voluntarily repatriate. Emphasis added. See UNHCR, Global Consultations on international protection/third track: local integration, 25 April 2002, document No. EC/GC/02/6, paragraphs 14–17.

4 UNHCR, Global Consultations on international protection/third track: local integration, 25 April 2002, document No. EC/GC/02/6, paragraph 5. The dimensions considered are the above mentioned: legal, economic and socio-cultural. As also the UNGA noted in 2012: '[The UNGA] reaffirms the right of return and the principle of voluntary repatriation, appeals to countries of origin and countries of asylum to create conditions that are conducive to voluntary repatriation, and recognizes that, *while voluntary repatriation remains the pre-eminent solution, local integration and third-country resettlement, where appropriate and feasible, are also viable options for dealing with the situation of African refugees who, owing to prevailing circumstances in their respective countries of origin, are unable to return home.*' See UNGA, Assistance to refugees, returnees and displaced persons in Africa, 20 December 2012, resolution No. A/RES/67/150, paragraph 21. Emphasis added.

5 Hathaway, J.C., *The Rights of Refugees Under International Law*, Cambridge, UK: Cambridge University Press, 2005, p. 978. At idem, footnote 277, the author quoted E. Michel affirming: '[O]fficial discourse on "integration" [. . .] lacks clarity.' In this regard, see also, for instance, Crisp, J., 'The local integration and local settlement of refugees: a conceptual and historical analysis', in UNHCR, *New Issues in Refugee Research*, research paper No. 102, 2004, p. 1, where the author contended that 'local integration' is: 'First, [. . .] a legal process, whereby refugees are granted a progressively wider range of rights and entitlements by the host state. Under the terms of the

health facilities, the possibilities of acquiring and disposing of property, and the capacity to travel with valid travel and identity documents. Realization of family unity is another aspect of local integration.[6]

The term 'assimilation' used in Article 34 of the 1951 Geneva Convention[7] is generally interpreted by the doctrine in the sense of integration into the cultural, economic and social life of the country and not as denoting any notion of coercion.[8] Likewise, the international community has always rejected the notion that refugees should be expected to abandon their own way of life, so as to become indistinguishable from nationals of the host community.[9]

Article 34 of the 1951 Geneva Convention contains two distinct obligations, one general and one specific. Contracting states are to facilitate integration and

1951 Refugee Convention, these include, for example, the right to seek employment, to engage in other income-generating activities, to own and dispose of property, to enjoy freedom of movement and to have access to public services such as education. The process whereby refugees gain and accumulate rights may lead to the acquisition of permanent residence rights and ultimately to the acquisition of citizenship in the country of asylum.' For an example of permanent residency as a form of integration, see the news: 'Zambia begins granting Angolan refugees permanent residency', 31 December 2012, document, available at: www.unhcr.org/50e162899.html, accessed 13 October 2014: 'Jose Pinto, a refugee for 33 years, can now call Zambia his permanent home after he and his family became the first former Angolan refugees to be granted permanent residency permits by Zambian authorities.'

6 UNHCR, Global Consultations on international protection/third track: local integration, 25 April 2002, document No. EC/GC/02/6, paragraph 6. In the regard of family unity S.J. Nawyn noted that: 'Some scholars have conducted research on the importance of family unity and maintaining family ties post-resettlement, but more work is needed particularly on transnational family relations post-resettlement. For example, the Somali Bantu resettlement produced a diaspora of usually tight-knit Bantu kin networks, presenting new challenges to the Bantu in maintaining family relations and rituals across great distances. The Tanzanian government's decision to grant citizenship to Burundian refugees has meant that those Burundians in Tanzania are not likely to be resettled with other family members in resettlement countries, solidifying the transnational status of families that had hoped to eventually reunite. The strategies that these Somali Bantu and Burundian families enact to maintain family relations, and the health of those families in the future will provide scholars evidence of both the positive and detrimental effects that resettlement can have on refugee families.' See Nawyn, S.J., 'Refugee resettlement policies and pathways to integration', in Gold, S.J. and Nawyn, S.J. (eds), *Routledge International Handbook of Migration Studies*, London/New York: Routledge, 2013, p. 115.

7 Article 34 of the 1951 Geneva Convention ('Naturalization') read: 'The Contracting States shall as far as possible facilitate the assimilation and naturalization of refugees. They shall in particular make every effort to expedite naturalization proceedings and to reduce as far as possible the charges and costs of such proceedings.'

8 In this regard, see, for instance, Da Costa, R., 'Rights of refugees in the context of integration: legal standards and recommendations', in UNHCR, *Legal and protection policy research series*, 2006, p. 24. A. Fielden, however, contended: 'The difference between assimilation and local integration should be clarified. The Refugee Convention uses the concept of assimilation alongside integration. UNHCR endorses local integration as a more useful term. [. . .] UNHCR thus promotes local integration, as opposed to assimilation, as one of the three "durable solutions" available to refugees.' See Fielden, A., op. cit. note 1, p. 2.

9 UNHCR, Global Consultations on international protection/third track: local integration, 25 April 2002, document No. EC/GC/02/6, p. 2, footnote No. 3.

naturalization in general and more specifically, to make every effort to expedite naturalization proceedings and reduce charges or costs of such proceedings.[10] Article 34 should be understood in a context in which the special situations of refugees impress upon contracting states the need to accord them rights and measures beyond those normally granted to other aliens and to assimilate their rights as much as possible to those of permanent residents or citizens.

In more detail, naturalization as a form of integration – also recommended several times by the UNHCR[11] – is also previewed by specific provisions in domestic legislation. One of the most explicit examples is given by Lesotho, section 14 of its 1985 Refugee Act (1983):

> The Minister [responsible for Interior and Chieftainship Affairs] may in consultation with the committee if application thereof is made to him/her by a refugee who satisfies him/her that he/she qualified under the schedule for naturalization grant such a refugee a certificate of naturalization.[12]

10 Grahl-Madsen, A., *Commentary on the Refugee Convention 1951: Articles 2–11, 13–37*, Geneva: UNHCR, 1997, p. 247. Mass-naturalization has been a common phenomenon in Sub-Saharan Africa especially in the 1960s, 1970s and 1980s. For a typical example of mass-naturalization in Sub-Saharan Africa, see Gasarasi, C.P., 'Mass-naturalization and further integration of Rwandese refugees in Tanzania: process, problems and prospects', in *Journal of Refugee Studies*, vol. 3, 1990, pp. 88–109. At p. 94, the author contended that: '[R]wandese refugees adopt a favorable attitude towards regularization of their stay in Tanzania and their eventual naturalization [. . .]', while at p. 103 the author continued: '[t]he indigenous population both in the vicinity of the settlements and across the country has generally shown no resentment towards the policy to naturalize the Rwandese.' By that time, the situation seemed to have changed. And to show the change I set out the following example: 'They [the government representatives] also highlighted local integration in Tanzania as another potential durable solution but said that a lot of work needed to be done to tackle the xenophobia faced by refugees in Tanzania', see JRS, dispatch No. 153, 8 July 2004. For a former naturalization, see the example of the 2,500 Angolans naturalized in Botswana in 1975 – one of the first mass-naturalizations of the country – in Zetterqvist, J., *Refugees in Botswana in the Light of International Law*, Uppsala: Scandinavian Institute of African Studies, 1990, p. 69.

11 In this regard, see the opinion by B. Geddo, UNHCR legal officer, in Salomons, M., 'Report of the three nations seminar for national Eligibility Committees of Zambia, Zimbabwe and Malawi, 11–12 April, 2001. Siavonga, Zambia', in *International Journal of Refugee Law*, vol. 13, 2001, p. 375: '[I]n cases where refugees cannot return home in the foreseeable future, naturalization may gather broad political support if it is clearly in the interest of the host country owing to the scale of the economic contribution made by refugees. It may also be an attractive policy option if full-fledged economic activity is hampered by restrictions on freedom of movement of refugees who are thus unable to reach larger markets and increase their production.' As witnessed by N.H. Goetz, a famous situation in which the UNHCR supported naturalization of refugees was in the mid-1960s with Rwandan refugees in Burundi but '[i]ntegration of the refugee population with the local population never stood a chance. Although the organizations and the Burundi government agreed that they would work toward the refugees becoming citizens, naturalization never happened. Further, the local population did not really benefit in any way from the program. There were only a few reported cases of the two populations interacting, and even fewer of mutual economic gain.' See Goetz, N.H., 'Towards self-sufficiency and integration: an historical evaluation of assistance programs for Rwandese refugees in Burundi, 1962–1965', in *New Issues in Refugee Research*, research paper No. 87, 2003, p. 20.

12 For a different example, see Zimbabwean Refugee Act No. 3, 1983 which provides in section 3 5) that a person shall not be a refugee for the purpose of this Act if 'he/she becomes a citizen

The national law of Sierra Leone contains a specific provision on 'local integration', generally underlining that it is a solution that '[s]hall be facilitated by the relevant state agencies, the Office of the United Nations High Commissioner for Refugees and other international and non-governmental agencies'.[13]

In South Africa, the procedure to be naturalized is complicated, and that is why, in practice, and in spite of the existence of a clear, legal pathway in order to gain citizenship, very few refugees are naturalized in that country.[14] Section 27 c) of the 1998 South African Refugee Act requires the refugee, as the first step in the of integration, to apply for appropriate documentation 'if the Standing Committee [for Refugee Affairs] certifies that he or she will remain a refugee indefinitely'.[15]

To the extent that integration can be also viewed as a stage which paves the way to naturalization, measures to facilitate integration have an important secondary or additional benefit, specifically that of enabling a possible naturalization process. This connection between integration and naturalization is particularly important in the case of refugees, who unlike other aliens, lack an effective nationality, and live in an atypical situation which is not considered sustainable for very long.[16]

There is no agreement by the doctrine, however, as to whether naturalization is fully synonymous with integration. Examining the situation of member countries of ECOWAS,[17] A. Adepoju and others have noted how refugees from other countries in the area have preferred a combination of secure residence and work entitlement, without having to give up the citizenship of their country of origin. This situation allows for the most part, the countries in the region not to grant a

of Zimbabwe or acquires the nationality of some other country and enjoys the protection of the country of his/her new nationality.' Section 12 1) also provides that '[s]ubject to the provisions of this act, every recognized refugee and every protected person within Zimbabwe shall be entitled to the rights and be subject to the duties contained in the articles of the 1951 Convention and the 1969 OAU Convention.' For a more recent example, see Article 45 of the 2006 Refugee Act. (Ugandan authorities have not been very clear on this. However, now the 2006 Refugee Act seems to hold the final definition.) See also, for instance, Article 14 of the 1992 Ghanaian Refugee Law; Article 17 of the 1989 Nigerian Decree, National Commission for Refugees; Article 12 of the 1991 Mozambique Act No. 21/1991 (Refugee Act).

13 Section 23 of the Sierra Leonean Refugees Protection Act, No. 6 of 2007, 30 August 2007.

14 Dass, D., Klaaren, J., Ramjathan-Keogh, K. and Khan, F., 'The civil and political rights of refugees and asylum-seekers in South Africa', in Khan, F. and Schreier (eds), *Refugee Law in South Africa*, Cape Town: Juta & Co., 2014, p. 218.

15 In full, section 25 c) of the South African Refugees Act No. 130, 2 December 1998 reads as follows: 'A refugee is c) is entitled to apply for an immigration permit in terms of the Aliens Control Act, 199 1, after five years' continuous residence in the Republic from the date on which he or she was granted asylum, if the Standing Committee certifies that he or she will remain a refugee indefinitely.'

16 Grahl-Madsen, A., *Commentary on the Refugee Convention 1951: Articles 2–11, 13–37*, op. cit. note 10, p. 245.

17 'ECOWAS is a regional group of fifteen countries, founded in 1975. Its mission is to promote economic integration in all fields of economic activity, particularly industry, transport, telecommunications, energy, agriculture, natural resources, commerce, monetary and financial questions, social and cultural matters.' See website of the ECOWAS at: www.comm.ecowas.int/sec/index.php?id=about_a&lang=en, accessed 10 October 2014.

double nationality to refugees coming from the same region.[18] In any event, the 2001 MoU between ECOWAS and the UNHCR remains silent on the possibility for refugees in the ECOWAS area to be naturalized by one of the member states of the sub-regional organization.[19]

In addition to the provision in the 1951 Geneva Convention, the 1950 UNHCR Statute and the Annex also contain provisions stipulating that this UN agency plays a role in the protection of refugees by assisting both governments and private organizations in the process of integration of recognized refugees within national communities. Specifically, the 1950 UNHCR Statute, in its paragraph 2 e), calls upon governments to promote the integration of refugees, in particular by facilitating their naturalization.[20] For instance, in 2000 the UNHCR played an important role in trying to integrate over 1,500 Rwandan and Burundian refugees in the Mwen Ditu area – DRC – with the opening of support schools and health centres for those refugees leaving the camp of Mbuji Maji.[21] More recently, in 2011, the UNHCR also sustained the integration of the old Burundians (who arrived in 1972) in Tanzania, providing for financial funding to the naturalized Burundians and cooperating with the local government to warrant that they can access services and receive the certificates of citizenship.[22]

Several ExCom conclusions[23] also provide guidance and recommendations on local integration being one of the durable solutions, despite historical scepticism

18 Adepoju, A., Boulton, A. and Levin, M., 'Promoting integration through mobility: free movement and the ECOWAS Protocol', in UNHCR, *New Issues in Refugee Research*, research paper No. 150, 2007, p. 20.

19 ECOWAS/UNHCR, Memorandum of Understanding between the Economic Community of West Africa States (ECOWAS) and the United Nations High Commissioner for Refugees (UNHCR), UNTS 1242, vol. 2165, p. 174. On 17 June 2015 The ECOWAS Community Court of Justice (ECCJ) and the UNHCR have signed an agreement to cooperate in improving the protection of the rights of refugees, asylum-seekers, and returnees. See: ECOWAS: 'ECOWAS Court, UNHCR sign pact on rights of refugees', 17 June 2015, available at: www.panapress.com/ECOWAS--ECOWAS-Court,-UNHCR-sign-pact-on-rights-of-refugees--15-630441519-32-lang2-index.html, accessed 18 June 2015: 'The MOU, to be implemented over three years (2015–2107) will also facilitate their collaboration in promoting the proper interpretation and application of relevant international, regional and national legal and policy instruments relating to the protection of the rights of these vulnerable persons.'

20 Paragraph 2 e) reads: '[The UNGA General Assembly] calls upon Governments to co-operate with the United Nations High Commissioner for Refugees in the performance of his/her functions concerning refugees falling under the competence of his/her Office, especially by: e) promoting the assimilation of refugees, especially by facilitating their naturalization.'

21 UNHCR, 'Integration of Rwandans and Burundi in the DRC', 11 July 2000, available at: www.unhcr.org/3ae6b8204.html, accessed 10 November 2014.

22 UNHCR, 'UNHCR reaffirms support for integration of 1972 Burundians in Tanzania', 29 August 2011, document, available at: www.unhcr.org/4e5baf2d6.html, accessed 10 November 2014. For another example see 'Liberian town sets aside land for local integration of Sierra Leoneans', 20 August 2008, document, available at: www.unhcr.org/48ac47a44.html, accessed 10 November 2014.

23 Among them, see ExCom, conclusion No. 29 (XXXIV), 'General conclusion on international protection', 1983; conclusion No. 79 (XLVII) 'General conclusion on international protection', 1996, conclusion No. 99 (LV), 'General conclusion on international protection', 2004. For instance, in

on this matter by many countries in Sub-Saharan Africa.[24] ExCom conclusion No. 50 notes the '[c]lose nexus between international refugee protection and durable solutions', and calls upon the High Commissioner for Refugees to continue efforts to provide international protection through voluntary repatriation, local integration and resettlement.[25] Further, ExCom conclusion No. 58 makes the connection between irregular movements of refugees who have already found protection in a country, and '[t]he absence of educational and employment possibilities [as well as] the non-availability of long-term durable solutions', including local integration.[26] ExCom conclusion No. 95 also mentions the crucial importance of achieving durable solutions for refugees, urging the continuation of efforts to work actively on local integration where appropriate and practicable, in addition to voluntary repatriation.[27]

Therefore, while a number of ExCom conclusions underline voluntary repatriation as the preferred solution when feasible, many of the conclusions also

the last conclusion mentioned, its paragraph y) clearly reads: '[The ExCom] encourages States and UNHCR, in consultation with other relevant actors, in considering local integration, where appropriate and when feasible, to use and take into account the profiles of groups of refugees within a broader refugee population bearing in mind the differing capacities of the refugee population, or segments thereof, and the States hosting them.'

24 For instance, a country like Namibia has historically opposed this solution. As has Liberia, although it has, in the last few years, become more positively inclined toward it, as 'Pact on good neighborhood, stability and solidarity' between the Mano River Union states – Guinea, Sierra Leone, Liberia – shows. See Fielden, A., op. cit. note 1, p. 9. About the conference we may also read: 'The conference was the first such forum for Mano River Union representatives from governments, security forces, and civil society to have such an honest dialogue. The fact of the meeting was more important than the actual substance of the discussions. Most significant perhaps was that the regional initiative was led by Guinea, with its history of isolation. It marked Guinea's effort to emerge from the shadows of its neighbors' civil wars. Many difficult issues were put on the table, including gross human rights violations, ongoing border issues, and airing the "dirty laundry" of wars, rebel incursions, and their aftermath. The atmosphere was friendly, warm, and "good neighborly." All agreed that it marked a very positive step in the right direction.' Document, available at: www.cablegatesearch.net/cable.php?id=06CONAKRY1711, paragraph 16), accessed 10 October 2014.

25 ExCom, conclusion No. 50 (XXXIX), 'General conclusion on international protection', 1998, where paragraph e) reads: '[The ExCom] noted the close nexus between international refugee protection and durable solutions and called upon the High Commissioner to continue his/her efforts to provide international protection through voluntary repatriation, local integration in countries of first asylum or resettlement in third countries.'

26 ExCom, conclusion No. 58 (XL), 'Problem of Refugees and Asylum-Seekers Who Move in an Irregular Manner from a Country in Which They Had Already Found Protection', 1989, where paragraph b) reads: 'Irregular movements of refugees and asylum-seekers who have already found protection in a country are, to a large extent, composed of persons who feel impelled to leave, due to the absence of educational and employment possibilities and the non-availability of long-term durable solutions by way of voluntary repatriation, local integration and resettlement.'

27 ExCom, conclusion No. 95 (LIV), 'General conclusion on international protection', 2003, where paragraph i) reads: '[The ExCom] reiterates the crucial importance of achieving durable solutions for refugees and urges States and UNHCR to continue their efforts in this regard to promote and facilitate, in conditions of safety and dignity, voluntary repatriation as the preferred solution, in addition to working proactively on local integration and resettlement opportunities where appropriate and feasible.'

ensure that all three durable solutions, including local integration, '[r]emain viable and important responses to refugee situations'[28] and that '[a] combination of solutions, taking into account the specific circumstances of each refugee situation, can help in achieving lasting solutions.'[29] This last recommendation has not always been put into practice, as in at least one documented case, when voluntary repatriation in Sub-Saharan Africa hampered plans for the integration of Angolans in Zambia.[30] This said, in 2014, according to the Zambian Department of Immigration, almost 6,000 Angolan former refugees were ready to be integrated in the country of asylum.[31]

In Sub-Saharan Africa, the minimum standards of treatment provided by the 1951 Geneva Convention, which specifically touches upon integration, are also endorsed by the 1969 OAU Convention with its paragraph 9 of the preamble, clearly affirming:

> [the] Recogni[tion] that the United Nations Convention of 28 July 1951, as modified by the Protocol of 31 January 1967, constitutes the basic and universal instrument relating to the status of refugees and reflects the deep concern of States for refugees and their desire to establish common standards for their treatment.

In addition, the 1969 OAU Convention contains a provision in which states undertake to '[u]se their best endeavors consistent with their respective legislations

28 ExCom, conclusion No. 85 (XLIX) 'General conclusion on international protection', 1998, where paragraph gg) reads: '[The ExCom] recalls conclusion No. 62 (XLI) which states that voluntary repatriation, local integration and resettlement, that is, the traditional solutions for refugees, all remain viable and important responses to refugee situations, even while voluntary repatriation is the preeminent solution.' Conclusion No. 62 (XLI) 'Note on international protection', 1990, section a) iv) clearly reads: '[High Commissioner's emphasis in the Note on International Protection on the following]: the fact that voluntary repatriation, local settlement or resettlement, that is, the traditional solutions for refugees, all remain viable and important responses to refugee situations, even while voluntary repatriation is the preeminent solution.'

29 ExCom, conclusion No. 87 (L), 'General conclusion on international protection', 1999, where paragraph r) reads: '[The ExCom] reaffirms that voluntary repatriation, local integration and resettlement are the traditional solutions for refugees, and that all remain viable and important responses to refugee situations; reiterates that voluntary repatriation, where and when feasible, remains the preferred solution in the majority of refugee situations; and notes that a combination of solutions, taking into account the specific circumstances of each refugee situation, can help achieve lasting solutions.'

30 Fielden, A., op. cit. note 1, pp. 11–12. At p. 12, the author underlined that: 'Moreover, according to UNHCR, government authorities have also been indicating that the remaining number of Angolan refugees is too big for local integration.'

31 Zambian Department of Immigration, '5,588 ex-Angolan Refugees ready for local integration', April 2014, available at: www.zambiaimmigration.gov.zm/index.php/latest-immigration-news/99–5588-exangolan-refugees-ready-for-local-integration, accessed 1 December 2014: 'About 5,588 ex-Angolan refugees out of 15,234 have been screened and signed for local integration based on criteria established under the government's strategic framework for the integration of former refugees, according to the Ministry of Home Affairs. And home affairs deputy minister Nickson Chilangwa says it is imperative that the media is engaged in local integration issues because some Zambians have "opposed" the approach without fully understanding what was involved.'

to receive refugees and to secure the settlement of [. . .] refugees', and to accord temporary residence when the refugee '[h]as not received the right to reside in any country'.[32] On the purpose of local integration, Article II6 also mentions this, the paragraph in question providing that: 'For reasons of security, countries of asylum shall, as far as possible, settle refugees at a reasonable distance from the frontier of their country of origin.'

In practice, such a provision often means that refugees are settled far away from their own ethnic group. In the early 1990s, the Burundian refugees in Tanzania were resettled a great distance from the border because of this provision.[33] More recently, in 2012, the UNHCR considered that the Yida refugee settlement in South Sudan was not safe for a stay of long duration by reason of its closeness to unstable boundaries. In spite of this recommendation, refugees preferred to remain close to their households in the Nuba Mountains, as, among other reasons, they had become familiar with the Yida landscape.[34]

If on the one hand Article II6 of the 1969 OAU Convention forces refugees to be relocated far from the settlement of their ethnic group, on the other, such a provision promotes more profound integration in the host country, with the refugees being compelled to enter into deeper contact with the host society.

In doctrine, attempts have been made to more explicitly define what 'integration' in developing countries consists of, on a practical level. Among other aspects, three main characteristics for a successful integration of refugees have been identified: a) the socio-cultural change they experience allows them to preserve an identity of their own and to adjust emotionally to their new situation; b) friction between host populations and refugees is not worse than within the host population itself;[35] c) refugees do not encounter more discrimination than exists between groups previously settled within the host society.[36]

32 Article II1 and III5 of the 1969 OAU Convention considered in Goodwin-Gill, G. and McAdam J., *The Refugee in International Law*, 3rd edn, Oxford: Oxford University Press, 2007, p. 491.

33 Chol, A.A., 'The influence of law and related factors in the integration of refugees in Tanzania', in *International Journal of Refugee Law*, vol. 4, 1992, pp. 177–8, where the author also quoted a local newspaper of the time affirming: 'Kagera region has 5 per cent of foreigners of its one million people. The Identification Act (No. 4, 1986) under which every national will be required to carry an identity card is hoped to ease the problem of unlawful immigrants. *De facto* refugees along the border are expected to be resettled.' As A. Fielden pointed out, Tanzanian policy towards Burundian refugees who have been living in planned settlements in three regions of Western Tanzania for over 35 years dramatically changed in 2007: 'Authorities have recently expressed willingness to consider the naturalization of these Burundians. The majority [. . .] have expressed their wish to become naturalized Tanzanian citizens.' See Fielden, A., op. cit. note 1, p. 10.

34 UNHCR, 'Border insecurity increasing concerns for refugees' safety in Yida, South Sudan', 27 March 2012, available at: www.unhcr.org/4f719a059.html, accessed 1 December 2014.

35 In this regard, K. Jacobsen noted that one decisive factor that contributes to making relations between refugees and host population better is the '[b]eliefs and expectations held by both the host community and the refugees, about the temporariness of the refugees' stay and the desirability of repatriation.' See Jacobsen, K., 'The forgotten solution: local integration for refugees in developing countries', in UNHCR, *New Issues in Refugee Research*, research paper No. 45, 2001, p. 19.

36 T. Kuhlman quoted in Dryden-Peterson, S. and Hovil, L., 'A remaining hope for durable solutions: local integration of refugees and their hosts in the case of Uganda', op. cit. note 3, p. 28.

In addition, the ExCom has emphasized individuals' characteristics that may assist in determining the circumstances in which local integration can represent an appropriate durable solution. They include:

i. refugees born in asylum countries who might otherwise become stateless; and/or
ii. refugees who, due to their personal circumstances including the reasons prompting their flight, are unlikely to be able to repatriate to their country of origin in the foreseeable future; and/or
iii. refugees who have established close family, social, cultural and economic links with their country of asylum, including those who already had, or have the capacity to attain, a considerable degree of socio-economic integration.[37]

Further, in the same conclusion, the ExCom:

> Affirms the particular importance of the legal dimension of integration, which entails the host State granting refugees a secure legal status and a progressively wider range of rights and entitlements that are broadly commensurate with those enjoyed by its citizens and, over time, the possibility of naturalizing, and in this respect:
>
> i. recognizes the relevance of the 1951 Convention and its 1967 Protocol and relevant human rights instruments as providing a useful legal framework for guiding the local integration process; and
> ii. recognizes further that in support of the legal process, host countries may need technical and financial support to adapt and revise their national legal and administrative frameworks to allow refugees equal enjoyment of rights, services and programs without discrimination.[38]

According to the above-stated considerations, Mozambican refugees could have been considered 'integrated' in South Africa during the 1990s, although their integration was mostly facilitated due to a range of local responses, rather than because of national legislation, which was inadequate.[39] In this sense, in 2006, the city of Cape Town committed themselves in a very serious way to the integration

37 ExCom, conclusion No. 104 (LVI), 'Local Integration', 2005, paragraph i).
38 Ibid., paragraph l).
39 Polzer, T., 'Adapting to changing legal frameworks: Mozambican refugees in South Africa', in *International Journal of Refugee Law*, vol. 19, 2007, pp. 22–50, note 2191, p. 28. At idem, the author added: '[I]nternational experience shows that locally integrated refugees, especially when there is a welcoming host community, are generally better off than those [for instance] confined to camps.' Among the local responses to integrate Mozambican refugees, the author cited the initiatives undertaken by the local chiefs in some provinces, such as the Gazankulu province, to favour their co-ethnics. As a means of integration the author also underlined the important role played by the 1995 and 1996 amnesties which were considered by the refugees as a long-awaited means of matching their social status with the appropriate legal status: see pp. 41–7 of T. Polzer's study.

of refugees through the Declaration on Refugees' Rights, which was signed by the UNHCR, the city's mayor, and Tutumike, a regional organization supporting refugees.[40]

Successful or not, T. Polzer has pointed out that such local South African mechanisms put into place to respond to unfavourable national laws should be understood as creating a relation between the refugees and the state, in the absence of other legal avenues and should be taken seriously by legal scholars.[41]

9.2 Why states in the region are currently reluctant to accept the local integration of refugees

In many Sub-Saharan African countries, integration often occurs very fluidly, with refugees settling without ever being fully separated from the local community, even when they are expected to live in camps. In this last situation, it is difficult to isolate them and there is movement in and out by both local people and refugees, as happened for instance in north-western Tanzania, where the town of Kigoma and the Lake Tanganyika shores were target areas of migration for Congolese on the other side of the lake. Refugees and locals mixed for purposes of entertainment, marriage, seasonal work and trade. Local people used refugee camps and settlements for the health facilities and markets.[42] In another and more recent (2009) case, integration – through naturalization – in Tanzania consisted simply in the return of a population to their ancestral land and, therefore, not halted by

40 City of Cape Town, 'City Signs Declaration of Refugee Rights, Cape Town Council Chamber', 20 June 2006, available at: www.capetown.gov.za/en/Pages/CitySignsDeclarationofRefugeeRights,CapeTownCouncilChamber,20June2006.aspx, accessed 8 November 2014: 'The declaration will help ensure that we offer fair treatment to all legitimate refugees. It also highlights the right of refugees to speedy and corruption free processing by the Home Affairs Department. This must be granted so that their status as refugees can be established. And it must be granted regardless of the political beliefs held by the individuals concerned.'

41 Polzer, T., op. cit. note 39, p. 50.

42 Jacobsen, K., 'The forgotten solution: local integration for refugees in developing countries', op. cit. note 35, p. 9. Tanzania is also the country where many Rwandese refugees have been naturalized in the late 1980s, a situation in which normal procedures were not followed. It was considered strange that the decision to naturalize came from higher authorities without the consent of the refugees themselves. But what was considered more frightening at that time was that Tanzanian law did not accommodate naturalization of refugees and a legal wrangle could ensue if a refugee who had been naturalized decided to declare him/herself a non-national. This situation aroused so much disappointment in the local population that it was avoided in the case of Burundians in the early 1990s. See Chol, A.A., op. cit. note 33, pp. 184–6. We note that in 1972, Burundi refugees contributed substantially in the growth of the Tanzanian economy. In this regard, see Fielden, A., op. cit. note 1, p. 3. Another example of harmonious relations between refugees and local community has been provided by C.R. Veney regarding several Coast Province camps (Marafa) in Kenya: 'A venture to reduce tensions between refugees and the local community resulted in more social and economic relations between the two communities because both groups [refugees and the local community] used the slaughterhouse and the meat was sold inside and outside the camps. [. . .] The market and water pump in the camp [Marafa] were tangible benefits to the local community and served to reduce tensions between refugees and

the central government in any way.[43] Congolese, fleeing Zaire during the attempt of the secession of Katanga in the 1970s, also mixed very well with Angolans during their stay in that country. After three decades of their arrival, the vast majority of Congolese had never seen their homeland, having been born in Angola and speaking Portuguese but not having yet obtained legal integration.[44]

The presence of Liberian refugees in the Ivory Coast in 2002 was found to have acted as an impetus for improved agricultural productivity while increasing pressure on scarce land.[45] In contrast, about 12,000 Ivorian refugees in 2005 integrated locally in the east of Liberia, while others chose Monrovia to make their own life in that country. Some refugees raised poultry, selling eggs at the local market. Others made bricks to bolster the supplies of building materials needed by the community hosting them.[46]

In eastern Sudan in 2002, the UNHCR's studies found that pressure on land to provide for inhabitants had increased, partially because of the protracted nature of settlements, while conversely there had been several improvements in the education and health sectors for the local population.[47] After the resolution of the first Sudanese conflict in 1972, significant numbers of former refugees remained in Uganda, where they fled at the outbreak of the conflict. These were mainly people who had integrated informally into the local populations and were able to negotiate or avoid the administrative expectation that they would return to Sudan. Although substantial numbers of Sudanese had also 'self-settled' in Uganda on this occasion, the changed political panorama at the local level made this kind of spontaneous settlement more difficult to negotiate. This being the case, it may be that, in the absence of government authorization for the local integration of any 'residual' refugee caseload, remaining in Uganda may be less simple in the 2000s than it was in 1972.[48]

the local community, but they also served as a social space for refugees and members of the local community.' See Veney, C.R., *Forced Migration in Eastern Africa: Democratization, Structural Adjustment, and Refugees*, Basingstoke: Palgrave MacMillan, 2007, p. 129.

43 UNHCR, 'Somali Bantus gain Tanzanian citizenship in their ancestral land', 3 June 2009, available at: www.unhcr.org/4a28cd886.html, accessed 1 December 2014: 'At first the government of Tanzania, with assistance from UNHCR, hosted the Somali refugees in Mkuyu camp, also in Tanga region. In March 2003, more than 3,000 refugees were transferred from there to Chogo, a newly-constructed settlement some 80 kilometers away, in a move towards naturalizing the Somali Bantus who wished to stay.'

44 UNHCR, 'Thirty years on, UNHCR seeks full integration for Congolese refugees in Angola', 21 March 2006, available at: www.unhcr.org/442003384.html, accessed 10 November 2014: 'There is no problem for cultural integration', Kopel Musengele, the Congolese coordinator for the Community Centre for Refugee Integration, said at his office in Luanda, 'The problem is legal integration.'

45 Mattner, M., 'Development actors and protracted refugee situations: progress, challenges, opportunities', in Loescher, G. *et al.* (eds), *Protracted Refugee Situations: Political, Human Rights and Security Implications*, New York: United Nations University Press, 2008, p. 110.

46 UNHCR, 'Ivorian refugees find novel ways to survive and thrive in Liberia', 18 August 2005, available at: www.unhcr.org/43049ef71.html, accessed 10 November 2014.

47 Mattner, M., op. cit. note 45, p. 110.

48 Kaiser, T., 'Sudanese refugees in Uganda and Kenya', in Loescher, G. (*et al.*) (eds), *Protracted Refugee Situations: Political, Human Rights and Security Implications*, New York: United Nations University Press, 2008, pp. 268–9.

As time goes by, African countries are more and more reluctant about accepting refugees to mix and integrate with local people. And, in the end, the potential success of local integration as a durable solution is largely dependent on the willingness of host governments to pursue this.[49]

Two of the main reasons for host governments' resistance to refugee settlement among the host community are security problems and resource burdens. During the 1980s, many host governments in Sub-Saharan Africa mentioned the limited capacity of their national economies to absorb refugees as the primary reason for their opposition to local integration, although this has been revealed not to always be true, as attested by the case of Mozambicans in the Zambian area of Ukwimi.[50] Host governments in Sub-Saharan Africa could not be expected to carry the burden of refugees, and they proposed the creation of local settlement structures, spatially segregated sites, which could be supported by international donors as the optimal solution.[51] Heavy burdens are also borne by host villages on numerous accounts, such as the case of thousands of Southern Senegalese arriving into Gambia from Casamance between 2009 and 2011. This may be among the least well known of cases but not for this reason is it less difficult to bear. The difficulty of bearing such a burden was augmented by the existing local famine that made it very difficult for the people fleeing from Casamance to integrate.[52]

49 Agblorti, S.K.M., 'Refugee integration in Ghana: the host community's perspective', in UNHCR, *New Issues in Refugee Research*, research paper No. 203, 2011, p. 2.

50 Dowty, A. and Loescher, G., 'Refugee flows as grounds for international action', in *International Security*, vol. 21, 1996, p. 47, footnote 11: 'Refugees are not always a burden on their local hosts; they may make a positive contribution to the economy in the areas where they settle. Refugees are survivors and often arrive in their new countries with skills, education, work practices, and personal resourcefulness that can have a highly positive impact on economic growth. For example, the arrival of 20, 000 exiled Mozambicans in the sparsely populated Zambian area of Ukwimi in the late 1980s transformed the economic prospects for this region. Substantial international assistance was poured into the area, allowing roads, schools, health centers, and agricultural extension services to be established. All these facilities were available for use by both the Mozambicans and local Zambians. Unfortunately, these examples are often the exception rather than the norm, as current practice forces refugees to live in camps and to rely on the distribution of food and health supplies rather than encouraging them to contribute to their host's economies.'

51 Kibreab, G., 'Local settlements in Africa: a misconceived option?', in *Journal of Refugee Studies*, vol. 2, 1989, p. 473. In this regard, see also Agblorti, S.K.M., op. cit. note 49, p. 8, where the author, about the Ghanaian situation pointed out that: '[i]n a situation where the level of poverty is relatively high especially in the rural areas of Ghana, any diversion [. . .] of resources to cater for the integration of refugees would be unpopular among the host population. This is likely to be one of the reasons why the government continues to shy away from openly promoting the idea of local integration as a durable solution for refugees in Ghana, especially those from Liberia who currently constitute the majority of the refugee population in Ghana.'

52 Hopkins, G., 'Casamance refugees in The Gambia: self-settlement and the challenges of integration', in UNHCR, *New Issues in Refugee Research*, research paper No. 220, 2011, p. 7: 'The common factor in host villages receiving new arrivals is that hosts welcome the refugees and share food, give clothes as many refugees arrive with only clothes they wear, and provide space in the host home for refugees to live. This may be for a day or two until the refugee locates family elsewhere, or may be for years, as was the case with a substantial number of respondents.'

Since the 1990s, security questions have added a similarly powerful reason for resistance from host countries. Within the host community, initial sympathy and readiness to help refugees often turns into resentment when they are perceived to aggravate problems. These threats and the resulting resentment increase when refugee numbers continue to grow, or when new waves of refugees arrive. According to anecdotal evidence, many people in Guinea believe that the *de facto* integration of Liberian and Sierra Leonean refugees that was permitted is linked to the rise in criminal activity, delinquency and drug proliferation which has plagued Guinea in recent years.[53] Guinea had been experiencing rising poverty and the imposition of structural adjustment programmes when the refugee influx began,[54] although A. Fielden affirmed that the prospects for local integration of Liberian and Sierra Leonean refugees would be good due to cultural similarities and common local languages[55] and ethnicities which should encourage cooperation between refugees and the host community.[56] However, in 2000, 'rebel' Guinean groups launched surprise attacks against the country from Liberia and Sierra Leone. Invoking the constitutional obligation to guarantee 'territorial integrity',[57] L. Conte, the President of Guinea, ordered that Liberian and Sierra-Leonean refugees be quartered in secured areas. He then proceeded to deliver a speech inciting soldiers and civilians to harass Sierra Leoneans in the country in order to unmask the attackers.[58] In later years, however, the desire of Sierra Leoneans to remain grew because Guinea was then considered by the same refugees as '[a] country that offered us hospitality'.[59]

And, under the leadership of A. Gutierres, the UNHCR has recently begun to explore opportunities for local integration of refugees in areas such as West Africa, a solution that in that area had been either largely ignored or criticized

53 In this sense, Mr. Zoumanigui, delegate of the country at the United Nations recently pointed out that Guinea had received in these last decades a large number of refugees, whose presence had entailed bad consequences for, *inter alia*, the environment, security, the economy and society as a whole. Declaration in UNGA, Third Committee, Summary record of the 39th meeting, 8 March 2005, document No. A/C.3/59/SR. 39, p. 5.

54 Jacobsen, K., 'The forgotten solution: local integration for refugees in developing countries', op. cit. note 35, p. 11.

55 Language is also one of the elements allowing the Togolese refugees to be 'well-integrated' in the Ghanaian city of Aflao. See UNHCR, 'African Union team finds Togolese refugees well integrated in Ghana', 25 May 2005, available at: www.unhcr.org/4295ee544.html, accessed 2 December 2014.

56 Fielden, A., op. cit. note 1, p. 8.

57 In Guinea, Article 4 of the Constitution du 23 décembre 1990, révisée par le Décret D/2002/48/PRG/SGG du 15 mai 2002, promulguant la Loi constitutionnelle adoptée par référendum du 11 novembre 2001, stipulates: 'La loi punit quiconque, par un acte de discrimination raciale, ethnique ou religieuse ou par un acte de propagande régionaliste, porte une atteinte grave à l'unité nationale, à la sécurité de l'Etat, à l'intégrité du territoire de la République ou au fonctionnement démocratique des institutions'.

58 Viljoen, F., *International Human Rights Law in Africa*, Oxford/New York: Oxford University Press, 2007, p. 259.

59 UNHCR, 'When going home is not an option: local integration in Guinea', 20 July 2005, available at: www.unhcr.org/42de5cbf4.html, accessed 2 December 2014.

in the past decades.[60] And since 2007, the UNHCR has helped the integration of Liberian refugees in Guinea.[61]

The ExCom has clearly emphasized that there is no obligation to accord a solution by way of local integration, even for countries party to the relevant refugee instruments. Local integration is regarded by ExCom as:

> A sovereign decision and an option to be exercised by states guided by their treaty obligations and human rights principles, and that the provisions of this conclusion are for the guidance of States and UNHCR when local integration is to be considered.[62]

It is also true that it has proven difficult to secure funding for local integration projects in spite of the fact that in Sub-Saharan Africa there is evidence to suggest that very large numbers of refugees are 'self-settled', supporting themselves without international assistance and living among the local population,[63] such is the case of many Somalis in South Africa.[64]

Donors are usually not attracted by longer-term activities encompassing refugee integration, and making refugees less visible is neither politically nor psychologically satisfying to national or international organizations. Host states also hold that, by limiting the potential for local settlement and integration, there is a greater possibility to promote repatriation,[65] a solution that is often preferred by the host countries in Sub-Saharan Africa, countries which often cannot sustain such a heavy burden, granting hospitality to people to whom they cannot effectively assure any standard of a normal life.[66] Kenyan policy, with the recent waves of

60 Mattner, M., op. cit. note 45, p. 134.

61 UNHCR, 'UNHCR helps Guinea ease the local integration of Liberian refugees', 16 August 2007, available at: www.unhcr.org/46c474702.html, accessed 1 December 2014: 'In Guinea, the UN Refugee Agency is working with the newly established National Commission for the Integration and Monitoring of Refugees to find durable solutions for those who remained behind. They launched an information campaign aimed at sensitizing refugees, the local authorities and the general public to the aim and goals of integration programmes for Liberians. The campaign has started in the southern Guinea Forestière region, where UNHCR is encouraging some 9,000 of the Liberians to opt for local integration, while advocating tolerance from Guineans and helping build confidence between refugees and the local population. To date, nearly 600 refugees have expressed their firm intention to be integrated in Guinea.'

62 ExCom, conclusion No. 104 (LVI), 'Local integration', 2005, first paragraph of the preamble.

63 Crisp, J., 'The local integration and local settlement of refugees: a conceptual and historical analysis', op. cit. note 5, p. 6.

64 UNHCR, 'Somali refugee community takes lead in local integration in South Africa', 19 March 2008, available at: www.unhcr.org/47e124214.html, accessed 1 December 2014: 'Over the years, many Somali refugees in South Africa have achieved substantial independence and self-sufficiency without the assistance of the UN refugee agency. These skilled traders have relied on cultural and religious ties and networks, business savvy, determination and single-mindedness to establish businesses and ensure their communities function on clearly formulated lines.'

65 Fielden, A., op. cit. note 1, p. 3.

66 In this sense, see for instance the intervention of Mr. Kapona, Zambian delegate at the UN excluding any kind of solution but voluntary repatriation for Angolan and Rwandese refugees in the country. His intervention is in UNGA, Third Committee, Summary record of the 41st meeting,

Sudanese, refugees throughout the 2010s, constitutes a good example of prevention of integration by host communities in the country of asylum[67] and makes it clear that while local integration is a viable solution, and one that could be offered by some African host countries, it is not feasible in others,[68] with countries like Malawi that are currently requested by the UNHCR to seriously consider locally integrating their refugees.[69]

9.3 The present status of resettlement

Resettlement that should have a 'humanitarian foundation'[70] implicates the selection and relocation of refugees from a country where they have looked for protection to a third country which has granted them with a permanent residence status. The new status should ensure protection against rejection, allowing a resettled refugee and his/her family to have access to civil, cultural, economic, political and social rights similar to those granted to nationals, also conceding to the prospect of ultimately becoming a naturalized citizen of the country of resettlement.[71]

5 December 2005, document No. A/C.3/60/SR. 41. His predecessor, Mr. Mpundu, in 2003 stressed the fact that the possible absorption of refugees in Zambia could pose many kinds of concerns. His intervention in UNGA, Third Committee, Summary record of the 32 meeting, 14 November 2003, document No. A/C.3/58/SR. 32. This happens notwithstanding that the OAU Council recently commended '[t]hat Member States that continue to ensure that social and economic rights of refugees are respected in particular through innovative local integration initiatives such as the Zambia Initiative.' See Council of Ministers (Executive Council), Decision on the situation of refugees, returnees and displaced persons, Doc.Ex.Cl/177 (VII), Decision No. Ex.Cl/Dec. 197 (VII), 28 June–2 July 2005, paragraph 7. Many other African delegates in the last years are on the same line as the Zambians. See, for instance, the speech held by Ms. Mohamed, Kenyan delegate at the UN who envisaged repatriation as the only viable solution for the plight of refugees that torments her country. Her intervention in UNGA, Third Committee, Summary record of the 33rd meeting, 7 November 2003, document No. A/C.3/58/SR. 33.

67 Kaiser, T., 'Sudanese refugees in Uganda and Kenya', op. cit. note 48, p. 257. In this regard, at idem, the author clarified: 'All refugees are restricted in camps, where they live in very difficult conditions and where hostile relations with the local host population are virtually guaranteed by the structural relationship they find themselves in. Regular round-ups take place of any refugees, only a small minority of whom is Sudanese, who have managed to slip through the net and remain in Nairobi.'

68 McBride, M., 'Anatomy of a resolution: the General Assembly in UNHCR history', in *UNHCR, New Issues in Refugee Research*, research paper No. 182, 2009, p. 35.

69 UN, 'UN thanks Malawi for hosting over 18,500 refugees and asylum seekers', 18 June 2014: 'We appeal to Malawi to consider providing local integration as a durable solution to some of these refugees who have been resident in this country for over ten years without a foreseeable lasting solution to their plight.' This document is available at: www.mw.one.un.org/un-commends-malawi-for-hosting-over-18500-refugees-and-asylum-seekers/, accessed 10 November 2014.

70 UNHCR, Progress Report on Resettlement, 6 June 2014, EC/65/SC/CRP.11, p. 7, available at: www.refworld.org/docid/543bba8a4.html, accessed 9 December 2014: 'UNHCR will continue to advocate for States to avoid restrictive selection criteria and to receive refugees recognized under UNHCR's mandate.'

71 UNHCR, Resettlement Handbook (revised edn July 2011), Geneva: UNHCR, 2011, p. 9. In this regard, see also UNGA, Assistance to refugees, returnees and displaced persons in Africa, 20 December 2012, resolution No. A/RES/67/150, paragraph 24: '[The UNGA] appeals to

Historically, resettlement has been contemplated for two main purposes: either because the first country of destination of an asylum-seeker/refugee is not able to provide protection, or because he/she wishes to settle in a different country that is not the first country of arrival.[72] It may also be promoted when it is evident that the individual refugee will likely not be able to return home in the future, is unable to integrate locally, or he/she has the opportunity for protection and integration elsewhere. As the motivation to resettle in this case is not based on a threat to the refugee's physical security, or a compelling protection claim, resettlement is considered after an assessment is made of the availability of space, the likelihood of acceptance, and the processing capacity of all parties involved.[73]

On several occasions, African regional authorities have formally encouraged resettlement as a durable solution, often through the help of international donors.[74] In this region, where M. Bedjaoui suggested that resettlement was, at least initially, mainly conceived for urban refugee students and/or intellectuals,[75] resettlement in a third country is often confused with 'reintegration', which is the process by which African refugees return to their own country and try to be re-integrated (or 'resettled') by local authorities along with the aid of sub-regional, regional or world organizations.[76] This confusion is sometimes also fed by national legislations, such as in Liberia, where the legislation on refugees provides for the existence of

the international community to respond positively, in the spirit of solidarity and burden- and responsibility-sharing, to the third-country resettlement needs of African refugees, notes in this regard the importance of using resettlement strategically, as part of situation-specific comprehensive responses to refugee situations, and to this end encourages States, the Office of the High Commissioner and other relevant partners to make full use of the Multilateral Framework of Understandings on Resettlement, where appropriate and feasible.'

72 Hathaway, J.C., *The Rights of Refugees Under International Law*, op. cit. note 5, p. 963.

73 UNHCR, 'Resettlement: an instrument of protection and a durable solution', in *International Journal of Refugee Law*, vol. 9, 1997, p. 670.

74 For instance, '[The Assembly of Heads of State and Government of the Organization of African Unity]: 2) appeals to the International donor community to development and aid-granting agencies, to the non-governmental organizations having refugee programs in Africa, to potential donors from friendly countries and organizations, to give serious consideration to the urgent needs of African countries of origin and asylum, to contribute generously to humanitarian, relief, rehabilitation and resettlement programs [. . .].' See African Union, Assembly of Heads of State and government, Second International Conference on Assistance to Refugees in Africa (ICARA II), resolution No. AHG/Res.114 (XIX), 6–12 June 1983, paragraph 2.

75 Bedjaoui, M., *L'Asile en Afrique*, Nairobi: All Africa Conference of Churches, 1979, p. 49. In this regard, G. Okoth-Obbo clarified: '[E]specially with respect to education, the Bureau was to record some notable successes in placing refugees in other African countries.' See Okoth-Obbo, G., 'Thirty years on: a legal review of the 1969 OAU Refugee Convention Governing the Specific Aspects of Refugee Problems in Africa', in *Refugee Survey Quarterly*, vol. 20, 2001, p. 93.

76 For instance, see JRS dispatch No. 115, 31 August 2004 entitled: 'Angola: lack of funds undermines resettlement process' where the word 'resettlement' clearly defines a re-integration process. Earlier, for the same country and the same meaning of the word 'resettlement': JRS dispatch No. 138, 9 September 2003: 'Return and resettlement in Angola'. At the institutional level, see African Union, Council of Ministers (Executive Council), Decision on the situation in the Democratic Republic of Congo, Decision No. CM/Dec.12 (LXXIV), 5–8 July 2001, paragraph 7: '[The Council] welcomes the adoption by the Political Committee, of the plans for disarmament, demobilization, reintegration, repatriation and resettlement of the armed

several organs in charge of 'resettlement', though reintegration is clearly the intended meaning.[77]

Resettlement in a third country generally serves three equally important functions: first, it is a tool to provide international protection and meet the special needs of individual refugees whose health, liberty, safety, life or other fundamental rights are at risk in the country where they have sought refuge.[78] In this sense, since 2000 and thanks to the effort made by the UNHCR to simplify the entire procedure, resettlement clearly has grown into a protection instrument identifying groups of individuals necessitating it as a lasting solution.[79]

In addition, resettlement constitutes today a durable solution for larger numbers or groups of refugees, alongside the other durable solutions of local integration and voluntary repatriation. Third, it represents a concrete expression of international solidarity and a responsibility-sharing mechanism, allowing countries to help share each other's burdens, and reduce problems impacting the country of first asylum.[80]

Among the durable solutions, resettlement in a third country is commonly indicated as the 'least preferred option' in Sub-Saharan Africa. This happens although a number of countries have also at times expressly accepted responsibility, such as the country of first admission, to accept a portion of asylum-seekers for local integration, provided that other countries, generally non-African albeit with some exceptions, could lighten the burden by offering appropriate resettlement opportunities.[81]

In this sense, Burkina Faso, in spite of its fragile economic situation, several years ago accepted resettlement of refugees on its territory and has considered this responsibility as part of burden-sharing in the framework of inter-African solidarity, seen as a supreme value in dealing with refugee issues on the continent.[82]

groups, and for the orderly withdrawal of all foreign forces from the DRC.' In Africa, but not exclusively in this continent, a third meaning of the word 'resettlement' refers to the internally displaced persons (IDPs), who are not the main object of this study. For a typical example in Sub-Saharan Africa, see Gebre, Y.D., 'Contextual determination of migration behaviors: the Ethiopian resettlement in light of conceptual constructs', in *Journal of Refugee Studies*, vol. 15, 2002, pp. 265–82. At p. 267 the author clearly explained his meaning of the word 'resettlement': 'During the mid-1980s the Ethiopian government relocated about 600, 000 people from drought-affected and over-populated regions of the country to different resettlement sites [. . .] located in north-western, western, and south-western parts of the country.'

77 Section 4 of the 1994 Liberian Refugee Act is dedicated to the 'Establishment of Liberia refugee, repatriation and resettlement commission'.

78 UNHCR, Global Consultations on international protection/third track: strengthening and expanding resettlement today: dilemmas, challenges and opportunities, 25 April 2002, document No. EC/GC/02/07, p. 1.

79 Nakashiba, H., 'Clarifying UNHCR resettlement: a few considerations from a legal perspective', in UNHCR, *New Issues in Refugee Research*, research paper No. 264, 2013, p. 3.

80 UNHCR, Global Consultations on international protection/third track: strengthening and expanding resettlement today: dilemmas, challenges and opportunities, 25 April 2002, document No. EC/GC/02/07, p. 1.

81 Goodwin-Gill, G. and McAdam J., op. cit. note 32, pp. 498–9. In this regard, UNHCR clearly affirmed that: '[R]esettlement benefits a small number of refugees; in 2010, only one per cent of the world's refugees directly benefited from resettlement.' See UNHCR, *60 Years and Still Counting: UNHCR Global Trends 2010*, Geneva: UNHCR, 2011, p. 17.

Benin, in order to strengthen international solidarity in search of durable solutions, has even signed an agreement with the UNHCR to set up a project for the resettlement of refugees on its territory.[83] From 1998 to 2003, approximately 130 refugees resettled in Benin, while in the same period 75 were resettled in Burkina Faso. According to the independent evaluation commissioned by the UNHCR, however, these resettlements resulted in failure: by March 2005, only 39 out of the 75 refugees remained in Burkina Faso and those who remained lived in an extreme condition of poverty.[84]

Considering the problem from the point of view of 'sender countries', the resettlement programme for Kenya was probably the largest in Sub-Saharan Africa. Between 1991 and 1998, almost 35,000 refugees were resettled to third countries from Kenya, with more refugees resettled from Kenya in 2000 than from any other African country. The slow pace of resettlement to third countries, however, has undermined the principle of burden-sharing, compelling Kenyan authorities to express concern over the burden involved in the protracted stay of refugees.[85]

9.4 The two forms of resettlement mentioned in the 1951 Geneva Convention and how they have been applied

In the 1951 Geneva Convention we can find two forms of resettlement denoted by Article 30 ('Transfer of assets')[86] and Article 31 2) ('Refugees unlawfully in the country of refuge').[87]

82 Burkinabe authorities stressed the fact that their country: '[g]rants priority to refugees of African origin and gives privilege to the physical and juridical protection of candidates' even if '[r]esettlement must not harm the interests of the country.' See UNHCR, Resettlement Handbook (revised September 2007), 1 November 2004, p. BKF/1.

83 UNHCR, Resettlement Handbook (revised September 2007), 1 November 2004, p. BEN/1. In Benin the admissibility for resettlement is determined on a legal and humanitarian basis by a Selection Committee. The Committee must ascertain that resettlement is the most appropriate solution for the candidate. See ibid., p. BEN/3.

84 Sandvik, K.B., 'A legal history: the emergence of the African resettlement candidate in international refugee management', in *International Journal of Refugee Law*, vol. 22, 2010, p. 39.

85 Kagwanja, P. and Juma, M., 'Somali refugees: protracted exile and shifting security frontiers', in Loescher, G. (*et al.*) (eds), *Protracted Refugee Situations: Political, Human Rights and Security Implications*, New York: United Nations University Press, 2008, p. 228. The authors took as an example the 3,000 Somali Benadir and the 12,000 Somali Bantu resettled in America in the early 2000s.

86 Article 30 of the 1951 Geneva Convention reads: '1) A Contracting State shall, in conformity with its laws and regulations, permit refugees to transfer assets which they have brought into its territory, to another country where they have been admitted for the purposes of resettlement. 2) A Contracting State shall give sympathetic consideration to the application of refugees for permission to transfer assets wherever they may be and which are necessary for their resettlement in another country to which they have been admitted.' Article 30 is entirely reproduced in the Namibian legislation (Article 30 of the Schedule of the Namibia Refugees (Recognition and Control) Act, 19 March 1999) as part of the 1951 Geneva Convention to be applied in the country.

87 Article 31 2) of the 1951 Geneva Convention reads: '2) The Contracting States shall not apply to the movements of such refugees [refugees coming directly from a territory where their life or

The importance of Article 30 in the case of resettlement of refugees is in the fact that it:

> [p]urports to regulate two types of transfers. The first is the transfer of those assets into the country of resettlement which the refugee has possessed before his/her arrival to, and independently from his/her sojourn in, the country which is to permit the transfer. This is the subject of paragraph 1. The second type of transfer relates to two types of assets [. . .] One subset of these assets is constituted by possessions which were acquired already in the country of first asylum while enjoying protection there and before resettlement occurs [. . .] The other subset comprises assets of the refugee located in other contracting states, irrespective of the moment and way of their acquisition.[88]

In addition, Article 31 2) can be considered in this section of the work because:

> Where contracting parties chose not to regularize such a refugee after recognition [provided for in Article 31 1)], they remain bound to offer the refugee the time and facilities needed to seek admission to other states.[89]

The rationale for Article 30, framed in mandatory terms in the interest of refugees, was to make clear that general rules must be applied to refugees, with the use of discretion. N. Robinson affirmed that the right of states parties to invoke their laws and regulations:

> do[es] not free a Contracting State from its obligation to permit the transfer of assets [. . .] even if it generally prohibits transfers in favor of other aliens or nationals, since the obligation is of a categorical nature: these words were inserted to regulate the manner of the transfer. In other words, the words ['in conformity with its laws and regulations'] require a refugee to obtain a license if such a document is required; they may in certain cases militate against total transfer at once if amounts of such magnitude cannot generally be exported in one lump sum; the transfer in certain currency may be subject to restrictions or can be made only through the intermediary of a certain agency or a payment union, if this is a general rule, etc. A state, however, cannot refuse to permit the transfer if all such formalities are complied with, on the grounds of lack of exchange or that other aliens or their own nationals do not enjoy the right of transfer.[90]

freedom was threatened] restrictions other than those which are necessary and such restrictions shall only be applied until their status in the country is regularized or they obtain admission into another country. The Contracting States shall allow such refugees a reasonable period and all the necessary facilities to obtain admission into another country.'

88 Nagy, B., 'Article 30', in Zimmermann, A. (ed.), *The 1951 Convention Relating to the Status of Refugees and its 1967 Protocol: A Commentary*, Oxford: Oxford University Press, 2011, pp. 1228–9.

89 Noll G., 'Article 31', in Zimmermann, A. (ed.), *The 1951 Convention Relating to the Status of Refugees and its 1967 Protocol: A Commentary*, Oxford: Oxford University Press, 2011, p. 1246.

90 Robinson, N., *Convention Relating to the Status of Refugees: Its History, Contents and Interpretation. A Commentary*, New York: Institute of Jewish Affairs, 1953, pp. 149–50.

J.C. Hathaway deemed this interpretation as inattentive to the reasons for amending Article 30 to include the provision on 'laws and regulations'. More specifically, a real worry was expressed that it would be too much to require refugees to exclusively abide by export 'formalities', because this could mean that the export of assets by a refugee could be undertaken with no substantive limits.[91] On this point, P. Weis has explicitly contended that the expression contained in Article 30 1) 'in conformity with its laws and regulations' does not mean that the application of those laws and regulations will conflict with the obligation contained in the same paragraph. Laws and regulations will therefore need to be applied in order to make the transfer feasible, although there could be several restraints including, for instance, that the transfer would occur in instalments or not in hard currency.[92]

Therefore, host governments are not legally prevented from applying substantive requirements on the export of refugees' assets but because it would conflict with the essential foundation of Article 30 of the 1951 Geneva Convention simply to apply all general rules with full intensity, state parties are legally bound to interpret and apply their general rules in a way facilitating the transfer of assets for resettling refugees.[93]

Sierra Leone is the only country on the continent that endorses the vision of the 1951 Geneva Convention by stipulating in its 2007 legislation:

> State authorities shall, in conformity with the laws of Sierra Leone, permit a refugee to transfer assets he/she has brought into Sierra Leone, to another country where he/she has been admitted for the purpose of resettlement.[94]

The drafters of the 1951 Geneva Convention also broadened the scope of Article 30 in a way, having the addition of paragraph 2 as a consequence. France, in particular, strove to conceive the 1951 Refugee Convention as an instrument to promote the right of refugees to transfer the assets held not only in the country from which resettlement is being carried out, but also held in any state party to the convention.[95]

Two important qualifications should be noted with regard to Article 30 as a whole: the proviso contained in the article does not imply establishing any general right of refugees to export their assets;[96] Article 30 can under no circumstance be

91 Hathaway, J.C., *The Rights of Refugees Under International Law*, op. cit. note 5, p. 969.

92 Weis, P., *The Refugee Convention, 1951/The travaux préparatoires analyzed, Cambridge International Document Series*, vol. 7, Cambridge/New York: Cambridge University Press, 1995, p. 277.

93 In this regard, A. Grahl-Madsen contended: 'Even [though] it was agreed to soften the original phraseology, it was clearly not the intention of the drafters to weaken the provision so much that it would make transfer of the assets concerned wholly subject to the discretion of the authorities.' See Grahl-Madsen, A., *Commentary on the Refugee Convention 1951: Articles 2–11, 13–37*, op. cit. note 10, p. 165.

94 Section 25 2) of the 2007 Refugees Protection Act of Sierra Leone.

95 Hathaway, J.C., *The Rights of Refugees Under International Law*, op. cit. note 5, p. 971.

96 In this regard, for instance, N. Robinson contended: 'It imposes an obligation upon contracting states to permit the transfer of assets of refugees, provided these assets have been brought in by

relied upon to justify granting that refugees' rights are inferior to those of other non-citizens.[97]

Finally, two different categories of obligations under Article 30 can also be identified. First, whatever assets a refugee has brought into the state where he/she presently lives should, in principle, be completely available for export by the refugee to his/her resettlement country. While the host state may apply its currency control and comparable regulations, it is bound to interpret those rules in the spirit of encouraging the presumed entitlement of a refugee to take whatever assets he/she had brought into it, out of the country of asylum. In this regard A. Grahl-Madsen concluded that:

> [T]he underlying idea is that a state shall be neither richer nor poorer as a result of the fact that a refugee has spent a transitory period in the country until he/she found a possibility for resettlement in another country.[98]

Second, whatever assets a refugee acquired in the original host state as well as assets held in other states parties, should also be made available for export to the resettlement state. However, the obligation of states parties concerning the export of these assets constitutes merely one of procedure. Although the 1951 Geneva Convention does not entail that governments should apply their domestic norms less strictly in the event that refugees resettle,[99] considering the ease with which a refugee may export his/her assets, in no case may a refugee be treated worse than other foreigners.[100]

the refugee and the transfer is made to another country where he/she has been admitted for resettlement. Thus no obligation exists in cases where the refugee leaves the country of his/her residence for a temporary stay abroad.' See Robinson, N., op. cit. note 90, p. 149, while A. Grahl-Madsen added: 'The Contracting States are not obliged to permit transfers of assets to any country of the refugee's choice, but merely to a country where the refugee concerned has been admitted for the purpose of resettlement.' See Grahl-Madsen, A., *Commentary on the Refugee Convention 1951: Articles 2–11, 13–37*, op. cit. note 10, p. 166.

97 In this regard, A. Grahl Madsen contended: 'Article 30 must be read in conjunction with article 7, paragraph 1. Should the regime establish for refugees by virtue of article 30 in any set of circumstances not correspond to the same treatment as is accorded to aliens generally, [the refugee] may invoke the provisions set forth in article 7, paragraph 1.' We note that Article 7 of the 1951 Geneva Convention deals with 'Exemption from reciprocity' and its paragraph 1 stipulates: '1) Except where this Convention contains more favorable provisions, a Contracting State shall accord to refugees the same treatment as is accorded to aliens generally.' See Grahl-Madsen, A., *Commentary on the Refugee Convention 1951: Articles 2–11, 13–37*, op. cit. note 10, p. 164.

98 Ibid., p. 166.

99 In at least one conclusion, the ExCom seems to have failed to make this distinction. In the framework of its leading statement of the duties which follow in the event of mass-influx of refugees, the ExCom opined that: '[a]sylum seekers who have been temporarily admitted pending arrangements for a durable solution standard [. . .] o) they should be permitted to transfer assets which they have brought into a territory to the country where the durable solution is obtained.' See ExCom, conclusion No. 22 (XXXII), 'Protection of asylum-seekers in situations of large-scale influx', 1981, paragraph II, sub-paragraph B, number 2 o).

100 Hathaway, J.C., *The Rights of Refugees Under International Law*, op. cit. note 5, p. 974.

By virtue of the obligation contained in Article 31 2), a refugee is legally entitled to an opportunity to come up with his/her own resettlement solution before being required to accept the government's option. More specifically, the refugee may insist upon a delay in his/her removal to enable him/her to pursue alternative resettlement options. Faced with this request, the host government must suspend pursuit of its own plan for a reasonable period, meaning the period required to obtain a visa by a refugee making reasonable efforts to obtain it, perhaps in this action helped by voluntary organizations or the UNHCR.[101] As affirmed by N. Robinson, the definition of 'reasonable period' must take into account all existing circumstances, including the time required to process a resettlement application for a person without a nationality and possessing given qualifications.[102]

In addition, the host country must ensure that the refugee has access to 'all the necessary facilities to obtain admission to another country'.[103] As a consequence, the refugee must not be constrained in his/her movement, and must be able to visit consulates of foreign countries, NGOs and/or UNHCR representatives.[104] When consulted, the UNHCR is committed to exploring regional solutions provided that the standards for refugee protection are maintained. Regional resettlement opportunities are, *a priori*, cheaper, and a concerted regional approach, wherever possible, will minimize the risk of creating poles of attraction for irregular movements, which are an impediment to refugee protection and assistance.

As the UNHCR noted, however, in Sub-Saharan Africa important refugee movements have already exacerbated economic and social problems. This situation undermines the abilities of local authorities to accept additional responsibilities such as protecting and integrating resettled refugees. In addition, an unstable security situation compromises the durability and quality of the protection that resettled refugees need.[105]

While not ruling out the possibility of keeping the refugee in provisional detention, the obligation provided in Article 31 2) of the 1951 Geneva Convention excludes confinement in a camp or even in remote locations, requiring the host country to allow the refugee to travel and to communicate with foreign interlocutors in order to be assisted in obtaining admission in a new country.[106]

Thus, the operation of a legal resettlement system presents two important criteria. The first one consists in the requirements of Article 31 2) that may prevent an effective development of the system in place. In effect, if the refugees to be removed are not restricted in their movements or even detained when they are

101 Weis, P., *The Refugee Convention, 1951/The travaux préparatoires analyzed*, op. cit. note 92, p. 304.

102 Robinson, N., op. cit. note 90, p. 155.

103 Article 31 2) of the 1951 Geneva Convention.

104 Weis, P., *The Refugee Convention, 1951/The travaux préparatoires analyzed*, op. cit. note 92, p. 304.

105 UNHCR, 'Resettlement: an instrument of protection and a durable solution', op. cit. note 73, p. 671.

106 Robinson, N., op. cit. note 90, p. 155.

under the authority of the country of destination, they must have the possibility to pursue their resettlement options. The second criterion consists in the quite meagre range of opportunities for these efforts and it finishes when lawful presence is established. At this point, the strict limitations on expulsion present in Article 32 of the 1951 Geneva Convention take over and most of the time do not allow enforced resettlement.[107]

Apart from the special steps required by Article 31 2) when a refugee's freedom of movement has been restrained, the country from which resettlement is considered is not generally compelled to take affirmative steps to assist him/her to secure a resettlement offer. In addition, in line with the drafters' commitment to preserving the sovereign right of states to choose which refugees should permanently be admitted to their territories, no state is obliged to extend an offer of resettlement to any refugee.[108] As seen above, the willingness of the country of resettlement evidently constitutes the 'decisive factor' as to whether or not a refugee can be resettled in its territory.[109] Along these lines, Mozambican legislation prevents forcing a candidate for asylum to look for asylum in another country[110] whereas, other African governments have facilitated the resettlement of refugees in third countries in the past, for instance by contributing towards paying the refugees' travel expenses.[111]

9.5 Final reflections on the institution of resettlement

In both political and practical terms, the importance of resettlement as a solution for refugees in Sub-Saharan Africa declined during the 1980s and 1990s. As recently as the late 1970s, resettlement was still highly valued by the international community. It was endorsed by the ExCom as the logical alternative solution when local integration of refugees was not possible.[112] At that point, the ExCom had

107 Hathaway, J.C., *The Rights of Refugees Under International Law*, op. cit. note 5, p. 966. In its footnote 216 the author explained that '[l]awful presence [. . .] is a status that is usually quickly acquired. Lawful presence includes authorized temporary presence; presence while undergoing refugee status assessment, including the exhaustion of appeals and reviews; and presence in a state party to the Convention which has opted either not to establish a procedure to verify refugee status, or to suspend the operation of such a procedure.'

108 Ibid., pp. 966–7.

109 Melander, G., 'Refugees with no country of asylum: strategies for third country resettlement', in Rogge, J.R. (ed.), *Refugees: A Third World Dilemma*, Totowa, NJ: Rowman and Littlefield, 1987, p. 40.

110 Article 15 of the 1991 Mozambique Refugee Act clearly reads: 'It shall be unlawful to send a candidate for the right of asylum to any country before a final ruling has been made on the petition for asylum.'

111 Declaration made by Mrs. Mbairo, delegate from Central African Republic at the UN, in 1981, UNGA, Third Committee, Summary record of the 55th meeting, 18 November 1981, document No. A/C.3/36/SR.55.

112 In the conclusion No. 2 (XXVII), 'Functioning of the Sub-Committee and general', 1976, at paragraph h, number ii) the ExCom: '[a]ppealed to states [. . .] to offer resettlement opportunities to those who had been unable to obtain permanent residence in the state of first-asylum.'

to coordinate efforts made by African countries to aid resettlement when the OAU created the Bureau for the Placement and Education of African Refugees (BPEAR)[113] in 1968 and renamed it the 'Bureau for Refugees, Displaced Persons and Humanitarian Assistance' in the early 1990s, although, in practice, its operations have not changed in spite of the change of nomenclature.[114] This organization, which establishes requests for resettlement and offers made by African states, has achieved several significant results. An example of these results consists in the promotion of the resettlement of refugees in some African countries that could help them to gain economic independence,[115] although the bureau has rarely mentioned the concept of 'resettlement' in its activities and it has not been clear until now if, by 'resettlement', the bureau meant all the time 'resettlement in a third country' or, rather, 'reintegration'.[116] In addition, for African states, the BPEAR was

113 The BPEAR, established by the OAU in 1968, following a resolution of the 1967 OAU Conference on the legal, economic and social aspects of the refugee crisis in Africa, is intended, among other aspects, to seek educational and economic opportunities for refugees in host countries, act as an information conduit for member countries and the international community, help asylum-seekers cope better with their present situation and eventual voluntary repatriation, and to work with the UNHCR, voluntary agencies, and member states pursuing the objectives established in the 1969 OAU Convention. Surprisingly, when the convention was promulgated in 1969, it made no mention of the BPEAR, either with respect to its role in education and training, or in relation to the protection of refugees. This is so in spite of the fact that item iv) of the Bureau's mandate refers to mediation between member states and the collection of reports on their activities regarding the refugee situation in their countries. For a broader commentary on the genesis and activities of the Bureau, see, for instance, Oloka-Onyango, J., 'The place and the role of the OAU Bureau for refugees in the African refugee crisis', in *International Journal of Refugee Law*, vol. 6, 1994, pp. 34–52. In this regard, see also Lawyers' Committee for Human Rights, *African Exodus: Refugee Crisis, Human Rights and the 1969 OAU Convention*, New York: Lawyers' Committee for Human Rights Editions, 1995, especially Chapter VII of their study where, at p. 164, the authors highlighted the fact that, about resettlement, the bureau should '[e]nsure that refugees do not suffer abuse and discrimination, and should also endeavor to publicize the rights of refugees to member states.'

114 Sharpe, M., 'Engaging with refugee protection? The Organization of African Unity and African Union since 1963', in *UNHCR, New Issues in Refugee Research*, research paper No. 226, 2011, p. 20.

115 Bedjaoui, M., op. cit. note 75, p. 50.

116 For instance, in the first time that it referred to the concept: '[The Council of Ministers of the Organization of African Unity]: requests the General Secretariat to convene as soon as possible a meeting of the Committee on Refugees established in 1964 to consider the current situation of refugees in Africa and the necessary measures to be taken with a view to their assistance and voluntary repatriation and their resettlement.' See OAU, Council of Ministers, resolution on the Bureau for the placement and education of African refugees, resolution No. CM/Res. 266 (XIX), 5–12 June 1972, paragraph 1. To show the fluidity of the expressions used, in another circumstance the Council clearly meant resettlement as 'local integration'. See Council of Ministers, Results of the International Conference on Assistance to Refugees in Africa, resolution, No. CM/Res. 916 (XXXVIII), 22–28 February 1982, paragraph 8: '[The Council of Ministers of the Organization of African Unity] calls on all African Governments to consider refugee situations so as to ensure through appropriate policies measures and the creation of the necessary conditions for the voluntary repatriation of Refugees to their countries of origin or their resettlement in the countries of asylum rehabilitation such that the prevailing situations are brought under control.'

intended to be a vehicle for generating spaces in the educational systems, while the OAU's objective was to resettle 'freedom fighters'. In contrast, the UNHCR saw the BPEAR as an opportunity to deal with difficult refugee situations without compromising its mission on the continent.[117]

But since the late 1980s and during the entire 1990s, the institution of resettlement in Africa has been deemed by the ExCom as only a secondary option, viable exclusively 'as a last resort when neither voluntary repatriation nor local integration is possible'.[118] More specifically, resettlement started out as an appropriate solution principally for '[i]ndividual refugees with special protection needs, including women at risk, minors, adolescents, elderly refugees, and survivors of torture'.[119] This situation also became known because there was no published research or data testing the real effectiveness of repatriations, perceived at that time as a social and spatial phenomenon, insufficiently understood.[120]

The Beninese policy of resettlement was conducted according to this aforementioned line of thinking. Authorities in Porto Novo and Cotonou[121] tended to favour resettlement for given categories of refugees and above all for those who could not be locally integrated. Therefore, it was quite clear that, for Beninese authorities, and in spite of what is stated in the 1951 Geneva Convention, resettlement is clearly subordinate to local integration and voluntary repatriation.[122] Even clearer is the position of the local authorities in Ouagadougou who extended the possibility of resettling refugees when they can be categorized as a 'refugee with no other durable solution'.[123]

117 Sandvik, K.B., op. cit. note 84, p. 37.

118 ExCom, conclusion No. 67 (XLII), 'Resettlement as an instrument of protection', 1991, paragraph g). See also what A. Aleinikoff contended in this regard: '[Starting with the 1980s] shrinking hope of resettlement combined with these theoretical considerations, have produced a fundamental rethinking of "solutions" to the refugee problem, with voluntary repatriation now considered the preferred durable solution.' See Aleinikoff, T.A., 'State-centered refugee law: from resettlement to containment', in *Michigan Journal of International Law*, vol. 14, 1992, p. 127. In this regard, see also IRIN, 'Refugees: resettlement still a last resort', 1 August 2012, available at: www.irinnews.org/report/95996/refugees-resettlement-still-a-last-resort, accessed 1 December 2014.

119 ExCom, conclusion No. 85 (XLIX), 'General conclusion on international protection', 1998, paragraph j). The same secondary role attributed to resettlement can also be found in other conclusions, as for instance, conclusion No. 67 (XLII), 'Resettlement as an instrument of protection', 1991; conclusion No. 71 (XLIV), 'General conclusion on international protection', 1993; conclusion No. 81 (XLVIII), 'General conclusion on international protection', 1997 where, at paragraph q) we may read: '[The ExCom] affirms that voluntary repatriation of refugees is the most preferred solution, when feasible; and calls upon countries of origin, countries of asylum, UNHCR, and the international community to take all necessary measures to enable refugees to exercise freely their right to return to their homes in safety and dignity.'

120 Chimni, B.S., 'From resettlement to involuntary repatriation: towards a critical history of durable solutions to refugee problems', in *Refugee Survey Quarterly*, vol. 23, 2004, p. 4.

121 As far as Porto Novo is the official capital of the country, Cotonou is the seat of the government.

122 UNHCR, Resettlement Handbook (revised September 2007), 1 November 2004, p. BEN/2.

123 Ibid., p. BKF/2. In addition, to stress how the resettlement is not really considered as the best option for the Burkinabe authorities, we note that 'no recourse is possible should a case be rejected.' See ibid., p. BFK/3.

The only clear example of national legislation in Sub-Saharan Africa dealing with resettlement seems to go in the direction of independent refugee protection if he/she will be allowed to finally settle in the country. Article 36 2) of the 1998 Tanzanian Refugee Act clearly reads:

> A refugee outside Tanzania may before entering Tanzania [. . .] apply to the Minister [responsible for refugee matters] for resettlement into Tanzania and *it is hereby prohibited that he/she shall not be allowed to enter Tanzania until his/her resettlement into Tanzania has been granted*,[124] the disobedience of which shall be an offence under this Act.[125]

J. Fredriksson noted, however, that the growing determination of states to manage refugee movement, and in particular to harmonize refugee protection with more general migration goals, may present a good opportunity for reinventing resettlement as a practicable option for many refugees living in the African continent:

> The time is ripe to discard the notion that there is a hierarchy of durable solutions, dubbing some as 'preferred' and others as 'undesirable'. Developing a clear policy on the intrinsic link between resettlement and the need for durable solutions will result in operational guidelines and criteria for this type of resettlement activity, which are now virtually absent from the UNHCR Resettlement Handbook. A reinvigorated debate about the role of resettlement for durable solution purposes is also timely in many states.[126]

One can hope that a renewed debate about the viability of a strong commitment to engage in refugee resettlement will provide us with the opportunity to return to the fundamental questions, the most important of which is whether this solution, openly envisaged by the 1951 Geneva Convention and in no sense treated as inferior to other options, may prove to be a vital means of ensuring the human dignity of refugees themselves. In this regard, the following affirmation, with its related final question, reflects the doubts about the situation in Sub-Saharan Africa:

> [As the] 'solution' pendulum swung from resettlement to repatriation, to the extent that policy documents began to refer to repatriation as the 'happiest' of durable solutions while resettlement was the 'least desirable' [, t]he question

124 Emphasis added.

125 In this regard, K. Kamanga noted: '[The Tanzanian Refugee Act] has confined itself to acknowledging only the [. . .] two known durable solutions: [. . .] repatriation and resettlement.' Resettlement as a third country in Tanzania is fully conceived, although practically not really applied. See Kamanga, K., 'The (Tanzania) Refugees Act of 1998: some legal and policy implications', in *Journal of Refugee Studies*, vol. 18, 2005, p. 108.

126 Fredriksson, J., 'Reinvigorating resettlement: changing realities demand changed approaches', in *Forced Migration Review*, vol. 13, 2002, p. 29.

remains: in whose eyes was it the 'happiest' solution – refugees, individual states or the international community, including UNHCR?'[127]

While several authors think that resettlement remains the least desirable solution for the refugees themselves,[128] in present-day Sub-Saharan Africa with its generally disastrous economies, lack of infrastructures, political instability and social tensions, the response to the question posed immediately above cannot be difficult to answer, and goes in the opposite direction to the above-mentioned idea, that resettlement remains the least desirable solution for the refugees themselves. The affirmation that every durable solution enhancing the life-situation of a refugee is well accepted by him/her can be questioned on a number of levels. The main problem is linked to the fact that the formulas used at the institutional level about the preference for this or that durable solution are often very vague. Take, for example: 'As repatriation was the preferred durable solution to the refugee problem [. . .].'[129] Nevertheless, it is true that of the three durable solutions, being voluntary repatriation, local settlement and third country resettlement, it is mainly the first two that seem to constitute rational options for the majority of African refugees. In this case, the governments are the ones ultimately deciding the destiny of refugees, reducing the three alternatives to political solutions, which can also be used as a domestic instrument to gain popular support for a political agenda.[130]

In a utopian vision, C. Mwalimu supported the idea of the African national state with a unique African citizenship that would be considered the permanent

127 Idem.

128 In this regard, R.L. Bach noted: 'Yet, third country resettlement is considered by most international agencies and observers, if not by the refugees themselves, to be the least desirable solution. The further the refugees are moved, the less likely they are ever to return home. And to return home is the cherished goal.' See Bach, R.L., 'Third country resettlement', in Loescher, G. and Monahan, L. (eds), *Refugees and International Relations*, New York: Oxford University Press, 1989, p. 313.

129 Declaration by Mr. Adenyake, Nigerian delegate at the UN in UNGA, Third Committee, Summary record of the 38th meeting, 29 November 2005, document No. A/C.3/60/SR.38.

130 Stein, B.N., 'ICARA II: burden sharing and durable solutions', in Rogge, J.R. (ed.), *Refugees: a Third World Dilemma*, Totowa, NJ-: Rowman & Littlefield, 1987, p. 56. Mr. Afande, former Kenyan delegate at the UN, clearly expressed that the idea of resettling refugees in Kenya was not so welcomed by the central government. Declaration by Mr. Afande in UNGA, Third Committee, Summary record of the 41st meeting, 11 November 1986, document No. A/C.3/41/SR.41. In other circumstances African delegates even excluded resettlement in a third country among the durable solutions admitted. As did several times Mr. Osman, Somali delegate at the UN in the 1980s. For instance, read his declaration in UNGA, Third Committee, Summary record of the 47th meeting, 16 November 1987, document No. A/C.3/42/SR.47. Mrs. Semambo-Kalema, the Ugandan delegate, considered resettlement in a third country as 'an alternative' if voluntary repatriation or local integration were impossible to put in practice. Read her declaration in UNGA, Third Committee, Summary record of the 46th meeting, 17 November 1989, document No. A/C.3/44/SR.46. To reinforce this vision with an opinion *a contrario*, we see, for instance, that Mrs. Sinegiorgis, Ethiopian delegate at the UN, clearly expressed the opinion that her government was in favour of resettling in a third country for the most part refugees who were on Ethiopian territory. Read her declaration in UNGA, Third Committee, Summary record of the 48th meeting, 18 November 1988, document No. A/C.3/43/SR. 48.

solution, making individuals accepted in every country of the continent.[131] If only one nationality existed, the number of refugees would decrease, because we would no longer see frontiers being crossed anymore, but the number of IDPs would conversely increase because 'one citizenship only' does not automatically mean fewer problems on the continent. The phenomenon of refugees is not a geographical one and, above all, if resettlement is carried out in a more developed country than the home country, resettlement rather than voluntary repatriation is by far the preferable solution for African refugees. For instance, if one person flees persecution from a place where he/she has no personal wealth, it is most likely that he/she will seek a new life in a place where he/she can also materially improve his/her life instead of going back to a place where, apart from fearing persecution, materially there is no possibility of doing anything to improve his/her existence. This idea has been shared also by a couple of hundreds of Congolese Brazzaville refugees in Gabon who, once the authority in Libreville ceased to consider them as refugees in November 2011, asked to be resettled in another country. In effect, former Congolese refugees in Gabon claimed a supposed fear of persecution, although since 2012 Congo Brazzaville could be substantially considered as an appeased country.[132]

In 2014, the DRC Refugee Contact Group[133] endorsed a sub-regional scheme to develop durable solutions for refugees from that country. That scheme consisted of a plan of action to increase the resettlement of Congolese refugees from various Sub-Saharan African countries and to encourage self-reliance activities of the refugees although none of the identified resettlement countries seem to be in Africa.[134]

131 Mwalimu, C., 'The legal framework on admission and resettlement of African refugees with an emphasis on Kenya, Tanzania, and Uganda', in *Emory International Law Review*, vol. 18, 2004, p. 491. To quote him, at idem: 'The notion of the African national state with a single block of African citizenship is the permanent solution to refugee problems on the continent.'

132 See 'Sit-in de réfugiés congolais au Gabon pour quitter le pays', 14 February 2012, document available at: www.rfi.fr/afrique/20120213-sit-in-refugies-congolais-gabon-quitter-le-pays-rdc, accessed 10 November 2014.

133 'Contact groups for individual priority situations can serve to facilitate collaboration among resettlement countries, host States and UNHCR, and can provide an effective vehicle to advance the strategic use of resettlement, helping to achieve solutions for refugees who remain in host countries, as well as for those who are resettled. Contact groups can promote multi-year commitments to ensure predictability and sustainability for resettlement efforts; they can also collaborate to strengthen protection mechanisms, including livelihoods and legal strategies, for refugees in host countries.' See UNHCR, Progress Report on Resettlement, 6 June 2014, EC/65/SC/CRP.11, paragraph 13, p. 7, available at: www.refworld.org/docid/543bba8a4.html, accessed 9 December 2014.

134 Ibid., paragraph 13, p. 5.

Conclusion

Concluding remarks on the peregrination of a persecuted human being in search of a safe haven in Sub-Saharan Africa: lessons learnt to face the future challenges

Upon the conclusion of our assessment of asylum-seeker and refugee protection in Sub-Saharan Africa, and although noting that, for the Asian African Legal Consultative Organization (AALCO), the phenomenon of refugees in Africa seems to have become not more urgent than the present situation of IDPs on the continent,[1] we think that it is more fruitful to point out the areas in need of improvement rather than the positive aspects, in order to elucidate the most prevalent lacunae as well as some remedies that could be useful to address them in order to make life easier for the persecuted man in search of a safe haven.

One clear example of these lacunae is certainly exemplified by the fact that many countries in Sub-Saharan Africa have taken and are still taking steps towards adopting policies, which often reveal an inconsistent approach to meeting obligations they have assumed under international law, but also under their own domestic laws.[2]

In addition, Sub-Saharan African countries have sometimes adopted laws that they are unable to enforce given their political situation. In this sense, the 2002 DRC refugee law, considering the difficult political situations the DRC has been going through conveys the most vivid example of this contradictory situation, a contradictory situation that can be perceived, for instance, in Guinea, as well.[3]

1 AALCO, *Yearbook of the Asian-African Legal Consultative Organization*, New Delhi: AALCO, vol. VIII, 2010, p. 478.

2 Lomo, Z., 'The struggle for protection of the rights of refugees and IDPs in Africa: making the existing international legal regime work', in *Berkeley Journal of International Law*, vol. 18, 2000, p. 279.

3 Canefe, N., 'The fragmented nature of the international refugee regime and its consequences: a comparative analysis of the applications of the 1951 Convention', in Simeon, J.C. (ed.) *Critical Issues in International Refugee Law*, Cambridge/New York: Cambridge University Press, p. 190. About the situation in Guinea, see, for instance: UN Human Rights Council, Report of the Working Group on the Universal Periodic Review: Guinea, 10 April 2015, A/HRC/29/6, available at: www.refworld.org/docid/5571693c4.html, accessed 1 June 2015. At paragraph 118.104, p. 19, Spain recommended the Guinean government to 'Intensify efforts in the fight against extrajudicial executions, rape and torture'.

It should also be noted that existing domestic laws and proposed refugee bills across the continent do not take into consideration the complex new realities posed by emerging circumstances, such as the war against terrorism.[4]

Domestic measures have often revealed inaptitude in response to the refugee crisis, in particular with regard to mass-influx situations that most likely require the establishment of special standardized procedures for either RSD or the protection of refugees. However, this gap is not so surprising, considering that Sub-Saharan African countries seem to lack a common jurisprudential approach to the question of refugees in the region.[5] Domestic courts, probably with the exception of South Africa, are not so keen on dealing with asylum-seeker and refugee issues and when they do so, they are often approached with distrust and prejudice.

On the other hand, on the continent, the distinction between 'political' refugee and 'economic' migrant is gradually becoming more and more blurred, principally in light of the economic structuring of this area of the world on the basis of local and internationally promoted labour migrations.[6] This kind of situation clearly affects the decisions of the judges, making their work more difficult. In effect, it would be more useful to analyze the asylum-seeker and refugee situation within a broader development context: this would alert us to the dangers of studying them separately. Asylum-seekers and refugees can be thus considered analogous to the visible 'top of the iceberg', where just below the 'water-line' there is a wider band of legal – or illegal – immigrants and exiles.[7] In Sub-Saharan Africa, in situations where economically motivated migrants may seek to take advantage of refugee channels, mass information programmes have been launched – but often without real success – in order to provide clearer public knowledge of refugee status. These programmes aim to discourage those who seek to use asylum channels for exclusively economic reasons, while keeping them open for people escaping persecution.[8] However, the patterns of migration can occasionally make it problematic to differentiate between the different groups of people on the move.

4 In this regard, two authors contended that: '[T]here is a marked gap between what refugee jurisprudence guarantees in the Guinean context and what actually happens in the daily life of refugees and asylum-seekers. In this particular case, the concern is not about the adaptation of international refugee law. It is about the lack of implementation, application and efficient monitoring of it from within the domestic domain, as well as the barring of international organizations from intervening in cases of malpractice.' See Juma, M.K. and Kagwanja, P.M., 'Securing refuge from terror: refugee protection in East Africa after September 11', in Steiner, N., Gibney, M. and Loscher, G., *Problems of Protection: The UNHCR, Refugees and Human Rights*, New York/London: Routledge, 2003, p. 234.

5 Aukot, E., 'Refugee protection in Africa: a developing country's dilemmas towards effective protection', in *East African Journal of Peace and Human Rights*, vol. 9, 2003, pp. 253–4. The author, Kenyan born, bemoaned the fact that this country lacked internal legislation for refugees. Finally, the first Kenyan Refugee Bill was approved in late December 2006 and the second in July 2011.

6 Jackson, J., 'Repatriation and reconstruction in Zimbabwe during the 1980s', in Allen, T. and Morsink, H. (eds), *When Refugees Go Home*, London: James Currey; Trenton, NJ: Africa World Press, 1994, p. 161.

7 Ibid., pp. 163–4.

8 Blavo, E.Q., *The Problems of Refugees in Africa: Boundaries and Borders*, Aldershot: Ashgate, 1999, p. 78.

Population flows are frequently mixed.[9] In Sub-Saharan Africa, a typical example of this is given by South Africa where foreign people move for a multiplicity of motives; some move to seek international protection while others for economic reasons.[10] The Zimbabweans represent well a model of 'mixed-migrants' in South Africa. Through testimony of political violence, the different stories of Zimbabweans in South Africa contribute to creating a portrait of a 'mixed flow' of people. The final representation is distant from the one-dimensional image of the 'illegal economic migrant', presented by the South African government and by the local media.[11]

African countries construe the notion of 'persecution' in a multiplicity of political ways suitable for their interests, in spite of the notion that the RSD should not be linked to any political idea.[12] For many African countries, asylum has become too broad, granting economic migrants an occasion to detour migration limitations, which would otherwise prevent their entry.[13] It is because of this reason that in recent years we have assisted in strengthening the severe asylum policies put in place by the African governments.

What we have also observed is that several international norms are weakly enforced on the continent or are not enforced at all. The most prominent example being the uncommon practical acceptance of *non-refoulement* related to any particular class of persons or type of risk; therefore, in our opinion, we cannot consider this principle as customary in Sub-Saharan Africa. In this sense, we would like to note that even UNGA resolutions could not be reliable as evidence of *opinio juris*, one of the two elements of a custom.[14] The persistent reluctance of the majority of countries in Sub-Saharan Africa to embrace a comprehensive legal duty to protect refugees against *refoulement* is also problematic because customary international legal training rightly gives particular attention to the views of states

9 UNHCR, 'Are refugees migrants? A dangerous confusion', speech by Ms. Erika Feller, Director of the Department of International Protection, SID lecture series Migration and Development: Challenges for a World on the Move, Amsterdam, 27 January 2004, p. 2, available at: www.refworld.org/docid/403603a24.html, accessed 25 January 2015.

10 UNHCR, *Submission by the United Nations High Commissioner for Refugees for the Office of the High Commissioner for Human Rights' Compilation Report – Universal Periodic Review: South Africa*, November 2011, p. 1, available at: www.refworld.org/docid/4ed724952.html, accessed 1 February 2015.

11 HRW, Neighbors in need: Zimbabweans seeking refuge in South Africa, 19 June 2008, pp. 29–30, available at: www.refworld.org/docid/485a184a2.html, accessed 2 February 2015.

12 Zetter, R., 'More labels, fewer refugees: remaking the refugee label in an era of globalization', in *Journal of Refugee Studies*, vol. 20, 2007, p. 184.

13 Glynn, I., 'The genesis and development of article 1 of the 1951 Refugee Convention', in *Journal of Refugee Studies*, vol. 25, 2012, p. 145.

14 Hathaway, J.C., 'Leveraging asylum', in *Texas International Law Journal*, vol. 45, 2010, p. 510. To support his thesis, the author quoted the ICJ in the: *Case concerning military and paramilitary activities in and against Nicaragua (Nicaragua v United States of America)*, judgment of 27 June 1986, in *ICJ Reports*, 1986, paragraphs 99–100, pp. 99–100: '*[o]pinio juris* may though with all due caution, be deduced from, *inter alia,* [. . .] *the attitude of states towards certain General Assembly resolutions*, [. . .] support of [regional conference] resolution[s] [. . .] [and] statements by state representatives.' Emphasis added.

'specially affected' by the phenomenon being regulated.[15] With Sub-Saharan Africa hosting a huge number of refugees, yet failing to affirm a duty to protect, the assertion of a universal *opinio juris* is particularly fragile.[16] In addition, in that region:

> Access to asylum procedures [is] occasionally problematic. [. . .] Sometimes screening or admissibility procedures effectively barred applicants from access to a substantive determination of their claim, including where a *prima facie* case appeared to exist. In some countries, reduced or lack of access to legal aid or to appropriate interpreters prevented or undermined effective presentation of cases. UNHCR and its partners worked with relevant counterparts to establish, reactivate and/or strengthen national eligibility procedures and improve decision-making.[17]

Recourse to durable solutions on the continent, especially voluntary repatriation, has given few tangible results relative to expectations and recent years have seen tragedy from this kind of solution,[18] with returnees who could not always enjoy the same rights as their compatriots, in spite of the efforts made by the African institutions to guarantee parity of treatment.[19]

The problem of asylum in Sub-Saharan Africa is mainly affected by the huge number of refugees; the insecurity created by the criminal behaviour of some of them, and clashes between refugees and local populations, this latter considering themselves to be discriminated against by national authorities *vis-à-vis* asylum-seekers and refugees.[20]

It seems, therefore, too easy to state that the unique solution to the plight of asylum-seekers and refugees in Sub-Saharan Africa is constituted by the elimination of the forces that generate this category of individuals. Although in the past, finding a concrete solution to the refugee plight was envisioned differently;

15 ICJ, *North Sea Continental Shelf Cases (Federal Republic of Germany v Denmark; Federal Republic of Germany v Netherlands)*, judgment of 20 February 1969, in *ICJ Reports*, 1969, paragraph 74, p. 43: '[S]tate practice, including that of states whose interests are specially affected, should have been both extensive and virtually in the sense of the provision invoked, and should moreover have occurred in such a way as to show a general recognition that a rule of law or legal obligation is involved.'

16 In this regard, J.C. Hathaway affirmed: '[T]here is a pervasive – perhaps even dominant – state practice that denies in one way or another, the right to be protected against *refoulement*.' See Hathaway, J.C., 'Leveraging asylum', op. cit. note 14, p. 516.

17 ExCom, Note on international protection, Geneva: UNHCR, 3–7 October 2005, document No. A/AC.96/1008, paragraph 18, p. 5.

18 See UNHCR, 'UNHCR chief says 2009 "worst" year for voluntary repatriation in two decades', 15 June 2010, available at: www.unhcr.org/4c11eadd9.html, accessed 10 November 2014.

19 In this sense see what was affirmed by the African Parliamentary Conference, 'Refugees in Africa: the challenges of protection and solutions', Program of Action, Cotonou, Benin, 1–3 June 2004, objective 6, p. 4, available at: www.ipu.org/splz-e/cotonou/action.pdf, accessed 2 January 2015: 'Take all measures to enable returnees to enjoy the same rights as their fellow citizens.'

20 Declaration by Ms. Mohamed, Kenyan delegate in UNGA, Third Committee, Summary record of the 33rd meeting, 7 November 2003, document No. A/C.3/58/SR.33, paragraph 13, p. 3.

rather than eradicating its causes,[21] a solution could only be found in the place where the refugees found shelter, because the causes that generated the refugee situation seemed insurmountable. This vision was far more pragmatic than the utopian vision to stop wars and persecutions.[22] For example, the proposition to introduce *jus soli* in the countries of refuge, replacing the concept of *jus sanguinis*, fits into this framework. This would allow future generations of refugees to acquire the nationality of their country of birth by law.[23] However, to date,[24] no Sub-Saharan African country seems to have adopted an unrestricted *jus soli* in its legislation.[25]

Both the UNHCR and the AU are aware of the importance of eliminating the root causes that create refugee flows, including the need to challenge the 'intolerance of the diversity'. That would mean persuading African countries to reinforce their nationhood, by strengthening 'nationalistic' sentiments, going beyond the preoccupations linked to the possible ethnic diversities of the local population.[26] For this reason, the AU and other regional and sub-regional organizations have tried to promote democratic governance, respect for human

21 In this regard M. Weiner argued that: '[t]he fundamental policy question for governments and international institutions still remains: what can be done to provide protection to a threatened people within their own country so they need not cross international borders?' See Weiner, M., 'Bad neighbors, bad neighborhoods: an inquiry into the causes of refugee flows', in *International Security*, vol. 21, 1996, p. 42.

22 Rubinstein, J.L., 'The refugee problem', in: *International Affairs*, vol. 15, 1936, pp. 719–20. At idem, the author proposed: '[t]o organise the right of asylum, and to assure the refugees of an undisturbed place in the community which has given them shelter. This is not a matter of philanthropy; it is a social and juridical question.'

23 Idem. As we may read: 'Citizenship at birth or *jus soli*, where citizenship is primarily acquired by the fact of being born in a territory over which the State maintains jurisdiction. In *jus soli* countries, citizenship is invariably acquired by descent as well. Citizenship through descent or *jus sanguinis*, where citizenship is acquired primarily through birth from parents having a specific citizenship. In *jus sanguinis* countries, citizenship may also be acquired by naturalization, marital status, or past or current residence. Policy changes in a number of *jus sanguinis* states are being made in favour of granting citizenship to children born to certain categories of immigrants, while at the same time modifying *jus soli* rules to limit birthright citizenship to children born to permanent immigrants. Information available at: www.iom.int/jahia/Jahia/about-migration/managing-migration/migration-and-citizenship/citizenship, accessed 20 November 2014.

24 20 February 2015.

25 Several sources indicate in Lesotho as a country where the *jus soli* has been adopted. However, Chapter IV, section 38 of the Constitution of Lesotho, adopted in 1993, amended 1996, 1997, 1998, 2001, and 2004, stipulates as follows: '38) Persons born in Lesotho after the coming into operation of the Constitution 1) Subject to the provisions of subsections 2) and (3), every person born in Lesotho after the coming into operation of this Constitution shall become a citizen of Lesotho. 2) Save as provided in subsection 3), a person shall not become a citizen of Lesotho by virtue of this section if at the time of his birth neither of his parents is a citizen of Lesotho, and – a) one or both of his parents possesses such immunity from suit and legal process as is accorded to the envoy of a foreign sovereign power accredited to Lesotho; or b) one or both of his parents is an enemy alien and the birth occurs in a place then under occupation by the enemy. 3) A person born in Lesotho on or after the coming into operation of this Constitution who is disqualified to become a citizen of Lesotho by virtue of subsection 2) of this section shall become a citizen of Lesotho if he would otherwise become stateless.'

26 AALCO, *Yearbook of the Asian-African Legal Consultative Organization*, New Delhi: AALCO, vol. VI, 2008, p. 609.

rights, and the enforcement of the African mechanism for the prevention, management and peaceful settlement of conflicts as an effective and incisive instrument to fight against the refugee plight that afflicts the entire continent.

J.C. Hathaway has affirmed that the concept of refugee status ends whenever the violence and other human rights abuses, which have provoked flight, are eradicated. According to this view, the refugee protection system is therefore intended more as a palliative regime for the protection of distressed people until a fundamental change of circumstances makes it safe for them to go home, rather than a mechanism to find more far-reaching solutions.[27] This is also a reminder that the notion of 'refugee' has always been malleable, having been defined and redefined numerous times by politicians and officials over the centuries.[28]

Both the UNHCR and AU were sometimes able to manage the situation in Sub-Saharan Africa, but this has not always been the case, as evident from the Great Lakes refugee crisis, where the UNHCR failed to implement the exclusion clauses of its legal mandate, nor did it manage to perform the necessary RSD.[29] Nevertheless, if the UNHCR fails in its actions, it is also because the agency has limits to them, limits determined by the international instruments. For instance, the drafters of the 1951 Refugee Convention declined to give the UNHCR a general right to facilitate the enforcement of refugee rights for states parties, the UNHCR having been entrusted only with the general duty of 'supervising the application of the provisions of [the] Convention.'[30] In spite of these limitations, there is no doubt that the UNHCR plays a crucial role in promoting respect for refugee rights in Sub-Saharan Africa. The UNHCR has persuaded most African governments to allow its physical presence in their jurisdiction, to meet refugees, and in general to be assured access to officials with the authority to respond to concerns *vis-à-vis* the treatment of people in need.[31] However, while the UNHCR protection officers in the field provide confidential compliance reports to their headquarters, states, on the other hand, are not required to submit their records to public scrutiny. Consequently, there is no forum that could require African governments to engage in the kind of dialogue of justification, normally practised under almost every other human rights instrument.[32]

27 Hathaway, J.C., 'Temporary protection of refugees: threat or solution?', in Handmaker, J., De La Hunt, L.A. and Klaaren, J. (eds), *Perspectives on Refugee Protection in South Africa*, Pretoria: Lawyers for Human Rights, 2001, p. 65.

28 Marfleet, P., *Refugees in a Global Era*, Basingstoke/New York: Palgrave Macmillan, 2006, p. 13.

29 Wagner, K., 'UNHCR's involvement in the Great Lakes refugee crisis', in *Pace International Law Review*, vol. 21, 2009, p. 386. At idem, the author pointed out: 'These failures were partially due to the UNHCR lack of preparation in having the full and necessary understanding of the social and political situations surrounding the Rwanda genocide.'

30 Article 35 1) of the 1951 Refugee Convention.

31 Kaelin, W., 'Supervising the 1951 Convention relating to the status of refugees: Article 35 and beyond', in Feller, E., Türk, V. and Nicholson, F. (eds), *Refugee Protection in International Law: UNHCR's Global Consultations on International Protection*, Cambridge, UK/New York/Geneva: Cambridge University Press and UNHCR, 2003, pp. 623–4.

32 Sohn, L.B., 'Human rights: their implementation and supervision by the United Nations', in Meron, T. (ed.), *Human Rights in International Law: Legal and Policy Issues*, Oxford: Clarendon Press, 1984. See, in particular, pp. 373–9.

The major problem regarding asylum-seeker and refugee protection under the main binding legal instruments is the failure to establish an independent supervisory mechanism, which, at least with regard to the 1951 Geneva Convention, is considered by J.C. Hathaway 'no more than an historical anomaly'. This failure may also be due to the fact that as refugee law has its own 'institutional guardian' in the High Commissioner for Refugees, any other mechanism for supervision would have been considered useless.[33] However, in a research undertaken in 2013, J. Whiteman and C. Nielsen concluded that:

> [T]here is no international body with full legitimacy, independence, participatory and operational capacity to provide authoritative guidance or particularized assessment of compliance in relation to the refugee Convention; that there is no lack of expertise, but a lack of optimal utilization of existing expertise at the international level; and that consistency and relevance of guidance and objectivity of assessment remain significant challenges in a system comprising a wide range of disparate decision-making, laws and policies.[34]

In addition, until now African states have been quite hesitant to introduce an independent and effective supervising body for their implementation of the 1951 Geneva Convention. In this respect, it would be essential to form an efficient system of liability, one that is impartial and autonomous.[35]

J.H.S. Milner has also suggested that a more comprehensive answer to the refugee crisis in Sub-Saharan Africa should place the issues into the:

> [C]ontext of North–South negotiations, including trade, aid, debt, governance, human rights, defense, and development. Incorporating asylum into this broader constellation of issues would not only recognize the full range of

33 Hathaway, J.C., *The Rights of Refugees Under International Law*, Cambridge: Cambridge University Press, 2005, p. 995.

34 Whiteman, J. and Nielsen, C., 'Lessons from supervisory mechanisms in international and regional law', in *Journal of Refugee Studies*, vol. 26, 2013, p. 385. In this regard, see also O'Bryne, K., 'Is there a need for better supervision of the refugee convention?', in *Journal of Refugee Studies*, vol. 26, 2013, pp. 349–54. In her attempt to find a mechanism of improved supervision of the 1951 Geneva Convention, A. Blackham contended that: 'First, it is essential that mechanisms be developed with regard to the different forms of supervision required under the Refugee Convention. [. . .] [D]ifferent forms of supervision will require different options for filling supervisory gaps. Second, the development of supervisory models should be criterion-focused, with an emphasis on addressing current gaps in each type of supervision and minimizing challenges related to existing supervisory mechanisms. Third, we recognize that some change models may appear confronting to states and UNHCR, and ambitious in the contemporary international context. However, we feel it is important to propose and discuss these models in the interests of facilitating dialogue around existing supervisory arrangements. At the same time, the success of any reform will be dependent on the support of UNHCR and states parties.'

35 AALCO, *Yearbook of the Asian-African Legal Consultative Organization*, New Delhi: AALCO, vol. VI, 2008, p. 610.

> factors that affect a state's asylum policies, but also create opportunities for the formulation of 'win-win' outcomes through the potential linking of asylum to wider benefits for the host state.[36]

Nevertheless, African states generating refugees generally do not wish to admit that they have caused the massive movement of people across borders. If they did such a thing, this would taint their image and affect their political and economic relations with other countries in the area.[37]

Crossing an international border to become an asylum-seeker and, possibly, a refugee is not an option for a vast number of individuals requiring protection; and the diffuse immobility of governments and their ineffective responses do not solve but exacerbate the problem of asylum for millions of Sub-Saharan Africans, because this means abandoning people whose fundamental human rights are being undermined. In contrast, whether an African state has a commitment to grant refugee rights through one of the main binding instruments on refugee protection, and whether the international community gives the necessary support to governments – which African countries constantly declare to lack – all refugee rights are indispensable components of state policy on refugee protection. In the absence of these rights, humane treatment of refugees is a lost cause and the good intentions of governments are eclipsed by other measures considered to be in the best interests of the local administration.[38]

An examination of the history of asylum in Sub-Saharan Africa from the beginning of the modern phenomenon dating back to the 1960s shows that there has been an alternation of 'help' and 'non-help', 'response' and 'non-response', constantly depending on the continental and international political climate, as well as the individuals in question.[39]

In some cases, as in Guinea, the granting of asylum has been used both as a means of stressing the failure of neighbouring regimes and as a cover for granting support to organizations or elements opposed to the bordering regime. In other cases, as in Tanzania, changing relations between the country of refuge and the country of origin resulted in the prioritization of regional relations over the needs of refugees, with Tanzania several years ago considered the worst country for refugees in Sub-Saharan Africa for neither allowing refugees to leave the camps, nor letting them work.[40] For countries like Kenya, the inability to resolve protracted refugee situations has been compounded by the neighbouring state of Somalia,

36 Milner, J.H.S., *Refugees, the State and the Politics of Asylum in Africa*, Basingstoke: Palgrave/Macmillan, 2009, p. 188.

37 Anand, R., *African Refugees: An Overview*, New Delhi: Khama, 1993, p. 88.

38 Blavo, E.Q., op. cit. note 8, p. 74.

39 Haddad, E., *The Refugee in International Society: Between Sovereigns*, Cambridge: Cambridge University Press, 2008, , pp. 213–14.

40 See the report: Too Many African Nations Fail Refugees, 2011, available at: www.refugees.org/refugee-voices/warehoused-refugees/too-many-african-nations-fail.html, accessed 10 November 2014.

which still in 2014 has no functioning central government,[41] although the 2013 Conference 'A New Deal for Somalia',[42] through the Somali Compact,[43] has tried to revitalize the peace process and to place back on the international scene a country that for a very long time has simply been considered a 'fragile state'.[44]

Moreover, asylum can be subjected to the total discretionary power of the local authority who grants it, as occurred in the past with the Refugee Commissioner in Botswana,[45] now considered several years ago one of the best places for asylum-seekers and refugees in Sub-Saharan Africa, along with Malawi.[46] As an example, there are occasions where certain aliens acquire refugee status because of their political value to the government. This enables such individuals to benefit also from assistance programmes provided by voluntary organizations, for instance those awarding scholarships for higher education, while refugees deserving this status lose such opportunities.[47]

In spite of the many adversities they are obliged to face, Sub-Saharan African asylum-seekers and refugees are generally considered to continue to preserve their integrity and honour, partly by a shared belief in the prospect of a better future. This was particularly evident, for instance, in the case of the Eritrean refugees in Sudan. The endurance shown by this particular group of people resulted from a strong conviction that one day in the future it would become possible to return home. Many of them enthusiastically participated in the liberation war and it was the dream of a free Eritrea that kept their hopes alive.[48]

41 Milner, J.H.S., op. cit. note 36, pp. 178–9.

42 A New Deal for Somalia, Brussels Conference, 16 September 2013, available at: http://eeas.europa.eu/archives/new-deal-for-somalia-conference/home.html, accessed 2 January 2015.

43 Available at: http://eeas.europa.eu/archives/new-deal-for-somalia-conference/sites/default/files/the_somali_compact.pdf, accessed 2 January 2015. Paragraphs 5 and 6 of the Somali Compact, p. 1, read as follows: 'The Somali Compact, a living document that reflects the ongoing process of transition and defines priority interventions to ensure the country stays on the path to long-term peace and state building. The Compact lays a strong foundation for building reliable, transparent, accountable and functioning state institutions, respectful of the fundamental rights, freedoms and equality of its citizens. In this respect, the establishment of local and regional administrations and federal units, in the spirit of the provisional Constitution, are key milestones for a vibrant and stable Somalia. The adoption of this Compact, which provides a new political, security and development architecture framing the future relations between Somalia, its people and the international community, embodies the spirit of our new partnership.'

44 In 2014, Somalia is still ranked as the second most 'fragile state' in the world, after South Sudan. The full ranking is available at: http://ffp.statesindex.org/rankings-2014, accessed 10 February 2015.

45 Botswana, Refugees (Recognition and Control Act), 5 April 1968, particularly Articles 3 through 5 on the establishment of the Refugee Advisory Committee.

46 See the report: Too Many African Nations Fail Refugees, 2011, available at: www.refugees.org/refugee-voices/warehoused-refugees/too-many-african-nations-fail.html, accessed 10 November 2014. The report is related to 2011.

47 Blavo, E.Q., op. cit. note 8, pp. 75–6.

48 Kibreab, G., 'Left in Limbo', in Allen, T. (ed.), *In Search of Cool Ground: War, Flight and Homecoming in Northeast Africa*, London: James Currey; Trenton, NJ: Africa World Press, 1996, p. 64. Regarding the situation of the Eritrean refugees in Sudan, see also, for instance, the analysis: 'Eritrea-Sudan: A forgotten refugee problem', 3 December 2009, available at: www.irinnews.org/Report/87300/ERITREA-SUDAN-A-forgotten-refugee-problem, accessed 10 January 2015: 'Eastern Sudan

A study carried out two decades ago made several recommendations to African governments for the implementation of refugee protection in Sub-Saharan Africa, recommendations which are still valid today, considering the less than effective action, or rather inaction, often demonstrated at government level. And if national governments can justify their inaction in relation to some of these recommendations – probably lacking the means to do a good job – we still would need to blame national authorities for not showing any substantial effort towards putting these recommendations into practice. Among the recommendations made at the time were the ratification of the main binding instruments on refugee protection (1951 Geneva Convention, 1967 New York Protocol, 1969 OAU Convention) 'without reservations'; and the establishment of training programmes for all those involved with refugees 'in international human rights standards and the protection of refugees under international law'. Furthermore: 'establishing programs to train security force personnel in the particular protection needs of refugees' and 'if necessary, establish[ment of] a specialized protection unit for refugees'; the establishment of 'independent mechanisms to receive and investigate complaints by refugees against security force personnel and other officials'; and 'ensur[ing] that all personnel crossing international borders purported to be refugees are disarmed'. The study also recommended for African governments: 'to carry out the requirements of international human rights law to prosecute those alleged to be responsible for gross violations of human rights'; 'while prohibiting armed activities by those purporting to be refugees, guarantee the right of refugees to participate in non-violent political activity and expression of their opinions'. It further recommended for governments to '[e]nsure that all refugees and asylum-seekers are issued with identity cards and are guaranteed freedom of movement within their country of asylum.'[49] By way of an example, the creation of mechanisms to protect refugees against abuse from security forces,[50] and, above

hosts more than 66,000 registered Eritrean refugees, the first of whom arrived in 1968 during the early years of Eritrea's war of independence against Ethiopia. [. . .] As they planned for their big escape to Europe or Israel, asylum-seekers dreamed of a better life in Sudan. But instead, thousands woke up to the realities of the grim camp conditions, lacking food security or proper healthcare, and sharing scarce resources with Sudanese nationals. On arrival at the reception center at Shagarab camp in Kassala state, near the Eritrean border, they are not immediately provided with proper shelter. Only when their refugee status is confirmed, which can take four to six weeks, are they able to move into tents or huts, which they often have to build themselves. [. . .] In 2002, the refugee status enjoyed by those who had fled the independence war, or subsequent conflict between Ethiopia and Eritrea, was revoked, on the grounds that the circumstances that led to their exodus no longer pertained. Although thousands of refugees returned to Eritrea, some refused to do so. [. . .] Some of the refugees moved to other cities in Sudan looking for employment. The government says there are about 40,000 refugees living in urban centers, sharing services and job opportunities with Sudanese nationals. Although UNHCR says the government has not rejected any Eritrean asylum-seekers, it does try to reduce the pull of the refugee camps to potential ones.'

49 Lawyers' Committee for Human Rights, *African Exodus: Refugee Crisis, Human Rights and the 1969 OAU Convention*, New York: Lawyers' Committee for Human Rights Editions, 1995, pp. 197–8.

50 For instance, see HRW, '"You are all terrorists" – Kenyan police abuse of refugees in Nairobi', 29 May 2013, available at: www.refworld.org/docid/51f121744.html, accessed 20 February

all, the freedom of movement guaranteed to refugees, represent two issues which appear to us to concern the majority of refugees on the continent at the moment. In this latest regard, the High Court of Kenya ruled in February 2015 that:

> [T]he right to enter, remain and reside anywhere in Kenya is constitutionally reserved to citizens and therefore there is no violation of the right to freedom of movement in requiring that refugees wishing to leave the camp obtain permission from the Camp Officer.[51]

In effect, one of the reasons obstructing development in refugee protection in Sub-Saharan Africa is due to how the present system of protection has managed to take for granted much of the refugee's security problem, by either pretending that the problem is not there or by assuming that it cannot be solved.[52] However, by being clear that the problem of refugee security cannot be solved through the elimination of refugee flows, it is easier to understand how the destiny of refugee protection in Sub-Saharan Africa greatly depends on the world's ability to deploy civilian and/or military police assets in order to promote regional security.[53]

The above recommendations have been mostly drawn on by the African Parliamentary Conference held in Cotonou in 2004, which issued a 'Program of Action' including the drafting of solid strategies to protect asylum-seekers and refugees and to find durable solutions for them. In this regard, and to confirm what we have stated up until now, Objective 2 of the programme aimed to guarantee that international treaties on refugee protection were not merely signed and adopted by countries but '[e]ffectively implemented through the enactment of national legislation and policies, including provisions penalizing violations of international humanitarian law'.[54] This latter case regards, for instance, the situation of ex-combatants, often finding themselves in camps mixed with the civilian population. An example of this kind is provided by the suspected 4,000 Liberian ex-combatants living in the Buduburam camp, home of 40,000 people

2015. At p. 12 we can read: 'Refugees told Human Rights Watch that police who abused them in Eastleigh used the threat of arrest and prosecution on terror charges – calling them "terrorists" – as an excuse to abuse and extort money from them.'

51 Kenya: High Court, *Coalition for Reform and Democracy and others v Republic of Kenya and others*, Petition No. 628 of 2014 consolidated with Petition No. 630 of 2014 and Petition No. 12 of 2015, 23 February 2015, paragraph 403, p. 195, available at: www.refworld.org/docid/54ecbdef4.html, accessed 24 February 2015.

52 Cuellar, M.-F., 'Refugee security and the organizational logic of legal mandates', in *Georgetown Journal of International Law*, vol. 37, 2005–06. Footnote 56: Cuellar, M.-F., op. cit. note 52, p. 723.

53 Ibid., pp. 711–12. At p. 716, the author explained: '[W]hile the three actors most immediately able to shape refugee security are UNHCR, the host state, and the refugees themselves, improvements in security depend on enhancing the capacity of UNHCR and refugees to assume a greater share of the security responsibility that is unlikely to be effectively discharged by anyone else.'

54 African Parliamentary Conference, 'Refugees in Africa: the challenges of protection and solutions', Program of Action, Cotonou, Benin, 1–3 June 2004.

in Ghana,[55] one of the many 'instant cities' located in Sub-Saharan Africa with problems of law enforcement, only infrequently addressed by the UNHCR or the host states.[56] This can be considered a typical case for the complementary application of international humanitarian law and international refugee law, with former combatants who can apply for asylum only if they have put down arms in a definitive way, and if they manage to pass the double screening of the clauses of inclusion and exclusion, although an accurate assessment of the case-by-case situation becomes very difficult, above all in situations of mass-influx.[57] However, despite the presence of national legislations, the existing policy of the Sub-Saharan countries towards an accurate evaluation of individual applicants for refugee status does not reflect the provisions outlined in the legislations. This often occurs because of the lack of available personnel, trained to successfully implement the provisions adopted in order to make the screening effective.[58]

In sum, at present we are witnessing a continuous deterioration of the institution of asylum across the continent, a deterioration that does not seem to have faltered in the past few years. The situation can probably be changed by these very same African nationals because there is a sentiment we could define as 'spiritual' among them, as has also been observed in a judgment concerning refugees on the continent:

> After all, we are all human beings and more importantly we are all children of one mother that is Africa the continent.[59]

It is clear that in an 'ideal world', refugees should not exist. In a 'semi-ideal world', refugees should have the right to decide their own destiny, preferably by, we believe, seeking refuge in a developed country where they can achieve what they were deprived of in their country of origin. Only in a second instance should they aim to go back to their hometown, which has possibly been left in ruin. In the real world, however, the reality that Sub-Saharan African refugees often confront is contradictory and unsatisfactory.

One of the solutions hoped for refugees in Sub-Saharan Africa is their integration into the host society. This solution, however, once not so difficult to achieve, has met increasing obstacles in its implementation, the most noticeable being discrimination, racism and xenophobia, as in South Africa where, in 2012,

55 News from Africa: 'Refugee camp: a security threat', December 2003, available at: www.newsfromafrica.org/newsfromafrica/articles/art_569.html, accessed 10 November 2014.

56 Cuellar, M.-F., op. cit. note 52, pp. 599 and 613.

57 Arenas-Hidalgo, N., 'Combatants and armed elements as refugees: the interplay between international humanitarian law and international refugee law', in Fernandez-Sanchez, P.A. (ed.), *The New Challenges of Humanitarian Law in Armed Conflicts. In Honor of Professor Juan Antonio Carillo-Salcedo*, Leiden: Martinus Nijhoff, 2005, p. 225.

58 AALCO, *Yearbook of the Asian-African Legal Consultative Organization*, New Delhi: AALCO, vol. VII, 2009, pp. 415–16.

59 Lilongwe Magistrate Court, *The Republic of Malawi v Abdul Rahman and Others (Somalians)*, judgment, Case No. 26 of 2005, 9 May 2005, p. 2.

police, employers and neighbours harassed urban asylum-seekers and refugees on a regular basis.[60] And the situation has not changed much since.[61]

African authorities, however, often commit to working with national media in campaigns to tackle these plights, through the promotion of peaceful coexistence between asylum-seekers, refugees and the local population.[62] Fear on both sides is perpetuated by misinformation; but, a point to take into consideration is that asylum-seekers and refugees are habitually hesitant to separate from the network forming their group. These challenges influence refugees' ability to preserve their identity and, thus, to integrate. If refugees successfully integrate, part of this process entails the safeguarding and mutual recognition of their distinctive identities, as is easily indicated by the model of integration as a 'two-way process'.[63] However, the phenomenon of the protracted refugee situation on the continent remains intact and, what we have seen for instance regarding Kenya, seems quite irresolvable now since the obvious solution of allowing refugees to leave camps and try to integrate in the local society is thwarted by the host countries. Tackling the plight of protracted situations such as these represents a crucial issue for Sub-Saharan Africa.[64]

Contributions of specifically African protection to the law governing refugee status cannot be denied – for instance, the broader definition of 'refugee' adopted by the 1969 OAU Convention, where the features of deliberateness and discrimination are not required and whose terminology responds to the humanitarian preoccupations typical of the area. Additionally, its recognition of the security implications of refugee flows makes it noteworthy, as well as its focus on the solutions. The legal provision on voluntary repatriation represents a pillar; and the promotion of a burden-sharing approach to assistance and protection of vulnerable people, along with all of these other elements listed, constitute several of the most significant examples of Africa's legal contributions to the refugee plight. Let us not forget the more completed elaboration of the principle of *non-refoulement*,

60 Anderson, J.L., 'Urban displacement and peacebuilding: an analysis of South African social cohesion interventions', in *UNHCR, New Issues in Refugee Research*, research paper No. 243, 2012, p. 5.

61 HRW, World Report 2015 – South Africa, 29 January 2015, available at: www.refworld.org/docid/54cf838015.html, accessed 20 February 2015: 'On June 19, 2014 security officials and police used excessive force to control a crowd of foreign nationals who were attempting to renew their permits at Marabastad reception office in Pretoria. Security officials and police attacked the unarmed crowd with whips and pepper spray.'

62 African Parliamentary Conference, 'Refugees in Africa: the challenges of protection and solutions', Program of Action, Cotonou, Benin, 1–3 June 2004, objective 11. The integration in the host society is supported by several scholars. See, for instance, Eze, O.C., 'The Convention Governing the Specific Aspects of Refugee Problems in Africa', in Yusuf, A.A. and Ouguergouz, F. (eds), *The African Union: Legal and Institutional Framework: A Manual on the Pan-African Organization*, Leiden/Boston, MA: Martinus Nijhoff, 2012, p. 517: 'But the better options [for African refugees] would appear to be integration by naturalization or assimilation in the local communities, where they would be accorded national treatment [. . .].'

63 Berry, S.E., 'Integrating refugees: the case for a minority rights based approach', in *International Journal of Refugee Law*, vol. 24, 2012, p. 11.

64 AALCO, *Yearbook of the Asian-African Legal Consultative Organization*, New Delhi: AALCO, vol. VI, 2008, p. 609.

in comparison with the analogous proviso of the 1951 Refugee Convention. The 1969 OAU Convention has not only played a big role in influencing African domestic refugee laws, it can also be seen as a legal pivot guaranteeing priorities that are not exclusively legal, but also political. This instrument has permitted, at least on paper, the establishment of a coherent and stable regime of asylum-seeker and refugee protection from a political point of view in a period in which chaos had been having the upper hand in refugee protection on the continent. In addition to this, we must not neglect the fact that the African model of protection based on the 1969 African Convention has influenced other regional systems, particularly the Inter-American one.[65]

Additionally, the 1981 Banjul Charter has reaffirmed the prohibition of forced exile, the mass-expulsion of foreigners, refugees included; and granted the right to 'seek and obtain asylum' to persecuted persons, thus creating an obligation for countries, parties to the charter, to use the asylum process in order to grant protection. Furthermore, the system put in place by the OAU/AU has also generated significant additional forms of protection for particularly vulnerable groups through the adoption of specific instruments protecting children and women.[66]

On the other hand, after a close look at the strictly legal aspects, this effort of the African legislator cannot be praised in full. Considering, for instance, that it has remained silent on the very common phenomenon of mass-influx,[67] it has thus obliged national governments to encourage the competent national authorities to work with the UNHCR to 'ensure a more effective emergency response.'[68] There is not, however, unanimous consensus by the doctrine on the fact the 1969 OAU Convention remains mute on issues dealing with mass-influx.[69] Moreover, the African system does not make any real mention of the many potential rights of asylum-seekers and refugees, which, although already mentioned in the 1951 Geneva Convention, could have been strongly reaffirmed in the African documents, in order to confer a more significant authority to the protection of the categories of the individuals in question. In addition, the African system lacks

65 AALCO, *Yearbook of the Asian-African Legal Consultative Organization*, New Delhi: AALCO, vol. VII, 2009, pp. 415–16. In this regard, see also Arboleda, E., 'Refugee definition in Africa and Latin America: the lessons of pragmatism', in *International Journal of Refugee Law*, vol. 3, 1991, pp. 185–207.

66 AALCO, *Yearbook of the Asian-African Legal Consultative Organization*, New Delhi: AALCO, vol. VII, 2009, pp. 404–6. OAU, African Charter on the Rights and Welfare of the Child, 11 July 1990, Document No. CAB/LEG/24.9/49 (1990); Protocol to the African Charter on Human and Peoples' Rights on the rights of women in Africa. Adopted by the 2nd Ordinary Session of the Assembly of the Union. Concluded in Maputo on 11 July 2003. Text: CAB/LEG/66.6 /Sept. 13, 2000.

67 Murray, R., *Human Rights in Africa: from the OUA to the African Union*, Cambridge: Cambridge University Press, 2004, p. 189.

68 African Parliamentary Conference, 'Refugees in Africa: the challenges of protection and solutions', Program of Action, Cotonou, Benin, 1–3 June 2004, objective 4.

69 For instance, A. Edwards explained that the African definition '[m]ay seem perfectly functional in cases of mass-influx where its humanitarian spirit governs its application.' See: Edwards, A., "Refugee status determination in Africa", in *African Journal of International and Comparative Law*, vol. 14, 2006, p. 211.

a supervisory body, which would also be desirable. Furthermore, the mandate of the *Special Rapporteur* on refugees, asylum-seekers and IDPs appointed by the ACHPR is quite narrow in comparison with the one of the UNHCR.[70]

On a final note, we would like to bring to mind the Latin saying '*faber est quisque faber fortunae suae*'.[71] Therefore, it should be up to the international community in general and African countries in particular to demonstrate their genuine good intentions of a political will to reinforce the strengths and eliminate the weaknesses of the protection system currently in effect in Sub-Saharan Africa, a political will with the ultimate aim of a better future for all refugees, because:

> Ultimately, the solution to the problems of refugees in Africa is not solely dependent on international and regional conventions but also on the collective conscience of African countries. In their efforts to solve the problems of refugees, African nations should hold high the well-known *dictum* of Fridjof Nansen [. . .] that 'love of man is practical policy'.[72]

70 In spite of several efforts, also corroborated by the appointment in 2004 of a *Special Rapporteur* on Refugees, Asylum Seekers and Internally Displaced Persons in Africa, the ACHPR's policy towards refugees was deemed incoherent and lacking coordination with other AU organs. This *Special Rapporteur*'s mandate was, among other aspects, to '[r]aise awareness and promote the implementation of the UN Convention on Refugees of 1951 as well as the 1969 OAU Convention Governing the Specific Aspects of Refugee Problems in Africa.' In this regard, see Murray, R., 'Refugees and internally displaced persons and human rights: the African system', in *Refugee Survey Quarterly*, vol. 24, 2005, p. 61; ACHPR, Resolution on the mandate of the *Special Rapporteur* on refugees, asylum seekers and internally displaced persons in Africa, resolution No. 72 (XXXVI), 2004, paragraph 1 g).

71 Appius Claudius Caecus, 280 BC. The English translation of this saying is '[E]veryone is the architect of his/her own success' and was affirmed in a famous speech he gave against *Cineas*, an envoy of *Pyrrhus of Epirus*, declaring that Rome would never surrender. This represents the first recorded political speech in Latin.

72 Blavo, E.Q., op. cit. note 8, pp. 78–9. For a detailed biography of Fridjof Nansen see, for instance, Huntford, R., *Nansen: The Explorer as Hero*, London: Abacus, 2001, p. 750.

Index